D0471672

NATIONAL OCCUPATIONAL CLASSIFICATION

INDEX OF TITLES

LM-248-12-92E

Disponible en français sous le titre
« Classification nationale des professions-
Index des appellations d'emplois. »

Canada	Groupe
Communication	Communication
Group	Canada
Publishing	Édition

©Minister of Supply and Services Canada 1993
Available in Canada through
your local bookseller
or by mail from
Canada Communication Group — Publishing
Ottawa, Canada K1A 0S9
Catalogue No. MP53-25/2-1993E
ISBN 0-660-14815-3
ISBN 0-660-14814-5 (set)

Reprint 1995

Alphabetical Index of Occupational Titles

The index of the National Occupational Classification (NOC) is an alphabetical listing of approximately 25,000 occupational titles. Each title is accompanied by the 4-digit code of the NOC unit group in which it is classified. The classification structure (major, minor and unit groups) begins on the following page. Descriptions of the unit groups are included in the separate publication, National Occupational Classification: Occupational Descriptions.

Scope of the Index

All occupational titles cited as example titles in the NOC unit group descriptions are included in the index, as well as thousands of additional titles.

Approximately 16,000 of these titles have been carried forward from the previous classification, the Canadian Classification and Dictionary of Occupations (CCDO). These are titles considered to be still in use. Additional titles were obtained during the various occupational research studies conducted for the NOC.

To assist users, the index includes both formally recognized occupational titles (for example, radiography technologist) and less formal titles that are in common usage (x-ray technician).

Some titles are "occupations" (for example, librarian; chef), while others are "specializations" (music librarian; pastry chef). Still others represent a range of jobs (furniture assembler; sawmill machine operator).

Inversions

Occupational titles appear in the index both in natural order (travel agent) and in inverted order (agent, travel). To facilitate the location of particular occupational titles, many inversions have been included.

However, when an occupational title is modified in several ways (criminal lawyer, tax lawyer and real estate lawyer) and all forms of the title are classified in the same NOC unit group, the index includes the modified titles in natural order and the generic title (lawyer) but does not include all the inversions. When the modified titles are classified in different NOC unit groups (chemical engineer, civil engineer and industrial engineer), inversions are included in the index to assist users in finding the appropriate unit group from the range of choices.

Restrictive Modifiers

Industry or subject matter modifiers are attached to many titles. This information is added to the title following a dash (customer service supervisor - retail; electrical mechanic - avionics) or a comma (design technologist, drafting; buffer, stone products). These modifiers should be considered when coding an occupational title.

Military Titles

Titles of military occupations are indicated by adding the modifier "military" after a dash (sonar operator - military) except in a very few cases where "military" appears in the title itself (military police officer; military engineering officer, civil).

When a military occupation includes more than one NOC unit group, the title has been given a restrictive modifier in brackets as well as the "military" modifier [medical officer (general practitioner) - military; medical officer (specialist) - military].

NOC Major, Minor and Unit Group Structure

MANAGEMENT OCCUPATIONS

Major Group 00
SENIOR MANAGEMENT OCCUPATIONS

001 Legislators and Senior Management

0011	Legislators
0012	Senior Government Managers and Officials
0013	Senior Managers - Financial, Communications Carriers and Other Business Services
0014	Senior Managers - Health, Education, Social and Community Services and Membership Organizations
0015	Senior Managers - Trade, Broadcasting and Other Services, n.e.c.*
0016	Senior Managers - Goods Production, Utilities, Transportation and Construction

Major Group 01-09
MIDDLE AND OTHER MANAGEMENT OCCUPATIONS

011 Administrative Services Managers

0111	Financial Managers
0112	Human Resources Managers
0113	Purchasing Managers
0114	Other Administrative Services Managers

012 Managers in Financial and Business Services

0121	Insurance, Real Estate and Financial Brokerage Managers
0122	Banking, Credit and Other Investment Managers
0123	Other Business Services Managers

013 Managers in Communication (Except Broadcasting)

0131	Telecommunication Carriers Managers
0132	Postal and Courier Services Managers

021 Managers in Engineering, Architecture, Science and Information Systems[1]

0210	Engineering, Science and Architecture Managers
0211	Engineering Managers
0212	Architecture and Science Managers
0213	Information Systems and Data Processing Managers

031 Managers in Health, Education, Social and Community Services

0311	Managers in Health Care
0312	Administrators in Post-Secondary Education and Vocational Training
0313	School Principals and Administrators of Elementary and Secondary Education
0314	Managers in Social, Community and Correctional Services

---

* n.e.c. = not elsewhere classified
[1] In data provided by Statistics Canada, unit groups 0211 and 0212 are combined to form *0210 Engineering, Science and Architecture Managers*.

041 Managers in Public Administration

0411   Government Managers in Health and Social Policy Development and Program Administration
0412   Government Managers in Economic Analysis, Policy Development and Program Administration
0413   Government Managers in Education Policy Development and Program Administration
0414   Other Managers in Public Administration

051 Managers in Art, Culture, Recreation and Sport

0511   Library, Archive, Museum and Art Gallery Managers
0512   Managers in Publishing, Motion Pictures, Broadcasting and Performing Arts
0513   Recreation and Sport Program and Service Directors

061 Sales, Marketing and Advertising Managers

0611   Sales, Marketing and Advertising Managers

062 Managers in Retail Trade

0621   Retail Trade Managers

063 Managers in Food Service and Accommodation

0631   Restaurant and Food Service Managers
0632   Accommodation Service Managers

064 Managers in Protective Service

0641   Commissioned Police Officers
0642   Fire Chiefs and Senior Firefighting Officers
0643   Commissioned Officers, Armed Forces[2]

065 Managers in Other Services

0651   Other Services Managers

071 Managers in Construction and Transportation

0711   Construction Managers
0712   Residential Home Builders and Renovators
0713   Transportation Managers

072 Facility Operation and Maintenance Managers[3]

0720   Facility Operation and Maintenance Managers
0721   Facility Operation Managers
0722   Maintenance Managers

081 Managers in Primary Production (Except Agriculture)

0811   Primary Production Managers (Except Agriculture)

---

[2] This unit group includes occupations unique to the armed forces. However, Statistics Canada data for this unit group includes all commissioned officers. (See introduction.)
[3] In data provided by Statistics Canada, unit groups 0721 and 0722 are combined to form *0720 Facility Operation and Maintenance Managers*.

091 Managers in Manufacturing and Utilities

    0911   Manufacturing Managers
    0912   Utilities Managers

BUSINESS, FINANCE AND ADMNISTRATION OCCUPATIONS

Major Group 11
PROFESSIONAL OCCUPATIONS IN BUSINESS AND FINANCE

111 Auditors, Accountants and Investment Professionals

    1111   Financial Auditors and Accountants
    1112   Financial and Investment Analysts
    1113   Securities Agents, Investment Dealers and Traders
    1114   Other Financial Officers

112 Human Resources and Business Service Professionals

    1121   Specialists in Human Resources
    1122   Professional Occupations in Business Services to Management

Major Group 12
SKILLED ADMINISTRATIVE AND BUSINESS OCCUPATIONS

121 Clerical Supervisors

    1211   Supervisors, General Office and Administrative Support Clerks
    1212   Supervisors, Finance and Insurance Clerks
    1213   Supervisors, Library, Correspondence and Related Information Clerks
    1214   Supervisors, Mail and Message Distribution Occupations
    1215   Supervisors, Recording, Distributing and Scheduling Occupations

122 Administrative and Regulatory Occupations

    1221   Administrative Officers
    1222   Executive Assistants
    1223   Personnel and Recruitment Officers
    1224   Property Administrators
    1225   Purchasing Agents and Officers
    1226   Conference and Event Planners
    1227   Court Officers and Justices of the Peace
    1228   Immigration, Unemployment Insurance and Revenue Officers

123 Finance and Insurance Administrative Occupations

    1231   Bookkeepers
    1232   Loan Officers
    1233   Insurance Adjusters and Claims Examiners
    1234   Insurance Underwriters
    1235   Assessors, Valuators and Appraisers
    1236   Customs, Ship and Other Brokers

124 Secretaries, Recorders and Transcriptionists

    1241   Secretaries (Except Legal and Medical)
    1242   Legal Secretaries
    1243   Medical Secretaries
    1244   Court Recorders and Medical Transcriptionists

Major Group 14
CLERICAL OCCUPATIONS

141 Clerical Occupations, General Office Skills

    1411   General Office Clerks
    1412   Typists and Word Processing Operators
    1413   Records and File Clerks
    1414   Receptionists and Switchboard Operators

142 Office Equipment Operators

    1421   Computer Operators
    1422   Data Entry Clerks
    1423   Typesetters and Related Occupations
    1424   Telephone Operators

143 Finance and Insurance Clerks

    1431   Accounting and Related Clerks
    1432   Payroll Clerks
    1433   Tellers, Financial Services
    1434   Banking, Insurance and Other Financial Clerks
    1435   Collectors

144 Administrative Support Clerks

    1441   Administrative Clerks
    1442   Personnel Clerks
    1443   Court Clerks

145 Library, Correspondence and Related Information Clerks

    1451   Library Clerks
    1452   Correspondence, Publication and Related Clerks
    1453   Customer Service, Information and Related Clerks
    1454   Survey Interviewers and Statistical Clerks

146 Mail and Message Distribution Occupations

    1461   Mail, Postal and Related Clerks
    1462   Letter Carriers
    1463   Couriers and Messengers

147 Recording, Scheduling and Distributing Occupations

    1471   Shippers and Receivers
    1472   Storekeepers and Parts Clerks
    1473   Production Clerks
    1474   Purchasing and Inventory Clerks
    1475   Dispatchers and Radio Operators
    1476   Transportation Route and Crew Schedulers

NATURAL AND APPLIED SCIENCES AND RELATED OCCUPATIONS

Major Group 21
PROFESSIONAL OCCUPATIONS IN NATURAL AND APPLIED SCIENCES

211 Physical Science Professionals

    2111   Physicists and Astronomers
    2112   Chemists
    2113   Geologists, Geochemists and Geophysicists
    2114   Meteorologists
    2115   Other Professional Occupations in Physical Sciences

212 Life Science Professionals

    2121   Biologists and Related Scientists
    2122   Forestry Professionals
    2123   Agricultural Representatives, Consultants and Specialists

213 Civil, Mechanical, Electrical and Chemical Engineers

    2131   Civil Engineers
    2132   Mechanical Engineers
    2133   Electrical and Electronics Engineers
    2134   Chemical Engineers

214 Other Engineers

    2141   Industrial and Manufacturing Engineers
    2142   Metallurgical and Materials Engineers
    2143   Mining Engineers
    2144   Geological Engineers
    2145   Petroleum Engineers
    2146   Aerospace Engineers
    2147   Computer Engineers
    2148   Other Professional Engineers, n.e.c.

215 Architects, Urban Planners and Land Surveyors

    2151   Architects
    2152   Landscape Architects
    2153   Urban and Land Use Planners
    2154   Land Surveyors

216 Mathematicians, Systems Analysts and Computer Programmers

    2161   Mathematicians, Statisticians and Actuaries
    2162   Computer Systems Analysts
    2163   Computer Programmers

Major Group 22
TECHNICAL OCCUPATIONS RELATED TO NATURAL AND APPLIED SCIENCES

221 Technical Occupations in Physical Sciences

2211   Applied Chemical Technologists and Technicians
2212   Geological and Mineral Technologists and Technicians
2213   Meteorological Technicians

222 Technical Occupations in Life Sciences

2221   Biological Technologists and Technicians
2222   Agricultural and Fish Products Inspectors
2223   Forestry Technologists and Technicians
2224   Conservation and Fishery Officers
2225   Landscape and Horticultural Technicians and Specialists

223 Technical Occupations in Civil, Mechanical and Industrial Engineering[4]

2230   Civil Engineering Technologists and Technicians and Construction Estimators
2231   Civil Engineering Technologists and Technicians
2232   Mechanical Engineering Technologists and Technicians
2233   Industrial Engineering and Manufacturing Technologists and Technicians
2234   Construction Estimators

224 Technical Occupations in Electronics and Electrical Engineering

2241   Electrical and Electronics Engineering Technologists and Technicians
2242   Electronic Service Technicians (Household and Business Equipment)
2243   Industrial Instrument Technicians and Mechanics
2244   Aircraft Instrument, Electrical and Avionics Mechanics, Technicians and
        Inspectors

225 Technical Occupations in Architecture, Drafting, Surveying and Mapping

2251   Architectural Technologists and Technicians
2252   Industrial Designers
2253   Drafting Technologists and Technicians
2254   Survey Technologists and Technicians
2255   Mapping and Related Technologists and Technicians

226 Other Technical Inspectors and Regulatory Officers

2261   Nondestructive Testers and Inspectors
2262   Engineering Inspectors and Regulatory Officers
2263   Inspectors in Public and Environmental Health and Occupational Health
        and Safety
2264   Construction Inspectors

---

[4] In data provided by Statistics Canada, unit groups 2231 and 2234 are combined to form *2230 Civil Engineering Technologists and Technicians and Construction Estimators.*

227 Transportation Officers and Controllers

2271 Air Pilots, Flight Engineers and Flying Instructors
2272 Air Traffic Control Occupations
2273 Deck Officers, Water Transport
2274 Engineer Officers, Water Transport
2275 Railway and Marine Traffic Controllers

HEALTH OCCUPATIONS

Major Group 31
PROFESSIONAL OCCUPATIONS IN HEALTH

311 Physicians, Dentists and Veterinarians

3111 Specialist Physicians
3112 General Practitioners and Family Physicians
3113 Dentists
3114 Veterinarians

312 Optometrists, Chiropractors and Other Health Diagnosing and Treating Professionals

3121 Optometrists
3122 Chiropractors
3123 Other Professional Occupations in Health Diagnosing and Treating

313 Pharmacists, Dietitians and Nutritionists

3131 Pharmacists
3132 Dietitians and Nutritionists

314 Therapy and Assessment Professionals

3141 Audiologists and Speech-Language Pathologists
3142 Physiotherapists
3143 Occupational Therapists
3144 Other Professional Occupations in Therapy and Assessment

315 Nurse Supervisors and Registered Nurses

3151 Head Nurses and Supervisors
3152 Registered Nurses

Major Group 32
TECHNICAL AND SKILLED OCCUPATIONS IN HEALTH

321 Medical Technologists and Technicians (Except Dental Health)

3211   Medical Laboratory Technologists and Pathologists' Assistants
3212   Medical Laboratory Technicians
3213   Animal Health Technologists
3214   Respiratory Therapists and Clinical Perfusionists
3215   Medical Radiation Technologists
3216   Medical Sonographers
3217   Cardiology Technologists
3218   Electroencephalographic and Other Diagnostic Technologists, n.e.c.
3219   Other Medical Technologists and Technicians (Except Dental Health)

322 Technical Occupations in Dental Health Care[5]

3220   Dental Technicians and Laboratory Bench Workers
3221   Denturists
3222   Dental Hygienists and Dental Therapists
3223   Dental Technicians

323 Other Technical Occupations in Health Care (Except Dental)

3231   Opticians
3232   Midwives and Practitioners of Natural Healing
3233   Registered Nursing Assistants
3234   Ambulance Attendants and Other Paramedical Occupations
3235   Other Technical Occupations in Therapy and Assessment

Major Group 34
ASSISTING OCCUPATIONS IN SUPPORT OF HEALTH SERVICES

341 Assisting Occupations in Support of Health Services[6]

3411   Dental Assistants
3412   Dental Laboratory Bench Workers
3413   Nurse Aides and Orderlies
3414   Other Aides and Assistants in Support of Health Services

OCCUPATIONS IN SOCIAL SCIENCE, EDUCATION, GOVERNMENT SERVICE AND RELIGION

Major Group 41
PROFESSIONAL OCCUPATIONS IN SOCIAL SCIENCE, EDUCATION, GOVERNMENT SERVICES AND RELIGION

411 Judges, Lawyers and Quebec Notaries

4111   Judges
4112   Lawyers and Quebec Notaries

---

[5] In data provided by Statistics Canada, unit groups 3223 and 3412 are combined to form *3220 Dental Technicians and Laboratory Bench Workers*. Hence, Statistics Canada data for major group 32 and for minor group 322 includes unit group 3412.
[6] In data provided by Statistics Canada, unit groups 3223 and 3412 are combined to form *3220 Dental Technicians and Laboratory Bench Workers*. Hence, Statistics Canada data for major group 34 and for minor group 341 does not include unit group 3412.

412 University Professors and Assistants

4121 University Professors
4122 Post-Secondary Teaching and Research Assistants

413 College and Other Vocational Instructors

4131 College and Other Vocational Instructors

414 Secondary and Elementary School Teachers and Counsellors

4141 Secondary School Teachers
4142 Elementary School and Kindergarten Teachers
4143 School and Guidance Counsellors

415 Psychologists, Social Workers, Counsellors, Clergy and Probation Officers

4151 Psychologists
4152 Social Workers
4153 Family, Marriage and Other Related Counsellors
4154 Ministers of Religion
4155 Probation and Parole Officers and Related Occupations

416 Policy and Program Officers, Researchers and Consultants[7]

4160 Health and Social Policy Researchers, Consultants and Program Officers
4161 Natural and Applied Science Policy Researchers, Consultants and Program Officers
4162 Economists and Economic Policy Researchers and Analysts
4163 Economic Development Officers and Marketing Researchers and Consultants
4164 Social Policy Researchers, Consultants and Program Officers
4165 Health Policy Researchers, Consultants and Program Officers
4166 Education Policy Researchers, Consultants and Program Officers
4167 Recreation and Sports Program Supervisors and Consultants
4168 Program Officers Unique to Government
4169 Other Professional Occupations in Social Science

Major Group 42
PARAPROFESSIONAL OCCUPATIONS IN LAW, SOCIAL SERVICES, EDUCATION AND RELIGION

421 Paralegals, Social Services Workers and Occupations in Education and Religion, n.e.c.[8]

4211 Paralegal and Related Occupations
4212 Community and Social Service Workers
4213 Employment Counsellors
4214 Early Childhood Educators
4215 Instructors and Teachers of Disabled Persons
4216 Other Instructors
4217 Other Religious Occupations

---

[7] In data provided by Statistics Canada, unit groups 4164 and 4165 are combined to form *4160 Health and Social Policy Researchers, Consultants and Program Officers.*
[8] In data provided by Statistics Canada, unit groups 4214 and 6473 are combined to form *6470 Early Childhood Educators and Assistants.* Hence, Statistics Canada data for major group 42 and for minor group 421 does not include unit group 4214.

Major Group 51
PROFESSIONAL OCCUPATIONS IN ART AND CULTURE

511 Librarians, Archivists, Conservators and Curators

5111   Librarians
5112   Conservators and Curators
5113   Archivists

512 Writing, Translating and Public Relations Professionals

5121   Writers
5122   Editors
5123   Journalists
5124   Professional Occupations in Public Relations and Communications
5125   Translators, Terminologists and Interpreters

513 Creative and Performing Artists

5131   Producers, Directors, Choreographers and Related Occupations
5132   Conductors, Composers and Arrangers
5133   Musicians and Singers
5134   Dancers
5135   Actors
5136   Painters, Sculptors and Other Visual Artists

Major Group 52
TECHNICAL AND SKILLED OCCUPATIONS IN ART, CULTURE, RECREATION AND SPORT

521 Technical Occupations in Libraries, Archives, Museums and Galleries

5211   Library and Archive Technicians and Assistants
5212   Technical Occupations Related to Museums and Galleries

522 Photographers, Graphic Arts Technicians and Technical Occupations in Motion Pictures, Broadcasting and the Performing Arts

5221   Photographers
5222   Film and Video Camera Operators
5223   Graphic Arts Technicians
5224   Broadcast Technicians
5225   Audio and Video Recording Technicians
5226   Other Technical Occupations in Motion Pictures, Broadcasting and the Performing Arts
5227   Support and Assisting Occupations in Motion Pictures, Broadcasting and the Performing Arts

523 Announcers and Other Performers

5231   Announcers and Other Broadcasters
5232   Other Performers

524 Creative Designers and Craftspersons

5241   Graphic Designers and Illustrating Artists
5242   Interior Designers
5243   Theatre, Fashion, Exhibit and Other Creative Designers
5244   Artisans and Craftspersons
5245   Patternmakers - Textile, Leather and Fur Products

525 Athletes, Coaches, Referees and Related Occupations

5251   Athletes
5252   Coaches
5253   Sports Officials and Referees
5254   Program Leaders and Instructors in Recreation and Sport

SALES AND SERVICE OCCUPATIONS

Major Group 62
SKILLED SALES AND SERVICE OCCUPATIONS

621 Sales and Service Supervisors

6211   Retail Trade Supervisors
6212   Food Service Supervisors
6213   Executive Housekeepers
6214   Dry Cleaning and Laundry Supervisors
6215   Cleaning Supervisors
6216   Other Service Supervisors

622 Technical Sales Specialists, Wholesale Trade

6221   Technical Sales Specialists, Wholesale Trade

623 Insurance and Real Estate Sales Occupations and Buyers

6231   Insurance Agents and Brokers
6232   Real Estate Agents and Salespersons
6233   Retail and Wholesale Buyers
6234   Grain Elevator Operators

624 Chefs and Cooks

6241   Chefs
6242   Cooks

625 Butchers and Bakers

6251   Butchers and Meat Cutters, Retail and Wholesale
6252   Bakers

626 Police Officers and Firefighters

6261   Police Officers (Except Commissioned)
6262   Firefighters

627 Technical Occupations in Personal Service

6271   Hairstylists and Barbers
6272   Funeral Directors and Embalmers

Major Group 64
INTERMEDIATE SALES AND SERVICE OCCUPATIONS

641 Sales Representatives, Wholesale Trade

6411   Sales Representatives, Wholesale Trade (Non-Technical)

642 Retail Salespersons and Sales Clerks

6421   Retail Salespersons and Sales Clerks

643 Occupations in Travel and Accommodation

6431   Travel Counsellors
6432   Pursers and Flight Attendants
6433   Airline Sales and Service Agents
6434   Ticket and Cargo Agents and Related Clerks (Except Airline)
6435   Hotel Front Desk Clerks

644 Tour and Recreational Guides and Amusement Occupations[9]

6441   Tour and Travel Guides
6442   Outdoor Sport and Recreational Guides
6443   Amusement Attraction Operators and Other Amusement Occupations

645 Occupations in Food and Beverage Service

6451   Maîtres d'hôtel and Hosts/Hostesses
6452   Bartenders
6453   Food and Beverage Servers

646 Other Occupations in Protective Service

6461   Sheriffs and Bailiffs
6462   Correctional Service Officers
6463   By-law Enforcement and Other Regulatory Officers, n.e.c.
6464   Occupations Unique to the Armed Forces[10]
6465   Other Protective Service Occupations

647 Childcare and Home Support Workers[11]

6470   Early Childhood Educators and Assistants
6471   Visiting Homemakers, Housekeepers and Related Occupations
6472   Elementary and Secondary School Teacher Assistants
6473   Early Childhood Educator Assistants
6474   Babysitters, Nannies and Parents' Helpers

---

[9] In data provided by Statistics Canada, unit groups 6443 and 6671 are combined to form *6670 Attendants in Amusement, Recreation and Sport.* Hence, Statistics Canada data for major group 64 and for minor group 644 does not include unit group 6443.
[10] This unit group only includes occupations unique to the armed forces. However, Statistics Canada data for this unit group includes all non-commissioned armed forces personnel. (See introduction.)
[11] In data provided by Statistics Canada, unit groups 4214 and 6473 are combined to form *6470 Early Childhood Educators and Assistants.* Hence, data for major group 64 and for minor group 647 includes unit group 4214.

648 Other Occupations in Personal Service

6481   Image, Social and Other Personal Consultants
6482   Estheticians, Electrologists and Related Occupations
6483   Pet Groomers and Animal Care Workers
6484   Other Personal Service Occupations

Major Group 66
ELEMENTAL SALES AND SERVICE OCCUPATIONS

661 Cashiers

6611   Cashiers

662 Other Sales and Related Occupations

6621   Service Station Attendants
6622   Grocery Clerks and Shelf Stockers
6623   Other Elemental Sales Occupations

663 Elemental Medical and Hospital Assistants

6631   Elemental Medical and Hospital Assistants

664 Food Counter Attendants and Kitchen Helpers

6641   Food Service Counter Attendants and Food Preparers
6642   Kitchen and Food Service Helpers

665 Security Guards and Related Occupations

6651   Security Guards and Related Occupations

666 Cleaners

6661   Light Duty Cleaners
6662   Specialized Cleaners
6663   Janitors, Caretakers and Building Superintendents

667 Other Attendants in Travel, Accommodation and Recreation[12]

6670   Attendants in Amusement, Recreation and Sport
6671   Attendants in Recreation and Sport
6672   Other Attendants in Accommodation and Travel (Except Airline Travel)

668 Other Elemental Service Occupations

6681   Dry Cleaning and Laundry Occupations
6682   Ironing, Pressing and Finishing Occupations
6683   Other Elemental Service Occupations

---

[12] In data provided by Statistics Canada, unit groups 6443 and 6671 are combined to form *6670 Attendants in Amusement, Recreation and Sport*. Hence, data for major group 66 and for minor group 667 includes unit group 6443.

TRADES, TRANSPORT AND EQUIPMENT OPERATORS AND RELATED OCCUPATIONS

Major Group 72-73
TRADES AND SKILLED TRANSPORT AND EQUIPMENT OPERATORS

721 Contractors and Supervisors, Trades and Related Workers

7211 Supervisors, Machinists and Related Occupations
7212 Contractors and Supervisors, Electrical Trades and Telecommunications Occupations
7213 Contractors and Supervisors, Pipefitting Trades
7214 Contractors and Supervisors, Metal Forming, Shaping and Erecting Trades
7215 Contractors and Supervisors, Carpentry Trades
7216 Contractors and Supervisors, Mechanic Trades
7217 Contractors and Supervisors, Heavy Construction Equipment Crews
7218 Supervisors, Printing and Related Occupations
7219 Contractors and Supervisors, Other Construction Trades, Installers, Repairers and Servicers

722 Supervisors, Railway and Motor Transportation Occupations

7221 Supervisors, Railway Transport Operations
7222 Supervisors, Motor Transport and Other Ground Transit Operators

723 Machinists and Related Occupations

7231 Machinists and Machining and Tooling Inspectors
7232 Tool and Die Makers

724 Electrical Trades and Telecommunication Occupations

7241 Electricians (Except Industrial and Power System)
7242 Industrial Electricians
7243 Power System Electricians
7244 Electrical Power Line and Cable Workers
7245 Telecommunications Line and Cable Workers
7246 Telecommunications Installation and Repair Workers
7247 Cable Television Service and Maintenance Technicians

725 Plumbers, Pipefitters and Gas Fitters

7251 Plumbers
7252 Steamfitters, Pipefitters and Sprinkler System Installers
7253 Gas Fitters

726 Metal Forming, Shaping and Erecting Occupations[13]

7261 Sheet Metal Workers
7262 Boilermakers
7263 Structural Metal and Platework Fabricators and Fitters
7264 Ironworkers
7265 Welders
7266 Blacksmiths and Die Setters

[13] In data provided by Statistics Canada, unit groups 7265 and 9515 are combined to form *9510 Welders and Soldering Machine Operators*. Hence, data for major group 72 and for minor group 726 does not include unit group 7265.

727 Carpenters and Cabinetmakers

7271 Carpenters
7272 Cabinetmakers

728 Masonry and Plastering Trades

7281 Bricklayers
7282 Cement Finishers
7283 Tilesetters
7284 Plasterers, Drywall Installers and Finishers and Lathers

729 Other Construction Trades

7291 Roofers and Shinglers
7292 Glaziers
7293 Insulators
7294 Painters and Decorators
7295 Floor Covering Installers

731 Machinery and Transportation Equipment Mechanics (Except Motor Vehicle)

7311 Construction Millwrights and Industrial Mechanics (Except Textile)
7312 Heavy-Duty Equipment Mechanics
7313 Refrigeration and Air Conditioning Mechanics
7314 Railway Carmen/women
7315 Aircraft Mechanics and Aircraft Inspectors
7316 Machine Fitters
7317 Textile Machinery Mechanics and Repairers
7318 Elevator Constructors and Mechanics

732 Motor Vehicle Mechanics

7321 Motor Vehicle Mechanics, Technicians and Mechanical Repairers
7322 Motor Vehicle Body Repairers

733 Other Mechanics

7331 Oil and Solid Fuel Heating Mechanics
7332 Electric Appliance Servicers and Repairers
7333 Electrical Mechanics
7334 Motorcycle and Other Related Mechanics
7335 Other Small Engine and Equipment Mechanics

734 Upholsterers, Tailors, Shoe Repairers, Jewellers and Related Occupations

7341 Upholsterers
7342 Tailors, Dressmakers, Furriers and Milliners
7343 Shoe Repairers and Shoemakers
7344 Jewellers, Watch Repairers and Related Occupations

735 Stationary Engineers and Power Station and System Operators

7351 Stationary Engineers and Auxiliary Equipment Operators
7352 Power Systems and Power Station Operators

736 Train Crew Operating Occupations

  7361   Railway and Yard Locomotive Engineers
  7362   Railway Conductors and Brakemen/women

737 Crane Operators, Drillers and Blasters

  7371   Crane Operators
  7372   Drillers and Blasters - Surface Mining, Quarrying and Construction
  7373   Water Well Drillers

738 Printing Press Operators, Commercial Divers and Other Trades and Related Occupations, n.e.c.

  7381   Printing Press Operators
  7382   Commercial Divers
  7383   Other Trades and Related Occupations

Major Group 74
INTERMEDIATE OCCUPATIONS IN TRANSPORT, EQUIPMENT OPERATION, INSTALLATION AND MAINTENANCE

741 Motor Vehicle and Transit Drivers

  7411   Truck Drivers
  7412   Bus Drivers and Subway and Other Transit Operators
  7413   Taxi and Limousine Drivers and Chauffeurs
  7414   Delivery Drivers

742 Heavy Equipment Operators

  7421   Heavy Equipment Operators (Except Crane)
  7422   Public Works Maintenance Equipment Operators

743 Other Transport Equipment Operators and Related Workers

  7431   Railway Yard Workers
  7432   Railway Track Maintenance Workers
  7433   Deck Crew, Water Transport
  7434   Engine Room Crew, Water Transport
  7435   Lock and Cable Ferry Operators and Related Occupations
  7436   Boat Operators
  7437   Air Transport Ramp Attendants

744 Other Installers, Repairers and Servicers

  7441   Residential and Commercial Installers and Servicers
  7442   Waterworks and Gas Maintenance Workers
  7443   Automotive Mechanical Installers and Servicers
  7444   Pest Controllers and Fumigators
  7445   Other Repairers and Servicers

745 Longshore Workers and Material Handlers

  7451   Longshore Workers
  7452   Material Handlers

Major Group 76
TRADES HELPERS, CONSTRUCTION LABOURERS AND RELATED OCCUPATIONS

761 Trades Helpers and Labourers

7611   Construction Trades Helpers and Labourers
7612   Other Trades Helpers and Labourers

762 Public Works and Other Labourers, n.e.c.

7621   Public Works and Maintenance Labourers
7622   Railway and Motor Transport Labourers

OCCUPATIONS UNIQUE TO PRIMARY INDUSTRY

Major Group 82
SKILLED OCCUPATIONS IN PRIMARY INDUSTRY

821 Supervisors, Logging and Forestry

8211   Supervisors, Logging and Forestry

822 Supervisors, Mining, Oil and Gas

8221   Supervisors, Mining and Quarrying
8222   Supervisors, Oil and Gas Drilling and Service

823 Underground Miners, Oil and Gas Drillers and Related Workers

8231   Underground Production and Development Miners
8232   Oil and Gas Well Drillers, Servicers, Testers and Related Workers

824 Logging Machinery Operators

8241   Logging Machinery Operators

825 Contractors, Operators and Supervisors in Agriculture, Horticulture and Aquaculture

8251   Farmers and Farm Managers
8252   Agricultural and Related Service Contractors and Managers
8253   Farm Supervisors and Specialized Livestock Workers
8254   Nursery and Greenhouse Operators and Managers
8255   Landscaping and Grounds Maintenance Contractors and Managers
8256   Supervisors, Landscape and Horticulture
8257   Aquaculture Operators and Managers

826 Fishing Vessel Masters and Skippers and Fishermen/women

8261   Fishing Masters and Officers
8262   Fishing Vessel Skippers and Fishermen/women

Major Group 84
INTERMEDIATE OCCUPATIONS IN PRIMARY INDUSTRY

841 Mine Service Workers and Operators in Oil and Gas Drilling

8411   Underground Mine Service and Support Workers
8412   Oil and Gas Well Drilling Workers and Services Operators

842 Logging and Forestry Workers

8421   Chainsaw and Skidder Operators
8422   Silviculture and Forestry Workers

843 Agriculture and Horticulture Workers

8431   General Farm Workers
8432   Nursery and Greenhouse Workers

844 Other Fishing and Trapping Occupations

8441   Fishing Vessel Deckhands
8442   Trappers and Hunters

Major Group 86
LABOURERS IN PRIMARY INDUSTRY

861 Primary Production Labourers

8611   Harvesting Labourers
8612   Landscaping and Grounds Maintenance Labourers
8613   Aquaculture and Marine Harvest Labourers
8614   Mine Labourers
8615   Oil and Gas Drilling, Servicing and Related Labourers
8616   Logging and Forestry Labourers

OCCUPATIONS UNIQUE TO PROCESSING, MANUFACTURING AND UTILITIES

Major Group 92
PROCESSING, MANUFACTURING AND UTILITIES SUPERVISORS AND SKILLED OPERATORS

921 Supervisors, Processing Occupations

9211   Supervisors, Mineral and Metal Processing
9212   Supervisors, Petroleum, Gas and Chemical Processing and Utilities
9213   Supervisors, Food, Beverage and Tobacco Processing
9214   Supervisors, Plastic and Rubber Products Manufacturing
9215   Supervisors, Forest Products Processing
9216   Supervisors, Textile Processing

922 Supervisors, Assembly and Fabrication

9221   Supervisors, Motor Vehicle Assembling
9222   Supervisors, Electronics Manufacturing
9223   Supervisors, Electrical Products Manufacturing
9224   Supervisors, Furniture and Fixtures Manufacturing
9225   Supervisors, Fabric, Fur and Leather Products Manufacturing
9226   Supervisors, Other Mechanical and Metal Product Manufacturing
9227   Supervisors, Other Products Manufacturing and Assembly

923 Central Control and Process Operators in Manufacturing and Processing

9231   Central Control and Process Operators, Mineral and Metal Processing
9232   Petroleum, Gas and Chemical Process Operators
9233   Pulping Control Operators
9234   Papermaking and Coating Control Operators

Major Group 94-95
PROCESSING AND MANUFACTURING MACHINE OPERATORS AND ASSEMBLERS

941 Machine Operators and Related Workers in Metal and Mineral Products Processing

9411   Machine Operators, Mineral and Metal Processing
9412   Foundry Workers
9413   Glass Forming and Finishing Machine Operators and Glass Cutters
9414   Concrete, Clay and Stone Forming Operators
9415   Inspectors and Testers, Mineral and Metal Processing

942 Machine Operators and Related Workers in Chemical, Plastic and Rubber Processing

9421   Chemical Plant Machine Operators
9422   Plastics Processing Machine Operators
9423   Rubber Processing Machine Operators and Related Workers
9424   Water and Waste Plant Operators

943 Machine Operators and Related Workers in Pulp and Paper Production and Wood Processing

9431   Sawmill Machine Operators
9432   Pulp Mill Machine Operators
9433   Papermaking and Finishing Machine Operators
9434   Other Wood Processing Machine Operators
9435   Paper Converting Machine Operators
9436   Lumber Graders and Other Wood Processing Inspectors and Graders

944 Machine Operators and Related Workers in Textile Processing

9441   Textile Fibre and Yarn Preparation Machine Operators
9442   Weavers, Knitters and Other Fabric-Making Occupations
9443   Textile Dyeing and Finishing Machine Operators
9444   Textile Inspectors, Graders and Samplers

945 Machine Operators and Related Workers in Fabric, Fur and Leather Products Manufacturing

9451   Sewing Machine Operators
9452   Fabric, Fur and Leather Cutters
9453   Hide and Pelt Processing Workers
9454   Inspectors and Testers, Fabric, Fur and Leather Products Manufacturing

946 Machine Operators and Related Workers in Food, Beverage and Tobacco Processing

9461   Process Control and Machine Operators, Food and Beverage Processing
9462   Industrial Butchers and Meat Cutters, Poultry Preparers and Related Workers
9463   Fish Plant Workers
9464   Tobacco Processing Machine Operators
9465   Testers and Graders, Food and Beverage Processing

947 Printing Machine Operators and Related Occupations

9471   Printing Machine Operators
9472   Camera, Platemaking and Other Pre-Press Occupations
9473   Binding and Finishing Machine Operators
9474   Photographic and Film Processors

948 Mechanical, Electrical and Electronics Assemblers

9481   Aircraft Assemblers and Aircraft Assembly Inspectors
9482   Motor Vehicle Assemblers, Inspectors and Testers
9483   Electronics Assemblers, Fabricators, Inspectors and Testers
9484   Assemblers and Inspectors, Electrical Appliance, Apparatus and Equipment Manufacturing
9485   Assemblers, Fabricators and Inspectors, Industrial Electrical Motors and Transformers
9486   Mechanical Assemblers and Inspectors
9487   Machine Operators and Inspectors, Electrical Apparatus Manufacturing

949 Other Assembly and Related Occupations

9491   Boat Assemblers and Inspectors
9492   Furniture and Fixture Assemblers and Inspectors
9493   Other Wood Products Assemblers and Inspectors
9494   Furniture Finishers and Refinishers
9495   Plastic Products Assemblers, Finishers and Inspectors
9496   Painters and Coaters, Manufacturing
9497   Plating, Metal Spraying and Related Operators
9498   Other Assemblers and Inspectors

951 Machining, Metalworking, Woodworking and Related Machine Operators[14]

9510   Welders and Soldering Machine Operators
9511   Machining Tool Operators
9512   Forging Machine Operators
9513   Woodworking Machine Operators
9514   Metalworking Machine Operators
9515   Welding, Brazing and Soldering Machine Operators
9516   Other Metal Products Machine Operators
9517   Other Products Machine Operators

Major Group 96
LABOURERS IN PROCESSING, MANUFACTURING AND UTILITIES

961 Labourers in Processing, Manufacturing and Utilities

9611   Labourers in Mineral and Metal Processing
9612   Labourers in Metal Fabrication
9613   Labourers in Chemical Products Processing and Utilities
9614   Labourers in Wood, Pulp and Paper Processing
9615   Labourers in Rubber and Plastic Products Manufacturing
9616   Labourers in Textile Processing
9617   Labourers in Food, Beverage and Tobacco Processing
9618   Labourers in Fish Processing
9619   Other Labourers in Processing, Manufacturing and Utilities

---

[14] In data provided by Statistics Canada, unit groups 7265 and 9515 are combined to form *9510 Welders and Soldering Machine Operators*. Hence, data for major group 95 and for minor group 951 <u>includes</u> unit group 7265.

Index

A

abattoir supervisor **9213**
able-bodied seaman/woman **7433**
able seaman/woman **7433**
abrasive belt cutter **9517**
abrasive coating machine operator **9414**
abrasive mixer – stone products **9414**
abrasive products kiln operator **9414**
abrasive reclaimer – mineral products
    manufacturing **9611**
abrasive sheets inspector **9619**
abrasive wheel maker, rubber **9414**
abrasive wheel moulder **9414**
abrasive wheel tester **9415**
abrasives furnace preparer – stone
    products **9414**
absorption operator **9232**
absorption plant operator **9232**
abstractor **4211**
academic dean – university or college **0312**
academic high school teacher **4141**
academic secondary school teacher **4141**
academic subjects teacher – community
    college, technical or vocational
    institute **4131**
academic superintendent **0313**
academic teacher – community college,
    technical or vocational institute **4131**
academic vice-president **0014**
accelerator physicist **2111**
access floor installer helper **7611**
access floor specialist carpenter **7271**
accessories overhaul technician, aircraft **7315**
accessory overhaul mechanic, aircraft **7315**
accident and sickness clerk – insurance **1434**
accident and sickness underwriter **1234**
accommodation analyst **1224**
accommodation co-ordinator **1224**
accommodation manager **0632**
accommodation officer **1224**
accommodation planning officer **1224**
accompanist **5133**
accordion repairer **7445**
account administrator – financial sector **1434**
account auditor **1111**
account checker **1431**
account executive, advertising **1122**
account executive – wholesale **6411**
account information clerk **1453**
account manager – banking **1232**
account officer – banking **1232**
account representative – financial sector **1434**
account representative – securities **1113**
account verification clerk **1431**
accountant **1111**
accountant supervisor **1111**
accounting and financial control chief **0111**

accounting and financial control
    director **0111**
accounting assistant **1431**
accounting/auditing clerk **1431**
accounting bookkeeper **1231**
accounting bookkeeping clerk **1231**
accounting clerk **1431**
accounting department manager **0111**
accounting director **0111**
accounting firm manager **0123**
accounting machine operator **1431**
accounting manager **0111**
accounting supervisor **1212**
accounting teacher – college or
    vocational institute **4131**
accounting teacher – high school **4141**
accounting technician **1111**
accounts clerk – financial sector **1434**
accounts manager, commercial
    mortgages **0122**
accounts payable and receivable clerk **1431**
accounts payable clerk **1431**
accounts payable supervisor **1212**
accounts receivable clerk **1431**
accounts receivable supervisor **1212**
accredited appraiser of the Canadian
    institute (AACI) **1235**
acetylene cutter – metal fabrication **9514**
acetylene cylinder preparer **9613**
acetylene plant attendant **9421**
acetylene torch operator – metal
    fabrication **9514**
acetylene welder **7265**
acid bottling machine tender **9619**
acid conditioning worker – primary
    metal processing **9611**
acid maker – pulp and paper **9432**
acid operator **9232**
acid operator, nitrocellulose **9232**
acid plant operator **9232**
acid pumper **9421**
acid tank cleaner **6662**
acid treater – oil field services **8412**
acid truck driver – oil field services **8412**
acidizer – oil field services **8412**
acoustic emission technician **2261**
acoustic emission tester **2261**
acoustical ceiling installer **7284**
acoustical engineer **2132**
acoustical tile and drywall installer **7284**
acoustical tile installer **7284**
acoustical tile surfacer **9517**
acoustics engineer **2132**
acoustics physicist **2111**
acquisitions editor **5122**
acrobat **5232**
acting teacher – private or studio **5135**
actor **5135**

actress **5135**
actuarial analyst **2161**
actuarial assistant **2161**
actuarial clerk **1434**
actuarial department manager **0212**
actuary **2161**
acupuncture assistant **3414**
acupuncture attendant **6631**
acupuncture, doctor of **3232**
acupuncturist **3232**
acute care co-ordinator – nursing **3151**
ad compositor, typesetting **1423**
ad writer **5121**
adapter, music **5132**
addiction social worker **4152**
addictions counsellor **4153**
addictions worker **4212**
adding machine operator **1431**
adding machine repairer **7445**
addressing clerk **1412**
addressing machine operator **1461**
adhesive bandage machine tender **9517**
adhesives engineer **2134**
adjudication and claims officer –
    immigration **1228**
adjudication and claims officer –
    unemployment insurance **1228**
adjudication officer – immigration **1228**
adjudication officer – unemployment
    insurance **1228**
adjudicator (except labour) **1228**
adjudicator, labour **1121**
adjuster, clock assembly **9498**
adjuster, insurance **1233**
adjuster, piano action **7445**
adjuster, watch balance wheel **9517**
adjustment clerk **1453**
administration manager **0114**
administrative analyst **1221**
administrative and financial officer **1221**
administrative assistant **1411**
administrative clerk **1441**
administrative clerk – military **1441**
administrative dietitian **3132**
administrative dietitian/nutritionist **3132**
administrative judge **4111**
administrative lawyer **4112**
administrative officer **1221**
administrative records department
    manager **0114**
administrative secretary **1241**
administrative services, chief **0114**
administrative services co-ordinator **1221**
administrative services director **0114**
administrative services manager **0114**
administrative services supervisor **1211**
administrative tribunal judge **0411**
administrator, art gallery **0511**

administrator, arts **0114**
administrator, band **1221**
administrator, board of education **0313**
administrator, chamber of commerce **0314**
administrator, child welfare services **0314**
administrator, city **0012**
administrator, court **1227**
administrator, credit and collection **1232**
administrator, database **2162**
administrator, dental health service **0311**
administrator, estate **1114**
administrator, financial **0111**
administrator, gallery **0511**
administrator, historic sites **0511**
administrator, hospital **0014**
administrator, house of commons **0414**
administrator, human resources **0112**
administrator, legislative assembly **0414**
administrator, museum **0511**
administrator, nursing **0311**
administrator of the court **1227**
administrator, pension plans **0111**
administrator, records **0114**
administrator, reservation **1221**
administrator, therapeutic services **0311**
administrator, vocational school **0312**
admissions director **0114**
admitting clerk **1414**
admitting department director **0114**
adoption project officer **4164**
adult echocardiographer **3216**
adult education program officer **4166**
adult education services director **0413**
adult education teacher, secondary
    school **4141**
advanced emergency medical assistant **3234**
advanced life support attendant **3234**
advanced life support co-ordinator **3234**
advertising account executive **1122**
advertising account manager **0611**
advertising agency broker **6411**
advertising agency president **0013**
advertising agent **6411**
advertising art director **5241**
advertising artist **5241**
advertising assistant **1452**
advertising button assembler **9498**
advertising clerk **1452**
advertising clerk supervisor **1213**
advertising collector **1435**
advertising consultant **1122**
advertising control clerk **1473**
advertising copywriter **5121**
advertising director **0611**
advertising editor **5122**
advertising illustrator **5241**
advertising layout designer **5241**
advertising manager **0611**

advertising space measurer **1452**
advertising specialist **1122**
advertising time sales representative **6411**
advertising writer **5121**
advisor, corporate development
    planning **1122**
advisor, law and corporate affairs **4112**
advisor, legal **4112**
advisor, public assistance **4164**
advisory counsel **4112**
advocate, legal **4112**
aerial crop duster **2271**
aerial photograph analyst **2255**
aerial photograph interpreter **2255**
aerial photograph technician **2255**
aerial photographer **5221**
aerial sprayer **2271**
aerial spraying assistant **7612**
aerial spraying lineman/woman **7612**
aerial survey pilot **2271**
aerial surveys flight supervisor **2271**
aero engine technician **7315**
aero engine technician – military **7315**
aero medical technician – military **3219**
aerobics instructor **5254**
aerodynamicist **2111**
aerodynamics engineer **2146**
aerological observer **2213**
aerological technician **2213**
aeromedical instructor – military **3219**
aeronautical draftsman/woman **2253**
aeronautical engineer **2146**
aeronautical technologist **2232**
aerospace engineer **2146**
aerospace engineer – design and
    development **2146**
aerospace engineer – flight operations **2146**
aerospace engineer – flight support **2146**
aerospace engineer – flight test **2146**
aerospace engineer – general **2146**
aerospace engineer – mass properties **2146**
aerospace engineer – materials and
    processes **2146**
aerospace engineer – military **2146**
aerospace engineer – structures **2146**
aerospace engineer – systems analysis **2146**
aerospace engineering head **0211**
aerospace engineering technician **2232**
aerospace engineering technologist **2232**
affirmative action advisor **4164**
agency marketing department manager **0611**
agent, apartment rental **1224**
agent, athlete **6411**
agent, booking – travel agency **6431**
agent, club lodge or society – food
    service **0631**
agent, correspondence school **6421**
agent, country grain elevator **6234**

agent, insurance **6231**
agent, real estate **6232**
agent, right of way **1235**
agent, securities **1113**
agent, ship cargo **6434**
agent, theatrical **6411**
agent, travel **6431**
ager tender – textiles **9443**
aging machine operator – textiles **9443**
agricultural advisor **2123**
agricultural association analyst **4161**
agricultural chemist **2112**
agricultural chemistry branch director **0212**
agricultural consultant **2123**
agricultural economist **4162**
agricultural engineer **2148**
agricultural engineering technician **2231**
agricultural equipment and supplies
    technical salesperson **6221**
agricultural equipment inspector **9486**
agricultural extension supervisor **2123**
agricultural issues lobbyist **4161**
agricultural livestock specialist **2123**
agricultural policy director –
    government services **0412**
agricultural products inspection
    supervisor **2222**
agricultural products inspector **2222**
agricultural representative **2123**
agricultural school teacher **4131**
agricultural scientist **2121**
agricultural soil and crop specialist **2123**
agricultural specialist **2123**
agricultural technician **2221**
agricultural technologist **2221**
agriculture implements assembly
    inspector **9486**
agriculture implements gear case
    assembler **9486**
agriculture machinery builder **7316**
agriculture professor – university **4121**
agriculturist **2123**
agrologist **2123**
agrology technician **2221**
agronomist **2123**
agronomy technician **2221**
aide, audiometric **3235**
aide, chiropractic **6631**
aide, communication – medical **3235**
aide, day-care **6473**
aide, emergency **3413**
aide, health care **3413**
aide, hospital **3413**
aide, library **5211**
aide, medical **3413**
aide, medical laboratory **3212**
aide, neuropsychiatric **3413**
aide, nursery – hospital **3413**

aide, nursery school **6473**
aide, nursing **3413**
aide, occupational therapy **6631**
aide, operating room **3413**
aide, patient care **3413**
aide, pharmacy **3414**
aide, physical therapy **6631**
aide, psychiatric **3413**
aide, school **6472**
aide, special care – nursing **3413**
aide, speech **3235**
aide, speech therapy **3235**
aide, supply processing and distribution – medical **6631**
aide, surgical **3413**
aide, ward – hospital **3413**
aileron fitter – aircraft assembly **9481**
air bag and tube curer – rubber manufacturing **9423**
air bag builder – rubber manufacturing **9423**
air brake hose builder – rubber manufacturing **9423**
air brake inspector, railway car **7314**
air breaker operator **7611**
air compressor repairer **7445**
air conditioner installer, window **7441**
air conditioning and refrigeration contractor **7216**
air conditioning and refrigeration mechanic **7313**
air conditioning contractor **7216**
air conditioning installer, window **7441**
air conditioning mechanic, commercial **7313**
air conditioning mechanic helper **7612**
air conditioning mechanic helper, commercial **7612**
air conditioning mechanic – window units **7332**
air conditioning systems draftsman/woman **2253**
air conditioning systems operator **7351**
air conditioning teacher – community college **4131**
air conditioning unit assembler **9484**
air conditioning unit tester **9484**
air-cooled engine assembler **9486**
air-cooled engine mechanic **7335**
air courier guard **6651**
air defence technician – military **6464**
air diver, commercial **7382**
air filter assembler **9498**
air force chaplain – military **4154**
air gun operator **7611**
air hammer operator – construction **7611**
air hammer operator – metal forgings **9512**
air navigator – military **2271**
air pilot **2271**
air pilots and navigators supervisor **2271**

air pollution field technician **2231**
air tool operator **7611**
air track drill operator – construction **7372**
air track drill operator helper **7611**
air traffic control assistant – military **2272**
air traffic control chief **2272**
air traffic control officer – military **2272**
air traffic controller **2272**
air transport ramp attendant **7437**
air transportation cargo handler **7437**
air treatment installer **7441**
air valve repairer – railway rolling stock **7445**
air weapons control officer – military **0643**
air weapons systems technician – military **6464**
airborne data acquisition specialist **2255**
airborne electronic sensor operator – military **6464**
airbrush artist **5223**
airbrush operator **9496**
airbrush painter **9496**
aircraft accessories mechanic **7315**
aircraft accessories repairman/woman **7315**
aircraft assembler **9481**
aircraft assembly foreman/woman **9226**
aircraft assembly inspection foreman/woman **9226**
aircraft assembly supervisor **9226**
aircraft avionics technician **2244**
aircraft bench assembler **9481**
aircraft body repairer **7315**
aircraft clay modeler **7383**
aircraft cleaner **7437**
aircraft composite technician **7315**
aircraft custom upholsterer **7341**
aircraft de-icer assembler – rubber manufacturing **9423**
aircraft design engineer **2146**
aircraft electrical equipment inspector and tester **2244**
aircraft electrical technician **2244**
aircraft electrician **2244**
aircraft electronic equipment inspector and tester **2244**
aircraft electronic equipment installer **2244**
aircraft engine assembly foreman/woman **7216**
aircraft engine fitter **7316**
aircraft engine mechanic **7315**
aircraft engine overhaul foreman/woman **7216**
aircraft engine tester **7315**
aircraft flight attendant **6432**
aircraft groomer **7437**
aircraft hydraulic equipment installation foreman/woman **9226**
aircraft hydraulics shop foreman/woman **7216**

aircraft hydraulics shop technician **7315**
aircraft hydraulics tester **7315**
aircraft inspector, assemblies and
    installations **9481**
aircraft inspector, assembly **9481**
aircraft inspector, mechanical systems **7315**
aircraft instrument inspector **2244**
aircraft instrument mechanic **2244**
aircraft instrument mechanic helper **7612**
aircraft instrument technician **2244**
aircraft jig and template maker **7232**
aircraft jig and tool builder **7232**
aircraft layout man/woman – sheet
    metal **7261**
aircraft machinist **7231**
aircraft maintenance engineer, avionics **2244**
aircraft maintenance engineer,
    mechanical systems **7315**
aircraft maintenance engineer,
    structures **7315**
aircraft mechanic, engine overhaul **7315**
aircraft mechanic, experimental **7315**
aircraft mechanic, flight test **7315**
aircraft mechanic foreman/woman –
    mechanical systems **7216**
aircraft mechanic helper **7612**
aircraft mechanic learner, mechanical
    systems **7315**
aircraft mechanic, mechanical systems **7315**
aircraft mechanical systems inspector **7315**
aircraft mechanics and repairers
    foreman/woman – mechanical
    systems **7216**
aircraft mock-up maker **7383**
aircraft painter **9496**
aircraft parts assembly repairer – plastic
    manufacturing **9495**
aircraft parts etcher **9511**
aircraft parts etching foreman/woman **9226**
aircraft parts packager **9619**
aircraft parts wrapper **9619**
aircraft patternmaker **7383**
aircraft pipe and tube fitter **9514**
aircraft plastic panelling assembler **9495**
aircraft plastic trim assembler **9495**
aircraft plumbing and hydraulics
    mechanic **7315**
aircraft power plant assembler/installer **9481**
aircraft production supply clerk **1473**
aircraft propeller repair foreman/woman **7216**
aircraft radar repair foreman/woman **7216**
aircraft ramp attendant **7437**
aircraft records clerk **1413**
aircraft refueler **7437**
aircraft repair inspector, mechanical
    systems **7315**
aircraft repairman/woman, mechanical
    systems **7315**

aircraft restoration technician **5212**
aircraft rigger – aircraft assembly **9481**
aircraft rigging and controls mechanic –
    aircraft assembly **9481**
aircraft rigging foreman/woman **9226**
aircraft sales representative **6221**
aircraft sealer – aircraft assembly **9481**
aircraft servicing foreman/woman **7216**
aircraft sheet metal technician **7315**
aircraft skin repairer **7315**
aircraft systems inspector **7315**
aircraft technician, mechanical systems **7315**
aircraft template maker **7383**
aircraft tester – aircraft assembly **9481**
aircraft tire tube builder – rubber
    manufacturing **9423**
aircraft upholsterer **7341**
aircraft welder **7265**
airframe assembler – aircraft assembly **9481**
airframe assembly foreman/woman **9226**
airframe fitter – aircraft assembly **9481**
airframe mechanic **7315**
airframe technician – military **7315**
airline baggage agent **6433**
airline captain **2271**
airline cargo agent **6433**
airline co-pilot **2271**
airline customer service instructor **4131**
airline customer service representative **6433**
airline dispatcher **2272**
airline division superintendent **0713**
airline fleet operations manager **0713**
airline food assembler **6641**
airline manager **0713**
airline pilot **2271**
airline pilot instructor **2271**
airline ramp manager **0713**
airline sales and service agent **6433**
airline sales and service agents
    supervisor **6216**
airline superintendent **0713**
airline test pilot **2271**
airplane pilot **2271**
airplane stewardess **6432**
airport cleaner **6661**
airport engineer **2131**
airport equipment maintenance repairer **7445**
airport fire chief **0642**
airport firefighter **6262**
airport limousine driver **7413**
airport limousine operator **7413**
airport manager **0721**
airport ramp attendant **7437**
airport road paving foreman/woman **7217**
airport security guard **6651**
airport services manager **0721**
airport terminal manager **0721**
airworthiness inspector **2262**

alarm investigator **6465**
alarm specialist **6465**
alarm system operator **1475**
alarm system sales representative **6411**
alarm systems installer **2242**
alarm systems technician **2242**
alcohol addiction counsellor **4153**
alderman/woman **0011**
algebra teacher – high school **4141**
algologist **2121**
aligner – electronics manufacturing **9483**
aligner tamper operator – railway **7432**
alkylation chief operator **9232**
alkylation operator **9232**
alkylation tower tender **9232**
all-terrain vehicle repairer **7334**
all-terrain vehicles inspector **9486**
allergist **3111**
alloy mixer – primary metal processing **9611**
alloy processor – primary metal
    processing **9611**
alpine guide **6442**
alteration man/woman **7342**
alterations dressmaker **7342**
alterations seamstress **7342**
alterations supervisor – clothing
    manufacturing **9225**
alterations woman/man **7342**
alterer, ladies garments **7342**
alterer, men's garments **7342**
alternate heating energy consultant **6221**
alternator tester **9485**
alum-liquor plant operator **9232**
alumina clarifier equipment helper **9611**
alumina clarifier equipment operator **9411**
alumina plant foreman/woman **9211**
alumina recovery equipment operator **9411**
alumina recovery helper **9611**
aluminium awning installer **7441**
aluminium awning maker **9498**
aluminium boat assembler **9491**
aluminium boat leak tester **9491**
aluminium door assembler **9498**
aluminium sheet cutter – metal
    fabrication **9514**
aluminium sheet trimmer – ductwork **9514**
aluminium siding installer **7441**
aluminium window assembler **9498**
aluminizing equipment operator –
    electronics manufacturing **9483**
aluminum briquetting equipment
    operator **9411**
aluminum casting machine operator –
    primary metal processing **9411**
aluminum cell process equipment tender **9411**
aluminum cell reconditioner **9411**
aluminum classifier **9411**
aluminum door and window installer **7441**

aluminum door installer **7441**
aluminum oxide controller **9411**
aluminum powder maker **9411**
aluminum products sales representative **6411**
aluminum sheet separator **9611**
aluminum siding salesperson **6421**
aluminum slurry pump tender **9411**
aluminum stretcher leveller operator **9411**
aluminum window installer **7441**
alumni executive director **0314**
amalgamator process equipment tender **9411**
amateur athlete **5251**
amateur athletic team coach **5252**
ambassador **0012**
ambulance attendant **3234**
ambulance attendant, chief **3234**
ambulance attendant trainee **3234**
ambulance dispatcher **1475**
ambulance driver **3234**
ambulance driver attendant **3234**
ambulance service field supervisor **3234**
ambulance service supervisor **3234**
ambulance service unit chief **3234**
ambulance technician **3234**
AME, avionics **2244**
AME, engines **7315**
AME, mechanical systems **7315**
AME, propellers **7315**
AME, rotorcraft **7315**
AME, structures **7315**
ammonia gas liquefier **9232**
ammonia plant operator **9232**
ammunition caster – foundry **9412**
ammunition foreman/woman **1215**
ammunition maker **9498**
ammunition manufacturing inspector **9498**
ammunition safety inspector **2262**
ammunition salvage inspector **9498**
ammunition storekeeper **1472**
ammunition storekeeper – military **1472**
ammunition technician – military **1472**
ammunition technician supervisor –
    military **1215**
ammunition worker **9498**
amplification audiologist **3141**
amplifier repairer **2242**
ampoule filler **9619**
ampoule inspector **9619**
amusement attraction operator **6443**
amusement concession operator **6443**
amusement machine routeman/woman **7414**
amusement park attendant **6671**
amusement ride attendant **6671**
amusement ride operator **6443**
anaesthesia, chief of **0311**
anaesthesia technologist **3214**
anaesthesiologist **3111**
anaesthetic orderly **3413**

anaesthetist **3111**
analog and amplifier design engineer **2133**
analysis supervisor, statistics **2161**
analyst, agricultural association **4161**
analyst, business – computer systems **2162**
analyst, business management **1122**
analyst, business methods **1122**
analyst, compensation-research **1121**
analyst, computer **2162**
analyst, computer systems **2162**
analyst, credit **1232**
analyst, economic **4162**
analyst, EDP **2162**
analyst, file systems **1122**
analyst, financial **1112**
analyst, fiscal **4162**
analyst, fitness **4167**
analyst, handwriting **4169**
analyst, information systems – computer
    systems **2162**
analyst, information technology **2162**
analyst, investment **1112**
analyst, job evaluation **1121**
analyst, loan **1232**
analyst, management **1122**
analyst, management information
    systems – computer systems **2162**
analyst, manufacturers' association **4163**
analyst, market – non-financial **4163**
analyst, marketing **4163**
analyst, methods and cost **1122**
analyst, methods and procedures **1122**
analyst, mines **2212**
analyst, money market **1112**
analyst, movement – medical **3144**
analyst, occupational supply **4164**
analyst, organizational **1122**
analyst, record systems **1122**
analyst, recreation **4167**
analyst, securities **1112**
analyst, software **2162**
analyst, sport **4167**
analyst, systems – computer systems **2162**
analyst, work study **1122**
analytical biochemist **2112**
analytical chemist **2112**
analytical statistician **2161**
analytical technician, chemical **2211**
anatomical pathologist **3111**
anatomical pathology technologist **3211**
anatomist **2121**
anatomist, veterinary **3114**
anatomy professor – university **4121**
anchor machine operator, railway **7432**
anesthesiologist **3111**
anesthetist **3111**
angle shear operator – metal fabrication **9514**
animal attendant **6483**

animal attendant, laboratory **6483**
animal attendant, zoo **6483**
animal breeder **8251**
animal care technician **3213**
animal care technologist **3213**
animal care worker **6483**
animal control inspector **6463**
animal control officer **6463**
animal control supervisor **6463**
animal control trapper **7444**
animal ecologist **2121**
animal eviscerator – meat packing **9462**
animal geneticist **2121**
animal groom – except horses **6483**
animal health inspector **2222**
animal health technician **3213**
animal health technologist **3213**
animal nutritionist **2121**
animal operating room attendant **3213**
animal pathologist **2121**
animal primary products inspector **2222**
animal scientist **2121**
animal skinner – meat packing **9462**
animal taxonomist **2121**
animal technologist **3213**
animal trainer – except horses or marine
    mammals **6483**
animation artist **5241**
animation camera operator **5223**
animation inker **5223**
animation painter **5223**
animator, graphic design and illustration **5241**
animator, recreation and sport **5254**
annealer – glass products manufacturing **9413**
annealer helper – primary metal
    processing **9611**
annealer – primary metal processing **9411**
annealing foreman/woman – primary
    metal processing **9211**
announcer **5231**
annuity representative, investments **1113**
anode adjuster **9415**
anode caster **9411**
anode caster – primary metal processing **9411**
anodizer **9497**
anodizing foreman/woman – primary
    metal processing **9211**
answering service operator **1414**
antenna assembler **9498**
antenna engineer **2133**
antenna installer **7441**
antenna installer apprentice **7441**
antenna rigger **7441**
antenna tuner inspector – electronics
    manufacturing **9483**
anthropologist **4169**
anthropology professor – university **4121**
anti-gambling section inspector – police **0641**

antibiotics fermenter **9232**
antique car restorer **7322**
antique dealer **0621**
antique vehicle restorer **7322**
antiquer **9494**
anvilsmith **7266**
apartment building maintenance worker **6663**
apartment building manager **1224**
apartment couple **6663**
apartment maintenance man/woman **6663**
apartment rental agent **1224**
apiarist **8251**
apiary worker **8431**
apiculturist **8251**
apparel design teacher – college or
    vocational institute **4131**
appeal officer – taxation **1228**
appellate court judge **4111**
apple grower **8251**
apple picker **8611**
apple sauce processor operator **9461**
appliance buyer **6233**
appliance repair clerk **1473**
appliance repair instructor – vocational
    school **4131**
appliance repair shop foreman/woman **7216**
appliance repair shop supervisor **7216**
appliance repairer apprentice **7332**
appliance repairer, production line **9484**
appliance salesperson **6421**
appliance service technician **7332**
appliance serviceman/woman
    apprentice **7332**
appliance servicer **7332**
appliance servicing teacher – vocational
    institute **4131**
appliance store manager **0621**
application clerk **1441**
application programmer **2163**
application reviewer – insurance **1434**
applications analyst – computer systems **2162**
applications programmer **2163**
applications sales engineer **6221**
applied arts teacher – community
    college **4131**
applied linguist **4169**
applied mathematician **2161**
applied meteorologist **2114**
applied statistician **2161**
appointment clerk **1414**
appraisal engineer **2131**
appraisal forester **2122**
appraisal technician **1235**
appraiser, customs **1228**
appraiser (except customs) **1235**
apprentice, barber **6271**
apprentice, bricklayer **7281**
apprentice carman/woman **7314**

apprentice, carpenter **7271**
apprentice, CATV technician – cable
    television **7247**
apprentice, cement finisher **7282**
apprentice, communication electrician –
    switching **7246**
apprentice, communication electrician –
    telephone **7246**
apprentice, construction electrician **7241**
apprentice, cook **6242**
apprentice, dental technician **3223**
apprentice, drafting technician **2253**
apprentice, dry cleaner **6681**
apprentice, drywall applicator **7284**
apprentice, electrician – construction **7241**
apprentice electrician –
    telecommunications equipment **7246**
apprentice, elevator mechanic **7318**
apprentice, embalmer **6272**
apprentice, firefighter **6262**
apprentice, floor covering installer **7295**
apprentice, gas fitter **7253**
apprentice, glazier **7292**
apprentice, hairdresser **6271**
apprentice, hairstylist **6271**
apprentice, heavy-duty equipment
    mechanic **7312**
apprentice, heavy-duty equipment
    operator **7421**
apprentice, industrial electrician **7242**
apprentice, industrial instrument
    mechanic **2243**
apprentice, industrial mechanic **7311**
apprentice, insulator **7293**
apprentice, ironworker **7264**
apprentice jeweller **7344**
apprentice, line maintainer – electric
    power systems **7244**
apprentice, lineman/woman – electric
    power systems **7244**
apprentice, lineman/woman –
    telecommunications **7245**
apprentice, marine electrician **7242**
apprentice marine engineer **2274**
apprentice, metal fabricator **7263**
apprentice, motor vehicle mechanic **7321**
apprentice moulder – foundry **9412**
apprentice, ocularist **3219**
apprentice, oil burner
    installer/maintainer **7331**
apprentice, optician **3231**
apprentice, painter and decorator **7294**
apprentice, pipefitter/steamfitter **7252**
apprentice, plasterer **7284**
apprentice, plumber **7251**
apprentice power dispatcher – electric
    power systems **7352**
apprentice, power engineer **7351**

apprentice, power system electrician **7243**
apprentice, pressman/woman – printing **7381**
apprentice, printing press operator **7381**
apprentice, refrigeration and air
    conditioning mechanic **7313**
apprentice, roofer **7291**
apprentice, ship's plater **7263**
apprentice, shipfitter **7263**
apprentice, sprinkler system installer **7252**
apprentice, stationary engineer **7351**
apprentice, steel fabricator **7263**
apprentice, structural metal and
    platework fabricator **7263**
apprentice, telephone
    switchman/woman **7246**
apprentice, tilesetter **7283**
apprentice, tool and die maker **7232**
apprentice, water well driller **7373**
apprenticeship training director –
    government services **0411**
approver, claims – insurance **1233**
aquaculture manager **8257**
aquaculture operator **8257**
aquaculture support worker **8613**
aquaculture technician **2221**
aquaculture worker **8613**
aquatic biologist **2121**
aquatic biology technician **2221**
aquatic biology technologist **2221**
arbitrager **0121**
arbitrator **1121**
arbor press tender – electrical equipment
    manufacturing **9487**
arborer **9498**
arboriculturist **2225**
arborist **2225**
arc cutter – metal fabrication **9514**
arc welder **7265**
arc welder, hand **7265**
arc welder, pipeline **7265**
arch cushion press operator – plastic
    manufacturing **9422**
archaeological consultant **4169**
archaeologist **4169**
archaeology curator **5112**
archaeology professor – university **4121**
archbishop **4154**
archdeacon **4154**
archeological field worker **4169**
archeological technician **4169**
archery bow maker **9498**
archery bow repairer **7445**
archery bow string maker **9498**
architect **2151**
architect, industrial and commercial
    buildings **2151**
architect, landscape **2152**
architect, naval **2148**

architect, residential buildings **2151**
architectural assistant **2251**
architectural design technician **2251**
architectural design technologist **2251**
architectural draftsman/woman **2253**
architectural draftsperson **2253**
architectural manager **0212**
architectural service manager **0212**
architectural standards specialist **2151**
architectural technician **2251**
architectural technologist **2251**
architectural technology instructor –
    college or vocational institute **4131**
archive attendant **5211**
archive director **0511**
archives assistant **5211**
archivist **5113**
archivist, assistant **5113**
archivist, chief **0511**
area co-ordinator – motor vehicle
    manufacturing **9221**
area development officer – government **4163**
area director, social services **0314**
area manager – banking, credit and
    investment **0122**
area manager, construction **0711**
area manager, family services **0314**
area manager, post office **0132**
area manager, property acquisitions **1224**
area manager, railway transport **0713**
area manager, retail chain **0621**
area retail manager – postal service **0132**
area sales manager **0611**
area superintendent – school system **0313**
arena manager **0721**
armature assembler – industrial
    electrical equipment **9485**
armature bander **9484**
armature coil former – industrial
    electrical equipment **9485**
armature coil winder – industrial electric
    equipment **9485**
armature connector – industrial
    electrical equipment **9485**
armature inspector – industrial electrical
    equipment **9485**
armature insulator – industrial electrical
    equipment **9485**
armature repairman/woman **7333**
armature tester **9487**
armature winder – industrial electrical
    equipment **9485**
armature winder/repairer **7333**
armature winder, small electric motor **9484**
armed forces chaplain – military **4154**
armour officer – military **0643**
armoured car driver **6651**
armoured car guard **6651**

armoured fighting vehicle operator –
    military **6464**
armoured vehicle crewmember –
    military **6464**
army chaplain – military **4154**
arranger, music **5132**
arrow assembler **9498**
arrow point assembler **9498**
art and photography model **5232**
art co-ordinator – education **4166**
art critic **5123**
art dealer **0621**
art department library clerk **1451**
art director, advertising **5241**
art director – motion picture,
    broadcasting and stage productions **5131**
art editor **5122**
art educator – museum **5124**
art gallery administrator **0511**
art gallery administrator, assistant **0511**
art gallery co-ordinator **0511**
art gallery curator **5112**
art gallery director **0511**
art gallery director, assistant **0511**
art gallery manager **0511**
art gallery manager, assistant **0511**
art gallery manager – retail **0621**
art instructor (except primary,
    secondary, post-secondary
    education) **5136**
art layout designer **5241**
art librarian **5111**
art metal worker helper **9619**
art restoration technician **5212**
art room supervisor **5241**
art sales consultant **6421**
art salesperson **6421**
art teacher – elementary school **4142**
art teacher (except primary, secondary,
    post-secondary education) **5136**
art teacher – secondary school **4141**
art teacher, spontaneous **3144**
art therapist **3144**
art therapist supervisor **3144**
art therapy consultant **3144**
art therapy teacher **3144**
art work assembler **5223**
articling student – law **4112**
artifact and fossil restorer **5112**
artifacts and fossils conservator **5112**
artifacts conservator **5112**
artificial breeding worker **8431**
artificial eye maker **3219**
artificial ice maker – rink **6671**
artificial inseminator **8252**
artificial limb assembler **3219**
artificial limb finisher **3219**
artificial limb maker **3219**

artificial marble setter **7283**
artificial pearl maker **9498**
artificial stone mason **7281**
artificial turf maker **9517**
artillery officer – military **0643**
artillery soldier – military **6464**
artilleryman/woman air defence –
    military **6464**
artilleryman/woman – military **6464**
artisan **5244**
artist, advertising **5241**
artist, commercial **5241**
artist, graphic **5241**
artist, story board **5241**
artist, tattoo **6482**
artist, visual art **5136**
artistic director, orchestra **5132**
artistic director, performing arts **5131**
arts administrator **0114**
arts and crafts leader – recreation and
    sport **5254**
arts and crafts program co-ordinator **4167**
arts and crafts teacher – secondary
    school **4141**
arts and crafts teacher – vocational **5244**
arts teacher – secondary school **4141**
asbestos board curer **9414**
asbestos cement insulation moulder **9414**
asbestos cement pipe bender **9414**
asbestos cement pipe curer **9414**
asbestos cement pipe gauger **9414**
asbestos cement pipe junction maker –
    concrete products **9414**
asbestos cement pipe machine lead hand **9414**
asbestos cement pipe machine setter **9414**
asbestos cement pipe spin former **9414**
asbestos cement pipe spin former helper **9414**
asbestos cement pipe tester **9414**
asbestos cement pipe valve operator **9414**
asbestos cement tile maker **9414**
asbestos crusherman/woman **9611**
asbestos drier **9411**
asbestos fibre inspector and tester **9415**
asbestos fibre preparer **7611**
asbestos grader **9415**
asbestos grinder **9611**
asbestos insulator **7293**
asbestos manufacturing foreman/woman **9211**
asbestos mixer **9414**
asbestos mould stripper **9611**
asbestos moulder **9611**
asbestos pipe insulation mixer **9414**
asbestos remover **7611**
asbestos screen tender **9411**
asbestos shingle assembler **9414**
asbestos shingle cutter **9414**
asbestos shingle inspector **9415**
asbestos shingle maker **9414**

asbestos shingle presser **9414**
asbestos worker – construction **7611**
asbestos worker – mineral and metal
    processing **9611**
asbestosboard machine operator **9414**
asbestosboard machinery setter **9414**
asbestosboard sander **9611**
asbestosboard shearer **9611**
asian studies professor – university **4121**
asian studies teacher – university **4121**
asphalt batch plant operator **7421**
asphalt engineer **2131**
asphalt grooving machine operator **7421**
asphalt heater tender **9421**
asphalt mixer **7611**
asphalt paving foreman/woman **7217**
asphalt paving labour foreman/woman **7217**
asphalt paving machine operator **7421**
asphalt plant drier tender **9421**
asphalt plant labourer – construction **7611**
asphalt plant operator **7421**
asphalt roller operator **7421**
asphalt roof slitter operator **9517**
asphalt roofer **7291**
asphalt roofing material mixer **9421**
asphalt shingler **7291**
asphalt spreader – manual **7611**
asphalt spreader operator **7421**
asphalt worker – road **7611**
assault pioneer – military **6464**
assayer **2212**
assembled furniture inspector **9492**
assembled wood products repairer **9493**
assembler, advertising button **9498**
assembler, air conditioner **9484**
assembler, aircraft **9481**
assembler, aircraft plastic panelling **9495**
assembler, aircraft structures and
    surfaces **9481**
assembler and wirer, electrical panels **9485**
assembler and wirer, motors and
    generators **9485**
assembler and wirer, switchgear **9485**
assembler, antenna **9498**
assembler, artificial limb **3219**
assembler, automobile **9482**
assembler, automotive engine **9486**
assembler, avionics equipment **9483**
assembler, ballast transformer **9484**
assembler, broom **9498**
assembler, brush and mop **9498**
assembler, cabinet **9492**
assembler, carbon brushes **9485**
assembler, clock **9498**
assembler, commercial refrigerator **9484**
assembler, commutator **9485**
assembler, convertible top – motor
    vehicle manufacturing **9482**

assembler, current transformers **9485**
assembler, desk **9492**
assembler, diesel engine **9486**
assembler, drawer **9492**
assembler, dry cell and battery **9487**
assembler, dry cell batteries **9487**
assembler, electric baseboard heaters **9484**
assembler, electric furnace **9486**
assembler, electric heaters **9484**
assembler, electric lamps **9484**
assembler, electric signs **9484**
assembler, electrical accessories **9484**
assembler, electrical appliances **9484**
assembler, electrical control panel **9485**
assembler, electrical equipment
    production **9484**
assembler, electrical meters **9484**
assembler, electrical switches **9484**
assembler, electrical wire group **9484**
assembler, electronic cash register **9483**
assembler, electronic keyboard
    machines **9483**
assembler – electronics manufacturing **9483**
assembler, eyeglass frames **9498**
assembler, filters **9498**
assembler, fixture **9492**
assembler, flat dry cell battery **9487**
assembler, fluorescent light fixtures **9484**
assembler, furniture **9492**
assembler, garden machinery **9486**
assembler, gas furnace **9486**
assembler, gear box **9486**
assembler, graphic arts **5223**
assembler, heavy current switches **9484**
assembler, heavy duty capacitors **9484**
assembler, heavy duty resistors **9484**
assembler, heavy duty transformer **9485**
assembler, hydraulic hoist **9486**
assembler, hydraulic pump **9486**
assembler, industrial brakes and AC
    motors **9485**
assembler, industrial storage battery
    plates **9487**
assembler/installer, metal building **7441**
assembler, interior finish trim – motor
    vehicle manufacturing **9482**
assembler, laminated core – industrial
    electrical equipment **9485**
assembler, large electrical appliance **9484**
assembler, laundry and dry cleaning **6681**
assembler, leather articles **9498**
assembler, light fixture **9484**
assembler, light material handling
    equipment **9486**
assembler, marine craft plastic panelling **9495**
assembler, mattress **9492**
assembler, motor and generator **9484**

assembler, motor control centres –
   industrial electrical equipment **9485**
assembler, motor vehicle lighting
   fixtures **9484**
assembler, motor vehicle manufacturing **9482**
assembler, motors and generators **9485**
assembler, office machines **9483**
assembler, orthopaedic apparel **3219**
assembler, outboard motor **9486**
assembler, panelboards – industrial
   electrical equipment **9485**
assembler, pens and pencils **9498**
assembler, plastic products **9495**
assembler, portable electrical appliance **9484**
assembler, prefabricated housing **9493**
assembler, quartz lamps **9484**
assembler, rotating field coils –
   industrial electrical equipment **9485**
assembler, rubber goods **9423**
assembler, sewing machine **9486**
assembler, shovel handle **9498**
assembler, small electric motor **9484**
assembler, small electrical products **9484**
assembler, small electrical transformer **9484**
assembler, spark plugs **9484**
assembler, sports headgear **9498**
assembler, storage battery **9487**
assembler – structural metal fabrication **7263**
assembler, switchgear and control panel
   – industrial electrical equipment **9485**
assembler, switchgear panels – industrial
   electrical equipment **9485**
assembler, switchgear racks – industrial
   electrical equipment **9485**
assembler tack welder **9515**
assembler, telecommunications
   equipment **9483**
assembler, thermostat **9484**
assembler, trailer **9486**
assembler, transformer accessories **9485**
assembler, transformer cores **9485**
assembler, transformer gas detector
   relays **9485**
assembler, transformer static plate **9484**
assembler, truck **9486**
assembler, whisk **9498**
assembler, wood products **9493**
assembler, wood sash and door **9493**
assembler, woodenware **9493**
assembly and test foreman/woman –
   electronics manufacturing **9222**
assembly fitter **7316**
assembly fitter, aircraft engine **7316**
assembly foreman/woman – motor
   vehicle manufacturing **9221**
assembly inspector, agriculture
   implements **9486**
assembly inspector, aircraft **9481**

assembly inspector – electronics
   manufacturing **9483**
assembly inspector – furniture
   manufacturing **9492**
assembly inspector – motor vehicle
   manufacturing **9482**
assembly inspector, paper products **9498**
assembly inspector – plastic
   manufacturing **9495**
assembly lead hand – electrical
   equipment manufacturing **9484**
assembly line expediter – electrical
   equipment manufacturing **9484**
assembly line operator, storage batteries **9487**
assembly line painter **9496**
assembly line repairer, appliances **9484**
assembly line set-up operator –
   electrical equipment manufacturing **9484**
assembly machine set-up person –
   electrical equipment manufacturing **9487**
assembly machine setter – electrical
   equipment manufacturing **9487**
assembly press operator **9517**
assembly press set-up operator **9517**
assembly quality upgrader – motor
   vehicle manufacturing **9482**
assembly repairer, plastics **9495**
assembly repairer, wood furniture **9492**
assembly repairman/woman, wood
   furniture **9492**
assembly station set-up operator
   electrical equipment manufacturing **9484**
assembly supervisor – electronics
   manufacturing **9222**
assembly tester – electronics
   manufacturing **9483**
assemblyman/woman, small electrical
   appliance **9484**
assessing officer – taxation **1228**
assessing unit head – taxation **1228**
assessment clerk **1431**
assessor (except tax) **1235**
assessor, tax **1228**
assignment clerk **1473**
assignment editor **5122**
assistant accountant, bank or financial
   institution **1212**
assistant accounting manager **0111**
assistant, acupuncture **3414**
assistant administrator, nursing **0311**
assistant animator **5241**
assistant appraiser **1235**
assistant, architectural **2251**
assistant, archives **5211**
assistant archivist **5113**
assistant art gallery administrator **0511**
assistant art gallery director **0511**
assistant art gallery manager **0511**

assistant, audio aid **3235**
assistant, audiometric **3235**
assistant, autopsy **3414**
assistant bank accountant **1212**
assistant bleacher operator – pulp and
    paper **9432**
assistant, blood donor clinic **6631**
assistant branch manager – banking,
    credit and investment **0122**
assistant brewer – food and beverage
    processing **9461**
assistant buyer **6233**
assistant camera operator **5222**
assistant cardiology supervisor **3217**
assistant chief health inspector **0411**
assistant chief inspector – police **0641**
assistant chief statistician – government
    services **0012**
assistant, chiropractic health **6631**
assistant, clinic – medical **6631**
assistant coating operator – pulp and
    paper **9433**
assistant, communication disorders **3235**
assistant, communication – medical **3235**
assistant construction manager **0711**
assistant cook **6242**
assistant crown attorney **4112**
assistant curator **5112**
assistant department manager – retail **0621**
assistant deputy fire chief **0642**
assistant deputy minister – government
    services **0012**
assistant deputy police chief **0641**
assistant deputy registrar – courts **1227**
assistant, dietary **3219**
assistant digester operator – pulp and
    paper **9432**
assistant director, art gallery **0511**
assistant director, economic policy
    analysis – government services **0412**
assistant director, education programs **0413**
assistant director, educational program
    support **0413**
assistant director, Elections Canada **0414**
assistant director, gallery **0511**
assistant director, health program –
    government services **0411**
assistant director, international trade
    policy – government services **0412**
assistant director, language programs **0413**
assistant director – motion pictures,
    broadcasting and stage productions **5226**
assistant director, museum **0511**
assistant director of archives **0511**
assistant director of nursing **0311**
assistant director of nursing services **0311**
assistant director of school services **0413**

assistant director, social program –
    government services **0411**
assistant director, special education
    services **0413**
assistant director, urban planning and
    development – government services **0212**
assistant, dispensary **3414**
assistant district superintendent **0313**
assistant driller, offshore drilling rig **8232**
assistant driller – oil and gas drilling **8232**
assistant, drug store dispensing **3414**
assistant, early childhood educator **6473**
assistant editor **5122**
assistant, emergency medical care **3234**
assistant engineer – water transport **2274**
assistant executive director – financial,
    communications and other business
    services **0013**
assistant executive director – goods
    production, utilities, transportation
    and construction **0016**
assistant executive director –
    government services **0012**
assistant executive director – health,
    education, social and community
    services and membership
    organizations **0014**
assistant executive director – trade,
    broadcasting and other services
    n.e.c. **0015**
assistant executive housekeeper **6213**
assistant financial analyst **1112**
assistant funeral director **6272**
assistant gallery administrator **0511**
assistant gallery director **0511**
assistant general agent – railway **0713**
assistant grain elevator manager **6234**
assistant grain inspector **2222**
assistant greenskeeper **8612**
assistant head nurse **3151**
assistant, hearing aid **3235**
assistant, herbal medicine **3414**
assistant historical park superintendent **0511**
assistant legal advisor **4112**
assistant, library **5211**
assistant mall manager **0721**
assistant manager, consumer credit **0122**
assistant manager, corporate services –
    banking **0122**
assistant manager, credit **0122**
assistant manager, hotel **0632**
assistant manager, operations – banking,
    credit and investment **0122**
assistant manager, restaurant **0631**
assistant manager – retail **0621**
assistant manager, traffic and
    transportation **0713**
assistant manager, travel agency **0621**

assistant – medical laboratory **3212**
assistant miller – food and beverage
    processing **9461**
assistant minister – religion **4154**
assistant museum administrator **0511**
assistant museum director **0511**
assistant, nursing **3413**
assistant nursing administrator **0311**
assistant, occupational therapy **6631**
assistant offshore drilling rig
    superintendent **8222**
assistant operator – chemical processing **9232**
assistant operator, printing press **7381**
assistant, ophthalmic **3235**
assistant, ophthalmic medical **3235**
assistant, orthopaedic **3414**
assistant, pathologists' **3211**
assistant, pathology **3211**
assistant paymaster **1432**
assistant personnel officer **1223**
assistant, pharmacy **3414**
assistant platform superintendent **8222**
assistant police commissioner **0641**
assistant postmaster **1214**
assistant press operator **7381**
assistant press secretary **5124**
assistant pressman/woman – printing **7381**
assistant principal **0313**
assistant professor, botany **4121**
assistant professor – university **4121**
assistant prosecuting officer **4112**
assistant, prosthetic **3219**
assistant pump operator, water treatment **9424**
assistant regional counsel **4112**
assistant regional manager – banking **0122**
assistant registrar – courts **1227**
assistant, social services **4212**
assistant, speech language **3235**
assistant, speech therapy **3235**
assistant superintendent of schools **0313**
assistant superintendent, railway **0713**
assistant supervisor, cardiology **3217**
assistant supervisor, ice cream
    processing **9213**
assistant, surgical – nursing **3233**
assistant, teacher's **6472**
assistant technician, autopsy **3414**
assistant tool pusher, offshore drilling
    rig **8222**
assistant traffic manager **0713**
assistant transmission lineman/woman –
    electric power systems **7244**
assistant transportation manager **0713**
assistant underwriter – insurance **1234**
assistant unit administrator – nursing **3151**
assistant, veterinary **3213**
assistant waiter/waitress **6453**
assistant warehouse manager **0721**

assistive listening device technician **3235**
associate chief justice **4111**
associate counsel **4112**
associate deputy judge **4111**
associate editor **5122**
associate lawyer **4112**
associate legal counsel **4112**
associate professor, linguistics **4121**
associate professor – university **4121**
associate registrar **0312**
associate superintendent, schools **0313**
association director **0314**
association executive **0314**
association executive director **0314**
association manager **0314**
astrologer **6484**
astrologist **6484**
astronomer **2111**
astronomy professor – university **4121**
astrophysicist **2111**
athlete **5251**
athletic equipment custodian **6671**
athletic facility manager **0721**
athletic judge **5253**
athletic therapist **3144**
athletic trainer, boxing **5252**
athletic trainer (except boxing) **3144**
athletics coach **5252**
athletics director **0513**
ATM guard **6651**
atmospheric chemist **2112**
atmospheric physicist **2114**
atomic fuel bundle assembler **9498**
atomic process engineer **2132**
atomizer operator **9611**
attaché **4168**
attendance checker **6671**
attendance counsellor **4143**
attendance records supervisor **1211**
attendant, advanced life support **3234**
attendant, ambulance **3234**
attendant, animal **6483**
attendant, animal operating room **3213**
attendant, archive **5211**
attendant, beauty salon **6683**
attendant, cafeteria/buffet **6641**
attendant, checkroom **6683**
attendant, child-care – elementary
    school **6472**
attendant, disabled person **6471**
attendant, drive-in theatre **6671**
attendant, emergency medical care **3234**
attendant, first aid **3234**
attendant, food service counter **6641**
attendant, fracture room **3414**
attendant, funeral **6683**
attendant, fur storage **6683**
attendant, gas bar (except self-serve) **6621**

attendant, gas station (except self-serve) **6621**
attendant, gate **6651**
attendant, hospital **3413**
attendant, infant transport **3234**
attendant, laundromat **6683**
attendant, laundry **6681**
attendant, lobster pound **8613**
attendant, locker room **6683**
attendant, marina **6621**
attendant, morgue **3414**
attendant, nursing **3413**
attendant, nursing home **3413**
attendant, parking lot **6683**
attendant, personal care **3413**
attendant, physiotherapy **6631**
attendant, plaster room **3414**
attendant, postmortem **3414**
attendant, recreation and sport **6671**
attendant, recreational facility **6671**
attendant, ride **6671**
attendant, service station **6621**
attendant, special care home **3413**
attendant, steam room **6683**
attendant, stockyard **8431**
attendant, sun tan studio **6683**
attendant, take-out service **6641**
attendant, technical – pathology **3211**
attendant, theatre **6683**
attendant, toll booth **6683**
attendant, tourist booth **6441**
attendant, turnstile **6683**
attendant, veterinary **6483**
attendant, visually impaired **6471**
attorney **4112**
attorney-at-law **4112**
attorney general **0011**
au pair **6474**
auction clerk **1441**
auctioneer **6411**
audio aid assistant **3235**
audio amplifier repairer – production **2241**
audio consultant – retail **6421**
audio engineer, electrical and
    electronics **2133**
audio engineer, recording studio **5225**
audio equipment salesperson **6421**
audio equipment store manager **0621**
audio operator **5225**
audio operator assistant **5225**
audio stereo technician **2242**
audio technician **5225**
audio/video service technician **2242**
audio-visual (A/V) assistant – motion
    pictures and broadcasting **5227**
audio-visual assistant – education **6472**
audio-visual equipment installer and
    repairer **2242**

audio-visual equipment repair
    supervisor **2242**
audio-visual manager **0512**
audio-visual materials assistant –
    education **6472**
audio-visual producer **5131**
audio-visual specialist **4166**
audio-visual technician **5225**
audiological technician **3235**
audiologist **3141**
audiology and speech language
    pathology, chief of **0311**
audiology and speech language
    pathology, director of **0311**
audiology clinician **3141**
audiology technician **3235**
audiometric aide **3235**
audiometric assistant **3235**
audiometric technician **3235**
audiometrist **3141**
audit and compliance director **0111**
audit clerk **1431**
audit machine operator **1431**
audit reviewer – taxation **1228**
audit unit head – taxation **1111**
auditing clerk **1431**
auditing department manager **0111**
auditing firm manager **0123**
auditor **1111**
auditor of accounts **1111**
auditor, public **1111**
auditor supervisor **1111**
aural habilitationist **3141**
aural rehabilitationist **3141**
author **5121**
author's agent **5124**
authorization clerk **1441**
auto assembly worker **9482**
auto care worker **6662**
auto dealership manager **0621**
auto driving instructor **4216**
auto glass glazier **7292**
auto glass repair shop manager **0621**
auto parts clerk – retail **1472**
auto parts inspector, machine shop **7231**
auto rustproofing shop manager **0621**
autobody mechanic **7322**
autobody repairer **7322**
autobody solderer **9515**
autobody technician **7322**
autoclave operator – chemical
    processing **9421**
autoclave tender – textiles **9443**
automated machine tools set-up
    operator **7231**
automated sphere polishing machine
    operator **9517**

automated storage and retrieval system operator **7452**
automated valve assembler **9498**
automated welding machine operator, flash butt process **9515**
automatic anchor applicator – railway **7432**
automatic bolt machine operator **9516**
automatic carton maker – paper converting **9435**
automatic casting machine operator – foundry **9412**
automatic coil machine operator **9516**
automatic coil winder – electrical equipment manufacturing **9487**
automatic component assembly machine operator – electronics manufacturing **9483**
automatic door system installer and servicer **7441**
automatic door system servicer **7441**
automatic garage door installer **7441**
automatic glass cutting table operator **9413**
automatic jiggerman – clay products **9414**
automatic lathe operator – clock **9517**
automatic machine polisher – metal fabrication **9612**
automatic moulding machine operator – foundry **9412**
automatic nailing machine operator – woodworking **9513**
automatic outsole cutter **9423**
automatic paint sprayer operator **9496**
automatic pallet equipment operator **7452**
automatic paper cutting machine operator – paper converting **9435**
automatic rubber sole buffer **9423**
automatic screw machine operator **9511**
automatic screw machine tender **9516**
automatic screwmaker **9516**
automatic seating gun operator – glass **9413**
automatic sewing machine operator – textiles **9442**
automatic shaper operator – woodworking **9513**
automatic substation operator – electric power systems **7352**
automatic teller machine (ATM) guard **6651**
automatic teller machine clerk **1434**
automatic transfer machine operator **9511**
automatic transmission mechanic – motor vehicle **7321**
automatic transmission technician – motor vehicle **7321**
automatic wheel line operator **9511**
automatic wire wrapping machine tender – electronics manufacturing **9483**
automobile accessories installer **9482**
automobile accessories installer and repairer **9482**

automobile accessories salesperson **6421**
automobile appraiser **1235**
automobile assembler **9482**
automobile assembly foreman/woman – motor vehicle manufacturing **9221**
automobile assembly painter **9496**
automobile body repairman/woman **7322**
automobile bumper straightener **7612**
automobile carrier driver **7411**
automobile checker – motor vehicle manufacturing **9482**
automobile dipper/painter **9496**
automobile engine tester – motor vehicle manufacturing **9482**
automobile final inspector – motor vehicle manufacturing **9482**
automobile inspector and tester – motor vehicle manufacturing **9482**
automobile insurance agent **6231**
automobile insurance salesman/woman **6231**
automobile leasing representative **6421**
automobile lubricator **7443**
automobile mechanic **7321**
automobile parts sales representative – wholesale **6411**
automobile production manager **0911**
automobile production spray painter **9496**
automobile production supply clerk **1473**
automobile racer **5251**
automobile repair shop manager **0621**
automobile salesperson **6421**
automobile service manager **0621**
automobile service mechanic **7321**
automobile tire builders foreman/woman **9214**
automobile transport driver **7411**
automobile underwriter **1234**
automobile upholsterer **7341**
automobile wrecker **7445**
automotive air conditioning mechanic **7321**
automotive assembler – motor vehicle manufacturing **9482**
automotive body mechanic **7322**
automotive body repairer **7322**
automotive body repairer/painter **7322**
automotive body shop foreman/woman **7216**
automotive body technician **7322**
automotive brake mechanic **7321**
automotive brake specialist **7321**
automotive builder – buses and trucks **9486**
automotive carburetor mechanic **7321**
automotive door panelling assembler – plastic manufacturing **9495**
automotive electrical mechanic **7321**
automotive electronic accessories installer and repairer **9482**
automotive engine accessories assembler **9486**

automotive engine assembler **9486**
automotive engine mechanic inspector **7321**
automotive engine quality control
    inspector **9482**
automotive engine repair
    foreman/woman **7216**
automotive engineer **2132**
automotive gear assembler **9486**
automotive generator and starter
    repairer **7333**
automotive machine shop
    foreman/woman **7211**
automotive machinist **7231**
automotive maintenance equipment
    servicer **7445**
automotive mechanic **7321**
automotive mechanical repairer **7321**
automotive muffler installer **7443**
automotive parts clerk – retail **1472**
automotive partsperson – retail **1472**
automotive radiator assembler **9498**
automotive radiator installer **7443**
automotive radiator mechanic **7321**
automotive radiator mechanic
    apprentice **7321**
automotive repair instructor – college or
    vocational institute **4131**
automotive rubber parts cutter **9423**
automotive service technician **7321**
automotive shock absorber installer **7443**
automotive spring installer **7443**
automotive technician – air conditioning
    system **7321**
automotive technician – automatic
    transmission systems **7321**
automotive technician – brakes systems **7321**
automotive technician – drive trains **7321**
automotive technician – electrical and
    electronic systems **7321**
automotive technician – engine and fuel
    systems **7321**
automotive technician – front-end
    systems **7321**
automotive technician – fuel system **7321**
automotive technician – standard
    transmission systems **7321**
automotive test shop supervisor **7216**
automotive tune-up and electrical
    systems apprentice **7321**
automotive wiring harness inspector –
    industrial electrical equipment **9485**
autopsy assistant **3414**
autopsy master **3211**
autopsy technician – health support
    services **3414**
autopsy technician – medical laboratory **3211**
autopsy technologist – health support
    services **3414**

autopsy technologist – medical
    laboratory **3211**
auxiliary equipment operator **7351**
auxiliary equipment operator – primary
    metal processing **9411**
auxiliary nursing supervisor **3151**
auxiliary operator – telephone systems **1424**
auxiliary plant operator **7351**
avalanche controller **2213**
avalanche observer **2213**
aviation and space curator **5112**
aviation school manager **0312**
aviation technician – military **7315**
avionic/electronic calibration specialist **2244**
avionics assembler **9483**
avionics engineer **2133**
avionics inspector **2244**
avionics instrument and accessory
    inspector **2244**
avionics mechanic **2244**
avionics specialist **2244**
avionics systems installer **2244**
avionics technician **2244**
avionics technician – military **2244**
awning and tent repairer **7445**
awning assembler **9498**
awning erector **7441**
awning installer **7441**
awning installer helper **7611**
awning maker, canvas **9498**
axle assembler – motor vehicle
    manufacturing **9482**
axle cutter **9511**
axle lathe operator **9511**
axminster carpet weaver **9442**

B

baby care worker **4214**
baby carriage assembler **9498**
baby carriage assembly foreman/woman **9227**
babysitter **6474**
baccarat dealer **6443**
back hoe operator **7421**
back padder **9619**
back strip machine tender – rubber
    manufacturing **9423**
back tender – cloth printing **9443**
back tender – paper machine **9234**
backfill plant operator – underground
    mining **8411**
backfiller – underground mining **8411**
background artist **5241**
backhoe mechanic **7312**
backplane and frame wiring operator **9483**
bacon curer **9461**
bacon grader **9465**
bacon inspector **2222**

bacteriological technician **2221**
bacteriological technologist **2221**
bacteriologist **2121**
bacteriology professor – university **4121**
bacteriology technician **2221**
bag boy/girl **6622**
bag builder, rubber **9423**
bag clerk **6622**
bag loader **9617**
bag maker, cellophane **9422**
bag maker, hand **9498**
bag maker – paper converting **9435**
bag making machine set up operator –
    paper converting **9435**
bag sewer, leather **9451**
bag sewer – textiles **9451**
baggage agent, airline **6433**
baggage agent (except airline) **6434**
baggage agent, railway **6434**
baggage handler, air transport **7437**
baggage handler (except airline) **6672**
baggage inspector – customs **1228**
baggage loader, air transport **7437**
baggage master **6672**
baggage porter **6672**
baggage porter, head **6216**
baggage tracer – airline **6433**
bagger – food and beverage processing **9617**
bagger, laundry and dry cleaning **6681**
bagging machine feeder **9619**
baghouse attendant **9611**
baghouse operator **9411**
bailiff **6461**
bake off equipment tender – food and
    beverage processing **9461**
bake pan greaser **9617**
bakelite mixer operator – plastic
    manufacturing **9422**
baker apprentice – retail trade **6252**
baker helper **9617**
baker – retail trade **6252**
baker, ship's **6252**
baker, specialty foods – retail trade **6252**
bakery clerk **6421**
bakery deliveryman/woman **7414**
bakery department manager **0621**
bakery divider – food and beverage
    processing **9617**
bakery foreman/woman **9213**
bakery labourer **9617**
bakery machinery mechanic **7311**
bakery manager – retail **0621**
bakery plant supervisor **9213**
bakery products bander **9617**
bakery products packager **9617**
bakery route salesman/woman **7414**
bakery supervisor – retail trade **6252**
baking machine operator, frozen dough **9461**

balalaika maker **5244**
balance clerk **1431**
balancing machine operator – small
    electric motors **9487**
balcony worker – glass manufacturing **9611**
bale breaker – textiles **9441**
bale checker – textiles **9616**
bale opener **9619**
baler – agriculture **8431**
baler, scrap metal – primary metal
    processing **9611**
baler tender **9619**
balerman/woman – pulp and paper **9433**
balerworker **9619**
baling machine operator **8431**
baling maching tender – rubber and
    plastic products **9615**
baling press tender – printing **9619**
ball and roller bearing assembly
    foreman/woman **9226**
ball bearings tester **9498**
ball mill foreman/woman – mineral
    products processing **9211**
ball mill helper **9611**
ball mill labourer **9611**
ball mill operator **9411**
ball stitcher – hand **9498**
ballast control operator – offshore
    drilling **8412**
ballast equalizer, railway **7432**
ballast regulator operator, railway **7432**
ballast transformer assembler **9484**
ballerina **5134**
ballet company director **0512**
ballet dancer **5134**
ballet teacher **5134**
ballistic technician **2211**
ballistician **2115**
ballistics examiner **2115**
balloon pilot **6442**
balloon printer **9471**
ballracker, billiards **6671**
ballroom dancing teacher **5134**
banbury machine operator – rubber
    manufacturing **9423**
banbury mixer operator – plastic
    manufacturing **9422**
banbury mixer operator – rubber
    manufacturing **9423**
banbury operator – plastic
    manufacturing **9422**
banbury operator – rubber
    manufacturing **9423**
banbury takeoff man/woman – plastic
    and rubber manufacturing **9615**
band administrator **1221**
band assembler – rubber manufacturing **9423**
band builder – rubber manufacturing **9423**

band chief **0011**

band conductor **5132**

band knitting machine operator **9442**

band leader **5132**

band manager, native band **0012**

band ripsaw operator – woodworking **9513**

band saw machine tender – woodworking **9513**

band saw operator – woodworking **9513**

band scroll saw operator – woodworking **9513**

band stock preparer – rubber manufacturing **9423**

bander, paper goods **9619**

banding machine tender, glassware **9413**

banding machine tender – tobacco products **9617**

banding machine tender – woodworking **9513**

bandoleer packer – explosives **7452**

bank branch accountant **1111**

bank branch manager **0122**

bank clerk **1434**

bank clerk supervisor **1212**

bank director **0122**

bank inspector **1114**

bank inspector general **0012**

bank manager **0122**

bank messenger **1463**

bank note designer **5241**

bank president **0013**

bank reserves auditor **1111**

bank runner **1463**

bank teller **1433**

banquet captain **6453**

banquet chef **6241**

banquet cook **6242**

banquet head waiter/waitress **6453**

banquet houseman/woman **6661**

banquet manager **0631**

banquet server **6453**

banquet waiter/waitress **6453**

bar attendant **6452**

bar helper **6642**

bar maid **6452**

bar manager **0631**

bar mill finisher – primary metal processing **9231**

bar porter **6642**

bar service waiter/waitress **6453**

bar steward **6452**

bar straightening machine operator – metal processing **9411**

barbed wire machine tender **9516**

barber **6271**

barber apprentice **6271**

barber shop manager **0651**

barge deckhand **7433**

barge loader **7451**

barkeeper **6452**

barker **6443**

barker operator – wood processing **9434**

barking machine cleaner – wood processing **9614**

barking machine operator – wood processing **9434**

barman/woman **6452**

barman/woman, beer **6452**

barn worker **8431**

barometer assembler **9498**

barrel assembler – machine **9513**

barrel builder, wood **9493**

barrel charrer **9619**

barrel cleaner – food and beverage processing **9617**

barrel cooper – woodworking **9513**

barrel filler – food and beverage processing **9617**

barrel header, wood **9493**

barrel inspector – wood **9493**

barrel maker, wood **9493**

barrel threader **9511**

barrister **4112**

barrister and solicitor **4112**

bartender **6452**

bartender helper **6642**

bartender supervisor **6452**

bartender, tap **6452**

base filler – electrical equipment **9487**

base filling machine operator – electronics manufacturing **9483**

base filling machine tender – electrical equipment manufacturing **9487**

baseball glove shaper **9619**

baseball maker **9498**

baseball manager/coach **5252**

baseball player **5251**

baseball scout **5252**

baseball team coach **5252**

baser **9483**

basin tender **9424**

basket filter tender – fish processing **9463**

basket machine operator – woodworking **9513**

basket maker, wood **9493**

basket weaver **5244**

basketball scout **5252**

basketball team coach **5252**

basketweave fence erector **7441**

basting sewing machine operator, automatic **9451**

batch drier tender helper **9613**

batch dyer – textiles **9443**

batch maker – primary metal processing **9611**

batch mixer – chemical processing **9421**

batch mixer, feed – food and beverage processing **9461**

batch plant tender – glass **9413**

batch process cook – pulp and paper **9233**
batch still operator **9421**
batch tester – rubber products
    manufacturing **9615**
bater – hide and pelt processing **9453**
bathtub refinisher **9496**
batik artisan **5244**
batter and dough mixer **9461**
batterboard setter **7611**
battery acid adjuster **9421**
battery acid dumper **9619**
battery assembler **9487**
battery case inspector and tester **9487**
battery charger – electrical equipment
    manufacturing **9487**
battery charger tester, heavy-duty **9487**
battery chargers machine operator **9487**
battery inspector, electrical **9487**
battery installer – motor vehicle
    manufacturing **9482**
battery lead burner **9515**
battery lead burner helper **9612**
battery lead burner operator **9515**
battery loader – textiles **9616**
battery maker **9487**
battery paste mixer **9421**
battery plate offbearer **9619**
battery plates inspector, electrical **9487**
battery repairer, production line **9487**
battery tester, electrical **9487**
batting machine tender – textiles **9441**
beachcomber **7436**
bead builder – rubber manufacturing **9423**
bead finisher – rubber manufacturing **9423**
bead forming machine operator – rubber
    manufacturing **9423**
bead picker – rubber products
    manufacturing **9615**
bead stringer **9498**
bead worker, hand **5244**
beading machine operator – rubber
    manufacturing **9423**
beaker tester **9413**
beam changer – textiles **9442**
beam department foreman/woman – hide
    and pelt **9225**
beam dyer – textiles **9443**
beam house worker – hide and pelt
    processing **9453**
beam setter – textiles **9441**
beam trawl fisherman/woman **8262**
beam warper – textiles **9441**
beamer helper – textiles **9441**
beamer – textiles **9441**
bearing assembler **9498**
bearing grinder **9511**
bearing inspector **9498**
beater engineer – pulp and paper **9233**

beater helper – pulp and paper **9614**
beater operator helper – pulp and paper **9614**
beater operator – pulp and paper **9432**
beater room foreman/woman – pulp and
    paper **9215**
beater room lead hand – pulp and paper **9233**
beater tender – chemical processing **9421**
beating machine tender – hide and pelt
    processing **9453**
beautician **6482**
beauty and charm course instructor **4216**
beauty care specialist **6482**
beauty culture operator **6482**
beauty culturist **6482**
beauty products consultant –
    door-to-door sales **6623**
beauty salon attendant **6683**
beauty salon inspector **6463**
beauty salon operator **6271**
beauty shop manager **0651**
beauty treatment operator **6482**
beaver trapper **8442**
bed and breakfast manager **0632**
bed and breakfast operator **0632**
bed assembler **9492**
bedspring stretcher **9492**
beef boner – meat packing **9462**
beef cattle farm worker **8431**
beef cattle herdsperson **8253**
beef cooler worker – meat packing **9462**
beef grader **9465**
beef marker – food and beverage
    processing **9617**
beef producer **8251**
beef trimmer – meat packing **9462**
beekeeper **8251**
beer dispensing equipment repairer **7445**
beer filter operator **9461**
beer maker **9461**
beer pasteurizer **9461**
beer sales representative, wholesale **6411**
beer sampler – food and beverage
    processing **9617**
beer server **6453**
beer store manager **0621**
beer store sales clerk **6421**
beer tester **9465**
beet pulp press tender **9461**
beet washer helper **9617**
behaviour therapy service director **0311**
behavioural modification psychologist **4151**
bell captain **6216**
bellhop **6672**
bellows maker **5244**
belly dancer **5134**
belt brander – rubber manufacturing **9423**
belt buffer, rubber **9423**
belt builder helper **9615**

belt builder, rubber **9423**
belt building foreman/woman – rubber
 manufacturing **9214**
belt cogger, rubber **9423**
belt edge stainer **9619**
belt laminator, hand – plastic
 manufacturing **9495**
belt maker operator **9517**
belt maker, rubber **9423**
belt repairer, industrial **7445**
belt sander – woodworking **9513**
beltman/woman **7452**
beltwagon operator – underground
 mining **8411**
bench and structural assembler **9481**
bench assembler – electrical appliances **9484**
bench assembler – electronics
 manufacturing **9483**
bench assembler – farm implements **9486**
bench assembler – wood products **9493**
bench blaster – underground mining **8231**
bench coremaker – foundry **9412**
bench die sinker **7232**
bench fitter – buses and trucks **9486**
bench fitter mechanic **9481**
bench grinder, hand – metal fabrication **9612**
bench grinder – metal fabrication **9612**
bench hand, bakery **6252**
bench hand, jewellery **9498**
bench hand, machine shop **9612**
bench hand, sheet metal mechanic **7261**
bench hand, wooden box **9493**
bench lacquer sprayer **9496**
bench loom wire weaver **9516**
bench machine operator – woodworking **9513**
bench machinist **7231**
bench moulder – dentures **3412**
bench moulder – foundry **9412**
bench moulder – jewellery **7344**
bench stamping die maker **7232**
bench, structural and airplane assembler **9481**
bench tool maker **7232**
bench worker, electrical appliances **9484**
bench worker, electronics
 manufacturing **9483**
bench worker, furniture manufacturing **9492**
bench worker, garment **9619**
bench worker, ophthalmic goods **3414**
benchman/woman – lumber **7383**
benchman/woman – meat packing **9462**
bender, lacrosse sticks – woodworking **9513**
bending machine operator helper – metal
 fabrication **9612**
bending machine operator – metal
 forgings **9512**
bending machine set-up operator – metal
 fabrication **9514**

bending machine tender – metal
 fabrication **9514**
bending press operator – metal
 fabrication **9514**
bending roll operator – metal
 fabrication **9514**
benefit and entitlement clerk –
 insurance **1434**
benefit control officer – unemployment
 insurance **1228**
benefits manager **0112**
benefits officer **1432**
benzol agitator operator **9232**
bereavement counsellor **4153**
berry picker **8611**
bessemer converter operator **9231**
bessemer furnace foreman/woman **9211**
best boy **5226**
bevel gear generator operator **9511**
beveler, glass **9413**
beveling machine feeder, glass **9413**
beveller operator, glass **9413**
beverage and bottle inspector **9465**
beverage canning machine operator **9461**
beverages inspector **9465**
bias cutter – rubber manufacturing **9423**
bias machine operator – rubber
 manufacturing **9423**
bias-ply cutter – rubber manufacturing **9423**
bible school teacher **4131**
bible worker **4217**
bibliographer – library **5111**
bicycle assembler **9498**
bicycle assembly foreman/woman **9227**
bicycle inspector **9498**
bicycle mechanic **7445**
bicycle rental attendant **6421**
bicycle repairer **7445**
bicycle shop manager **0621**
bicycle tour guide **6441**
bicycles salesperson **6421**
bilingual service co-ordinator **1221**
bill collector **1435**
bill complaints investigator **1453**
bill distributor **1463**
billboard erector **7441**
billet grinder – primary metal
 processing **9611**
billet heater **9411**
billet helper – primary metal processing **9611**
billet mill roller **9231**
billiard and bowling equipment installer
 repairer **7445**
billiard ball maker **9517**
billiard cloth inspector **9498**
billiard cue maker **9513**
billiard parlour attendant **6671**
billiard player **5251**

billiard table assembler **9492**
billiard table repairer **7445**
billiard table servicer **7445**
billing clerk **1431**
billing machine operator **1431**
billing supervisor **1212**
billrate clerk **1471**
bin attendant **7452**
bin cleaner – food and beverage
    processing **9617**
bin filler **7452**
binder and finisher – printing **9473**
binder, machine – printing **9473**
binder operator – agriculture **8431**
binder – printing **9473**
bindery assistant – printing **9619**
bindery foreman/woman – printing **7218**
bindery helper – printing **9619**
bindery machine feeder – printing **9619**
bindery operator – printing **9473**
bindery supervisor – printing **7218**
bindery worker **9473**
binding sewing machine operator **9451**
binding stitcher – footwear
    manufacturing **9451**
bingo caller **6671**
bingo floor attendant **6671**
bingo floorman/woman **6671**
bingo games supervisor **6216**
bingo hall attendant **6671**
binman/woman **7452**
biochemical and biotechnical engineer **2134**
biochemical engineer **2134**
biochemist (except medical) **2112**
biochemist, medical **3111**
biochemistry professor – university **4121**
biochemistry technician (except
    medical) **2211**
biochemistry technologist (except
    medical) **2211**
biochemistry technologist – medical
    laboratory **3211**
biogeographer **4169**
biographer **5121**
biological and agricultural science
    statistician **2161**
biological chemist **2112**
biological illustrator **5241**
biological laboratory technologist **2221**
biological research department chief **0212**
biological scientist **2121**
biological technician **2221**
biological technologist **2221**
biologist **2121**
biology professor – university **4121**
biology teacher – high school **4141**
biomechanics professor – university **4121**

biomedical and laboratory equipment
    repairer **2241**
biomedical engineer **2148**
biomedical engineer, clinical **2148**
biomedical engineer, research and
    development **2148**
biomedical engineering technologist **2241**
biometrician **2161**
biophysicist **2111**
biostatistician **2161**
biostratigrapher **2113**
biotechnical engineer **2134**
biotechnology engineer **2134**
bird breeder **8251**
biscuit packer **9617**
bishop **4154**
bisque cleaner **9619**
bisque kiln operator – clay products **9414**
bisque kilnman/woman – clay products **9414**
bisque placer – mineral products
    manufacturing **9611**
bite bloc former – dentures **3412**
bitumen extraction plant operator **9232**
bituminous paving labourer **7611**
black light inspector **2261**
black powder grainer and glazer **9421**
black powder press tender **9421**
black top raker **7611**
black top spreader **7611**
blackboard eraser maker **9619**
blackboard maker **9498**
blackjack dealer **6443**
blacksmith – agriculture **7383**
blacksmith, farm **7383**
blacksmith helper **9612**
blacksmith – manufacturing **7266**
bladder moulder – rubber manufacturing **9423**
blade man/woman **7421**
blade operator **7421**
blanching machine tender **9461**
blanket weaver **9442**
blast furnace foreman/woman **9211**
blast furnace helper **9611**
blast furnace keeper **9411**
blast furnace operator **9231**
blast furnace tapper **9411**
blaster – construction **7372**
blaster foreman/woman – mining and
    quarrying **8221**
blaster helper – underground mining **8411**
blaster – quarrying **7372**
blaster – surface mining **7372**
blaster – underground mining **8231**
blasting cap assembler **9498**
bleach plant foreman/woman – pulp and
    paper **9215**
bleach plant operator – pulp and paper **9233**
bleacher helper – textiles **9616**

bleacher operator – food and beverage processing **9461**
bleacher operator – pulp and paper **9233**
bleacher tender – pulp and paper **9432**
bleacher – textiles **9443**
bleaching foreman/woman – textiles **9216**
bleaching machine operator – textiles **9443**
bleaching range operator – textiles **9443**
bleaching solution maker **9421**
blender and packer – food and beverage processing **9617**
blender – chemical processing **9421**
blender, margarine **9461**
blender operator – chemical processing **9421**
blender operator – food and beverage processing **9461**
blender operator – oil field services **8412**
blender operator – plastic manufacturing **9422**
blender, petroleum **9232**
blending machine tender – textiles **9441**
blindsticher sewing machine operator **9451**
blister former – plastic manufacturing **9495**
blister packer **9619**
block cuber – concrete, clay and stone products **9414**
block machine operator – concrete, clay and stone product **9414**
block making machine operator – concrete, clay and stone products **9414**
block sander and glazer **9496**
block splitter – sawmill **9431**
blocker, flat glass **9413**
blocker – laundry and dry cleaning **6682**
blockholer – underground mining **8231**
blood bank technologist **3211**
blooming mill roller **9231**
blow moulder operator – plastic manufacturing **9422**
blow moulding foreman/woman – rubber and plastic manufacturing **9214**
blow moulding machine operator – plastic manufacturing **9422**
blow moulding process operator – plastic manufacturing **9422**
blow moulding team leader – plastic manufacturing **9422**
blow torch operator **9515**
blower operator, insulation **7611**
blue leather grader **9454**
blueprint blocker **9471**
blueprint developer **9471**
blueprint trimmer – printing **9619**
blueprinter helper – printing **9619**
blueprinting machine operator **9471**
blues singer **5133**
bo'sun, fishing vessel **8261**
board hammer operator – metal forgings **9512**

board of education administrator **0313**
board of education inspector **4166**
boarder – textiles **9443**
boarding house keeper **0632**
boarding kennel operator **8251**
boarding machine tender – hide and pelt processing **9453**
boarding machine tender – textiles **9443**
boarding room fixer – textile manufacturing **7317**
boardman/woman – chemical processing **9232**
boat and marine equipment salesperson **6421**
boat and ship insulator **7293**
boat assembler **9491**
boat assembler, aluminum **9491**
boat assembly repairer **9491**
boat builder, quartz – stone products **9414**
boat building apprentice **7271**
boat carpenter **7271**
boat crane operator **7371**
boat cruise reservation agent **6434**
boat cruise ticket agent **6434**
boat dealer **0621**
boat dispatcher **1475**
boat inspector **9491**
boat joiner **7271**
boat loader **7451**
boat motor installer **9491**
boat propeller repairman/woman **7445**
boat rental attendant **6671**
boat tour guide **6441**
boatbuilder, wood **9491**
boatswain, fishing vessel **8261**
boatswain – military **7433**
boatswain – water transport **7433**
bobbin changer – textiles **9616**
bobbin cleaner – textiles **9616**
bobbin collector – textiles **9616**
bobbin drier – textiles **9443**
bobbin sorter – textiles **9616**
bobbin stripper – textiles **9441**
bobbin winder – textiles **9441**
bobcat operator **7421**
bobsled coach **5252**
body and fender repairer, automobile **7322**
body and fender repairman/woman, automobile **7322**
body assembler – motor vehicle manufacturing **9482**
body frame inspector – motor vehicle manufacturing **9482**
body repairer apprentice, motor vehicle **7322**
body repairer helper, automobile **7612**
body repairer, motor vehicle **7322**
bodyguard (except police) **6651**
bodyguard – police **6261**
boiler and machinery inspector **2262**
boiler and machinery underwriter **1234**

boiler and pipe insulator **7293**
boiler cleaner **6662**
boiler inspector **2262**
boiler installation inspector **2264**
boiler installer **7262**
boiler insulator **7293**
boiler operator **7351**
boiler operator helper **9613**
boiler painter **9496**
boiler repairman/woman **7262**
boiler shop mechanic **7262**
boiler tender – ship **7434**
boiler tester **2261**
boiler – textiles **9443**
boiler water tester **9613**
boiler welder **7265**
boilerhouse helper **9613**
boilerhouse operator **7351**
boilermaker **7262**
boilermaker, apprentice **7262**
boilermaker, erection and repair **7262**
boilermaker, erection and repair
    apprentice **7262**
boilermaker helper **9612**
boilermaker helper, erection and repair **9612**
boilermaker, maintenance **7262**
bologna maker **9461**
bolt header operator **9516**
bolt loader – sawmill **9614**
bolt machine operator **9516**
bolt maker **9516**
bolt sawyer – sawmill **9431**
bolt threader **9511**
bolt threading machine operator **9511**
bolter operator – food and beverage
    processing **9461**
bolterman/woman – sawmill **9431**
bond broker **1113**
bond dealer **1113**
bond manager **0121**
bond trader **1113**
bond underwriter **1114**
bonding machine operator, glass **9413**
bonding machine tender – textiles **9443**
bonding press tender – rubber
    manufacturing **9423**
boner, garment and hosiery **9619**
boner, meat **9462**
book binder, machine **9473**
book caser, hand **5244**
book critic **5123**
book cutting machine operator **9473**
book editor **5122**
book finisher **9473**
book mender **5244**
book publicist **5124**
book publishing manager **0512**
book repairer **5244**

book return library clerk **1451**
book reviewer **5123**
book salesperson **6421**
book sewing machine operator **9473**
book store clerk **6421**
book store manager **0621**
book trimmer **9473**
bookbinder, hand **5244**
bookbinding machine operator **9473**
booker – rubber manufacturing **9615**
booker – tobacco processing **9464**
booking agent, sales **6411**
booking agent, travel agency **6431**
booking clerk **1414**
bookkeeper **1231**
bookkeeper accountant **1231**
bookkeeper and accounting clerk
    supervisor **1212**
bookkeeping clerk **1231**
bookkeeping machine operator **1431**
bookkeeping supervisor **1212**
bookkeeping teacher – college or
    vocational school **4131**
bookmobile clerk **1451**
bookmobile driver **7414**
bookmobile librarian **5111**
boom conveyor operator **7421**
boom crane operator **7371**
boom grip **5227**
boom master – logging **8211**
boom microphone positioner **5227**
boom truck crane operator **7363**
boom worker – logging **8616**
boom worker – mill-pond **8616**
boomboat operator **7436**
boomman/woman **8616**
boot and shoe foreman/woman **9225**
boot and shoe grader **9454**
boot and shoe inspector **9454**
boot and shoe matcher **9619**
boot and shoe perforator **9619**
boot and shoe sorter **9454**
boot and shoe sprayer **9496**
boot cutter, rubber **9423**
boot maker, rubber **9423**
boot repairer **7343**
bootmaker **7343**
borer – woodworking **9513**
boring machine operator – metal
    machining **9511**
boring machine operator –
    woodworking **9513**
boring mill operator – concrete products **9414**
boring mill operator – metal machining **9511**
boring mill set-up operator – metal
    machining **9511**
boss carpenter **7215**
boss plumber **7213**

botanical technician **2221**
botanical technologist **2221**
botanist **2121**
botany professor – university **4121**
bottle caser – food and beverage
    processing **9617**
bottle checker – food and beverage
    processing **9617**
bottle filler **9617**
bottle inspector – glass products
    manufacturing **9413**
bottle labeller – food and beverage
    processing **9617**
bottle machine operator **9413**
bottle maker operator **9413**
bottle sorter **9619**
bottle tester **9413**
bottle washer – food and beverage
    processing **9617**
bottle washing machine tender – food
    and beverage processing **9617**
bottler **9617**
bottling foreman/woman **9213**
bottling line attendant – food and
    beverage processing **9617**
bottling machine operator – food and
    beverage processing **9461**
bottling supervisor – food and beverage
    processing **9213**
bottom cager – underground mining **8411**
bottom machine tender – woodworking **9513**
bottom wheeler **9619**
bouncer **6651**
bouquet designer **6421**
bowker – textiles **9443**
bowl blank boring and finishing machine
    operator **9513**
bowl lathe tender **9513**
bowling alley attendant **6671**
bowling instructor **5254**
box assembler, wood **9493**
box bander **7452**
box blank former, wood **9493**
box blank machine feeder **9619**
box blank machine operator **9517**
box blank repairer – woodworking **9513**
box boy/girl **6622**
box cutter – paper converting **9435**
box factory labourer **9619**
box finisher – paper converting **9435**
box gluer – paper converting **9435**
box inspector, wood **9493**
box labeller **9619**
box machine operator – food and
    beverage processing **9461**
box maker operator **9435**
box maker, wood **9493**

box making foreman/woman – paper
    converting **9215**
box marker **9619**
box office cashier **6611**
box packer **9619**
box printer **9471**
box printing machine operator **9471**
box sealer **9619**
box sealing machine operator **9517**
box spring assembler **9619**
box spring frame assembler **9492**
box stitcher – food and beverage
    processing **9617**
boxcar loader **7452**
boxer **5251**
boxing promoter **5124**
boxing trainer **5252**
BPX clerk **1461**
brace maker **3219**
bracelet assembler **9498**
brachytherapy technologist **3215**
braid maker – textiles **9442**
braid pattern setter **7317**
braid weaver – textiles **9442**
braider operator – rubber manufacturing **9423**
braiding machine tender – rubber
    manufacturing **9423**
braiding machine tender – textiles **9442**
braille and talking books library clerk **1451**
braille computer translations specialist **1423**
braille data entry clerk **1423**
braille duplicator **9471**
braille impressing machine operator **9471**
braille keyboard operator **1423**
braille stereograph machine operator **1423**
braille transcription technician **1423**
braillewriter operator **1423**
brake assembler – motor vehicle
    manufacturing **9482**
brake drum lathe operator **9511**
brake inspector, railway car **7314**
brake mechanic, automotive **7321**
brake operator helper – metal
    fabrication **9612**
brake press operator **9514**
brake setter – metalworking **9514**
brake shop manager **0621**
brake worker – yard **7362**
brakeman/woman **7362**
brakeman/woman – yard **7362**
branch accountant – bank **1111**
branch clearing clerk -financial sector **1434**
branch exchange repairer –
    telecommunications **7246**
branch library clerk **1451**
branch manager – administration **0114**
branch manager – banking, credit and
    investment **0122**

branch manager, insurance sales **0121**
branch manager, real estate sales **0121**
brand recorder **1441**
brass caster **9412**
brass or bronze chaser **7344**
brattice builder – underground mining **8411**
brazer, furnace **9515**
brazer, gas **9515**
brazer, resistance **9515**
brazing machine feeder **9619**
brazing machine operator **9515**
brazing machine setter **9515**
bread baker – retail trade **6252**
bread deliverer **7414**
bread inspector **2222**
bread pan greaser – food and beverage processing **9617**
bread route driver **7414**
bread slicer operator **9461**
bread tester **9465**
breaker feeder – textiles **9441**
breaker tank attendant – food and beverage processing **9461**
breaker tender – textiles **9443**
breakerman/woman – pulp and paper **9432**
breakfast cook **6242**
breeder – domestic animals **8251**
breeder (except domestic animals) **8251**
brewer – food and beverage processing **9461**
brewer supervisor **9213**
breweries kettle tender – food and beverage processing **9461**
breweries stillman/woman – beverage processing **9461**
brewery pumpman/woman **9461**
brewery technician **2211**
brewery worker **9617**
brewhouse operator **9461**
brewmaster **0911**
briar bowl turner – woodworking **9513**
brick and tile batch mixer **9611**
brick and tile crusher operator **9411**
brick and tile foreman/woman **9211**
brick and tile inspector **9415**
brick and tile kiln cleaner **9611**
brick and tile making machine operator – clay products **9414**
brick and tile tester **9415**
brick baker **9414**
brick burner **9414**
brick chimney builder **7281**
brick cleaner **7611**
brick cutter – clay products **9414**
brick cutting machine operator – clay products **9414**
brick grader **9415**
brick kiln operator **9414**
brick kilnman/woman **9414**

brick machine set-up operator – clay products **9414**
brick maker – clay products **9414**
brick moulder – clay products **9414**
brick moulder, hand – clay products **9414**
brick moulding machine operator – clay products **9414**
brick presser – clay products **9414**
brick presser operator – clay products **9414**
brick setter **7281**
bricklayer **7281**
bricklayer apprentice **7281**
bricklayer foreman/woman **7219**
bricklayer – furnace lining **7281**
bricklayer helper **7611**
bricklayer – kiln repair **7281**
bricklayer – ladle repair **7281**
bricklayer – refractory brick **7281**
bricklayer – residential **7281**
bricklayer – smokestacks **7281**
bricklayer supervisor **7219**
bricklaying contractor **7219**
brickmason **7281**
brickmason – kiln repair **7281**
brickmason's helper **7611**
bridal sales consultant **6421**
bridge and building construction manager **0711**
bridge and building inspector **2264**
bridge and girder plater **7263**
bridge and highway construction-gang foreman/woman **7217**
bridge attendant, canal lock systems **7435**
bridge building foreman/woman **7214**
bridge building foreman/woman, railway **7214**
bridge carpenter **7271**
bridge construction superintendent **0711**
bridge crane operator **7371**
bridge design technician **2231**
bridge engineer **2131**
bridge gang worker – construction **7611**
bridge inspector – construction and maintenance **2264**
bridge keeper – lock systems **7435**
bridge maintenance boss **7214**
bridge operator – lock systems **7435**
bridge painter **7294**
bridge painters foreman/woman **7219**
bridgeman/woman – lock systems **7435**
bridgemaster – lock systems **7435**
brief writer, law **4211**
brine equipment tender **9232**
brine maker – mineral products processing **9411**
brine mixer operator – food and beverage processing **9461**
briner, fish – fish processing **9618**

briquetting machine operator **9411**
brisket cutter – meat packing **9462**
British Columbia notary public **4211**
broacher, production **9511**
broaching machine operator **9511**
broaching machine set-up operator **9511**
broadcast clerk **1441**
broadcast engineer **5224**
broadcast interference inspector **2262**
broadcast journalist **5123**
broadcast technician **5224**
broadcast transmitter operator **5224**
broadcaster **5231**
broadcasting corporation president **0015**
broadcasting director **5131**
broadcasting equipment salesperson **6221**
broadcasting manager **0512**
broadcasting news analyst **5123**
broadcasting news editor **5122**
broadcasting producer **5131**
broadcasting traffic clerk **1473**
broadloom installer **7295**
broiler cook **6242**
broiler producer **8251**
broke beater tender – pulp and paper **9432**
broke hustler – pulp and paper **9614**
broker, advertising agency **6411**
broker, cargo **1236**
broker, customs house **1236**
broker, gas **1236**
broker, information **1236**
broker, insurance **6231**
broker, investments **1113**
broker, oil lease **1236**
broker, ship **1236**
broker, yacht **1236**
brokerage clerk **1434**
brokerage manager – investments **0121**
bronze plater operator **9497**
bronzer tender – printing **9473**
broom assembler **9498**
broom cleaner and cutter **9619**
broom maker **9498**
broom stitcher **9498**
broom stitching machine operator **9517**
broomcorn dyer **9517**
brother – religion **4217**
brown stock washer helper – pulp and
    paper **9614**
brown stock washer – pulp and paper **9432**
brown sugar maker **9461**
brush and mop assembler **9498**
brush coater operator – concrete
    products **9414**
brush cutter – forestry **8422**
brush finisher **9498**
brush lacing and trimming operator –
    electrical equipment manufacturing **9487**

brush machine tender – textiles **9443**
brush maker, hand **9498**
brush maker operator **9517**
brush making foreman/woman **9227**
brush making machine operator **9517**
brush material preparer **9498**
brush painter, production **9496**
brusher and shearer – textiles **9443**
brusher – underground mining **8411**
brushing machine operator – hide and
    pelt processing **9453**
brushing operator – textiles **9443**
bryologist **2121**
bucker – logging **8421**
bucket chucker – woodworking **9513**
bucket lathe operator **9513**
bucket stave assembler **9493**
bucketwheel excavator operator **7421**
bucketwheel operator **7421**
buckle maker **9619**
buckle strap machine tender – rubber
    manufacturing **9423**
buckshot swage operator **9516**
budget accountant **1111**
budget accounting supervisor **1111**
budget clerk **1431**
budget supervisor **1212**
buffer, flat glass **9413**
buffer, furniture **9494**
buffer, leather – hide and pelt
    processing **9453**
buffer, rubber footwear parts **9423**
buffer, rubber products **9423**
buffer, shoe parts **9619**
buffer, stone products **9414**
buffet waiter/waitress **6453**
buffing and lacquering foreman/woman
    – furniture and fixtures
    manufacturing **9224**
buffing machine operator – shoe
    manufacturing **9619**
buffing machine tender – metal
    fabrication **9612**
buffing operator – plastic manufacturing **9495**
buggy operator – construction **7611**
buggy operator – primary metal
    processing **9611**
buggy operator skinner **7421**
buggy scraper operator **7421**
buhr mill operator – food and beverage
    processing **9461**
builder and welder, stator and rotor
    cores – industrial electrical
    equipment **9485**
building and house wrecker **7611**
building caretaker **6663**
building carpenter **7271**

building cleaning and maintenance
   supervisor **6215**
building cleaning supervisor **6215**
building construction estimator **2234**
building construction general contractor **0711**
building construction general manager **0016**
building construction inspector **2264**
building construction superintendent **0711**
building electrician **7241**
building exterior cleaner **6662**
building foreman/woman, wood framing **7215**
building handyman/woman **6663**
building inspector **2264**
building inspector – electrical wiring **2264**
building inspector – safety **2264**
building inspector – structure **2264**
building insulator **7293**
building maintenance manager **0722**
building maintenance services sales
   representative **6411**
building maintenance supervisor **7219**
building maintenance worker **6663**
building materials technician **2231**
building mover contractor **7217**
building painter **7294**
building sander **6662**
building services manager **0722**
building services worker **6663**
building space planner **5242**
building stonecutter, stone products **9414**
building superintendent **6663**
building supplies purchasing manager **0113**
building supplies salesperson **6421**
building systems operator **7351**
building wrecker **7611**
building wrecking contractor **7217**
building wrecking foreman/woman **7217**
buildings and bridge engineer **2131**
buildings, vehicles and supplies
   manager **0114**
built-up flat roofer **7291**
built-up roofer **7291**
bulb coater, picture tube **9483**
bulb mount assembler – electronics
   manufacturing **9483**
bulb planter **8612**
bulb prep operator – electronics
   manufacturing **9483**
bulk blender – tobacco processing **9464**
bulk goods truck driver **7411**
bulk materials loader operator **7452**
bulk materials unloader **7452**
bulk milk driver grader **7411**
bulk sausage stuffing machine operator –
   food and beverage processing **9461**
bulker blender – tobacco processing **9464**
bullard multiple spindle operator **9511**
bulldozer driver **7421**

bulldozer operator **7421**
bullet and cartridge case inspector **9498**
bullet cutter and former **9516**
bullet maker **9516**
bullet moulder – foundry **9412**
bulletin board fabricator **9498**
bumper operator, aircraft **9612**
buncher, cigar **9464**
bundle wrapper **9619**
bundler **9619**
bungee jump attendant **6671**
bunk skidder operator **8241**
bureau chief, news agency **0512**
burglar alarm system installer and
   servicer **2242**
burn unit co-ordinator – nursing **3151**
burn unit nursing supervisor **3151**
burner operator – petroleum **9232**
burning table operator – metal
   fabrication **9514**
burnisher – hide and pelt processing **9453**
burnisher – metalworking **9612**
burnishing machine operator – footwear
   manufacturing **9517**
bursar **0111**
bus and transport mechanic **7321**
bus and truck mechanic **7321**
bus and truck repair foreman/woman **7216**
bus assembler **9486**
bus boy/girl **6642**
bus cleaner **6662**
bus company manager **0713**
bus dispatcher **7222**
bus driver **7412**
bus information clerk **1453**
bus inspector **7222**
bus mechanic **7321**
bus parcel express clerk **1461**
bus parts inspector **9486**
bus refueler **6621**
bus scheduler **1476**
bus ticket agent **6434**
bus tour guide **6441**
bus transportation service co-ordinator **1453**
bus washer **6662**
bush pilot **2271**
busher – primary metal processing **9611**
bushing assembler, high voltage
   transformers **9485**
bushing assembler, small transformer
   manufacturing **9484**
bushing core winder – industrial
   electrical equipment **9485**
bushing tender **9619**
business administration professor –
   university **4121**
business administration teacher –
   community college **4131**

business agent, computers **6221**
business agent, labour union **1121**
business agent, theatrical **6411**
business analyst, computer systems **2162**
business and commercial machines
    assembly foreman/woman **9222**
business and economics statistician **2161**
business association general manager **0014**
business broker **1235**
business college instructor **4131**
business college manager **0312**
business college teacher **4131**
business/commerce subject secondary
    school teacher **4141**
business consultant **1122**
business development officer –
    government **4163**
business economist **4162**
business editor **5122**
business equipment representative **6411**
business establishment investigator –
    security **6465**
business forms sales representative **6411**
business issues lobbyist **4163**
business law teacher – business college **4131**
business machine servicer **2242**
business machines tester **9483**
business management analyst **1122**
business management consultant **1122**
business manager, non-profit
    organization **0114**
business manager, sales and advertising **0611**
business manager, theatrical **6411**
business methods analyst **1122**
business programmer **2163**
business programmer chief **2163**
business receptionist **1414**
business representative – club, lodge or
    society **1221**
business representative, labour
    organization **1121**
business school general manager **0014**
business school manager **0312**
business services manager **0123**
business services officer **1221**
business services purchasing officer **1225**
business subjects teacher – vocational
    school **4131**
business systems analyst – computer
    systems **2162**
business systems specialist – computer
    systems **2162**
business teacher – secondary school **4141**
business telephone equipment installer
    and repairer **7246**
business valuation officer **1235**
business valuator **1235**
busker **5232**

butcher **9462**
butcher apprentice **6251**
butcher, industrial **9462**
butcher, retail and wholesale **6251**
butcher shop clerk **6421**
butler **6683**
butter grader **9465**
butter inspector **2222**
butter maker **9461**
butter packer **9617**
butter sampler **9617**
butter wrapper **9617**
butterfat tester **9465**
button assorter **9619**
button machine operator **9517**
button machine set-up man/woman **9517**
button machine setter **9517**
button marker **9619**
button moulder operator **9517**
button press operator **9517**
button sewer, machine **9451**
button sorting machine feeder **9619**
button stayer **9451**
buttonhole finisher **9451**
buttonhole machine operator **9451**
buttonhole maker **9451**
buttonhole stayer **9451**
buttons inspector **9498**
buyer – manufacturing and processing **1225**
buyer, media time and space **1225**
buyer – retail and wholesale **6233**
by-law clerk **1441**
by-law enforcement officer **6463**

C

CA **1111**
CA student **1111**
cab driver, taxicab **7413**
cabinet assembler – furniture
    manufacturing **9492**
cabinet inspector – furniture
    manufacturing **9492**
cabinet minister **0011**
cabinetmaker **7272**
cabinetmaker apprentice **7272**
cabinetmaker foreman/woman –
    furniture and fixtures manufacturing **9224**
cabinetmaker/patternmaker **7272**
cabinetmaker's helper **7611**
cable armourer **9516**
cable coding machine tender – electrical
    equipment manufacturing **9487**
cable contractor **7212**
cable engineer **2133**
cable ferry deckhand **7435**
cable ferry operator **7435**
cable ferry operator, manual **7435**

cable hooker – logging **8616**

cable installation and repair foreman/woman – telecommunications **7212**

cable installer and repairer – electric power systems **7244**

cable installer, electrical power **7244**

cable installer helper **7612**

cable installer – telecommunications **7245**

cable insulator **9516**

cable insulator helper **9619**

cable jointer – electric power systems **7244**

cable line worker **7612**

cable repair technician – telecommunications **7245**

cable repairer – electric power systems **7244**

cable repairer helper – telecommunications **7612**

cable repairer – telecommunications **7245**

cable servicer, television **7247**

cable skidder operator **8421**

cable splicer – electric power systems **7244**

cable splicer helper **7612**

cable splicer – telecommunications **7245**

cable splicing foreman/woman – telecommunications **7212**

cable station tester – telecommunications **7246**

cable television installer **7247**

cable television repairer **7247**

cable tester – telecommunications **7245**

cable tool driller – water well **7373**

cable transfer clerk **1473**

cable TV converter and decoder equipment repairer **2242**

cable TV/pay TV salesperson **6421**

cable yarding operator **8241**

cableman/woman – electric power systems **7244**

cableman/woman helper **7612**

cablevision servicer **7247**

CAD designer, printed circuit boards **2253**

CAD technologist **2253**

cadastral surveyor **2154**

CADD/CAM equipment installer – household and business equipment **2242**

CADD/CAM repair technician **2242**

caddie **6671**

caddie master, golf **5254**

cadet, police **6261**

cadmium galvanizer **9411**

cadmium plant operator **9411**

cadmium recoverer **9411**

cadmium zinc leacher **9411**

cafeteria/buffet attendant **6641**

cafeteria cashier **6611**

cafeteria cook **6242**

cafeteria manager **0631**

cafeteria supervisor – food services **6212**

cage maker – wire products manufacturing **9516**

cage tender – underground mining **8411**

caisson compressor operator **7351**

cake baker – retail trade **6252**

cake decorator – retail trade **6252**

cake icer **6252**

cake press operator – plastic manufacturing **9422**

cake wrapper **9617**

calciner – mineral products processing **9411**

calculation clerk – financial sector **1434**

calculus teacher – high school **4141**

caleche driver **6441**

caleche operator **6441**

calendar operator – pulp and paper **9433**

calender feeder – plastic and rubber manufacturing **9615**

calender helper – textiles **9616**

calender let-off operator – plastic manufacturing **9422**

calender let-off operator – rubber manufacturing **9423**

calender machine operator – rubber manufacturing **9423**

calender machine tender – textiles **9443**

calender man/woman – pulp and paper **9433**

calender operator, multi-roll – plastic manufacturing **9422**

calender operator – plastic manufacturing **9422**

calender operator – rubber manufacturing **9423**

calender warmer – rubber manufacturing **9423**

calender wind-up tender – plastic manufacturing **9422**

calender wind-up tender – rubber manufacturing **9423**

calendering foreman/woman – rubber and plastic manufacturing **9214**

calendering machine tender – plastic manufacturing **9422**

calendering machine tender – rubber manufacturing **9423**

calf skinner – meat packing **9462**

calibration tester **2241**

calibrator, electrical controls **9484**

calibrator, scientific instrument **7383**

calibrator, torque wrench **7445**

calibrator, wire wound resistors **9483**

calisthenics instructor **5254**

calligrapher **5241**

camera assembler **9498**

camera assembly inspector **9498**

camera crane operator **5227**

camera equipment salesperson **6421**

camera operator, colour separation –
  printing **9472**
camera operator, graphic arts **9472**
camera operator, motion picture **5222**
camera operator, photogravure **9472**
camera operator – printing **9472**
camera operator, video **5222**
camera repairer **7445**
camera repairman/woman **7445**
camera salesperson **6421**
camera store manager **0621**
camming machine operator **9511**
camp co-ordinator **4167**
camp cook **6242**
camp cook helper **6642**
camp counsellor **5254**
camp director **4167**
camp ground supervisor **6216**
camp leader **5254**
camp lunchman/woman **6641**
camp manager **0632**
camp waiter/waitress **6453**
campaign consultant **5124**
campaign manager **0611**
campground attendant **6671**
campground cleaner **6661**
campground manager **0632**
campground operator **0632**
campground worker **6671**
campsite labourer **6661**
campus maintenance manager **0722**
can doffer – textiles **9616**
can filler – fish processing **9463**
can filling machine operator – fish
  processing **9463**
can filling machine operator – food and
  beverage processing **9461**
can forming machine operator **9516**
can inspector – food and beverage
  processing **9465**
can turner **9617**
Canada lands surveyor **2154**
Canadian forces chaplain – military **4154**
Canadian residential appraiser (CRA) **1235**
Canadian Security Intelligence Service
  (CSIS) investigation officer **6261**
canal equipment mechanic **7311**
canal lock operator **7435**
canal lock tender **7435**
canal lockman/woman **7435**
canal operator **7435**
canal superintendent **0721**
cancer research technician **3212**
candied fruit processor **9461**
candle maker, hand **5244**
candle making foreman/woman **9227**
candle wrapping machine tender **9619**
candy cutting machine tender **9461**

candy dipper, hand – food and beverage
  processing **9617**
candy maker **9461**
candy maker helper **9617**
candy making machine tender **9461**
candy packer **9617**
candy puller and roller **9461**
candy rolling machine operator **9461**
candy sales clerk **6421**
caner, custom furniture **5244**
canine team member – police **6261**
canned and bottled foods inspector **9465**
canned goods cook **9461**
canned milk sterilizer **9461**
cannery manager **0911**
cannery worker – food and beverage
  processing **9617**
canoe assembler **9491**
canoe builder **5244**
canoe camp operator **0632**
canoe canvasser **9491**
canoe repairer **5244**
canoeing guide **6442**
cant loader – wood processing **9614**
canteen driver **7414**
canteen manager **0631**
canteen operator **0631**
canteen service district manager **0631**
canteen supervisor **6212**
cantilever crane operator **7371**
cantor **4217**
canvas canoe waterproofer **9491**
canvas cover repairer **7445**
canvas cutter – fabric products
  manufacturing **9452**
canvas goods assembler **9498**
canvas goods inspector **9454**
canvas goods pattern designer and
  patternmaker **5245**
canvas goods sewing machine operator **9451**
canvas layer-out – textile products **5245**
canvas patternmaker **5245**
canvas products manufacturing
  foreman/woman **9225**
canvas products sales representative **6411**
canvasser – retail **6623**
capacitor assembler **9483**
capacitor inspector **9483**
capacitor treating tank operator **9483**
capon grader, food and beverage
  processing **9465**
caponizing service contractor **8252**
capping machine tender, dry cell –
  electrical equipment manufacturing **9487**
capsule filler – chemical processing **9421**
capsule machine operator – chemical
  processing **9421**
captain, factory freezer trawler **8261**

captain, ferryboat **2273**
captain, fire **6262**
captain, fishing vessel **8261**
captain – mining **8221**
captain, offshore fishing vessel **8261**
captain, passenger ship **2273**
captain, self-propelled drilling rig **2273**
captain waiter/waitress **6453**
captain waiter/waitress, formal service **6453**
captain – water transport **2273**
car assembler **9482**
car care worker **6662**
car checker, railway **7622**
car controller, railway **7431**
car dealer **0621**
car dealership manager **0621**
car dispatcher, coal mine **1475**
car distributor, railway **7431**
car examiner – motor vehicle
    manufacturing **9482**
car greaser, railway **7431**
car hop, drive-in restaurant **6453**
car inspector – motor vehicle
    manufacturing **9482**
car inspector, railway **7314**
car jockey **6683**
car leasing representative **6421**
car letterer, railway **9496**
car loader **7452**
car lot attendant **6683**
car lubricator, railway **7431**
car mechanic **7321**
car oiler, railway **7431**
car painter and letterer, railway **9496**
car painter – manufacturing **9496**
car park cashier **6611**
car rental agent **6421**
car rental servicer **7443**
car repairer apprentice, railway **7314**
car repairer helper, railway **7612**
car repairer, railway **7314**
car repossessor **6461**
car retarder operator, railway **7431**
car salesperson **6421**
car scrubber **6662**
car seat assembler **9498**
car servicer **6621**
car shunter, railway **7431**
car stacker – wood processing **9614**
car stenciller, railway **9496**
car storage attendant **6683**
car unloader **7452**
car varnisher, railway **9496**
car wash attendant **6662**
car wash manager **0651**
car wash supervisor **6215**
car washer **6662**
caramel equipment operator **9461**

carbide press tender **9516**
carbide tool maker **7232**
carbide tool worker **9516**
carbon black furnace operator **9232**
carbon black pelletizer **9421**
carbon brush assembler **9485**
carbon brush inspector **9484**
carbon brush maker **9485**
carbon coater machine operator **9435**
carbon dioxide truck operator – oil field
    services **8412**
carbon press operator **9411**
carbon products inspector **9484**
carbon rod inserter, machine **9619**
carbonation equipment operator – food
    and beverage processing **9461**
carbonator – food and beverage
    processing **9461**
carbonizer tender – textiles **9443**
carburetor assembler **9486**
carburetor assembly inspector **9486**
carcass splitter – meat packing **9462**
carcass washer – food and beverage
    processing **9617**
carcass weigher – food and beverage
    processing **9617**
card cutter – textiles **9442**
card filer **1413**
card fixer – textile manufacturing **7317**
card grinder – textile manufacturing **7317**
card lacer – textiles **9442**
card operator – textiles **9441**
card punch operator **1422**
card reader **6484**
card room supervisor – textiles **9216**
card setter – textile manufacturing **7317**
card shop clerk **6421**
card sorter **1422**
card stripper – textiles **9441**
card tape converter operator **1422**
card tender – textiles **9441**
cardboard lining machine tender – paper
    converting **9435**
carder helper – textiles **9619**
carder – textiles **9441**
cardiac sonographer **3216**
cardiac stress technologist **3217**
cardinal **4154**
carding machine cleaner – textiles **9616**
carding machine fixer – textile
    manufacturing **7317**
carding machine tender – textiles **9441**
cardiologist **3111**
cardiology nurse technician **3152**
cardiology supervisor **3217**
cardiology technician **3217**
cardiology technologist **3217**
cardiology technologist – military **3217**

cardiopulmonary technician **3214**
cardiothoracic surgeon **3111**
cardiovascular and thoracic surgeon **3111**
cardiovascular perfusion supervisor **3214**
cardiovascular perfusion technologist **3214**
cardiovascular perfusionist **3214**
cardiovascular surgeon **3111**
cardiovascular technologist **3217**
career counsellor **4213**
caregiver, babysitting **6474**
caretaker, building **6663**
caretaker, park **8256**
cargo agent, airline **6433**
cargo agent (except airline) **6434**
cargo agent, marine **6434**
cargo agent, ship **6434**
cargo attendant, air transport **7437**
cargo broker **1236**
cargo checker **7452**
cargo handler, air transport **7437**
cargo handling supervisor **7217**
cargo loader, air transport **7437**
cargo location clerk **1471**
cargo surveyor **2262**
carillonneur **5133**
carman/woman helper **7612**
carman/woman, railway **7314**
carnalite flux maker **9611**
carpenter **7271**
carpenter apprentice **7271**
carpenter, building additions **7271**
carpenter/contractor **7215**
carpenter foreman/woman **7215**
carpenter helper **7611**
carpenter inspector **2264**
carpenter joiner **7271**
carpenter lead hand **7271**
carpenter, maintenance **7271**
carpenter, manufactured homes **7271**
carpenter, prefabricated structure **7271**
carpenter, railway rolling stock **7271**
carpenter, renovation **7271**
carpenter, rough **7271**
carpenter's assistant **7611**
carpenter, stage **7271**
carpenter, studio **7271**
carpenter supervisor **7215**
carpentry contractor **7215**
carpentry repairman/woman **7271**
carpentry supervisor **7215**
carpet binder **9451**
carpet cleaner **6662**
carpet cleaning service manager **0651**
carpet cleaning supervisor **6215**
carpet drying machine tender **9443**
carpet inspector **9444**
carpet inspector supervisor **9216**
carpet installer **7295**

carpet layer **7295**
carpet layer helper **7611**
carpet loom fixer – textile
    manufacturing **7317**
carpet mechanics helper **7611**
carpet sewer **9451**
carpet tape machine tender **9517**
carpet weaver **9442**
carrier driver **7452**
cartage and storage salesperson **6411**
cartage company manager **0713**
cartographer **2255**
cartographic compiler **2255**
cartographic draftsman/woman **2255**
cartographic engineer **2131**
cartographic technician **2255**
cartographic technologist **2255**
carton assembler – paper converting **9435**
carton bander **9617**
carton filler **9619**
carton forming machine feeder **9614**
carton forming machine operator **9435**
carton forming machine repairer **7311**
carton labeller **9619**
carton marker **9619**
carton package stapler **9617**
carton packaging machine tender **9617**
carton packaging machine tender,
    tobacco **9617**
carton stamper **9619**
carton wrapper **9619**
cartoon background artist **5223**
cartoon embroidery enlarger **5245**
cartoonist **5241**
cartridge assembler **9498**
cartridge filler operator **9517**
cartridge flux maker **9611**
cartridge inspector **9498**
cartridge loader machine operator **9517**
carver **5244**
carver, machine – woodworking **9513**
carver, native art **5244**
carver, totem pole **5244**
cascade blender – tobacco processing **9464**
case aide, social services **4212**
case filler **9619**
case fitter – furniture manufacturing **9492**
case hardener – primary metal
    processing **9411**
case maker, hand **5244**
case maker, leather **9498**
case maker, wood **9493**
case making machine tender **9473**
case management consultant **4152**
case management social worker **4152**
case manager – corrections **4155**
case packer **9619**
case review officer – immigration **1228**

case stacker – food and beverage
    processing **9617**
case work consultant **4152**
case worker **4152**
caser – tobacco processing **9617**
casework supervisor **4152**
cash coupon clerk **1431**
cash receipts supervisor **1212**
cash register repairer **7445**
cash register servicer **7445**
cashier **6611**
cashier supervisor **6211**
cashier/wrapper **6611**
casing cooker – tobacco processing **9464**
casing grader – food and beverage
    processing **9465**
casing line set-up operator **9473**
casing machine operator – food and
    beverage processing **9461**
casing machine operator – tobacco
    processing **9464**
casing machine tender – tobacco
    processing **9464**
casing mixer – tobacco processing **9464**
casing salter – food and beverage
    processing **9617**
casing shirrer – food and beverage
    processing **9617**
casing stripper – food and beverage
    processing **9617**
cask maker **9513**
casket assembler, metal **9492**
casket assembler, wood **9492**
casket inspector **9493**
casket inspector, wood **9493**
casket liner **9619**
casket maker, wood **9492**
casket trimmer **9619**
casket upholsterer **7341**
cassette recorder technician **2242**
cast room technician **3414**
caster and moulder – dental ceramics **3412**
caster, brick and tile – clay products **9414**
caster – concrete products **9414**
caster jewellery – foundry **9412**
caster, metal – foundry **9412**
caster – plastics **9422**
casting agent **5226**
casting cleaner **9611**
casting director **5226**
casting helper **9611**
casting house labourer **9611**
casting inspector – foundry **9415**
casting machine operator – foundry **9412**
casting machine operator – primary
    metal processing **9411**

casting operations supervisor – primary
    metal and mineral products
    processing **9211**
casting operator – foundry **9412**
casting recording clerk **1473**
casting room foreman/woman **9211**
casting room operator – plastic
    manufacturing **9422**
casting tester – primary metal and
    mineral products processing **9415**
casting trimmer **9611**
casual worker – public works **7621**
casualty actuary **2161**
casualty insurance adjuster **1233**
casualty underwriter **1234**
cat breeder **8251**
cat operator **7421**
cat skinner **7421**
catalogue agent – retail **6421**
catalogue compiler **1452**
catalogue illustrator **5241**
cataloguer – library **5111**
cataloguer – museum **5212**
catalyst operator, gasoline **9232**
caterer cook **6242**
caterer helper **6642**
caterer waiter/waitress **6453**
catering service manager **0631**
catering supervisor **6212**
caterpillar operator **7421**
caterpillar servicer **7443**
caterpillar tractor repairer **7312**
cathode coater – electronics
    manufacturing **9483**
cathode loader **9611**
cathode ray tube processing equipment
    setter **9483**
catsup maker **9461**
cattle buyer **6233**
cattle dealer **0611**
cattle herdsperson **8253**
cattle killer **9462**
cattle ranch foreman/woman **8253**
cattle ranch labourer **8431**
cattle ranch worker **8431**
cattle rancher **8251**
cattle relief **8253**
CATV construction technician –
    telecommunications **7245**
CATV technician apprentice – cable
    television **7247**
CATV technician – cable television **7247**
caulker – construction **7611**
caustic cell operator **9232**
caustic operator **9432**
CCP **3214**
cedar shingler **7291**
CÉGEP instructor **4131**

CÉGEP teacher **4131**
ceiling installer **7248**
cell biologist **2121**
cell maintainer – primary metal and mineral products processing **9411**
cell operations foreman/woman – primary metal and mineral products processing **9211**
cell operator **9232**
cell operator helper – chemical processing **9613**
cell room operator, chlor-alkali plant **9232**
cell tester – primary metal processing **9415**
cellarman/woman, winery – food and beverage processing **9461**
cellarmaster **9213**
cellist **5133**
cello maker **5244**
cellophane bag machine operator – plastic manufacturing **9422**
cellophane bag maker – plastic manufacturing **9422**
cellophaner – tobacco products **9617**
cellular phone installer **7246**
cellular physiologist **2121**
cellular telephone installer **7246**
cellular telephone technician **7246**
cellulose film caster **9421**
cellulose film rewinder **9421**
cement applicator – shoe manufacturing **9619**
cement block maker – concrete products **9414**
cement block moulder – concrete products **9414**
cement finisher **7282**
cement finisher apprentice **7282**
cement finisher foreman/woman **7219**
cement gun nozzle operator **7611**
cement gun operator **7611**
cement inspector **2264**
cement loader and sacker **7452**
cement mason **7282**
cement mason, highways and streets **7282**
cement mason, maintenance **7282**
cement miller **9411**
cement mixer driver **7411**
cement mixer – mineral and metal processing **9411**
cement mixer operator – construction **7611**
cement pipe machine operator – concrete products **9414**
cement plant inspector **9415**
cement processing foreman/woman **9211**
cement processing supervisor **9211**
cement production pumpman/woman **9411**
cement pump operator **7611**
cement truck driver – construction **7411**
cement truck driver – oil field services **8412**
cement truck loader **7452**

cementation equipment operator **9411**
cementer, hand – plastic and rubber manufacturing **9615**
cementer, hand – shoe manufacturing **9619**
cementer helper, oil well **8615**
cementer, knife parts **9619**
cementer machine operator – rubber manufacturing **9423**
cementer – oil field services **8412**
cementer operator – rubber manufacturing **9423**
cementer, plastics **9495**
cementer, rubber tire and tube **9423**
cementer, tire repair – rubber manufacturing **9615**
cementing equipment operator – oil field services **8412**
cemetery foreman/woman **8256**
cemetery labourer **8612**
cemetery manager **0651**
cemetery worker **8612**
census clerk **1454**
census commissioner **0012**
census enumerator **1454**
census worker **1454**
central air conditioning installer **7313**
central air conditioning mechanic **7313**
central air conditioning servicer **7313**
central control caster – primary metal processing **9231**
central control operator – cement manufacturing **9231**
central control room operator – electric power systems **7352**
central control room operator – primary metal and mineral products processing **9231**
central office equipment inspector – telecommunications **7246**
central office equipment installer – telecommunications **7246**
central office equipment maintainer – telecommunications **7246**
central office equipment repairer – telecommunications **7246**
central office frame servicer – telecommunications **7246**
central office power room operator – electric power systems **7352**
central office technician – telecommunications **7246**
central operator – telephone systems **1424**
central service room worker **6631**
central supply aide **6631**
central supply clerk **1472**
central supply room supervisor – hospital **6631**

central supply room technician –
    hospital **6631**
centralized traffic controller – railway **2275**
centri-cleaner tender – pulp and paper **9432**
centrifugal casting machine operator **9412**
centrifugal casting machine tender –
    foundry **9412**
centrifugal extractor – textiles **9443**
centrifugal tender – food and beverage
    processing **9461**
centrifuge operator – textiles **9443**
centrifuge tender – chemical processing **9421**
centrifuge tender – fish processing **9463**
centrifuge tender – meat packing **9617**
CEO – financial, communications and
    other business services **0013**
CEO – goods production, utilities,
    transportation and construction **0016**
CEO – health, education, social and
    community services and membership
    organizations **0014**
CEO – trade, broadcasting and other
    services n.e.c. **0015**
ceramic and enamel refinisher **9496**
ceramic artist **5244**
ceramic enameler **9496**
ceramic mouldmaker – foundry **9412**
ceramic sprayer **9496**
ceramic teacher **5244**
ceramic tile installer **7283**
ceramic tile press operator – concrete
    products **9414**
ceramic tilesetter **7283**
ceramics and glass conservator **5112**
ceramics engineer **2142**
ceramist, dental **3223**
cereal baker – food and beverage
    processing **9461**
cereal cleaner **9461**
cereal cleaning equipment operator **9461**
cereal coating operator **9461**
cereal cooker and extruder operator **9461**
cereal maker – food and beverage
    processing **9461**
cereal oven tender **9461**
cerlox binder operator – printing **9473**
certified aircraft technician **7315**
certified aircraft technician, mechanical
    systems **7315**
certified athletic therapist **3144**
certified audiologist **3141**
certified avionics technician **2244**
certified clinical perfusionist **3214**
certified dental assistant **3411**
certified dental technician **3223**
certified general accountant **1111**
certified hearing aid audiologist **3141**
certified intra-oral dental assistant **3411**

certified iridologist **6484**
certified load planner, airline **6433**
certified management accountant **1111**
certified nursing assistant **3233**
certified orthotist **3219**
certified prosthetist **3219**
certified prosthetist/orthotist **3219**
certified reflexologist **3232**
certified rolfer **3232**
certified rolfing movement teacher **3232**
cesspool cleaner **6662**
CFO – financial, communications and
    other business services **0013**
CFO – goods production, utilities,
    transportation and construction **0016**
CFO – health, education, social and
    community services and membership
    organizations **0014**
CFO – trade, broadcasting and other
    services n.e.c. **0015**
CGA **1111**
chain builder – textiles **9442**
chain conveyor tender – sawmill **9614**
chain inspector **9516**
chain link fence erector **7441**
chain link fence machine operator **9516**
chain maker, hand **9498**
chain making machine operator **9516**
chain making machine tender **9516**
chain testing machine tender **9516**
chainer – textiles **9616**
chainman/woman, pile driving **7611**
chainman/woman, surveying **7612**
chainman/woman – textiles **9442**
chainman/woman – wood processing **9614**
chainsaw operator – logging **8421**
chair assembler **9492**
chair caner – furniture manufacturing **9492**
chair inspector – furniture
    manufacturing **9492**
chair leveler – woodworking **9513**
chair, metropolitan council **0011**
chair, regional municipality **0011**
chair sander **9619**
chair seat planer tender **9513**
chair trimmer **9619**
chair upholsterer **7341**
chairman/woman – financial,
    communications and other business
    services **0013**
chairman/woman – goods production,
    utilities, transportation and
    construction **0016**
chairman/woman – government services **0012**
chairman/woman – health, education,
    social and community services and
membership organizations **0014**

chairman/woman – trade, broadcasting and other services n.e.c. **0015**

chairman/woman – university department **4121**

chairperson – arts and culture association **0014**

chairperson – education association **0014**

chairperson – financial, communications and other business services **0013**

chairperson – food sciences department **4121**

chairperson – goods production, utilities, transportation and construction **0016**

chairperson – government services **0012**

chairperson – health, education, social and community services and membership organizations **0014**

chairperson – physics department **4121**

chairperson – scientific association **0014**

chairperson – trade, broadcasting and other services n.e.c. **0015**

chairperson – university department **4121**

chalk moulder – mineral products processing **9611**

chambermaid **6661**

chamfering machine tender **9516**

chancellor – education **0014**

chancellor – religion **4154**

chandelier maker **9516**

channel operator – foundry **9412**

channeler – footwear manufacturing **9517**

chaplain **4154**

chaplain – military **4154**

char filter tender – food and beverage processing **9461**

char kiln tender – food and beverage processing **9461**

char kiln tender helper – food and beverage processing **9617**

charcoal artist **5136**

charcoal burner **9421**

charge account audit clerk **1431**

charge account clerk **1431**

charge hand, machine fitters **7316**

charge hand, machine shop **7231**

charge operator – telephone systems **1424**

charge technologist – autopsy services **3211**

charge technologist – electrocardiography **3217**

charge weigher – primary metal processing **9611**

charger – electrical equipment manufacturing **9487**

charger, glass **9413**

charger helper **9611**

charging car operator **9411**

charging machine operator **9411**

charging room operator – electrical equipment manufacturing **9487**

charitable organization executive director **0014**

charm course instructor **4216**

chart clerk **1454**

chart plotter **2213**

charter boat operator **7436**

charter bus driver **7412**

charter pilot **2271**

chartered accountant **1111**

chartered financial analyst **1112**

chartered herbalist **3232**

chartered quantity surveyor **2234**

chartered ship broker **1236**

charworker **6661**

chaser, jewellery **7344**

chaser – logging **8421**

chassis assembler – electronics manufacturing **9483**

chassis assembler – motor vehicle manufacturing **9482**

chassis assembly inspector – motor vehicle manufacturing **9482**

chassis inspector – motor vehicle manufacturing **9482**

chassis installer – electronics manufacturing **9483**

chauffeur **7413**

chauffeur, private household **7413**

check-in agent (except airline) **6434**

check pilot **2271**

check weigher, mine **8614**

checker, attendance **6671**

checker, drafting **2253**

checker, electrical appliance assembly **9484**

checker/inspector, golf ball – rubber manufacturing **9615**

checker – laundry and dry cleaning **6681**

checkerer, small arms **9513**

checkerman/woman, fishing vessel **8441**

checkroom attendant **6683**

cheese blender – food and beverage processing **9461**

cheese cooker **9461**

cheese cutter **9617**

cheese factory worker **9617**

cheese grader **9465**

cheese maker **9461**

cheese maker helper **9617**

chef **6241**

chef de cuisine **6241**

chef de partie **6241**

chef, saucier **6241**

chemical analyst **2211**

chemical applicator, lawn care **8612**

chemical engineer **2134**

chemical engineer, design and development **2134**
chemical engineer, production **2134**
chemical engineer, research **2134**
chemical engineering professor – university **4121**
chemical engineering technician **2211**
chemical engineering technologist **2211**
chemical laboratory analyst **2211**
chemical laboratory technician **2211**
chemical mixer – photographic processing **9474**
chemical oceanographer **2113**
chemical operator – chemical processing **9421**
chemical operator – pulp and paper **9432**
chemical physicist **2111**
chemical plant labourer **9613**
chemical plant machine operator **9421**
chemical plant service mechanic **7311**
chemical preparation operator – pulp and paper **9432**
chemical process analyst **2211**
chemical process batching operator **9232**
chemical process engineer **2134**
chemical process equipment mechanic **7311**
chemical process equipment mechanic helper **7612**
chemical process operator **9232**
chemical process operator, batching **9232**
chemical process technologist **2211**
chemical process unit operator **9232**
chemical processing machine builder **7316**
chemical processing supervisor **9212**
chemical research division manager **0212**
chemical research engineer **2134**
chemical research technician **2211**
chemical research technologist **2211**
chemical roaster **9232**
chemical sales representative **6221**
chemical services operator – oil field services **8412**
chemical spectroscopist **2112**
chemical technician **2211**
chemical technician, heavy water plant and nuclear generating station **2211**
chemical technologist **2211**
chemical technology instructor – vocational institute **4131**
chemical technology teacher – vocational institute **4131**
chemical truck operator – oil field services **8412**
chemical unit foreman/woman **9212**
chemist **2112**
chemistry professor – university **4121**
chemistry researcher **2112**
chemistry statistician **2161**

chemistry teacher – high school **4141**
chenille tender – textiles **9443**
cheque control clerk **1431**
chewing gum batch mixer **9617**
chick sexer **8431**
chicken farmer **8251**
chicken plucker **9462**
chicken take out attendant **6641**
chicle centrifuge operator – food and beverage processing **9461**
chief, accounting and financial control **0111**
chief administrative officer – government services **0012**
chief, administrative services **0114**
chief air traffic controller **2272**
chief ambulance attendant **3234**
chief architect **2151**
chief – archives **0511**
chief archivist **5113**
chief, bilateral relations **0414**
chief, biological research department **0212**
chief buyer **6233**
chief canvasser – retail **6211**
chief chemical engineer **2134**
chief civil engineer **2131**
chief, claims and benefit control – unemployment insurance **0411**
chief, classification and compensation **0112**
chief cruiser **2223**
chief customer supervisor – gas service **7213**
chief detective – police **0641**
chief diagnostic medical sonographer **3216**
chief dietitian **0311**
chief draftsman/woman **2253**
chief, economic analysis – government services **0412**
chief, economic policy analysis – government services **0412**
chief electoral officer **0012**
chief electrical engineer **2133**
chief electrician **7212**
chief electrician, drilling rig **7212**
chief electroencephalographic technologist **3218**
chief electromyography technologist **3218**
chief electronic engineer **2133**
chief EMG technologist **3218**
chief, employment equity **0112**
chief engineer, coast guard vessel **2274**
chief engineer, drilling and recovery **2145**
chief engineer, electric power **2133**
chief engineer, fishing vessel **2274**
chief engineer – radio & television broadcasting **2133**
chief engineer, self propelled drilling rig **2274**
chief engineer – water transport **2274**

chief, enquiries and services –
  unemployment insurance **0411**
chief estimator – construction **2234**
chief executive – financial,
  communications and other business
  services **0013**
chief executive – goods production,
  utilities, transportation and
  construction **0016**
chief executive officer, deputy –
  financial, communications and other
  business services **0013**
chief executive officer, deputy – goods
  production, utilities, transportation
  and construction **0016**
chief executive officer, deputy – health,
  education, social and community
  services and membership
  organizations **0014**
chief executive officer, deputy – trade,
  broadcasting and other services
  n.e.c. **0015**
chief executive officer – financial,
  communications and other business
  services **0013**
chief executive officer – goods
  production, utilities, transportation
  and construction **0016**
chief executive officer – health,
  education, social and community
  services and membership
  organizations **0014**
chief executive officer – manufacturing
  company **0016**
chief executive officer – telephone
  company **0013**
chief executive officer – trade,
  broadcasting and other services
  n.e.c. **0015**
chief executive officer – vacation tour
  operation **0015**
chief executive – trade, business and
  other services n.e.c. **0015**
chief, federal-provincial relations **0414**
chief, financial and administrative
  services **0114**
chief financial officer – advertising
  agency **0013**
chief financial officer (CFO) –
  educational institution **0014**
chief financial officer – financial,
  communications and other business
  services **0013**
chief financial officer – goods
  production, utilities, transportation
  and construction **0016**
chief financial officer – health,
  education, social and community

services and membership
  organizations **0014**
chief financial officer – professional
  sports club **0015**
chief financial officer – trade,
  broadcasting and other services
  n.e.c. **0015**
chief financial officer – urban transit
  system **0016**
chief, fire department **0642**
chief flying instructor **2271**
chief, forest resource analysis –
  government services **0412**
chief host/hostess **6451**
chief, immigration appeals and litigation
  – government services **0411**
chief inspector – police **0641**
chief, intergovernmental affairs **0414**
chief, international relations –
  government **0414**
chief justice **4111**
chief justice, associate **4111**
chief librarian **0511**
chief – library **0511**
chief lighting technician **5226**
chief maintenance engineer – aircraft
  mechanical systems **7216**
chief, maintenance support services **0722**
chief, management services division **0114**
chief marine engineer, factory freezer
  trawler **2274**
chief marine engineer – water transport **2274**
chief mechanical engineer **2132**
chief, native band **0011**
chief of anaesthesia **0311**
chief of audiology and speech language
  pathology **0311**
chief of cardiology **0311**
chief of dermatology **0311**
chief of diagnostic imaging **0311**
chief of diagnostic radiology **0311**
chief of emergency medicine **0311**
chief of endocrinology **0311**
chief of gastroenterology **0311**
chief of haematology **0311**
chief of infectious diseases **0311**
chief of laboratory medicine **0311**
chief of medicine **0311**
chief of nephrology **0311**
chief of neurology **0311**
chief of obstetrics/gynaecology **0311**
chief of occupational therapy **0311**
chief of ophthalmology **0311**
chief of pathology **0311**
chief of pediatrics **0311**
chief of pharmacy **0311**
chief of physiotherapy **0311**
chief of protocol **0414**

chief of psychiatry **0311**
chief of psychology **0311**
chief of radiation oncology **0311**
chief of respirology **0311**
chief of rheumatology **0311**
chief of staff – hospital **0311**
chief of surgery **0311**
chief of urology **0311**
chief, office of health promotion –
    government services **0411**
chief officer, coast guard vessel **2273**
chief officer, ship **2273**
chief officer, ship operations **2273**
chief, official languages **0112**
chief operating officer – engineering
    firm **0013**
chief operating officer – financial,
    communications and other business
    services **0013**
chief operating officer – goods
    production, utilities, transportation
    and construction **0016**
chief operating officer – health,
    education, social and community
    services and membership
    organizations **0014**
chief operating officer – trade,
    broadcasting and other services
    n.e.c. **0015**
chief operator, area dispatch – electric
    power systems **7352**
chief operator, batching process **9232**
chief operator – chemical processing **9232**
chief operator, continuous process **9232**
chief operator, synthesis **9232**
chief orthoptist **3123**
chief pathologists' assistant **3211**
chief perfusionist **3214**
chief petroleum engineer **2145**
chief photographer **5221**
chief pilot **2271**
chief pilot, helicopter **2271**
chief process engineer **2134**
chief, purchasing **0113**
chief, railway police **0641**
chief, regional pay centre –
    unemployment insurance **0411**
chief respiratory technologist **3214**
chief, revenue accounting and controls
    section **0111**
chief scaler **2223**
chief security guard **6651**
chief sheriff **6461**
chief, social development program –
    government services **0411**
chief, staff relations **0112**
chief, staff training and development **0112**
chief, staffing **0112**

chief stage electrician **5226**
chief stationary engineer **9212**
chief statistician – government services **0012**
chief steward, ship **6432**
chief substation operator **9212**
chief superintendent, police **0641**
chief superintendent, schools **0313**
chief technician, chemical processing **9232**
chief technologist, nuclear medicine **3215**
chief technologist, radiation therapy **3215**
chief technologist, radiography **3215**
chief telephone operator **1211**
chief train dispatcher **2275**
chief, training **0112**
chief wine steward **6453**
child and family counsellor **4153**
child care attendant – elementary school **6472**
child care programs planning officer **4164**
child care teacher – community college **4131**
child care worker assistant **6473**
child care worker, day-care **4214**
child care worker (except day-care) **4212**
child consultant **4153**
child health care programs planning
    officer **4165**
child psychologist **4151**
child specialist **3111**
child welfare policy analyst **4164**
child welfare services administrator **0314**
child welfare social worker **4152**
child welfare worker **4212**
children's aid investigator **4152**
children's aid society director **0314**
children's counsellor **4153**
children's nurse, private household **6474**
children's services librarian **5111**
children's wear salesperson **6421**
chiller operator – chemical processing **9421**
chiller tender – chemical processing **9421**
chimney cleaner **6662**
chimney sweep **6662**
china and crystal salesperson **6421**
china packer – clay products **9611**
chinese medical practitioner **3232**
chinese medicine, doctor of **3232**
chip bin attendant – wood processing **9614**
chip dump operator – wood processing **9614**
chip mixing machine tender – wood
    processing **9434**
chip screen tender – wood processing **9434**
chip silo attendant – wood processing **9614**
chip spreader labourer **7611**
chipper, flat glass **9413**
chipper/grinder – metal fabrication **9612**
chipper machine knife setter – pulp and
    paper **9614**
chipper operator – wood processing **9434**
chipper, pottery and porcelain **9414**

chipping machine operator – logging **8241**
chiropodist **3123**
chiropractic aide **6631**
chiropractic doctor **3122**
chiropractic health assistant **6631**
chiropractor **3122**
chisel grinder – metal products **9612**
chlorination plant operator **9232**
chlorine plant foreman/woman **9212**
chlorine plant operator **9232**
chocolate coater – food and beverage
    processing **9461**
chocolate moulder, machine **9461**
chocolate packer, hand **9617**
chocolate processing helper **9617**
chocolate refiner **9461**
chocolate temperer **9461**
choir director **5132**
choir leader **5132**
choirmaster **5132**
choke setter – logging **8616**
choke winder – electronics
    manufacturing **9483**
chokerman/woman – logging **8616**
choral director **5132**
chore hand – agriculture **8431**
choreographer **5131**
chorister **5133**
chorus dancer **5134**
christian sciences worker **4217**
christmas tree farm operator **8254**
christmas tree shearer **8432**
chromium plater operator **9497**
chub sausage machine tender **9461**
chucking and boring machine operator –
    woodworking **9513**
chucking machine operator –
    woodworking **9513**
chucking machine set-up operator **9511**
chuckwagon driver **5251**
church caretaker **6663**
church organist **5133**
church secretary **1241**
church worker **4217**
churn drill operator – water well **7373**
chute blaster – underground mining **8231**
chute loader – underground mining **8411**
chute operator – underground mining **8411**
cider maker **9461**
cigar bander **9617**
cigar brander **9617**
cigar bunch maker **9464**
cigar buncher **9464**
cigar drier **9464**
cigar filler, mixer and shredder **9464**
cigar inspector **9465**
cigar maker, hand **9464**
cigar maker, machine **9464**

cigar moulder, hand **9464**
cigar roller, hand **9464**
cigar wrapper **9617**
cigar wrapping machine tender **9617**
cigarette filter machine tender **9464**
cigarette holder maker **9498**
cigarette inspector **9465**
cigarette inspector foreman/woman **9213**
cigarette machine drum repairer **7445**
cigarette machine tender **9464**
cigarette maker **9464**
cigarette packer **9617**
cigarette packing machine tender **9617**
cigarette roller **9464**
cigarette stamper **9464**
cigarette tester **9465**
cigarette tipper **9464**
cigarette vendor **6623**
cinder block machine operator –
    concrete products **9414**
cinder block mason **7281**
cinder crane operator **7371**
cinder snapper **9611**
cinematographer **5131**
cipher expert **4161**
cipher expert – military **4161**
circuit board assembler **9483**
circuit breaker assembler **9484**
circuit breaker fitter – industrial
    electrical equipment **9485**
circuit breaker mechanic **7333**
circuit design engineer **2133**
circuit designer – railway **2241**
circular distributor **1463**
circular knitter **9442**
circular saw operator – concrete, clay
    and stone products **9414**
circular saw operator – sawmill **9431**
circular saw operator – woodworking **9513**
circular sawyer – stone products **9414**
circulation assistant – library **5211**
circulation clerk – library **1451**
circulation clerk, newspaper **1452**
circulation manager **0611**
circus performer **5232**
citizenship court judge **1227**
citizenship officer **4164**
city administrator **0012**
city alderman **0011**
city attorney **4112**
city clerk **0012**
city collector – taxation **1228**
city controller **0011**
city councillor **0011**
city councilman/woman **0011**
city editor **5122**
city manager **0012**
city medical officer of health **0411**

city planner 2153
city solicitor 4112
city superintendent 0012
city supervisor 0012
city surveyor 2154
civil aviation medical officer 3112
civil draftsman/woman 2253
civil draftsperson 2253
civil emergency measures co-ordinator 1221
civil engineer 2131
civil engineering design technologist 2231
civil engineering division manager 0211
civil engineering professor – university 4121
civil engineering soil technologist 2231
civil engineering technician 2231
civil engineering technologist 2231
civil inspection engineer 2131
civil lawyer 4112
civil technician 2231
cladder 7441
cladding assembler – primary metal processing 9611
claim adjuster supervisor 1212
claim approver – insurance 1233
claim attorney 4112
claim clerk – insurance 1434
claim clerk, lost or damaged goods 1453
claim examiner – insurance 1233
claim investigator – insurance 1233
claims accountant 1111
claims adjudicator – unemployment insurance 1228
claims adjuster – insurance 1233
claims collector 1435
claims representative – insurance 1233
clam digger 8613
clam dredge operator 8262
clam fisherman/woman 8262
clam shucker – fish processing 9463
clam shucking machine tender – fish processing 9463
clam steamer – fish processing 9463
clamp carrier 9493
clamp carrier man/woman 9493
clamp remover – wood products 9619
clamper, transformer assembly 9485
clamping machine tender – woodworking 9513
clarifying equipment tender – food and beverage processing 9461
classical dance instructor 5134
classical dancer 5134
classical languages secondary school teacher 4141
classics professor – university 4121
classification clerk, personnel 1442
classification clerk, records 1413
classification counsellor 4155

classification officer, correctional institution 4155
classification officer, human resources 1121
classification policy advisor 1121
classification specialist 1121
classified advertising clerk 1452
classifier helper – primary metal and mineral products processing 9611
classifier – library 5111
classifier operator 9411
classifier, records 1413
clay insulator builder – clay products 9414
clay pipe bender 9414
clay preparation foreman/woman 9211
clay press operator 9414
clay press worker 9611
clay products grader 9415
clay shop foreman/woman 9211
clay slate bed maker 9414
clay slip mixer 9414
clay structure moulder and installer 9414
clay temperer – clay products 9414
clay turner – clay products 9414
clay works moulder – clay products 9414
clayware driller – clay products 9414
clean up crew worker 6661
clean up sander – woodworking 9513
cleaner 6661
cleaner and presser, laundry and dry cleaning 6681
cleaner and repairer, venetian blinds 6662
cleaner, building exterior 6662
cleaner, campground 6661
cleaner, carpet 6662
cleaner, chimney 6662
cleaner, drain-roto 6662
cleaner/drier, grain – food and beverage processing 9461
cleaner, electronic components 9483
cleaner, filter – chemical processing 9613
cleaner, fireplace 6662
cleaner, freight car 6662
cleaner, furnace 6662
cleaner, heavy duty 6663
cleaner, hospital 6661
cleaner, hotel/motel 6661
cleaner, industrial plant 6663
cleaner, laboratory equipment 6662
cleaner, laundry and dry cleaning 6681
cleaner, light duty 6661
cleaner, lodge 6661
cleaner, porcelain enamel 9619
cleaner, rest room 6661
cleaner, room 6661
cleaner, rug 6662
cleaner, septic tank 6662
cleaner, sewer pipe – manual 7621
cleaner, still – chemical processing 9613

cleaner, swimming pool **6662**
cleaner, tank **6662**
cleaner, textile machine **9616**
cleaner, tire – rubber manufacturing **9615**
cleaner, vehicle **6662**
cleaner, ventilation system **6662**
cleaner, window **6662**
cleaning and classifying operator –
    tobacco processing **9464**
cleaning and maintenance supervisor **6215**
cleaning compounds mixer **9421**
cleaning lady **6661**
cleaning machine operator **6681**
cleaning products salesperson,
    door-to-door **6623**
cleaning services general manager **0015**
cleaning services sales representative **6411**
cleaning supervisor **6215**
clearance diver – military **7382**
clearance diving technician – military **6464**
clearing clerk **1431**
clearing saw operator – forestry **8422**
cleat notcher – woodworking **9513**
clemency officer **4155**
clergyman **4154**
clerical assistant **1411**
clerical supervisor **1211**
clerk, aircraft records **1413**
clerk, cable transfer **1473**
clerk, city **0012**
clerk, classification **1413**
clerk, county **0012**
clerk, court **1443**
clerk/crier, court **1443**
clerk, customer service **1453**
clerk – financial sector **1434**
clerk, front desk **6435**
clerk, front office **6435**
clerk, general office **1411**
clerk, hospital records **1413**
clerk, hotel **6435**
clerk, insurance **1434**
clerk, law **4211**
clerk, library **1451**
clerk, mail **1461**
clerk, mail distributing **1461**
clerk, mail room **1461**
clerk, maintenance service **1453**
clerk, meter records **1413**
clerk, municipal **0012**
clerk, night **6435**
clerk of probate **1227**
clerk of proceedings – courts **1227**
clerk of process – courts **1443**
clerk of scales – race track **5253**
clerk of the committee, legislative
    assembly committee **0414**
clerk of the course – harness racing **5253**

clerk of the court **1227**
clerk of the crown and peace – courts **1227**
clerk of the crown – courts **1227**
clerk of the house of commons **0012**
clerk of the legislative assembly **0414**
clerk of the privy council **0012**
clerk of works – construction **2234**
clerk, post office **1461**
clerk, postal **1461**
clerk, rail express **1461**
clerk, records **1413**
clerk, reservations **6435**
clerk, retail sales **6421**
clerk, room **6435**
clerk/stenographer **1411**
clerk, supermarket **6622**
clerk, technical records **1413**
clerk, town **0012**
clerk, township **0012**
clerk, travel information **6431**
clerk/typist **1412**
clerk, village **0012**
client service clerk **1453**
climate data processor **2213**
climate service specialist **2213**
climate service technician **2213**
climatological technician **2213**
climatologist **2114**
climbing crane operator **7371**
climbing tower crane operator **7371**
clinic assistant – medical **6631**
clinic director – medical **0311**
clinic nurse **3152**
clinical assistant **3414**
clinical audiologist **3141**
clinical biomedical engineer **2148**
clinical chemist **2112**
clinical co-ordinator, nuclear medicine **3215**
clinical co-ordinator, physical therapy **3142**
clinical co-ordinator, radiation therapy **3215**
clinical co-ordinator, radiography **3215**
clinical dietitian **3132**
clinical engineer **2148**
clinical hypnotherapist **3232**
clinical immunologist **3111**
clinical immunologist and allergist **3111**
clinical immunology technologist **3211**
clinical instructor, cardiovascular
    perfusion **3214**
clinical instructor, clinical perfusion **3214**
clinical instructor, nuclear medicine **3215**
clinical instructor, radiation therapy **3215**
clinical instructor, radiography **3215**
clinical instructor, respiratory therapy **3214**
clinical lab technologist **3211**
clinical laboratory helper **6631**
clinical medicine, director of **0311**
clinical nurse specialist **3152**

clinical nutritionist **3132**
clinical occupational therapist **3143**
clinical occupational therapy specialist **3143**
clinical orthoptist **3123**
clinical pathologist **3111**
clinical pathologist, speech-language **3141**
clinical perfusion supervisor **3214**
clinical perfusionist **3214**
clinical pharmacist **3131**
clinical pharmacologist **3111**
clinical psychologist **4151**
clinical specialist, physical therapy **3142**
clinician, hearing **3141**
clinician, speech **3141**
clinician, speech and hearing **3141**
clipper operator – wood processing **9434**
clipping marker **1452**
cloakroom attendant **6683**
clock and watch assembler **9498**
clock and watch finisher **9498**
clock and watch inspection
    foreman/woman **9227**
clock assembler **9498**
clock finisher **9498**
clock hairspring calibrator **9498**
clock repairer **7344**
clock repairman/woman **7344**
clock shop clerk **6421**
clock spring assembler **9498**
clock staker **9498**
clocker – race track **5253**
clockmaker **9498**
closed circuit television installer **2242**
closed circuit TV sewer inspector **2264**
closer, sewing **9451**
closer sewing machine operator **9451**
cloth baler – textile **9619**
cloth bleacher **9443**
cloth bleaching range tender **9443**
cloth buffing disk assembler **9619**
cloth carrier **9616**
cloth cutter – fabric products
    manufacturing **9452**
cloth cutter, hand **9619**
cloth cutting machine operator – fabric
    products manufacturing **9452**
cloth doubling machine operator **9443**
cloth drier **9443**
cloth dyeing range tender **9443**
cloth dyer **9443**
cloth examiner **9444**
cloth feeder **9616**
cloth finisher **9443**
cloth finishing range operator **9443**
cloth folder, hand **9616**
cloth framer **9616**
cloth grader **9444**
cloth hauler **9616**

cloth inspector **9444**
cloth layer **9619**
cloth measurer **9444**
cloth measuring machine tender **9444**
cloth mender **9451**
cloth mercerizer operator **9443**
cloth neutralizer **9443**
cloth offbearer **9616**
cloth printer **9443**
cloth printing machine helper **9443**
cloth printing machine tender **9443**
cloth processing range tender **9443**
cloth ribber **9442**
cloth shade maker **9443**
cloth shrinker **9443**
cloth sorter **9444**
cloth steamer **9443**
cloth stretcher and drier **9443**
cloth tester **9444**
cloth turner **9616**
cloth washer – textiles **9443**
cloth weaver **9442**
cloth winder **9616**
clothes dryer assembler, electric **9484**
clothes presser – laundry and dry
    cleaning **6682**
clothing buyer **6233**
clothing cutter – clothing manufacturing **9452**
clothing design teacher – college or
    vocational institute **4131**
clothing designer **5243**
clothing factory manager **0911**
clothing inspector **9454**
clothing ironer – laundry and dry
    cleaning **6682**
clothing manufacturing foreman/woman **9225**
clothing plant labourer **9619**
clothing purchasing manager **0113**
clothing salesperson **6421**
clothing store manager **0621**
clown **5232**
club agent – food service **0631**
club car attendant **6453**
club steward **6453**
clubhouse attendant **6683**
clutch assembler **9486**
clutch assembly inspector – motor
    vehicle **9486**
clutch inspector **9486**
clutch preassembler **9486**
clutch rebuilder **9486**
CMA **1111**
CMD **3232**
CMHC inspector **2264**
CNC lathe operator – metal machining **9511**
CNC machining tool operator **9511**
CNC profile mill operator **9511**
CNC technologist **2233**

CNC woodworking machine tool
    operator **9513**
co-ordinator, aquatic programs **4167**
co-ordinator, art gallery **0511**
co-ordinator, assembly – motor vehicle
    manufacturing **9221**
co-ordinator, bilingual services **1221**
co-ordinator, civil emergency measures **1221**
co-ordinator, compensation and benefits **1121**
co-ordinator, conference **1226**
co-ordinator, convention **1226**
co-ordinator, day-care co-op **4214**
co-ordinator, employee relations **1121**
co-ordinator, employment equity **1121**
co-ordinator – gallery **0511**
co-ordinator, human resources **1121**
co-ordinator, infection control –
    hospital **3152**
co-ordinator, labour relations **1121**
co-ordinator, municipal recycling **4161**
co-ordinator – museum **0511**
co-ordinator, native centre **4212**
co-ordinator – nursing **3151**
co-ordinator of court services **1227**
co-ordinator of nursing services **3151**
co-ordinator of social work **4152**
co-ordinator of technical services –
    telecommunications **0131**
co-ordinator, office services **1221**
co-ordinator, profit planning **1122**
co-ordinator, recreation **4167**
co-ordinator, special education **4166**
co-ordinator, standards **1122**
co-ordinator, tourism – government **4163**
co-ordinator, waste management **4161**
co-ordinator, women's centre **4212**
co-ordinator, women's shelter **4212**
co-ordinator, word processing **1211**
co-pilot **2271**
coach **5252**
coach assembler **9486**
coach, athletics **5252**
coach, life skills **4212**
coach repairer, railway **7314**
coach, sports **5252**
coal breaker **9411**
coal conveyor operator, surface mining **7452**
coal dumper **7452**
coal furnace installer **7331**
coal geologist **2113**
coal handler **7452**
coal hauler (except underground
    mining) **7411**
coal hauler – underground mining **8411**
coal mine car dispatcher **1475**
coal mine foreman/woman **8221**
coal miner **8231**
coal mining production manager **0811**

coal sampler **8614**
coal screener **9411**
coal separator **9411**
coal wheeler **7452**
coarse salt equipment operator **9411**
coast guard officer **6261**
coastal engineer **2131**
coat and hat checker **6683**
coater, asphalt **9421**
coater operator – metal plating **9497**
coater operator – textiles **9443**
coating and embossing labourer **9619**
coating and embossing unit operator –
    textiles **9443**
coating compound mixer – chemical
    processing **9421**
coating equipment operator **9496**
coating line operator, glass **9413**
coating machine feeder – chemical
    processing **9613**
coating machine feeder – plastic and
    rubber manufacturing **9615**
coating machine operator, production **9496**
coating machine operator – textiles **9443**
coating machine operator, tin plate **9496**
coating machine tender – chemical
    processing **9421**
coating machine tender – product
    manufacturing **9496**
coating machine tender – textiles **9443**
coating mixer – chemical processing **9421**
coating oven tender, production **9496**
coating room foreman/woman – pulp and
    paper **9215**
coatings chemist **2112**
coatings engineer **2134**
cobbler **7343**
cocktail waiter/waitress **6453**
cocoa bean processor **9461**
cocoa bean roaster **9461**
cocoa mill operator **9461**
cocoa nib grinder **9461**
cocoa press mill helper **9617**
COD clerk **1431**
coding clerk **1454**
coding machine tender – electrical
    equipment manufacturing **9487**
coffee blender **9461**
coffee blending machine feeder **9617**
coffee grinder **9461**
coffee roaster **9461**
coffeemaker assembler **9484**
coffin and casket fitter **9492**
cognitive psychologist **4151**
coil adjuster – electrical equipment
    manufacturing **9484**
coil assembler – electronics
    manufacturing **9483**

coil assembler – industrial electrical
    equipment **9485**
coil bander – primary metal processing **9611**
coil builder – industrial electrical
    equipment **9485**
coil clamper, transformer assembly **9485**
coil connector/repairer **7333**
coil finisher – electrical equipment
    manufacturing **9484**
coil former, heavy duty – industrial
    electrical equipment **9485**
coil inspector – electronics
    manufacturing **9483**
coil installer, motor and generator –
    industrial electrical equipment **9485**
coil machine operator **9516**
coil maker – industrial electrical
    equipment **9485**
coil rewind machine tender **9516**
coil shaper – industrial electrical
    equipment **9485**
coil spring dipper **9496**
coil spring grinder **9612**
coil spring machine tender **9516**
coil taper – electrical equipment
    manufacturing **9484**
coil taper, hand – industrial electrical
    equipment **9485**
coil winder and repairer **7333**
coil winder, automatic – electrical
    equipment **9484**
coil winder, manual-feed – electrical
    equipment manufacturing **9484**
coil winder, transformers **9485**
coil winding foreman/woman –
    electronics manufacturing **9222**
coil winding machine operator **9483**
coil winding machine tender, automatic
    – electrical equipment **9484**
coiled tubing operator – oil field
    services **8412**
coiler equipment operator **9411**
coiler, hot wound springs **9516**
coiler – primary metal processing **9611**
coin dealer **0621**
coin machine mechanic **7445**
coin machine repairer **7445**
coin machine servicer **7445**
coin wash attendant **6683**
coke grinder **9411**
coke inspector – primary metal
    processing **9415**
coke loader – primary metal processing **9611**
coke oven operator **9411**
coke ovens foreman/woman **9211**
coke plant by-products operator **9231**
coke sampler and tester – primary metal
    processing **9415**

coke screen tender **9411**
coke screening foreman/woman **9211**
cold drown operator – metal forgings **9512**
cold end operator, glass **9413**
cold foods chef **6241**
cold mill feeder – primary metal
    processing **9611**
cold mill inspector – primary metal
    processing **9415**
cold mill operator – primary metal
    processing **9231**
cold patcher – asphalt **7611**
cold press operator – metal forgings **9512**
cold press tender – woodworking **9513**
cold roll catcher – primary metal
    processing **9611**
cold steel roller **9411**
cold storage checker **7622**
cold storage manager **0651**
collaborator, encyclopedia **5121**
collating machine operator – printing **9473**
collator/inserter – printing **9619**
collator – printing **9619**
collection agent **1435**
collection centre manager **0122**
collection clerk **1435**
collection clerk supervisor **1212**
collection legal assistant **4211**
collection manager **0122**
collection officer (except taxation) **1435**
collection officer – taxation **1228**
collection unit head – government
    services **1228**
collections agent – government services **1228**
collections investigation officer **1435**
collections manager **0111**
collections paralegal **4211**
collections supervisor **1212**
collector **1435**
college chancellor **0014**
college department chairperson, trade
    programs **4131**
college laboratory assistant **4122**
college of applied arts and technology
    instructor **4131**
college of applied arts and technology
    teacher **4131**
college president **0014**
college principal **0312**
college provost **0312**
college registrar **0312**
college teacher **4131**
college teaching assistant **4122**
collet maker **9517**
colour analyst, fashion **6481**
colour and large copier operator **9471**
colour artist **5241**
colour coder, component insertion **9483**

colour consultant, fashion **6481**
colour copier operator **9471**
colour editing terminal operator –
    printing **9472**
colour film analyzer **9474**
colour grinder **9421**
colour matcher – chemical processing **9421**
colour matcher – textiles **9444**
colour mixer, chemical processing **9421**
colour mixer, textile **9443**
colour picture tube assembler **9483**
colour printer – photographic
    processing **9472**
colour scanner operator – printing **9472**
colour separation assistant, scanning **9472**
colour separation camera operator –
    printing **9472**
colour separator, scanning machine –
    printing **9472**
colour weigher and mixer **9421**
colourer, hides **9453**
colourist, photography **5223**
colourist, textile **9443**
column operator – chemical processing **9232**
columnist **5123**
columnist, entertainment **5123**
columnist, fashion **5123**
columnist, political **5123**
columnist, society **5123**
columnist, sports **5123**
comb fixer – textile manufacturing **7317**
comb maker **9498**
comb setter – textile manufacturing **7317**
comber – textiles **9441**
combination man/woman –
    telecommunications **7246**
combination mechanic, heavy
    equipment **7312**
combination packing machine tender **9617**
combination welder **7265**
combine operator **8431**
combiner machine operator – pulp and
    paper **9433**
combining and drawing machine tender
    – textiles **9441**
combustion tester, furnace – primary
    metal processing **9415**
comedian **5135**
comic **5135**
comis waiter/waitress **6453**
commander, police detachment **0641**
commanding officer, coast guard vessel **2273**
commanding officer – police **0641**
commanding officer – water transport **2273**
commentator **5123**
commentator, news **5123**
commentator, radio **5123**
commerce teacher – secondary school **4141**

commercial agent – wholesale **6411**
commercial air conditioning mechanic **7313**
commercial air conditioning mechanic
    helper **7611**
commercial air-diver **7382**
commercial airline pilot **2271**
commercial and industrial equipment
    and supplies sales representative **6221**
commercial art teacher – college or
    vocational institute **4131**
commercial artist **5241**
commercial banking account officer **1232**
commercial banking manager **0122**
commercial bias tire builder **9423**
commercial building painter **7294**
commercial construction manager **0711**
commercial design artist **5241**
commercial development officer –
    government **4163**
commercial diver **7382**
commercial draftsman/woman **2253**
commercial law clerk **4211**
commercial lawyer **4112**
commercial legal assistant **4211**
commercial paralegal **4211**
commercial photographer **5221**
commercial pilot **2271**
commercial press operator **7381**
commercial property manager **1224**
commercial real estate salesperson **6232**
commercial refrigeration mechanic **7313**
commercial refrigerator assembler **9484**
commercial sales representative,
    technical **6221**
commercial salesperson – wholesale **6411**
commercial sewing machine operator **9451**
commercial subjects teacher –
    community college **4131**
commercial transport inspector **6463**
commercial transport vehicle mechanic **7321**
commercial traveller – wholesale **6411**
commercial underwriter **1234**
commercial vehicle driver instructor **4131**
commercial vehicle enforcement officer **6463**
commissary agent, airline **6433**
commission agent, livestock **6411**
commission broker manager –
    investments **0121**
commission steward **5253**
commissionaire – security **6651**
commissionaires supervisor **6216**
commissioned land surveyor **2154**
commissioned salesperson – retail **6421**
commissioner, deputy – government
    services **0012**
commissioner – government services **0012**
commissioner of affidavits **1227**
commissioner of inquiries **0012**

commissioner of marriages **1227**
commissioner of police **0012**
commissioner, territorial **0011**
committee clerk **1222**
commodities trader **1113**
commodities trading manager **0121**
communication aide, medical **3235**
communication assistant, medical **3235**
communication clerks supervisor **1211**
communication disorder specialist **3141**
communication disorders assistant **3235**
communication electrician, switching **7246**
communication electrician, telephone **7246**
communication electrician, toll **7246**
communication equipment sales
    representative **6221**
communication instructor, medical **3235**
communication operator **1475**
communication service co-ordinator **1221**
communication specialist – health **3141**
communication systems technician –
    military **7246**
communication technician, construction **7245**
communication technician, line **7245**
communications adviser **5124**
communications and electronics
    engineer **2133**
communications and electronics
    engineer – military **2133**
communications consultant **5124**
communications director **0611**
communications electrician –
    telecommunications **7246**
communications engineer **2133**
communications equipment assembler **9483**
communications equipment assembly
    foreman/woman – electronics
    manufacturing **9222**
communications equipment repairer –
    avionics **2244**
communications equipment repairer –
    household and business equipment **2242**
communications equipment restoration
    technician **5212**
communications equipment testing
    foreman/woman – electronics
    manufacturing **9222**
communications foreman/woman **7212**
communications manager, public
    relations **0611**
communications manager –
    telecommunications **0131**
communications officer **5124**
communications policy researcher **4161**
communications specialist **5124**
communications teacher – community
    college **4131**
communications technician – military **7246**

communications technologist **2241**
communicator **1475**
communicator research – military **6464**
communicologist **3141**
community and urban planner **2153**
community antenna television
    technician **7247**
community arts co-ordinator **0314**
community based occupational therapist **3143**
community case management officer **4155**
community centre co-ordinator **4212**
community centre worker **4212**
community college dean **0312**
community college department head **4131**
community college instructor **4131**
community college president **0014**
community college registrar **0312**
community college teacher **4131**
community development officer **4164**
community development worker **4212**
community dietitian **3132**
community health nurse **3152**
community information officer **5124**
community liaison worker **4212**
community medicine specialist **3111**
community museum technician **5212**
community nutritionist **3132**
community occupational therapist **3143**
community organization worker **4212**
community organizer **4164**
community pharmacist **3131**
community planner **2153**
community planning director –
    government services **0411**
community planning teacher –
    community college **4131**
community program consultant,
    recreation **4167**
community recreation consultant **4167**
community recreation planner **2153**
community rehabilitation manager –
    government services **0411**
community relations officer – police **6261**
community school principal **0313**
community service worker **4212**
community services officer – police **6261**
community social development officer **4164**
community worker **4212**
commutator assembler – industrial
    electrical equipment **9485**
compact disc player assembler **9483**
compact disc player inspector and tester **9483**
compact disc sales clerk **6421**
companion **6471**
companion animal veterinarian **3114**
company chauffeur **7413**
company physician **3112**
company trainer **4131**

comparison shopper **6623**
compass assembler **9498**
compassman/woman – surveying **7612**
compensation adjuster – insurance **1233**
compensation agent **1453**
compensation and benefits co-ordinator **1121**
compensation manager **0112**
compensation officer **1121**
compensation research analyst **1121**
compiler **1452**
complaint adjuster **1453**
complaint clerk **1453**
complaint operator – telephone systems **1424**
complaint service technician – telecommunications **7246**
compliance inspector, buildings **2264**
component assembler – electronics manufacturing **9483**
component inserting machine operator **9483**
component lead former **9483**
components inspector – electronics manufacturing **9483**
composer **5132**
composing machine operator, linotype **1423**
composing room proofreader **1452**
composing room supervisor – printing **7218**
composite and sheet metal repairer, aircraft **7315**
composite technician, aircraft **7315**
composition floor layer **7295**
composition mixer – chemical processing **9421**
composition roofer **7291**
compositor operator, typesetting **1423**
compositor, typesetting **1423**
compound worker **9421**
compounder – chemical processing **9421**
compounder, latex **9421**
compounder – plastic manufacturing **9422**
compounding foreman/woman – rubber and plastic manufacturing **9214**
compression air and gas regulator assembler **9498**
compressed gas plant maintenance mechanic **7311**
compressed gas plant worker **9613**
compressed gases tester **2211**
compression moulder – plastic manufacturing **9422**
compression moulding foreman/woman – rubber and plastic manufacturing **9214**
compression moulding machine operator – plastic manufacturing **9422**
compression moulding operator – plastic manufacturing **9422**
compression plastic moulder **9422**
compressor fitter **7316**
compressor operator, caisson **7351**

compressor operator, gas processing **9232**
compressor operator, natural gas **9232**
compressor station foreman/woman **9212**
compressor stations manager **0912**
comptroller **0111**
comptroller general of Canada **0012**
computer aided designer **2253**
computer aided dispatch clerk **1475**
computer aided electro-mechanical design draftsman/woman **2253**
computer aided manufacturing repair technician – household and business equipment **2242**
computer analyst **2162**
computer applications engineer **2147**
computer applications manager **0213**
computer assisted design draftsman/woman **2253**
computer assisted drafting instructor – college or vocational institute **4131**
computer assisted machinist **7231**
computer audit specialist **1111**
computer communications technician **2241**
computer consultant **2162**
computer cutter **9452**
computer education director **0413**
computer engineer **2147**
computer equipment installer **2242**
computer equipment repairer **2242**
computer equipment technician – household and business equipment **2242**
computer facility manager **0213**
computer field service technician **2242**
computer graphics analyst **2162**
computer graphics designer **5241**
computer graphics specialist **2162**
computer hardware engineer **2147**
computer inspector/tester **2241**
computer marketing development, sales director **0611**
computer numerically controlled machining tool operator **9511**
computer operator **1421**
computer operator supervisor **1211**
computer peripheral equipment operator **1421**
computer products dealer – retail **0621**
computer programmer **2163**
computer programming instructor – college or vocational institute **4131**
computer salesperson – retail **6421**
computer science college teacher **4131**
computer science professor – university **4121**
computer search librarian **5111**
computer service technician **2242**
computer software engineer **2147**
computer software sales representative **6221**
computer store manager **0621**
computer system operations manager **0213**

computer systems development manager **0213**
computer systems engineer **2147**
computer systems manager **0213**
computer systems sales representative **6221**
computer tape librarian **1421**
computer technician, software **2163**
computer technologist, hardware **2241**
computer telecommunications specialist **2147**
computer trainer **4131**
computer training instructor **4131**
computer training representative **4131**
computer typesetter **1423**
computerized information processor **1422**
computerized information systems
    manager **0213**
computerized panel saw tender **9513**
computing services company president **0013**
computing systems analyst **2162**
concentrator foreman/woman – primary
    metal and mineral products
    processing **9211**
concert singer **5133**
concession manager **0621**
conciliation officer **1121**
conciliator **1121**
concrete and cement finishing
    contractor **7219**
concrete batch plant operator – cement
    manufacturing **9411**
concrete block machine operator **9414**
concrete block maker **9414**
concrete block pourer **7611**
concrete block setter **7281**
concrete breaker **7611**
concrete engineer **2131**
concrete finisher **7282**
concrete finisher helper **7611**
concrete fittings maker **9414**
concrete float maker **7611**
concrete floor finisher **7282**
concrete former helper **7611**
concrete forms carpenter **7271**
concrete grooving machine operator **7421**
concrete gun operator **7611**
concrete hydraulic press operator **9414**
concrete inspector **2264**
concrete laying gang foreman/woman **7217**
concrete mason **7282**
concrete mixer caster **9611**
concrete mixer helper **7611**
concrete mixer operator – concrete
    manufacturing **9411**
concrete mixer operator helper –
    highway construction **7611**
concrete mixing truck driver **7411**
concrete moulder **9414**
concrete patcher/finisher **7282**
concrete paver operator helper **7611**

concrete paving foreman/woman **7217**
concrete paving labour gang
    foreman/woman **7217**
concrete paving labourer **7611**
concrete paving machine operator **7421**
concrete pipe machine tender **9414**
concrete pipe tester **9415**
concrete polisher **7282**
concrete pourer – construction **7611**
concrete products foreman/woman **9211**
concrete products inspector **9415**
concrete products salesperson –
    wholesale **6411**
concrete products tester **9415**
concrete pump operator **7611**
concrete smoother/finisher **7282**
concrete spin caster **9414**
concrete spinning machine operator **9414**
concrete sprayer **7611**
concrete spreader operator **7421**
concrete technician **2231**
concrete vibrator – manual **7611**
concrete waterproofer, construction **7611**
concrete wheeler **7452**
condenser setter – primary metal
    processing **9411**
condenser winder – electronics
    manufacturing **9483**
conditioner tender – textiles **9443**
conductor, orchestra **5132**
conductor, railway **7362**
conductor, yard **7362**
conduit installer – electric power
    systems **7244**
cone and wafer machine tender **9461**
cone assembler – electronics
    manufacturing **9483**
cone maker – food and beverage
    processing **9461**
cone winder – textiles **9441**
confection labourer – food and beverage
    processing **9617**
confection syrup maker **9461**
confectionery cooker **9461**
confectionery manager **0621**
conference and meeting planner **1226**
conference centre manager **0721**
conference co-ordinator **1226**
conference facilitator **1122**
conference interpreter **5125**
conference planner **1226**
conference services officer **1226**
connecting rod borer **9511**
connector assembler – electrical
    equipment manufacturing **9484**
consecutive interpreter **5125**
conservation and protection enforcement
    officer **2263**

conservation and restoration technician **5212**
conservation officer **2224**
conservation technician – forestry **2223**
conservationist – art objects **5112**
conservator **5112**
conservator – art gallery **5112**
console assembler – electronics manufacturing **9483**
console operator – cement manufacturing **9231**
console operator – computer **1421**
console operator – food and beverage processing **9461**
constable **6261**
construction and maintenance electrician **7241**
construction and maintenance technician – military **2231**
construction area manager **0711**
construction assistant manager **0711**
construction blaster **7372**
construction boilermaker **7262**
construction camp cook **6242**
construction campsite attendant **6663**
construction cost consultant **2234**
construction cost estimator **2234**
construction crane operator **7371**
construction division manager **0711**
construction driller **7372**
construction electrical contractor **7212**
construction electrician **7241**
construction engineer **2131**
construction engineering procedures technician – military **2231**
construction engineering technician – military **2231**
construction equipment mechanic **7312**
construction equipment mechanic helper **7612**
construction equipment repairman/woman **7312**
construction equipment sales representative **6221**
construction estimator **2234**
construction foreman/woman, residential **7215**
construction general manager **0016**
construction helper **7611**
construction highway inspector **2264**
construction inspector **2264**
construction labourer **7611**
construction labourer and helper **7611**
construction lineman/woman – electric power systems **7244**
construction manager **0711**
construction manager, industrial **0711**
construction material estimator **1473**
construction millwright **7311**
construction operations manager **0711**

construction painter **7294**
construction painters foreman/woman **7219**
construction permit clerk **1441**
construction progress clerk **1473**
construction project manager **0711**
construction project superintendent **0711**
construction safety officer **2264**
construction superintendent **0711**
construction supervisor, residential **7215**
construction supervisor – underground mining and quarrying **8221**
construction technician, CATV **7245**
construction technician, civil engineering **2231**
construction technician – telecommunications **7245**
construction technologist **2231**
construction trades helper **7611**
construction worker **7611**
consul **0012**
consultant, advertising **1122**
consultant, art therapy **3144**
consultant, business **1122**
consultant, computer **2162**
consultant, data processing **2162**
consultant dietitian **3132**
consultant, drug and alcohol abuse **4165**
consultant, education **4166**
consultant, fashion **6481**
consultant – financial **1112**
consultant, fitness **4167**
consultant, health care **4165**
consultant, health care planning **4165**
consultant, health labour force planning **4165**
consultant, heritage languages education **4166**
consultant, home care program **4165**
consultant, human resources **1121**
consultant, information technology **2162**
consultant, labour relations **1121**
consultant, management **1122**
consultant, management information systems – computer systems **2162**
consultant, marketing **4163**
consultant, mental health programs **4165**
consultant, mortgage **1232**
consultant, natural and applied science **4161**
consultant – nursing **3152**
consultant nutritionist **3132**
consultant, organizational analysis **1122**
consultant, personal image **6481**
consultant, recreation **4167**
consultant, school subjects **4166**
consultant, security **6465**
consultant, social policy **4164**
consultant, social services **4164**
consultant, social services planning **4164**
consultant, special education **4166**

consultant, teaching **4166**
consultant, tourism – government **4163**
consultant, training and development **4131**
consultant, travel **6431**
consultant, wedding services **6481**
consulting agrologist **2123**
consulting architect **2151**
consulting civil engineer **2131**
consulting engineer, coal preparation **2142**
consulting forester **2122**
consulting geologist **2113**
consulting geophysicist **2113**
consulting industrial engineer **2141**
consulting mechanical engineer **2132**
consulting mining engineer **2143**
consulting notary (Quebec) **4112**
consumer advisor **4164**
consumer affairs inspector **2262**
consumer credit officer **1232**
consumer loan officer **1232**
consumer products service technician **2242**
consumer sales representative **6411**
consumer services representative **1453**
contact lens dispenser **3231**
contact lens fitter **3231**
contact lens technician **3231**
contact printer **9472**
container designer **2252**
container manufacturing manager **0911**
container washer, machine – food and
    beverage processing **9617**
contemporary art curator **5112**
content analyst, editor **5122**
continuity person – motion pictures and
    broadcasting **5227**
continuous casting operator – primary
    metal processing **9231**
continuous digester operator – pulp and
    paper **9233**
continuous dyeing machine operator –
    textiles **9443**
continuous felt drier operator – textiles **9443**
continuous glue machine operator –
    printing **9473**
continuous mining machine operator **8231**
continuous mixing operator – rubber
    manufacturing **9423**
continuous press tender – textiles **9443**
continuous process cook – pulp and
    paper **9233**
continuous process foreman/woman –
    chemical processing **9212**
contortionist **5232**
contour grinder, machine – concrete,
    clay and stone products **9414**
contour grinding machine operator –
    concrete, clay and stone products **9414**
contour sander operator – woodworking **9513**

contract analyst – purchasing **1225**
contract claims examiner **1225**
contract clerk, administrative **1441**
contract clerk – financial sector **1434**
contract clerk – law **4211**
contract counsel **4112**
contract management officer –
    purchasing **1225**
contract manager **0113**
contract negotiator – purchasing **1225**
contracting officer – purchasing **1225**
contractor – agricultural service **8252**
contractor, air conditioning **7216**
contractor, air conditioning and
    refrigeration **7216**
contractor, asphalt roofing **7219**
contractor, bricklaying **7219**
contractor, bricklaying and masonry **7219**
contractor/carpenter **7215**
contractor, carpentry **7215**
contractor, concrete and cement
    finishing **7219**
contractor, construction ironwork **7214**
contractor, decorating **7219**
contractor, drywalling **7219**
contractor, electrical **7212**
contractor, electrical installation **7212**
contractor, electrical systems **7212**
contractor, electrical wiring installation **7212**
contractor/electrician **7212**
contractor, excavating **7217**
contractor/excavator **7217**
contractor, floor covering **7219**
contractor, general construction **0711**
contractor, glazing **7219**
contractor, heating and air conditioning
    systems **7216**
contractor, heating system installation
    and repair **7216**
contractor, heating systems **7216**
contractor, home builder **0712**
contractor, home renovation **0712**
contractor, insulation **7219**
contractor, logging **8211**
contractor, metal roofing **7219**
contractor, painting **7219**
contractor, paperhanging **7219**
contractor, pipefitting **7213**
contractor, plastering **7219**
contractor, plumbing **7213**
contractor, refrigeration **7216**
contractor, residential homes **0712**
contractor, roofing **7219**
contractor, sheet metal work **7214**
contractor, silviculture **8211**
contractor, sprinkler systems **7213**
contractor, stone masonry **7219**
contractor, structural steel erecting **7214**

contractor, terrazzo finishing **7219**

contractor, tile, terrazo and marble
    setting **7219**

contractor, tilesetting **7219**

contractor, water well drilling **7217**

contractor, welding **7214**

contractor, wood shingle roofing **7219**

contractors' estimator **2234**

contracts administrator – purchasing **1225**

contributing editor **5122**

control analyst, metallurgical **2212**

control analyst, real-time systems **2147**

control board operator – telephone
    systems **1424**

control chemist **2112**

control clerk, data processing **1422**

control clerk – financial sector **1434**

control clerk, hotel and restaurant **1431**

control clerk, production **1473**

control operator, broadcasting **5224**

control operator, paper machine **9234**

control panel assembler – industrial
    electrical equipment **9485**

control panel operator – chemical
    processing **9232**

control panel technician – industrial
    electrical equipment **9485**

control panel tester **2241**

control room editor **5122**

control room operator – electric power
    systems **7352**

control room operator – food and
    beverage processing **9461**

control room operator, nuclear **7352**

control room operator, offshore drilling **8412**

control room operator – pulp and paper **9233**

control room operator, trainee – electric
    power systems **7352**

control system tester **2241**

control systems engineer **2133**

control technician, nuclear generating
    station and heavy water plant **2243**

control tower operator, railway **7431**

controller, corporate – financial,
    communications and other business
    services **0013**

controller, corporate – goods production,
    utilities, transportation and
    construction **0016**

controller, corporate – health, education,
    social and community services and
    membership organizations **0014**

controller, corporate – trade,
    broadcasting and other services
    n.e.c. **0015**

controller, financial **0111**

controller, network **1421**

controller, oil movement **9232**

controller, subway **7222**

controls assembler, aircraft **9481**

convenience store clerk **6421**

convenience store manager **0621**

convention centre manager **0721**

convention co-ordinator **1226**

conversion substation operator – electric
    power systems **7352**

converter foreman/woman – primary
    metal and mineral products
    processing **9211**

converter unit operator – chemical
    processing **9232**

convertible top assembler – motor
    vehicle manufacturing **9482**

conveyance clerk **4211**

conveyancer **4211**

conveyor belt attendant **7452**

conveyor belt foreman/woman – rubber
    manufacturing **9214**

conveyor belt operator (except
    underground mines) **7452**

conveyor belt splicer – rubber
    manufacturing **9423**

conveyor cleaner – pulp and paper **9614**

conveyor console operator **7452**

conveyor line worker – electronics
    manufacturing **9483**

conveyor man/woman **7452**

conveyor operator, (except underground
    mines) material handling **7452**

conveyor operator – primary and mineral
    products processing **9611**

conveyor operator – underground
    mining **8411**

conveyor oven operator – food and
    beverage processing **9461**

conveyor repairer **7311**

conveyor repairman/woman **7311**

conveyor tender, (except underground
    mines) material handling **7452**

conveyor tender – tobacco processing **9464**

conveyor washer tender **9619**

convict guard **6462**

convoy guard **6651**

cook **6242**

cook apprentice **6242**

cook, domestic **6242**

cook, first **6242**

cook, fishing and merchant vessel **6242**

cook, foreign foods **6242**

cook helper – food and beverage
    processing **9617**

cook, institution **6242**

cook, kosher foods **6242**

cook, meats – food and beverage
    processing **9461**

cook – pulp and paper **9233**

cook's first helper – pulp and paper **9432**
cook's helper **6642**
cook's helper, camp **6642**
cook, small establishment **6242**
cook tank operator – food and beverage
 processing **9461**
cook, third **6242**
cookee, logging camp **6642**
cooker – chemical processing **9421**
cooker, offal – food and beverage
 processing **9461**
cooking school manager **0651**
cooking teacher – secondary school **4141**
cooler operator – fish processing **9618**
cooler shell assembler – plastic
 manufacturing **9495**
cooler tender – tobacco processing **9464**
cooling machine tender – food and
 beverage processing **9461**
cooling system operator **7351**
cooling unit assembler – electrical
 equipment manufacturing **9484**
cooper foreman/woman **9227**
cooper header operator, wood **9513**
cooper header, wood **9513**
cooper operator – woodworking **9513**
cooperage headings sawyer **9513**
cooperage labourer **9619**
cooperage set-up man/woman, wood **9513**
cooperage setter-up, wood **9513**
copper billet piercer **9411**
copper briquetting machine operator **9411**
copper caster – foundry **9412**
copper coater **9497**
copper dust collector **9611**
copper etcher – printing **9472**
copper flotation operator **9411**
copper melter **9411**
copper ore slime treater **9411**
copper plate engraver **5244**
copper plater operator **9497**
copper refinery operator **9231**
coppersmith **7261**
coppersmith foreman/woman **7214**
copy camera operator **9474**
copy chief **5122**
copy editor **5122**
copy holder **1452**
copy lathe tender **9513**
copy marker, typesetting **1423**
copy runner **1463**
copy, staple and glue machine operator **9471**
copy stylist, graphic arts **5223**
copy stylist, typesetting **1423**
copy typist **1412**
copyist **5132**
copyright clearance supervisor **1213**
copyright clerk **1441**

copyright manager **0512**
copyright manager, publishing **0512**
copywriter **5121**
cordwood cutter **8421**
core and shaft assembler, small electric
 motor **9484**
core assembler – industrial electrical
 equipment **9485**
core blower machine operator – foundry **9412**
core builder, small transformers **9484**
core cutter – paper converting **9435**
core drill operator – construction,
 surface mining and quarrying **7372**
core drill operator – underground
 mining **8231**
core inspector – foundry **9415**
core lapper, transformers **9485**
core layer – wood processing **9434**
core laying machine tender – wood
 processing **9434**
core machine operator – foundry **9412**
core making machine operator –
 foundry **9412**
core mounter **9619**
core oven tender – foundry **9412**
core pipe extractor **9619**
core room foreman/woman – pulp and
 paper **9215**
core room foundry labourer **9611**
core room set-up man/woman – foundry **9412**
core sand mixer operator – foundry **9412**
core setter – foundry **9412**
core stacker, transformers **9485**
core winder – paper converting **9435**
coremaker – foundry **9412**
coremaker, machine – foundry **9412**
coremaker – paper converting **9435**
coremaker, transformer **9485**
coremaking foreman/woman – foundry **9211**
coremaking foreman/woman – paper
 converting **9215**
coremaking machine tender, dry battery
 – electrical equipment
 manufacturing **9487**
cork insulation installer **7293**
cork tipper, cigarette **9464**
corker **9617**
corks and bottle caps inspector **9498**
corn chips cook **9461**
corn cooker – food and beverage
 processing **9461**
corn dough machine tender **9461**
corn flakes roller – food and beverage
 processing **9461**
corn germ preparer – food and beverage
 processing **9461**
corn products germ drier **9461**
corn products pressman/woman **9461**

corn products starch presser **9461**

corn sugar crystallizer operator **9461**

corn sugar filter operator **9461**

corn sugar refinery operator **9461**

corn syrup cooler and decolourizer **9461**

corn syrup maker **9461**

corncob pipe assembler **9498**

corner store clerk **6421**

coroner **4165**

corporate and litigation law clerk **4211**

corporate banking centre manager **0122**

corporate banking vice president – banking **0013**

corporate budgeting and analysis manager **0111**

corporate chef **6241**

corporate controller – financial, communications and other business services **0013**

corporate controller – goods production, utilities, transportation and construction **0016**

corporate controller – health, education, social and community services and membership organizations **0014**

corporate controller – mortgage brokerage firm **0013**

corporate controller – restaurant chain **0015**

corporate controller – social services institution **0014**

corporate controller – trade, broadcasting and other services n.e.c. **0015**

corporate counsel **4112**

corporate development planning adviser **1122**

corporate finance legal assistant **4211**

corporate finance manager **0111**

corporate image consultant **6481**

corporate law clerk **4211**

corporate legal assistant **4211**

corporate paralegal **4211**

corporate pilot **2271**

corporate planner **1122**

corporate records legal assistant **4211**

corporate risk department manager **0111**

corporate sales manager **0611**

corporate secretary **1222**

corporate securities law clerk **4211**

corporate security officer **6465**

corporate traffic manager **0713**

corporate transportation manager **0713**

corporate trust services manager **0122**

corporation lawyer **4112**

corporation notary (Quebec) **4112**

corporation paralegal **4211**

corral boss **8253**

correctional facility guard **6462**

correctional institution director **0314**

correctional institution guard **6462**

correctional officer **6462**

correctional officer supervisor **6462**

correctional service officer **6462**

correspondence clerk **1452**

correspondence clerk supervisor **1213**

correspondence file clerk **1413**

correspondence review clerk **1452**

correspondence school agent **6421**

correspondence school instructor **4131**

correspondence school tutor **4131**

correspondence teacher, elementary school **4142**

correspondence teacher, high school **4141**

correspondent, foreign **5123**

correspondent, news **5123**

corrosion engineer **2142**

corrosion resistant metal sprayer **9497**

corrugated asbestosboard former **9414**

corrugated box cutter – paper converting **9435**

corrugated fastener driver – woodworking **9513**

corrugating machine operator – paper converting **9435**

corrugator operator knifeman/woman – paper converting **9435**

corrugator operator – paper converting **9435**

corrugator, sheet metal **9514**

cosmetic surgeon **3111**

cosmetician **6482**

cosmetics and perfume maker **9421**

cosmetics and toiletries salesperson – retail **6421**

cosmetics demonstrator – retail **6623**

cosmetologist **6482**

cosmic ray physicist **2111**

cosmologist **2111**

cost accountant **1111**

cost accounting clerk **1431**

cost accounting supervisor **1111**

cost and royalty manager, publishing **0512**

cost clerk **1431**

cost engineer **2141**

cost estimating clerk **1431**

cost estimator, construction **2234**

cost estimator, manufacturing **2233**

cost supervisor **1212**

costing clerk **1431**

costume designer **5243**

costume supervisor **5226**

costumer **5226**

cottage cheese maker **9461**

cotton ball machine tender **9441**

cottrell helper – primary metal processing **9611**

cottrell treater **9411**

council member, native band **0011**

council secretary – government services **0012**
councillor **0011**
councilman/woman, city **0011**
counsel **4112**
counselling psychologist **4151**
counselling services director **0314**
counsellor, addiction **4153**
counsellor-at-law **4112**
counsellor, attendance **4143**
counsellor, camp **5254**
counsellor, educational **4143**
counsellor, family **4153**
counsellor, general **4153**
counsellor, guidance **4143**
counsellor, investment **1112**
counsellor/lawyer **4112**
counsellor, loan **1232**
counsellor, marriage **4153**
counsellor, mental retardation **4212**
counsellor, occupations **4213**
counsellor, outplacement **4213**
counsellor, pre-retirement **4153**
counsellor, rehabilitation **4153**
counsellor, relocation **4213**
counsellor, school **4143**
counsellor, securities **1112**
counsellor, substance abuse **4153**
counsellor, travel **6431**
counsellor, vocational **4213**
counter attendant, cafeteria **6641**
counter attendant, lunchroom **6641**
counter clerk, bakery **6421**
counter clerk, deli **6421**
counter clerk, meats **6421**
counter clerk, parts **1472**
counter clerk – retail **6421**
counter enquiries clerk **1453**
counter representative, car rental **6421**
counter services agent, airline **6433**
counter services agent (except airline) **6434**
counter services agent, railway **6434**
counter sinker **9511**
country club grounds supervisor **8256**
country elevator manager **6234**
country grain elevator agent **6234**
country grain elevator manager **6234**
country grain elevator operator **6234**
country inn operator **0632**
country surveyor **2154**
county attorney **4112**
county clerk **0012**
county court clerk **1443**
county court judge **4111**
county court registrar **1227**
county engineer **2131**
county judge **4111**
coupler, railway **7431**
coupling machine tender **9517**

coupon clerk – financial sector **1434**
coupon redemption clerk **6421**
courier **1463**
courier service driver **1463**
courier service manager **0132**
courier services sales representative **6411**
courier supervisor **1214**
course co-ordinator **1441**
court administrator **1227**
court bailiff **6461**
court clerk **1443**
court clerk/crier **1443**
court clerk supervisor **1227**
court interpreter **5125**
court martial judge – military **0643**
court monitor **1244**
court of Queen's bench justice **4111**
court officer **1227**
court recorder **1244**
court registrar **1227**
court reporter **1244**
court reporting instructor – college or vocational institute **4131**
court stenographer **1244**
court supervisor **1227**
courtesy desk clerk **1453**
courtroom clerk **1443**
courtroom officer **1227**
couturier **5243**
cover designer **5241**
coverage and interpretation officer – taxation **1228**
coverer, luggage **9619**
covering machine operator – printing **9473**
cow-calf operator **8251**
cowboy **8431**
cowhand **8431**
cowpuncher **8431**
CP **3214**
crab fisherman/woman **8262**
crabbing machine tender – textiles **9443**
cracker and cookie machine operator **9461**
cracker operator – rubber manufacturing **9423**
craft instructor **5244**
craft school manager **0651**
crafts teacher – elementary school **4142**
craftsman/woman **5244**
craftsperson **5244**
crane and claw operator – logging **8241**
crane and hoisting equipment operator **7371**
crane chaser **7611**
crane crew foreman/woman **7217**
crane fitter **7316**
crane greaser **7443**
crane hooker **7611**
crane inspector **2262**
crane ladle pourer **9411**
crane oiler **7443**

crane operator **7371**
crane operator apprentice **7371**
crane operator, drilling rig **7371**
crane operator, pile-driver **7371**
crane repairer **7312**
crank shaft assembler – motor vehicle
    manufacturing **9482**
crash firefighter **6262**
crate builder, wood **9493**
crate liner **9619**
crate maker, wood **9493**
crate marker **9619**
crater **9619**
crawler crane operator **7371**
crawler track servicer **7443**
crawler tractor operator **7421**
crayon making machine tender **9517**
crayon moulder **9619**
cream cheese maker **9461**
cream grader **9465**
cream inspector **2222**
cream sampler – food and beverage
    processing **9617**
creaser – garment and fabric **9517**
creative arts administrator **0114**
credit advisor, veterans' land act **4212**
credit agency inspector **1114**
credit analyst **1232**
credit and accounts manager **0122**
credit and collection administrator **1232**
credit and collection clerk **1435**
credit and collection department
    manager **0122**
credit and collection supervisor **1212**
credit applicant interviewer – financial
    sector **1434**
credit approval and market development
    manager **0122**
credit bureau sales representative **6411**
credit card authorization clerk **1441**
credit card die cutter operator – printing **9473**
credit clerk **1434**
credit clerk supervisor **1212**
credit investigation officer **1232**
credit investigator **1434**
credit manager **0122**
credit officer **1232**
credit supervisor **1212**
credit union manager **0122**
credit union teller **1433**
credit unions examiner **1114**
credit vice-president – banking **0013**
cree teacher – elementary school **4142**
cremator **6683**
crematorium manager **0651**
creping machine operator – paper
    converting **9435**
crest designer **5243**

crew chief – aircraft maintenance **7216**
crew leader, forest fire suppression **2223**
crew leader, industrial painter **9496**
crew schedule supervisor **1215**
crew scheduler, transportation **1476**
crewman/woman – military **6464**
crewperson, custom harvest **8431**
cribber, grain elevator **7452**
crime prevention constable **6261**
criminal law clerk **4211**
criminal law legal assistant **4211**
criminal law paralegal **4211**
criminal lawyer **4112**
criminologist **4169**
criminology professor – university **4121**
crimping machine tender **9517**
crimping machine tender – electrical
    equipment manufacturing **9487**
cripple worker – footwear
    manufacturing **9498**
crisis counsellor **4153**
crisis intervention worker **4212**
critic **5123**
critical care medicine specialist **3111**
critical care nurse **3152**
critical care nursing supervisor **3151**
critical care physician **3111**
crochet machine operator **9442**
crocheter, hand **5244**
crop certification inspector **2222**
crop duster **2271**
crop dusting contractor **8252**
crop dusting service manager **8252**
crop farm labourer **8431**
crop farmer **8251**
crop harvesting contractor **8252**
crop research scientist **2121**
crop scientist **2121**
crop specialist **2123**
cropper – textiles **9443**
cropsprayer machine operator **8431**
cross cut saw operator – woodworking **9513**
crossing guard **6651**
crossword puzzle maker **5121**
crown and bridge dental technician **3223**
crown assembly machine set-up
    operator **9517**
crown assets disposal officer **1221**
crown attorney **4112**
crown attorney, assistant **4112**
crown corporation counsel **4112**
crown counsel **4112**
crown lands forester **2122**
crown law officer **4112**
crown prosecutor **4112**
crucible furnace operator **9411**
crucible pourer **9411**
cruiser **2223**

cruising technician – forestry **2223**
crusher and blender operator **9411**
crusher control room operator **9231**
crusher equipment operator **9411**
crusher operator – tobacco processing **9464**
crusher operator – underground mining **8411**
crusher setter **9411**
crusher worker – primary metal and
    mineral products processing **9611**
crushing and grinding operations
    foreman/woman – primary metal and
    mineral products processing **9211**
crushing machine tender – food and
    beverage processing **9461**
crushing operations helper **9611**
crutcher operator – chemical processing **9421**
cryogenic engineering technologist **2232**
cryogenics engineer **2132**
cryogenics physicist **2111**
cryolite recovery equipment operator **9411**
cryptanalyst **4161**
crystal ball reader **6484**
crystal calibrator – electronics
    manufacturing **9483**
crystal dicing saw operator **9483**
crystal final tester – electronics
    manufacturing **9483**
crystal finisher – electronics
    manufacturing **9483**
crystal frequency measurer – electronics
    manufacturing **9483**
crystal glassware salesperson – retail **6421**
crystal inspector – electronics
    manufacturing **9483**
crystal lapper **9483**
crystal physicist **2111**
crystal processing foreman/woman –
    electronics manufacturing **9222**
crystal unit assembler **9483**
crystal unit tester **9483**
crystallizer tender – chemical
    processing **9421**
crystallizer tender – food and beverage
    processing **9461**
CSIS investigation officer **6261**
CTC operator – railway **2275**
cub reporter **5123**
cucumber picker **8611**
cullet crusher tender, glass **9413**
cultivator operator **8431**
cultural activities leader **5254**
cupboard installer, kitchen and vanity **7441**
cupola charger – primary metal and
    mineral processing **9611**
cupola furnace operator – foundry **9412**
cupola furnace operator – primary metal
    processing **9411**
cupola helper **9611**

cupola operator – concrete, clay and
    stone products **9414**
cupola operator – foundry **9412**
cupola spray reliner **7611**
cupola tapper **9611**
curate **4154**
curator **5112**
curator director **0511**
curatorial assistant **5212**
curb builder – manual **7611**
cure operator – rubber manufacturing **9423**
cured tire repairer **9423**
curer – food and beverage processing **9461**
curer, rubber **9423**
curer, tobacco **8431**
curing bin tender – food and beverage
    processing **9461**
curing foreman/woman – rubber
    manufacturing **9214**
curing machine operator – rubber
    manufacturing **9423**
curing man/woman – rubber
    manufacturing **9423**
curing press set-up operator – rubber
    manufacturing **9423**
curing press tender – rubber
    manufacturing **9423**
curing pressman/woman – rubber
    manufacturing **9423**
currency sorter **1431**
current account teller – financial
    services **1433**
current accounts clerk **1434**
current accounts supervisor **1212**
current planner, land use **2153**
current transformer coil winder **9485**
curriculum consultant **4166**
curriculum developer **4166**
curriculum development director,
    education **0413**
curriculum planner **4166**
curtain and drapery presser – laundry
    and dry cleaning **6682**
curtain rod assembler **9498**
cushion and cover inspector **9454**
cushion cementer – shoe manufacturing **9619**
cushion filler – furniture assembly **9619**
cushion stuffer **9619**
custodian, athletic equipment **6671**
custodian, building **6663**
custodian supervisor **6215**
custom bracelet maker **7344**
custom brooch maker **7344**
custom combine operator **8252**
custom combining contractor **8252**
custom cue maker and repairer **9513**
custom cue maker and
    repairman/woman **9513**

custom desk maker, wood **7272**
custom drapery salesperson **6421**
custom electrical panel assembler **9485**
custom feed miller – food and beverage
  processing **9461**
custom feed miller helper **9617**
custom feed preparer – food and
  beverage processing **9461**
custom frame and mirror assembler **7272**
custom fur joiner **7342**
custom furrier **7342**
custom harvest crewperson **8431**
custom harvester **8252**
custom house manager **0123**
custom jewellery mounter **7344**
custom locket maker **7344**
custom moulder, metal casting –
  foundry **9412**
custom operator, crop spraying **8252**
custom operator, farm machinery **8252**
custom piano case maker **7272**
custom screw machine operator **9511**
custom sewer, women's garments **7342**
custom sheet metal fabricator **7261**
custom shoemaker **7343**
custom tailor **7342**
custom upholsterer **7341**
custom wood furniture maker **7272**
custom wooden desk maker **7272**
customer accounts supervisor **1212**
customer engineer, communications **2133**
customer gas servicer **7253**
customer relations clerk **1453**
customer sales agent, airline **6433**
customer sales and service agent (except
  airline) **6434**
customer service agent, airline **6433**
customer service agent, bus terminal **6434**
customer service clerk, insurance **1453**
customer service clerk, retail **1453**
customer service manager, automobiles **0621**
customer service manager – retail **0621**
customer service officer, bank **1433**
customer service representative –
  financial services **1433**
customer service representative,
  insurance **1453**
customer service representative, retail **1453**
customer service supervisor, bank or
  financial institution **1212**
customer service supervisor – housing
  construction **7219**
customer service supervisor – retail **6211**
customs appraiser **1228**
customs baggage inspector **1228**
customs broker **1236**
customs brokerage clerk supervisor **1212**
customs clearing agent **1236**

customs clerk **1441**
customs clerk supervisor **1211**
customs collector **1228**
customs consultant **1236**
customs examiner **1228**
customs excise clerk **1441**
customs excise examiner **1228**
customs excise superintendent **1228**
customs house broker **1236**
customs inspection supervisor **1228**
customs inspector **1228**
customs investigator **1228**
customs manager – government services **0412**
customs officer **1228**
customs specialist **1236**
cut off saw operator – sawmill **9431**
cut off saw operator – woodworking **9513**
cutlery and tool etcher **9511**
cutlery assembly inspector **9498**
cutlery maker **9498**
cutlery maker operator **9517**
cutter, aluminum sheet – ductwork **9514**
cutter helper – pulp and paper **9614**
cutter – leather products manufacturing **9452**
cutter – logging **8421**
cutter – meat packing **9462**
cutter operator – concrete, clay and
  stone products **9414**
cutter operator – printing **9473**
cutter, plastics **9495**
cutter, rubber **9423**
cutter, shoe parts – footwear
  manufacturing **9452**
cutter, tobacco leaf **9464**
cutting and creasing press operator –
  paper converting **9435**
cutting and printing machine setup
  operator **9443**
cutting department foreman/woman –
  fabric, fur and leather products
  manufacturing **9225**
cutting machine fixer – textile
  manufacturing **7317**
cutting machine operator – clothing
  manufacturing **9452**
cutting machine operator – printing **9473**
cutting machine operator, rubber **9423**
cutting machine operator – textile
  products manufacturing **9517**
cutting machine operator – underground
  mining **8231**
cutting machine tender – textile products
  manufacturing **9517**
cutting room foreman/woman – fabric,
  fur and leather products
  manufacturing **9225**
cutting torch operator – metal
  fabrication **9514**

cylinder assembler, flexographic printing **9472**
cylinder coater – clay products **9414**
cylinder engraver – printing **9472**
cylinder filler **9461**
cylinder grinder – metal machining **9511**
cylinder head assembler **9486**
cylinder honer – metal machining **9511**
cylinder machine operator – pulp and paper **9234**
cylinder painter – printing **9472**
cylinder plater/grinder – metal processing **9497**
cylinder preparer, carbon tissue – printing **9472**
cylinder preparer – printing **9472**
cylinder press operator – printing **7381**
cylinder pressman/woman – printing **7381**
cylinder printing press set-up operator **7381**
cylinder roll fabricator **9516**
cylinder sander feeder – woodworking **9513**
cylinder tender – clay products **9414**
cytogeneticist **2121**
cytogenetics technologist – medical laboratory **3211**
cytotechnologist – medical laboratory **3211**

D

dado operator – woodworking **9513**
dado saw operator – woodworking **9513**
dairy bacteriologist **2121**
dairy cattle breeder **8251**
dairy chemist **2112**
dairy clerk **6421**
dairy cream tester **9465**
dairy equipment repairer **7311**
dairy farm couple **8431**
dairy farm foreman/woman **8253**
dairy farm labourer **8431**
dairy farm manager **8251**
dairy farm worker **8431**
dairy farmer **8251**
dairy hand **8431**
dairy helper **9617**
dairy herdsperson **8253**
dairy inspector **9465**
dairy moisture tester **9465**
dairy plant engineer **2148**
dairy plant manager **0911**
dairy producer **8251**
dairy products inspector **2222**
dairy products specialty maker **9461**
dairy products technician **2221**
dairy relief **8253**
dairy route salesman/woman **7414**
dairy sampler – food and beverage processing **9617**

dairy scientist **2121**
dairy technologist **2221**
dairy tester **9465**
dairy worker, storage **7452**
dam construction inspector **2264**
damage repair estimator, automobile **7322**
dampproofer helper **7611**
dams engineer **2131**
dance company director **0512**
dance instructor **5134**
dance/movement therapist **3144**
dance/movement therapy researcher **3144**
dance therapist **3144**
dance therapist registered **3144**
dance therapist, supervisor **3144**
dancer **5134**
dancing instruction salesperson **6421**
dancing teacher **5134**
danish seine fisherman/woman **8262**
dark room technician – photographic processing **9474**
data centre manager **0213**
data control clerk **1422**
data entry clerk **1422**
data entry operator **1422**
data entry supervisor **1211**
data entry verifier operator **1422**
data processing and systems analysis manager **0213**
data processing co-ordinator **1211**
data processing consultant **2162**
data processing director **0213**
data processing manager **0213**
data processing planning manager **0213**
data processing sales representative **6221**
data processing teacher – college or vocational institute **4131**
data processing teacher – high school **4141**
data processor **1422**
data technician – geophysics **2212**
data transmission systems, design engineer **2133**
database administrator **2162**
database librarian **5111**
database manager **2162**
dating service consultant **6481**
day camp counsellor **5254**
day-care aide **6473**
day-care helper **6473**
day-care planning services director – government services **0411**
day-care supervisor **4214**
day-care teacher **4214**
day-care worker **4214**
day-care worker's assistant **6473**
day clerk, hotel **6435**
DC **3122**

de-icer kit preparer – rubber
    manufacturing **9423**
deacon – religion **4217**
dealer, antiques **0621**
dealer – wholesale or retail **0621**
dean, faculty of arts **0312**
dean of adult education **0312**
dean of graduate studies **0312**
dean of science **0312**
dean of student activities **0312**
dean of students **0312**
dean of technical and technological
    program **0312**
dean, school of technology **0312**
death claim clerk **1434**
debarker operator – wood processing **9434**
debrancher operator **8241**
decal applier **9496**
decal operator **9496**
decating machine tender – textiles **9443**
deck builder **7441**
deck hand – ship **7433**
deck installer **7441**
deck officer **2273**
deck officer cadet **2273**
deck officer – self-propelled barges **2273**
deck officer – self-propelled oil rigs **2273**
deck officer – water transport **2273**
decker tender – pulp and paper **9432**
deckerman/woman – pulp and paper **9432**
deckhand, fishing vessel **8441**
deckhand, gillnetter **8441**
deckhand, offshore trawler **8441**
deckhand, seiner **8441**
deckman/woman – underground mining **8411**
decorating consultant **6421**
decorating contractor **7219**
decorating foreman/woman – furniture
    and fixtures manufacturing **9224**
decorating kiln operator – clay products **9414**
decorating machine operator, glass **9413**
decorating machine tender – clay
    products **9414**
decorator and painter **7294**
decorator and painter helper **7611**
decorator – furniture finishing and
    refinishing **9494**
decorator operator, glass **9413**
decorator/plasterer **7284**
decorators foreman/woman **7219**
deed recorder **1227**
deed registrar **1227**
defect trimmer – woodworking **9513**
dehairing machine dropper – meat
    packing **9462**
dehorning services contractor **8252**
dehydrating press tender – chemical
    processing **9421**

dehydrator, grain – food and beverage
    processing **9461**
dehydrator tender, peat moss **9411**
delicatessen clerk **6421**
delicatessen manager – retail **0621**
delimber and buncher operator **8241**
delimber operator **8241**
deliverer, mail **1462**
deliverer, parcels **1463**
delivery checker **1473**
delivery driver **7414**
delivery driver, fast food **7414**
delivery drivers foreman/woman **7222**
delivery drivers superintendent **7222**
delivery drivers supervisor **7222**
delivery person, courier service **1463**
delivery room supervisor – nursing **3151**
delivery service sales agent **6411**
delivery services sales representative **6411**
delivery truck driver **7414**
delivery truck helper **7622**
deliveryman/woman, bakery **7414**
demographer **2161**
demolition contractor **7217**
demolition driver **5251**
demolition worker **7611**
demonstrator, department of agriculture **2123**
demonstrator, laboratory –
    post-secondary **4122**
demonstrator – retail **6623**
demurrage clerk **1431**
dent remover and repairer, automobile **7322**
dental amalgam processor **9411**
dental assistant **3411**
dental assistant program teacher –
    community college **4131**
dental associate officer – military **0311**
dental ceramic caster **3412**
dental ceramic moulder **3412**
dental ceramist **3223**
dental claims clerk **1434**
dental clinical assistant **3411**
dental clinical assistant (dental assistant)
    – military **3411**
dental clinical assistant (dental
    technician) – military **3223**
dental equipment and supplies
    salesperson **6221**
dental equipment installer servicer **7441**
dental equipment maintenance
    technician – military **7441**
dental equipment technician **7441**
dental health service administrator **0311**
dental hygienist **3222**
dental hygienist – military **3222**
dental hygienist program teacher –
    college or vocational institute **4131**
dental instrument assembler **9498**

dental laboratory bench worker **3412**
dental laboratory technician **3223**
dental laboratory technician – military **3223**
dental mechanic **3221**
dental mechanic apprentice **3221**
dental nurse **3222**
dental office receptionist **1414**
dental officer – military **3113**
dental prosthesis maker **3223**
dental receptionist **1414**
dental surgeon **3113**
dental technician **3223**
dental technician apprentice **3223**
dental technician supervisor **3223**
dental therapist **3222**
dental therapist – military **3222**
dentist **3113**
dentist, veterinary **3114**
dentistry professor – university **4121**
denture bench moulder **3412**
denture finisher **3412**
denture mechanic **3221**
denture packer **3412**
denture setter **3412**
denture technician **3221**
denture therapist **3221**
denture trimmer-polisher **3412**
denture waxer **3412**
denture waxer – metal framework **3412**
denturist **3221**
denturologist **3221**
department chairperson – community
    college **4131**
department chairperson – university **4121**
department chief, social services **0314**
department director, welfare
    organization **0314**
department head – community college **4131**
department head, dental hygienist
    program **4131**
department head, geography **4121**
department head, retail store **6211**
department head – secondary school **4141**
department head, social services **0314**
department head – university **4121**
department manager, food store **0621**
department manager – retail **0621**
department manager, security **0114**
department store clerk **6421**
department store information clerk **1453**
department store manager **0621**
department store president **0015**
department store supervisor **6211**
department supervisor – retail **6211**
department technician, electrical **2241**
departmental accountant **1111**
departmental solicitor **4112**
deposit clerk **1431**

depot clerk, transit system **1476**
deputy chief executive officer –
    financial, communications and other
    business services **0013**
deputy chief executive officer – goods
    production, utilities, transportation
    and construction **0016**
deputy chief executive officer – health,
    education, social and community
    services and membership
    organizations **0014**
deputy chief executive officer – life
    insurance company **0013**
deputy chief executive officer – trade,
    broadcasting and other services
    n.e.c. **0015**
deputy city solicitor **4112**
deputy clerk, house of commons **0414**
deputy clerk, legislative assembly **0414**
deputy commissioner – government
    services **0012**
deputy court registrar **1227**
deputy fire chief **0642**
deputy judge **4111**
deputy judge, associate **4111**
deputy justice **4111**
deputy minister – government services **0012**
deputy municipal clerk **0012**
deputy police chief **0641**
deputy provincial secretary –
    government services **0012**
deputy registrar – courts **1227**
deputy sheriff **6461**
deputy superintendent, schools **0313**
dermatologist **3111**
dermatology, chief of **0311**
derrick worker – oil and gas drilling **8412**
derrickhand, offshore drilling **8412**
derrickhand – oil and gas drilling **8412**
derrickman/woman – oil and gas
    drilling **8412**
descriptive toxicologist **2121**
design and development engineer,
    electrical and electronic **2133**
design and drafting technologist **2253**
design and lettering stamper – printing **9473**
design checker **2253**
design cutter, jewellery **7344**
design draftsperson **2253**
design engineer, electrical **2133**
design engineer, mechanical **2132**
design engineer, oil-well equipment **2132**
design engineer, radio and television
    broadcasting **2133**
design technician **2253**
design technologist, drafting **2253**
design technologist, electrical and
    electronics **2241**

designated ship broker **1236**
designer, clothing **5243**
designer, display **5243**
designer, exhibit **5243**
designer, furniture **2252**
designer, graphic **5241**
designer, heating **2232**
designer, industrial **2252**
designer, industrial products **2252**
designer, machine **2232**
designer, mechanical engineering
    equipment **2232**
designer, mould **2232**
designer, museum **5243**
designer, package **2252**
designer, textile **5243**
designer, theatrical **5243**
designer, tool and die **2232**
desk assembler **9492**
desk clerk, hotel **6435**
desk officer – police **6261**
desk sander – woodworking **9513**
desktop compositor **1423**
desktop publishing operator **1423**
desktop publishing specialist **1423**
desma laster – plastic manufacturing **9495**
desma laster – rubber manufacturing **9423**
dessert preparer **6641**
desulphurizer operator **9232**
detachment commander – police **0641**
detail assembler – aircraft assembly **9481**
detail draftsman/woman **2253**
detail inspector – aircraft assembly **9481**
detail programmer **2163**
detail shaper – woodworking **9513**
detailer **2253**
detective agency manager **0123**
detective, counterfeit and forgery
    section **6261**
detective inspector – police **0641**
detective, narcotics squad **6261**
detective – police **6261**
detective, private **6465**
detective, vice squad **6261**
detention attendant **6462**
detention centre director **0314**
detention guard **6462**
detention home worker **4212**
detergent chemist **2112**
detonator and fuse assembler **9498**
developer printer machine tender **9474**
developing machine operator –
    photographic processing **9474**
development control officer **6463**
development economist **4162**
development engineer, biomedical **2148**
development geologist **2113**

development mechanic – aircraft
    assembly **9481**
development miner **8231**
development service worker **4212**
development technologist –
    telecommunications **2241**
developmental biologist **2121**
developmental geneticist **2121**
developmental psychologist **4151**
devulcanizer tender **9421**
dewaterer equipment operator **9411**
dewaterer tender – primary metal
    processing **9411**
dextrine maker – food and beverage
    processing **9461**
diagnostic audiologist **3141**
diagnostic cardiac sonographer **3216**
diagnostic imaging, chief of **0311**
diagnostic imaging technologist **3218**
diagnostic instrument sales
    representative **6221**
diagnostic medical radiation
    technologist **3215**
diagnostic medical sonographer **3216**
diagnostic medical sonographer, chief **3216**
diagnostic radiography technologist **3215**
diagnostic radiological technician **3215**
diagnostic radiological technologist **3215**
diagnostic radiologist **3111**
diagnostic radiology, chief of **0311**
diagnostic technician – motor vehicle **7321**
diagnostic ultrasound technologist **3216**
dial plant superintendent –
    telecommunications **0131**
diamond abrasive wheel maker **9414**
diamond cutter **7344**
diamond drill operator – surface mining
    and quarrying **7372**
diamond drill runner – underground
    mining **8231**
diamond driller helper – underground
    mining **8411**
diamond driller – underground mining **8231**
diamond drilling foreman/woman **8221**
diamond drilling technician **2212**
diamond expert **7344**
diamond grader **7344**
diamond grinder, glass finishing **9413**
diamond powder mixer – stone products **9414**
diamond saw maker **7232**
diamond selector **7344**
diamond setter **7344**
diamond tool maker **7232**
diamond wheel edger, glass finishing **9413**
diamond wheel moulder and finisher **9414**
diaper machine tender – paper
    converting **9435**
dice maker **9498**

dicing machine tender – plastic manufacturing **9495**
dicta-typist **1412**
dictaphone servicer **7445**
dictating machine servicer **7445**
dictionary editor **5122**
die attacher – electronics manufacturing **9483**
die barber **7232**
die casting foreman/woman – foundry **9211**
die casting machine operator **9412**
die casting machine set-up man/woman – foundry **9412**
die casting machine setter – foundry **9412**
die casting machine tender – foundry **9412**
die casting supervisor **9211**
die cut platen press operator **9473**
die cutter – fabric, fur and leather products **9452**
die cutter, jewellery **7232**
die cutter, metalworking **7232**
die cutting machine operator – paper products **9435**
die cutting or numbering press operator – printing **9473**
die designer **2232**
die finisher **7232**
die fitter **7232**
die machine operator – metal forgings **9512**
die maker **7232**
die maker, bench, stamping **7232**
die maker, jewellery **7232**
die maker, wire-drawing **7232**
die press operator – plastic manufacturing **9495**
die reamer **7232**
die repairer **7232**
die repairman/woman **7232**
die setter **7266**
die sinker **7232**
die sinker, bench **7232**
die stamper – printing **9471**
die storage clerk **1472**
dielectric and induction heaters assembler – electronics manufacturing **9483**
diesel electrician – railway **7242**
diesel engine assembler **9486**
diesel engine assembly foreman/woman **9226**
diesel engine erector **9486**
diesel engine mechanic apprentice **7312**
diesel engine mechanic, heavy equipment **7312**
diesel engine operator, stationary **7351**
diesel engine repairman/woman – railway **7312**
diesel engine tester **9486**
diesel engineer, design and research **2132**
diesel engineer, railway **7361**

diesel generating station operator – electric power systems **7352**
diesel locomotive repairman/woman **7312**
diesel mechanic apprentice **7312**
diesel mechanic, heavy equipment **7312**
diesel mechanic helper **7612**
diesel plant operator – electric power systems **7352**
diet clerk **1454**
diet kitchen cook **6242**
diet kitchen food service supervisor **6212**
dietary aide, hospital **6631**
dietary assistant **3219**
dietary cook **6242**
dietary technician **3219**
dietary technologist **3219**
dietetic intern **3132**
dietetic researcher **3132**
dietetics, director of **0311**
dietitian **3132**
dietitian, chief **0311**
dietitian, consultant **3132**
dietitian/nutritionist **3132**
differential assembler **9486**
diffuser operator – food and beverage processing **9461**
diffusion furnace operator – electronics manufacturing **9483**
digester cook – pulp and paper **9233**
digester equipment operator **9411**
digester operator – chemical processing **9421**
digester operator – pulp and paper **9233**
digger – construction **7611**
digital circuit design engineer **2133**
digital computer operator **1421**
digital electronic technician **2241**
digitizer – textile, leather and fur products **5245**
dimension planner – woodworking **9513**
dinghy assembler **9491**
dingman/woman, autobody **7322**
dining car steward **6453**
dining car waiter/waitress **6453**
dining establishment managing supervisor **0631**
dining room attendant **6642**
dining room captain **6453**
dining room cashier **6611**
dining room host/hostess **6451**
dining room manager **0631**
dining room steward **6453**
dinosaur operator – clay products **9414**
diorama maker – museums and galleries **5212**
dip and bake operator – electrical equipment manufacturing **9487**
dip soldering machine operator – electronics manufacturing **9483**
dip tank attendant **9496**

dip tank tender – wood processing **9434**

diplomat **4168**

diplomatic historian **4169**

dipper and coater operator – metal plating **9497**

dipper/baker attendant **9496**

dipper, coating tank **9496**

dipping machine tender – rubber manufacturing **9423**

dipping tank tender **9496**

direct distributor – retail **6623**

direct fire support vehicle driver – military **6464**

direct fire support vehicle gunner – military **6464**

direct mail specialist **1122**

direct sales instructor **4131**

directional driller – oil and gas drilling **8232**

directional drilling operator – oil and gas drilling **8232**

director, accounting and financial control **0111**

director, administration and property management services **0114**

director, administrative services **0114**

director, admissions **0114**

director, admitting department **0114**

director, adult education services **0413**

director, advertising **0611**

director, agricultural chemical branch **0212**

director, agricultural policy – government services **0412**

director, agricultural products market development – government services **0412**

director, agricultural representatives **0212**

director, apprenticeship training – government services **0411**

director, archive **0511**

director, art gallery **0511**

director, athletics **0513**

director, audit and compliance **0111**

director, ballet company **0512**

director, behaviour therapy service **0311**

director, broadcasting **5131**

director, business development – government services **0412**

director, cabinet liaison **0414**

director, cabinet relations **0414**

director, camp **4167**

director, casting **5226**

director, children's aid society **0314**

director, clinic – medical **0311**

director, commercial analysis – government services **0412**

director, communications **0611**

director, community centre **0314**

director, community economic development – government services **0412**

director, community planning – government services **0411**

director, community programs **0314**

director, computer education **0413**

director, computer technology school **0312**

director, consumer information **0314**

director, correctional services **0314**

director, counselling services **0314**

director, curriculum development – education **0413**

director, data processing **0213**

director, day-care planning services – government services **0411**

director, detention centre **0314**

director, distribution **0721**

director, distribution systems – utilities **0912**

director, economic and trade analysis – government services **0412**

director, economic development – government services **0412**

director, economic policy analysis – government services **0412**

director, education inspection services **0413**

director, education policy analysis and research **0413**

director, education research and information **0413**

director, educational program support **0413**

director, election finances **0414**

director, election planning **0414**

director, Elections Canada **0414**

director, electrical power transmission operations **0912**

director, elementary education **0413**

director, elementary school education **0413**

director, employee benefits **0112**

director, employment equity **0112**

director, employment equity program – government services **0411**

director, energy market analysis – government services **0412**

director, energy policy – government services **0412**

director, engineering quality control department **0211**

director, engineering research and development **0211**

director, environmental health services – government services **0411**

director, excise-tax programs **0412**

director, executive – financial, communications and other business services **0013**

director, executive – health, education, social and community services and membership organizations **0014**

director, family and children's services – government services **0411**

director, family benefits – government services **0411**

director, family resources **0314**

director, farm products marketing – government services **0412**

director, federal-provincial relations **0414**

director, finance **0111**

director, finance and administration **0114**

director, financial evaluations **0111**

director, financial planning and reporting **0111**

director, financing and administration **0111**

director, first-aid **0311**

director, fisheries policy – government services **0412**

director, fitness administration – government **0513**

director fitness programs **0513**

director, flight operations **0713**

director, forestry policy – government services **0412**

director, funeral **6272**

director – gallery **0511**

director general – government services **0012**

director general – health, education, social and community services and membership organizations **0014**

director, health care insurance plan – government services **0411**

director, health education – government services **0411**

director, health information and promotion – government services **0411**

director, heritage language program **0413**

director, home care services **0311**

director, homemaker services – government services **0411**

director, horse racing **0513**

director, hotel **0632**

director, housing policy and development – government services **0411**

director, human resources **0112**

director, human resources development **0112**

director, immigration and settlement – government services **0411**

director, industrial development – government services **0412**

director, industry, trade and technology – government services **0412**

director, inspection services, education **0413**

director, intergovernmental affairs **0414**

director, international relations, government **0414**

director, investment sales **0121**

director, laboratory **0212**

director, labour relations **0112**

director, language training **0112**

director, laundry service **0651**

director, learning programs, adult education **0413**

director, learning programs, early childhood education **0413**

director, learning programs, elementary education **0413**

director, learning programs, secondary education **0413**

director, legal department **0114**

director, legislative services **0414**

director – library **0511**

director, local health services – government services **0411**

director, logistics **0713**

director, management information systems (MIS) **0213**

director, media relations **0611**

director, medical **0311**

director, membership education **0314**

director, microeconomic policy development – government services **0412**

director, motion picture **5131**

director – museum **0511**

director, natural resources policy – government services **0412**

director, nursing services **0311**

director, occupational health **0311**

director, oceanographic research **0212**

director of accounting **0111**

director of athletics and recreation **0513**

director of audiology and speech language pathology **0311**

director of clinical medicine **0311**

director of community service **0314**

director of conservation, museum **0511**

director of correctional treatment and training **0314**

director of counselling **0314**

director of dietetics **0311**

director of education, correctional institution **0313**

director of facilities management **0722**

director of guidance services **0314**

director of laboratory medicine **0311**

director of logistics **0713**

director of mining **0811**

director of nursing registry **0123**

director of occupational therapy **0311**

director of operations, housing department **0314**

director of operations, manufacturing **0911**

director of operations, transport **0713**

director of photography **5131**

director of physiotherapy **0311**

director of professional services – medical **0311**

director of public welfare **0314**

director of recreation **0513**

director of rehabilitation **0311**
director of research – forestry **0212**
director of research – manufacturing **0212**
director of research – mining **0212**
director of research – securities broker **0121**
director of research, university or
  college **0312**
director of school services **0413**
director of student affairs **0312**
director of surgery **0311**
director of traffic **0713**
director of transportation **0713**
director of waste management **0912**
director of water distribution **0912**
director of water pollution control **0912**
director of water supply **0912**
director, opera company **0512**
director, operational planning **0114**
director, organizational methods
  analysis **0123**
director, organizational planning and
  development **0123**
director, parks administration **0412**
director, parliamentary services **0414**
director, pay and benefits **0112**
director, pay processing division –
  government services **0112**
director, pay services **0112**
director, personnel **0112**
director, personnel and industrial
  relations **0112**
director, personnel services **0112**
director, pharmacy **0311**
director, planning and urban renewal –
  government services **0212**
director, policy and planning, education
  programs **0413**
director – post secondary education **0413**
director, prisoner rehabilitation society **0314**
director – private vocational school **0312**
director, procurement operations **0113**
director, psychological services **0314**
director, psychology **0311**
director, public affairs **0611**
director, public health nursing **0311**
director, public relations **0611**
director, purchasing **0113**
director, quality assurance **0211**
director, radio **5131**
director, radio operations **0512**
director, recreation centre **0513**
director, recruiting **0112**
director, rehabilitation services –
  medical **0311**
director, religious education **0314**
director, residential services – treatment
  centre **0311**
director, sales and marketing **0611**

director – school for the blind **0313**
director – school for the hearing
  impaired **0313**
director – school inspection **0413**
director – school of nursing **0312**
director – school of technology **0312**
director, second language program **0413**
director – secondary school education **0413**
director – secretarial college **0312**
director, settlement programs –
  government services **0411**
director, social services, policy, planning
  and research – government services **0411**
director, social surveys – government
  services **0411**
director, social work **0314**
director, special education program **0413**
director, sport administration –
  government **0513**
director, stage **5131**
director, statistical department **0212**
director, student assistance program **0413**
director, supply management **0113**
director, survey research – government
  services **0411**
director, switching systems **0131**
director, taxation programs **0412**
director – technical school **0312**
director, television **5131**
director, theatre company **0512**
director, therapeutic services –
  psychiatric hospital **0311**
director, tourism development –
  government services **0412**
director, tourism promotion –
  government services **0412**
director, trade development –
  government services **0412**
director, trade liaison – government
  services **0412**
director – trade school **0312**
director, training institute **0312**
director, transmission operations **0912**
director, transportation management **0713**
director, transportation policy –
  government services **0412**
director, urban planning and
  development – government services **0212**
director, veteran's services **0314**
director, video **5131**
director – vocational school **0312**
director, volunteer services **0314**
director, welfare administration –
  government services **0411**
director, welfare organization **0314**
director, young offender services **0314**
director, zoo **0212**
director, zoological park **0212**

directory assistance operator – telephone system **1424**
directory clerk **1452**
directory compiler **1452**
disability claim clerk – insurance **1434**
disability claim examiner – insurance **1233**
disabled person's attendant **6471**
disabled persons instructor **4215**
disaster relief claims adjuster **1233**
disbursement clerk **1431**
disc flanging operator – metal fabrication **9514**
disc jockey **5231**
discharge door attendant **9411**
discount clerk – financial sector **1434**
discussion group leader – post-secondary **4122**
dish maker – clay products **9414**
dishwasher **6642**
dishwasher assembler **9484**
dishwasher installer **7441**
dishwasher repairer **7332**
dishwashing machine operator **6642**
disk cutter, wood products **9513**
disk flange operator – metal fabrication **9514**
dispatch operator – railway **2275**
dispatcher, 911 **1475**
dispatcher, bus **7222**
dispatcher, fire department **1475**
dispatcher, flights **2272**
dispatcher, gas **9232**
dispatcher, gas service crews **1475**
dispatcher, mail service **1475**
dispatcher, mine **1475**
dispatcher, mobile equipment **1475**
dispatcher, motor vehicles **1475**
dispatcher, newspapers **1475**
dispatcher, oil **9232**
dispatcher, oil well services **1475**
dispatcher, plant **1475**
dispatcher, police **1475**
dispatcher, radio **1475**
dispatcher, taxi **1475**
dispatcher, tow-truck **1475**
dispatcher, truck **1475**
dispatcher, utilities maintenance crews **1475**
dispensary assistant **3414**
dispensary department manager **3131**
dispenser, contact lens **3231**
dispenser, ophthalmic **3231**
dispenser, optical **3231**
dispensing assistant, drug store **3414**
dispensing optician **3231**
display advertising sales representative **6411**
display balloon maker **9498**
display designer **5243**
display maker – museums and galleries **5212**
display officer – museums and galleries **5212**

display supervisor **5243**
displays and controls design engineer **2133**
disposal plant operator **9424**
disposal worker – warehouse **7452**
dissolver precipitator **9232**
distillation foreman/woman – chemical processing **9212**
distillation operator **9232**
distillation operator helper – chemical processing **9613**
distilled liquors rectifier – food and beverage processing **9461**
distilled liquors stillman/woman **9461**
distiller, wood distillation and charcoal **9421**
distilleries cooker **9461**
distilleries press operator **9461**
distilleries yeast maker **9461**
distillery grinder operator **9461**
distillery manager **0911**
distribution centre manager **0721**
distribution clerk **1471**
distribution control operator – electric power systems **7352**
distribution design technologist, lines **2241**
distribution director **0721**
distribution engineer **2133**
distribution maintenance worker – utilities **7442**
distribution manager, gas **0912**
distribution manager, sales **0611**
distribution manager, storage and warehousing **0721**
distribution operations manager – utilities **0912**
distribution operations manager – warehousing **0721**
distribution planning engineer – electrical **2133**
distribution planning technologist **2241**
distribution system dispatcher apprentice – electric power systems **7352**
distribution systems director – utilities **0912**
district agricultural specialist **2123**
district agriculturist **2123**
district and surrogate court judge **4111**
district court judge **4111**
district court registrar **1227**
district director, post office **0132**
district director, social services **0314**
district engineer **2131**
district fire chief **0642**
district forester **2122**
district gas serviceman/woman **7253**
district grain elevator manager **6234**
district inspector – fisheries **2224**
district manager – canteen service **0631**
district manager, solid waste **0912**
district manager – telecommunications **0131**

district manager, telephone company **0131**
district manager – unemployment
    insurance **0411**
district representative, government
    agricultural service **2123**
district representative – wholesale **6411**
district sales manager (except insurance
    and real estate) **0611**
district sales manager, insurance **0121**
district sales manager, real estate **0121**
district sales representative **6411**
district school superintendent **0313**
district sheriff **6461**
district supervisor, insurance office **6231**
districtman/woman –
    telecommunications **7246**
ditch cleaner – construction **7611**
ditch construction inspector **2264**
ditcher operator **7421**
ditching foreman/woman **7217**
ditching machine operator **7421**
diver **7382**
diver, commercial **7382**
diver helper **7612**
dividend clerk – financial sector **1434**
dividing machine tender – food and
    beverage processing **9461**
diving contractor **7382**
diving specialist **7382**
diving supervisor **7382**
division fire chief **0642**
division manager, petroleum
    distribution **0912**
division superintendent, railway **0713**
divisional diving supervisor – police **6261**
divisional sales manager **0611**
divisional superintendent – schools **0313**
DJ **5231**
DO **3123**
dobby loom drawer-in **9442**
dobby loom weaver **9442**
dock builder/installer **7441**
dock carpenter **7271**
dock foreman/woman – marine cargo **7217**
dock foreman/woman – shipbuilding **9226**
dock hand **7451**
dock labourer, warehouse **7622**
dock supervisor – shipbuilding **9226**
dockman/woman, truck transport **7452**
dockmaster – shipbuilding **9226**
dockworker **7451**
doctor, chiropractic **3122**
doctor, family **3112**
doctor, medical **3112**
doctor, naturopathic **3123**
doctor of acupuncture **3232**
doctor of chinese medicine **3232**
doctor of chiropractic **3122**

doctor of homeopathic therapeutics **3232**
doctor of homeopathy **3232**
doctor of naturopathic medicine **3123**
doctor of optometry **3121**
doctor of oriental medicine **3232**
doctor of osteopathic medicine **3123**
doctor of osteopathy **3123**
doctor of podiatric medicine **3123**
doctor, osteopathic **3123**
doctor's office nurse **3152**
doctor's office receptionist **1414**
doctor, specialist **3111**
document clerk **1413**
document examiner **2211**
document restorer **5112**
document restorer technician **5212**
documentation clerk **1441**
documents conservator **5112**
doffer – textiles **9616**
dog breeder **8251**
dog catcher **6463**
dog groomer **6483**
dog grooming establishment manager **0651**
dog handler **6483**
dog kennel manager **8251**
dog master – police **6261**
dog trainer **6483**
dog warden **6463**
dogsledding guide **6442**
doll assembly repairer **9498**
doll maker – manufacturing **9498**
dollmaker, hand **5244**
dolly operator – motion pictures and
    broadcasting **5227**
domestic and rural electrician **7241**
domestic housekeeper **6471**
domestic maid **6661**
domestic operations vice-president –
    banking **0013**
domestic servant **6661**
domestic sewing machine operator **9451**
domestic window air conditioner
    installer **7441**
domestic window air conditioner
    mechanic **7332**
domestic window air conditioner
    repairer **7332**
dominion carillonneur **5133**
door adjuster – motor vehicle
    manufacturing **9482**
door and deck lid adjuster – motor
    vehicle manufacturing **9482**
door and sash assembly foreman/woman **9227**
door assembler – motor vehicle
    manufacturing **9482**
door assembler, wood **9493**
door attendant **6683**

door finisher – wood products manufacturing **9493**
door fitter – furniture manufacturing **9492**
door fitter – motor vehicle manufacturing **9482**
door frame installer **7611**
door hang machine operator – woodworking **9513**
door hanger – motor vehicle manufacturing **9482**
door installer **7441**
door installer, overhead **7441**
door maker, wood **9493**
door paneler – motor vehicle manufacturing **9482**
door patcher, wood **9493**
door salesperson **6421**
door sander **9619**
door-to-door sales supervisor **6211**
door-to-door salesperson **6623**
doorkeeper, hotel **6672**
doorman/woman **6683**
dope machine operator, pipelines **7611**
doper – fabric products **5245**
dot etcher – printing **9472**
double needle sewing machine operator **9451**
double needle stitcher **9451**
doubling machine tender – textiles **9441**
dough feeder – food and beverage processing **9617**
dough kneading machine tender **9461**
dough maker **9461**
dough roller **9617**
dough weigher **9617**
doughnut machine tender **9461**
doughnut maker **9461**
doughnut shop clerk **6421**
dovetail machine operator – woodworking **9513**
dowel machine operator – woodworking **9513**
dowel machine set-up operator – woodworking **9513**
dowel machine tender **9513**
dowel pointer – woodworking **9513**
dowelling machine tender – woodworking **9513**
downhand welder, pipeline **7265**
downhole loader – underground mining **8231**
downhole tool operator – oil and gas drilling **8232**
dozer operator **7421**
DPM **3123**
drafter **2253**
drafting instructor – community college **4131**
drafting supervisor **2253**
drafting teacher – community college **4131**
drafting technician **2253**
drafting technologist **2253**

draftsman/woman, air-conditioning systems **2253**
draftsman/woman, architectural **2253**
draftsman/woman, architectural apprentice **2253**
draftsman/woman, cartographic **2255**
draftsman/woman, civil **2253**
draftsman/woman, commercial **2253**
draftsman/woman, computer aided design **2253**
draftsman/woman, electrical **2253**
draftsman/woman, electro-mechanical **2253**
draftsman/woman, electronic **2253**
draftsman/woman, geological **2253**
draftsman/woman, geophysical **2253**
draftsman/woman, heating and ventilating **2253**
draftsman/woman, hull – shipbuilding and repair **2253**
draftsman/woman, hydraulic machinery **2253**
draftsman/woman, map **2255**
draftsman/woman, marine **2253**
draftsman/woman, mechanical **2253**
draftsman/woman, mechanical apprentice **2253**
draftsman/woman, mine **2253**
draftsman/woman, one-tenth scale **2253**
draftsman/woman, petroleum exploration **2253**
draftsman/woman, process piping **2253**
draftsman/woman, refrigeration systems **2253**
draftsman/woman supervisor **2253**
draftsman/woman, tool design **2253**
draftsperson, general drafting **2253**
dragline crane operator **7371**
dragline oiler **7443**
dragline operator, crane **7371**
dragline operator helper **7611**
dragline runner **7421**
dragsaw operator – sawmill **9431**
drain roto servicer – public works **7422**
drain tile auger machine operator – clay products **9414**
drainage design engineer **2131**
drama coach **5135**
drama critic **5123**
drama professor – university **4121**
drama teacher – high school **4141**
dramatic arts historian **4169**
dramatic arts teacher – private or studio **5135**
dramatic reader **5135**
draper **9454**
drapery and upholstery salesperson **6421**
drapery cleaner, laundry and dry cleaning **6681**
drapery hanger **7441**
drapery header **9451**
drapery heading maker **9451**

drapery labourer **9619**
drapery pleater, machine **9517**
drapery sewer **9451**
draughtsman/woman, general **2253**
draw string inserter – garment
    manufacturing **9619**
drawer assembler **9492**
drawer fitter **9492**
drawer helper – primary metal
    processing **9611**
drawer-in, loom **9442**
drawer-in loom helper **9442**
drawer-in – textiles **9442**
drawing-in machine operator – textiles **9442**
drawing instrument assembler **9498**
drawing kiln operator, glass forming **9413**
drawing machine tender – textiles **9441**
drawings file clerk **1413**
dredge captain **2273**
dredge deckhand **7611**
dredge mate **2273**
dredge mechanic **7312**
dredge operator **7421**
dredge runner **7421**
dredge worker **7611**
dredgemaster **7217**
dress finisher **9619**
dress repair foreman/woman – clothing
    manufacturing **9225**
dressage and stunt horse trainer **8253**
dressage instructor **5254**
dresser – motion pictures, broadcasting
    and stage productions **5227**
dresser – textiles **9441**
dressing and sauce mixer **9461**
dressings mixer operator – food and
    beverage processing **9461**
dressmaker **7342**
dressmaking department
    foreman/woman **9225**
drier, asbestos **9411**
drier fireman/woman – stone products **9414**
drier operator – chemical processing **9421**
drier operator – mineral and metal
    processing **9411**
drier operator – textiles **9443**
drier tender **9421**
drier tender helper – chemical
    processing **9613**
drier tender, wood particles **9434**
drier – textiles **9443**
drift miner **8231**
drill and ream mechanic – aircraft
    assembly **9481**
drill grinder – metal products **9612**
drill operator, glass **9413**
drill operator – woodworking **9513**
drill press operator – metal machining **9511**

drill press operator's helper **9612**
drill press operator – stone products **9414**
drill press operator – woodworking **9513**
drill press set-up operator – metal
    machining **9511**
drill press set-up operator,
    multiple-spindle **9511**
drill press set-up operator, tape control **9511**
drill punch tender – paper converting **9435**
drill stem tester – oil and gas drilling **8232**
driller – construction **7372**
driller, drift – underground mining **8231**
driller helper, churn drill **7611**
driller helper – underground mining **8411**
driller helper, water well **7611**
driller, long hole – underground mining **8231**
driller, offshore drilling rig **8232**
driller – oil and gas drilling **8232**
driller, optical goods – non-prescription **9517**
driller, quarrying **7372**
driller, raise – underground mining **8231**
driller, rotary raise – underground
    mining **8231**
driller – surface mining **7372**
driller – underground mining **8231**
driller, water well apprentice **7373**
drilling and milling machine operator –
    metal machining **9511**
drilling and recovery petroleum
    engineer **2145**
drilling engineer, oil and gas **2145**
drilling fluid technician, offshore
    drilling rig **2212**
drilling foreman/woman – mining and
    quarrying **8221**
drilling machine operator – construction **7372**
drilling machine operator – underground
    mining **8231**
drilling rig chief electrician **7212**
drilling rig dynamic positioning
    operator **8412**
drilling rig radio operator **1475**
drilling superintendent, oil and gas **0811**
drive-in attendant – food services **6641**
drive-in theatre attendant **6671**
driver, ambulance **3234**
driver, bulk milk truck **7411**
driver, bus **7412**
driver, concrete mixing truck **7411**
driver – fast food service **7414**
driver – funeral services **7413**
driver, hearse **7413**
driver helper **7622**
driver – light trucks **7414**
driver, public passenger transit **7412**
driver, road oiling truck – public works **7422**
driver's licence examiner **4216**
driver-salesman/woman **7414**

driver-salesmen/women supervisor **7222**
driver/salesperson **7414**
driver, school bus **7412**
driver – small vans **7414**
driver, sprinkling truck – public works **7422**
driver, taxicab **7413**
driving examiner **4216**
driving instructor, commercial vehicles **4131**
driving instructor, driving school **4216**
driving school manager **0651**
drop forge hand **9512**
drop forge operator **9512**
drop forger **9512**
drop hammer forger **9512**
drop hammer helper **9612**
drop hammer operator – metal forgings **9512**
drop-in centre worker **4212**
drop-pinning machine operator –
    textiles **9442**
drop sorter operator – wood processing **9434**
dross furnace operator **9231**
dross skimmer **9611**
drug addiction counsellor **4153**
drug and alcohol abuse consultant **4165**
drug and toilet goods weigher **9421**
drug information pharmacist **3131**
drug investigator – police **6261**
drug squad inspector – police **0641**
drug store clerk **6421**
drug store delivery driver **7414**
drug store dispensing assistant **3414**
drug store manager **0621**
druggist **3131**
drum barker tender – wood processing **9434**
drum builder, rubber **9423**
drum filler, liquefied gases **9421**
drum painter **9496**
drum sander – woodworking **9513**
drummer **5133**
dry battery coremaking machine tender **9487**
dry battery inspector – electrical
    equipment manufacturing **9487**
dry cans operator – textiles **9443**
dry cell and battery assembler **9487**
dry cell assembly machine feeder –
    electrical equipment manufacturing **9487**
dry cell battery tester – electrical
    equipment manufacturing **9487**
dry cell remover **9619**
dry cell sealer – electrical equipment
    manufacturing **9487**
dry cell tuber, machine – electrical
    equipment manufacturing **9487**
dry chain off-bearer – wood processing **9614**
dry chainman/woman – wood
    processing **9614**
dry charge machine operator – electrical
    equipment manufacturing **9487**

dry cleaner **6681**
dry cleaner apprentice **6681**
dry cleaner helper **6681**
dry cleaning driver **7414**
dry cleaning foreman/woman **6214**
dry cleaning machine operator helper **6681**
dry cleaning plant manager **0651**
dry cleaning production supervisor **6214**
dry cleaning service manager **0651**
dry cleaning supervisor **6214**
dry curer – food and beverage
    processing **9617**
dry end tender, cellulose film **9421**
dry explosive mixer **9421**
dry goods salesperson **6421**
dry house attendant – chemical
    processing **9421**
dry ice maker **9421**
dry moulder, metal casting – foundry **9412**
dry pan operator – stone products **9414**
dry plaster mixer **9414**
dry press operator – clay products **9414**
dry products mixer – stone products **9414**
dry starch maker helper **9461**
dry starch operator – food and beverage
    processing **9461**
dry starch worker – food and beverage
    processing **9461**
drydock worker **7435**
dryer tender – tobacco processing **9464**
drying drum tender – food and beverage
    processing **9461**
drying kiln operator – wood processing **9434**
drying machine helper – textiles **9616**
drying machine operator – laundry and
    dry cleaning **6681**
drying machine operator – tobacco
    processing **9464**
drying machine tender – clay products **9414**
drying machine tender – textiles **9443**
drying machine tender, yarn **9443**
drywall and acoustical installer helper **7611**
drywall and acoustical mechanic **7284**
drywall and lather applicator **7284**
drywall applicator **7284**
drywall applicator apprentice **7284**
drywall contractor **7219**
drywall finisher **7284**
drywall finisher apprentice **7284**
drywall hanger **7284**
drywall helper **7611**
drywall installer **7284**
drywall mechanic **7284**
drywall sander **7611**
drywall taper **7284**
DTP operator **1423**
DTR **3144**

dual action hammer operator – metal forgings **9512**
dubbing machine operator **5225**
duct installer **7441**
duct layer **7611**
dude wrangler **6442**
dulse gatherer **8613**
dumb waiter installer/repairer **7318**
dump truck driver **7411**
dumper, material handling **7452**
duplicator punch operator – metal fabrication **9514**
dust brush assembler **9498**
dust mop maker **9498**
dust operator **9411**
dust operator helper – primary metal processing **9611**
dust remover – primary metal processing **9611**
dye chemist **2112**
dye department foreman/woman – textiles **9216**
dye house foreman/woman – hide and pelt processing **9225**
dye house helper – textiles **9616**
dye maker **9421**
dye mixer **9443**
dye penetrant tester **2261**
dye range operator – textiles **9443**
dye reel tender – textiles **9443**
dye room supervisor – textiles **9216**
dye technician **2211**
dye tub tender – textiles **9443**
dyeing and finishing machine loader – textiles **9616**
dyeing and finishing technologist **2211**
dyeing machine tender – textiles **9443**
dyer – laundry and dry cleaning **6681**
dyer – textiles **9443**
dynamic positioning operator, offshore drilling **8412**
dynamo operator, hydro electric station **7352**

E

e-line operator – oil field services **8232**
ear muff assembler **9498**
ear, nose and throat specialist **3111**
ear specialist **3111**
early childhood educator **4214**
early childhood educator assistant **6473**
early childhood program staff **4214**
early childhood program staff assistant **6473**
early childhood services teacher – elementary school **4142**
early childhood supervisor **4214**
earth mover tire builder **9423**
earth moving equipment operator **7421**

eavestrough contractor **7219**
eavestrough installer **7441**
ECG technologist **3217**
echocardiography technologist sonographer **3216**
echoencephalographic technician **3218**
ecological research manager **0212**
ecological technician **2221**
ecological technologist **2221**
ecologist **2121**
econometrician **4162**
economic analyst **4162**
economic and trade analysis director – government services **0412**
economic botanist **2121**
economic development director – government services **0412**
economic development officer – government **4163**
economic geographer **4169**
economic historian **4169**
economic research supervisor **4162**
economic researcher **4162**
economics professor – university **4121**
economics teacher – community college **4131**
economics teacher – high school **4141**
economist **4162**
economist, natural resources **4162**
eddy current technician **2261**
eddy current tester **2261**
edge bander operator – woodworking **9513**
edge bander – woodworking **9513**
edge gluer – wood processing **9434**
edge grinder, ophthalmic lens **3414**
edger, glass **9413**
edger operator, automatic – sawmill **9431**
edger operator, glass **9413**
edger – sawmill **9431**
edger, table top – woodworking **9513**
edgerman/woman – sawmill **9431**
edging machine feeder, glass **9413**
edible oil pumper – food and beverage processing **9461**
edible oil refiner – food and beverage processing **9461**
edible oil refiner helper **9617**
editing clerk **1452**
editor **5122**
editor, acquisitions **5122**
editor, advertising **5122**
editor, assignments **5122**
editor, book **5122**
editor, business **5122**
editor, city **5122**
editor, control room **5122**
editor, copy **5122**
editor, editorial page **5122**
editor, film **5131**

Index

editor, financial **5122**
editor-in-chief **0512**
editor, journal **5122**
editor, magazine **5122**
editor, manuscript **5122**
editor, map **2255**
editor, news **5122**
editor, newspaper **5122**
editor, picture **5122**
editor, production **5122**
editor, publications **5122**
editor, sound **5225**
editor, special features **5122**
editor, sports **5122**
editor, telecommunications **5122**
editor, videotape **5225**
editorial assistant **1452**
editorial cartoonist **5241**
editorial chief **0512**
editorial clerk **1452**
editorial writer, newspaper **5123**
EDP analyst **2162**
EDP applications programmer **2163**
EDP graphics specialist **2162**
EDP manager **0213**
EDP services sales representative **6221**
EDP specialist **2162**
education consultant **4166**
education courses salesperson **6421**
education director **0413**
education inspection services director **0413**
education officer, museum **5124**
education policy analysis and research
    director **0413**
education policy analyst **4166**
education policy consultant **4166**
education policy manager **0413**
education policy officer **4166**
education professor – university **4121**
education program co-ordinator **4166**
education program officer **4166**
education program planner **4166**
education rector **0014**
education research and information
    director **0413**
education research officer **4166**
education researcher **4166**
education statistician **2161**
educational audiologist **3141**
educational counsellor **4143**
educational director, public health
    nursing **0411**
educational psychologist **4151**
educational resources assistant **6472**
educational resources technician **6472**
educational sociologist **4169**
EEG technologist **3218**
eel culture technician **2221**

eel farmer **8257**
efficiency engineer **2141**
EFP camera operator **5222**
egg candler **8431**
egg gatherer **8431**
egg grader **8431**
egg grading machine tender **8431**
egg grading station labourer **8431**
egg grading station manager **8252**
egg inspector **8431**
egg processing machine tender **8431**
egg producer **8251**
election campaign manager **0611**
election enumerator **1454**
election finances director **0414**
elections officer – government services **4168**
electric air conditioning assembler **9484**
electric appliance assembler **9484**
electric appliance service technician **7332**
electric arc furnace operator – primary
    metal processing **9411**
electric bulb maker **9487**
electric cable manufacturing
    foreman/woman **9223**
electric cable splicer – electric power
    systems **7244**
electric cable splicer helper **7612**
electric circuit breaker assembler **9484**
electric circuit breaker assembly tester **9484**
electric clock assembler **9484**
electric clock components inspector **9484**
electric clothes drier assembler **9484**
electric crane operator **7371**
electric dolly operator **7452**
electric dragline operator **7371**
electric dry cell assembly
    foreman/woman **9223**
electric dryer repairer **7332**
electric fan assembler **9484**
electric furnace assembler **9486**
electric furnace operator – foundry **9412**
electric furnace operator – primary
    metal and mineral products
    processing **9411**
electric gantry crane operator **7371**
electric household appliance inspector **9484**
electric lamp maker **9484**
electric lamp parts inspector **9484**
electric lantern maker **9484**
electric lawn mower repairer **7332**
electric lawnmower inspector and tester **9484**
electric line operator – oil field services **8232**
electric locomotive operator **7361**
electric meter installer – electric power
    systems **7244**
electric meter reader **1454**
electric meter repairer **7333**
electric meter repairer apprentice **7333**

electric meter setter – electric power
    systems **7244**
electric meter technician **7333**
electric meter tester – industrial
    electrical assembler **9485**
electric monorail crane operator **7371**
electric motor assembler **9485**
electric motor repair foreman/woman **7216**
electric motor repairer **7333**
electric motor repairer and tester **7333**
electric motor repairer helper **7612**
electric motor repairman/woman **7333**
electric motor tester **9485**
electric motor testing foreman/woman **9223**
electric motor winder/repairer **7333**
electric mule operator **7452**
electric power and wire communications
    labourer **7612**
electric power company president **0016**
electric power inspector and tester
    supervisor **7212**
electric power manager **0912**
electric power plant manager **0912**
electric range assembler **9484**
electric refrigerator assembler **9484**
electric refrigerator servicer **7332**
electric sign assembler **9484**
electric sign erector **7441**
electric sign repairer **7445**
electric signal repairer, railway **7242**
electric spotwelder **9515**
electric stove assembler **9484**
electric switch assembler **9484**
electric toaster inspector **9484**
electric tool repairman/woman **7332**
electric toy repairer **7445**
electric truck operator **7452**
electric truck servicer **7443**
electrical accessories assembler **9484**
electrical and electronic aerospace
    engineer **2133**
electrical and electronic research
    engineer **2133**
electrical appliance assembly
    foreman/woman **9223**
electrical appliance installer **7441**
electrical appliance servicer **7332**
electrical appliances assembler **9484**
electrical battery charger **9487**
electrical battery plate stacker, machine **9487**
electrical battery plate washer and drier **9487**
electrical battery repairer – production
    line **9487**
electrical bulb inspector and tester **9487**
electrical construction foreman/woman **7212**
electrical continuity tester **9485**
electrical contractor **7212**

electrical control equipment fitter
    assembler **9485**
electrical controls calibrator **9484**
electrical controls inspector **9484**
electrical design engineer **2133**
electrical drafting supervisor **2253**
electrical draftsman/woman **2253**
electrical draftsperson **2253**
electrical/electronic technician –
    avionics **2244**
electrical energy installation inspector **2264**
electrical engineer **2133**
electrical engineering design
    technologist **2241**
electrical engineering manager **0211**
electrical engineering professor –
    university **4121**
electrical engineering technician **2241**
electrical engineering technologist **2241**
electrical equipment assembler **9484**
electrical equipment base filler **9487**
electrical equipment engineer **2133**
electrical equipment impregnator **9487**
electrical equipment installation and
    repair foreman/woman **7212**
electrical equipment manufacturing
    inspector **9484**
electrical estimator – construction **2234**
electrical fitter – industrial electrical
    equipment **9485**
electrical fixtures installer **7241**
electrical foreman/woman **7212**
electrical fuse maker **9487**
electrical generating system technician –
    military **7351**
electrical generating systems technician
    (power stations) – military **7352**
electrical golf cart servicer **7443**
electrical industrial equipment sales
    representative **6221**
electrical inspector **2264**
electrical inspector, aircraft **2244**
electrical inspector, locomotive **9485**
electrical inspector – manufacturing **9484**
electrical installation inspector **2264**
electrical instrument mechanic **7333**
electrical insulator tester **9619**
electrical light bulb maker **9487**
electrical light bulb tester **9487**
electrical light fixtures assembler **9484**
electrical machinist **7231**
electrical mechanic – avionics **2244**
electrical mechanic (except avionics) **7333**
electrical mechanic helper **7612**
electrical mechanic, meter repair **7333**
electrical mechanic, switchgear repair **7333**
electrical mechanic, trainee **7333**
electrical mercury switch assembler **9484**

electrical mercury switch assembly tester **9484**
electrical meter assembler **9484**
electrical motor inspector **9485**
electrical motor shop foreman/woman **7216**
electrical plant engineer **2133**
electrical plug maker **9487**
electrical power system operator **7352**
electrical powerhouse electrician **7243**
electrical products labourer **9619**
electrical relay tester and adjuster **9484**
electrical repairer, crane maintenance **7242**
electrical repairer, industrial **7242**
electrical repairer, machine shop **7242**
electrical research engineer **2133**
electrical safety inspector **2264**
electrical station power distribution inspector **7352**
electrical superintendent **0722**
electrical supervisor – drilling rig **7212**
electrical switchgear inspector **9485**
electrical switchgear wireperson **9485**
electrical switchmaker **9484**
electrical systems planning engineer **2133**
electrical technician – military **7242**
electrical technician (power system) – military **7243**
electrical tester, manufacturing **9484**
electrical transformer repairer **7333**
electrical wire group assembler – electronics manufacturing **9483**
electrical wire insulation tester **9484**
electrical wirer, automotive **9482**
electrical wirer, construction **7241**
electrical wiring inspector **2264**
electrical wiring inspector supervisor **7212**
electrical wiring installation contractor **7212**
electrical wiring installer **7241**
electrician, aircraft **2244**
electrician apprentice **7241**
electrician, building construction **7241**
electrician – construction **7241**
electrician, construction and maintenance **7241**
electrician/contractor **7212**
electrician – electric power systems **7243**
electrician, electrical powerhouse – electric power systems **7243**
electrician, electrical substation – electric power systems **7243**
electrician foreman/woman **7212**
electrician helper – automotive **7612**
electrician helper – construction **7611**
electrician helper – powerhouse **7612**
electrician, industrial **7242**
electrician, institution **7241**
electrician, marine equipment **7242**

electrician, meter installation – electric power systems **7244**
electrician – military **7241**
electrician, plant maintenance **7242**
electrician, rail transport **7242**
electrician, residential construction **7241**
electrician, shipyard **7242**
electrician, stage **5226**
electrician, telecommunications equipment **7246**
electrician, telecommunications equipment, apprentice **7246**
electrician, trouble shooter **7241**
electricity and magnetism physicist **2111**
electricity sales representative **6221**
electro-chemical machining tool operator **9511**
electro-former **9497**
electro-mechanical draftsperson **2253**
electro-mechanical technician – military **2241**
electro-technician – aircraft and missiles avionics **2244**
electro-technician, aircraft avionics preflight **2244**
electro-technician, certified aircraft avionics preflight **2244**
electro-technician, certified missile avionics preflight **2244**
electro-technician, missile – avionics **2244**
electrocardiographic technician **3217**
electrocardiographic technologist **3217**
electrocardiography technician **3217**
electrocardiology technician **3217**
electrochemical engineer **2134**
electrochemist **2112**
electrode installer **9487**
electroencephalograph technologist **3218**
electroencephalographic technician **3218**
electroencephalographic technologist **3218**
electroencephalographic technologist, chief **3218**
electrogalvanizer **9497**
electrogalvanizing machine operator – primary metal processing **9411**
electrologist **6482**
electrologist technician **6482**
electrolysis instructor – college or vocational institute **4131**
electrolysis operator **6482**
electrolysis tester – electrical equipment manufacturing **9484**
electrolytic anode changer **9487**
electrolytic cell cleaner **9613**
electrolytic cell maker – concrete products **9414**
electrolytic cell repairer – industrial electric equipment **9485**

electrolytic cell tester – primary metal
  processing **9415**
electrolytic cleaner operator – primary
  metal processing **9411**
electrolytic de-scaler – primary metal
  processing **9411**
electrolytic etcher **9511**
electrolytic refiner helper – primary
  metal and mineral products
  processing **9611**
electrolytic refinery process operator **9231**
electrolytic tank tender **9497**
electromechanical technology teacher –
  college or vocational institute **4131**
electromedical equipment technician **2241**
electrometallurgical engineer **2142**
electromyography technician **3218**
electromyography technologist **3218**
electromyography technologist, chief **3218**
electron microscopy technologist –
  medical laboratory **3211**
electroneurophysiology technologist **3218**
electronic accessories overhaul and
  repair mechanic – avionics **2244**
electronic cash register assembler **9483**
electronic cash register servicer **2242**
electronic components cleaner **9483**
electronic components purchasing
  manager **0113**
electronic components tester –
  electronics manufacturing **9483**
electronic control assembler **9483**
electronic data processing (EDP)
  manager **0213**
electronic data processing systems
  analyst **2162**
electronic data terminal operator **1422**
electronic draftsman/woman **2253**
electronic draftsperson **2253**
electronic engineer **2133**
electronic equipment installation and
  repair supervisor **2242**
electronic equipment repairer **2242**
electronic field production (EFP) camera
  operator **5222**
electronic formatter **1423**
electronic games repairer **2242**
electronic games technician – household
  and business equipment **2242**
electronic gluing machine tender –
  woodworking **9513**
electronic inspection foreman/woman –
  electronics manufacturing **9222**
electronic instrument maker **9483**
electronic music equipment installer and
  repairer **2242**
electronic news gathering (ENG) camera
  operator **5222**

electronic news gathering (ENG) editor **5225**
electronic office machines assembler **9483**
electronic organ assembler **9483**
electronic organ repairer **2242**
electronic peripheral equipment
  assembler **9483**
electronic pre-press technician **9472**
electronic products mounter –
  electronics manufacturing **9483**
electronic prototype technologist **2241**
electronic research engineer **2133**
electronic sign maker operator **9471**
electronic technician, drilling rig **2241**
electronic technician, fire alarm **2242**
electronic technician – household and
  business equipment **2242**
electronic technology teacher –
  community college **4131**
electronic typewriter repairer **2242**
electronic unit inspector – electronics
  manufacturing **9483**
electronic warfare operator – military **6464**
electronic warfare technician – military **6464**
electronics assembler **9483**
electronics, community antenna
  television apprentice **7441**
electronics design technologist **2241**
electronics engineer **2133**
electronics engineering design
  technologist **2241**
electronics engineering technician **2241**
electronics engineering technologist **2241**
electronics equipment assembler **9483**
electronics equipment repairer –
  hospital **2241**
electronics inspector, aircraft **2244**
electronics inspector – manufacturing **9483**
electronics inspector, missiles **2244**
electronics manufacturing
  foreman/woman **9222**
electronics manufacturing technician **2241**
electronics manufacturing technologist **2241**
electronics mechanic – avionics **2244**
electronics salesperson **6421**
electronics scientist **2111**
electronics technician, engineering **2241**
electronics technologist, physics
  department **2241**
electronics tester **9483**
electroplater, metal **9497**
electroplater operator **9497**
electroplater – production **9497**
electroplating foreman/woman **9226**
electrostatic painter **9496**
electrostatic painting line tender **9496**
electrostatic painting machine set-up
  operator **9496**

electrostatic separator tender – primary metal processing **9411**

elemental worker – food and beverage processing **9617**

elemental worker – municipal **7621**

elemental worker – packaging **9619**

elementary education director **0413**

elementary particle physicist **2111**

elementary particle theorist **2111**

elementary program school teacher **4142**

elementary school education director **0413**

elementary school librarian **4142**

elementary school principal **0313**

elementary school reading clinician **4142**

elementary school substitute teacher **4142**

elementary school supply teacher **4142**

elementary school teacher **4142**

elementary school teacher – special education **4142**

elevating grader operator **7421**

elevating scraper operator **7421**

elevator adjuster **7318**

elevator builder **7318**

elevator constructor **7318**

elevator constructor helper **7612**

elevator constructor/mechanic **7318**

elevator erector **7318**

elevator inspector **2262**

elevator installer **7318**

elevator mechanic **7318**

elevator mechanic apprentice **7318**

elevator mechanic helper **7612**

elevator operator **6683**

elevator repair mechanic **7318**

elevator repairer **7318**

elevators maintenance service supervisor **7216**

elpo tank attendant **9496**

ema **3234**

embalmer **6272**

embalmer apprentice **6272**

embalmer's apprentice **6272**

embalming teacher – college or vocational institute **4131**

emblem fuser operator – clothing manufacturing **9619**

embosser operator – textile **9517**

embossing calender operator – pulp and paper **9433**

embossing calender tender – textiles **9443**

embossing/encoding machine tender – printing **9473**

embossing/imprinting machine operator **9471**

embossing machine operator – footwear **9517**

embossing machine operator – printing **9471**

embossing machine operator – textile **9517**

embossing machine operator – woodworking **9513**

embossing machine tender – explosives manufacturing **9516**

embossing machine tender – woodworking **9513**

embossing press operator – printing **9473**

embossing printer **9471**

embroiderer, hand **5244**

embroiderer, machine **9442**

embroidery designer **5243**

embroidery frame, mounter **9619**

embroidery machine operator **9442**

embroidery patternmaker **5245**

embroidery supervisor – fabric products **9225**

embryologist **2121**

EMCA **3234**

emergency admitting clerk **1414**

emergency aide **3413**

emergency line repairer – electric power systems **7244**

emergency medical assistant **3234**

emergency medical attendant **3234**

emergency medical care assistant **3234**

emergency medical care attendant **3234**

emergency medical dispatcher **1475**

emergency medical technician **3234**

emergency medicine, chief of **0311**

emergency medicine specialist **3111**

emergency paramedic **3234**

emergency physician **3111**

emergency repairer, transit vehicle **7383**

emergency road servicer, motor vehicle **7443**

emergency servicer – electric power systems **7244**

emergency vehicle dispatcher **1475**

emergentologist **3111**

emery grading operator – stone products **9414**

EMG lab technician **3218**

EMG technician **3218**

EMG technologist **3218**

EMG technologist, chief **3218**

employee benefits manager **0112**

employee benefits officer **1121**

employee fitness consultant **4167**

employee insurance clerk **1434**

employee relations co-ordinator **1121**

employee relations manager **0112**

employee relations officer **1121**

employees representative **1121**

employment advisor **1121**

employment agencies general manager **0013**

employment agency manager **0123**

employment clerk **1442**

employment counsellor assistant **1442**

employment counsellor – government services **4213**

employment counsellor supervisor **4213**

employment equity co-ordinator **1121**

employment equity manager **0112**

employment equity officer **1121**
employment initiatives co-ordinator **4164**
employment interviewer **1223**
employment manager **0112**
employment practices officer **1121**
employment recruiter **1223**
employment services officer **4213**
employment specialist **4213**
employment staffing officer **1223**
employment standards specialist **4164**
employment supervisor **1223**
EMT **3234**
EMT – P **3234**
enamel applier, jewellery **9498**
enamel baker – manufacturing **9497**
enamel burner – glass products **9413**
enamel decorator, jewellery **9498**
enamel dipper **9496**
enameler – electrical equipment **9496**
enameler – industrial painting and coating **9496**
enameler, ship and boat building **9496**
enameller, hand **5244**
enamelling furnace operator – glass products **9413**
enamelling machine tender **9496**
enamellist **5244**
enamelware paint baker – glass products **9413**
encapsulator – electrical equipment manufacturing **9487**
encyclopedia collaborator **5121**
encyclopedia salesperson, door-to-door **6623**
end bore operator – woodworking **9513**
end matcher, sash and door – woodworking **9513**
end roller – primary metal processing **9411**
end trim and bore machine operator – woodworking **9513**
endocrinologist **3111**
endocrinology, chief of **0311**
endodontist **3113**
energy conservation engineer **2132**
energy (from waste) plant operator **7351**
energy policy analyst **4161**
energy policy director – government services **0412**
enforcement officer – forestry **2223**
ENG camera operator **5222**
ENG editor **5225**
engine accessories assembly foreman/woman **9226**
engine accessories inspector **9486**
engine accessories overhaul mechanic **7315**
engine assembler, gasoline **9486**
engine assembly foreman/woman (except aircraft) **9226**
engine block tester – motor vehicle manufacturing **9482**

engine dispatcher – railway **2275**
engine dress assembler – motor vehicle manufacturing **9482**
engine dynamometer tester **9486**
engine fitter, aircraft **7316**
engine fitter helper **7612**
engine fitter, ship **7316**
engine generator set assembler **9484**
engine hostler **7361**
engine inspector, aircraft **7315**
engine inspector – motor vehicle manufacturing **9482**
engine installer – motor vehicle manufacturing **9482**
engine lathe set-up operator **9511**
engine mechanic, aircraft **7315**
engine mechanic – motor vehicle **7321**
engine overhaul inspector, aircraft mechanical systems **7315**
engine rebuilding shop foreman/woman **9226**
engine room crew, ship **7434**
engine technician, aircraft mechanical systems **7315**
engine tester, aircraft **7315**
engine tester – motor vehicle manufacturing **9482**
engine testing foreman/woman (except aircraft) **9226**
engineer, acoustics and vibration **2132**
engineer, aeronautical **2146**
engineer, aerospace **2146**
engineer, agricultural **2148**
engineer, automotive **2132**
engineer, bio-technology **2134**
engineer, biochemical **2134**
engineer, biomedical **2148**
engineer, ceramics **2142**
engineer, chemical **2134**
engineer, civil **2131**
engineer, computer **2147**
engineer, computer integrated manufacturing **2141**
engineer, electrical **2133**
engineer, electronic **2133**
engineer, electronics **2133**
engineer, environmental **2131**
engineer, food processing **2148**
engineer, food technology **2148**
engineer, forest **2122**
engineer, geological **2144**
engineer, geophysical **2144**
engineer, geotechnical **2144**
engineer, hydrogeological **2144**
engineer, industrial **2141**
engineer, industrial hygiene **2134**
engineer, instrument **2133**
engineer, instrument and control **2133**
engineer, manufacturing **2141**

engineer, marine and naval **2148**
engineer, materials **2142**
engineer, mechanical **2132**
engineer, metallurgical **2142**
engineer, mineral **2143**
engineer, mining **2143**
engineer, municipal **2131**
engineer, naval **2148**
engineer, nuclear **2132**
engineer, nuclear operations **2132**
engineer officer, fishing vessel **2274**
engineer officer – water transport **2274**
engineer, optical communications **2133**
engineer, petroleum **2145**
engineer, power **7351**
engineer, power generation **2132**
engineer, process **2134**
engineer, pulp and paper **2134**
engineer, railway locomotive **7361**
engineer's assistant **7622**
engineer, software **2147**
engineer, soil **2144**
engineer, solid waste management **2131**
engineer, stationary **7351**
engineer, structural **2131**
engineer, surveying **2131**
engineer, systems **2147**
engineer, textile **2148**
engineer trainee, railway **7361**
engineer, tugboat **2274**
engineering and architecture professor –
    university **4121**
engineering and scientific programmer **2163**
engineering assistant, mechanical
    equipment **2232**
engineering clerk **1441**
engineering department inspector, local
    government **2262**
engineering department manager **0211**
engineering depreciation evaluator **2141**
engineering design technician **2253**
engineering design technologist **2253**
engineering draftsman/woman **2253**
engineering firm president **0013**
engineering geologist **2144**
engineering group manager **0211**
engineering inspector **2262**
engineering manager **0211**
engineering meteorologist **2114**
engineering physicist **2148**
engineering psychologist **4151**
engineering quality control department
    director **0211**
engineering quality control manager **0211**
engineering research and development
    director **0211**
engineering scientist **2148**
engineering supplies salesperson **6221**

engineering survey technician **2254**
engineering survey technologist **2254**
engineering test pilot **2271**
engineering vice president – financial,
    communications and other business
    services **0013**
engineering vice president – goods
    production, utilities, transportation
    and construction **0016**
engineering vice president – trade,
    broadcasting and other services
    n.e.c. **0015**
English as a second language teacher
    (except elementary, high school or
    university) **4131**
English as second language teacher –
    elementary school **4142**
English as second language teacher –
    high school **4141**
English literature high school teacher **4141**
English teacher – business college **4131**
English teacher – secondary school **4141**
engraver, decorative **5244**
engraver, hand **5244**
engraver, monuments **9414**
engraver, pantograph **5244**
engraver, printing cylinders **9472**
engraver, printing plates **9472**
engraver, stonework **9414**
engraving machine operator **9517**
enquiries clerk **1453**
enrobing machine operator – food and
    beverage processing **9461**
entering machine operator – textiles **9442**
entertainer **5232**
entomological technician **2221**
entomological technologist **2221**
entomologist **2121**
entremetier **6241**
enumerator **1454**
envelope machine tender – paper
    converting **9435**
envelope maker, hand **9498**
envelope maker operator **9435**
envelope making machine setter – paper
    converting **9435**
environment planner **2153**
environmental and occupational
    toxicologist **2121**
environmental biologist **2121**
environmental chamber fitter/assembler **9484**
environmental chemist **2112**
environmental consultant **4161**
environmental engineer **2131**
environmental engineer, chemical **2134**
environmental epidemiologist **2161**
environmental geologist **2113**
environmental group director **0314**

environmental health inspector **2263**

environmental health inspector
  supervisor **2263**

environmental health officer **2263**

environmental health officer supervisor **2263**

environmental impact analyst **4161**

environmental issues lobbyist **4161**

environmental lobbyist **4161**

environmental officer **2263**

environmental science manager **0212**

environmental technician **2231**

environmental toxicologist **2121**

enzyme chemist **2112**

enzyme injector – food and beverage
  processing **9462**

enzymologist **2121**

epidemiologist **2161**

epidemiologist, veterinary **3114**

epidemiology and community medicine
  specialist **3111**

epidemiology worker – medical
  laboratory **3212**

epoxy coating machine operator –
  electrical equipment manufacturing **9487**

epoxy encapsulator – electrical
  equipment manufacturing **9487**

epoxy pouring machine operator **9517**

epoxy pouring operator **9517**

equalizer operator, woodworking **9513**

equine veterinarian **3114**

equipment chief – telecommunications **0131**

equipment cleaner – chemical
  processing **9613**

equipment development technician **2232**

equipment installer & repairer –
  telecommunications **7246**

equipment inventory clerk **1474**

equipment maintenance technician –
  electronics **2241**

equipment operator, heavy duty **7421**

equipment operator, railway **7432**

equipment restorer – museum **5212**

equity trader **1113**

erecting engineer **2131**

erector, neon sign **7441**

erector, pre-cast concrete **7264**

erector, scaffold **7611**

erector, sign **7441**

erector, steel stud – non bearing walls **7611**

ergonomist **4161**

escalator inspector **2262**

escalator installer **7318**

escalator repairer **7318**

escalator repairman/woman **7318**

escort interpreter **5125**

escort, tour or travel **6441**

essayist **5121**

establishment guide **6441**

estate administrator **1114**

estate and trust administrator **1114**

estate secretary **1242**

esthetic service manager **0651**

esthetician **6482**

estimator, construction **2234**

estimator, electrical – construction **2234**

estimator, jewellery **7344**

estimator, material **1473**

estimator, mechanical – construction **2234**

estimator, media **1225**

estimator, trade contractor –
  construction **2234**

etcher, aircraft parts **9511**

etcher and plater, quartz crystal **9483**

etcher, cutlery and tool **9511**

etcher, electrolytic **9511**

etcher, firearms **9511**

etcher, gravure – printing **9472**

etcher helper, gravure – printing **9619**

etcher, iron foundry **9511**

etcher, jewellery and silverware **9511**

etcher, photoengraving **9472**

etcher, platemaking **9472**

etcher, printed circuit board **9483**

etching corrector – printing **9472**

ethnic food cook **6242**

ethnic relations constable – police **6261**

ethnographer **4169**

ethnologist **4169**

ethnology curator **5112**

etiquette consultant **6481**

eto storeman/woman, railway **7452**

etymologist **4169**

evaluation officer, job creation and
  employment services **4164**

evangelist **4154**

evaporator operator – chemical
  processing **9421**

evaporator tender – pulp and paper **9432**

event co-ordinator **1226**

event planner **1226**

evergreen grower **8254**

evergreens picker **8612**

evidence photographer **5221**

evidence technician – police **6261**

eviscerator, animal – meat packing **9462**

evoked potential technologist **3218**

ex officio judge **4111**

ex officio justice **4111**

examiner, citizenship registration **1228**

examiner, claims – insurance **1233**

examiner, credit unions **1114**

examiner, financial institutions **1114**

excavating and grading labour
  foreman/woman **7217**

excavating contractor **7217**

excavating equipment mechanic **7312**

excavation labourer **7611**
excavation worker **7611**
excavations superintendent **7217**
excavator foreman/woman **7217**
excavator operator **7421**
exchange clerk **1453**
exchange installer and repairer – telecommunications **7246**
exchange operator – telephone system **1424**
exchange tester – telecommunications **7246**
excise duty agent **1228**
excise duty officer **1228**
excise duty supervisor **1228**
excise examiner **1228**
excise tax collection supervisor **1228**
excise tax collector **1228**
excise tax inspector **1228**
executive administrator, government agency **0012**
executive administrator, government department **0012**
executive assistant **1222**
executive chef **6241**
executive director, alumni association **0314**
executive director – arts association **0014**
executive director, assistant – financial, communications and other business services **0013**
executive director, assistant – goods production, utilities, transportation and construction **0016**
executive director, assistant – health, education, social and community services and membership organizations **0014**
executive director, assistant – trade, broadcasting and other services n.e.c. **0015**
executive director, association **0314**
executive director, automobile association **0015**
executive director – craft guild **0014**
executive director – crafts association **0014**
executive director, credit union **0013**
executive director – environmental association **0014**
executive director – financial, communications and other business services **0013**
executive director – goods production, utilities, transporation and construction **0016**
executive director, government services **0012**
executive director – health, education, social and community services and membership organizations **0014**
executive director – health services institution **0014**
executive director, museum **0511**

executive director – non-government organization **0014**
executive director, non-government organization (NGO) **0314**
executive director, nurses' association **0314**
executive director – professional association **0014**
executive director – recreation association **0014**
executive director, teachers' federation **0314**
executive director – trade, broadcasting and other services n.e.c. **0015**
executive director – voluntary organization **0014**
executive director ymca **0513**
executive general manager – health, education, social and community services and membership organizations **0014**
executive general manager – trade, broadcasting and other services n.e.c. **0015**
executive housekeeper **6213**
executive housekeeping, assistant **6213**
executive housekeeping manager **6213**
executive officer, firefighters **0642**
executive pilot **2271**
executive producer, film and video **0512**
executive recruiter **1223**
executive secretary **1241**
executive sous-chef **6241**
executive vice-president – financial, communications and other business services **0013**
executive vice-president – goods production, utilities, transportation and construction **0016**
executive vice president – health, education, social and community services and membership organizations **0014**
executive vice-president – metal and metal products wholesaler **0015**
executive vice-president – railway **0016**
executive vice-president – real estate agency **0013**
executive vice-president – trade, broadcasting and other services n.e.c. **0015**
executor, estate **1114**
exerciser, racehorse **8431**
exhaust and sealing machine operator **9483**
exhibit designer **5243**
exhibit officer – museum **5212**
exhibit preparator **5212**
exhibition and display designer **5243**
exotic dancer **5232**
expanded duty dental hygienist **3222**

expanded duty dental nurse **3222**
expander, metalworking **9514**
expansion joint builder – rubber
    manufacturing **9423**
expansion joint finisher – rubber
    manufacturing **9423**
expediter **1473**
expediter, purchasing **1473**
expenditure clerk **1431**
experimental aircraft mechanic **7315**
experimental farm superintendent **0212**
experimental home economist **4164**
experimental physicist **2111**
experimental psychologist **4151**
experimental test pilot **2271**
experimental tire manufacturing
    inspector **9423**
exploration engineer, mines **2143**
exploration geologist **2113**
exploration geophysicist **2113**
explosives and ammunition magazine
    foreman/woman **1215**
explosives and ammunition magazine
    keeper **1472**
explosives and ammunition magazine
    keeper – military **1472**
explosives engineer **2134**
explosives handler **7452**
explosives mixer **9421**
explosives packer **7452**
explosives senior operator **9232**
explosives truck driver **7411**
export booking clerk **1471**
export clerk **1441**
export documentation clerk **1441**
export sales manager **0611**
export traffic clerk **1441**
export traffic manager **0713**
export traffic supervisor **1215**
exporter **6411**
express handler (except airlines) **7452**
express mail clerk **1461**
extensible conveyor belt assembler –
    underground mining **8411**
extension forester **2122**
extension home economist **4164**
extension officer, museum **5124**
extension ranger – forestry **2223**
extension technician – forestry **2223**
exterior cladder **7441**
exterior cladder helper **7611**
exterior plasterer **7284**
exterior trailer finisher **9486**
exterior trimmer, building **7441**
exterminating service supervisor **7219**
exterminator, pests **7444**
extra, performing arts **5135**
extracorporeal circulation technologist **3214**

extracorporeal technician **3214**
extracorporeal technologist **3214**
extract maker – food and beverage
    processing **9461**
extractive metallurgist **2142**
extractor machine tender – textiles **9443**
extractor operator, laundry and dry
    cleaning **6681**
extruded metal coiler tender – primary
    metal processing **9411**
extruder machine operator – rubber
    manufacturing **9423**
extruder operator – concrete, clay and
    stone products **9414**
extruder operator – plastic
    manufacturing **9422**
extruder operator – rubber
    manufacturing **9423**
extruding foreman/woman – primary
    metal and mineral products
    processing **9211**
extruding machine operator helper –
    plastic and rubber manufacturing **9615**
extruding machine operator – plastic
    manufacturing **9422**
extruding machine operator – rubber
    manufacturing **9423**
extrusion finisher – rubber
    manufacturing **9423**
extrusion foreman/woman – rubber and
    plastic manufacturing **9214**
extrusion helper – primary metal
    processing **9611**
extrusion machine operator – plastic
    manufacturing **9422**
extrusion press operator – primary metal
    processing **9411**
eye specialist **3111**
eyeglass fitter **3231**
eyeglass frame assembler **9498**
eyeglass frame cutter **9498**
eyeglass frame inspector and sorter **9498**
eyeglass frame trimmer **9619**
eyeglass pad cementer **9619**

F

fabric cutter – fabric products
    manufacturing **9452**
fabric design technologist **2233**
fabric designer **5243**
fabric dyer **9443**
fabric estimator **1473**
fabric examiner **9444**
fabric grader **9444**
fabric inspector **9444**
fabric marker **9452**
fabric repairer **9451**

fabric salesperson **6421**
fabric store manager **0621**
fabric washer **9443**
fabrication welder **7265**
fabricator, microelectronic circuits **9483**
fabricator, plastics **9495**
fabricator, platework **7263**
fabricator, structural metal **7263**
fabricator, structural steel **7263**
face boss – underground mining **8221**
faceman/woman, coal mine **8231**
facer operator – woodworking **9513**
facial treatment operator **6482**
facilitator, conference **1122**
facilities man/woman –
    telecommunications **7246**
facilities manager – telecommunications **0131**
facility maintenance manager **0722**
facility operation manager **0721**
facsimile equipment installer **7246**
facsimile operator **1411**
factory cleaner **6663**
factory helper **9619**
factory labourer **9619**
factory maintenance man/woman **6663**
factory shoe repairer **9498**
factory superintendent **0911**
factory tour guide **6441**
faculty administrator **0312**
faculty of arts dean **0312**
faith healer **4217**
faller and bucker – logging **8421**
faller – logging **8421**
family and children's services director –
    government services **0411**
family and estates lawyer **4112**
family counsellor **4153**
family court judge **4111**
family court registrar **1227**
family court supervisor **1227**
family doctor **3112**
family law clerk **4211**
family law legal assistant **4211**
family law paralegal **4211**
family physician **3112**
family planning counsellor **4153**
family service worker **4212**
family services area manager **0314**
family social worker **4152**
family violence prevention program
    advisor **4164**
fancy stitch machine operator **9451**
fancy wire drawer – jewellery
    manufacturing **9517**
farebox collector **6683**
farebox servicer **7445**
farm blacksmith **7383**
farm boss **8253**

farm consultant **2123**
farm couple **8431**
farm economist **4162**
farm equipment repair foreman/woman **7216**
farm foreman/woman **8253**
farm hand **8431**
farm implements bench assembler **9486**
farm irrigating system contractor **8252**
farm labourer **8431**
farm machinery assembler **9486**
farm machinery inspection
    foreman/woman **9226**
farm machinery operator **8431**
farm machinery salesperson **6221**
farm management consultant **2123**
farm manager **8251**
farm produce grading service contractor **8252**
farm supervisor **8253**
farm tractor mechanic **7312**
farm tractor repairer **7312**
farm underwriter **1234**
farm vacation operator **0632**
farm worker **8431**
farmer (except nursery and fish) **8251**
farmer, nursery **8254**
farrier **7383**
fashion and wardrobe consultant **6481**
fashion co-ordinator **5243**
fashion colour consultant **6481**
fashion columnist **5123**
fashion consultant **6481**
fashion designer **5243**
fashion illustrator **5241**
fashion model **5232**
fashion show commentator **5231**
fashion teacher – community college **4131**
fast food delivery driver **7414**
fast food preparer **6641**
fast-food service worker **6641**
fastener, shoe parts **9517**
fats and oils loader **7452**
feature editor **5122**
feature reporter **5123**
feature writer **5121**
federal and intergovernmental affairs
    research officer – government
    services **4168**
federal appeal court justice **4111**
federal court justice **4111**
federal-provincial relations director **0414**
federal-provincial relations manager **0414**
federal-provincial relations officer **4168**
federal supreme court justice **4111**
federal trial court justice **4111**
feed and flour mills general manager **0016**
feed mill loader **7452**
feed miller – food and beverage
    processing **9461**

feed mixer – food and beverage
    processing **9461**
feed products sales representative **6411**
feed tester – food and beverage
    processing **9465**
feeder – chemical processing **9613**
feeder mill operator – rubber
    manufacturing **9423**
feeder – printing **9619**
feeder switchboard operator apprentice –
    electric power systems **7352**
feeder switchboard operator – electric
    power systems **7352**
feeder, textile machine **9616**
feeder – wood processing **9614**
feedlot foreman/woman **8253**
feedlot manager **8251**
feedlot operator **8251**
feedlot worker **8431**
feller buncher operator **8241**
feller delimber operator **8241**
feller forwarder operator **8241**
feller – logging **8421**
felt drier – textiles **9443**
felt finishing room foreman/woman, felt
    hat manufacturing **9225**
felt making machine operator **9442**
felt repairer, papermaking **7311**
felting machine tender **9442**
fence builder **7441**
fence contractor **7219**
fence erector **7441**
fence installer **7441**
fence making machine operator **9516**
fermentation inspector, wineries **9465**
fermentation operator – food and
    beverage processing **9461**
fermenter, antibiotics **9232**
fermenter – tobacco processing **9464**
fermentologist **2112**
ferris wheel operator **6443**
ferry boat deck hand **7433**
ferry superintendent **0713**
ferry terminal worker **7435**
ferryboat captain **2273**
ferryboat master **2273**
ferryboat operator **2273**
fertilizer maker, phosphate process **9232**
festival organizer **1226**
fiber strap machine tender **9517**
fibre classer **9441**
fibre examiner – textiles **9444**
fibre glass lay-up worker – plastic
    manufacturing **9495**
fibre grader – textiles **9444**
fibre inspector – textiles **9444**
fibre mixer **9441**
fibre optic cable splicer **7245**

fibre optics technician **2241**
fibre washer **9441**
fibreglass binder mixer **9421**
fibreglass boat assembler **9491**
fibreglass boat assembly repairer **9491**
fibreglass boat foreman/woman **9227**
fibreglass boat inspector and finisher **9491**
fibreglass filter assembler **9495**
fibreglass forming machine repairer **7311**
fibreglass inspector **9495**
fibreglass insulation installer **7293**
fibreglass laminator **9495**
fibreglass lay-up man/woman **9495**
fibreglass machine operator **9422**
fibreglass moulder **9422**
fibreglass oven helper **9611**
fibreglass plastics foreman/woman **9214**
fibreglass spraying machine operator **9422**
fibreglass tester **9415**
fiction writer **5121**
field adjuster – insurance **1233**
field agent – insurance **6231**
field and vegetable crop labourer **8431**
field artilleryman/woman – military **6464**
field auditor – financial **1111**
field auditor – taxation **1228**
field coil taper – industrial electric
    equipment **9485**
field crop foreman/woman **8253**
field crop technician **2221**
field crop technologist **2221**
field director, manufacturing **0911**
field engineer equipment – military **7421**
field engineer – military **6464**
field engineer, radio and television **2133**
field foreman/woman, nursery **8256**
field inspector, construction **2264**
field measurement hand, utilities **7442**
field mechanic, heavy equipment **7312**
field mechanic helper **7612**
field office supervisor – forestry **2223**
field officer, veterans' affairs **4212**
field operator, nuclear generating station
    – electric power systems **7352**
field operator – pulp and paper **9432**
field reporter **5123**
field representative – housing **4164**
field representative – insurance **6231**
field sales manager **0611**
field salesperson – wholesale **6411**
field service adviser – agriculture **2123**
field service agent – agriculture **2123**
field service manager – postal and
    courier service **0132**
field service technician – household and
    business equipment **2242**
field supervisor, ambulance service **3234**

field supervisor, occupational health and safety **2263**

field supervisor, oil well services **8222**

field technologist – geophysics **2212**

field technologist, petroleum **2212**

fifth class stationary engineer **7351**

fifth hand – pulp and paper **9614**

figure skater **5251**

figure skating judge **5253**

filament coater **9497**

filament stem inspector – electronics manufacturing **9483**

filament tester – electronics manufacturing **9483**

file and classification clerk **1413**

file clerk **1413**

file clerks supervisor **1211**

file cutter – metal machining **9511**

file maker – metal machining **9511**

file systems analyst **1122**

filer, hand – metal fabrication **9612**

filer, jewellery **9498**

filer, photograph – library **1451**

fill foreman/woman – underground mining **8221**

filler, liquefied gases **9421**

fillet chopper – fish processing **9463**

filleting machine operator – fish processing **9463**

filleting machine setter – fish processing **9463**

filling carrier – textiles **9616**

filling machine set-up man **9461**

filling machine setter **9461**

filling machine tender – electrical equipment manufacturing **9487**

filling station attendant **6621**

film assembler – printing **9472**

film camera operator **5222**

film counter clerk **6421**

film cutter – film processing **9619**

film developer **9474**

film developer foreman/woman **7218**

film developing machine tender **9474**

film director **5131**

film editor **5131**

film facilities supervisor **5226**

film file clerk **1413**

film location manager **5226**

film mounter – film processing **9619**

film numberer – film processing **9619**

film printer foreman/woman **7218**

film printer, photographic **9474**

film printing machine operator **9474**

film printing machine tender **9474**

film processing foreman/woman **7218**

film processing machine operator **9474**

film processing supervisor **7218**

film processing technician **9474**

film processing unit assembler **9498**

film processor **9474**

film producer **5131**

film production manager **0512**

film quality inspector **5227**

film rental clerk **6421**

film sizer – printing **9472**

film splicer **9474**

film stripper/assembler – printing **9472**

film stripper specialist – printing **9472**

film technician **5225**

film vault clerk – library **1451**

filmmaker **5131**

films and recordings library clerk **1451**

filter assembler – electronics manufacturing **9483**

filter assembler, oil **9498**

filter cigarette machine tender **9464**

filter cleaner – chemical processing **9613**

filter leaves cleaner – primary metal and mineral products processing **9611**

filter plant foreman/woman – primary metal and mineral products processing **9211**

filter plant operator, water treatment **9424**

filter press tender – chemical processing **9421**

filtering attendant – primary metal and mineral products processing **9611**

filterman/woman – pulp and paper **9432**

filtration helper – chemical processing **9613**

final assembler, electrical control panel **9485**

final assembler, garment **9619**

final assembly inspector – aircraft assembly **9481**

final assembly tester – electronics manufacturing **9483**

final inspector, automobile – motor vehicle manufacturing **9482**

final inspector, furniture assembly **9492**

final inspector, garments **9454**

final inspector, snowmobile **9486**

final inspector, truck trailer **9486**

final inspector, watch assembly **9498**

finance and administration, director **0114**

finance and administration vice-president – financial, communications and other business services **0013**

finance and administration vice-president – goods production, utilities, transportation and construction **0016**

finance and administration vice-president – health, education, social and community services and membership organizations **0014**

finance and administration
    vice-president – trade, broadcasting
    and other services n.e.c. **0015**
finance and credit administrator,
    international banking **1114**
finance clerk **1431**
finance clerk – military **1431**
finance vice president – financial,
    communications and other business
    services **0013**
finance vice president – goods
    production, utilities, transportation
    and construction **0016**
finance vice president – health,
    education, social and community
    services and membership
    organizations **0014**
finance vice president – trade,
    broadcasting and other services
    n.e.c. **0015**
financial accountant **1111**
financial accounting supervisor **1212**
financial administrator **0111**
financial analyst **1112**
financial assistance co-ordinator –
    college or university **1221**
financial assistance officer **4212**
financial assistance worker **4212**
financial broker **1113**
financial brokerage manager **0121**
financial clerk **1434**
financial consultant **1112**
financial control manager **0111**
financial control officer **1111**
financial director **0111**
financial economist **4162**
financial editor **5122**
financial evaluations director **0111**
financial institutions inspector **1114**
financial investigator **1114**
financial manager **0111**
financial planner **1114**
financial reporter **5123**
financial services salesperson **6411**
financial statistician **2161**
fine art administrator **0114**
fine arts and polychromes conservator **5112**
fine arts archivist **5113**
fine arts professor – university **4121**
fine arts teacher – college **4131**
fine arts teacher – high school **4141**
fingerprint classifier **1413**
fingerprint classifier supervisor **1215**
fingerprint clerk **1413**
finish carpenter **7271**
finish carpenters foreman/woman **7215**
finish grinder – metal products
    manufacturing **9612**

finish photographer **5221**
finish planer operator – woodworking **9513**
finish plasterer **7284**
finish sander, furniture **9619**
finished product inspector – electronics
    manufacturing **9483**
finisher, artificial limb **3219**
finisher, cement **7282**
finisher, concrete **7282**
finisher – concrete, clay and stone
    products **9414**
finisher, concrete floors **7282**
finisher, concrete products **7282**
finisher, drywall **7284**
finisher/grinder – plastic manufacturing **9495**
finisher – laundry and dry cleaning **6682**
finisher, plastic products **9495**
finisher, plastic sheets **9495**
finisher – primary metal processing **9411**
finisher – pulp and paper **9433**
finisher – textiles **9443**
finishing carpenter **7271**
finishing department foreman/woman –
    fabric, fur and leather products
manufacturing **9225**
finishing foreman/woman – plastic
    manufacturing **9214**
finishing foreman/woman – printing **7218**
finishing foreman/woman – rubber
    manufacturing **9214**
finishing inspector – primary metal and
    mineral products processing **9415**
finishing inspector – textiles **9444**
finishing machine operator – furniture
    manufacturing **9494**
finishing machine operator – printing **9473**
finishing machine operator – textiles **9443**
finishing range operator – textiles **9443**
finishing room foreman/woman – fabric,
    fur and leather products
    manufacturing **9225**
finishing room foreman/woman –
    furniture and fixtures manufacturing **9224**
finishing supervisor – printing **7218**
finishing supervisor – textiles **9216**
finishing trimmer – footwear
    manufacturing **9619**
fire alarm electronic technician **2242**
fire alarm operator **1475**
fire alarm system installer and servicer **2242**
fire boss **8221**
fire brick layer **7281**
fire captain **6262**
fire chief **0642**
fire chief, industrial **0642**
fire control operator – military **6464**
fire control systems technician, land –
    military **2241**

fire control technician, electronic – military **2241**
fire control technician – military **6464**
fire control technician, optronic – military **2241**
fire crew leader – forestry **2223**
fire crewman/woman **8422**
fire department dispatcher **1475**
fire equipment repairer **7445**
fire equipment servicer **7445**
fire equipment servicer helper **7612**
fire extinguisher repairer **7445**
fire hose curer, rubber **9423**
fire hose maker, rubber **9423**
fire inspector **6262**
fire insulator **7293**
fire insurance adjuster **1233**
fire insurance agent **6231**
fire insurance salesman/woman **6231**
fire lieutenant **6262**
fire marshal **0012**
fire patrol pilot **2271**
fire prevention engineer **2141**
fire protection insulator **7293**
fire protection piping installer **7252**
fire protection technician **2233**
fire safety inspector – non-government **6465**
fire sprinkler fitter **7252**
fire suppression crew foreman/woman – forestry **8211**
fire suppression crewman/woman **8422**
fire suppression officer – forestry **2223**
fire underwriter **1234**
firearm section inspector – police **0641**
firearms assembly foreman/woman **9227**
firearms cleaner **9612**
firearms etcher **9511**
firearms examiner **2115**
firearms expert **2115**
firearms fitter **9486**
firearms machining inspector **7231**
firearms model maker machinist **7231**
firebrick helper **7611**
firecontrolman/woman – military **6464**
firefighter **6262**
firefighter apprentice **6262**
firefighter, communication **6262**
firefighter, fire safety inspection **6262**
firefighter, fire safety inspection – military **6464**
firefighter hat assembler **9498**
firefighter lieutenant **6262**
firefighter – military **6262**
firefighter, shipboard **6262**
firefighter, structural **6262**
firefighter, structural – military **6262**
firefighter, training **6262**
firefighting instructor **4131**

fireplace brick mason **7281**
fireplace cleaner **6662**
fireproofing applicator **7284**
fireproofing plasterer **7284**
fireworks handler **5227**
fireworks maker **9498**
fireworks pyrotechnic assembler **9498**
first aid attendant **3234**
first aid director **0311**
first aid nurse **3152**
first class power engineer **7351**
first class stationary engineer **7351**
first cook **6242**
first engineer, factory freezer trawler **2274**
first engineer, self-propelled drilling rig **2274**
first mate, ferryboat **2273**
first mate, fishing vessel **8261**
first mate, foreign going **2273**
first mate, home trade **2273**
first mate, inland water **2273**
first mate, self-propelled drilling rig **2273**
first mate, ship **2273**
first officer, airplane **2271**
first pressman/woman – printing **7381**
first secretary, foreign service **4168**
first sous-chef **6241**
first watchkeeping engineer, coast guard vessel **2274**
first watchkeeping officer, coast guard vessel **2273**
fiscal analyst **4162**
fiscal clerk **1431**
fish and chips cook – fish processing **9463**
fish and chips preparer **6641**
fish and fish products inspector **2222**
fish and game warden **2224**
fish and wildlife officer **2224**
fish bin worker – fish processing **9618**
fish boner – fish processing **9463**
fish briner – fish processing **9618**
fish broiler – fish processing **9463**
fish by-products processor **9463**
fish cake former – fish processing **9463**
fish cake maker – fish processing **9463**
fish camp operator **0632**
fish canning machine operator – fish processing **9463**
fish cleaner and cutter – fish processing **9463**
fish cleaning machine tender – fish processing **9463**
fish cook – fish processing **9463**
fish culler **9618**
fish culture manager **8257**
fish culture operator **8257**
fish curer – fish processing **9463**
fish cutting machine operator – fish processing **9463**

fish cutting machine setter – fish
    processing **9463**
fish dipper – fish processing **9618**
fish dresser – fish processing **9463**
fish drier and grinder tender – fish
    processing **9463**
fish drier tender – fish processing **9463**
fish egg processor – fish processing **9463**
fish farm helper **8613**
fish farm manager **8257**
fish farm operator **8257**
fish farm technologist **2221**
fish farm worker **8613**
fish farmer **8257**
fish flaker – fish processing **9618**
fish freezer worker – fish processing **9618**
fish freezing and storage
    foreman/woman **9213**
fish fryer – fish processing **9463**
fish grader **9465**
fish handler – fish processing **9618**
fish hatchery attendant **8613**
fish hatchery manager **8257**
fish hatchery operator **8257**
fish hatchery tagger **8613**
fish hatchery technician **2221**
fish hatchery worker **8613**
fish header – fish processing **9463**
fish icer – fish processing **9618**
fish inspector **2222**
fish monger **6623**
fish net making machine operator **9517**
fish offal processor – fish processing **9463**
fish oil separator – fish processing **9463**
fish packer – fish processing **9618**
fish paste grinder – fish processing **9463**
fish pickler – fish processing **9618**
fish plant machine operator – fish
    processing **9463**
fish plant manager **0911**
fish preparation foreman/woman **9213**
fish presser operator – fish processing **9463**
fish processing labourer **9618**
fish processing machine feeder tender **9463**
fish processing machine operator **9463**
fish processing plant labourer **9618**
fish processing plant worker **9463**
fish processor **9463**
fish product inspector **2222**
fish products inspection supervisor **2222**
fish products maker – fish processing **9463**
fish racker – fish processing **9618**
fish reduction foreman/woman **9213**
fish roe technician **2221**
fish salter – fish processing **9618**
fish skinner operator – fish processing **9463**
fish smoker – fish processing **9463**
fish sorter **9618**

fish splitter – fish processing **9463**
fish stick machine tender – fish
    processing **9463**
fish tagger **8613**
fish trimmer – fish processing **9463**
fish washer – fish processing **9618**
fisheries analyst **4161**
fisheries area supervisor **2224**
fisheries inspector **2224**
fisheries observer **2224**
fisheries policy director – government
    services **0412**
fisheries technician **2221**
fisheries technologist **2221**
fisherman/woman **8262**
fishery bacteriological technician **2221**
fishery bacteriological technologist **2221**
fishery bacteriologist **2121**
fishery officer **2224**
fishing guide **6442**
fishing lure designer **5243**
fishing master **8261**
fishing operations manager **0811**
fishing reel assembler **9498**
fishing rod assembler **9498**
fishing rod finisher **9498**
fishing tackle maker **9498**
fishing tool operator – oil field services **8232**
fishing vessel boatswain **8261**
fishing vessel captain **8261**
fishing vessel deckhand **8441**
fishing vessel master **8261**
fishing vessels appraiser **1235**
fit-up welder **7265**
fitness co-ordinator **4167**
fitness consultant **4167**
fitness instructor **5254**
fitness leader **5254**
fitness leadership consultant **4167**
fitness policy analyst **4167**
fitter, aircraft engine **7316**
fitter and adjuster – motor vehicle
    manufacturing **9482**
fitter and assembler, AC and DC motors **9485**
fitter apprentice – structural steel and
    platework **7263**
fitter/assembler – electrical control
    equipment **9485**
fitter/assembler, environmental chamber **9484**
fitter/assembler – industrial electrical
    equipment **9485**
fitter/assembler – structural metal **7263**
fitter, coffin and casket **9492**
fitter, contact lens **3231**
fitter, eyeglass **3231**
fitter, firearms **9486**
fitter, gas main **7253**
fitter, glass frame **3231**

fitter, heavy equipment **7316**
fitter, heavy machinery **7316**
fitter helper – construction **7611**
fitter, lead hand – structural metal and
    platework **7263**
fitter, locomotive **7316**
fitter, machine **7316**
fitter, machinery manufacturing **7316**
fitter – metal fabrication **7263**
fitter, platework **7263**
fitter, production equipment **7316**
fitter, railway coach **7316**
fitter, sprinkler system **7252**
fitter, structural metal **7263**
fitter, structural steel **7263**
fitter, surgical **3219**
fitter, surgical appliances **3219**
fitter/tester, welded assembly – aircraft
    assembly **9481**
fitter-up, furniture **9492**
fitter/welder – structural metal and
    platework **7263**
fitting lathe operator – concrete
    products **9414**
fitting room inspector – fabric products **9454**
fixer, boarding room – textile
    manufacturing **7317**
fixer, textile machine **7317**
fixture assembler **9492**
fixture designer **2252**
flag making machine operator **9517**
flagman/woman – construction **7611**
flaker operator – wood processing **9434**
flaker tender – chemical processing **9421**
flaking roll tender – food and beverage
    processing **9461**
flame annealing machine tender –
    primary metal processing **9411**
flame brazing machine operator **9515**
flame brazing machine setter **9515**
flame cutter helper **9612**
flame cutter – metal fabrication **9514**
flame cutting machine operator – metal
    fabrication **9514**
flame cutting operator – metal
    fabrication **9514**
flame cutting tracer machine operator –
    metal fabrication **9514**
flap curer, rubber **9423**
flap presser, rubber **9423**
flare assembler **9498**
flarer, wood products **9513**
flash butt welder **7265**
flat bed press operator – plastic
    manufacturing **9422**
flat dry cell battery assembler **9487**
flat dry cell machine tender – electrical
    equipment manufacturing **9487**

flat knitter **9442**
flat optical element maker –
    non-prescription **9517**
flat roofer **7291**
flatbed truck driver **7411**
flatwork finisher – laundry and dry
    cleaning **6682**
flatwork folder – laundry and dry
    cleaning **6682**
flatwork foreman/woman – laundry and
    dry cleaning **6214**
flatwork ironer – laundry and dry
    cleaning **6682**
flavour maker – food and beverage
    processing **9461**
flavour maker – tobacco processing **9464**
flavour man/woman – tobacco
    processing **9464**
flavourer – tobacco processing **9464**
flavouring mixer – tobacco processing **9464**
flea market concession operator **0621**
fleecer – textiles **9443**
fleecing machine operator – textiles **9443**
fleet manager, transportation **0713**
fleet sales representative **6411**
flesher, hand – hide and pelt processing **9453**
fleshing machine tender – hide and pelt
    processing **9453**
fletcher – arrow **9498**
flexible plate engraver – printing **9472**
flexible printing plate mounter **9472**
flexo-folder operator – paper converting **9435**
flexographic mounter/proofer – printing **9472**
flexographic press operator – printing **7381**
flexographic pressman/woman –
    printing **7381**
flexographic printing cylinder
    assembler **9472**
flight agent **6433**
flight attendant **6432**
flight attendant instructor **4131**
flight crew scheduler **1476**
flight dispatcher **2272**
flight engineer **2271**
flight engineer officer – military **2271**
flight operation inspector **2262**
flight operations aerospace engineer **2146**
flight operations director **0713**
flight operations manager **0713**
flight operations officer **2272**
flight purser **6432**
flight schedule design manager, airline **0713**
flight scheduler **0713**
flight scheduler manager **0713**
flight service director **6432**
flight service specialist **2272**
flight simulator instructor **4131**
flight steward **6432**

flight steward instructor **4131**
flight stewardess **6432**
flight supervisor, aerial surveys **2271**
flight test inspector, mechanical systems **7315**
float chief operator – glass forming **9413**
float clerk **1411**
float operator – glass forming **9413**
floating crane operator **7371**
flocking machine tender **9443**
flood damage inspector, construction **2264**
floor and wall covering installer,
    residential **7295**
floor attendant, bingo **6671**
floor attendant – printing **9619**
floor cleaner **6661**
floor coverer helper **7611**
floor covering contractor **7219**
floor covering foreman/woman **7219**
floor covering inset cutter – plastic
    manufacturing **9495**
floor covering installer **7295**
floor covering installer apprentice **7295**
floor covering mechanic **7295**
floor covering mechanic's helper **7611**
floor covering salesperson **6421**
floor covering supervisor **7219**
floor coverings and draperies store
    manager **0621**
floor director – broadcasting **5226**
floor finisher **7441**
floor framer, buses and trucks **9486**
floor helper – textiles **9616**
floor inspector – motor vehicle
    manufacturing **9482**
floor layer **7295**
floor layer's helper **7611**
floor layer, terrazzo **7283**
floor manager – broadcasting **5226**
floor manager – retail **0621**
floor mat press tender – plastic
    manufacturing **9422**
floor mat press tender – rubber
    manufacturing **9423**
floor moulder, sand – foundry **9412**
floor sander **7441**
floor sander and finisher **7441**
floor sander and finisher helper **7611**
floor sander and polisher **7441**
floor sheeting layer **7295**
floor sweeper **6661**
floor systems carpenter **7271**
floor tile layer **7295**
floor trader, commodity exchange **1113**
floor trader, stock exchange **1113**
floor worker, bindery **9619**
floor worker, parachutes **9619**
floor worker, printing room **9619**
flooring grader – wood processing **9436**

floorman/woman, hat finishers – fabric,
    fur and leather products
    manufacturing **9225**
floorman/woman, offshore drilling rig **8615**
floorman/woman – oil and gas drilling **8615**
floorman/woman – retail store **6465**
floorwalker – retail store **6465**
floral arranger **6421**
floriculturist **2225**
florist – retail **0621**
flotation cell helper – primary metal and
    mineral products processing **9611**
flotation cell tender – metal processing **9411**
flour blender operator – food and
    beverage processing **9461**
flour inspector **2222**
flour miller **9461**
flour milling team supervisor **9213**
flour mixer helper **9617**
flour purifier **9461**
flour stock man/woman – plastic and
    rubber manufacturing **9615**
flour stock worker – rubber
    manufacturing **9615**
flow coat dip painter **9496**
flow controller, hydro electric station **7352**
flower grower **8254**
flower maker, hand **5244**
flue cleaner – utilities **9613**
flue dust labourer – primary metal and
    mineral products processing **9611**
fluid mechanics engineer **2132**
fluids physicist **2111**
fluorescent light fixtures assembler **9484**
fluorescent penetrant inspector **2261**
fluorescent screen former **9483**
fluoroscope tester **2261**
fluorspar flux maker – primary metal
    processing **9611**
fluorspar recovery operator **9411**
fluting machine operator – laundry and
    dry cleaning **6682**
fluting machine operator –
    woodworking **9513**
flutist **5133**
flux mixing machine tender – metal
    processing **9411**
flyer distributor **1463**
flying instructor **2271**
flying school manager **0312**
flying shear operator – metal fabrication **9514**
flyman/woman **5227**
foam cushion production repairer –
    plastic manufacturing **9495**
foam cushion reinforcer – plastic
    manufacturing **9495**
foam machine operator – electrical
    equipment manufacturing **9487**

foam plastic spraying machine operator **9422**
foam products inspection
    foreman/woman – rubber
    manufacturing **9214**
foam rubber goods inspector **9423**
foam rubber maker **9423**
foam rubber mattress inspector **9423**
foam rubber mixer **9423**
foamed insulation applicator **7293**
focus puller **5227**
foil roller helper **9611**
foil separator – primary metal
    processing **9611**
foil stamp platen press operator **9473**
foil winding machine operator – primary
    metal processing **9411**
folded gasket maker – rubber
    manufacturing **9423**
folder, laundry **6681**
folder – laundry and dry cleaning **6682**
folder operator – printing **9473**
folderman/woman – printing **9619**
folding machine feeder – printing **9619**
folding machine operator – garment
    manufacturing **9517**
folding machine operator – printing **9473**
folding machine tender – laundry and
    dry cleaning **6682**
folding machine tender – paper
    converting **9435**
folding machine tender – textiles **9443**
folk dancing teacher **5134**
folk singer **5133**
folkloric dancer **5134**
food and beverage control clerk **1431**
food and beverage manager **0631**
food and beverage processing
    foreman/woman **9213**
food and beverage processing grader **9465**
food and beverage production manager **0911**
food and beverage server **6453**
food and nutrition consultant **4164**
food animal veterinarian **3114**
food assembler **6641**
food bacteriological technician **2221**
food bacteriological technologist **2221**
food bacteriologist **2121**
food buyer **6233**
food chemist **2112**
food colouring equipment operator **9461**
food controller **1431**
food cooling pan tender **9617**
food counter attendant **6641**
food damage inspector **2263**
food delivery driver **7414**
food demonstrator – retail **6623**
food finisher **6641**
food flavouring equipment tender **9461**

food inspector **9465**
food mixing machine tender **9461**
food packaging equipment assembly
    inspector **9486**
food packaging inspector **9465**
food preparer **6641**
food processing engineer **2148**
food processing equipment cleaner **9617**
food processing labourer **9617**
food processing machine fitter **7316**
food processing plant manager **0911**
food production manager **0911**
food products sales representative **6411**
food purchasing manager **0113**
food science professor – university **4121**
food scientist **2121**
food service attendant **6641**
food service driver **7414**
food service sales representative **6411**
food service supervisor **6212**
food service supervisor, hospital **6212**
food services manager **0631**
food services officer, base – military **0631**
food store cashier **6611**
food store manager **0621**
food store supervisor **6211**
food stylist **5243**
food technician **2211**
food technologist **2211**
food technology engineer **2148**
food tester **2211**
food testing foreman/woman – food and
    beverage processing **9213**
foot knitter **9442**
foot specialist **3123**
football coach **5252**
football player **5251**
football scout **5252**
footman/woman – underground mining **8411**
footwear finishing foreman/woman **9225**
footwear manufacturing
    foreman/woman **9225**
footwear mould press feeder – rubber
    manufacturing **9615**
footwear salesperson **6421**
footwear sewer **9451**
footwear sorter – rubber products
    manufacturing **9615**
forage crop farmer **8251**
force grinder – rubber manufacturing **9423**
forced air furnace installer **7331**
foreclosures law clerk **4211**
foreclosures legal assistant **4211**
foreclosures paralegal **4211**
foreign banking arrangements officer **1114**
foreign broadcast translator **5125**
foreign correspondent **5123**

foreign currency accounts adjuster –
   financial sector **1434**
foreign exchange clerk – financial
   sector **1434**
foreign exchange teller – financial
   services **1433**
foreign exchange trader **1113**
foreign going master **2273**
foreign invoice clerk **1431**
foreign news broadcasting editor **5122**
foreign remittance clerk – financial
   sector **1434**
foreign service officer **4168**
foreman/woman, abattoir **9213**
foreman/woman, air conditioning and
   refrigeration mechanics **7216**
foreman/woman, air conditioning
   mechanics **7216**
foreman/woman, aircraft assembly **9226**
foreman/woman, aircraft engine
   assemblers **7216**
foreman/woman, aircraft engine fitters **7216**
foreman/woman, aircraft hydraulics
   repair shop **7216**
foreman/woman, aircraft maintenance
   mechanics – mechanical systems **7216**
foreman/woman, aircraft mechanics and
   inspectors – mechanical systems **7216**
foreman/woman, aircraft mechanics and
   repairers – mechanical systems **7216**
foreman/woman, aircraft painters **9226**
foreman/woman, aircraft parts etching **9226**
foreman/woman, aircraft radar repair **7216**
foreman/woman, annealing – primary
   metal processing **9211**
foreman/woman, anodizing – primary
   metal processing **9211**
foreman/woman, appliance repair shop **7216**
foreman/woman, asphalt paving **7217**
foreman/woman, asphalt roofers **7219**
foreman/woman, assemblers – rubber
   and plastic manufacturing **9214**
foreman/woman, assembly mechanics **7216**
foreman/woman, automobile mechanics **7216**
foreman/woman, automobile tire
   builders **9214**
foreman/woman, automotive body repair
   shop **7216**
foreman/woman, automotive service
   mechanics **7216**
foreman/woman, baby carriage
   assembly **9227**
foreman/woman, bakery – food and
   beverage processing **9213**
foreman/woman, baking and
   confectionery making **9213**
foreman/woman, ball and roller bearings
   assembly **9226**

foreman/woman, beam department –
   hide and pelt processing **9225**
foreman/woman, beater room – pulp and
   paper **9215**
foreman/woman, beef boning and
   cutting **9213**
foreman/woman, beef dressing **9213**
foreman/woman, belt building – rubber
   manufacturing **9214**
foreman/woman, bench assemblers –
   wood products **9227**
foreman/woman, bicycle assembly **9227**
foreman/woman, bindery – printing **7218**
foreman/woman, blasters – construction **7217**
foreman/woman, blasters – quarrying **8221**
foreman/woman, blasters – surface
   mining **8221**
foreman/woman, blasting – mining and
   quarrying **8221**
foreman/woman, bleaching – textiles **9216**
foreman/woman, blow moulding –
   rubber and plastic manufacturing **9214**
foreman/woman, boiler and pipe
   insulators **7219**
foreman/woman, boilermakers **7214**
foreman/woman, boilermakers, platers,
   and structural metal workers **7214**
foreman/woman, box making – paper
   converting **9215**
foreman/woman, bricklayers **7219**
foreman/woman, brush making **9227**
foreman/woman, buffing and lacquering
   – furniture and fixtures
   manufacturing **9224**
foreman/woman, building construction
   inspectors **2264**
foreman/woman, building insulators **7219**
foreman/woman, bus and truck repair **7216**
foreman/woman, business and
   commercial machines assembly **9222**
foreman/woman, cabinet and wood
   furniture makers **9224**
foreman/woman, cabinetmakers –
   furniture manufacturing **9224**
foreman/woman, cable installations **7212**
foreman/woman, cablevision
   technicians **7212**
foreman/woman, calendering – rubber
   and plastic manufacturing **9214**
foreman/woman, candle making **9227**
foreman/woman, candy making
   department **9213**
foreman/woman, canvas products
   manufacturing **9225**
foreman/woman, carpenters **7215**
foreman/woman, casting operations **9211**

foreman/woman cell operations –
    primary metal and mineral
    processing **9211**
foreman/woman, cement processing **9211**
foreman/woman, cemetery **8256**
foreman/woman, char house – food and
    beverage processing **9213**
foreman/woman, chemical **9212**
foreman/woman, chocolate candies
    processing **9213**
foreman/woman, chocolate refining **9213**
foreman/woman, clay, glass and stone
    furnace and kiln operations **9211**
foreman/woman, clock and watch
    assembly **9227**
foreman/woman, clothing
    manufacturing **9225**
foreman/woman, coal and coke crushing
    and grinding **9211**
foreman/woman, coating and
    calendering occupations – chemical
    processing **9212**
foreman/woman, coffee roasting **9213**
foreman/woman, coke screening **9211**
foreman/woman, compounding – rubber
    and plastic manufacturing **9214**
foreman/woman, compression moulding
    – rubber and plastic manufacturing **9214**
foreman/woman, concrete finishers **7219**
foreman/woman, concrete form builders **7215**
foreman/woman, concrete paving **7217**
foreman/woman, concrete products **9211**
foreman/woman, construction
    electricians **7212**
foreman/woman, construction
    electricians and repair workers **7212**
foreman/woman, construction inspectors **2264**
foreman/woman, controlling and
    recording instruments assembly **9227**
foreman/woman, converter – primary
    metal and mineral products
    processing **9211**
foreman/woman, conveyor belt building
    – rubber manufacturing **9214**
foreman/woman, coppersmiths **7214**
foreman/woman, coremaking – foundry **9211**
foreman/woman, coremaking – paper
    converting **9215**
foreman/woman, cosmetics processing **9212**
foreman/woman, crane crew **7217**
foreman/woman, crushing and grinding
    occupations, chemicals and related
    materials **9212**
foreman/woman, crushing and grinding
    operations – primary metal and
    mineral products processing **9211**
foreman/woman, curing room – tobacco
    processing **9213**

foreman/woman, curing – rubber
    manufacturing **9214**
foreman/woman, cutlery manufacturing **9227**
foreman/woman, dairy farm workers **8253**
foreman/woman, dairy products
    processing **9213**
foreman/woman, demolition **7217**
foreman/woman, desk assembly –
    furniture and fixtures manufacturing **9224**
foreman/woman, diamond drilling **8221**
foreman/woman, dipped rubber goods **9214**
foreman/woman, distilling **9213**
foreman/woman, dredging equipment
    operators **7217**
foreman/woman, drilling and blasting –
    construction **7217**
foreman/woman, dry starch – food
    processing **9213**
foreman/woman, drywall applicators **7219**
foreman/woman, drywall installers **7219**
foreman/woman, dye department –
    textiles **9216**
foreman/woman, electric motor and
    generator assembly **9223**
foreman/woman, electric motor testing **9223**
foreman/woman, electrical appliance
    assembly **9223**
foreman/woman, electrical battery
    manufacturing **9223**
foreman/woman, electrical construction **7212**
foreman/woman, electrical dry cell
    assembly **9223**
foreman/woman, electrical equipment
    fabricating and assembling
    occupations **9223**
foreman/woman, electrical equipment
    installation and repair **7212**
foreman/woman, electrical equipment
    manufacturing **9223**
foreman/woman, electrical mechanics **7216**
foreman/woman, electrical motor
    assembly **9223**
foreman/woman, electrical power line
    and cable workers **7212**
foreman/woman, electrical switchgear
    assembly **9223**
foreman/woman, electrical transformer
    assembly **9223**
foreman/woman, electricians **7212**
foreman/woman, electronic assembly **9222**
foreman/woman, electronic equipment
    fabricating and assembling **9222**
foreman/woman, electronic inspection –
    electronics manufacturing **9222**
foreman/woman – electronics
    manufacturing **9222**
foreman/woman, electroplating **9226**
foreman/woman, elevator constructors **7219**

foreman/woman, elevator mechanics **7216**
foreman/woman, engine assembly (except aircraft) **9226**
foreman/woman, excavating equipment operators **7217**
foreman/woman, excavating, grading and related occupations **7217**
foreman/woman, extruding – primary metal processing **9211**
foreman/woman, extruding – rubber and plastic manufacturing **9214**
foreman/woman, extrusion – rubber and plastic manufacturing **9214**
foreman/woman, fabric, fur and leather products manufacturing **9225**
foreman/woman, farm **8253**
foreman/woman, farm equipment repair **7216**
foreman/woman, feed milling **9213**
foreman/woman, feedlot **8253**
foreman/woman, fiberglass boats **9214**
foreman/woman, fibre insulators **7219**
foreman/woman, fibreglass plastics **9214**
foreman/woman, field crop and vegetable workers **8253**
foreman/woman, film developer **7218**
foreman/woman, film printer **7218**
foreman/woman, film processor **7218**
foreman/woman, final assembly and test – electronics manufacturing **9222**
foreman/woman, finish carpenters **7215**
foreman/woman, finishing and trimming – rubber and plastic manufacturing **9214**
foreman/woman, finishing department – textiles **9216**
foreman/woman, finishing – plastic manufacturing **9214**
foreman/woman, finishing – printing **7218**
foreman/woman, finishing – rubber manufacturing **9214**
foreman/woman, fire protection equipment installers **7213**
foreman/woman, fireams assembly **9227**
foreman/woman, fireproofing plasterers **7219**
foreman/woman, fish canning, curing and packing occupations **9213**
foreman/woman, fish freezing **9213**
foreman/woman, fish freezing and storage **9213**
foreman/woman, fish preparation **9213**
foreman/woman, fish reduction **9213**
foreman/woman, flour and grain milling occupations **9213**
foreman/woman, flour milling **9213**
foreman/woman, foam insulators **7219**
foreman/woman, foam products inspection – rubber manufacturing **9214**
foreman/woman, food and beverage processing **9213**
foreman/woman, food testing – food and beverage processing **9213**
foreman/woman, footwear inspection – rubber manufacturing **9214**
foreman/woman, footwear manufacturing **9225**
foreman/woman, forestry **8211**
foreman/woman, forge shop **9226**
foreman/woman, forging machine operators **9226**
foreman/woman, form builders **7215**
foreman/woman, framers **7215**
foreman/woman, freight terminal **7217**
foreman/woman, fruit and vegetable canning, preserving and packing occupations **9213**
foreman/woman, fruit farm workers **8253**
foreman/woman, fruit grading **9213**
foreman/woman, fur dressing – hide and pelt processing **9225**
foreman/woman, fur hat making department **9225**
foreman/woman, furnace installers **7216**
foreman/woman, furnace operations – primary metal and mineral products processing **9211**
foreman/woman, furniture assemblers **9224**
foreman/woman, furniture assembly **9224**
foreman/woman, furniture finishers – furniture and fixtures manufacturing **9224**
foreman/woman furniture inspectors – furniture and fixtures manufacturing **9224**
foreman/woman, furriers **9225**
foreman/woman, galvanizing **9226**
foreman/woman, garden tractor assembly **9226**
foreman/woman, garment manufacturing **9225**
foreman/woman, gas fitters **7213**
foreman/woman, general carpenters **7215**
foreman/woman glass grinders and polishers **9211**
foreman/woman, glass installers **7219**
foreman/woman, glass processing **9211**
foreman/woman, glaziers **7219**
foreman/woman, glove manufacturing **9225**
foreman/woman, gluing – furniture and fixtures manufacturing **9224**
foreman/woman, grading equipment operators **7217**
foreman/woman, groundskeeping **8256**
foreman/woman, ham curing **9213**
foreman/woman, hatchery workers **8253**
foreman/woman, heating plant **9212**
foreman/woman, heating systems mechanics **7216**
foreman/woman, heavy agricultural machinery assembly **7216**

foreman/woman, heavy construction equipment assembly **7216**

foreman/woman, heavy duty equipment mechanics **7216**

foreman/woman, heavy duty equipment operators **7217**

foreman/woman, heavy equipment assembly **7216**

foreman/woman heavy equipment mechanics **7216**

foreman/woman, heavy farm equipment assembly **7216**

foreman/woman, heavy machinery assembly **7216**

foreman/woman, helicopter maintenance – mechanical systems **7216**

foreman/woman, hide and pelt processing occupations **9225**

foreman/woman, hide curing – food and beverage processing **9213**

foreman/woman, hide house – hide and pelt processing **9225**

foreman/woman, highway construction **7217**

foreman/woman, highway construction inspectors **2264**

foreman/woman, house moving **7217**

foreman/woman, ice cream making **9213**

foreman/woman, industrial blacksmiths **7214**

foreman/woman, industrial electrical systems **7212**

foreman/woman, industrial electricians **7212**

foreman/woman, industrial, farm and construction machinery mechanics and repairers **7216**

foreman/woman, industrial machinery manufacturing **7216**

foreman/woman, industrial mechanics **7216**

foreman/woman, industrial truck assembly **9226**

foreman/woman, injection moulding – rubber and plastic manufacturing **9214**

foreman/woman, ink preparation – chemical processing **9212**

foreman/woman, inspecting occupations, wood machining **9224**

foreman/woman, inspecting, testing and grading – primary metal and mineral products processing **9211**

foreman/woman, inspection – textiles **9216**

foreman/woman, inspectors, graders, samplers and testers – fabric, fur and leather products manufacturing **9225**

foreman/woman, insulators **7219**

foreman/woman, ironworkers **7214**

foreman/woman, jam and jelly processing **9213**

foreman/woman, jewellery and silverware manufacturing workers **9227**

foreman/woman, jewellery manufacturing **9227**

foreman/woman, jewellery repairing – manufacturing **9227**

foreman/woman, labourers and other elemental workers – construction **7217**

foreman/woman, labourers – primary metal and mineral products processing **9211**

foreman/woman, laminating – furniture and fixtures manufacturing **9224**

foreman/woman, lamp shade fabrication **9227**

foreman/woman, landscaping **8256**

foreman/woman, laundry and dry cleaning **6214**

foreman/woman, lay out and marking – fabric, fur and leather products manufacturing **9225**

foreman/woman, lead refining **9211**

foreman/woman, leather finishing – hide and pelt processing **9225**

foreman/woman, leather products manufacturing **9225**

foreman/woman lens grinders and polishers **9227**

foreman/woman, light industrial, farm and construction machinery assembly **9226**

foreman/woman, light material handling equipment assembly **9226**

foreman/woman light rail transit operator **7222**

foreman/woman, line and cable repairers – electrical power line **7212**

foreman/woman, loading and moving **7217**

foreman/woman, locomotive inspectors **7216**

foreman/woman, loft **9226**

foreman/woman, logging **8211**

foreman/woman, logging road construction **7217**

foreman/woman, longshore workers **7217**

foreman/woman, luggage assembly – fabric, fur and leather products manufacturing **9225**

foreman/woman, lumber grading **9215**

foreman/woman, machine builders **7216**

foreman/woman, machine fitters **7216**

foreman/woman, machine shop **7211**

foreman/woman, machine shop inspectors **7211**

foreman/woman, machine tool operators **7211**

foreman/woman, machining and tooling inspectors **7211**

foreman/woman, machining inspectors **7211**

foreman/woman, machining tool operators **7211**

foreman/woman, machinists **7211**

foreman/woman, machinists and machine
   tool set-up operators 7211
foreman/woman, maintenance
   carpenters 7215
foreman/woman, maintenance
   electricians 7212
foreman/woman, manufacturing
   machinery assembly 7216
foreman/woman, marble setters 7219
foreman/woman, marine electricians 7212
foreman/woman, marine service – engine
   repair 7216
foreman/woman, marking and cutting
   occupations 9225
foreman/woman, matting inspection –
   rubber manufacturing 9214
foreman/woman, mattress
   manufacturing 9225
foreman/woman, meat cutting plant 9213
foreman/woman, mechanical equipment
   repair inspectors 7216
foreman/woman, mechanical inspectors 7216
foreman/woman, mechanics 7216
foreman/woman, melting and roasting –
   primary metal and mineral products
   processing 9211
foreman/woman, metal buffing 9226
foreman/woman, metal casting,
   moulding and coremaking 9211
foreman/woman, metal extruding and
   drawing 9211
foreman/woman, metal fabricators 7214
foreman/woman, metal fitters 7214
foreman/woman, metal furniture
   assembly 9224
foreman/woman, metal heat treating –
   primary metal processing 9211
foreman/woman, metal machining
   inspection 7211
foreman/woman, metal mould and
   pattern makers 7211
foreman/woman, metal products
   inspection and testing 9226
foreman/woman, metal rolling 9211
foreman/woman, metal roofers 7219
foreman/woman, metal smelting,
   converting and refining 9211
foreman/woman, metalworking machine
   operators 9226
foreman/woman, milk production 9213
foreman/woman, millinery – fabric, fur
   and leather products manufacturing 9225
foreman/woman, milling plant – primary
   metal and mineral product
   processing 9211
foreman/woman, millroom – rubber
   manufacturing 9214

foreman/woman, millwork assemblers –
   wood manufacturing 9227
foreman/woman, millwork assembly 9227
foreman/woman, mirror silvering 9227
foreman/woman, mixing and separating
   operations – primary metal and
   mineral products processing 9211
foreman/woman, mixing – rubber and
   plastic manufacturing 9214
foreman/woman, mobile home assembly 9226
foreman/woman, motor vehicle body
   repairers 7216
foreman/woman, motor vehicle
   manufacturing 9221
foreman/woman, motor vehicle
   mechanics and repairers 7216
foreman/woman, motor vehicle repair
   shop 7216
foreman/woman, motorcycle mechanics 7216
foreman/woman mould shop –
   machining 7211
foreman/woman, moulded rubber
   footwear 9214
foreman/woman, moulding – foundry 9211
foreman/woman, moulding – rubber and
   plastic manufacturing 9214
foreman/woman, musical instrument
   manufacturing 9227
foreman/woman, natural gas plant 9212
foreman/woman, nursery and related
   workers 8256
foreman/woman, office machine
   repairers 7216
foreman/woman, offset press – printing 7218
foreman/woman, oil and gas well
   drilling 8222
foreman/woman, oil and natural gas well
   services 8222
foreman/woman, oil burner mechanics 7216
foreman/woman, oilfield construction 7217
foreman/woman, optical instruments
   manufacturing 9227
foreman/woman, opticopy and stripping
   – printing 7218
foreman/woman, orchard 8253
foreman/woman, paint department –
   aircraft manufacturing 9226
foreman/woman, paint department –
   furniture and fixture manufacturing 9224
foreman/woman, paint department –
   heavy equipment manufacturing 9226
foreman/woman, paint department –
   heavy truck, bus and trailer
   manufacturing 9226
foreman/woman, paint department –
   machinery manufacturing 9226
foreman/woman, paint department –
   metal products manufacturing 9226

foreman/woman, paint department –
motor vehicle manufacturing **9221**
foreman/woman, paint department –
plastic products **9214**
foreman/woman, paint department –
railway rolling stock **9226**
foreman/woman, paint department –
rubber products **9214**
foreman/woman, paint department – ship
building **9226**
foreman/woman, paint department –
transport equipment manufacturing
(except motor vehicles) **9226**
foreman/woman, paint shop – motor
vehicle manufacturing **9221**
foreman/woman, painters and
decorators **7219**
foreman/woman, painters – appliance
manufacturing **9226**
foreman/woman, painters – construction **7219**
foreman/woman, painters – metal
products **9226**
foreman/woman, painters – transport
equipment manufacturing (except
motor vehicles) **9226**
foreman/woman, paper inspectors – pulp
and paper **9215**
foreman/woman, paper machine – pulp
and paper **9215**
foreman/woman, paper product
fabricating and assembling **9215**
foreman/woman, paperhangers **7219**
foreman/woman, papermaking and
finishing **9215**
foreman/woman, park **8256**
foreman/woman, paving **7217**
foreman/woman, paving, surfacing and
related occupations **7217**
foreman/woman PCB fabrication **9222**
foreman/woman, photographic
equipment assembly **9227**
foreman/woman, photographic
processing and finishing **7218**
foreman/woman, pilot plant **9212**
foreman/woman, pipefitters **7213**
foreman/woman, pipefitters, plumbers
and related workers **7213**
foreman/woman, pipeline construction **7217**
foreman/woman, pipeline inspectors **2264**
foreman/woman, plasterers **7219**
foreman/woman, plastic products
manufacturing **9214**
foreman/woman, plastic shop **9214**
foreman/woman, plastics inspectors **9214**
foreman/woman, plate shop **7214**
foreman/woman, platework fabricators **7214**
foreman/woman, plumbers **7213**

foreman/woman, plywood inspection –
wood processing **9215**
foreman/woman, plywood making **9215**
foreman/woman, pot room – primary
metal and mineral products
processing **9211**
foreman/woman, poultry farm workers **8253**
foreman/woman, poultry graders **9213**
foreman/woman, poultry preparers **9213**
foreman/woman, power station
operators **9212**
foreman/woman, power systems
electricians **7212**
foreman/woman, pre-fab housing
assemblers **9227**
foreman/woman, precision instrument
mechanics and repairers **7216**
foreman/woman, precision instruments
and related equipment assembly **9227**
foreman/woman prep department – metal
fabrication **9226**
foreman/woman, pressroom – printing **7218**
foreman/woman – primary metal and
mineral products processing **9211**
foreman/woman, printed circuit board
fabrication **9222**
foreman/woman, printing press and
machines mechanics **7216**
foreman/woman, pulp processing – pulp
and paper **9215**
foreman/woman, pumping and blending **9212**
foreman/woman, pumping and pipeline
equipment operating **9212**
foreman/woman, quarry **8221**
foreman/woman, quenching – primary
metal processing **9211**
foreman/woman, rail transport
equipment repairers **7216**
foreman/woman, railway car inspectors **7216**
foreman/woman, railway car
maintenance **7216**
foreman/woman, railway
carmen/women **7216**
foreman/woman, railway equipment
maintenance inspectors **7216**
foreman/woman, railway gang **7217**
foreman/woman, railway maintenance of
way **7217**
foreman/woman, railway rolling stock
assembly **7216**
foreman/woman, railway section and
track workers **7217**
foreman/woman, railway transport
operating occupations **7221**
foreman/woman, ranch **8253**
foreman/woman, refinery unit **9212**
foreman/woman, refractory bricklayers **7219**

foreman/woman, refrigeration and air-conditioning equipment insulators **7219**

foreman/woman, refrigeration mechanics **7216**

foreman/woman, rendering plant workers **9213**

foreman/woman, retread tire inspection **9214**

foreman/woman, roll building – rubber manufacturing **9214**

foreman/woman, rubber hose building **9214**

foreman/woman, rubber hose inspection and testing **9214**

foreman/woman, rubber inspectors **9214**

foreman/woman, rubber products manufacturing **9214**

foreman/woman, sanitary service **9212**

foreman/woman, sash and door shop **9227**

foreman/woman, sawmill **9215**

foreman/woman, scales assembly **9227**

foreman/woman, scrap preparation – primary metal and mineral products processing **9211**

foreman/woman, sewage disposal **9212**

foreman/woman, sewer installers **7217**

foreman/woman, sewing machine operators **9225**

foreman/woman, sheet metal workers **7214**

foreman/woman, shingle mill – wood processing **9215**

foreman/woman, shipbuilding carpenters **7215**

foreman/woman, silverware department **9227**

foreman/woman, sintering plant – primary metal and mineral products processing **9211**

foreman/woman, slaughtering and meat packing workers **9213**

foreman/woman, small engine assembly **9226**

foreman/woman, small engine repair **7216**

foreman/woman, smelter – primary metal and mineral products processing **9211**

foreman/woman, snow blower tractor assembly **9226**

foreman/woman, snowmobile assembly **9226**

foreman/woman, snowtrack – rubber manufacturing **9214**

foreman/woman, spikemaking **9227**

foreman/woman, sports equipment manufacturing **9227**

foreman/woman, sprinkler systems installers **7213**

foreman/woman, stage properties **5226**

foreman/woman, stained glass glaziers **7219**

foreman/woman, stair builders **7215**

foreman/woman, steamfitters **7213**

foreman/woman, steel fitters – metal fabrication **7214**

foreman/woman, steel riggers **7214**

foreman/woman, stitching department – fabric, fur and leather products manufacturing **9225**

foreman/woman, stock preparation – rubber manufacturing **9214**

foreman/woman, stone masons **7219**

foreman/woman, stone processing **9211**

foreman/woman, structural metal erectors **7214**

foreman/woman, structural metal fabricators **7214**

foreman/woman, structural steel workers **7214**

foreman/woman, stucco plasterers **7219**

foreman/woman subway motorman/woman **7222**

foreman/woman, sugar filter house **9213**

foreman/woman, sugar processing workers **9213**

foreman/woman, surface mine **8221**

foreman/woman, switchgear assembly **9223**

foreman/woman, systems test – electronics manufacturing **9222**

foreman/woman, tankhouse – primary metal and mineral products processing **9211**

foreman/woman, tapper operations – mineral and metal processing **9211**

foreman/woman, tea blending plant **9213**

foreman/woman, telecommunication installers and repairers **7212**

foreman/woman, telephone installation **7212**

foreman/woman, tempering – primary metal processing **9211**

foreman/woman, terrazzo workers **7219**

foreman/woman, textile mechanics **7216**

foreman/woman, textile processing **9216**

foreman/woman – textiles **9216**

foreman/woman, thermoforming – plastic manufacturing **9214**

foreman/woman, thermostats assembly **9227**

foreman/woman, threshing department – tobacco processing **9213**

foreman/woman, tilesetters **7219**

foreman/woman, tipping department – tobacco processing **9213**

foreman/woman, tire building **9214**

foreman/woman, tire finishing **9214**

foreman/woman, tire inspection **9214**

foreman/woman, tire retread **9214**

foreman/woman, tire stock preparation **9214**

foreman/woman, tire tubes **9214**

foreman/woman, tobacco curing room **9213**

foreman/woman, tobacco processing occupations **9213**

foreman/woman, tobacco processing workers **9213**
foreman/woman, tool and die inspectors **7211**
foreman/woman, tool and die makers **7211**
foreman/woman, tooling inspectors **7211**
foreman/woman, toy assembly **9227**
foreman/woman, transformer repair shop **7216**
foreman/woman, treating plant – wood processing **9215**
foreman/woman truck drivers **7222**
foreman/woman, underground mine **8221**
foreman/woman, upholsterers – fabric, fur and leather products manufacturing **9225**
foreman/woman, uranium processing **9211**
foreman/woman urban transit system **7222**
foreman/woman, v-belt – rubber manufacturing **9214**
foreman/woman, vegetable farm workers **8253**
foreman/woman, vegetable oil milling **9213**
foreman/woman, veneer – wood processing **9215**
foreman/woman, vineyard **8253**
foreman/woman, viscose filtration – chemical processing **9212**
foreman/woman, vulcanizing – rubber manufacturing **9214**
foreman/woman, waferboard – wood processing **9215**
foreman/woman, wash house – food and beverage processing **9213**
foreman/woman, water and sanitation utilities equipment operating occupations **9212**
foreman/woman, water purification plant **9212**
foreman/woman, water well drilling **7217**
foreman/woman, waterproofers **7219**
foreman/woman weaver **9216**
foreman/woman, welders **7214**
foreman/woman, wet starch – food and beverage processing **9213**
foreman/woman, wire drawing – primary metal processing **9211**
foreman/woman wood machining occupations **9224**
foreman/woman, wood patternmaking occupations **7215**
foreman/woman, wood shingle roofers **7219**
foreman/woman, wood treating plant **9215**
foreman/woman, wooden barrelmakers **9227**
foreman/woman, wooden box maker **9227**
foreman/woman, wooden truss makers – manufacturing **9227**
foreman/woman, woodenware assemblers **9227**
foreman/woman, woodworking machine department **9224**
foreman/woman, woodworking machine operators – furniture and fixtures manufacturing **9224**
foreman/woman, wrecking crew **7217**
foreman/woman, zoo **2221**
forensic chemist **2112**
forensic examiner, alcohol **2211**
forensic examiner, hair and fibre **2221**
forensic lab analyst **2211**
forensic pathologist **3111**
forensic photographer **5221**
forest assistant, nursery **8432**
forest ecologist **2121**
forest economist **4162**
forest engineer **2122**
forest engineering technician **2223**
forest engineering technologist **2223**
forest extension technician **2223**
forest fire officer **2223**
forest fire ranger **2223**
forest fire suppression crew leader **2223**
forest fire technician **2223**
forest firefighter **8422**
forest firefighting crew leader **2223**
forest inventory resource officer **2223**
forest inventory technician **2223**
forest management supervisor **2223**
forest nursery forester **2122**
forest nursery worker **8432**
forest officer **2223**
forest operations manager **0811**
forest operations supervisor **8211**
forest pathologist **2121**
forest planning technician **2223**
forest products technologist **2211**
forest protection officer **2223**
forest ranger – forestry **2223**
forest ranger – wildlife management **2224**
forest resource technician **2223**
forest survey technician **2223**
forest technician **2223**
forest technologist **2223**
forest worker **8421**
forest worker – logging **8421**
forester **2122**
forestry and logging manager **0811**
forestry conservation contractor **8211**
forestry conservation worker **8422**
forestry crew co-ordinator **2223**
forestry crew person **8422**
forestry crew supervisor **8211**
forestry crewman/woman **8422**
forestry extension technician **2223**
forestry foreman/woman **8211**
forestry labourer **8616**
forestry machinery sales representative **6221**

forestry patrol pilot **2271**

forestry policy director – government services **0412**

forestry professor – university **4121**

forestry protection officer **2223**

forestry spray pilot **2271**

forestry superintendent **2122**

forestry supervisor **8211**

forestry technician **2223**

forestry technologist **2223**

forestry worker **8422**

forge header operator, steel shot **9512**

forge helper **9612**

forge manipulator operator **9512**

forge shop foreman/woman **9226**

forge shop machinery mechanic **7311**

forging air hammer operator **9512**

forging die maker **7232**

forging inspector **2261**

forging machine operator **9512**

forging machine set-up man/woman **9512**

forging machine setter **9512**

forging press operator **9512**

forging press tender **9512**

forging roll operator **9512**

fork lift truck operator **7452**

form builders foreman/woman **7215**

form carpenter **7271**

form remover – construction **7611**

form setter, metal – construction **7611**

form stripper – construction **7611**

formal service waiter/waitress **6453**

formal waiter/waitress **6453**

formation fracturing operator – oil field services **8412**

formatter operator, typesetting **1423**

former, pottery and porcelain – clay products **9414**

forming line operator, hardboard **9434**

forming machine operator – metal fabrication **9514**

forming machine operator, particle board **9434**

forming press operator – metal fabrication **9514**

forming roll operator helper **9619**

forming roll set-up operator – metal fabrication **9514**

forming roll tender – metal fabrication **9514**

forming room operator – electrical equipment manufacturing **9487**

forming specialist, glass **9413**

forms analyst **5241**

forms control clerk **1441**

forms designer **5241**

forms management analyst **5241**

forms management officer **1221**

formula room worker – medical **6631**

formula weigher – rubber and plastic manufacturing **9615**

formulation technician **2211**

formulations blender operator – chemical processing **9421**

formulations blender operator, pesticides **9421**

fortune teller **6484**

forwarder operator – logging **8241**

forwarder – printing **9619**

foster father **6471**

foster mother **6471**

foster parent **6471**

foundation dampproofer helper **7611**

foundation drill operator – construction **7372**

foundation drill operator helper **7611**

foundation engineer **2131**

foundation garment fitter **7342**

foundation garment inspector **9454**

foundation technologist **2231**

foundation waterproofer – construction **7611**

foundry engineer **2142**

foundry flask maker, wood **9493**

foundry foreman/woman **9211**

foundry furnace operator **9412**

foundry helper – primary metal processing **9611**

foundry laboratory technician **2212**

foundry labourer, core room **9611**

foundry manager **0911**

foundry mould finisher **9619**

foundry mould maker **9412**

foundry sand mixer **9412**

foundry supervisor **9211**

foundry worker **9412**

foundry worker – primary metal processing **9611**

fountain attendant **6641**

fountain pen inspector **9498**

fountain pen maker **9498**

fourdrinier machine operator – pulp and paper **9234**

fourth class power engineer **7351**

fourth class stationary engineer **7351**

fourth engineer – water transport **2274**

fourth hand – pulp and paper **9433**

foxer, footwear **9517**

foxer, rubber goods **9423**

frac driver – oil field services **8412**

fractionator operator **9232**

fracture room attendant **3414**

fracturing supervisor – oil field services **8222**

frame assembler – motor vehicle manufacturing **9482**

frame assembler, wood furniture **9492**

frame builder, buses and trucks **9486**

frame fitter – museums and galleries **5212**

frame maker, eyeglasses **9498**

frame maker – furniture manufacturing **9492**
frame operator – textiles **9441**
frame spinner – textiles **9441**
frame table operator – woodworking **9513**
frame wirer, telephones **7246**
framer carpenter **7271**
framer helper **7611**
framer – laundry and dry cleaning **6682**
framer – telecommunications **7246**
framers foreman/woman **7215**
framework finisher, denture **3412**
framing carpenter **7271**
framing consultant – retail **6421**
framing technician **5212**
frazer – woodworking **9513**
frazing machine operator – woodworking **9513**
freelance film maker **5131**
freelance video maker **5131**
freeze-dry food processor **9461**
freeze tumbler tender – rubber manufacturing **9423**
freezer operator – food and beverage processing **9461**
freezer worker – food and beverage processing **9617**
freight adjuster – insurance **1233**
freight agent (except airline) **6434**
freight agent, railway **6434**
freight attendant, air transport **7437**
freight car checker – railway **7622**
freight car cleaner **6662**
freight car loader **7452**
freight car service inspector **2262**
freight car unloader **7452**
freight checker **1471**
freight company manager **0713**
freight elevator operator **6683**
freight forwarder **0713**
freight forwarding clerk **1441**
freight forwarding sales representative **6411**
freight forwarding supervisor **1215**
freight forwarding technician **1215**
freight handler (except airlines) **7452**
freight handling foreman/woman **7217**
freight loader (except airlines) **7452**
freight loading foreman/woman **7217**
freight railway engineer **7361**
freight rate clerk **1431**
freight receiver **1471**
freight representative **6411**
freight sales agent **6411**
freight scheduling supervisor **1215**
freight shipper **1471**
freight supervisor **1215**
freight traffic agent **6411**
freight traffic co-ordinator **1215**
freight traffic manager **0713**

freight traffic supervisor **1215**
freight train brakeman/woman **7362**
freight train conductor **7362**
freight train engineer **7361**
freight truck driver **7411**
freight unloader (except airlines) **7452**
French as a second language teacher – (except elementary, high school or university) **4131**
French as second language teacher – elementary school **4142**
French as second language teacher – high school **4141**
French immersion teacher – elementary school **4142**
French pastry baker – retail trade **6252**
French pleater – laundry and dry cleaning **6682**
French teacher – elementary school **4142**
French teacher, secondary school **4141**
frequency measurer, crystal processing **9483**
frit dispenser **9483**
front clerk **6435**
front desk cashier **6611**
front desk clerk **6435**
front desk manager, hotel **0632**
front end brakeman/woman **7362**
front end loader operator **7421**
front-end mechanic **7321**
front line supervisor, cable workers **7212**
front line supervisor, power line maintenance **7212**
front office clerk **6435**
front office manager, hotel **0632**
frosting maker – food and beverage processing **9461**
frozen dinner assembler – food and beverage processing **9617**
frozen fish cutter – fish processing **9463**
frozen food packer **9617**
frozen meat cutter **9617**
fruit and vegetable canning and preserving foreman/woman **9213**
fruit and vegetable cleaner **9617**
fruit and vegetable grader **9465**
fruit and vegetables inspector **2222**
fruit buyer **6233**
fruit canner – food and beverage processing **9461**
fruit cook – food and beverage processing **9461**
fruit examiner – agriculture **8431**
fruit farm labourer **8431**
fruit farm worker **8431**
fruit farmer **8251**
fruit grading foreman/woman **9213**
fruit grower **8251**
fruit harvester **8611**

fruit inspector **9465**
fruit mixer – food and beverage
 processing **9461**
fruit packer – agriculture **8611**
fruit peeler – food and beverage
 processing **9617**
fruit picker **8611**
fruit preparer – food and beverage
 processing **9617**
fruit preserver – food and beverage
 processing **9461**
fruit press tender **9461**
fruit sorter – agriculture **8611**
fruit thinner **8431**
fruit tree pruner **8431**
fry cook – food and beverage
 processing **9461**
fry marker – fishing **8613**
fryer operator – food and beverage
 processing **9461**
fuel and sand operator – railway
 transport **7622**
fuel filter assembler **9498**
fuel gas treater **9232**
fuel log maker – wood processing **9434**
fuel oil truck driver **7411**
fuel pump assembler **9486**
fuel rod assembler **9498**
fuel system maintenance
 foreman/woman **7216**
fuel tank builder, rubber **9423**
fuel tank finisher and repairer, rubber **9423**
fuel technician **2211**
fuels engineer **2134**
full professor – university **4121**
fuller – textiles **9443**
fulling mill operator – textiles **9443**
fume scrubber operator **9411**
fumigator, pests **7444**
fun house operator **6443**
fund raiser **5124**
fund raising campaign manager **0611**
fund raising consultant **5124**
funeral attendant **6683**
funeral chauffeur **7413**
funeral director **6272**
funeral director, assistant **6272**
funeral driver **7413**
funeral services general manager **0015**
funnel coater – electronics
 manufacturing **9483**
fur blender **9453**
fur blocker **9498**
fur blower **9441**
fur buyer **6233**
fur cleaner, laundry and dry cleaning **6681**
fur cleaning foreman/woman **6214**
fur cleaning plant manager **0651**

fur cutter **9452**
fur designer **5243**
fur dresser – hide and pelt processing **9453**
fur dressing foreman/woman – hide and
 pelt processing **9225**
fur drummer machine operator – laundry
 and dry cleaning **6681**
fur farm worker **8431**
fur farmer **8251**
fur floor worker – hide and pelt
 processing **9453**
fur garment patternmaker **5245**
fur glazer – laundry and dry cleaning **6682**
fur goods sewer **9451**
fur grader **9454**
fur ironer glazer – laundry and dry
 cleaning **6682**
fur ironer – laundry and dry cleaning **6682**
fur ironing machine operator – laundry
 and dry cleaning **6682**
fur lusterizer – laundry and dry cleaning **6682**
fur matcher – fur products
 manufacturing **9454**
fur patternmaker **5245**
fur products manufacturing
 foreman/woman **9225**
fur ranch labourer **8431**
fur remodeler **7342**
fur repair estimator **7342**
fur repairman/woman **7342**
fur salesperson **6421**
fur sewer **9451**
fur sewing machine operator **9451**
fur shaving machine tender – hide and
 pelt processing **9453**
fur sorter **9454**
fur sorter, hat **9454**
fur steamer **6681**
fur storage attendant **6683**
fur tailor **7342**
fur trader **6411**
fur trapper **8442**
furnace boiler operator **7351**
furnace brick mason, industrial **7281**
furnace charger **9411**
furnace charger – primary metal
 processing **9611**
furnace cleaner **6662**
furnace cleaner – primary metal and
 mineral products processing **9611**
furnace combustion tester – primary
 metal processing **9415**
furnace converter **7331**
furnace electrode inspector **9484**
furnace feeder – primary metal and
 mineral products processing **9611**

furnace foreman/woman, melting and roasting – primary metal and mineral products processing **9211**

furnace helper – primary metal and mineral products processing **9611**

furnace installer and repairer **7331**

furnace loader – primary metal and mineral products processing **9611**

furnace maintenance mechanic **7331**

furnace mechanic **7331**

furnace operations foreman/woman – primary metal and mineral products processing **9211**

furnace operator – foundry **9412**

furnace operator – primary metal and mineral products processing **9411**

furnace repairer **7331**

furnace repairer helper **7612**

furnace repairman/woman **7331**

furnace skimmer – primary metal and mineral products processing **9611**

furnace solderer **9515**

furnace tapper – primary metal processing **9611**

furniture and fixtures assembler **9492**

furniture and fixtures manufacturing inspector **9492**

furniture and wooden objects conservator **5112**

furniture appraiser **1235**

furniture assembler **9492**

furniture assembler, metal **9492**

furniture assembler, wood **9492**

furniture assembly foreman/woman **9224**

furniture buffer **9494**

furniture cabinetmaker **7272**

furniture caner **9492**

furniture checker **9492**

furniture crater **9619**

furniture designer **2252**

furniture enameler **9494**

furniture factory manager **0911**

furniture finisher **9494**

furniture finisher and repairer **9494**

furniture finishes inspector **9492**

furniture fitter-up **9492**

furniture inspector **9492**

furniture inspectors foreman/woman **9224**

furniture joiner **9492**

furniture loader **7452**

furniture mover **7452**

furniture mover helper **7622**

furniture packer **9619**

furniture parts inspector **9492**

furniture polisher – furniture finishing **9494**

furniture refinisher **9494**

furniture sales consultant – retail trade **6421**

furniture salesperson **6421**

furniture shipping inspector **9492**

furniture store manager **0621**

furniture stripper **9494**

furniture upholsterer **7341**

furniture van driver **7411**

furrier **7342**

furriers supervisor **9225**

fuse maker – chemical processing **9421**

fuselage fitter – aircraft assembly **9481**

fusing furnace loader – mineral products manufacturing **9611**

futures research services manager **0121**

futures trader **1113**

G

g.p. **3112**

g.s.t collection officer **1228**

gaffer **5226**

gallery administrator **0511**

gallery administrator, assistant **0511**

gallery co-ordinator **0511**

gallery director **0511**

gallery director, assistant **0511**

galosh maker, rubber **9423**

galvanizer helper **9619**

galvanizing foreman/woman **9226**

galvanizing machine operator **9497**

gambling table operator **6443**

game concession operator **6443**

game officer **2224**

game show host **5231**

game trapper **8442**

game warden **2224**

games booth operator **6443**

gandy dancer, railway transport **7432**

gang foreman/woman, bridge and highway construction **7217**

gang foreman/woman, concrete laying **7217**

gang foreman/woman, construction **7217**

gang press operator – rubber manufacturing **9423**

gang ripsaw operator – woodworking **9513**

gang sawyer – sawmill **9431**

gang sawyer – stone products manufacturing **9414**

gang sawyer – woodworking **9513**

gantry crane operator **7371**

garage door installer **7441**

garage foreman/woman **7216**

garage jockey **6683**

garage manager, automobile repairs **0621**

garage mechanic **7321**

garage supervisor **7216**

garbage collection inspector **6463**

garbage collector **7621**

garbage receptacles maintainer **7621**

garbage truck driver – public works **7422**

garbage truck loader **7621**
garbageman/woman **7621**
garde-manger, chef **6241**
garden centre manager – retail trade **0621**
garden machinery assembler **9486**
garden supplies sales clerk **6421**
garden tractor repairer **7335**
gardening helper **8612**
gardner, landscape **2225**
garment and hosiery boner **9619**
garment bagger **9619**
garment braider – garment
    manufacturing **9451**
garment cleaner – laundry and dry
    cleaning **6681**
garment designer **5243**
garment dyer – laundry and dry
    cleaning **6681**
garment final inspector **9454**
garment fitter **7342**
garment folder **9619**
garment fringer – garment
    manufacturing **9619**
garment inspector **9454**
garment looper **9442**
garment marker **9452**
garment mender **9619**
garment packer **9619**
garment parts sorter **9619**
garment patternmaker **5245**
garment price marker **6622**
garment sorter **9619**
garment steamer **9619**
garment waterproofer **9619**
garnett machine tender – textiles **9441**
gas and arc welder **7265**
gas and steam distribution engineer **2132**
gas appliance servicer **7253**
gas bar attendant (except self-serve) **6621**
gas bar attendant, self-serve **6611**
gas bar cashier, self-serve **6611**
gas brazer **9515**
gas broker **1236**
gas charger, refrigeration equipment **9484**
gas chromatographer **2211**
gas compressor operator **9232**
gas controller **9232**
gas customer servicer **7253**
gas dispatcher **9232**
gas distribution foreman/woman **9212**
gas distribution general manager **0016**
gas distribution inspector **7442**
gas distribution manager **0912**
gas field battery operator **9232**
gas field operator **9232**
gas fitter **7253**
gas fitter apprentice **7253**
gas fitter helper – utilities **9613**

gas fitter/installer **7253**
gas fitter trainee **7253**
gas fitters, foreman/woman **7213**
gas furnace assembler **9486**
gas jockey **6621**
gas leak inspector **7442**
gas leak surveyor **7442**
gas line fitters foreman/woman **7213**
gas liquefaction and regasification plant
    operator **9232**
gas maintenance man/woman **7442**
gas mask maker, rubber **9423**
gas meter assembler **9498**
gas meter installer **7442**
gas meter reader **1454**
gas meter repairer **7445**
gas meter repairer helper **7612**
gas meter servicer **7445**
gas meter tester **7445**
gas odorization and safety person **7442**
gas pipefitter **7253**
gas pipelayer – construction **7611**
gas plant foreman/woman **9212**
gas plant operator **9232**
gas pressure regulator **9232**
gas processing compressor operator **9232**
gas range serviceman/woman **7253**
gas recovery operator **9232**
gas refrigerator serviceman/woman **7253**
gas regulator **7442**
gas service crew dispatcher **1475**
gas service foreman/woman **7213**
gas service supervisor **7213**
gas serviceman/woman **7253**
gas servicer **7253**
gas servicer helper – utilities **9613**
gas-shielded arc welder **7265**
gas station attendant (except self-serve) **6621**
gas station manager **0621**
gas supply operations manager **0912**
gas tester – oil field services **8232**
gas treating unit operator **9232**
gas truck driver **7411**
gas utility labourer **9613**
gas utility man/woman **9613**
gas welder **7265**
gas well operator **9232**
gas works trouble man/woman **7253**
gas works trouble shooter **7253**
gasket cutter, rubber **9423**
gasket finisher, rubber **9423**
gasket gluer, rubber **9423**
gasket maker, rubber **9423**
gasoline catalyst operator **9232**
gasoline engine assembler **9486**
gasoline pump calibrator **9486**
gasoline pump tester **9486**
gasoline truck operator **7411**

gastroenterologist **3111**
gastroenterology, chief of **0311**
gate attendant **6651**
gate attendant, campground **6671**
gateman/woman **6651**
gathering machine feeder – printing **9619**
gathering machine operator – printing **9473**
gathering machine set-up operator – printing **9473**
gauge maker, tool and die **7232**
gauge setter/machinist **7231**
gauger, oil **9232**
gauger, semiconductor material – electronics manufacturing **9483**
gauze pad machine tender **9517**
gear box assembler **9486**
gear cutting machine set-up operator **9511**
gear cutting machine tender **9511**
gear grinder **9511**
gear hobber **9511**
gear inspector/machinist **7231**
gear lapping machine set-up operator **9511**
gear milling machine operator **9511**
gear roller grinder **9511**
gear room keeper **1472**
gear shaper set-up operator **9511**
gear shaver set-up operator **9511**
gear tester/machinist **7231**
gear train assembler **9486**
gearcase assembler, agriculture implements **9486**
gelatine blending machine tender **9461**
gelatine evaporator filter operator **9461**
gelatine extractor tender **9461**
gelatine powder mixer **9461**
gelatine stock cooker **9617**
gem cutter **7344**
gem expert **7344**
gemologist **7344**
general accountant **1111**
general agent, railway transport **0713**
general assembler and light machine operator – electronics manufacturing **9483**
general assembly supervisor – motor vehicle manufacturing **9221**
general building contractor **0711**
general carpenters foreman/woman **7215**
general construction foreman/woman **7217**
general construction superintendent **0711**
general construction supervisor **7217**
general contractor, construction **0711**
general cook **6242**
general counsel **4112**
general duty nurse **3152**
general economist **4162**
general farm worker **8431**
general foreman/woman – building construction **7215**

general foreman/woman – residential construction **7215**
general helper – small electrical appliance assembly **9619**
general insurance representative **6231**
general labourer – light fixture assembly **9619**
general labourer – municipal **7621**
general labourer – public works **7621**
general machinist **7231**
general manager – cleaning service **0015**
general manager – financial, communications and other business services **0013**
general manager – goods production, utilities, transportation and construction **0016**
general manager – government services **0012**
general manager – health, education, social and community services and membership organizations **0014**
general manager – membership organization **0014**
general manager, professional athletic team **0513**
general manager – real estate management company **0013**
general manager, sales – trade, broadcasting and other services n.e.c. **0015**
general manager – trade, broadcasting and other services n.e.c. **0015**
general manager – trucking company **0016**
general office clerk **1411**
general office clerks supervisor **1211**
general office worker **1411**
general pathologist **3111**
general practice dentist **3113**
general practice physician **3112**
general practitioner **3112**
general production operator – motor vehicle manufacturing **9482**
general repairer and adjuster – motor vehicle manufacturing **9482**
general sales manager – trade, broadcasting and other services n.e.c. **0015**
general secretary – government services **0012**
general secretary, ymca **0513**
general solicitor **4112**
general superintendent, construction **0711**
general supervisor, assembly – motor vehicle manufacturing **9221**
general supervisor – building construction **7215**
general supervisor – residential construction **7215**
general surgeon **3111**

general ticket and information clerk, airline **6433**

general traffic manager **0713**

general transportation manager **0713**

general welder **7265**

generating station operator – electric power systems **7352**

generation substation operator – electric power systems **7352**

generator repairman/woman **7333**

generator tester – industrial electrical equipment **9485**

geneticist **2121**

geneticist – medical **3111**

geochemical manager **0212**

geochemical technician **2211**

geochemical technologist **2211**

geochemist **2113**

geodetic engineer **2131**

geodetic survey technician **2254**

geodetic survey technologist **2254**

geographer **4169**

geographic information system (GIS) technician **2255**

geographic information system (GIS) technologist **2255**

geography professor – university **4121**

geography teacher – high school **4141**

geological draftsman/woman **2253**

geological engineer **2144**

geological engineering technician **2212**

geological engineering technologist **2212**

geological manager **0212**

geological mapping technician **2255**

geological prospecting technologist **2212**

geological survey technician **2212**

geological technician **2212**

geological technologist **2212**

geologist **2113**

geology professor – university **4121**

geology technical assistant **2212**

geometry teacher – high school **4141**

geomorphologist **2113**

geophysic instrument assembler – electronics manufacturing **9483**

geophysical draftsman/woman **2253**

geophysical engineer **2144**

geophysical equipment operator, airborne **2212**

geophysical manager **0212**

geophysical observer **2212**

geophysical prospecting technologist **2212**

geophysical survey technician **2212**

geophysical survey technologist **2212**

geophysical technician **2212**

geophysical technologist **2212**

geophysicist **2113**

geophysics professor – university **4121**

geotechnical engineer **2144**

geriatric activities co-ordinator **4167**

geriatric activities leader **5254**

geriatric medicine specialist **3111**

geriatric social worker **4152**

geriatrician **3111**

geriatrics nursing supervisor **3151**

geriatrist – medical **3111**

germ separator operator – food and beverage processing **9461**

german teacher – high school **4141**

gerontologist **4169**

gift shop clerk **6421**

gift shop manager **0621**

gig machine operator – textiles **9443**

gill net fisherman/woman **8262**

GIS forester **2122**

GIS technician **2255**

GIS technologist **2255**

glaciologist **2113**

glass and metal mechanic **7292**

glass bender **9413**

glass beveler **9413**

glass beveler tender **9413**

glass blower **5244**

glass blowing lathe operator **9413**

glass blowing machine operator **9413**

glass breaker **9413**

glass buffer **9413**

glass calibrator **7383**

glass chemist **2112**

glass chipper **9413**

glass cleaner **6662**

glass containers tester **9415**

glass cut off machine operator **9413**

glass cut off machine unloader **7452**

glass cutter, hand **9413**

glass cutter operator **9413**

glass cutting foreman/woman **9211**

glass decorator operator **9413**

glass drawing machine operator **9413**

glass drill tender **9413**

glass edge finisher, hand **9413**

glass edger **9413**

glass edger tender **9413**

glass engraver **5244**

glass engraving foreman/woman **9211**

glass etcher **9413**

glass finisher **9611**

glass finishing machine operator **9413**

glass forming foreman/woman **9211**

glass forming machine operator **9413**

glass forming machine operator helper **9611**

glass forming machine set-up person **9413**

glass forming machine setter **9413**

glass forming machine setter assistant **9413**

glass frame fitter **3231**

glass furnace foreman/woman **9211**

glass furnace operator **9413**
glass grinder **9413**
glass grinders and polishers
   foreman/woman **9211**
glass grinding machine feeder **9413**
glass heater **9413**
glass helper – mineral products
   manufacturing **9611**
glass inspector **9415**
glass installation and repair contractor **7219**
glass installer apprentice **7292**
glass installer/glazier **7292**
glass installer, structural **7292**
glass laminator **9413**
glass lathe operator **9413**
glass manufacturing glazer **9413**
glass marker **9413**
glass melter **9413**
glass mixer **9413**
glass mould cleaner **9413**
glass moulder **9413**
glass packer **9611**
glass polisher **9413**
glass polisher tender **9413**
glass press and blow machine operator **9413**
glass presser **9413**
glass pressing machine operator **9413**
glass processing foreman/woman **9211**
glass sander, belt **9413**
glass setter **7292**
glass setter helper **7611**
glass stopper grinder **9413**
glass tank furnace operator **9413**
glass temperer **9413**
glass worker – glass products
   manufacturing **9413**
glass worker helper **7611**
glassware banding machine tender **9413**
glassware grinder **9413**
glassworker, hand **5244**
glaze maker – clay products **9414**
glazier **7292**
glazier and metal mechanic **7292**
glazier apprentice **7292**
glazier, curtain wall **7292**
glazier, exterior walls **7292**
glazier helper **7611**
glazier, plate glass **7292**
glazier, stained glass **7292**
glazier, structural glass **7292**
glazier supervisor **7219**
glazier, window sash and frame **7292**
glaziers foreman/woman **7219**
glazing contractor **7219**
gliding instructor **4131**
glost kiln operator – clay products **9414**
glove and mitten examiner **9454**
glove cutter **9452**

glove designer **5243**
glove knitter **9442**
glove liner **9619**
glove maker, rubber **9423**
glove pairer **9619**
glove turner, hand **9619**
glue blender **9421**
glue bonding machine tender –
   woodworking **9513**
glue clamp operator, wood products **9493**
glue jointer operator – woodworking **9513**
glue machine operator – woodworking **9513**
gluer **9498**
gluer, assembly line – wood products
   manufacturing **9493**
gluer – furniture manufacturing **9492**
gluer, wood products **9493**
gluing and folding machine operator –
   printing **9473**
gluing machine operator – rubber
   manufacturing **9423**
gluten settler – food and beverage
   processing **9617**
glycerine refinery operator **9232**
go-cart assembler **9486**
go-cart repairer **7335**
go-cart ride attendant **6671**
goal judge **5253**
gold assayer **2212**
gold leaf stamper – printing **9473**
gold prospector **2212**
gold recoverer **9411**
goldsmith **5244**
golf ball assembler **9423**
golf ball maker **9423**
golf ball vulcanizer **9423**
golf club adjuster **9498**
golf club assembler **9498**
golf club facer, wood **9493**
golf club head finisher, wood **9493**
golf club inspector **9498**
golf club maker, custom **9498**
golf club repairer **7445**
golf course labourer **8612**
golf course starter **6671**
golf course superintendent **2225**
golf course worker **8612**
golf instructor **5254**
golf pro **5254**
golf professional **5254**
golf range attendant **6671**
golfer **5251**
gondola operator **6671**
gospel worker **4217**
gouger, lacrosse sticks – woodworking **9513**
gourmet cooking instructor –
   non-vocational **4216**
government agency senior administrator **0012**

government leader **0011**
government logistician **2161**
government property manager **1224**
governor general **0011**
gradall operator **7421**
grade school teacher **4142**
grade tamper – construction **7611**
grader, fabric **9444**
grader, fish **9465**
grader fitter **7316**
grader – food and beverage processing **9465**
grader, hosiery **9444**
grader, lumber **9436**
grader, meat **9465**
grader operator **7421**
grader, sash and door **9493**
grader, seed corn **9465**
grader, smoking pipe **9493**
grader tallyman/woman – wood processing **9436**
grader – textiles **9444**
grader, veneer and plywood – wood processing **9436**
grader – wood processing **9436**
graderman/woman – pulp and paper **9433**
grading equipment mechanic **7312**
graduate assistant – post secondary **4122**
graduate nurse **3152**
grafter **8431**
grain broker **1113**
grain cleaner **9461**
grain cleaning machine operator – food and beverage processing **9461**
grain commissioner **0012**
grain conveyor operator **7452**
grain cooker – food and beverage processing **9461**
grain elevator agent **6234**
grain elevator maintenance mechanic **7311**
grain elevator manager **6234**
grain elevator manager, country elevator **6234**
grain elevator operator **6234**
grain farm labourer **8431**
grain farm worker **8431**
grain farmer **8251**
grain handler **7452**
grain inspection supervisor **2222**
grain inspector **2222**
grain meal processor – food and beverage processing **9461**
grain merchandiser **6411**
grain miller **9461**
grain mixer – food and beverage processing **9461**
grain roaster **9461**
grain sample miller **9461**
grain sampler **9465**

grain tester **2222**
grain thresher **8431**
grain trader **1113**
grain trading manager **0121**
grain weigher **7622**
grainer – furniture finishing and refinishing **9494**
graining machine operator – tannery **9453**
graining press operator – chemical processing **9421**
granite carver **9414**
granite cutter **9414**
granite polisher, hand **9414**
granite polisher, machine **9414**
granular aluminium caster – foundry **9412**
granulating machine tender – tobacco processing **9464**
granulator machine operator – chemical processing **9421**
granulator tender – food and beverage processing **9461**
granulator – tobacco processing **9464**
grape grower **8251**
graphic artist **5241**
graphic arts camera operator **9472**
graphic arts teacher – college **4131**
graphic arts technician **5223**
graphic design instructor – college or vocational institute **4131**
graphic design sales representative **6411**
graphic designer **5241**
graphics analyst, computer **2162**
graphics specialist, computer **2162**
graphics specialist, e.d.p. **2162**
graphoanalyst **4169**
graphologist **6484**
grapple operator **7421**
grapple operator – logging **8241**
grapple skidder operator **8421**
grapple yarder hooktender **8211**
grapple yarder operator **8241**
grass cutter **8612**
grated cheese maker **9461**
grave digger **8612**
gravel hauler **7411**
gravel roofer **7291**
gravel screener **9611**
gravel truck driver **7411**
gravity data technician **2212**
gravure proof press operator – printing **7381**
grease maker **9232**
greaser, engine room **7434**
greaser, heavy truck **7443**
greaser, journal box **7431**
greek teacher – high school **4141**
green chainman/woman – wood processing **9614**
green lumber grader **9436**

green sorter – wood processing **9614**
green tire inspector **9423**
green tire lubricator **9423**
green tire repairer **9423**
greenhouse farmer **8254**
greenhouse florist **8432**
greenhouse foreman/woman **8256**
greenhouse manager **8254**
greenhouse operator **8254**
greenhouse supervisor **8256**
greenhouse worker **8432**
greenhouse worker, crew chief **8256**
greens superintendent **2225**
greens worker **8612**
greensaw off-bearer – wood processing **9614**
greenware driller – clay products **9414**
greenware finisher – clay products **9414**
greenware turner operator – clay
    products **9414**
greeting card assembler **9498**
greige cloth examiner **9444**
grid caster operator – foundry **9412**
grid gauger – electronics manufacturing **9483**
grid inspector – electrical equipment
    manufacturing **9484**
grid inspector – electronics
    manufacturing **9483**
grid operator – electronics
    manufacturing **9483**
grief counsellor **4153**
grill cook **6242**
grinder and sharpener – metal
    fabrication **9612**
grinder, asbestos **9611**
grinder/chipper – metal fabrication **9612**
grinder – concrete, clay and stone
    products **9414**
grinder/deburrer – metal fabrication **9612**
grinder feeder – pulp and paper **9614**
grinder loader – pulp and paper **9432**
grinder operator – plastic manufacturing **9422**
grinder operator – pulp and paper **9432**
grinder operator – rubber manufacturing **9423**
grinder, precision **9511**
grinder set-up operator **9511**
grinder tender – chemical processing **9421**
grinder, tobacco leaf **9464**
grinder/trimmer – metal fabrication **9612**
grinderman/woman – pulp and paper **9432**
grinding and classifier tender **9411**
grinding and floatation operator **9411**
grinding and packing foreman/woman –
    chemical processing **9212**
grinding machine operator, hardboard **9434**
grinding mill operator – primary metal
    processing **9231**
grinding stone sharpener **9414**
grip **5227**

gristmill operator – food and beverage
    processing **9461**
grizzly worker – underground mining **8614**
grocer **0621**
groceries deliverer **7414**
grocery clerk **6622**
grocery clerk supervisor **6211**
grocery packer **6622**
grocery store baker **6252**
grocery store butcher **6251**
grocery store cashier **6611**
groceteria cashier **6611**
groom **8431**
groomer, aircraft **7437**
groomer, pet **6483**
groove grinder, glass **9413**
groover operator – woodworking **9513**
grooving machine operator **7421**
grooving machine operator –
    woodworking **9513**
ground hand – telecommunications **7612**
ground school instructor **4131**
ground transportation driver **7412**
ground worker – pile driving **7611**
ground worker – power lines **7612**
ground worker – telecommunications **7612**
grounds keeper **8432**
grounds keeper supervisor **8256**
grounds maintenance contractor **8255**
grounds maintenance manager **8255**
grounds maintenance worker **8612**
groundsman/woman **8612**
groundwater geologist **2113**
groundwood pulp tester **9432**
group accounting manager **0111**
group counsellor employment **4213**
group home counsellor **4153**
group home worker **4212**
group insurance clerk **1434**
group insurance representative **6231**
group leader, drafting **2253**
group leader, electrical mechanics **7333**
group leader, forging machine operator **9512**
group leader, industrial painter **9496**
group leader – large electrical appliance
    assembly **9484**
group leader, machine fitters **7316**
group leader, mechanical assemblers **9486**
group leader – small electrical appliance
    assembly **9484**
group life claim examiner – insurance **1233**
group representative – insurance **6231**
group sales representative, travel **6411**
group social worker **4152**
group underwriter – insurance **1234**
grout machine operator **7611**
grouter **7611**
grower, evergreens **8254**

grower, flower **8254**

grower's adviser – agriculture **2123**

grower, shrubs **8254**

guard, armoured car **6651**

guard – correctional institution **6462**

guard, security **6651**

guest home worker **6661**

guest house operator **0632**

guest service agent **6435**

guest services manager **0632**

guidance counsellor **4143**

guidance director **0314**

guidance head **4143**

guidance services technician –
    education **4212**

guide, establishment **6441**

guide, horse drawn sightseeing tour **6441**

guide, hunting and fishing **6442**

guide, mountain climbing **6442**

guide – museum **5212**

guide, outfitting **6442**

guide, rafting **6442**

guide setter – metal processing **9411**

guide, sightseeing **6441**

guide, travel **6441**

guide, whitewater **6442**

guillotine operator – printing **9473**

guitar maker **5244**

guitar player **5133**

guitar repairer **7445**

gum cutter – rubber footwear **9423**

gum sheeting and scoring machine
    operator – food and beverage
    processing **9461**

gun assembler **9486**

gun assembler, television picture tubes **9483**

gun perforator – oil field services **8232**

gun repairer **7383**

gun stock checkerer **9513**

gun stock fitter – woodworking **9513**

gun stock shaper, wood products **9513**

gun subassembler **9486**

guniter – construction **7611**

gunner – military **6464**

gunsmith **7383**

gymnast, remedial **3144**

gymnastics coach **5252**

gymnastics instructor **5254**

gynaecologist **3111**

gyproc applicator **7284**

gyproc maker **9414**

gypsum calciner **9411**

gypsum lather **7284**

gyroscope repairer **7445**

gyroscope repairman/woman **7445**

H

habilitationist, aural **3141**

habitat management technician **2221**

haematological pathologist **3111**

haematologist **3111**

haematology, chief of **0311**

haematology technologist – medical
    laboratory **3211**

hair and fibre examiner, forensic **2221**

hair care specialist **6271**

hair colour technician **6271**

hair dryer assembler **9484**

hair dyer **6271**

hair removal specialist **6482**

hair replacement consultant **6482**

hair replacement technician **6482**

hairdresser **6271**

hairdresser apprentice **6271**

hairdressing instructor – college or
    vocational institute **4131**

hairdressing salon manager **0651**

hairdressing teacher – college or
    vocational institute **4131**

hairstyling salon manager **0651**

hairstylist **6271**

hairstylist apprentice **6271**

halftone camera operator – printing **9472**

halfway house manager **0314**

halfway house supervisor **4212**

halfway house worker **4212**

hall cleaner **6661**

ham curer **9461**

ham cutter **9462**

ham grader **9465**

ham presser **9617**

ham sawyer – meat packing **9462**

hammer driver – forging **9512**

hammer man/woman – metal forgings **9512**

hammer mill tender – concrete, clay and
    stone products **9414**

hammer mill tender – food and beverage
    processing **9461**

hammer operator – metal forgings **9512**

hammersmith **7266**

hammersmith – jewellery **7344**

hamper maker, wood **9493**

hand bonder, rubber footwear **9423**

hand buffer – metal fabrication **9612**

hand bundler – wood processing **9614**

hand cutter – clothing manufacturing **9452**

hand cutter – fabric, fur and leather
    products manufacturing **9452**

hand finisher – laundry and dry
    cleaning **6682**

hand fish net maker **9498**

hand fur cleaner **6681**

hand icer, bakery **6252**

hand inserter – printing **9619**
hand ironer – laundry and dry cleaning **6682**
hand lacer **9498**
hand lapper **9511**
hand leather cutter – leather products manufacturing **9452**
hand lens beveler – non prescription **9517**
hand lens edger – non prescription **9517**
hand liner fisherman/woman **8262**
hand luggage inspector **6651**
hand moulder – clay products **9414**
hand net maker **9498**
hand packager **7452**
hand packer, food store **6622**
hand pad gluer **9619**
hand pleater – garment manufacturing **9498**
hand presser – laundry and dry cleaning **6682**
hand screen printer – textiles **9443**
hand shellfish processor – fish processing **9463**
hand skeiner – textiles **9616**
hand sprayer **8432**
hand stitcher, shoes **9498**
hand stonecutter **9414**
hand tennis net maker **9498**
hand tool repairman/woman **7445**
hand tools manufacturing foreman/woman **9227**
hand touch-up painter, production **9496**
hand trimmer – garment manufacturing **9619**
hand trimmer – shoe manufacturing **9619**
hand truck operator **7452**
hand washer – laundry and dry cleaning **6681**
handbag designer **5243**
handbag maker, leather **9498**
handbag manufacturing foreman/woman **9225**
handbill passer **1463**
handbook writer **5121**
handle mounter **9619**
handler, material **7452**
handwriting analyst **4169**
handwriting analyst, scientific **4169**
handwriting expert **4169**
handwriting expert, forensic **2211**
handyman/woman **6663**
hang-up blaster – underground mining **8231**
hansard reporter **1244**
harbour master **0721**
harbour pilot **2273**
harbour police chief **0641**
harbour police officer **6261**
harbour policeman/woman **6261**
hard hat assembler **9498**
hardboard coating line checker **9498**
hardboard grinding machine operator **9434**
hardboard pressman/woman – wood processing **9434**
hardboard spray coating machine tender **9496**

hardener – primary metal processing **9411**
hardhat diver **7382**
hardness tester – primary metal processing **9415**
hardrock miner **8231**
hardrock miner apprentice **8231**
hardware assembler **9498**
hardware buyer **6233**
hardware engineer **2147**
hardware installer – furniture manufacturing **9492**
hardware mounter – furniture manufacturing **9492**
hardware purchasing manager **0113**
hardware store clerk **6421**
hardware store manager **0621**
hardwood faller and bucker **8421**
hardwood floor covering installer **7295**
harness and cable fabricator – electronics manufacturing **9483**
harness cleaner – textiles **9616**
harness maker, leather **9452**
harness race driver **5251**
harness racing starter **5253**
harness tier – textiles **9442**
harpist **5133**
harpoon fisherman/woman **8262**
harpsichord builder **5244**
harvest hand **8611**
harvester machine operator **8431**
hat and cap eyelet machine operator **9517**
hat and cap maker foreman/woman **9225**
hat and cap parts bundler **9619**
hat and cap perforator **9619**
hat assembler, fabric **9498**
hat brusher **9619**
hat check attendant **6683**
hat designer **5243**
hat inspector **9454**
hat liner **9619**
hat sewer, factory **9451**
hat sizer **9619**
hat sorter **9619**
hat sweatband flanger **9619**
hat treater **9619**
hat trimming department foreman/woman **9225**
hatchery helper **8613**
hatchery manager **8251**
hatchery producer **8251**
hatchery worker **8431**
hatmaking machine operator **9517**
hatter **6681**
haulageman/woman – underground mining **8411**
hazardous waste inspector – environmental health **2263**
hazzan **4217**

head, accounting section **1212**
head air traffic controller **2272**
head baggage porter **6216**
head baker – retail trade **6252**
head, billing unit **1212**
head boner – meat packing **9462**
head brakeman/woman **7362**
head, building services **0722**
head butcher – retail and wholesale **6251**
head buyer **6233**
head caretaker **6215**
head cashier **6211**
head charger **9231**
head chef **6241**
head cleaner **6215**
head coach **5252**
head correctional officer **6462**
head custodian **6215**
head dispatcher **1215**
head end technician – cable television **7247**
head, facilities maintenance **0722**
head, guidance department **4143**
head, home economics department –
    secondary school **4141**
head janitor **6215**
head lamps adjuster – motor vehicle
    manufacturing **9482**
head librarian **0511**
head maid **6215**
head matron **6462**
head miller, feed and flour mill **9213**
head mixer, bakery **9213**
head nurse **3151**
head of cataloguing **0511**
head of wardrobe **5226**
head office underwriter – insurance **1234**
head, park maintenance **8256**
head preparator **5212**
head, property section **1224**
head refrigerating engineer **9212**
head saw operator – sawmill **9431**
head sawyer – sawmill **9431**
head, science department, secondary
    school **4141**
head shipper **1215**
head teller – financial services **1433**
head train dispatcher **2275**
head waiter/waitress **6453**
header machine operator, metal **9516**
header operator, wood cooperage **9513**
header, wood barrel **9513**
heading machine tender – woodworking **9513**
headings sawyer, cooperage **9513**
headline writer **5123**
headliner installer – motor vehicle
    manufacturing **9482**
headman/woman – underground mining **8411**

headmaster, private school **0313**
headquarters duty officer – police **6261**
headrig operator – sawmill **9431**
headwelder, electric welding pipe mill **7214**
healer, faith **4217**
health aide **6631**
health and dental claim examiner –
    insurance **1233**
health and safety instructor **4131**
health and safety officer **2263**
health and welfare manager –
    government services **0411**
health care administration officer
    (management) – military **0311**
health care administration officer
    (program officer) – military **4165**
health care aide **3413**
health care association program officer **4165**
health care consultant **4165**
health care planner **4165**
health care planning consultant **4165**
health care planning officer **4165**
health care researcher **4165**
health club manager **0721**
health commissioner **0012**
health economist **4162**
health education teacher – secondary
    school **4141**
health labour force planning consultant **4165**
health librarian **5111**
health officer supervisor **2263**
health physicist **2111**
health policy development officer **4165**
health policy research analyst **4165**
health promotion program officer **4165**
health record unit supervisor **1211**
health records administrator **0114**
health records supervisor **1211**
health records technician **1413**
health research officer **4165**
health standards inspector **2263**
health studio manager **0651**
health technology teacher – college **4131**
hearing aid assistant **3235**
hearing aid earpiece maker **9517**
hearing aid inspector – electronics
    manufacturing **9483**
hearing aid repairer **2242**
hearing aid sales consultant **6421**
hearing aid salesperson **6421**
hearing aid specialist **3235**
hearing aid technician **3235**
hearing aid technician – household and
    business equipment **2242**
hearing assessment technician **3235**
hearing clinician **3141**
hearing impaired instructor **4215**
hearing impaired teacher **4215**

hearing specialist **3141**

hearse driver **7413**

heart specialist **3111**

heat and frost insulator **7293**

heat curer – textiles **9443**

heat seal equipment operator – electrical equipment manufacturing **9487**

heat seal press pad assembler – furniture assembly **9619**

heat sensor assembler **9498**

heat shield maker, aircraft **9498**

heat treat operator – primary metal processing **9411**

heat treat technician **2212**

heat treater helper **9619**

heat treating inspector – metal processing **9415**

heater, coke ovens **9411**

heater, glass **9413**

heater helper – primary metal processing **9611**

heater operator – metal forgings **9512**

heater/planer operator **7421**

heater – primary metal processing **9411**

heating and air conditioning contractor **7216**

heating and air conditioning mechanic helper **7612**

heating and cooling mechanic **7313**

heating and ventilation equipment tender **7351**

heating designer **2232**

heating element coil former operator **9487**

heating engineer **2132**

heating mechanic **7331**

heating service mechanic **7331**

heating stationary engineer **7351**

heating systems contractor **7216**

heating systems installer **7331**

heating systems mechanic **7331**

heating systems servicer **7331**

heating systems technician **7331**

heating technician **7331**

heating ventilating and air conditioning engineer **2132**

heating, ventilation and air conditioning (HVAC) mechanic **7313**

heavy-duty capacitor assembler **9484**

heavy-duty cleaner **6663**

heavy duty coil former – industrial electrical equipment **9485**

heavy-duty electrical battery charger tester **9487**

heavy-duty equipment mechanic **7312**

heavy-duty equipment mechanic apprentice **7312**

heavy-duty equipment operator **7421**

heavy-duty equipment operator apprentice **7421**

heavy-duty equipment servicer **7443**

heavy-duty mechanic foreman/woman **7216**

heavy-duty press set-up operator – metal fabrication **9514**

heavy-duty resistor assembler **9484**

heavy-duty slip roll operator – metal fabrication **9514**

heavy-duty transformer assembler **9485**

heavy equipment greaser **7443**

heavy equipment inspector – repairer **7312**

heavy equipment mechanic **7312**

heavy equipment operator **7421**

heavy equipment sales representative **6221**

heavy equipment servicer **7443**

heavy forger **9512**

heavy machinery fitter **7316**

heavy media tender – mineral and metal processing **9411**

heavy mobile equipment repairer **7312**

heavy mobile equipment repairman/woman **7312**

heavy mobile logging equipment mechanic **7312**

heavy mobile mining equipment mechanic **7312**

heavy truck driver **7411**

heavy trucks salesperson **6221**

heavy water plant control technician **2243**

heavy water steam plant operator **7351**

hebrew teacher – elementary school **4142**

heel cutter – rubber footwear **9423**

heel maker **9517**

heel maker – rubber footwear **9423**

heel seat fitter **9517**

heel shaper – shoe manufacturing **9619**

heel trimming machine operator – footwear manufacturing **9517**

heliarc welder **7265**

helicopter assembly foreman/woman **9226**

helicopter assembly supervisor **9226**

helicopter flying instructor **2271**

helicopter inspector, mechanical systems **7315**

helicopter maintenance foreman/woman – mechanical systems **7216**

helicopter mechanic **7315**

helicopter pilot **2271**

helminthologist **2121**

helper, awning installer **7611**

helper, bar **6642**

helper, bindery **9619**

helper, blaster – underground mining **8411**

helper, blood donor clinic **6631**

helper, boilermaker **9612**

helper, bricklayer **7611**

helper, cable installation and repair – telecommunications **7612**

helper, cable splicer **7612**

helper, carman/woman **7612**
helper, carpenter **7611**
helper, carpet layer **7611**
helper, cement finisher **7611**
helper – chemical processing **9613**
helper, construction **7611**
helper, construction trades **7611**
helper, day-care **6473**
helper, diver **7612**
helper, driller – underground mining **8411**
helper, dry cleaner **6681**
helper, electric motor testing **9619**
helper, electrician – construction **7611**
helper, elevator mechanic **7612**
helper, engine fitter **7612**
helper, floor covering installer **7611**
helper, glazier **7611**
helper, industrial mechanic **7612**
helper, insulation hoseman **7611**
helper, insulator **7611**
helper, ironworker **7611**
helper, laundry **6681**
helper, mechanic **7612**
helper – medical laboratory **3212**
helper, metal roofer – construction **7611**
helper, millwright **7612**
helper, miner **8614**
helper, motor vehicle body repairer **7612**
helper, motor vehicle mechanic **7612**
helper, nursery school **6473**
helper, occupational therapy **6631**
helper, oil burner installer **7611**
helper, oil burner technician **7612**
helper, oil well cementer **8615**
helper, painter **7611**
helper, physiotherapy **6631**
helper, pipeworker – underground
    mining **8614**
helper, plasterer **7611**
helper, plumber **7611**
helper, press **9619**
helper – primary metal and mineral
    products processing **9611**
helper – printing **9619**
helper, raise miner **8411**
helper, reeled tubing operator – oil field
    services **8615**
helper, roofer **7611**
helper – rubber manufacturing **9615**
helper, sheet metal worker –
    construction **7611**
helper, sheet metal worker – industrial **9612**
helper, small engine mechanic **7612**
helper, teacher's **6472**
helper – textiles **9616**
helper, tile layer **7611**
helper, tile setter **7611**
helper, timber and steel prop setter **8614**

helper, tree surgeon **8612**
helper, waterproofer **7611**
helper, wireline – oil field services **8615**
hematological pathologist **3111**
hematologist **3111**
hemmer sewing machine operator **9451**
herb practitioner **3232**
herbal medicine assistant **3414**
herbal practitioner **3232**
herbal specialist **3232**
herbalist **3232**
herbarium curator **5112**
herbologist **3232**
herbology practitioner **3232**
herder – stockyards **8431**
herdsman/woman **8253**
herdsperson **8253**
heritage language program director **0413**
heritage planner, land use **2153**
herpetologist **2121**
hide and pelt processing inspector **9454**
hide and pelt processing worker **9453**
hide and skin preparer **9453**
hide beamer – hide and pelt processing **9453**
hide grader **9454**
hide house foreman/woman – hide and
    pelt processing **9225**
hide processing worker **9453**
hide sorter **9454**
hide stretcher **9453**
high commissioner **0012**
high density operator – wood processing **9434**
high rigger, theatre **5227**
high school librarian **4141**
high school library teacher **4141**
high school principal **0313**
high school teacher **4141**
high school teacher, physical education **4141**
high school teacher, religious and moral
    education **4141**
high school teacher, sciences **4141**
high school teacher, special education **4141**
high school teacher, substitute **4141**
high school teacher, supply **4141**
high sheriff **6461**
high speed printer operator **9471**
high temperature physicist **2111**
high voltage lineman/woman – electric
    power systems **7244**
high voltage power transformer repairer **7333**
highway and bridge maintenance road
    boss **7217**
highway and street cement mason **7282**
highway commissioner **0012**
highway concrete mixer operator helper **7611**
highway construction boss **7217**
highway construction foreman/woman **7217**
highway construction general manager **0016**

highway construction inspector **2264**
highway construction manager **0711**
highway construction materials, testing technician **2231**
highway engineer **2131**
highway line painter **7621**
highway maintenance foreman/woman **7217**
highway maintenance worker **7611**
highway patrol officer **6261**
highway patrolman/woman **6261**
highway radio/telephone operator **1475**
highway scale operator **6463**
highway snow removal equipment operator **7422**
highway technician **2231**
hinger, wood box **9493**
histologist **2121**
histology technologist – medical laboratory **3211**
histopathologist **3111**
historian **4169**
historic site interpreter **5212**
historic sites administrator **0511**
historical archivist **5113**
historical artifacts conservator **5112**
historical demographer **4169**
historical geographer **4169**
historical interpreter **5212**
historical park superintendent **0511**
historical park superintendent, assistant **0511**
historical site technician **5212**
historical village supervisor **5212**
historical village technician **5212**
history museum interpreter **5212**
history professor – university **4121**
history teacher – college **4131**
history teacher – high school **4141**
histotechnology technologist – medical laboratory **3211**
hobbing machine setter **9511**
hockey association general manager **0015**
hockey coach **5252**
hockey player **5251**
hockey scout **5252**
hockey stick assembler **9493**
hockey stick inspector/grader **9493**
hog breeder **8251**
hog buyer **6233**
hog farm foreman/woman **8253**
hog farm worker **8431**
hog killer **9462**
hog machine tender – wood processing **9614**
hog operation supervisor **8253**
hog producer **8251**
hogshead assembler – wood products **9493**
hogshead cooper **9513**
hogshead filler and packer – tobacco products **9617**

hogshead inspector – tobacco processing **9465**
hoist operator – underground mining **8411**
hoisting and lifting equipment assembly foreman/woman **9226**
hoisting engineer **7371**
hole saw tender – woodworking **9513**
holistic practitioner **3232**
hollow ware buffing machine tender **9517**
hologram imprinting machine tender **9473**
holographic technician **2241**
holographic technologist **2241**
holter monitor technologist **3217**
holter scanning technologist **3218**
home builder **0712**
home care program consultant **4165**
home care service manager **0651**
home care services director **0311**
home care therapist **3143**
home care worker **6471**
home cleaner **6661**
home decorating consultant – retail **6421**
home demonstrator – retail **6623**
home economics department head – secondary school **4141**
home economics teacher – elementary school **4142**
home economics teacher – secondary school **4141**
home economist **4164**
home health aide **6471**
home inspector **2264**
home lighting technician **2241**
home mission worker – religion **4217**
home renovation contractor **0712**
home renovator **0712**
home support worker **6471**
home trade master **2273**
homemaker helper, rest home **6661**
homemaker services director **0314**
homemaker services director – government services **0411**
homeopath **3232**
homeopathic physician **3232**
homeopathic practitioner **3232**
homeopathist **3232**
homeopathy, doctor of **3232**
homogenizer operator – food and beverage processing **9461**
hone operator – metal machining **9511**
honey grader and blender **9465**
honey processing equipment operator **9461**
honing machine operator – metal machining **9511**
honing machine set-up operator **9511**
hood fitter – motor vehicle manufacturing **9482**
hook and rig supervisor – logging **8211**

hook tender – logging **8211**
hooker/laster – rubber manufacturing **9423**
hoop driving machine operator –
    woodworking **9513**
hoop maker, machine – metal
    fabrication **9514**
hoop making machine operator **9516**
hoop riveting machine operator **9516**
hoopnet fisherman/woman **8262**
hop farm foreman/woman **8253**
hop picking machine operator **8431**
horizontal boring mill set-up operator **9511**
horizontal earth boring machine helper **7611**
horizontal earth boring machine
    operator **7421**
horizontal resaw operator **9513**
horn player **5133**
horse breaker **8431**
horse breeder **8251**
horse-drawn vehicle, sightseeing tour
    guide **6441**
horse identifier **5253**
horse plating inspector – race track **5253**
horse race timer **5253**
horse racing director **0513**
horse racing starter **5253**
horse stable foreman/woman **8253**
horse trainer **8253**
horseman/woman, show **8251**
horseshoer **7383**
horticultural contractor **8254**
horticultural greenhouse operator **8254**
horticultural technician **2225**
horticultural technologist **2225**
horticulture and landscaping instructor –
    school of horticulture **4131**
horticulture specialist **2225**
horticulture worker supervisor **8256**
horticulturist **2225**
hose builder, rubber **9423**
hose building foreman/woman – rubber
    manufacturing **9214**
hose curer, open steam **9423**
hose curer – rubber products
    manufacturing **9423**
hose cutter and brander operator –
    rubber manufacturing **9423**
hose maker, hand – rubber
    manufacturing **9423**
hose maker machine operator – rubber
    manufacturing **9423**
hoseman/woman – insulation **7611**
hosiery boarder **9443**
hosiery folder **9616**
hosiery inspector **9444**
hosiery knitter **9442**
hosiery knitting machine tender **9442**
hosiery looper – textiles **9442**

hosiery pairer **9444**
hosiery seamer – textiles **9442**
hosiery sizer **9444**
hospital administrator **0014**
hospital admissions director **0114**
hospital admitting clerk **1414**
hospital admitting clerks supervisor **1211**
hospital aide **3413**
hospital attendant **3413**
hospital baker **6252**
hospital cleaner **6661**
hospital cook **6242**
hospital delivery room supervisor –
    nursing **3151**
hospital druggist **3131**
hospital engineer, stationary **7351**
hospital equipment sales representative **6221**
hospital executive director **0014**
hospital executive housekeeper **6213**
hospital floor supervisor – nursing **3151**
hospital food service supervisor **6212**
hospital hygienist – nursing **3152**
hospital information clerk **1453**
hospital insurance clerk **1434**
hospital nurse **3152**
hospital orderly **3413**
hospital pharmacist **3131**
hospital porter **3413**
hospital records clerk **1413**
hospital television rental attendant **6421**
hospital tray line worker **6641**
host/hostess, restaurant or cocktail
    lounge **6451**
host/hostess, ski resort **6441**
host/hostess, television or radio **5231**
hostel co-ordinator **4212**
hostess/host, food service **6451**
hostler, railway **7361**
hostler, transit system **7443**
hostler, truck **7443**
hot air balloonist **6442**
hot-dip galvanizer – metal plating **9497**
hot dog vendor **6623**
hot glass worker – mineral products
    processing **9611**
hot metal crane operator **7371**
hot mill roller – primary metal
    processing **9231**
hot moulder – foundry **9412**
hot press operator – clay products **9414**
hot press operator – metal forgings **9512**
hot press operator – wood processing **9434**
hot press tender – woodworking **9513**
hot strip mill finisher – primary metal
    processing **9411**
hot strip mill rougher – primary metal
    processing **9411**
hot water heater contractor **7219**

hot water heater installer **7441**
hot wound spring coiler **9516**
hotbed lever – primary metal processing **9611**
hotel accommodations sales executive **6411**
hotel and restaurant inspector – public
    health **2263**
hotel assistant manager **0632**
hotel baker **6252**
hotel carpenter **7271**
hotel cleaner **6661**
hotel clerk **6435**
hotel clerks supervisor **6216**
hotel director **0632**
hotel executive housekeeper **6213**
hotel food and beverage service
    manager **0631**
hotel front desk clerk **6435**
hotel general manager **0015**
hotel information clerk **1453**
hotel management instructor – college **4131**
hotel management teacher – college **4131**
hotel manager **0632**
hotel managing supervisor **6216**
hotel night auditor **6435**
hotel purchasing officer **1225**
hotel seamstress **7342**
hotel valet **6683**
hothouse flower grower **8254**
hothouse worker **8432**
hotwalker, horse **6483**
house carpenter **7271**
house cleaner **6661**
house detective **6465**
house maid **6661**
house mover contractor **7217**
house of commons administrator **0414**
house of commons committee officer **4168**
house painter **7294**
house trailer assembly foreman/woman **9226**
house trailer salesperson **6421**
household electrical appliance
    repairman/woman **7332**
housekeeper **6471**
housekeeper, executive **6213**
housekeeping aide **6661**
housekeeping director **6213**
housekeeping maid **6661**
housekeeping manager **6213**
housekeeping manager, assistant **6213**
housekeeping supervisor **6215**
houseman/woman **6661**
houseparent **4212**
houseparent, halfway house **4212**
housesitter **6683**
housewares salesperson **6421**
housing construction manager **0711**
housing development officer **1224**
housing inspector, rehabilitation **2264**

housing officer **1224**
housing officer, public housing **4164**
housing policy analyst **4164**
housing project manager **1224**
housing rehabilitation specialist **0712**
housing renovator **0712**
hovercraft master **2273**
hull draftsman/woman – shipbuilding
    and repair **2253**
hull inspector **9491**
hull surveyor **9491**
hull technician – military **7263**
human kineticist **4167**
human physiologist **2121**
human resource planning consultant **1121**
human resource planning manager **0112**
human resources administrator **0112**
human resources and organizational
    development vice president financial,
    communications and other business
    services **0013**
human resources and organizational
    development vice president – health,
    education, social and community
    services and membership
    organizations **0014**
human resources and organizational
    development vice president goods
    production, utilities, transportation
    and construction **0016**
human resources and organizational
    development vice president trade,
    broadcasting and other services
    n.e.c. **0015**
human resources assistant **1442**
human resources clerk **1442**
human resources co-ordinator **1121**
human resources manager **0112**
human resources officer **1223**
human resources policy analyst **1121**
human resources research officer **1121**
human resources, vice president –
    financial, communications and other
    business services **0013**
human resources, vice president – goods
    production, utilities, transportation
    and construction **0016**
human resources, vice president –
    health, education, social and
    community services and membership
    organizations **0014**
human resources, vice president – trade,
    broadcasting and other services
    n.e.c. **0015**
human rights commission officer **4164**
human rights officer – government
    services **4164**
humane officer – humane society **6463**

humane society inspector **6463**
humane society officer **6463**
humanities professor – university **4121**
humidifier tender – wood processing **9434**
humidifying systems operator **7351**
humourist **5121**
hunter **8442**
hunting and fishing guide **6442**
hunting and fishing lodge manager **0632**
hunting camp operator **0632**
hunting guide **6442**
hunting guns salesperson **6421**
HVAC engineer **2132**
HVAC mechanic **7313**
HVAC mechanics foreman/woman **7216**
HVAC technologist **2232**
hybrid circuit assembler – electronics
    manufacturing **9483**
hybrid inspector – electronics
    manufacturing **9483**
hydrant and valve maintenance worker **7442**
hydrate scale reclaimer – primary metal
    processing **9611**
hydrate thickener operator **9411**
hydrator operator **9421**
hydraulic barker operator – wood
    processing **9434**
hydraulic chair assembler **9492**
hydraulic engineer **2131**
hydraulic engineer, mechanical **2132**
hydraulic excavator operator **7421**
hydraulic hoist assembler **9486**
hydraulic installer – aircraft **9481**
hydraulic machinery draftsman/woman **2253**
hydraulic mechanic **7315**
hydraulic press operator – metal
    fabrication **9514**
hydraulic press tender – woodworking **9513**
hydraulic pump assembler **9486**
hydraulic roof support mover –
    underground mining **8411**
hydraulic unit repairer **7445**
hydraulic unit repairman/woman **7445**
hydraulics inspector, aircraft **7315**
hydraulics mechanic, aircraft **7315**
hydraulics technician, aircraft **7315**
hydraulics tester, aircraft **7315**
hydraxtor tumble dryer tender – laundry
    and dry cleaning **6681**
hydro electric generating station
    operator **7352**
hydro electric station chief operator **9212**
hydro electricity sales representative **6221**
hydro plant operator **7352**
hydro president **0016**
hydrochemist **2113**
hydrogen braze furnace operator **9515**
hydrogen furnace tender – clay products **9414**

hydrogen process operator **9232**
hydrogenation operator – food and
    beverage processing **9461**
hydrogeological engineer **2144**
hydrogeologist **2113**
hydrogeology engineer **2144**
hydrographic engineer **2131**
hydrographic survey technician **2212**
hydrographic survey technologist **2212**
hydrographic surveyor **2113**
hydrologist **2113**
hydrology technician **2212**
hydrometallurgical engineer **2142**
hydrometallurgist **2142**
hydrometer assembler **9498**
hydroponics grower **8254**
hydroponics operator **8254**
hydroponics technician **2225**
hydroponics worker **8432**
hydrostatic tester **2261**
hygiene professor – university **4121**
hygiene technician – military **2263**
hygienist, dental **3222**
hygienist, hospital nursing **3152**
hypnotherapist **3232**
hypnotist **5232**
hyster driver **7452**

I

ice cream counter attendant **6641**
ice cream decorator **9461**
ice cream maker **9461**
ice cream novelty maker **9461**
ice cream vendor **6623**
ice cutting machine tender **9517**
ice maker **9517**
ice maker, rink **6671**
ice manufacturing storage worker **9619**
ice observer **2213**
ice patroller, arena **6671**
ice sculptor **5136**
ice service specialist **2213**
icer, fishing vessel **8441**
ichthyological technician **2221**
ichthyological technologist **2221**
ichthyologist **2121**
icing dipper – food and beverage
    processing **9617**
icing machine operator – food and
    beverage processing **9461**
icing mixer – food and beverage
    processing **9461**
ICU nurse **3152**
identification clerk **1442**
identification officer – police **6261**
identifier, horse **5253**
igniter assembler **9498**

illuminating engineer **2133**
illusionist **5232**
illustrator **5241**
illustrator, artistic **5241**
illustrator, scientific or medical **5241**
illustrator, technical **2253**
image co-ordinator **6481**
image consultant **6481**
image processing operator – printing **9472**
imam **4154**
immigration agent – government services **1228**
immigration and settlement director – government services **0411**
immigration appeals manager – government services **0411**
immigration appeals officer **1228**
immigration consultant **1228**
immigration enforcement officer **1228**
immigration examiner **1228**
immigration examining officer **1228**
immigration inspector **1228**
immigration lawyer **4112**
immigration officer **1228**
immigration policy analyst **4164**
immunohematology technologist – medical laboratory **3211**
immunologist **2121**
immunologist, clinical **3111**
immunology technologist – medical laboratory **3211**
impact hammer operator – metal forgings **9512**
impersonator **5232**
implementation officer **1221**
import clerk **1441**
import documentation clerk **1441**
import freight clerk **1471**
import traffic clerk **1441**
import traffic manager **0713**
import traffic supervisor **1215**
importer **6411**
impregnator and drier – electronics manufacturing **9483**
impregnator corrugator, plastic sheets **9422**
impregnator, electrical equipment **9487**
impression die press operator – metal fabrication **9514**
imprinting machine tender, plastics **9422**
in-charge flight attendant **6432**
in-circuit test operator **9483**
in-flight service manager **6432**
in-hole drill operator – underground mining **8231**
in-house legal counsel **4112**
in-process assembly inspector – motor vehicle manufacturing **9482**

in-process inspector – electric equipment manufacturing **9484**
incinerator foreman/woman **9212**
incinerator plant tender **9619**
incising machine tender – wood processing **9434**
income maintenance director **0314**
income maintenance officer **4212**
income tax adjuster **1111**
income tax advisor **1111**
income tax consultant **1111**
income tax investigator **1111**
income tax return preparer **1431**
income tax specialist **1111**
incubator tender **8431**
independent living instructor **4212**
independent paralegal **4211**
indian affairs development officer **4164**
indium refiner **9411**
indoor tanning studio attendant **6683**
induction brazer operator **9515**
induction brazer, production **9515**
induction furnace operator – foundry **9412**
induction furnace operator – mineral and metal processing **9411**
induction machine tender – primary metal processing **9411**
induction solderer **9515**
industrial accountant **1111**
industrial and commercial buildings architect **2151**
industrial and manufacturing production manager **0911**
industrial arts teacher – elementary school **4142**
industrial arts teacher – secondary school **4141**
industrial audiologist **3141**
industrial audiometric technician **3235**
industrial back-hoe operator **7421**
industrial bacteriological technician **2221**
industrial bacteriological technologist **2221**
industrial bacteriologist **2121**
industrial battery assembler **9487**
industrial belt repairer **7445**
industrial blacksmiths foreman/woman **7214**
industrial boilermaker **7262**
industrial building construction manager **0711**
industrial butcher **9462**
industrial butcher helper **9617**
industrial chemist **2112**
industrial cleaner **6663**
industrial coater – manufacturing **9496**
industrial construction manager **0711**
industrial construction painter **7294**
industrial construction safety inspector **2264**
industrial design consultant **2252**

industrial designer **2252**
industrial development officer –
    government **4163**
industrial door installer **7441**
industrial economist **4162**
industrial efficiency engineer **2141**
industrial electric equipment assembler **9485**
industrial electric equipment fabricator **9485**
industrial electric equipment inspector **9485**
industrial electrical repairer **7242**
industrial electrical systems
    foreman/woman **7212**
industrial electrician **7242**
industrial electrician apprentice **7242**
industrial electrician leadhand **7242**
industrial electricians foreman/woman **7212**
industrial engineer **2141**
industrial engineering analyst **2233**
industrial engineering department
    manager **0211**
industrial engineering professor –
    university **4121**
industrial engineering technician **2233**
industrial engineering technologist **2233**
industrial engines and equipment
    partsperson **6421**
industrial equipment sales engineer **6221**
industrial fire chief **0642**
industrial firefighter **6262**
industrial forester **2122**
industrial furnace brick mason **7281**
industrial furnace bricklayer **7281**
industrial gas servicer **7253**
industrial geographer **4169**
industrial heat exchanger boilermaker **7262**
industrial hoist mechanic **7311**
industrial hygiene engineer **2134**
industrial hygiene technologist **2211**
industrial hygienist **4161**
industrial instrument mechanic **2243**
industrial instrument mechanic
    apprentice **2243**
industrial instrument repairer helper **7612**
industrial instrument technician **2243**
industrial instrumentation teacher –
    vocational institute **4131**
industrial lawyer **4112**
industrial locomotive engineer **7361**
industrial machinery mechanics
    foreman/woman **7216**
industrial machinery sales
    representative **6221**
industrial maintenance manager **0722**
industrial maintenance painter **7294**
industrial meat chopper **9462**
industrial meat cutter **9462**
industrial mechanic **7311**
industrial mechanic apprentice **7311**

industrial mechanic, petroleum refinery **7311**
industrial meteorologist **2114**
industrial motor winder/repairer **7333**
industrial needle machine
    setter/operator **9516**
industrial needle maker **9516**
industrial nurse **3152**
industrial order completion clerk **1473**
industrial oven brick mason **7281**
industrial painter – construction **7294**
industrial painter – maintenance **7294**
industrial pharmacist **3131**
industrial photographer **5221**
industrial physician **3112**
industrial plant cleaner **6663**
industrial plant cleaning
    foreman/woman **6215**
industrial process control equipment
    repairer **2243**
industrial product painter **9496**
industrial products designer **2252**
industrial property manager **1224**
industrial psychologist **4151**
industrial radiographer (rt) **2261**
industrial registered nurse **3152**
industrial relations economist **4162**
industrial relations manager **0112**
industrial relations officer **1121**
industrial safety engineer **2141**
industrial safety instructor **4131**
industrial safety officer – occupational
    health and safety **2263**
industrial sociologist **4169**
industrial statistician **2161**
industrial storage battery plate
    assembler **9487**
industrial supplies sales representative **6221**
industrial tools sales representative **6411**
industrial trade economist **4162**
industrial truck mechanic **7334**
industrial truck operator **7452**
industrial washing machine tender **9619**
industrial waste control inspector **2263**
industrial waste treatment engineer **2134**
industrial waste treatment plant
    operator **9424**
infant transport attendant **3234**
infantry officer – military **0643**
infantry soldier – military **6464**
infantryman/woman – military **6464**
infants' day-care worker **4214**
infection control co-ordinator – hospital **3152**
infection control nurse **3152**
infection control officer – hospital **3152**
infection surveillance nurse **3152**
infectious diseases, chief of **0311**
infectious diseases specialist **3111**
infertility specialist **3111**

inflated ball moulder **9517**

information and communications
    manager **0611**

information and reference librarian **5111**

information broker **1236**

information clerk **1453**

information clerk supervisor **1213**

information clerk, travel **6431**

information co-ordinator **5124**

information officer **5124**

information operator – telephone system **1424**

information service manager **0611**

information systems analyst – computer
    systems **2162**

information systems manager **0213**

information systems, vice president –
    financial, communications and other
    business services **0013**

information systems, vice president –
    goods production, utilities,
    transportation and construction **0016**

information systems, vice president –
    health, education, social and
    community services and membership
    organizations **0014**

information systems, vice president –
    trade, broadcasting and other services
    n.e.c. **0015**

information technology analyst **2162**

infra-red tester **2261**

infra-red thermographer **2261**

infrared technician **2261**

ingot buggy operator **9411**

ingot cladder **9611**

ingot header **9411**

ingredients scaler and dispenser – food
    and beverage processing **9461**

inhalation technician **3214**

inhalation technologist **3214**

inhalation therapist **3214**

inhalation therapy technician **3214**

inhalation therapy technologist **3214**

injectable operator **9232**

injection moulder operator – plastic
    manufacturing **9422**

injection moulding foreman/woman –
    rubber and plastic manufacturing **9214**

injection moulding machine operator –
    plastic manufacturing **9422**

injection moulding operator – plastic
    manufacturing **9422**

injection moulding process operator –
    plastic manufacturing **9422**

injection moulding technician **2233**

injection plastic moulder **9422**

ink evaluation pressman/woman –
    printing **7381**

ink matcher **9421**

ink purifier **9421**

ink sketcher **5136**

inker and painter, animation **5223**

inland waters master **2273**

inlayer, woodworking **9492**

inn manager **0632**

inn operator **0632**

inner tube checker – rubber
    manufacturing **9615**

inner tube inserter – rubber
    manufacturing **9615**

inner tube repairer – rubber
    manufacturing **9615**

inner tube skiver – rubber
    manufacturing **9615**

innkeeper **0632**

inorganic chemist **2112**

insect physiologist **2121**

inserter – printing **9619**

inserting machine operator – printing **9473**

inserting machine tender **1461**

inshore fisherman/woman **8262**

insole filler **9619**

insole moulding machine tender **9517**

insole tacking machine operator **9517**

insole tape machine operator **9517**

inspecting machine tender – textiles **9444**

inspecting, testing, grading and sampling
    foreman/woman – primary metal and
    mineral products processing **9211**

inspection centre supervisor, fruit and
    vegetables **2222**

inspection services director – education **0413**

inspector, AC and DC motors **9485**

inspector/adjuster, piano action **9498**

inspector – air carrier maintenance **2262**

inspector – air transport **2262**

inspector, aircraft assembly **9481**

inspector, aircraft fabrication **9481**

inspector, aircraft production **9481**

inspector, all-terrain vehicles **9486**

inspector – ammunition manufacturing **9498**

inspector, ampoule **9619**

inspector and finisher, fibreglass boats **9491**

inspector and tester, AC and DC motors **9485**

inspector and tester, aircraft electrical
    equipment **2244**

inspector and tester, aircraft electronic
    equipment **2244**

inspector and tester, battery case –
    electrical equipment manufacturing **9487**

inspector and tester, electric lawnmower **9484**

inspector and tester, electric
    snowblower **9484**

inspector and tester, electrical lamps **9484**

inspector and tester, meteorological
    equipment **7383**

inspector, assembled furniture **9492**

inspector, assembly – furniture manufacturing **9492**

inspector, assembly line – electric equipment manufacturing **9484**

inspector, automotive wiring harness **9485**

inspector, avionics **2244**

inspector, bank **1114**

inspector, black light **2261**

inspector – board of education **4166**

inspector, body in white – motor vehicle manufacturing **9482**

inspector, boiler installation **2264**

inspector, building **2264**

inspector, bus **7222**

inspector, bus parts **9486**

inspector, buttons **9498**

inspector – by-law enforcement **6463**

inspector, canned foods **9465**

inspector, carbon products **9484**

inspector carman/woman, railway **7314**

inspector, chassis assembly – motor vehicle manufacturing **9482**

inspector, CMHC **2264**

inspector, components – electronics manufacturing **9483**

inspector, construction **2264**

inspector, contagious animal diseases **2222**

inspector, corks and bottle caps **9498**

inspector, credit agency **1114**

inspector, customs **1228**

inspector/dispatcher, bus **7222**

inspector – education **4166**

inspector, electric appliance manufacturing **9484**

inspector, electric clock components **9484**

inspector, electrical **2264**

inspector – electrical appliance assembly **9484**

inspector, electrical battery plates **9487**

inspector, electrical control panel **9485**

inspector, electrical controls assembly **9484**

inspector, electrical dry battery **9487**

inspector, electrical dry cell battery **9487**

inspector, electrical lamp parts **9484**

inspector, electrical light bulbs **9487**

inspector, electrical motor **9485**

inspector, electrical station – power distribution **7352**

inspector, electrical switchboards and panels **9485**

inspector, electrical switchgear **9485**

inspector, electrical switchgear panels **9485**

inspector, electricity and gas meters **2262**

inspector electronic unit – electronics manufacturing **9483**

inspector – electronics manufacturing **9483**

inspector, engineering department **2262**

inspector, environmental health **2263**

inspector – fabric products manufacturing **9454**

inspector, financial institutions **1114**

inspector, finished vehicle – motor vehicle manufacturing **9482**

inspector, fire safety – non-government **6465**

inspector, fish and fish products **2222**

inspector, fisheries **2224**

inspector, flight test **7315**

inspector, flood damage **2263**

inspector, fluorescent penetrant **2261**

inspector – food and beverage processing **9465**

inspector – food packaging **9465**

inspector, forgings **9512**

inspector, foundation garments **9454**

inspector, fruit and vegetables **2222**

inspector – fur products manufacturing **9454**

inspector, furniture **9492**

inspector, furniture assembly **9492**

inspector, furniture finishes **9492**

inspector – furniture manufacturing **9492**

inspector, garment **9454**

inspector, gas distribution **7442**

inspector, gas leaks **7442**

inspector general of banks **0012**

inspector/grader, fish **2222**

inspector/grader, hockey stick **9493**

inspector/grader, seconds **9454**

inspector, grain **2222**

inspector, ground transit **7222**

inspector, hazardous waste – environmental health **2263**

inspector, health standards **2263**

inspector – home construction **2264**

inspector, hotel and restaurant – public health **2263**

inspector, hull **9491**

inspector, in-process assembly – motor vehicle manufacturing **9482**

inspector, jewellery assembly **9498**

inspector, knitting **9444**

inspector – large transformer manufacturing **9485**

inspector – laundry and dry cleaning **6681**

inspector, lead acid battery parts **9487**

inspector, leaf springs **9514**

inspector, leather goods **9454**

inspector, livestock **2222**

inspector, loom **9444**

inspector, machine shop **7231**

inspector, machining **7231**

inspector, matchbooks **9498**

inspector, meat **2222**

inspector, metal fabricating **9514**

inspector, metal parts **9514**

inspector, milk **2222**

inspector, motor and generator **9485**

inspector, motor vehicle **2262**
inspector – municipal law enforcement **6463**
inspector – munitions manufacturing **9498**
inspector, nondestructive evaluation **2261**
inspector, nondestructive examination **2261**
inspector, occupational safety **2263**
inspector, oil pipe **2261**
inspector, optical goods **3414**
inspector, paper products **9435**
inspector – PCB fabrication **9483**
inspector, pharmaceuticals and toiletries **2211**
inspector, piano assembly **9498**
inspector – pipeline construction **2264**
inspector, plant products **2222**
inspector, plastic and painted panels –
    motor vehicle manufacturing **9482**
inspector, plastic products **9495**
inspector, plumbing **2264**
inspector, police **0641**
inspector, pollution control **2263**
inspector, prestressed concrete **2264**
inspector – primary metal and mineral
    products processing **9415**
inspector, printed circuit board
    assembly **9483**
inspector, private branch exchange –
    telecommunications **7246**
inspector, product – furniture
    manufacturing **9492**
inspector, public health **2263**
inspector, pulp **9432**
inspector, quality control – wood
    products manufacturing **9493**
inspector, radiator -motor vehicle
    manufacturing **9482**
inspector, rail dangerous goods **2263**
inspector, refrigeration unit **9484**
inspector, rehabilitation housing **2264**
inspector, reinforced concrete **2264**
inspector, repair and overhaul **7315**
inspector/repairer, heavy equipment **7312**
inspector – rubber manufacturing **9423**
inspector – safety and health **2263**
inspector, sanitary department –
    environmental health **2263**
inspector, sash and door **9493**
inspector, seat belt assembly **9498**
inspector, sewage disposal –
    environmental health **2263**
inspector – sewer construction **2264**
inspector, sheet paper **9433**
inspector – slaughtering and meat
    processing plant **2222**
inspector, slide fastener **9498**
inspector, small electrical appliances **9484**
inspector, soap and toilet goods **9498**
inspector, structural iron work **2264**
inspector, structural steel **2264**

inspector – textiles **9444**
inspector, tin can **9516**
inspector, tool and gauge **7231**
inspector, transit system **7222**
inspector, trim and hardware – motor
    vehicle manufacturing **9482**
inspector/trimmer, moulded rubber **9423**
inspector – tunnel construction **2264**
inspector, ultra-violet light **2261**
inspector, umbrella **9498**
inspector, veterinary **3114**
inspector, water **2263**
inspector, weights and measures **2262**
inspector, winding – large electric
    motors manufacturing **9485**
inspector, wire products **9516**
inspector, wood machining **9493**
inspector – wood processing **9436**
inspector, wood sash and door **9493**
inspector, wooden boat assembly **9491**
installation and repair technician –
    telecommunications **7246**
installation foreman/woman –
    telecommunications **7212**
installation helper –
    telecommunications **7612**
installation manager –
    telecommunications **0131**
installation superintendent –
    telecommunications **0131**
installation technician, cable television **7247**
installer, aircraft electronic equipment **2244**
installer, aluminium awning **7441**
installer, aluminum door **7441**
installer, aluminum windows **7441**
installer and repairer, electronic music
    equipment **2242**
installer and repairer, furnace **7331**
installer and repairer – household and
    business equipment **2242**
installer, automatic door system **7441**
installer, automatic garage door **7441**
installer, automotive shock absorber **7443**
installer, automotive spring **7443**
installer, awning **7441**
installer, electrical cables – electric
    power systems **7244**
installer, electrical meters – electric
    power systems **7244**
installer – electronics manufacturing **9483**
installer, elevator **7318**
installer, fence **7441**
installer, fire protection piping **7252**
installer, forced air furnace **7331**
installer, gas meter **7442**
installer helper – power cable systems **7612**
installer, household appliance **7441**
installer, hydraulics – aircraft assembly **9481**

installer, insulation **7293**
installer, kitchen cabinet **7441**
installer, muffler **7443**
installer, radiator **7443**
installer, recreational equipment **7441**
installer, seats – construction **7611**
installer, septic system **7441**
installer, septic tank **7441**
installer/servicer – dental equipment **7441**
installer, siding **7441**
installer, solid fuel heaters **7331**
installer, sprinkler system **7252**
installer, swimming pool **7441**
installer, switch network **7246**
installer – telecommunications **7246**
installer, telecommunications line **7245**
installer, water meter **7441**
installer, window air conditioner **7441**
installer, wood burners **7331**
installer, wooden window sash **7441**
instalment collector **1435**
instant coffee drier **9461**
instant coffee extractor operator **9461**
instant powdered foods equipment
    operator **9461**
institution case management officer **4155**
institution guard **6462**
institutional cook **6242**
institutional food sales representative **6411**
instructor, airline attendants **4131**
instructor, auto driving **4216**
instructor, ballet **5134**
instructor, baton twirling **5134**
instructor, beauty and charm **4216**
instructor, beauty culture school **4216**
instructor, bowling **5254**
instructor, bridge **5254**
instructor – business college **4131**
instructor – CÉGEP **4131**
instructor, charm course **4216**
instructor – college **4131**
instructor – college of applied arts and
    technology **4131**
instructor – commercial college **4131**
instructor, communication – medical **3235**
instructor, correspondence school **4131**
instructor, crafts **5244**
instructor, dancing **5134**
instructor, department of agriculture **2123**
instructor, developmentally delayed **4215**
instructor, diagnostic medical
    sonography **3216**
instructor, disabled persons **4215**
instructor, firefighting **4131**
instructor, fitness **5254**
instructor, flight attendants **4131**
instructor, flying **2271**
instructor for visually impaired **4215**

instructor, ground school **4131**
instructor, health and safety **4131**
instructor, hearing impaired **4215**
instructor, heavy equipment operators **4131**
instructor, industrial safety **4131**
instructor – language school **4131**
instructor, life skills **4212**
instructor, mentally handicapped **4215**
instructor – modelling and finishing
    school **4216**
instructor, orientation and mobility **4215**
instructor, physical training **5254**
instructor, police **4131**
instructor, pursers **4131**
instructor, recreation **5254**
instructor, self-improvement course **4216**
instructor, sewing – non-vocational **4216**
instructor, small boat navigation **4216**
instructor, sports **5254**
instructor – technical institute **4131**
instructor – technological institute **4131**
instructor – vocational institute **4131**
instructor – vocational school **4131**
instrument and control engineer **2133**
instrument and electrical technician,
    industrial **2243**
instrument cluster assembler – motor
    vehicle manufacturing **9482**
instrument electrical technician –
    military **2244**
instrument engineer **2133**
instrument engineer, electrical **2133**
instrument inspector, aircraft **2244**
instrument inspector and tester, avionics **2244**
instrument maintenance mechanic **2243**
instrument maker, optical **9498**
instrument man/woman – surveying **2254**
instrument mechanic apprentice,
    industrial **2243**
instrument mechanic, avionics **2244**
instrument mechanic helper – utilities **7612**
instrument mechanic, industrial **2243**
instrument mechanic – utilities **2243**
instrument overhaul and repair
    mechanic, avionics **2244**
instrument overhaul technician,
    avionics **2244**
instrument panel assembler – motor
    vehicle manufacturing **9482**
instrument panel electrical tester –
    motor vehicle manufacturing **9482**
instrument repairer apprentice,
    industrial **2243**
instrument repairer, industrial **2243**
instrument sterilizer – medical **6631**
instrument technician, industrial **2243**
instrumental music teacher **5133**
instrumental musician **5133**

instrumentalist **5133**
instrumentation and control engineer **2133**
instrumentation mechanic, industrial **2243**
instrumentation technician, industrial **2243**
insulating contractor **7219**
insulation applicator **7293**
insulation blanket maker **9498**
insulation blower helper **7611**
insulation blower operator **7611**
insulation cutter and former – electrical
    equipment manufacturing **9484**
insulation installer **7293**
insulation installer – electrical
    equipment manufacturing **9484**
insulation machine operator **9516**
insulation mat machine operator – stone
    products **9414**
insulation mechanic **7293**
insulation packer **9611**
insulation panel maker **9517**
insulation salesperson – wholesale **6411**
insulation supervisor **7219**
insulator **7293**
insulator apprentice **7293**
insulator helper **7611**
insulator tester **9619**
insulator tester, electrical **9619**
insulator tester, mechanical **9619**
insulators foreman/woman **7219**
insurance actuary **2161**
insurance adjuster **1233**
insurance agent **6231**
insurance appraiser **1235**
insurance broker **6231**
insurance claims manager **0121**
insurance clerk **1434**
insurance collector **1435**
insurance company general manager **0013**
insurance inspector **1233**
insurance inspector, loss prevention **2262**
insurance law clerk **4211**
insurance lawyer **4112**
insurance legal assistant **4211**
insurance manager **0121**
insurance office district supervisor **6231**
insurance officer – unemployment
    insurance **1228**
insurance paralegal **4211**
insurance rater **1434**
insurance sales agent **6231**
insurance sales representative **6231**
insurance sales supervisor **6231**
insurance salesman/woman **6231**
insurance underwriter **1234**
integral systems technician – military **2244**
integrated circuit assembler **9483**
integrated logistics manager **0713**
intellectual property lawyer **4112**

intelligence officer (management) –
    military **0643**
intelligence officer (non-management) –
    military **6464**
intelligence operator – military **6464**
intensive care nurse **3152**
interbank arrangements officer **1114**
interest clerk **1434**
intergovernmental affairs director **0414**
intergovernmental affairs manager **0414**
intergovernmental affairs officer **4168**
interior and exterior wall erector helper **7611**
interior decorator – retail **6421**
interior design assistant **5242**
interior design teacher – college or
    vocational institute **4131**
interior design technician **5242**
interior designer **5242**
interior drywall installer **7284**
interior finish carpenter **7271**
interior finish trim assembler – motor
    vehicle manufacturing **9482**
interior finishing helper **7611**
interior plantscaper **8432**
interior plantscaping contractor **8255**
interior space designer **5242**
interior systems installer **7284**
interior systems mechanic **7284**
interior trailer finisher **9486**
interior trimmer carpenter **7271**
interlibrary loan clerk **1451**
interlocking stone contractor **7219**
interlocking stone installer **7441**
intermediate computer operator **1421**
intermediate underwriter – insurance **1234**
intern, dietetic **3132**
intern, general practice **3112**
intern, specialist **3111**
internal audit services manager **0111**
internal auditor – financial **1111**
internal auditor supervisor – financial **1111**
internal combustion engine assembler **9486**
internal combustion engineer **2132**
internal medicine specialist **3111**
international aid and development
    project officer **4164**
international aid and development
    researcher **4164**
international banking manager **0122**
international operations vice president –
    banking **0013**
international relations chief –
    government **0414**
international relations director –
    government **0414**
international relations specialist **4164**
international trade economist **4162**

international trade policy manager –
    government services 0412
international traffic manager 0713
internist 3111
internist, veterinary 3114
interpretation visitor services
    co-ordinator – government 4163
interpreter 5125
interpreter for the deaf 5125
interpreter, historic site 5212
interpreter – museum 5212
interpreting machine operator 1422
interpretive dancer 5134
interpretive naturalist 2121
interview clerk 1454
interviewer, survey or poll 1454
intra-oral dental assistant 3411
Inuit art sculptor 5136
inventory clerk 1474
inventory control clerk 1474
inventory control manager 0114
inventory control officer, base –
    military 0114
inventory control supervisor 1215
inventory control technician 2233
inventory manager 0114
invertebrate zoologist 2121
invertebrate zoology curator 5112
investigation clerk, financial 1431
investigations officer – postal service 6465
investigative inspector – police 0641
investigative reporter 5123
investigator, air conditioning and
    ventilation 2232
investigator, bill complaints 1453
investigator, business establishment 6465
investigator, police 6261
investigator, private 6465
investigator, railway 6261
investigator, taxation 1228
investment analyst 1112
investment broker 1113
investment caster – foundry 9412
investment clerk 1431
investment counsellor 1112
investment dealer 1113
investment economist 4162
investment manager 0121
investment manager – banking, credit
    and investment 0122
investment officer 1112
investment salesman/woman 1113
investment underwriter 1114
invoice and order checker 1474
invoice clerk 1431
invoice control clerk 1474
ion exchange operator 9231
iridologist 6484

irish moss gatherer 8613
iron brazer 9515
iron caster – foundry 9412
iron erector 7264
iron foundry etcher 9511
iron moulder – foundry 9412
iron pellet hardness tester – metal
    processing 9415
iron worker – bridge construction 7264
iron worker – curtain wall installation 7264
iron worker – metal tank erecting 7264
iron worker – metal wall framing 7264
iron worker – metal wall installation 7264
iron worker, ornamental 7264
iron worker, reinforcing steel 7264
iron worker – steel construction 7264
iron worker – steel door setting 7264
ironer glazer, fur – laundry and dry
    cleaning 6682
ironer – laundry and dry cleaning 6682
ironworker 7264
ironworker apprentice 7264
ironworker helper 7611
ironworkers foreman/woman 7214
irrigation and drainage engineer 2131
irrigation district manager 0912
irrigation engineer 2131
irrigation foreman/woman – agriculture 8253
irrigation inspector – construction 2264
irrigation labourer 8431
irrigation specialist 2123
irrigation worker 8431
irrigator, row 8431
irrigator, sprinkler system 8431
irrigator, wheel line system 8431
italian teacher – high school 4141

J

jack hammer operator 7611
jack ladder tender 9614
jack leg drill operator – underground
    mining 8231
jack operator – underground mining 8411
jacket coremaker – foundry 9412
jacket designer 5243
jacquard card cutter – textiles 9442
jacquard card lacer – textiles 9442
jacquard loom fixer – textile
    manufacturing 7317
jacquard loom pattern changer 9442
jacquard loom weaver 9442
jacquard machine operator 9442
jail guard 6462
jailer 6462
jam processor operator 9461
janitor 6663
janitor, head 6215

janitorial couple **6663**
janitorial services manager **0651**
jewel setter **7344**
jeweller **7344**
jeweller apprentice **7344**
jeweller cleaner **9517**
jewellery and silverware etcher **9511**
jewellery annealer **9517**
jewellery assembler **9498**
jewellery assembly inspector **9498**
jewellery case assembler **9498**
jewellery design cutter **7344**
jewellery designer **5243**
jewellery die maker **7232**
jewellery enameler **9498**
jewellery engraver **5244**
jewellery estimator **7344**
jewellery filer **9498**
jewellery maker, hand **5244**
jewellery model maker **7344**
jewellery moulder **7344**
jewellery parts assembler **9498**
jewellery salesperson **6421**
jewellery sample maker **7344**
jewellery solderer **9498**
jewellery soldering machine tender **9517**
jewellery store manager **0621**
jewellery strip roller **9517**
jewellery turner **9498**
jib crane operator **7371**
jig and form maker **7232**
jig and template maker, aircraft **7232**
jig and tool builder, aircraft **7232**
jig bore tool maker **7232**
jig borer tape control machining
     operator **9511**
jig builder – metal products
     manufacturing **7232**
jig builder – motor vehicle
     manufacturing **7232**
jig builder – wood products
     manufacturing **7272**
jig maker **7232**
jig tender – primary metal processing **9411**
jig welder fitter **7265**
jigger operator, automatic – clay
     products **9414**
jigger operator – clay products **9414**
jigger operator helper **9611**
jigger operator, supermarket **7452**
jigger operator – textiles **9443**
jiggerman/woman, automatic – clay
     products **9414**
jiggerman/woman – clay products **9414**
jigsaw operator – woodworking **9513**
jitney driver – material handling **7452**
job analyst **1121**
job and wage analyst **1121**

job compositor – typesetting **1423**
job evaluation analyst **1121**
job evaluation and salary research
     manager **0112**
job evaluation supervisor **1121**
job evaluator **1121**
job moulder – foundry **9412**
job order clerk – manufacturing **1473**
job order clerks supervisor **1215**
job press feeder – printing **9619**
job printer **7381**
jockey **5251**
jockey, car **6683**
jockey, garage **6683**
jockey room custodian **6671**
jockey valet **6671**
jogger – printing **9619**
joiner – railway rolling stock **7271**
joiner, sewing machine operator **9451**
joiner – shipbuilding **7271**
joiners foreman/woman – shipbuilding **7215**
joint sawyer – concrete, clay and stone
     products **9414**
jointer operator – woodworking **9513**
jointer – woodworking **9513**
jollier – clay products **9414**
journal box greaser **7431**
journal clerk **1431**
journal editor **5122**
journal entry audit clerk **1431**
journalism professor – university **4121**
journalism teacher – college **4131**
journalist **5123**
journeyman/woman boilermaker **7262**
journeyman/woman bricklayer **7281**
journeyman/woman cabinetmaker **7272**
journeyman/woman carpenter **7271**
journeyman/woman cement finisher **7282**
journeyman/woman construction
     electrician **7241**
journeyman/woman cook **6242**
journeyman/woman drywall installer **7284**
journeyman/woman elevator constructor **7318**
journeyman/woman elevator mechanic **7318**
journeyman/woman floor covering
     installer **7295**
journeyman/woman floor mechanic **7295**
journeyman/woman gas fitter **7253**
journeyman/woman glazier **7292**
journeyman/woman heavy-duty
     equipment mechanic **7312**
journeyman/woman industrial
     electrician **7242**
journeyman/woman industrial mechanic **7311**
journeyman/woman insulator **7293**
journeyman/woman iron worker **7264**
journeyman/woman lather **7284**
journeyman/woman machinist **7231**

journeyman/woman motor vehicle body repairer **7322**

journeyman/woman painter and decorator **7294**

journeyman/woman plasterer **7284**

journeyman/woman plumber **7251**

journeyman/woman refrigeration and air conditioning mechanic **7313**

journeyman/woman roofer **7291**

journeyman/woman sheet metal worker **7261**

journeyman/woman sprinkler system installer **7252**

journeyman/woman steamfitter – pipefitter **7252**

journeyman/woman stonemason **7281**

journeyman/woman telecommunication lines **7245**

journeyman/woman tilesetter **7283**

journeyman/woman tool and die maker **7232**

journeyman/woman water well driller **7373**

ju-jitsu instructor **5254**

judge, administrative tribunal **0411**

judge, citizenship court **1227**

judge – law **4111**

judge, sports **5253**

judge, standardbred – racetrack **5253**

judge, tribunal **0411**

judicial administrator **1227**

judicial clerk **1443**

judicial court administrator **1227**

judicial officer – courts **1227**

judo instructor **5254**

juggler **5232**

juice blender **9617**

juke box mechanic **7445**

jumbo drill operator helper – underground mining **8411**

jumbo drill operator – underground mining **8231**

junior computer operator **1421**

junior engineer – water transport **2274**

junior estimator – construction **2234**

junior financial analyst **1112**

junior hockey coach **5252**

junior mate, ship **2273**

junior mechanic, aircraft mechanical systems **7315**

junior office clerk **1411**

junior underwriter – insurance **1234**

justice **4111**

justice of the peace **1227**

juvenile court judge **4111**

K

karate instructor **5254**

keeper, grounds **8432**

keg maker, wood **9493**

kennel attendant **6483**

kennel keeper **6483**

kennel manager **8251**

kennel operator **8251**

kennelman/woman **6483**

keno dealer **6443**

kettle charger **9411**

kettle operator – chemical processing **9421**

kettle tender – chemical processing **9421**

kettle tender – primary metal processing **9411**

kettle tender – textiles **9443**

key account manager, sales **0611**

key cutter **9516**

key grip **5226**

key punch operator **1422**

key tape operator **1422**

keyboard operator – typesetting **1423**

keyboardist **5133**

keyseater operator **9511**

kier boiler tender – textiles **9443**

kiln cleaner – primary metal and mineral products processing **9611**

kiln fireman/woman – clay products **9414**

kiln helper – mineral products manufacturing **9611**

kiln labourer **9611**

kiln operator, malt house – food and beverage processing **9461**

kiln operator – primary metal and mineral products processing **9411**

kiln operator – wood processing **9434**

kiln setter – mineral products manufacturing **9611**

kiln workers foreman/woman – clay products **9211**

kilnman/woman, periodic – clay products **9414**

kilnman/woman tunnel – clay products **9414**

kinanthropologist **4167**

kindergarten teacher **4142**

kinesiologist **4167**

kiosk information clerk **1453**

kiosk sales clerk **6421**

kitchen cupboard and vanity installer **7441**

kitchen designer **5242**

kitchen helper **6642**

kitchen porter **6642**

kitchen steward **6212**

kitchen systems installer **7441**

knife assembler **9498**

knife blade polisher **9516**

knife grinder **9612**

knife sharpener **9612**

knife shop clerk **6421**

knitted fabric inspector **9444**

knitter **9442**

knitter, hand **5244**

knitter helper **9616**

knitter, wire mesh **9516**
knitting foreman/woman **9216**
knitting inspector **9444**
knitting machine adjuster – textile
    manufacturing **7317**
knitting machine fixer – textile
    manufacturing **7317**
knitting machine mender **9442**
knitting machine operator **9442**
knitting machine tender **9442**
knitting pattern setter – textile
    manufacturing **7317**
knotting machine operator – textiles **9442**
knurling machine operator, pen and
    pencil **9517**
kosher cook **6242**
kosher inspector, food and beverage
    processing **9465**

L

lab operator, wafer fabrication –
    electronics manufacturing **9483**
lab technician, EMG **3218**
lab technician, ophthalmic – retail **3414**
lab technician, optical – retail **3414**
label brander **9619**
label cutter – paper converting **9435**
label cutting machine tender **9517**
label heat tacker **9619**
label printer **9471**
laboratory animal attendant **6483**
laboratory animal technician **3213**
laboratory animal veterinarian **3114**
laboratory assistant, college **4122**
laboratory assistant, university **4122**
laboratory chemist **2112**
laboratory clerk **1473**
laboratory demonstrator –
    post-secondary **4122**
laboratory director **0212**
laboratory equipment cleaner **6662**
laboratory equipment installer **7441**
laboratory furnishings installer **7441**
laboratory maintenance supervisor,
    anatomical pathology **3414**
laboratory medicine, chief of **0311**
laboratory medicine, director of **0311**
laboratory physical sciences technician **2241**
laboratory physical sciences
    technologist **2241**
laboratory supervisor, chemical **2211**
laboratory technician, biochemistry **2211**
laboratory technician, chemical **2211**
laboratory technician, veterinary **3213**
laboratory technologist, chemical **2211**
laboratory technology professor –
    university **4121**

laboratory tester **2211**
laboratory tester – chemical processing **2211**
laboratory tester – pulp and paper **2211**
labour adjudicator **1121**
labour affairs officer **4164**
labour affairs officer, occupational
    health and safety **2263**
labour conciliator **1121**
labour economist **4162**
labour foreman/woman, asphalt paving **7217**
labour foreman/woman, excavating and
    grading **7217**
labour gang foreman/woman **7217**
labour gang foreman/woman, asphalt
    paving **7217**
labour gang foreman/woman, concrete
    paving **7217**
labour law clerk **4211**
labour law legal assistant **4211**
labour law paralegal **4211**
labour lawyer **4112**
labour market analysis director –
    government services **0412**
labour organization agent **1121**
labour organization business
    representative **1121**
labour organization manager **0314**
labour organization negotiator **1121**
labour organization president **0014**
labour organizer **1121**
labour policy analyst **4164**
labour relations board officer **1121**
labour relations clerk **1442**
labour relations co-ordinator **1121**
labour relations manager **0112**
labour relations officer **1121**
labour relations returning officer **1121**
labour relations specialist **1121**
labour standards officer, occupational
    health and safety **2263**
labour union business agent **1121**
labourer, bakery – food and beverage
    processing **9617**
labourer – bindery **9619**
labourer, bituminous paving **7611**
labourer, box factory **9619**
labourer, candle manufacturing **9619**
labourer, cannery – fish processing **9618**
labourer, chemical plant **9613**
labourer – chemical processing **9613**
labourer, concrete paving **7611**
labourer, construction **7611**
labourer crew leader – public works **7621**
labourer – egg grading station **8431**
labourer – electric power and wire
    communications **7612**
labourer – electrical products
    manufacturing **9619**

labourer, excavation **7611**
labourer – farm **8431**
labourer, felt goods **9616**
labourer, fish plant – fish processing **9618**
labourer, fish processing plant **9618**
labourer – food and beverage processing **9617**
labourer – footwear manufacturing **9619**
labourer – furniture manufacturing **9619**
labourer, furrier shop **9619**
labourer – gas utility **9613**
labourer, general – manufacturing **9619**
labourer, general – quarry **7611**
labourer, golf course **8612**
labourer, grounds maintenance **8612**
labourer – hide and pelt processing **9619**
labourer, laundry **6681**
labourer, logging and forestry **8616**
labourer – material handling **7452**
labourer, meat packing plant **9617**
labourer, mine **8614**
labourer, municipal **7621**
labourer, oil field **8615**
labourer – packaging company **9619**
labourer, padding **9619**
labourer, paint plant **9613**
labourer – paper converting **9614**
labourer, park maintenance **8612**
labourer, paving operations **7611**
labourer, petroleum refinery **9613**
labourer – plastic manufacturing **9615**
labourer, plywood and veneer plant **9614**
labourer – primary metal and mineral
    products processing **9611**
labourer – printing **9619**
labourer, public works **7621**
labourer – pulp and paper **9614**
labourer – rubber manufacturing **9615**
labourer – sanitary service **7621**
labourer, sawmill **9614**
labourer, shellfish – fish processing **9618**
labourer – shellfish processing **9618**
labourer, shipyard **9619**
labourer – shoe manufacturing **9619**
labourer – shore dredging **7611**
labourer, starch factory – food and
    beverage processing **9617**
labourer – steel production **9611**
labourer, syrup processing plant **9617**
labourer – textiles **9616**
labourer – tobacco processing **9617**
labourer, underground – construction **7611**
labourer – warehousing and storage **7452**
labourer, wood preserving plant **9614**
labourer – wood processing **9614**
labourer, woollen mill **9616**
labourer, yeast plant **9617**
lace weaver **9442**
lacer – sporting equipment **9619**

lacquer maker **9421**
lacquer sprayer **9496**
lacquer sprayer, bench **9496**
lacquer sprayer, products **9496**
lacrosse scout **5252**
lacrosse stick bender – woodworking **9513**
lacrosse stick gouger – woodworking **9513**
lacrosse stick lacer **9498**
lacrosse stick maker – woodworking **9513**
lacrosse team coach **5252**
ladder assembler **9493**
ladder assembler, wood **9493**
ladder builder, wood **9493**
ladle crane operator **7371**
ladle operator – primary metal
    processing **9411**
ladle pourer – primary metal processing **9411**
lag bolt machine tender – woodworking **9513**
lamb feedlot worker **8431**
lamb grader **9465**
laminated asbestos products inspector **9415**
laminated beam inspector **9493**
laminated bowl machine tender **9513**
laminating foreman/woman – furniture
    and fixtures manufacturing **9224**
laminating machine operator **9473**
laminating machine operator – pulp and
    paper **9433**
laminating machine tender – paper
    converting **9435**
laminating machine tender – plastic
    manufacturing **9422**
laminating machine tender – rubber
    manufacturing **9423**
laminating press tender – woodworking **9513**
lamination stacker – industrial electrical
    equipment **9485**
lamination stacking machine tender –
    electrical equipment manufacturing **9487**
laminator, boat assembly **9491**
laminator, hand – furniture
    manufacturing **9492**
laminator machine operator – rubber
    manufacturing **9423**
laminator, plastic **9495**
laminator, television picture tube **9483**
lamp filament processer **9487**
lamp keeper – underground mining **8411**
lamp shade assembler **9498**
lamp shade maker, paper **9498**
lamp shade sewer **9498**
land based sealer **8442**
land drainage engineer **2131**
land economist **4162**
land electrical and mechanical engineer
    – military **2133**
land information system (LIS)
    technician **2255**

land information system (LIS)
    technologist **2255**
land ordnance engineer – military **2132**
land survey technician **2254**
land survey technologist **2254**
land surveyor **2154**
land titles clerk **4211**
land use planner **2153**
land use technician **2231**
landfill scale operator **9613**
landfill weigh scale attendant **9613**
landing bucker – logging **8421**
landingman/woman – logging **8421**
landlady **6663**
landlord **6663**
landscape architect **2152**
landscape architectural technician **2225**
landscape architectural technologist **2225**
landscape architecture manager **0212**
landscape design contractor **8255**
landscape designer **2225**
landscape gardener **2225**
landscape labourer **8612**
landscape maintenance contractor **8255**
landscape painter **5136**
landscape service contractor **8255**
landscape specialist **2225**
landscape technician **2225**
landscape worker **8612**
landscaper **2225**
landscaping contractor **8255**
landscaping foreman/woman **8256**
landscaping instructor – college **4131**
landscaping manager **8255**
landsman/woman, oil and gas **1225**
language instructor – language school **4131**
language pathologist **3141**
language-speech pathologist **3141**
language teacher, elementary school **4142**
language training director **0112**
languages co-ordinator – education **4166**
languages professor – university **4121**
lap machine tender – textiles **9441**
lap truing machine tender **9511**
lap winder tender – textiles **9441**
lapidary **7344**
lapper, hand **9474**
lapper tender – textiles **9441**
lapper – textiles **9441**
lapper, wallpaper – paper converting **9435**
lapping machine operator **9511**
lapping machine set-up operator **9511**
lapping machine tender **9511**
lard renderer – food and beverage
    processing **9461**
large power transformer coil winder **9485**
larry car operator **9411**

laser assembler – electronics
    manufacturing **9483**
laser beam welder **7265**
laser printer operator **9471**
laser technician **2241**
laser trimmer operator – electronics
    manufacturing **9483**
laser tube assembler **9498**
laser welding operator **9515**
last lathe tender – woodworking **9513**
last pattern grader **5245**
last remodeler – woodworking **9513**
last repairman/woman – woodworking **9513**
last turner – woodworking **9513**
laster – footwear manufacturing (except
    rubber) **9517**
latex carpet backing department
    foreman/woman **9216**
latex coagulation operator **9421**
latex coating machine operator –
    textiles **9443**
latex ribbon machine operator – rubber
    manufacturing **9423**
latex thread machine operator – rubber
    manufacturing **9423**
latex thread spooler – rubber
    manufacturing **9615**
lathe machining operator **9511**
lathe operator – concrete products **9414**
lathe operator – metal machining **9511**
lathe operator – woodworking **9513**
lathe sander – woodworking **9513**
lathe spotter – wood processing **9434**
lathe turner – woodworking **9513**
lather **7284**
lather applicator **7284**
lather apprentice **7284**
lather foreman/woman **7219**
lather-interior systems mechanic **7284**
latin teacher – high school **4141**
launch captain **7436**
launch master **7436**
launch operator **7436**
launderer **6681**
laundromat attendant **6683**
laundry and dry cleaning general
    manager **0015**
laundry and dry cleaning manager **0651**
laundry attendant **6681**
laundry finisher **6682**
laundry folder **6681**
laundry foreman/woman **6214**
laundry helper **6681**
laundry labourer **6681**
laundry machine mechanic, commercial **7311**
laundry machine operator **6681**
laundry manager **0651**
laundry production supervisor **6214**

laundry route driver **7414**
laundry service manager **0651**
laundry service sales representative **6411**
laundry supervisor **6214**
laundry tub maker – concrete products **9414**
laundry worker **6681**
law clerk **4211**
law clerk, supreme court **4112**
law clerk to judge **4211**
law enforcement teacher – community
    college **4131**
law librarian **5111**
law partner **4112**
law professor – university **4121**
law reporter **5123**
lawn and garden supplies salesperson **6421**
lawn care manager **8255**
lawn care specialist **2225**
lawn care supervisor **8256**
lawn maintenance contractor **8255**
lawn mower **8612**
lawn mower mechanic, gasoline
    powered **7335**
lawn mower repairer, electric **7332**
lawn mower repairer, gasoline powered **7335**
lawnmower assembler, electric **9484**
lawyer **4112**
lay assistant – teaching **6472**
layaway clerk **1453**
layer out developer – structural metal
    and platework **7263**
layer out, machine shop **9511**
layer out, sheet metal **7261**
layer out, structural metal and
    platework **7263**
layer up – textiles **9616**
layout and marking foreman/woman –
    fabric, fur and leather products
manufacturing **9225**
layout artist **5241**
layout designer **5241**
layout marker – cabinetmaking **7272**
layout marker, machine shop **9511**
layout marker, structural metal **7263**
layout person, animation **5241**
layup machine operator – wood
    processing **9434**
layup man/woman, fibreglass **9495**
layup worker, fibreglass **9495**
layup worker – garment manufacturing **9619**
layup worker, plastics **9495**
leaching operator – primary metal
    processing **9411**
lead acid battery filler, electrical **9487**
lead acid battery parts inspector **9487**
lead acid battery plate maker, electrical **9487**
lead acid battery production tester –
    electrical equipment manufacturing **9487**

lead acid storage battery plate former –
    electrical equipment manufacturing **9487**
lead acid storage battery tester –
    electrical equipment manufacturing **9487**
lead and copper refiner **9411**
lead burner **9515**
lead caster – foundry **9412**
lead casting machine operator – primary
    metal processing **9411**
lead coater operator **9497**
lead dust treater **9411**
lead extruder **9411**
lead fabricator **9514**
lead former – electrical equipment
    manufacturing **9487**
lead hand assembler – furniture
    manufacturing **9492**
lead hand assembler – wood products
    manufacturing **9493**
lead hand, assembly mechanics/fitters **7316**
lead hand, automatic sewing machine
    operators **9442**
lead hand, electrical mechanics **7333**
lead hand, forging machine operators **9512**
lead hand, industrial painters **9496**
lead hand – large electrical appliance
    assembly **9484**
lead hand, mechanical assemblers **9486**
lead hand, pipe maintenance workers **7442**
lead hand – small electrical appliance
    assembly **9484**
lead lineman/woman – electric power
    system **7244**
lead lineman/woman – electric power
    systems **7244**
lead operator, blow moulding – plastic
    manufacturing **9422**
lead operator – chemical processing **9232**
lead operator, injection moulding –
    plastic manufacturing **9422**
lead oxide maker – chemical processing **9421**
lead oxide mill tender – chemical
    processing **9421**
lead placer helper – pile driving **7611**
lead pony rider **8431**
lead reclaimer – primary metal
    processing **9611**
lead refiner **9411**
lead refining foreman/woman **9211**
lead shot caster – foundry **9412**
lead stripping machine operator – rubber
    manufacturing **9423**
lead wheel operator **9411**
leaded glass glazier **7292**
leader of opposition **0011**
leaf spring inspector **9514**
leaf spring maker – metal fabrication **9514**
leak inspector, gas mains **7442**

leak locator, gas mains **7442**
leak repairer – wood products **9619**
leak tester, aluminum boats **9491**
leakage tester, gas mains **7442**
lease and title clerk **4211**
lease worker – textiles **9442**
leasehand – oil and gas drilling **8615**
leasing agent, automobiles **6421**
leasing agent, signs and displays **6411**
leasing and development officer, public
    works **1224**
leasing clerk, storage facility **6421**
leasing co-ordinator, property **1224**
leasing machine tender – textiles **9442**
leasing manager – real estate **0121**
leasing representative, automobiles **6421**
leasing services – sales representative **6411**
leather bag maker **9498**
leather belt maker **9619**
leather buffer – hide and pelt processing **9453**
leather case maker **9498**
leather chemist **2112**
leather cleaner – laundry and dry
    cleaning **6681**
leather cutter – leather footwear
    manufacturing **9452**
leather dyer – hide and pelt processing **9453**
leather finisher – dry cleaning **6682**
leather finishing foreman/woman – hide
    and pelt processing **9225**
leather garment cutter – manufacturing **9452**
leather garment sewer **9451**
leather garment sewing machine
    operator **9451**
leather glove examiner **9454**
leather glove repairer **9451**
leather glove worker **9619**
leather goods inspector **9454**
leather goods production sprayer **9496**
leather goods salesperson **6421**
leather goods store manager **0621**
leather grader **9454**
leather inspector **9454**
leather marker **9452**
leather measurer – hide and pelt
    processing **9453**
leather polisher – hide and pelt
    processing **9453**
leather pressman/woman **9452**
leather processing labourer – hide and
    pelt processing **9619**
leather products manufacturing
    foreman/woman **9225**
leather products patternmaker **5245**
leather purse maker **9498**
leather riveter – footwear
    manufacturing **9517**

leather sander – hide and pelt
    processing **9453**
leather scraper – hide and pelt
    processing **9453**
leather sewer **9451**
leather sewing machine operator **9451**
leather sorter **9454**
leather stainer – hide and pelt
    processing **9453**
leather stock inspector **9454**
leather stretcher – hide and pelt
    processing **9453**
leather stripping machine tender –
    leather products manufacturing **9452**
leather tanneries inspector **9454**
leather trunk maker **9452**
leather worker, hand **5244**
lecturer – university **4121**
ledger clerk **1431**
ledger clerk – financial sector **1434**
ledger control clerk – financial sector **1434**
ledger control officer – financial sector **1434**
legal advisor **4112**
legal advisor, assistant **4112**
legal assistant **4211**
legal assistant program teacher –
    college **4131**
legal counsel **4112**
legal counsel, associate **4112**
legal firm manager **0123**
legal officer – military **4112**
legal researcher **4211**
legal secretarial program teacher –
    college or vocational institute **4131**
legal secretary **1242**
legal services officer – courts **1227**
legal stenographer **1242**
legal survey assistant **2254**
legal survey technician **2254**
legal survey technologist **2254**
legal surveyor **2154**
legal technician **4211**
legal terminologist **5125**
legislative advisor **4112**
legislative assistant **1222**
legislative committee officer **4168**
legislative counsel **4112**
legislator **0011**
lehr attendant, glass **9413**
lehr operator, glass **9413**
lehr tender, glass **9413**
leisure consultant **4167**
leisure counsellor **4167**
leisure services co-ordinator **4167**
lending services officer **1232**
lending services trainee **1232**
lens blank marker **9619**
lens block cleaner **9619**

lens blocker **9619**
lens cutter, ophthalmic goods **3414**
lens edger feeder – non-prescription **9517**
lens edger, hand – non prescription **9517**
lens edger tender – non-prescription **9517**
lens grinder, ophthalmic **3414**
lens grinding machine tender –
   non-prescription **9517**
lens hardener **9619**
lens marker, ophthalmic **3414**
lens mounter **9498**
lens polisher operator –
   non-prescription **9517**
lens polishing machine operator –
   non-prescription **9517**
lens silverer operator **9517**
lensomiter operator – non-prescription **9517**
letter carrier **1462**
letter carrier supervisor **1214**
lettering artist **5223**
letterpress foreman/woman – printing **7218**
letterpress proof press operator –
   printing **7381**
level boss – underground mining **8221**
level brusher – underground mining **8411**
level man/woman – surveying **2254**
level operator – surveying **2254**
leveler operator – woodworking **9513**
leverman/woman – wood processing **9614**
lexicographer **5121**
LHD operator – underground mining **8231**
liability adjuster – insurance **1233**
liability clerk – financial sector **1434**
liability underwriter **1234**
liaison officer **1221**
liaison officer, native land claims **4168**
librarian **5111**
librarian, chief **0511**
librarian – elementary school **4142**
librarian, head **0511**
librarian – high school **4141**
library aid **5211**
library assistant **5211**
library clerk **1451**
library clerk supervisor **1213**
library consultant **5111**
library director **0511**
library page **1451**
library science professor – university **4121**
library supervisor **5111**
library technical assistant **5211**
library technician **5211**
licence clerk **1441**
licence inspector **6463**
licensed cook **6242**
licensed customs broker **1236**
licensed dental assistant **3411**
licensed midwife **3232**

licensed nursing assistant **3233**
licensed practical nurse **3233**
lie detector examiner **6465**
lieutenant, firefighter **6262**
lieutenant-governor **0011**
lieutenant, police **0641**
life actuary **2161**
life insurance agent **6231**
life insurance representative **6231**
life insurance salesman/woman **6231**
life sciences professor – university **4121**
life sciences program manager **0212**
life sciences teacher – university **4121**
life skills coach **4212**
life skills instructor **4212**
life underwriter **6231**
lifeguard **5254**
lift driver **7452**
lift jack operator **7452**
lift scoop operator **7452**
lift truck mechanic **7334**
lift truck operator **7452**
light agricultural and farm equipment
   assembly foreman/woman **9226**
light agricultural machinery assembler **9486**
light agricultural machinery assembly
   foreman/woman **9226**
light construction equipment assembler **9486**
light construction machinery assembly
   foreman/woman **9226**
light duty cleaner **6661**
light farm equipment assembler **9486**
light, heat and power sales engineer **6221**
light industrial truck assembler **9486**
light material handling equipment
   assembler **9486**
light rail transit operator **7412**
light station keeper **7435**
light truck assembler – motor vehicle
   manufacturing **9482**
lighthousekeeper **7435**
lighting assistant **5227**
lighting designer **5243**
lighting fixtures sales representative –
   wholesale **6411**
lighting fixtures wirer **9484**
lighting salesperson **6421**
lighting technician **5226**
lighting technologist **2241**
lightkeeper **7435**
lightning cable installer **7441**
lightning rod erector helper **7611**
lightning rod installer **7441**
lime kiln helper – mineral products
   processing **9611**
lime kiln operator – mineral and metal
   processing **9411**
lime kiln operator – pulp and paper **9432**

lime mixer operator **9414**
lime mixing machine tender **9411**
lime preparation foreman/woman **9211**
lime slaker **9611**
limer – hide and pelt processing **9453**
limestone burner **9411**
limestone burner helper – mineral
    products processing **9611**
limestone spreader – underground
    mining **8614**
limnologist **2121**
limousine driver **7413**
line and cable contractor **7212**
line and frame pole worker, wood
    products **9513**
line and frame poleman/woman –
    woodworking **9513**
line and station installer, telephone **7246**
line assembly utility man/woman –
    electrical manufacturing **9484**
line construction engineer **2133**
line editor **5122**
line fisherman/woman **8262**
line foreman/woman – electrical **7212**
line foreman/woman –
    telecommunications **7212**
line inspector – railway transportation **7432**
line inspector – telecommunications **7245**
line installer and repairer –
    telecommunications **7245**
line installer – telecommunications **7245**
line installer, telephone – military **7245**
line locate man/woman – utilities **7442**
line locater – utilities **7442**
line maintainer apprentice – electric
    power systems **7244**
line maintainer – electric power systems **7244**
line packer **9617**
line painting machine operator,
    highways and roads **7621**
line patroller – electric power systems **7244**
line repairer – electric power systems **7244**
line repairer – telecommunications **7245**
line servicer – electric power systems **7244**
line technician – telecommunications **7245**
line travel heater operator – pipeline **7611**
line truck operator **7411**
linehorse operator **8241**
lineman/woman apprentice –
    telecommunications **7245**
lineman/woman – electric power
    systems **7244**
lineman/woman, electric street car **7244**
lineman/woman helper – power and
    communication lines **7612**
lineman/woman – military **7245**
lineman/woman – telecommunications **7245**

lineman/woman trainee – electric power
    systems **7244**
lineman/woman, trainee – electric power
    systems **7244**
linen rental control clerk **6421**
linen room attendant **1472**
linen supply clerk **1472**
liner installer, pipelines **7611**
liner machine operator – paper
    converting **9435**
liner replacer – ore processing
    equipment **7612**
lineshandler, canal lock systems **7435**
linesman/woman, canal lock systems **7435**
linesman/woman, sports **5253**
lineup adjuster – motor vehicle
    manufacturing **9482**
lineup editor **5122**
lineup examiner **9472**
lineup man/woman – motor vehicle
    manufacturing **9482**
lineworker – electric power systems **7612**
linguist **4169**
linguistic anthropologist **4169**
linguistics professor – university **4121**
lining inserter, skates **9619**
lining machine tender **9496**
lining sewer **9451**
lining stitcher **9451**
link cutter – garment manufacturing **9619**
link wire machine set-up operator **9516**
link wire machine tender **9516**
links machine knitter **9442**
linoleum floor installer **7295**
linoleum floor layer **7295**
linoleum floor tile backer **9422**
linoleum floor tile calendar operator **9422**
linoleum inspector **9495**
linotype operator – typesetting **1423**
linotype repairer **7311**
linseed oil extractor **9461**
lint roller brush assembler **9498**
liquefaction plant operator **9232**
liquid fertilizer truck driver **7411**
liquid fuels engineer **2134**
liquid loader **7452**
liquid mixerman/woman, photographic
    chemicals **9421**
liquid penetrant technician **2261**
liquid sugar operator **9461**
liquor blender – food and beverage
    processing **9461**
liquor board licence inspector **6463**
liquor commissioner **0012**
liquor controller **1431**
liquor gallery tender – food and
    beverage processing **9461**
liquor licence inspector **6463**

liquor maker – pulp and paper **9432**
liquor sales representative, wholesale **6411**
liquor store manager **0621**
liquor store sales clerk **6421**
liquor store supervisor **6211**
liquor tester – food and beverage
    processing **9465**
LIS technician **2255**
LIS technologist **2255**
literary agent **6411**
literary editor **5122**
literary translator **5125**
literary writer **5121**
literature professor – university **4121**
litho artist **5241**
lithographic offset press feeder **9619**
lithographic platemaker **9472**
lithographic press feeder, sheet metal **9619**
lithographic press operator – printing **7381**
lithographic press operator, sheet metal **7381**
lithographic pressman/woman – printing **7381**
lithographic pressman/woman, sheet
    metal **7381**
lithographic printer **7381**
litigation law clerk **4211**
litigation legal assistant **4211**
litigation paralegal **4211**
litigation secretary **1242**
litigator **4112**
live-in caregiver **6474**
livery foreman/woman **8253**
livestock breeding service manager **8252**
livestock buyer **6233**
livestock commission agent **6411**
livestock dealer **0611**
livestock driver **8431**
livestock exchange manager **8252**
livestock farmer **8251**
livestock inspector **2222**
livestock killer **9462**
livestock labourer **8431**
livestock sales representative –
    wholesale **6411**
livestock weigher **8431**
livestock worker, foreman/woman **8253**
livestock yard attendant **8431**
livestock yardman/woman **8431**
living unit officer **4212**
LNA **3233**
load control agent, airline **6433**
load control supervisor, airline **1215**
load dispatcher apprentice – electric
    power systems **7352**
load dispatcher – electric power systems **7352**
load-haul-dump unit operator –
    underground mining **8231**
load planner, airline **6433**
load tester supervisor, electrical **7212**

loader, cement truck **7452**
loader – chemical processing **9613**
loader, liquids **7452**
loader, logging truck **8241**
loader operator – construction **7421**
loader operator – logging **8241**
loader, railway car **7452**
loaderman/woman, diesel – underground
    mining **8231**
loading bridge operator **7435**
loading dock foreman/woman **7217**
loading foreman/woman – logging **8211**
loading head operator – underground
    mining **8411**
loading inspector – chemical processing **9421**
loading machine operator – powder
    charging **9517**
loading machine operator – underground
    mining **8231**
loading pocket operator – underground
    mining **8411**
loading shovel oiler **7443**
loan advisor **1232**
loan agent **1232**
loan analyst **1232**
loan and credit manager **0122**
loan clerk **1434**
loan collector **1435**
loan counsellor **1232**
loan inspector **1232**
loan officer **1232**
loan supervisor, finance **1232**
loan supervisor, library **1213**
loans manager **0122**
lobby group chief executive officer **0014**
lobby porter **6672**
lobbyist, agricultural issues **4161**
lobbyist, business issues **4163**
lobbyist, environmental issues **4161**
lobbyist, native issues **4164**
lobster culture technician **2221**
lobster farmer **8257**
lobster fisherman/woman **8262**
lobster pound attendant **8613**
lobster processor – fish processing **9463**
local manager, social services **0314**
local registrar **1227**
location manager – motion pictures and
    broadcasting **5226**
locator **1435**
lock assembler **9498**
lock expert **7383**
lock fitter **7383**
lock maker **9498**
lock repairer **7383**
lock repairman/woman **7383**
lock setter **7383**

locker plant attendant – food and
    beverage processing **9461**
locker room attendant **6683**
lockerman/woman – marine cargo
    handling **7451**
lockmaster **7435**
locksmith **7383**
locomotive builder **7316**
locomotive crane operator **7371**
locomotive craneman/woman **7371**
locomotive dispatcher – railway
    transport **2275**
locomotive engine servicer **7431**
locomotive engineer – railway transport **7361**
locomotive erecting shop
    foreman/woman **7216**
locomotive hostler **7361**
locomotive mechanic **7312**
locomotive painter **9496**
locomotive repairman/woman, diesel **7312**
locomotive servicer **7431**
lodging house managing supervisor **6216**
loft rigger, boat assembly **9491**
loftsman/woman – aircraft
    manufacturing **7383**
loftsman/woman – shipbuilding **7383**
log analyst **2212**
log boom tugboat deck hand **7433**
log builder **7271**
log buyer **6233**
log cooker – wood processing **9434**
log cut off operator – sawmill **9431**
log cut off sawyer – sawmill **9431**
log cutter **8421**
log deck tender **9614**
log driver **8616**
log gang sawyer – sawmill **9431**
log grader **2223**
log hauler **7411**
log home carpenter **7271**
log loader **8241**
log loader operator **8241**
log loading machine operator **8241**
log processor operator – logging **8241**
log rider **8616**
log salvager **7436**
log scaler **2223**
log technician **2212**
log transfer tender **9614**
log truck driver **7411**
log yarding boss **8211**
logger **8421**
logging and perforating operator – oil
    field services **8232**
logging camp baker **6252**
logging contractor **8211**
logging crane operator **8241**
logging engineer, oil well **2145**

logging equipment salesperson **6221**
logging foreman/woman **8211**
logging labourer **8616**
logging machinery fitter **7316**
logging machinery operator **8241**
logging production manager **0811**
logging supervisor **8211**
logging tractor operator **8421**
logging truck driver **7411**
logging truck loader **8241**
logistics director **0713**
logistics manager **0713**
logistics officer (administration) –
    military **0114**
logistics officer (food service) –
    military **0631**
logistics officer (transportation) –
    military **0713**
logopedist **3141**
lollipop maker **9461**
long distance bus driver **7412**
long distance operator – telephone
    system **1424**
long distance truck driver **7411**
long haul driver **7411**
long haul driver, groceries **7411**
long haul tractor trailer driver **7411**
long hole blaster – underground mining **8231**
long range planner, land use **2153**
long term care aide **3413**
longliner, fisherman/woman **8262**
longshore worker **7451**
longshoreman/woman **7451**
longwall coal shearer operator **8231**
loom changer **7317**
loom cleaner **9616**
loom doffer – textiles **9616**
loom fixer – textile manufacturing **7317**
loom inspector **9444**
loom mechanic – textile manufacturing **7317**
loom operator **9442**
loom pattern changer **7317**
loom preparer **7317**
loom repairer – textile manufacturing **7317**
loom repairman/woman – textile
    manufacturing **7317**
loom setter, wire weaving **9516**
loom starter **7317**
loom technician – textile manufacturing **7317**
loom tender – rubber manufacturing **9423**
loom threader, machine **9442**
loom weaver **9442**
loom winder tender **9441**
looper fixer – textile manufacturing **7317**
looper – textiles **9442**
loss control representative **2233**
loss examiner – insurance **1233**
loss prevention insurance inspector **2262**

loss prevention officer – retail **6465**
loss prevention technologist **2233**
lost and found clerk **1453**
lost claims clerk **1453**
lost or damaged goods claim clerk **1453**
lost wax caster – foundry **9412**
lottery kiosk clerk **6421**
lottery sales representative – retail **6421**
lottery, supervisor – government
    services **6463**
lounge supervisor/bartender **6452**
lounge waiter/waitress **6453**
louver router operator – woodworking **9513**
louvered fence erector **7441**
low bed trailer driver **7411**
low rise residential home builder **0712**
low voltage equipment engineer **2133**
LPN **3233**
lube technician **7443**
lubricating equipment salesperson **6221**
lubrication engineer **2132**
luge coach **5252**
luggage attendant, air transport **7437**
luggage attendant (except airline) **6672**
luggage binding assembler – plastic
    products manufacturing **9495**
luggage checker (except airline) **6434**
luggage coverer **9619**
luggage designer **5243**
luggage handle maker **9619**
luggage repairer **7445**
luggage shell bonder operator **9517**
lumber buyer **6233**
lumber feeder – wood processing **9614**
lumber grader **9436**
lumber grading foreman/woman – wood
    processing **9215**
lumber handler – building supplies **7452**
lumber handler – wood processing **9614**
lumber inspector **9436**
lumber kiln operator **9434**
lumber marker **9436**
lumber mill manager **0911**
lumber piler – building supplies **7452**
lumber sales representative – wholesale **6411**
lumber salvager – wood processing **9614**
lumber sizer operator – sawmill **9431**
lumber sorter, machine **9434**
lumber stocker, material handling **7452**
lumber straightener – wood processing **9614**
lumber tailer – wood processing **9614**
lumber tallyman/woman **1473**
lumber tier – wood processing **9614**
lumber unloader, material handling **7452**
lumberjack **8421**
lump maker – tobacco processing **9464**
lump roller – tobacco processing **9464**
lunch room supervisor **6472**

lunchroom, counterman/woman **6641**
lusterer – textiles **9443**
luterman/woman, coke ovens **9611**
lyricist **5132**

M

macaroni press operator **9461**
machine assembly mechanic/fitter –
    industrial machinery assembly **7316**
machine builder **7316**
machine carver – woodworking **9513**
machine clothing replacer –
    papermaking **7311**
machine compositor – typesetting **1423**
machine coremaker **9412**
machine designer **2232**
machine embroiderer **9442**
machine engraver **5244**
machine feeder **9619**
machine fitter **7316**
machine fitter, agricultural machinery **7316**
machine fixer, textile – textile
    manufacturing **7317**
machine fur cleaner **6681**
machine helper – primary metal and
    mineral products processing **9611**
machine marble polisher – stone
    products **9414**
machine moulder – foundry **9412**
machine operator, automatic – textiles **9442**
machine operator, binding and finishing **9473**
machine operator, chemical plant **9421**
machine operator – clay products **9414**
machine operator – concrete, clay and
    stone forming **9414**
machine operator – concrete products **9414**
machine operator – electrical apparatus
    manufacturing **9487**
machine operator – electrical appliance
    manufacturing **9487**
machine operator, electrical appliances **9487**
machine operator – electrical equipment
    manufacturing **9487**
machine operator – electronics
    manufacturing **9483**
machine operator – fish processing **9463**
machine operator – food and beverage
    processing **9461**
machine operator, furniture finishing **9494**
machine operator – garment
    manufacturing **9451**
machine operator – glass forming and
    finishing **9413**
machine operator helper – plastic
    manufacturing **9615**
machine operator helper – rubber
    manufacturing **9615**

machine operator – hide and pelt
  processing **9453**
machine operator – laundry and dry
  cleaning **6681**
machine operator, leather gloves **9451**
machine operator, light bulbs **9487**
machine operator, metal machining **9511**
machine operator, metalworking **9514**
machine operator – mineral and metal
  processing **9411**
machine operator, miniature bulbs **9487**
machine operator – motor vehicle
  assembly **9482**
machine operator, painting and coating –
  manufacturing **9496**
machine operator – paper converting **9435**
machine operator – papermaking and
  finishing **9433**
machine operator – photographic and
  film processing **9474**
machine operator – plastics processing **9422**
machine operator – plating and metal
  spraying **9497**
machine operator, printing **9471**
machine operator, pulp mill **9432**
machine operator – rubber processing **9423**
machine operator, sewing **9451**
machine operator, small electric motor
  assembly **9487**
machine operator – stone products **9414**
machine operator – textile dyeing and
  finishing **9443**
machine operator – textile fibre and yarn
  preparation **9441**
machine operator – tobacco processing **9464**
machine operator – welding, brazing and
  soldering **9515**
machine operator, woodworking **9513**
machine pad gluer – paper converting **9435**
machine pie maker **9461**
machine plug moulder – tobacco
  processing **9464**
machine presser – laundry and dry
  cleaning **6682**
machine processing accountant **1111**
machine set up operator – electric
  equipment manufacturing **9487**
machine set-up operator – electrical
  equipment manufacturing **9487**
machine setter, metalworking **9514**
machine shop bench hand **9612**
machine shop electrical repairer **7242**
machine shop foreman/woman **7211**
machine shop helper **9612**
machine shop inspector **7231**
machine shop layer out **9511**
machine shop store clerk **1472**
machine shop supervisor **7211**

machine skiver – leather products
  manufacturing **9517**
machine stacker operator – electrical
  equipment manufacturing **9487**
machine stone polisher **9414**
machine stripper – tobacco processing **9464**
machine tender, nut and bolt **9516**
machine tool designer **2232**
machine tool grinding foreman/woman **7211**
machine tool operator **9511**
machine tool operator foreman/woman **7211**
machine tool set-up man/woman **7231**
machine tool set-up operator **7231**
machine tool setter **7231**
machine vending service sales
  representative **6411**
machine washer – laundry and dry
  cleaning **6681**
machine welder **7265**
machined parts inspector **7231**
machinery mechanic – boilerhouse **7311**
machinery mechanic – powerhouse **7311**
machinery salesperson **6221**
machining and tooling inspector **7231**
machining inspector **7231**
machining operator, vertical **9511**
machining set-up operator **7231**
machining supervisor **7211**
machining tool foreman/woman **7211**
machining tool operator **9511**
machining tracer operator **9511**
machinist **7231**
machinist apprentice **7231**
machinist, ballistic laboratory **7231**
machinist, experimental **7231**
machinist foreman/woman **7211**
machinist – military **7231**
machinist, model maker **7231**
machinist, NC **7231**
machinist – numerically controlled
  machine tools **7231**
machinist, precision **7231**
maestro **5132**
magazine editor **5122**
magazine foreman/woman, explosives **1215**
magazine keeper **1472**
magazine keeper – military **1472**
magazine sales representative –
  wholesale **6411**
magazine shop clerk **6421**
magazine subscription solicitor **6623**
magician **5232**
magistrate court judge **4111**
magnaflux inspector **2261**
magnetic flame cutting machine operator
  – metal fabrication **9514**
magnetic observer **2212**
magnetic particle technician **2261**

magnetic particle tester **2261**
magnetic separator operator – primary
    metal processing **9411**
magnetic tape operator **1421**
magnetic tester **2261**
magnetism physicist **2111**
magnometer assembler – electronics
    manufacturing **9483**
maid **6661**
mail and postal clerks supervisor **1214**
mail carrier **1462**
mail carrier, special delivery **1462**
mail carriers supervisor **1214**
mail clerk **1461**
mail collector **1462**
mail counter clerk **1461**
mail deliverer **1462**
mail distributing clerk **1461**
mail handler **1461**
mail order clerk **1441**
mail order filler **6622**
mail processing equipment mechanic **7311**
mail processing plant manager **0132**
mail processing plant superintendent **0132**
mail room assistant **1461**
mail room clerk **1461**
mail room supervisor **1214**
mail service courier **7414**
mail sorter **1461**
mail truck driver – heavy truck **7411**
mailer **1461**
mailing list compiler **1452**
mailing machine operator **1461**
main bearing borer **9511**
maintainer, central office equipment –
    telecommunications **7246**
maintainer, mobile home **7441**
maintainer, oil-drilling rig **7311**
maintainer, voltage regulator – electric
    power systems **7243**
maintenance and repair plumber **7251**
maintenance and service superintendent **0722**
maintenance boilermaker **7262**
maintenance carpenter **7271**
maintenance carpenter helper **7611**
maintenance electrician **7242**
maintenance electricians
    foreman/woman **7212**
maintenance inspector – construction **2264**
maintenance lineman/woman – electric
    power systems **7244**
maintenance machine shop
    foreman/woman **7211**
maintenance machinist **7231**
maintenance man/woman, building **6663**
maintenance manager **0722**
maintenance mechanic – commercial
    laundry **7311**

maintenance mechanic – compressed gas
    plant **7311**
maintenance mechanic, elevators **7318**
maintenance mechanic – factory **7311**
maintenance mechanic foreman/woman,
    production machinery **7216**
maintenance mechanic, industrial
    machinery **7311**
maintenance mechanic – mill **7311**
maintenance mechanic, plant machinery **7311**
maintenance mechanic, production
    machinery **7311**
maintenance mechanic – utilities **7311**
maintenance mechanic – water treatment
    plants **7311**
maintenance millwright **7311**
maintenance of way foreman/woman **7217**
maintenance of way inspector, railway **7432**
maintenance painter **7294**
maintenance pipefitter **7252**
maintenance plumber **7251**
maintenance repairman/woman, gas
    mains **7442**
maintenance service clerk **1441**
maintenance superintendent **0722**
maintenance supervisor, laboratory,
    anatomical pathology **3414**
maintenance supervisor – processing and
    packaging equipment **7216**
maintenance supervisor – production
    equipment **7216**
maintenance supervisor –
    telecommunications lines **7212**
maintenance technician – cable
    television **7247**
maintenance technician, NDT **2261**
maintenance technician, nondestructive
    test **2261**
maintenance utility worker **7442**
maintenance welder **7265**
maintenance worker, building **6663**
maintenance worker, campground **6671**
maintenance worker, parks **8612**
maintenance worker, water mains **7442**
maintenance worker, waterworks **7442**
maître d' **6451**
maître d'hôtel **6451**
major electrical appliance repairer **7332**
major electrical appliance servicer **7332**
make-up artist – motion pictures,
    broadcasting and stage productions **5226**
make-up consultant **6481**
maker, artificial eye **3219**
maker, artificial limb **3219**
maker, brace **3219**
maker, surgical belt **3219**
malt drier tender – food and beverage
    processing **9461**

malt house operator – food and beverage
  processing **9461**
malt house worker **7452**
malt roaster **9461**
maltster – food and beverage processing **9461**
mammalogist **2121**
mammalogy technician **2221**
mammalogy technologist **2221**
mammography technologist **3215**
management accountant **1111**
management analyst **1122**
management consultant **1122**
management consulting service manager **0123**
management engineer **2148**
management information systems analyst
  – computer systems **2162**
management information systems (MIS)
  manager **0213**
management seminar leader **4131**
management services division, chief **0114**
management services officer, base –
  military **0114**
management trainee, consumer credit **0122**
management trainee – retail **0621**
manager, accommodation services **0632**
manager, accounting **0111**
manager, accounting firm **0123**
manager, actuarial department **0212**
manager, administration **0114**
manager, administrative records **0114**
manager, administrative services **0114**
manager, administrative support
  services **0114**
manager, advertising **0611**
manager, agency marketing department **0611**
manager, agricultural programs –
  government services **0412**
manager, air freight **0713**
manager, airline current schedule
  planning **0713**
manager, airport **0721**
manager, architectural **0212**
manager, architectural service **0212**
manager, arena **0721**
manager, art gallery **0511**
manager, association **0314**
manager, athletic facility **0721**
manager, audio-visual department **0512**
manager, auditing department **0111**
manager, auditing firm **0123**
manager, aviation school **0312**
manager, bank **0122**
manager, barber shop **0651**
manager, beauty shop **0651**
manager, bed and breakfast **0632**
manager, boarding or lodging house **0632**
manager, book publishing **0512**

manager, branch administration –
  banking, credit and investment **0122**
manager, buildings, vehicles and
  supplies **0114**
manager, business college **0312**
manager, cabinet liaison **0414**
manager, cabinet relations **0414**
manager, camp **0632**
manager, campaign **0611**
manager, campground **0632**
manager, car wash **0651**
manager, carpet cleaning service **0651**
manager, catering service **0631**
manager, cemetery **0651**
manager, chemical research division **0212**
manager, child welfare services –
  government services **0411**
manager, circulation **0611**
manager, city **0012**
manager, civil engineering division **0211**
manager, claim services **0121**
manager, cold storage **0651**
manager, collection and delivery
  operation – postal service **0132**
manager, collection centre **0122**
manager, collections **0111**
manager, commercial development –
  postal and courier service **0132**
manager, communications **0611**
manager, communications –
  telecommunications **0131**
manager, community centre **0314**
manager, community rehabilitation –
  government services **0411**
manager, compensation **0112**
manager, computer and related services **0213**
manager, computer applications **0213**
manager, computer facility **0213**
manager, computer system operations **0213**
manager, computer systems **0213**
manager, computer systems
  development **0213**
manager, computerized information
  systems **0213**
manager, conference centre **0721**
manager, construction **0711**
manager, convention facilities **0721**
manager, cooking school **0651**
manager, copyright and royalties **0512**
manager, corporate accounts – banking,
  credit and investment **0122**
manager, corporate banking centre **0122**
manager, corporate budgeting and
  analysis **0111**
manager, corporate finance **0111**
manager, corporate policy – education **0413**
manager, corporate risk department **0111**
manager, corporate trust services **0122**

manager, correspondence and public
  enquiries **0611**
manager, counselling service **0314**
manager, courier service **0132**
manager, court services **1227**
manager, credit and collection **0122**
manager, credit card centre **0122**
manager, credit union **0122**
manager, crematorium **0651**
manager, custom house **0123**
manager, custom tailoring shop **0621**
manager, customs – government
  services **0412**
manager, dance school **0651**
manager, data centre **0213**
manager, data process planning **0213**
manager, data processing **0213**
manager, data processing and systems
  analysis **0213**
manager, database **2162**
manager, department store **0621**
manager, detective agency **0123**
manager, dispensary department **3131**
manager, distillery **0911**
manager, distribution **0721**
manager, distribution and warehousing **0721**
manager, distribution centre **0721**
manager, distribution operations –
  utilities **0912**
manager, distribution services **0721**
manager, dog kennel **8251**
manager, drilling operations **0811**
manager, driving school **0651**
manager, dry cleaning plant **0651**
manager, dry cleaning service **0651**
manager, earth stations –
  telecommunications **0131**
manager, ecological research **0212**
manager, EDP **0213**
manager, education policy **0413**
manager, education policy development **0413**
manager, education program
  administration **0413**
manager, egg grading station **8252**
manager, electric generating station **0912**
manager, electric power **0912**
manager, electrical generating plant **0912**
manager, electronic data processing **0213**
manager, employee benefits **0112**
manager, employee relations **0112**
manager, employment agency **0123**
manager, engineering **0211**
manager, engineering services **0211**
manager, environmental science **0212**
manager, esthetic services **0651**
manager, export programs – government
  services **0412**
manager, export sales **0611**

manager, farm **8251**
manager, farm produce packing service **8252**
manager, federal-provincial relations **0414**
manager, fertilizing service –
  agriculture **8252**
manager, finance **0111**
manager, financial control **0111**
manager, financial planning and
  analysis **0111**
manager, financial planning and
  reporting **0111**
manager, fish culture **8257**
manager, fish farm **8257**
manager, fish hatchery **8257**
manager, fisheries programs –
  government services **0412**
manager, fishing operations **0811**
manager, food and beverage **0631**
manager, food safety programs –
  government services **0411**
manager, food services **0631**
manager, forestry and logging **0811**
manager, forestry operations **0811**
manager, forestry programs –
  government services **0412**
manager, freight division **0713**
manager, freight traffic **0713**
manager, fur cleaning plant **0651**
manager, gas field operations **0811**
manager, gas supply operations **0912**
manager, general – financial,
  communications and other business
  services **0013**
manager, general – goods production,
  utilities, transportation and
  construction **0016**
manager, general – health, education,
  social and community services and
  membership organizations **0014**
manager, general – trade, broadcasting
  and other services n.e.c. **0015**
manager, goods and services tax **0412**
manager, grain elevator **6234**
manager, grain market analysis –
  government services **0412**
manager, greenhouse **8254**
manager, group home **0314**
manager, hair styling salon **0651**
manager, hairdressing salon **0651**
manager, halfway house **0314**
manager, health and welfare –
  government services **0411**
manager, health club **0721**
manager, health manpower planning –
  government services **0411**
manager, health program operations –
  government services **0411**

manager, health strategies – government
  services **0411**
manager, health studio **0651**
manager, home care service **0651**
manager, hotel **0632**
manager, hotel food and beverage
  service **0631**
manager, hotel front desk **0632**
manager, hotel front office **0632**
manager, human resource planning **0112**
manager, human resources **0112**
manager, immigration appeals –
  government services **0411**
manager, industrial construction **0711**
manager, industrial engineering
  department **0211**
manager, industrial relations **0112**
manager, information service **0611**
manager, information systems **0213**
manager, inn **0632**
manager, insurance **0121**
manager, intergovernmental affairs **0414**
manager, internal audit services **0111**
manager, international banking **0122**
manager, international traffic **0713**
manager, irrigation district **0912**
manager, janitorial services **0651**
manager, job evaluation and salary
  research **0112**
manager, laboratory **0212**
manager, labour organization **0314**
manager, landscape architecture **0212**
manager, landscaping **8255**
manager, laundry and dry cleaning **0651**
manager, laundry service **0651**
manager, lawn care service **8255**
manager, leasing – real estate **0121**
manager, legal firm **0123**
manager, liability trading **0121**
manager, life sciences program **0212**
manager, livestock program
  development **0212**
manager, loans **0122**
manager, logistics **0713**
manager, mail operations **0132**
manager, maintenance **0722**
manager, maintenance and service **0722**
manager, management consulting
  service **0123**
manager, management information
  systems **0213**
manager, manufacturers' association **0314**
manager, manufacturing **0911**
manager, marina **0721**
manager, market research service **0123**
manager, marketing **0611**
manager, mathematical services **0212**
manager, media relations **0611**

manager, medical records **0114**
manager, men's hostel **0314**
manager, messenger service **0132**
manager, methods and procedures **0123**
manager, mines **0811**
manager, MIS **0213**
manager, modelling school **0651**
manager, mortgage **0122**
manager, mortgage brokers **0121**
manager, municipal taxation **0412**
manager, music school **0651**
manager, native band **0012**
manager, native centre **0314**
manager, network installation –
  telecommunications **0131**
manager, networks –
  telecommunications **0131**
manager, newspaper **0512**
manager, non-government organization
  (NGO) **0314**
manager, nursery **8254**
manager, nursing registry **0123**
manager, occupational health and safety **0112**
manager of accounting department **0111**
manager of auditing department **0111**
manager of mining operations **0811**
manager of waterworks operations **0912**
manager, oil well servicing **0811**
manager, operations – banking, credit
  and investments **0122**
manager, operations planning – solid
  waste **0912**
manager, other business services **0123**
manager, patient registration **0114**
manager, payroll service **0123**
manager, peat bog **0811**
manager, pension and benefits **0112**
manager, pension services **0111**
manager, personal trust **0122**
manager, personnel **0112**
manager, personnel agency **0123**
manager, personnel consulting service **0123**
manager, pest control service **0651**
manager, pet care services **0651**
manager, pet grooming establishment **0651**
manager, petroleum geology department **0212**
manager, petroleum research – securities
  broker **0121**
manager, pharmacy department **3131**
manager, photographic studio **0621**
manager, physical sciences program **0212**
manager, pipeline construction **0711**
manager, pipelines **0912**
manager, plant maintenance **0722**
manager, plant operations – postal
  service **0132**
manager, postal offices **0132**
manager, postal zone **0132**

manager, printing **0911**
manager, private investigation and
    security service **0123**
manager, procurement **0113**
manager, production **0911**
manager, production engineering **0211**
manager, production operations **0911**
manager, production – railway rolling
    stock **0911**
manager, professional athletic team **0513**
manager, program services, education **0413**
manager, promotions **0611**
manager, public utilities **0912**
manager, public works **0414**
manager, purchasing **0113**
manager, purchasing contracts **0113**
manager, quality assurance **0211**
manager, quarrying **0811**
manager, radio station **0512**
manager, rail transportation **0713**
manager, raw materials production **0811**
manager, real estate **0121**
manager, real estate office **0121**
manager, real estate sales **0121**
manager, realty taxation **0412**
manager, recreational campground **0632**
manager, recreational facility **0721**
manager, regional economic services –
    government services **0412**
manager, regional taxation **0412**
manager, research department **0212**
manager, reservations **0632**
manager, residential cleaning service **0651**
manager, resort **0632**
manager, restaurant **0631**
manager, retail sales **0621**
manager, retail store **0621**
manager, revenue programs –
    government services **0412**
manager, rooms **0632**
manager, rural development program **0212**
manager, salary research and
    administration **0112**
manager, sales and marketing **0611**
manager, sales distribution **0611**
manager, sauna **0651**
manager, school board services **0413**
manager, school of art **0651**
manager, school of technology **0312**
manager, seasonal resort **0632**
manager, securities and investment **0121**
manager, security **0114**
manager, security department **0114**
manager, security service **0123**
manager, septic tank service **0651**
manager, sewage disposal **0912**
manager, sewage plant **0912**
manager, sewage treatment plant **0912**

manager, shoe repair service **0651**
manager, shopping mall **0721**
manager, social services planning –
    government services **0411**
manager, space programs –
    telecommunications **0131**
manager, sports facility **0721**
manager, stadium **0721**
manager, staff training and development **0112**
manager, statistical service **0212**
manager, student residence **0632**
manager, support services **0114**
manager, survey research – government
    services **0411**
manager, survey research service **0123**
manager, swimming pool maintenance
    service **0651**
manager, systems – computer systems **0213**
manager, systems development –
    computer systems **0213**
manager, tanning salon **0651**
manager, tax policy research –
    government services **0412**
manager, taxation **0412**
manager, technical school **0312**
manager, telecommunications
    engineering **0211**
manager, telecommunications services **0131**
manager, television station **0512**
manager, tennis court **0721**
manager, theatre **0651**
manager, tobacco warehouse **0721**
manager, tourism development –
    government services **0412**
manager, tourism research – government
    services **0412**
manager, trade school **0312**
manager, trading floor **0121**
manager, traffic **0713**
manager, traffic engineering **0211**
manager trainee, consumer credit
    services **0122**
manager trainee, restaurant **0631**
manager trainee, retail **0621**
manager, training and development **0112**
manager, transfer company **0713**
manager, transmission lines **0912**
manager, transportation **0713**
manager, transportation and traffic **0713**
manager, transportation programs –
    government services **0412**
manager, travel and relocation
    department **0713**
manager, tree service **8255**
manager, truck wash **0651**
manager, trust company **0122**
manager, turkish bath houses **0651**
manager, underwriting department **0121**

manager, university residence **0632**
manager, urban transit system **0713**
manager, video production company **0512**
manager, vocational rehabilitation unit **0314**
manager, wage and salary
    administration **0112**
manager, warehouse **0721**
manager, warehousing **0721**
manager, water works **0912**
manager, weed control service –
    agriculture **8252**
manager, weight loss clinic **0651**
manager, wholesale establishment **0621**
manager, window washing service **0651**
manager, women's centre **0314**
manager, woodlands **0811**
manager, youth hostel **0632**
managing bartender **6452**
managing director, insurance **0121**
managing director, real estate sales **0121**
managing editor, newspaper or
    periodical **0512**
managing supervisor, building **1224**
managing supervisor, construction camp **6216**
managing supervisor, customer service **0621**
managing supervisor, dining
    establishment **0631**
managing supervisor, food concession **6212**
managing supervisor, real estate **0121**
managing supervisor, recreation
    establishments **0513**
managing supervisor, retail **0621**
managing supervisor, trailer park **6216**
managing supervisor, wholesale
    establishment **0611**
mandolin maker **5244**
mandrel operator, pipeline **7611**
mandrell builder – rubber
    manufacturing **9423**
mangle roller operator **9411**
mangle tender – textiles **9443**
manicurist **6482**
manifest clerk **1441**
manipulator machine operator – primary
    metal processing **9411**
manipulator operator – metal forgings **9512**
mannequin artist **5223**
mannequin assembler **9498**
mannequin mould maker **9495**
mannequin moulder – plastic
    manufacturing **9422**
mannequin painter **9496**
manual arts therapist **3235**
manual asphalt layer – road paving **7611**
manual lead caster – foundry **9412**
manufactured home assembler **9493**
manufactured home production worker,
    wood **9493**

manufactured housing production
    worker, wood **9493**
manufacturers' agent – wholesale **6411**
manufacturers' association analyst **4163**
manufacturers' association manager **0314**
manufacturers' representative –
    wholesale **6411**
manufacturing company chief executive
    officer **0016**
manufacturing cost estimator **2233**
manufacturing engineer **2141**
manufacturing field director **0911**
manufacturing job order clerk **1473**
manufacturing machinery fitter **7316**
manufacturing manager **0911**
manufacturing operations manager **0911**
manufacturing operator – electronics
    manufacturing **9483**
manufacturing painter **9496**
manufacturing technician – chemical
    processing **9232**
manufacturing technician – industrial
    engineering **2233**
manufacturing technologist **2233**
manuscript editor **5122**
map clerk **1441**
map draftsman/woman **2255**
map editor **2255**
map reproduction technician – military **2255**
maple products foreman/woman –
    agriculture **8253**
maple syrup maker **8431**
maple syrup producer **8251**
mapping engineer **2131**
mapping pilot **2271**
mapping technician **2255**
maraschino cherry processor – food and
    beverage processing **9461**
marble carver **9414**
marble cutter **9414**
marble layer **7281**
marble mason **7281**
marble mechanic **7281**
marble polisher, hand **9414**
marble polisher, machine **9414**
marble setter **7281**
marble setter helper **7611**
margarine clarifier – food and beverage
    processing **9461**
margarine processor **9461**
margin clerk – financial sector **1434**
marina attendant **6621**
marina manager **0721**
marina operator **0721**
marina worker **6621**
marine biologist **2121**
marine boilermaker **7262**
marine cargo agent **6434**

marine cargo surveyor **2262**
marine claims adjuster **1233**
marine damage surveyor **2262**
marine drafting supervisor **2253**
marine draftsman/woman **2253**
marine draftsman/woman, electrical **2253**
marine draftsperson **2253**
marine electrician **7242**
marine electrician apprentice **7242**
marine electrician helper **7612**
marine electrician – military **7242**
marine engine mechanic **7311**
marine engine mechanic apprentice **7311**
marine engine oiler **7434**
marine engineer **2148**
marine engineer apprentice **2274**
marine engineer, chief – water transport **2274**
marine engineer, mechanical **2132**
marine engineer officer cadet **2274**
marine engineer officer, coast guard
      vessel **2274**
marine engineer officer – water
      transport **2274**
marine engineering artificer – military **7434**
marine engineering mechanic – military **7434**
marine engineering technician,
      mechanical **2232**
marine engineering technician –
      military **7434**
marine engineering technologist **2232**
marine equipment electrician **7242**
marine geologist **2113**
marine geoscience technologist **2212**
marine insurance adjuster **1233**
marine mammal trainer **2221**
marine operations manager **0713**
marine pipefitter **7252**
marine plant gatherer **8613**
marine plastic craft panelling assembler **9495**
marine plumber **7251**
marine service foreman/woman – engine
      repair **7216**
marine steamfitter **7252**
marine superintendent **0713**
marine surveyor **2262**
marine systems engineer **2148**
marine traffic controller **2275**
marine traffic regulator **2275**
marine underwriter **1234**
marine wireman/woman **7242**
marionette handler **5232**
marital counsellor **4153**
maritime engineer – military **2148**
maritime engineering officer – military **2148**
maritime surface and sub surface officer
      – military **2273**
marker and cutter, upholstery **9452**
marker – laundry and dry cleaning **6681**

marker, lumber **9436**
marker – primary metal processing **9611**
marker, shoe parts **9619**
market analyst, non-financial **4163**
market development manager **0611**
market gardener **8251**
market research analyst **4163**
market research service manager **0123**
market researcher **4163**
marketing analyst **4163**
marketing consultant **4163**
marketing executive **0611**
marketing manager **0611**
marketing project officer **4163**
marketing teacher – college or
      vocational institute **4131**
marketing vice president – financial,
      communications and other business
      services **0013**
marketing vice president – goods
      production, utilities, transportation
      and construction **0016**
marketing vice president – health,
      education, social and community
      services and membership
      organizations **0014**
marketing vice president – trade,
      broadcasting and other services
      n.e.c. **0015**
markup person, typesetting **1423**
marquetry worker **9492**
marriage consultant **4153**
marriage counsellor **4153**
marriage therapist **4153**
marshal, fire **0012**
marshmallow maker **9461**
martial arts instructor **5254**
marzipan maker **9461**
mash drier – food and beverage
      processing **9461**
mash operator – food and beverage
      processing **9461**
mashgiach – food and beverage
      processing **9465**
mask operator – electronics
      manufacturing **9483**
masker **9619**
mason, artificial stone **7281**
mason, brick **7281**
mason, cement **7282**
mason, concrete **7282**
mason, marble **7281**
mason, refractory **7281**
mason's helper **7611**
mason, stone **7281**
mason, terrazzo **7283**
masonry and bricklaying contractor **7219**
masonry inspector **2264**

masonry products erector **7281**
masonry silo erector **7281**
mass spectrometer technician **2211**
massage therapist **3235**
massager **6482**
masseur/masseuse **6482**
master chef **6241**
master console operator **1421**
master control equipment operator **5224**
master control room (MCR) technician **5224**
master, dredge **2273**
master dyer – textiles **2211**
master, ferryboat **2273**
master, fishing vessel **8261**
master glass blower **5244**
master machinist **7211**
master mariner **2273**
master mechanic, mining equipment **7311**
master of ceremonies **5231**
master operator – chemical processing **9232**
master plumber **7251**
master record cutter **5225**
master, self-propelled drilling rig **2273**
master, ship **2273**
master tailor **7342**
master – water transport **2273**
mat packer **9619**
match head maker **9421**
matchbook inspector **9498**
matcher – furniture finishing and
    refinishing **9494**
matcher operator – woodworking **9513**
mate, fishing vessel **8261**
mate, self-propelled drilling rig **2273**
mate, ship **2273**
mate – water transport **2273**
material and services purchasing
    manager **0113**
material checker **1473**
material clerks supervisor **1215**
material co-ordinator **1473**
material control co-ordinator **1215**
material control manager **0114**
material control officer – military **0114**
material estimator **1473**
material estimator – construction **1473**
material handler **7452**
material handler, heavy materials **7452**
material handler, light materials **7452**
material handling equipment
    salesperson **6221**
material keeper **1472**
material management officer **1225**
material manager **0113**
material mender **9451**
materialman/woman – underground
    mining **8411**
materials and testing engineer, civil **2131**

materials engineer **2142**
materials handling technician **2233**
materials scientist **2115**
materials technician – military **7263**
materials testing technician **2231**
materials testing technologist **2231**
materiel purchasing officer **1225**
mathematical biophysicist **2111**
mathematical economist **4162**
mathematical services manager **0212**
mathematical statistician **2161**
mathematician **2161**
mathematician, applied **2161**
mathematician, research **2161**
mathematics co-ordinator – education **4166**
mathematics department head –
    secondary school **4141**
mathematics professor – university **4121**
mathematics teacher – high school **4141**
mathematics teacher – vocational
    institute **4131**
matron **6462**
matron, head **6462**
matting checker/inspector – rubber
    manufacturing **9615**
matting inspection foreman/woman –
    rubber manufacturing **9214**
mattress assembler – furniture
    manufacturing **9492**
mattress inspector **9454**
mattress maker **9492**
mattress manufacturing foreman/woman **9225**
mattress sewing machine operator **9442**
mayor **0011**
MC **5231**
MCR technician **5224**
MD **3112**
meal clerk, hospital **6641**
meals-on-wheels co-ordinator **4212**
measuring instrument repairer,
    industrial **2243**
meat boner **9462**
meat buyer **6233**
meat canner **9461**
meat chef **6241**
meat chopper – food and beverage
    processing **9461**
meat chopper – meat packing **9462**
meat clerk, supermarket **6421**
meat cook – food and beverage
    processing **9461**
meat counter clerk **6421**
meat curer **9461**
meat cutter apprentice – meat packing **9462**
meat cutter – meat packing **9462**
meat cutter – retail and wholesale **6251**
meat department supervisor **6211**
meat dresser – meat packing **9462**

meat drier **9617**

meat grader **9465**

meat grinder – food and beverage processing **9461**

meat hygiene inspector **2222**

meat inspection supervisor **2222**

meat inspector **2222**

meat manager, food store **0621**

meat mixer **9461**

meat mould sealer **9617**

meat moulder – food and beverage processing **9461**

meat packager **9617**

meat portion cutter – meat packing **9462**

meat portion cutter – retail and wholesale **6251**

meat, poultry and fish chef **6241**

meat roll tier – food and beverage processing **9462**

meat salter **9617**

meat sawyer – meat packing **9462**

meat tenderizer – food and beverage processing **9462**

meat trimmer – meat packing **9462**

meat vacuum wrapper **9617**

meat washer **9617**

meat wrapper **9617**

mechanic, aircraft maintenance **7315**

mechanic, aircraft mechanical systems **7315**

mechanic, automobile **7321**

mechanic, automotive **7321**

mechanic, backhoe **7312**

mechanic, bus **7321**

mechanic, canal equipment **7311**

mechanic, car **7321**

mechanic, central air conditioning **7313**

mechanic, chemical process equipment **7311**

mechanic, circuit breaker **7333**

mechanic, commercial air conditioning **7313**

mechanic, dental **3221**

mechanic, denture **3221**

mechanic, electrical **7333**

mechanic, elevator **7318**

mechanic, farm equipment **7312**

mechanic, gas pipe **7253**

mechanic, heating and cooling **7313**

mechanic, heavy equipment **7312**

mechanic, heavy equipment – diesel engine **7312**

mechanic helper, heavy equipment **7612**

mechanic, HVAC **7313**

mechanic, industrial **7311**

mechanic, locomotive **7312**

mechanic, maintenance – compressed gas plant **7311**

mechanic, maintenance – grain elevator **7311**

mechanic, maintenance – industrial machinery **7311**

mechanic, maintenance – industrial plants **7311**

mechanic, maintenance – plant machinery **7311**

mechanic, maintenance – water treatment plants **7311**

mechanic, mechanical – utilities **7311**

mechanic, mobile logging equipment **7312**

mechanic, mobile mining equipment **7312**

mechanic, motor vehicle **7321**

mechanic, oil drill rig **7311**

mechanic, optical lab – retail **3414**

mechanic, orthopaedic **3219**

mechanic, refrigeration **7313**

mechanic, refrigeration and air conditioning **7313**

mechanic's helper – automotive **7612**

mechanic, side boom **7312**

mechanic, small engine **7335**

mechanic, small equipment **7335**

mechanic, stationary farm equipment **7311**

mechanic, textile machines **7317**

mechanic, tile **7283**

mechanic, tractor **7312**

mechanic, truck **7321**

mechanical and fuel systems overhaul and repair mechanic, aircraft **7315**

mechanical artist **5223**

mechanical assistant, engine room **7434**

mechanical design draftsman/woman **2253**

mechanical draftsman/woman **2253**

mechanical draftsperson **2253**

mechanical engineer **2132**

mechanical engineer, gas utilization **2132**

mechanical engineering design technologist **2232**

mechanical engineering development technologist **2232**

mechanical engineering equipment designer **2232**

mechanical engineering manager **0211**

mechanical engineering professor – university **4121**

mechanical engineering technician **2232**

mechanical engineering technologist **2232**

mechanical equipment engineering assistant **2232**

mechanical equipment repair inspector foreman/woman **7216**

mechanical estimator – construction **2234**

mechanical fitter **7316**

mechanical harvester operator – logging **8241**

mechanical insulator tester **9619**

mechanical maintainer, heavy water plant **7311**

mechanical maintainer, nuclear generating station **7311**

mechanical maintenance engineer **2132**

mechanical maintenance foreman/woman
  – utilities **7216**
mechanical maintenance supervisor **7216**
mechanical maintenance supervisor –
  manufacturing **7216**
mechanical meter repairer **7445**
mechanical power engineer **2132**
mechanical pump assembler **9486**
mechanical repairer, motor vehicle **7321**
mechanical superintendent **0722**
mechanical sweeper operator – public
  works **7422**
mechanical system technician – military **7351**
mechanical systems inspector, aircraft
  repair and overhaul **7315**
mechanical technologist **2232**
mechanical technology teacher –
  technological institute **4131**
mechanical trades contractor –
  construction **7213**
mechanical trades supervisor –
  construction **7213**
mechanical tree processor operator –
  logging **8241**
mechanical upgrader – motor vehicle
  manufacturing **7321**
mechanics physicist **2111**
media advertising manager **0611**
media buyer **1225**
media co-ordinator **5124**
media estimator **1225**
media events co-ordinator **5124**
media relations director **0611**
media relations officer **5124**
media time and space buyer **1225**
media time sales representative **6411**
mediator **1121**
medic clerk, drilling rig **3234**
medic, drilling rig **3234**
medical aide **3413**
medical and surgical claim clerk –
  insurance **1434**
medical assistant (paramedic) – military **3234**
medical assistant (registered nursing
  assistant) – military **3233**
medical assistant (supporting health
  services) – military **3414**
medical associate officer – military **0311**
medical bacteriologist **3111**
medical biochemist **3111**
medical biophysicist **2111**
medical chemist **2112**
medical claims assessor – insurance **1233**
medical clinic assistant **6631**
medical clinic director **0311**
medical dicta typist **1244**
medical director **0311**
medical doctor **3112**

medical engineering biophysicist **2111**
medical equipment and supplies
  salesperson **6221**
medical genetics specialist **3111**
medical illustrator **5241**
medical instrumentation sales engineer **6221**
medical laboratory aid **3212**
medical laboratory assistant **3212**
medical laboratory equipment repairer **2241**
medical laboratory helper **3212**
medical laboratory technical assistant **3212**
medical laboratory technician **3212**
medical laboratory technologist **3211**
medical librarian **5111**
medical material handler **6631**
medical microbiologist **3111**
medical missionary **3112**
medical office assistant **1414**
medical officer, civil aviation **3112**
medical officer (general practitioner) –
  military **3112**
medical officer of health, city **0411**
medical officer (specialist) – military **3111**
medical oncologist **3111**
medical orderly **3413**
medical parasitologist **3111**
medical pathologist **3111**
medical photographer **5221**
medical physicist **2111**
medical physiologist **3111**
medical radiation technologist **3215**
medical radiographer **3215**
medical receptionist **1414**
medical records clerk **1413**
medical records department manager **0114**
medical records program teacher –
  community college **4131**
medical records supervisor **1211**
medical records technician **1413**
medical sciences professor – university **4121**
medical secretary **1243**
medical social worker **4152**
medical sociologist **4169**
medical sonographer **3216**
medical sonographer – military **3216**
medical statistician **2161**
medical stenographer **1243**
medical supply attendant **1472**
medical supply clerk **1472**
medical technologist – laboratory **3211**
medical technology teacher –
  technological institute **4131**
medical terminologist **5125**
medical transcriber **1244**
medical transcriptionist **1244**
medical vice president – health **0014**
medical warden, drilling rig **3234**
medicine, chief of **0311**

medicine professor – university **4121**
medium **6484**
meeting planner **1226**
melter – foundry **9412**
melter tender – food and beverage
    processing **9461**
melting and roasting operations
    foreman/woman – primary metal and
    mineral products processing **9211**
member of house of assembly **0011**
member of legislative assembly **0011**
member of national assembly **0011**
member of parliament **0011**
member of provincial parliament **0011**
member of territorial council **0011**
membership education director **0314**
membership sales representative **6411**
membership secretary **1241**
membership services manager **0314**
memorial designer **5243**
memorial salesperson **6421**
mender, garment **9451**
mender, textile products **9451**
mental health counsellor **4153**
mental health programs consultant **4165**
mental health worker **4212**
mental retardation counsellor **4212**
mental retardation worker **4212**
mental telepathist **6484**
mercerizer machine operator – textiles **9443**
mercerizer – textiles **9443**
merchandise purchasing manager **0113**
merchandiser **6233**
merchandising clerk supervisor **1212**
merchant **0621**
merchant miller – food and beverage
    processing **9461**
mercury recoverer – chemical
    processing **9421**
merry-go-round operator **6443**
mesh welding machine operator **9515**
mess cook **6242**
mess waiter/waitress **6453**
message relayer, telegrams **1463**
messenger **1463**
messenger service manager **0132**
messenger supervisor **1214**
metabolic unit cook **6242**
metal and roasting department
    supervisor **9211**
metal and woodworking machinery
    manufacturing foreman/woman **7216**
metal arts worker **5244**
metal awning maker operator **9516**
metal band saw operator **9511**
metal blade sharpener operator **9516**
metal bluing cleaner – metal fabrication **9612**
metal bonding equipment operator **9516**

metal buffer **9612**
metal buffing foreman/woman **9226**
metal building assembler/installer **7441**
metal cabinet assembler **9492**
metal cable maker operator **9516**
metal casket assembler **9492**
metal caster – foundry **9412**
metal casting finisher **9612**
metal chair assembler **9492**
metal cleaner **9612**
metal cleaner, immersion **9612**
metal cleaner – metal fabrication **9612**
metal coating equipment operator **9497**
metal cut off saw operator **9514**
metal dealer **0611**
metal dental technician **3223**
metal dipper operator **9497**
metal door frame assembler **9498**
metal electro plating inspector **9497**
metal electroplater **9497**
metal engraver **5244**
metal extruder operator **9411**
metal fabricating inspector **9514**
metal fabricating machine operator **9514**
metal fabricating shop helper **9612**
metal fabrication air grinder **9612**
metal fabrication fitter helper **9612**
metal fabricator apprentice **7263**
metal fabricator – structural metal and
    platework **7263**
metal fence erector **7441**
metal filer, hand **9612**
metal finish and touch up repairer –
    motor vehicle manufacturing **7322**
metal finisher – motor vehicle
    manufacturing **7322**
metal fitter, structural **7263**
metal floor lamp maker **9516**
metal forging inspector **9512**
metal forming machine set-up operator **9514**
metal forming machine tender **9514**
metal frame moulder helper **9612**
metal furniture assembler **9492**
metal furniture assembly
    foreman/woman **9224**
metal furniture inspector **9492**
metal furniture model maker **7261**
metal furniture patternmaker **7261**
metal furniture repairer **9494**
metal grinder operator – production **9511**
metal hardness tester – primary metal
    processing **9415**
metal heater – primary metal processing **9411**
metal inspector – primary metal
    processing **9415**
metal lather **7284**
metal locker assembler **9492**

metal machining inspection foreman/woman **7211**

metal mixer helper – primary metal processing **9611**

metal mould and pattern makers foreman/woman **7211**

metal mould finisher **7232**

metal mould maker **7232**

metal nut former **9516**

metal nut maker **9516**

metal organ pipe maker **9516**

metal parts inspector **9514**

metal patternmaker **7232**

metal physicist **2111**

metal pickler **9612**

metal pipe compressor **9514**

metal pipe cutter machine operator **9516**

metal pipe cutter operator **9516**

metal plating equipment operator **9497**

metal pointer – primary metal processing **9411**

metal polisher, automatic machine **9516**

metal polisher helper **9612**

metal pourer helper – primary metal processing **9611**

metal pourer – metal processing **9411**

metal power saw operator **9514**

metal prep lead hand – structural metal and platework **7263**

metal processing products inspector **9415**

metal products inspection and testing foreman/woman **9226**

metal reclaimer **9411**

metal reclamer – primary metal processing **9611**

metal repairer – motor vehicle manufacturing **7322**

metal roaster **9411**

metal rolling foreman/woman **9211**

metal roofer **7291**

metal roofing contractor **7219**

metal saw tooth grinder **9511**

metal sawing machine operator **9514**

metal screened door and window maker **9516**

metal sculptor **5136**

metal shipwright **7263**

metal smelter **9411**

metal solderer **9515**

metal spinner **9514**

metal spinning lathe tender **9516**

metal spray operator **9497**

metal spring former operator **9514**

metal stamping press operator **9514**

metal strength tester – primary metal processing **9415**

metal structure erector **7264**

metal table assembler **9492**

metal table saw operator **9514**

metal trim erector helper **7611**

metal twisting machine tender **9516**

metal upgrader – motor vehicle manufacturing **7322**

metal X-Ray operator **2261**

metallizer operator **9497**

metallographer **2115**

metallurgical control analyst **2212**

metallurgical engineer **2142**

metallurgical engineering professor – university **4121**

metallurgical engineering technician **2212**

metallurgical engineering technologist **2212**

metallurgical laboratory technician **2212**

metallurgical technologist **2212**

metallurgist, extractive **2142**

metallurgist, physical **2115**

metallurgy professor – university **4121**

metals conservator **5112**

metals technician – military **7261**

metalworker, hand **5244**

metalworking cable maker **9516**

metalworking die cutter **7232**

metalworking expander **9514**

metalworking machine helper **9612**

metalworking machine operator **9514**

metalworking machine set-up man/woman **9514**

metalworking machine set-up operator **9514**

metalworking machine setter **9514**

metalworking machinery mechanic **7311**

metalworking shearer **9514**

metalworking threader **9514**

metalworking weaver **9516**

meteorological aide **2213**

meteorological equipment inspector and tester **7383**

meteorological inspector **2213**

meteorological technician **2213**

meteorological technician – military **2213**

meteorologist **2114**

meteorology officer – military **2114**

meteorology professor – university **4121**

meter assembler **9498**

meter engineer **2133**

meter installer – electric power systems **7244**

meter installer supervisor – electrical **7212**

meter reader **1454**

meter records clerk **1413**

meter servicer **7445**

meter shop foreman/woman **7216**

metering technologist **2241**

methods and cost analyst **1122**

methods and procedures analyst **1122**

methods and procedures analyst supervisor **1122**

methods and procedures manager **0123**

methods designer **2233**

methods engineer **2141**
metrologist **2111**
metrology engineer **2133**
metrology technician **2241**
MHA **0011**
mica capacitor assembler **9483**
mica classifier – mineral products processing **9415**
mica crusher **9411**
mica plate layer **9411**
mica press tender **9411**
mica processing foreman/woman **9211**
mica products maker **9484**
mica sheet laminator **9411**
mica sheet salvager **9411**
mica splitter **9411**
mica trimmer **9411**
microbiological technician **2221**
microbiologist **2121**
microbiologist, medical **3111**
microbiologist, veterinary **3114**
microbiology quality control technologist **2221**
microbiology technologist **2221**
microbiology technologist – medical laboratory **3211**
microcomputer salesperson – retail **6421**
microelectronic fabrication operator **9483**
microfilm camera operator **1413**
microfilm operator **1413**
microfilm records searcher **1413**
microfilmer **1413**
micropaleontologist **2113**
microprocessor design and application engineer **2133**
microwave facilities manager – telecommunications **0131**
microwave maintenance technician **2241**
microwave physicist **2111**
microwave system foreman/woman **7212**
microwave systems engineer **2133**
microwave transmission systems engineer **2133**
midwife **3232**
mig welder **7265**
military dental officer **3113**
military engineer **2131**
military engineering officer, civil **2131**
military historian **4169**
military pilot **2271**
military police officer **6261**
military policeman/woman **6261**
milk deliverer **7414**
milk drier – food and beverage processing **9461**
milk grader **9465**
milk hauler, tank truck **7411**
milk inspector **2222**

milk pasteurizer – food and beverage processing **9461**
milk powder grinder **9617**
milk processing equipment operator **9461**
milk receiver/tester **9465**
milk sampler **9617**
milking machine salesperson **6221**
milking machine tender **8431**
milking services contractor **8252**
milkman/woman **7414**
mill carpenter **7271**
mill charger – chemical processing **9613**
mill control operator – primary metal processing **9231**
mill electrician **7242**
mill grinder – rubber manufacturing **9423**
mill helper – primary metal and mineral products processing **9611**
mill manager **0911**
mill mechanic helper **7612**
mill mixer – rubber manufacturing **9423**
mill roll grinder – metal fabrication **9612**
mill superintendent **0911**
mill tender – chemical processing **9421**
mill tender – clay products **9414**
mill tender – rubber manufacturing **9423**
milled rubber cooler **9615**
miller – food and beverage processing **9461**
miller, salt **9411**
miller, wood flour **9434**
milliner **7342**
millinery floorman/woman – fabric, fur and leather products manufacturing **9225**
millinery maker **7342**
millinery salesperson **6421**
milling equipment operator – mineral and metal processing **9411**
milling machine operator – metal machining **9511**
milling machine set-up operator – metal machining **9511**
milling machine setter **7231**
milling plant foreman/woman – primary metal and mineral products processing **9211**
millroom foreman/woman – rubber manufacturing **9214**
millroom operator – rubber manufacturing **9423**
millstone cutter operator – stone products **9414**
millwork assembler – wood products manufacturing **9493**
millwright apprentice **7311**
millwright, construction **7311**
millwright foreman/woman **7216**
millwright helper **7612**
millwright, industrial **7311**

mime **5135**
mimic **5232**
mincemeat maker **9461**
mine captain **8221**
mine carpenter **7271**
mine check weigher **8614**
mine construction worker **8411**
mine design engineer **2143**
mine development engineer **2143**
mine development technologist **2212**
mine dispatcher **1475**
mine draftsman/woman **2253**
mine drilling foreman/woman **8221**
mine electrician **7242**
mine examiner **2263**
mine foreman/woman **8221**
mine helper **8614**
mine hoist machinery mechanic **7311**
mine hoist repairer **7311**
mine labourer **8614**
mine layout engineer **2143**
mine manager **0811**
mine mechanic **7311**
mine motorman/woman **8411**
mine planning engineer **2143**
mine production engineer **2143**
mine production technician **2212**
mine safety engineer **2143**
mine safety inspector **2263**
mine superintendent **0811**
mine supervisor **8221**
mine survey technician **2212**
mine survey technologist **2212**
mine timberman/woman **8411**
mine ventilation engineer **2143**
miner **8231**
miner apprentice **8231**
miner helper **8614**
miner operator **8231**
mineral dressing engineer **2143**
mineral engineer **2143**
mineral sampler – primary metal and
    mineral products processing **9415**
mineral technician **2212**
mineral technologist **2212**
mineral technology teacher – college of
    applied arts and technology **4131**
mineralogist **2113**
mineralogy technician **2212**
mines analyst **2212**
mines exploration engineer **2143**
mini golf attendant **6671**
mini van assembler – motor vehicle
    manufacturing **9482**
miniature bulb maker **9487**
minicomputer systems programmer **2163**
mining engineer **2143**
mining engineering technician **2212**

mining engineering technologist **2212**
mining equipment sales engineer **6221**
mining equipment sales representative **6221**
mining geologist **2113**
mining machine operator **8231**
mining machinery fitter **7316**
mining machinery mechanic **7311**
mining rescue instructor **4131**
mining shovel oiler **7443**
mining shovel operator **7421**
mining survey technician **2212**
mining survey technologist **2212**
mining technologist **2212**
minister, deputy – government services **0012**
minister – government **0011**
minister – religion **4154**
ministerial assistant **1222**
mink tail slitter – fur products
    manufacturing **9452**
minor waters master **2273**
mint refiner – primary metal processing **9411**
mirror and picture frame maker **9492**
mirror assembler **9498**
mirror framer **9498**
mirror maker **9413**
mirror painter **9496**
mirror silverer **9496**
mirror silvering equipment operator **9496**
mirror silvering foreman/woman **9227**
mirror wall installer **7292**
MIS manager **0213**
missionary **4217**
missionary doctor **3112**
missionary, medical **3112**
missionary nurse **3152**
mitre saw tender – woodworking **9513**
mixed farmer **8251**
mixer and extruder, modelling clay **9414**
mixer, asphalt roofing material **9421**
mixer, bakelite – plastic manufacturing **9422**
mixer caster, concrete **9414**
mixer – chemical processing **9421**
mixer – concrete, clay and stone
    products **9414**
mixer, dressings and sauces **9461**
mixer/drier tender, wood particles **9434**
mixer, dry plaster **9414**
mixer, explosives **9421**
mixer, fertilizer **9421**
mixer, foam rubber **9423**
mixer, gunite – construction **7611**
mixer helper – primary metal and
    mineral products processing **9611**
mixer, music or sound **5225**
mixer operator – chemical processing **9421**
mixer operator – concrete products **9414**
mixer operator, dry foods **9461**
mixer operator, lime **9414**

mixer operator, molten metal **9411**
mixer tender – chemical processing **9421**
mixer – tobacco processing **9464**
mixing and separating operations foreman/woman – primary metal and mineral
products processing **9211**
mixing machine tender, plasterboard **9414**
mixing operator – pulp and paper **9233**
mixing plant foreman/woman – primary metal and mineral products processing **9211**
MLA **0011**
MNA **0011**
mobile broadcast equipment operator **5224**
mobile canteen driver **7414**
mobile canteen service supervisor **7222**
mobile caterer **7414**
mobile chipper operator – logging **8241**
mobile crane operator **7371**
mobile disc jockey **5231**
mobile equipment dispatcher **1475**
mobile equipment repairer helper **7612**
mobile farm equipment mechanic **7312**
mobile farm equipment mechanic apprentice **7312**
mobile farm machinery repairer **7312**
mobile generator operator **7351**
mobile home assembly foreman/woman **9226**
mobile home equipment servicer **7441**
mobile home salesperson **6421**
mobile home servicer **7441**
mobile inspector, transit **7222**
mobile radio broadcast supervisor **5224**
mobile radio installer – telecommunications **7246**
mobile radio technician – telecommunications **7246**
mobile support equipment operator (buses) – military **7412**
mobile support equipment operator (chauffeurs) – military **7413**
mobile support equipment operator (dispatchers) – military **1475**
mobile support equipment operator (heavy equipment) – military **7421**
mobile support equipment operator (trucks) – military **7411**
mobile transceiver inspector – electronics manufacturing **9483**
mobilift operator **7452**
moccasin sewer **9451**
model **5232**
model and mould maker – concrete products **7383**
model and mould maker, plaster **9414**
model maker, aircraft **7383**
model maker, jewellery **7344**

model maker machinist **7231**
model maker, metal furniture **7261**
model maker, pottery **9414**
model maker, sheet metal **7261**
model maker, ship **7383**
model maker, tool and die **7232**
model maker, wood **7272**
modelling school manager **0651**
moderator – religion **4154**
modern languages teacher – college **4131**
modern languages teacher – secondary school **4141**
modification mechanic, aircraft mechanical systems **7315**
modular housing wood fabricator **9493**
module tender – tobacco processing **9464**
mohel **4217**
molasses mixer **9461**
molasses wort processor **9461**
mole operator **7421**
mole operator helper **7611**
molecular biologist **2121**
molecular biophysicist **2111**
molecular geneticist **2121**
molecular physiologist **2121**
molten metal sampler – primary metal processing **9415**
molybdenum flotation operator **9411**
molybdenum leaching plant operator **9411**
molybdenum roaster operator **9231**
money counter **6611**
money market analyst **1112**
money market investments supervisor **1212**
money market trader **1113**
money order clerk **1461**
money sorting machine operator **1431**
money trader **1113**
monitor, court **1244**
monitoring station operator **1475**
monk **4217**
monorail crane operator **7371**
monument carver – stone products **9414**
monument engraver – stone products **9414**
monument erector **7611**
monument inspector – mineral products processing **9415**
monument letterer – stone products **9414**
monument sculptor **5136**
monument setter **7611**
mop maker **9498**
morality officer – police **6261**
morgue attendant **3414**
morgue technician **3414**
mortar mixer **9414**
mortarman/woman – military **6464**
mortgage and consumer credit manager **0122**
mortgage broker **1114**
mortgage broker manager **0121**

mortgage clerk **1434**
mortgage consultant **1232**
mortgage manager **0122**
mortgage officer **1232**
mortgage/real estate legal assistant **4211**
mortgage/real estate paralegal **4211**
mortician **6272**
mortiser operator – woodworking **9513**
mortising machine operator – woodworking **9513**
mortuary supervisor **3414**
mosaic tile worker **7283**
mosaicer **2255**
motel cleaner **6661**
motel manager **0632**
motel managing supervisor **6216**
mother's helper **6474**
mother superior **4217**
motion picture camera operator **5222**
motion picture director **5131**
motion picture film developer **9474**
motion picture film examiner – photographic processing **9474**
motion picture film printer **9474**
motion picture musical director **5132**
motion picture producer **5131**
motion picture projectionist **5227**
motor and chassis inspector – motor vehicle manufacturing **9482**
motor and generator assembler **9484**
motor and generator coil installer **9485**
motor and generator inspector **9485**
motor and generator subassemblies painter **9496**
motor assembler, gasoline **9486**
motor boat assembler **9491**
motor boat captain **7436**
motor boat mechanic **7335**
motor boat operator **7436**
motor installer, boat **9491**
motor installer – motor vehicle manufacturing **9482**
motor launch operator **7436**
motor repairer – motor vehicle manufacturing **7321**
motor scooter repairer **7334**
motor transport manager **0713**
motor transport regulations officer **2262**
motor transportation inspector **2262**
motor vehicle and equipment sales representative – wholesale **6411**
motor vehicle assembler – motor vehicle manufacturing **9482**
motor vehicle assembly plant manager **0911**
motor vehicle body repairer **7322**
motor vehicle body repairer apprentice **7322**
motor vehicle body repairer foreman/woman **7216**

motor vehicle body repairer/painter **7322**
motor vehicle body technician **7322**
motor vehicle bureau clerk **1441**
motor vehicle claim adjuster – insurance **1233**
motor vehicle cylinder grinder **9511**
motor vehicle diesel engine mechanic **7321**
motor vehicle dispatcher **1475**
motor vehicle fuel and electric systems mechanic apprentice **7321**
motor vehicle fuel conversion technician **7321**
motor vehicle inspection and testing foreman/woman – motor vehicle manufacturing **9221**
motor vehicle inspector **2262**
motor vehicle jig builder **7232**
motor vehicle jockey **6683**
motor vehicle leasing representative **6421**
motor vehicle machinist apprentice **7231**
motor vehicle manufacturing painter **9496**
motor vehicle mechanic **7321**
motor vehicle mechanic apprentice **7321**
motor vehicle mechanic helper **7612**
motor vehicle mechanics supervisor **7216**
motor vehicle model maker **7383**
motor vehicle parts apprentice **1472**
motor vehicle parts stock clerk **1472**
motor vehicle partsman/woman **1472**
motor vehicle repair co-ordinator **1473**
motor vehicle repair painter apprentice **7322**
motor vehicle repair shop manager **0621**
motor vehicle repairer (truck and transport) **7321**
motor vehicle salesperson **6421**
motor vehicle steering, suspension and brakes mechanic apprentice **7321**
motor vehicle technician **7321**
motor vehicle transmission mechanic **7321**
motor vehicle transmission mechanic apprentice **7321**
motor vehicles defects investigator **2262**
motor winder – industrial electrical equipment **9485**
motorcycle driving instructor **4216**
motorcycle mechanic **7334**
motorcycle patrolman/woman **6261**
motorcycle repair apprentice **7334**
motorcycle repairer **7334**
motorcycle repairman/woman **7334**
motorcycle salesperson **6421**
motorman/woman – oil and gas drilling **8412**
motorman/woman – underground mining **8411**
mould and core machinist **7231**
mould bonding machine tender – foundry **9412**
mould caster – foundry **9412**

mould cleaner – rubber manufacturing **9615**
mould closer – foundry **9612**
mould design engineer **2132**
mould designer **2232**
mould filler – plastic and rubber
    manufacturing **9615**
mould finisher – foundry **9612**
mould helper – primary metal
    processing **9611**
mould laminator – plastic
    manufacturing **9495**
mould machine operator – rubber
    manufacturing **9423**
mould maker, aircraft **7232**
mould maker – clay products **9414**
mould maker, metal **7232**
mould-making machinist **7231**
mould polisher, glass **9413**
mould preparer – plastic and rubber
    manufacturing **9615**
mould shop foreman/woman –
    machining **7211**
mould stamper **9511**
mould stripper – concrete products
    manufacturing **9611**
mould stripper – plastic manufacturing **9495**
mould supplier, rubber **1473**
mould waxer – plastic and rubber
    manufacturing **9615**
mould waxer – plastic manufacturing **9495**
moulded footwear inspection
    foreman/woman – rubber and plastic
    manufacturing **9214**
moulded overshoe maker – rubber
    manufacturing **9423**
moulded plastic and rubber trimmer **9615**
moulded plastic finisher **9495**
moulded plastic inspector **9495**
moulded plastic product trimmer **9495**
moulded products finisher – plastic
    manufacturing **9495**
moulded products stripper – plastic and
    rubber products manufacturing **9615**
moulded products stripper – plastic
    manufacturing **9495**
moulded pulp products foreman/woman **9215**
moulded rubber footwear
    foreman/woman **9214**
moulder, bench – foundry **9412**
moulder – chemical processing **9421**
moulder – clay works **9414**
moulder, compression – plastic
    manufacturing **9422**
moulder – concrete products **9414**
moulder, fibreglass **9422**
moulder, floor – foundry **9412**
moulder, injection – plastic
    manufacturing **9422**

moulder operator – plastic
    manufacturing **9422**
moulder, sports balls **9517**
moulder – stone products **9414**
moulder, sweep – foundry **9412**
moulder – wood products **9513**
moulder – woodworking **9513**
moulding and coremaking machine
    set-up man/woman – foundry **9412**
moulding and coremaking machines
    setter – foundry **9412**
moulding cutter, wood products **9513**
moulding foreman/woman – foundry **9211**
moulding machine offbearer – rubber
    manufacturing **9615**
moulding machine operator – food and
    beverage processing **9461**
moulding machine operator, injection –
    plastic manufacturing **9422**
moulding machine operator –
    woodworking **9513**
moulding plasterer **7284**
moulding press tender – rubber
    manufacturing **9423**
moulding sand mixer – foundry **9412**
mouldmaker apprentice **7232**
mouldmaker, manual – foundry **9412**
mouldmaker, smelter – foundry **9412**
mouldman/woman – rubber
    manufacturing **9423**
mount operator – electronics
    manufacturing **9483**
mountain climbing guide **6442**
mountain guide **6442**
mountaineering guide **6442**
mounted police constable **6261**
mounted policeman/woman **6261**
mounter – electronics manufacturing **9483**
movement analyst – medical **3144**
movement therapist **3144**
movie critic **5123**
movie director **5131**
movie producer **5131**
movie theatre cashier **6611**
movie usher **6683**
moving company manager **0713**
moving van driver **7411**
moving van helper **7622**
moving walkway installer/repairer **7318**
MP **0011**
MPP **0011**
mucker operator – construction **7421**
mucker – underground mining **8231**
mucking machine operator –
    construction **7421**
mucking machine operator –
    underground mining **8231**
mud engineer **2145**

mud jack operator **7611**
mud man/woman – petroleum drilling **2212**
muffler installer **7443**
muffler shop manager **0621**
mule fixer – textile manufacturing **7317**
multiculturalism project officer **4164**
multifocal lens assembler **9498**
multimachine operator – metal
    machining **9511**
multimachine operator trainee – metal
    machining **9511**
multineedle sewing machine operator **9451**
multioperator – printing **9471**
multiple extruder operator – plastic
    manufacturing **9422**
multiple punch press operator – metal
    fabrication **9514**
multiple spindle drill press operator **9511**
multiple spindle screw machine
    operator **9511**
multiroll calender operator – plastic
    processing **9422**
multiroll calender operator – rubber
    manufacturing **9423**
multiservice operator – oil field
    services **8222**
municipal administrator **0012**
municipal assessor **1235**
municipal clerk **0012**
municipal clerk, deputy **0012**
municipal engineer **2131**
municipal engineering assistant **2231**
municipal labourer **7621**
municipal law enforcement officer **6463**
municipal maintenance equipment
    operator **7422**
municipal office clerk **1441**
municipal park planner **2153**
municipal planner **2153**
municipal recreation manager **0513**
municipal recycling co-ordinator **4161**
municipal servicer – drain roto **7422**
municipal solicitor **4112**
munition manufacturing inspector **9498**
munitions assembler **9498**
munitions handler **7452**
mural painter **5136**
museum administrator **0511**
museum administrator, assistant **0511**
museum cataloguer **5212**
museum co-ordinator **0511**
museum curator **5112**
museum director **0511**
museum director, assistant **0511**
museum educator **5124**
museum executive director **0511**
museum exhibit designer **5243**
museum exhibit officer **5212**

museum extension officer **5124**
museum guide **5212**
museum interpreter **5212**
museum manager **0511**
museum preparator **5212**
museum registrar **5212**
museum technician **5212**
mushroom grower **8251**
mushroom picker **8611**
music adapter **5132**
music arranger **5132**
music co-ordinator – education **4166**
music critic **5123**
music director **5132**
music editor, recording studio **5225**
music librarian **5111**
music librarian – broadcasting **5226**
music librarian's assistant **5211**
music mixer **5225**
music officer – military **5133**
music professor – university **4121**
music program planner, radio **5226**
music teacher – elementary school **4142**
music teacher – high school **4141**
music teacher – private, conservatory or
    studio **5133**
music therapist **3144**
music therapist, supervisor **3144**
music therapy researcher **3144**
musical director **5132**
musical instrument and supplies
    salesman **6421**
musical instrument maker **9498**
musical instrument repairer **7445**
musical instrument tester **7445**
musical instrument tube bender **9514**
musician **5133**
musician – military **5133**
muskrat trapper **8442**
mussel farmer **8257**
mussel grower **8257**
mussel harvester **8613**
mutual fund broker **1113**
mutual fund manager – financial
    brokerage **0121**
mutual fund sales agent **1113**
mutual fund sales representative **1113**
mycological technician **2221**
mycological technologist **2221**
mycologist **2121**

N

nail making machine set up operator **9516**
nail making machine tender **9516**
nailing machine operator –
    woodworking **9513**
nails and lashes applicator **6482**

nameplate engraver **5244**
nanny **6474**
naphthalene clarifier **9232**
napper adjuster – textile manufacturing **7317**
napper grinder – textile manufacturing **7317**
napper tender – textiles **9443**
narcotics stock clerk **1472**
narrator **5135**
narrow fabrics examiner **9444**
national account manager, sales **0611**
national sales manager **0611**
national sales manager – real estate **0121**
national team coach **5252**
native affairs officer **4164**
native art carver **5244**
native band chief **0011**
native band council member **0011**
native band government leader **0011**
native band manager **0012**
native centre, co-ordinator **4212**
native craftwork instructor **5244**
native employment program officer **4164**
native government leader **0011**
native issues lobbyist **4164**
native land claims liaison officer **4168**
native outreach worker **4212**
natural gas compressor operator **9232**
natural gas engineer **2145**
natural gas sales representative **6221**
natural history specimens conservator **5112**
natural resource officer **2224**
natural resource planner **4161**
natural resource policy analyst **4161**
natural resources economist **4162**
natural resources technician **2223**
natural science curator **5112**
naturalist **2121**
naturopath **3123**
naturopathic doctor **3123**
naturopathic medicine, doctor of **3123**
nautical instrument maker – electronics
    manufacturing **9483**
naval acoustics operator – military **6464**
naval architect **2148**
naval combat information operator –
    military **6464**
naval electronic sensor operator –
    military **6464**
naval electronics technician, acoustics –
    military **2241**
naval electronics technician,
    communications – military **2241**
naval electronics technician – military **6464**
naval electronics technician, systems –
    military **2241**
naval electronics technician, tactical –
    military **2241**
naval engineer **2148**

naval radio operator – military **6464**
naval signalman – military **6464**
naval weapons technician – military **6464**
navigation aid inspector – electronics
    manufacturing **9483**
navigation officer, coast guard vessel **2273**
navigation officer, fishing vessel **8261**
navigation officer – water transport **2273**
navy chaplain – military **4154**
NC/CNC machining tool operator **9511**
NC machine operator, machining **9511**
NC machinist **7231**
ND **3123**
NDT maintenance technician **2261**
necklace assembler **9498**
needle board repairer – textile
    manufacturing **7317**
needle loom operator **9442**
needle loom weaver **9442**
needleworker, hand **5244**
negative cutter – film processing **9474**
negative merger – printing **9472**
negative restorer **9474**
negative retoucher **9474**
negative spotter – film processing **9474**
negative spotter – printing **9472**
negotiator **1121**
negotiator, collective agreements **1121**
negotiator, contract – purchasing **1225**
negotiator, labour organization **1121**
neighbourhood planner **2153**
neighbourhood worker **4212**
nematologist **2121**
neon sign builder **9484**
neon sign erector **7441**
neon sign installer **7441**
neon sign maker **9484**
neon sign pumper **9413**
neon sign repairer **7445**
neon sign tube bender **9413**
neon tube bender **9413**
neon tube pumper **9413**
neonatologist **3111**
neoprene sprayer operator – plastic
    manufacturing **9422**
nephrologist **3111**
nephrology, chief of **0311**
nerve specialist **3111**
net applicator – plastic manufacturing **9495**
net knitting machine operator **9442**
net mender **7445**
net repairer **7445**
net repairman/woman **7445**
net weaver **9442**
netmender, fishing vessel **8441**
network controller **1421**
network engineer **2133**
network engineer, electrical **2133**

network operations manager –
    telecommunications 0131
network operator 1421
network reporter 5123
network, services manager –
    telecommunications 0131
neuroelectrophysiology technologist 3218
neurological surgeon 3111
neurologist 3111
neurology, chief of 0311
neuropathologist 3111
neuropsychiatric aide 3413
neuropsychiatrist 3111
neuropsychologist 4151
neurosurgeon 3111
neutralizer, corn starch 9617
neutralizer – textiles 9443
new car mechanic 7321
new car preparer 9482
new car service mechanic 7321
new home salesperson 6232
news analyst – broadcasting 5123
news camera operator 5222
news commentator 5123
news department manager 0512
news editor 5122
news editor – broadcasting 5122
news photographer 5221
news reader 5231
news reporter 5123
news vendor – street sales 6623
newscaster 5231
newspaper advertisement tailer 1452
newspaper carrier 1463
newspaper copy rater 1452
newspaper correspondent 5123
newspaper critic 5123
newspaper delivery driver 7414
newspaper delivery supervisor 6211
newspaper editor 5122
newspaper illustrator 5241
newspaper manager 0512
newspaper page assembler 1423
newspaper press operator 7381
newspaper pressman/woman 7381
newspaper reporter 5123
newspaper sales supervisor 6211
newspaper vendor 6623
newspaper writer 5123
newsstand clerk 6421
NGO manager 0314
nib finisher – metal fabrication 9612
nibbling machine operator – jewellery
    manufacturing 9517
nibbling machine operator – metal
    fabrication 9514
nickel plater 9497
night auditor 6435

night clerk 6435
night clerk supervisor – hotel 6216
night supervisor – hotel 6216
night supervisor, telephone system 1211
night watchman/woman 6651
911 dispatcher 1475
nipper – underground mining 8411
nitrocellulose maker 9232
nitrogen operator – oil field services 8412
nitrogen plant operator 9232
nitrogen truck operator – oil field
    services 8412
nitroglycerine nitrator operator 9232
nitroglycerine separator 9232
NMR spectroscopist 2112
NMR technician, chemical 2211
noise abatement engineer 2131
noise abatement technician 2231
non-government organization (NGO)
    manager 0314
non-registered electrocardiography
    technician 3217
nondestructive evaluation tester 2261
nondestructive examiner 2261
nondestructive inspector 2261
nondestructive test technician 2261
nondestructive tester (NDT) 2261
nose specialist 3111
notary in partnership (Quebec) 4112
notary public, British Columbia 4211
notary public (outside Quebec) 4211
notary, Quebec 4112
notcher operator – woodworking 9513
novelist 5121
novelties designer 5243
novelties sales representative –
    wholesale 6411
novelty shoe lacer – footwear
    manufacturing 9498
novice – religion 4217
nozzle worker – pile driving 7611
nuclear chemist 2112
nuclear control room operator 7352
nuclear design engineer 2132
nuclear engineer 2132
nuclear engineering technician 2232
nuclear engineering technologist 2232
nuclear fuel processor 9231
nuclear generating station operator –
    electric power systems 7352
nuclear magnetic resonance
    spectroscopist 2112
nuclear medicine clinical co-ordinator 3215
nuclear medicine specialist 3111
nuclear medicine technician 3215
nuclear medicine technologist 3215
nuclear operations engineer 2132
nuclear physician 3111

nuclear physicist **2111**
nuclear power station machinery
   mechanic **7311**
nuclear reactor control room operator –
   electric power systems **7352**
nuclear reactor operator – electric power
   systems **7352**
nuclear reactor physicist **2111**
nuclear technologist **2232**
nucleonic controller repairer **2243**
nucleonics instrument assembler **9483**
nuisance control trapper **7444**
numbering machine operator – printing **9473**
numerical control drilling machine
   operator **9511**
numerical control machine tool operator **9511**
numerical control tool programmer **2233**
numismatist **0621**
nun **4217**
nurse **3152**
nurse aide **3413**
nurse clinician **3152**
nurse, dental **3222**
nurse, geriatric **3152**
nurse/midwife **3232**
nurse (non-supervisory) – military **3152**
nurse practitioner **3152**
nurse (supervisor) – military **3151**
nurse technician **3152**
nursemaid – domestic **6474**
nursery aide – hospital **3413**
nursery farmer **8254**
nursery foreman/woman **8256**
nursery manager **8254**
nursery operator **8254**
nursery school aide **6473**
nursery school helper **6473**
nursery school teacher **4214**
nursery supervisor **8256**
nursery technician, forestry **2223**
nursery worker **8432**
nursery worker, crew chief **8256**
nurseryman/woman **8254**
nurses' association executive director **0314**
nursing administrator **0311**
nursing advisor **3152**
nursing assistant, non-registered **3413**
nursing assistant, registered **3233**
nursing attendant **3413**
nursing care co-ordinator **3151**
nursing consultant **3152**
nursing counsellor **3152**
nursing evaluator **3152**
nursing home attendant **3413**
nursing home inspector **2263**
nursing instructor – community college **4131**
nursing orderly **3413**
nursing professor – university **4121**

nursing registry manager **0123**
nursing registry supervisor **1211**
nursing researcher **3152**
nursing service aide **3413**
nursing services director **0311**
nursing sister **3152**
nursing supervisor **3151**
nursing unit administrator **3151**
nursing unit co-ordinator **3151**
nursing unit supervisor **3151**
nursing vice president – health **0014**
nut and bolt packer **9612**
nut maker, metal **9516**
nut mixer operator **9461**
nut roasting equipment operator **9461**
nut sorter – food and beverage
   processing **9617**
nutrition and dietetics researcher **3132**
nutritional chemist **2112**
nutritionist **3132**

O

oar maker – woodworking **9513**
oats miller **9461**
observer, fisheries **2224**
observer helper – gravity prospecting **8615**
observer helper – seismic prospecting **8615**
observer, seismic prospecting **2212**
obstetrical nursing supervisor **3151**
obstetrician **3111**
obstetrician/gynaecologist **3111**
obstetrics/gynaecology, chief of **0311**
obstetrics nurse **3152**
occasional teacher – elementary school **4142**
occupational analyst **1122**
occupational counsellor **4213**
occupational health and safety manager **0112**
occupational health consultant – nurse **3152**
occupational health director **0311**
occupational health nurse **3152**
occupational health officer **2263**
occupational health physician **3112**
occupational health supervisor **2263**
occupational hygienist **4161**
occupational medicine specialist **3111**
occupational physician **3111**
occupational safety inspector **2263**
occupational safety officer **2263**
occupational supply analyst **4164**
occupational therapist **3143**
occupational therapy aide **6631**
occupational therapy, chief of **0311**
occupational therapy, director of **0311**
occupational therapy helper **6631**
occupational therapy technician **6631**
ocean and lake container transportation
   sales representative **6411**

ocean engineer **2131**
ocean freight co-ordinator **1215**
ocean freight manager **0713**
ocean freight technician **1215**
oceanographer **2113**
oceanographic chemist **2112**
oceanographic operator – military **6464**
oceanographic research director **0212**
oceanography professor – university **4121**
ocular prosthetician **3219**
ocularist **3219**
ocularist apprentice **3219**
oculist **3111**
OD **3121**
odorization technician – chemical
    processing **9421**
off-the-road tire builder **9423**
offbearer – printing **9619**
offbearer, textile machine **9616**
office administration clerk **1441**
office administrator **1221**
office assistant **1411**
office auditor – taxation **1228**
office automation co-ordinator **1221**
office cashier **6611**
office chair assembler **9492**
office cleaner **6661**
office clerk **1411**
office clerk supervisor **1211**
office co-ordinator **1221**
office equipment purchasing manager **0113**
office equipment purchasing officer **1225**
office equipment sales representative –
    technical **6221**
office equipment sales representative –
    wholesale (non-technical) **6411**
office equipment salesperson – retail **6421**
office equipment service technician **2242**
office furniture sales representative –
    wholesale **6411**
office machine operators supervisor **1211**
office machine repairer **2242**
office machine repairer apprentice **2242**
office machine repairers
    foreman/woman **7216**
office manager **1221**
office messenger **1463**
office nurse **3152**
office receptionist **1414**
office services co-ordinator **1221**
office space planner **5242**
office supervisor, clerical **1211**
office supplies store manager **0621**
officer, account – banking **1232**
officer, adjudication – immigration **1228**
officer, adjudication – unemployment
    insurance **1228**
officer, adult education program **4166**

officer, band council **4168**
officer, by-law enforcement **6463**
officer, commercial development –
    government **4163**
officer, community relations – police **6261**
officer, conservation **2224**
officer, corporate security **6465**
officer, court **1227**
officer, credit **1232**
officer, deck – water transport **2273**
officer, economic development –
    government **4163**
officer, election commission **4168**
officer, engineer – water transport **2274**
officer, environmental health **2263**
officer, federal-provincial relations **4168**
officer, financial control **1111**
officer, fishery **2224**
officer, foreign service **4168**
officer, game **2224**
officer, health care planning **4165**
officer, health policy development **4165**
officer, house of commons committee **4168**
officer, human rights **4164**
officer, immigration **1228**
officer, immigration and demographic
    analysis **4164**
officer-in-charge, weather station **2213**
officer, industrial development –
    government **4163**
officer, infection control – hospital **3152**
officer, intergovernmental affairs **4168**
officer, investigations – postal service **6465**
officer, legislative committee **4168**
officer, legislative council **4168**
officer, loan **1232**
officer, mortgage **1232**
officer, municipal law enforcement **6463**
officer, navigation – water transport **2273**
officer, occupational safety **2263**
officer, office of the speaker **4168**
officer, official languages commission **4168**
officer, official languages education **4166**
officer, organization and methods **1122**
officer, postal inspection **6465**
officer, premier's office **4168**
officer, prime minister's office **4168**
officer, privy council office **4168**
officer, protocol **4168**
officer, public inquiry **4168**
officer, public relations **5124**
officer, regional council **4168**
officer, regional economic development
    agency **4163**
officer, royal commission **4168**
officer, rulings – taxation **1111**
officer, security analysis – postal
    service **6465**

officer, senate committee **4168**
officer, standing or select committee **4168**
officer, task force **4168**
officer, taxation **1228**
officer, territorial council **4168**
officer, tourism development –
    government **4163**
officer, tribunal **4168**
officer, unemployment insurance **1228**
officer, unemployment insurance policy
    analysis **4164**
official languages co-ordinator **1221**
official languages manager **0112**
official languages promotion officer **4168**
offline printing and finishing machine
    operator **9471**
offset duplicating machine operator **9471**
offset lithographic platemaker **9472**
offset lithographic proof press operator –
    printing **7381**
offset lithography foreman/woman –
    printing **7218**
offset multilith operator – printing **9471**
offset press foreman/woman – printing **7218**
offset press operator – printing **7381**
offset pressman/woman – printing **7381**
offset printer **7381**
offshore diver **7372**
offshore driller **8232**
offshore drilling rig superintendent **8222**
oil and gas field production manager **0811**
oil and gas law clerk **4211**
oil and gas legal assistant **4211**
oil and gas paralegal **4211**
oil and gas production engineer **2145**
oil and solid full heating mechanic **7331**
oil blender **9232**
oil burner installer **7331**
oil burner installer/maintainer
    apprentice **7331**
oil burner maintainer **7331**
oil burner maintainer helper **7612**
oil burner mechanic **7331**
oil burner mechanic apprentice **7331**
oil burner mechanic helper **7612**
oil burner servicer **7331**
oil burner technician **7331**
oil changer – motor vehicle service **7443**
oil clarifier tender – food and beverage
    processing **9461**
oil controller **9232**
oil dispatcher **9232**
oil distributor **6411**
oil exploration test equipment repairer **2241**
oil field pumper **9232**
oil filter assembler **9498**
oil furnace installer **7331**
oil lease broker **1236**

oil painter **5136**
oil pipe inspector **2261**
oil pipe tester **2261**
oil pipeline pumpman/woman **9232**
oil pump station mechanic **7311**
oil refiner **9232**
oil refinery equipment sales
    representative **6221**
oil spreader operator – public works **7422**
oil tool maintenance mechanic **7311**
oil tool repairer **7311**
oil transport driver **7411**
oil well cementer – oil field services **8412**
oil well drilling manager **0811**
oil well equipment design engineer **2132**
oil well logging engineer **2145**
oil well perforator **8232**
oil well service dispatcher **1475**
oil well services field supervisor **8222**
oil well services sales engineer **6221**
oil well servicing manager **0811**
oiler and greaser – crane and dragline **7443**
oiler, heavy truck **7443**
oiler, industrial machinery **7612**
oiler, marine **7434**
oiler, stationary engine **7612**
ombudsman – government services **0012**
on-line realtime systems programmer **2163**
oncologist **3111**
oncologist, pediatric **3111**
oncology nurse **3152**
oncology technologist **3215**
oncology technologist, radiation therapy **3215**
open end spinner – textiles **9441**
open end technician – textile
    manufacturing **7317**
open hearth furnace foreman/woman **9211**
open hearth furnace helper – primary
    metal processing **9611**
open hearth furnace labourer – primary
    metal processing **9611**
open hearth furnace operator **9231**
open pit blaster **7372**
open pit driller **7372**
opener tender – textiles **9441**
opening and blending operator – textiles **9441**
opening machine feeder – rubber
    products manufacturing **9615**
opera company director **0512**
opera singer **5133**
operating engineer, heavy equipment **7421**
operating engineer, stationary **7351**
operating room aide **3413**
operating room assistant (medical
    laboratory technician) – military **3212**
operating room assistant – military **3233**
operating room assistant (supporting
    health services) – military **3414**

operating room head nurse **3151**

operating room nurse **3152**

operating room supervisor – nursing **3151**

operating room technician – nursing **3233**

operating systems programmer **2163**

operating technician – chemical processing **9232**

operational meteorologist **2114**

operations and transmission services manager – telecommunications **0131**

operations co-ordinator, property management **1224**

operations director, transport **0713**

operations forester **2122**

operations manager, credit card company **0122**

operations manager, forestry **0811**

operations manager, maintenance **0722**

operations manager, manufacturing **0911**

operations manager, marine transportation **0713**

operations manager, publishing or broadcasting **0512**

operations manager, ship management **0713**

operations manager, telecommunications **0131**

operations officer, administration **1221**

operations research analyst **2161**

operations research technologist **2233**

operations researcher **2161**

operations technician, weather station **2213**

operations vice president – financial, communications and other business services **0013**

operations vice president – goods production, utilities, transportation and construction **0016**

operations vice president – health, education, social and community services and membership organizations **0014**

operations vice president – trade, broadcasting and other services n.e.c. **0015**

operator, amusement ride **6443**

operator, asphalt plant **7421**

operator/assembler, electrical appliances **9484**

operator, bindery **9473**

operator, bleaching range – textiles **9443**

operator, boiler **7351**

operator, bookbinding machine **9473**

operator, bus **7412**

operator, cable yarding **8241**

operator, capacitor assembly **9483**

operator, carbon press **9411**

operator, catalytic conversion **9232**

operator, chainsaw – logging **8421**

operator, chemical process unit **9232**

operator, chemical processing machine **9421**

operator, chlorination plant **9232**

operator, coating machine – pulp and paper **9234**

operator, coke oven door **9411**

operator, computer **1421**

operator, computer peripheral equipment **1421**

operator, console **1421**

operator dryer and cooler – tobacco processing **9464**

operator, dyeing range – textiles **9443**

operator – electrical equipment manufacturing **9487**

operator, electrical power system **7352**

operator, elevator **6683**

operator, feller buncher **8241**

operator, ferris wheel **6443**

operator, finishing range – textiles **9443**

operator, fish culture **8257**

operator, fish farm **8257**

operator, fish hatchery **8257**

operator, fork lift truck **7452**

operator, forming room – electrical equipment manufacturing **9487**

operator, forwarder – logging **8241**

operator, fun house **6443**

operator, games booth **6443**

operator, gas field **9232**

operator, hand truck **7452**

operator, head saw – sawmill **9431**

operator, heavy construction equipment **7421**

operator, heavy water chemical process **9232**

operator, integrated circuit assembly **9483**

operator – liquid waste treatment plant **9424**

operator, log loading machine **8241**

operator, logging machinery **8241**

operator, lumber kiln **9434**

operator, machine – electrical equipment manufacturing **9487**

operator, master console **1421**

operator, mechanical harvester – logging **8241**

operator, mixer – chemical processing **9421**

operator, network **1421**

operator, palletizer **7452**

operator, paper converting machine **9435**

operator, paper machine **9234**

operator, peripheral **1421**

operator, petroleum refinery **9232**

operator, planer – sawmill **9431**

operator, planer – woodworking **9513**

operator, plywood press **9434**

operator, power station – electric power systems **7352**

operator, press – electrical equipment manufacturing **9487**

operator, ready-mix concrete – cement
    manufacturing **9411**
operator, resaw – sawmill **9431**
operator, sawing machine –
    woodworking **9513**
operator, sewage plant **9424**
operator, shooting gallery **6443**
operator, skidder – logging **8421**
operator, slasher – logging **8241**
operator, snowmaking equipment **6671**
operator, steam plant **7351**
operator, steel spar **8241**
operator, streetcar **7412**
operator, subway **7412**
operator, switchboard **1414**
operator, system **1421**
operator, tamper **7611**
operator, telephone answering service **1414**
operator, telephone system **1424**
operator, test desk –
    telecommunications **7246**
operator, transfer and turntable –
    railway **7431**
operator, urban transit **7412**
operator, waste water treatment plant **9424**
operator, water purification plant **9424**
operator, water treatment plant **9424**
operator, woodworking machine **9513**
operator, word processor **1412**
ophthalmic assistant **3235**
ophthalmic dispenser **3231**
ophthalmic lab technician – retail **3414**
ophthalmic lens bench worker **3414**
ophthalmic lens cutter **3414**
ophthalmic lens grinder **3414**
ophthalmic lens grinder and polisher **3414**
ophthalmic lens inspector **3414**
ophthalmic medical assistant **3235**
ophthalmic medical technician **3235**
ophthalmic medical technologist **3235**
ophthalmic technician **3235**
ophthalmic technologist **3235**
ophthalmological technician **3235**
ophthalmologist **3111**
ophthalmology, chief of **0311**
opinion polling statistician **2161**
optical dispensary manager **0621**
optical dispenser **3231**
optical draftsman/woman **2253**
optical element cleaner **9619**
optical element coater –
    non-prescription **9517**
optical glass etcher **9517**
optical goods driller – non-prescription **9517**
optical goods prescription clerk **1472**
optical instrument assembler **9498**
optical instruments assembly
    foreman/woman **9227**

optical lab technician – retail **3414**
optical mechanic **3414**
optical mirror coater operator **9517**
optical spectroscopist **2112**
optical systems engineer –
    telecommunications **2133**
optical technician **3414**
optician **3231**
optician, dispensing **3231**
optician's apprentice **3231**
optician, student **3231**
opticopy keypunch operator – printing **9472**
opticopy machine operator – printing **9472**
opticopy offline programmer – printing **9472**
opticopy program tape preparer –
    printing **9472**
optics physicist **2111**
optics technologist **2241**
options trader **1113**
optometric technician **6631**
optometrist **3121**
optometrist assistant **6631**
optometry, doctor of **3121**
oral and maxillofacial surgeon **3113**
oral pathologist **3113**
oral radiologist **3113**
oral surgeon **3113**
orator **5135**
orchard worker **8431**
orchestra conductor **5132**
orchestrator **5132**
order clerk **1441**
order filler **6622**
order picker **6622**
order typist **1412**
orderly **3413**
ordinary seaman/woman **7433**
ore buyer **6233**
ore crushing equipment operator **9411**
ore crushing helper – primary metal and
    mineral products processing **9611**
ore drier operator **9411**
ore grinding equipment operator **9411**
ore milling foreman/woman **9211**
ore milling machine operator **9411**
ore milling supervisor **9211**
ore processing equipment mechanic **7311**
ore processing equipment repairer
    helper **7612**
ore processing labourer – primary metal
    and mineral products processing **9611**
ore roaster **9411**
ore sample tester – primary metal and
    mineral products processing **9415**
ore sampler – primary metal and mineral
    products processing **9415**
ore screener **9411**

ore separator – primary metal and
   mineral products processing **9411**
orepass tender – underground mining **8411**
organ pipe maker, metal **9516**
organ tuner **7445**
organic chemist **2112**
organic mass spectroscopist **2112**
organist **5133**
organization and methods analyst
   supervisor **1122**
organization and methods officer **1122**
organization and methods researcher **1122**
organizational analysis consultant **1122**
organizational analyst **1122**
organizational methods analysis director **0123**
organizational methods analysis
   manager **0123**
organizational planning and
   development director **0123**
organizational psychologist **4151**
organizer, special events **1226**
organometallic chemist **2112**
oriental medical practitioner **3232**
oriental rug repairer **7445**
orientation and mobility instructor **4215**
ornamental caster – foundry **9412**
ornamental glass production worker **9413**
ornamental iron erector helper **7611**
ornamental iron worker **7264**
ornamental ironwork apprentice **7264**
ornamental metal worker helper **7611**
ornamental metal worker – metal
   fabrication **9514**
ornamental plasterer **7284**
ornamenter – furniture finishing and
   refinishing **9494**
ornithological technician **2221**
ornithological technologist **2221**
ornithologist **2121**
ornithology curator **5112**
orthodontic band maker **3412**
orthodontic technician **3223**
orthodontist **3113**
orthopaedic apparel assembler **3219**
orthopaedic assistant **3414**
orthopaedic mechanic **3219**
orthopaedic physician assistant **3414**
orthopaedic shoe repairman/woman **7343**
orthopaedic shoe salesperson **6421**
orthopaedic shoemaker **7343**
orthopaedic surgeon **3111**
orthopaedic technician **3414**
orthopaedic technologist **3414**
orthopaedist **3111**
orthoptist **3123**
orthotic technician **3219**
orthotist **3219**
osteopath **3123**

osteopathic physician **3123**
osteopathy, doctor of **3123**
OT **3143**
otolaryngologist **3111**
otologist **3111**
otorhinolaryngologist **3111**
ottertrawl fisherman/woman **8262**
outboard motor assembler **9486**
outboard motor assembly
   foreman/woman **9226**
outboard motor inspector and tester **9486**
outboard motor installer **9491**
outboard motor mechanic **7335**
outboard motor mechanic apprentice **7335**
outboard motor prototype tester **9486**
outdoor illuminating engineer **2133**
outfitter **6442**
outfitting guide **6442**
outplacement consultant **4213**
outplacement counsellor **4213**
outplacement relocation specialist **4213**
outpost nurse **3152**
outreach counsellor **4213**
outreach program co-ordinator **4213**
outreach program counsellor **4213**
outside-plant engineer **2133**
oven loader – chemical processing **9613**
oven operator, electrodes **9421**
oven operator – food and beverage
   processing **9461**
oven tender **9496**
overcaster – garment manufacturing **9451**
overhaul planner **1473**
overhauler, textile machine **7317**
overhead crane operator **7371**
overhead distribution engineer **2133**
overhead door installer **7441**
overlock sewing machine operator **9451**
overseamer – garment manufacturing **9451**
oxidation operator, nitric acid **9232**
oxyacetylene cutter – metal fabrication **9514**
oxyacetylene welder **7265**
oxygen furnace foreman/woman –
   primary metal and mineral products
   processing **9211**
oxygen furnace operator – primary metal
   processing **9231**
oxygen plant operator **9232**
oxygen therapist **3214**
oxygen therapy technician **3214**
oxygen therapy technologist **3214**
oxyhydrogen welder **7265**
oyster canner – fish processing **9463**
oyster culture technician **2221**
oyster farmer **8257**
oyster grower **8257**
oyster picker **8613**
oyster shucker – fish processing **9463**

oyster washer tender – fish processing **9463**
oyster worker **8613**

P

P Ag **2123**
pacemaker assembler – electronics
    manufacturing **9483**
pack boy/girl **6622**
package designer **2252**
package lift operator **7452**
package underwriter **1234**
packager, aircraft parts **9619**
packager, bakery products **9617**
packager, hand **7452**
packager, laundry and dry cleaning **6681**
packager, machine **9619**
packager, poultry **9617**
packaging container designer **2252**
packaging machine adjuster **9461**
packaging machine mechanic **7311**
packaging machine operator – chemical
    processing **9421**
packaging manufacturing plant manager **0911**
packaging supervisor – food and
    beverage processing **9213**
packaging tester **9498**
packer, fruit – agriculture **8611**
packer, liquid **9617**
packer, vegetable – agriculture **8611**
packing machine setup operator **9461**
pad extractor tender – textiles **9443**
pad gluer, machine – paper converting **9435**
padded dashboard maker – plastic
    manufacturing **9495**
padding cutter **9619**
padding labourer **9619**
padding machine operator – textiles **9442**
padding machine tender – textiles **9443**
paddle maker – woodworking **9513**
paddock judge – race track **5253**
paddock plater – race track **5253**
paediatric audiologist **3141**
paediatrician **3111**
paediatrics nurse **3152**
paedodontist **3113**
page **1463**
page compositor **1423**
page designer **5241**
page, library **1451**
paint baker, enamelware – glass
    products **9413**
paint baker, industrial **9496**
paint brush final assembler **9498**
paint control operator **9496**
paint dipper, industrial **9496**
paint finisher, industrial **9496**
paint maker **9421**

paint making foreman/woman **9212**
paint mixer **9421**
paint mixer, industrial **9496**
paint operator, industrial **9496**
paint plant labourer **9613**
paint processing foreman/woman **9212**
paint room attendant **9496**
paint salesperson **6421**
paint sprayer, industrial **9496**
paint sprayer operator **9496**
paint sprayer operator, automatic **9496**
paint store manager **0621**
paint stripper **9619**
paint systems attendant **9496**
paint systems operator **9496**
paint technician **2211**
paint varnish dipper/operator **9496**
painter, aircraft **9496**
painter and decorator **7294**
painter and decorator apprentice **7294**
painter and decorator helper **7611**
painter and paperhanger **7294**
painter, animation **5223**
painter, artistic **5136**
painter, automobile assembly **9496**
painter, boiler **9496**
painter – commercial construction **7294**
painter, construction **7294**
painter/decorator **7294**
painter, drum **9496**
painter, electrostatic **9496**
painter/finisher, production **9496**
painter foreman/woman, construction **7219**
painter foreman/woman, shipyard **9226**
painter/helper, construction **7611**
painter helper, shipyard **9619**
painter – industrial construction **7294**
painter, industrial construction
    apprentice **7294**
painter, industrial products **9496**
painter, locomotive **9496**
painter, maintenance **7294**
painter, motor and generator
    subassemblies **9496**
painter, motor vehicle repair **7322**
painter – residential construction **7294**
painter, shipyard **9496**
painter, sign **5223**
painter, traffic signs **5223**
painter, tumbling barrel **9496**
painting and wallpaper contractor **7219**
painting contractor **7219**
painting decorator **7219**
painting line tender, electrostatic **9496**
painting machine operator **9496**
painting machine tender **9496**
painting supervisor – construction **7219**
painting teacher **5136**

paintings conservator **5112**
paintings restorer **5112**
paintings restorer technician **5212**
paleobotanist **2113**
paleoecologist **2113**
paleontologist **2113**
paleontology technician **2212**
pallet maker, wood **9493**
palletizer **7452**
palletizer operator **7452**
palynologist **2113**
palynology technician **2212**
pan greaser – food and beverage
    processing **9617**
pan operator – food and beverage
    processing **9461**
panel coverer – furniture assembly **9619**
panel groover operator – wood
    processing **9434**
panel inspector – wood processing **9436**
panel instrument repairer, industrial **2243**
panel matcher **9493**
panel operator – chemical processing **9232**
panel raiser operator – woodworking **9513**
panel sanding machine operator – wood
    processing **9434**
panel saw operator – woodworking **9513**
panelboard assembler – industrial
    electric equipment **9485**
panelboard operator – primary metal and
    mineral products processing **9231**
panelboard operator – pulp and paper **9234**
pantograph burner – metal fabrication **9514**
pantograph engraver **5244**
pantograph flame cutter – metal
    fabrication **9514**
pantograph machine patternmaker **7261**
pantograph setter **9472**
pantographer **9472**
pantry worker – food and beverage
    processing **9461**
paper bag machine operator **9435**
paper bag machine tender **9435**
paper box machine operator **9435**
paper box machine tender **9435**
paper box maker – paper converting **9435**
paper boy/girl **1463**
paper coating machine operator **9234**
paper cone winder – paper converting **9435**
paper conservator **5112**
paper consultant, sales **6411**
paper converting machine operator **9435**
paper cup machine tender – paper
    converting **9435**
paper cutter – paper converting **9435**
paper feeder, press **9619**
paper finishing machine operator **9433**
paper foreman/woman – pulp and paper **9215**

paper grader **9433**
paper jogger operator – pulp and paper **9433**
paper lamp shade maker **9498**
paper latcher – construction **7611**
paper machine back tender **9234**
paper machine foreman/woman – pulp
    and paper **9215**
paper machine operator **9234**
paper machine tender **9234**
paper machine winderman/woman **9433**
paper maker **9234**
paper mill foreman/woman **9215**
paper mill manager **0911**
paper platemaker – printing **9472**
paper products inspector **9435**
paper punch press tender – paper
    converting **9435**
paper securities designer **5241**
paper sheet counter – printing **9619**
paper slitter operator **9435**
paper twister tender – paper converting **9435**
paperhanger **7294**
paperhanger helper **7611**
paperhanging contractor **7219**
paperhanging decorator **7219**
papermaker, hand **5244**
papermaking and finishing machine
    operator **9433**
parachute folder **9619**
parachute inspector – fabric products **9454**
parachute stringer **9498**
paralegal **4211**
paramedic **3234**
paramedical equipment repairer **2241**
parasitologist **2121**
parasitologist, veterinary **3114**
parcel checker **6683**
parcel post clerk **1461**
parcel processing plant manager **0132**
parchment lamp shade maker **9498**
parent, foster **6471**
parent's helper **6474**
parent therapist **4153**
parish priest **4154**
park attendant **6671**
park caretaker **8256**
park foreman/woman **8256**
park maintenance labourer **8612**
park naturalist **2121**
park planner, municipal **2153**
park ranger **2224**
park receptionist **6671**
park section head, arboriculture **8256**
park superintendent – government
    services **0412**
park supervisor, grounds maintenance **8256**
park worker **8612**
parking co-ordinator **1221**

parking control officer **6463**
parking garage operator **0621**
parking lot attendant **6683**
parking lot operator **0621**
parking lot supervisor **6216**
parking meter collector **7621**
parking meter repairer **7445**
parking meter servicer **7445**
parking valet **6683**
parks administration director **0412**
parks and recreation forester **2122**
parliamentary assistant **1222**
parole board chairman **0012**
parole officer **4155**
parole supervisor **4155**
parquetry floor layer **7295**
particle board foreman/woman **9215**
particle board forming machine operator **9434**
particle board grader – wood processing **9436**
particle board line operator **9434**
particle board press line operator **9434**
particle board sizing saw tender **9434**
partition assembly machine operator –
  paper converting **9435**
partition slotter machine tender – paper
  converting **9435**
parts and assemblies typewriter
  inspector **9483**
parts clerk **1472**
parts clerks supervisor **1215**
parts counter clerk – retail **1472**
parts lister **1472**
parts manager – retail **0621**
parts supervisor **1215**
parts supplier **1472**
parts technician **1472**
partsperson **1472**
party chief, land surveying **2154**
passenger agent, airline **6433**
passenger agent (except airline) **6434**
passenger and freight rates analyst **1114**
passenger attendant, cruise line **6672**
passenger attendant, ship **6672**
passenger bias tire builder **9423**
passenger elevator operator **6683**
passenger operations manager, railway **0713**
passenger sales agent, airline **6433**
passenger service director **6432**
passenger ship captain **2273**
passenger tire builder **9423**
passenger train brakeman/woman **7362**
passenger train conductor **7362**
passenger train engineer **7361**
passport clerk **1441**
passport issuer **1441**
pasta chef **6241**
pasta maker **9461**
paste-up artist **5223**

pasteurizer operator – food and beverage
  processing **9461**
pasting machine operator – electrical
  equipment manufacturing **9487**
pastor **4154**
pastoral animator **4217**
pastoral associate officer – military **4217**
pastry chef **6241**
pastry cook **6242**
pastry cook's helper **9617**
pastry wrapper **9617**
pasture managing supervisor **8253**
patcher, laundry and dry cleaning **6681**
patcher operator – wood processing **9434**
patcher, wooden door **9493**
patching machine operator – laundry and
  dry cleaning **6681**
patent agent **4161**
patent agent, registered **4161**
patent counsel **4112**
patent lawyer **4112**
patent searcher **4161**
patent solicitor **4112**
pathologist, anatomical **3111**
pathologist, animal **2121**
pathologist, clinical **3111**
pathologist, forensic **3111**
pathologist, forest **2121**
pathologist, general **3111**
pathologist, hematological **3111**
pathologist, language **3141**
pathologist, medical **3111**
pathologist, oral **3113**
pathologist, plant **2121**
pathologist, post-mortem **3111**
pathologist, speech **3141**
pathologist, speech – language **3141**
pathologist, surgical **3111**
pathologist, veterinary **3114**
pathologists' assistant **3211**
pathology assistant **3211**
pathology, chief of **0311**
pathology technician **3211**
patient billing clerk **1431**
patient care aide **3413**
patient care co-ordinator – nursing **3151**
patio builder **7441**
patio installer **7441**
patissier/pastry chef **6241**
patrol judge – race track **5253**
patrol officer – police **6261**
patrol officer, traffic **6261**
patrol pilot **2271**
patroller – textiles **9442**
patrolman/woman, pipeline **7442**
patrolman/woman, security **6651**
pattern card preparer – textiles **9442**
pattern changer, jacquard looms **9442**

pattern cutter **9452**
pattern designer and pattern maker, canvas goods **5245**
pattern designer and patternmaker – textile, leather and fur products **5245**
pattern engineer **2132**
pattern illustrator **2253**
pattern modifier – textile, leather and fur products **5245**
pattern moulder – foundry **9412**
pattern perforating machine operator **5245**
pattern puncher – textiles **9442**
pattern repairman – foundry **7271**
pattern setter, braid **7317**
pattern weaver **9442**
patternmaker and upholsterer, aircraft **7341**
patternmaker – envelopes **7383**
patternmaker, metal **7232**
patternmaker, metal apprentice **7232**
patternmaker, metal furniture **7261**
patternmaker, pantograph machine **7261**
patternmaker, plaster – aircraft **7383**
patternmaker, shoe **5245**
patternmaker – textile, leather and fur products **5245**
patternmaker/upholsterer **7341**
patternmaker, wood **7272**
patternmarker – fabric products **5245**
patternshop foreman/woman – machining **7211**
pavement line painter **7611**
pavement striper **7611**
paver operator **7421**
paving and stone block maker – concrete and stone products **9414**
paving contractor **7217**
paving equipment mechanic **7312**
paving gang road boss **7217**
paving inspector, road **2264**
pawnbroker **0621**
pay accounts clerk **1432**
pay advisor **1432**
pay and benefits administrator **1432**
pay and benefits clerk **1432**
pay and benefits manager **0112**
pay and benefits supervisor **1212**
pay clerk **1432**
pay verifier **1432**
payloader operator **7421**
paymaster **1212**
payment entry clerk **1422**
payment processing unit supervisor **1212**
payroll clerk **1432**
payroll machine operator **1432**
payroll officer **1432**
payroll service manager **0123**
payroll supervisor **1212**

PBX & PABX inspector – telecommunications **7246**
PBX & PABX installer – telecommunications **7246**
PBX & PABX repairer – telecommunications **7246**
PCA clerk – financial sector **1434**
PCB fabrication inspector **9483**
PCB fabrication machine operator **9483**
PCB in-circuit test machine and repair operator **9483**
peace activist **4164**
peace officer **6261**
peace researcher **4164**
peanut blanching machine tender **9461**
peanut butter maker **9461**
pearl cutter **7344**
pearl ear ring maker **9498**
pearl maker **9498**
pearl setter **7344**
peat bog manager **0811**
peat digger **7612**
peat moss cutter, hand **7612**
peat moss cutting machine operator **7421**
peat moss dehydrator tender **9411**
peat moss gatherer, hydraulic **7421**
peat moss gathering machine operator **7421**
pedestal drill operator **9511**
pediatric audiologist **3141**
pediatric dentist **3113**
pediatric echocardiographer **3216**
pediatric general surgeon **3111**
pediatric oncologist **3111**
pediatrician **3111**
pediatrics, chief of **0311**
pedicurist **6482**
pedologist **2115**
pellet grinder – metal fabrication **9612**
pellet maker – foundry **9412**
pellet mill worker – food and beverage processing **9617**
pellet press tender – primary metal processing **9411**
pellet segregator – primary metal processing **9411**
pelletizer, plastics **9421**
pelt dresser **9453**
pelt dyer – hide and pelt processing **9453**
pelt grader – hide and pelt processing **9454**
pelt processing worker **9453**
pelt shearer **9453**
pelt stretcher – hide and pelt processing **9453**
pen and pencil assembler **9498**
pen and pencil inspector **9498**
pencil grooving machine tender **9513**
pencil maker operator **9517**
pencil making machine setter **9517**
pencil making machine tender **9517**

pencil rounding machine tender **9513**
pencil tipping machine feeder **9619**
penologist **4169**
penrider **8431**
pension plan administrator **0111**
pension plan clerk – insurance **1434**
pension services manager **0111**
perch operator – textiles **9444**
percher – textiles **9444**
percussion instrument repairer **7445**
percussionist **5133**
perfect binder machine operator –
    printing **9473**
perfect binder setup operator **9473**
perforating machine tender – printing **9473**
perforator helper – oil field services **8615**
perforator, oil well **8232**
perforator operator – printing **9473**
performance artist **5136**
performance controller **2262**
performing arts administrator **0114**
perfume maker **9421**
perfusionist **3214**
periodic kiln operator – clay products **9414**
periodic kilnman/woman – clay
    products **9414**
periodicals clerk – library **1451**
periodicals librarian **5111**
periodicals sales representative **6411**
periodontist **3113**
peripheral operator **1421**
perlite expander control operator –
    mineral products processing **9231**
permanent mould operator – foundry **9412**
permastone installer **7281**
permission manager, publishing **0512**
permit clerk **1441**
personal aide **6471**
personal banking account officer **1232**
personal banking representative **1232**
personal banking vice president –
    banking **0013**
personal care attendant **3413**
personal computer salesperson – retail **6421**
personal financial planner **1114**
personal image consultant **6481**
personal image counsellor **6481**
personal improvement consultant **6481**
personal lines clerk – insurance **1434**
personal loans officer **1232**
personal secretary **1241**
personal servant **6683**
personal shopper **6623**
personal skills instructor **4212**
personal style co-ordinator **6481**
personal trust manager **0122**
personal trust officer **1114**
personal wardrobe consultant **6481**

personnel administration manager **0112**
personnel administration officer
    (administrative) – military **1221**
personnel administration officer
    (management) – military **0114**
personnel administrator **1223**
personnel advisor **1223**
personnel agency manager **0123**
personnel assistant **1442**
personnel clerk **1442**
personnel clerks supervisor **1211**
personnel consulting service manager **0123**
personnel interviewer **1223**
personnel manager **0112**
personnel officer **1223**
personnel recruiter **1223**
personnel research officer **1121**
personnel selection officer **1223**
personnel selection officer – military **1223**
personnel services clerk **1442**
personnel services manager **0112**
personnel standards officer **1121**
personnel supervisor **1223**
personnel training and development
    manager **0112**
personnel vice president – financial,
    communications and other business
    services **0013**
personnel vice president – goods
    production, utilities, transportation
    and construction **0016**
personnel vice president – health,
    education, social and community
    services and membership
    organizations **0014**
personnel vice president – trade,
    broadcasting and other services
    n.e.c. **0015**
pest control operator **7444**
pest control representative **7444**
pest control service manager **0651**
pest control technician **7444**
pest controller **7444**
pest fumigator **7444**
pesticide mixer **9421**
pet food cook – food and beverage
    processing **9461**
pet groomer **6483**
pet grooming salon manager **0651**
pet sitter **6483**
pet sitting service manager **0651**
pet store manager **0621**
pet store salesperson **6421**
petrochemical engineer **2134**
petrochemical engineering technician **2211**
petrochemical engineering technologist **2211**
petrochemical laboratory technologist **2211**
petrographer **2113**

petroleum chemist **2112**
petroleum distribution manager **0912**
petroleum engineer **2145**
petroleum engineer, completion **2145**
petroleum engineer, drilling and recovery **2145**
petroleum engineer, production **2145**
petroleum engineering technician **2212**
petroleum engineering technologist **2212**
petroleum field technologist **2212**
petroleum geologist **2113**
petroleum geology department manager **0212**
petroleum geology technologist **2212**
petroleum process operator **9232**
petroleum processing foreman/woman **9212**
petroleum products sales representative **6411**
petroleum refiner **9232**
petroleum refineries process engineer **2134**
petroleum refinery labourer **9613**
petroleum research technologist **2211**
petroleum reservoir engineer **2145**
petroleum technician **2212**
petrologist **2113**
petrology technician **2212**
petrophysicist **2113**
pharmaceutical bacteriologist **2121**
pharmaceutical buyer **6233**
pharmaceutical chemist **2112**
pharmaceutical compounding foreman/woman **9212**
pharmaceutical inspector **2211**
pharmaceutical operator **9232**
pharmaceutical processing operator **9232**
pharmaceutical sales representative **6221**
pharmaceutical salesperson **6221**
pharmaceuticals and toiletries inspector **2211**
pharmaceuticals and toiletries inspector supervisor **9212**
pharmacist **3131**
pharmacist consultant **3131**
pharmacist – military **3131**
pharmacological chemist **2112**
pharmacologist, clinical **3111**
pharmacologist (except clinical and veterinary) **2121**
pharmacologist, veterinary **3114**
pharmacy aide **3414**
pharmacy assistant **3414**
pharmacy, chief of **0311**
pharmacy clerk **6421**
pharmacy department manager **3131**
pharmacy, director **0311**
pharmacy manager **3131**
pharmacy professor – university **4121**
pharmacy supply assistant **3414**
pharmacy technical assistant **3414**
pharmacy technician **3414**
philatelist **0621**

philologist **4169**
philosopher **4169**
philosophy professor – university **4121**
phonograph record inspector **9495**
photo archivist **5113**
photo cartographer **2255**
photo developer **9474**
photo developer printer **9474**
photo editor **5122**
photo finisher **9474**
photo finishing equipment repairer **7445**
photo lab technician **9474**
photo processor **9474**
photo stencil maker **5223**
photo technician **9474**
photo tracer burner – metal fabrication **9514**
photocomposing machine tender **1423**
photocopy machine technician **2242**
photocopy operator, colour **9471**
photoelectric sorting machine repairer **2242**
photoengraver – printing **9472**
photoengraving etcher – printing **9472**
photoengraving plate finisher – printing **9472**
photoengraving platemaker – printing **9472**
photogeologist **2113**
photogrammetric engineer **2131**
photogrammetric technician **2255**
photogrammetric technologist **2255**
photogrammetrist **2255**
photograph developer **9474**
photograph enlarger **9474**
photograph filer – library **1451**
photograph inspector **9474**
photograph mounter **9474**
photograph retoucher **5223**
photographer **5221**
photographer's assistant **6683**
photographer's helper **6683**
photographic aide **6683**
photographic airbrush artist **5223**
photographic and film processing supervisor **7218**
photographic colourist **5223**
photographic equipment and supplies salesperson **6421**
photographic equipment assembler **9498**
photographic equipment assembly inspector **9498**
photographic film processor **9474**
photographic printer **9474**
photographic processor **9474**
photographic services, sales representative **6411**
photographic studio clerk **6421**
photographic studio manager **0621**
photographic technician – military **5221**
photographs conservator **5112**
photography equipment store manager **0621**

photography technician **5221**
photogravure camera operator – printing **9472**
photojournalist **5221**
photomicrographer **5221**
photoresist printer – electronics manufacturing **9483**
phototypesetter **1423**
phototypesetter operator **1423**
phototypesetter terminal operator **1423**
phrenologist **6484**
physiatrist **3111**
physical aerodynamicist **2111**
physical and health education teacher – secondary school **4141**
physical anthropologist **4169**
physical chemist **2112**
physical education and recreation instructor – military **5254**
physical education and recreation officer (director) – military **0513**
physical education and recreation officer (supervisor) – military **4167**
physical education co-ordinator – education **4166**
physical education programs director **0513**
physical education teacher – elementary school **4142**
physical education teacher – secondary school **4141**
physical geographer **4169**
physical medicine and rehabilitation specialist **3111**
physical metallurgical engineer **2142**
physical metallurgical technician **2212**
physical metallurgical technologist **2212**
physical metallurgist **2115**
physical oceanographer **2113**
physical rehabilitation technician **3235**
physical research chemist **2112**
physical science and engineering statistician **2161**
physical sciences professor – university **4121**
physical sciences program manager **0212**
physical therapist **3142**
physical therapy attendant **6631**
physical therapy officer – military **3142**
physical training director **0513**
physical training instructor **5254**
physician, community medicine **3112**
physician, community preventive medicine **3112**
physician, company **3112**
physician, emergency **3111**
physician, family **3112**
physician, general practice **3112**
physician, homeopathic **3232**
physician, homoeopathic **3232**
physician, industrial **3112**

physician, occupational health **3112**
physician of infectious diseases **3111**
physician, osteopathic **3123**
physician's office nurse **3152**
physician, specialist **3111**
physician, sports medicine **3111**
physicist **2111**
physics professor – university **4121**
physics teacher – high school **4141**
physiological chemist **2112**
physiologist (except medical and veterinary) **2121**
physiologist, medical **3111**
physiologist, veterinary **3114**
physiology professor – university **4121**
physiotherapist **3142**
physiotherapy aide **6631**
physiotherapy attendant **6631**
physiotherapy, chief of **0311**
physiotherapy, director of **0311**
physiotherapy helper **6631**
physiotherapy supervisor **3142**
physiotherapy technician **3235**
phytopathologist **2121**
pianist **5133**
piano action adjuster **7445**
piano action assembler **9498**
piano action regulator **7445**
piano and organ bench worker **9498**
piano and organ refinisher **9494**
piano assembler **9498**
piano assembly inspector **9498**
piano back assembler **9498**
piano case assembler **9498**
piano repairer **7445**
piano subassembler **9498**
piano teacher **5133**
piano technician **7445**
piano tone regulator **7445**
piano tuner **7445**
pick remover – textiles **9616**
pick up machine operator **7452**
picker, fruit or vegetable **8611**
picker tender – textiles **9441**
picker – textiles **9441**
picking machine operator – textiles **9441**
pickle maker **9461**
pickler and dipper, jewellery **9619**
pickler – food and beverage processing **9461**
pickler – hide and pelt processing **9453**
pickler, meat **9461**
pickler operator helper **9619**
pickler operator – primary metal processing **9411**
pickling plant manager **0911**
pickling solution injector – food and beverage processing **9461**
pictorial artist **5136**

picture editor **5122**
picture enlarger – photographic processing **9474**
picture frame assembler – furniture and fixtures manufacturing **9492**
picture framer **5212**
picture framing consultant **6421**
picture tube assembler **9483**
picture tube screen aluminizer **9483**
picture tube tester – electronics manufacturing **9483**
pie dough roller **9461**
pie filling cooker **9461**
pie filling mixer **9461**
pie maker, machine **9461**
piece hauler – textiles **9616**
pieceworker – logging **8421**
pieceworker – silviculture **8422**
pier foreman/woman **7217**
piercing mill operator – primary metal processing **9411**
pig caster – primary metal processing **9411**
pig iron pourer **9411**
pile driver operator's helper **7611**
pile driver winch operator **7421**
pile driving chainman/woman **7611**
pile driving crane operator **7371**
pile fabric finisher **9443**
pile finishing machine tender – textiles **9443**
piler, pulpwood **8616**
piler – wood processing **9614**
pill maker operator **9517**
pilot, airline **2271**
pilot instructor **2271**
pilot – military **2271**
pilot plant foreman/woman – chemical processing **9212**
pilot plant technician **2211**
pilot plant technologist **2211**
pilot plant tender **9232**
pilot, remote sensing **2271**
pilot, ship **2273**
pin maker – metal products **9516**
pin maker – wood products **9513**
pin setter, bowling **6671**
pin setter – textile manufacturing **7317**
pinball machine driver/servicer **7414**
pinning machine operator – textiles **9442**
pipe aligner – pipeline construction **7611**
pipe bending machine operator – metal fabrication **9514**
pipe coater/painter **9496**
pipe coremaker – foundry **9412**
pipe doper, construction **7611**
pipe finisher – clay products **9414**
pipe fittings moulder – concrete products **9414**
pipe grader **9619**

pipe inspector **2261**
pipe installer, radiator **7252**
pipe insulator **7293**
pipe junction maker – concrete products **9414**
pipe laying contractor **7217**
pipe organ builder **5244**
pipe organ erector **7441**
pipe organ installer **7441**
pipe organ tuner and repairer **7445**
pipe spray painter **9496**
pipe tester – concrete products **9414**
pipe tester – nondestructive testing **2261**
pipe threader **9511**
pipe threading machine operator **9511**
pipefitter **7252**
pipefitter foreman/woman **7213**
pipefitter foreman/woman – ships **7213**
pipefitter helper – construction **7611**
pipefitter helper – shipbuilding **7612**
pipefitter, railway car and locomotive **7252**
pipefitter – shipbuilding **7252**
pipefitter/steamfitter **7252**
pipefitter/steamfitter apprentice **7252**
pipefitter, turbines **7252**
pipefitting contractor **7213**
pipelayer – construction **7611**
pipelayer, drainage systems **7611**
pipelayer irrigation **7611**
pipelayer operator **7421**
pipeline caulker **7611**
pipeline compressor station operator **9232**
pipeline construction inspector **2264**
pipeline construction manager **0711**
pipeline construction superintendent **0711**
pipeline construction supervisor **7217**
pipeline engineer, civil **2131**
pipeline foreman/woman **9212**
pipeline foreman/woman – construction **7217**
pipeline gauger **9232**
pipeline inspector **2261**
pipeline inspectors foreman/woman, construction **2264**
pipeline maintenance worker **7442**
pipeline manager **0912**
pipeline mandrel operator **7611**
pipeline patrol pilot **2271**
pipeline patrolman/woman **7442**
pipeline pump station operator **9232**
pipeline rehabilitation worker **7442**
pipeline service truck driver **7443**
pipeline surveyor **2154**
pipeline transport engineer **2134**
pipeline trouble shooter **7442**
pipeline welder **7265**
pipeline welder helper **7611**
pipeline worker – construction **7611**
pipeworker helper – underground mining **8614**

pipeworker – underground mining **8411**
piping draftsman/woman **2253**
piping engineer **2132**
piping sewing machine operator **9451**
piston and valve maker **9511**
pit boss **6443**
pit bottom worker **7611**
pit moulder – foundry **9412**
pizza cook **6242**
pizza delivery driver **7414**
placement officer **1223**
placer geologist **2113**
placing judge – race track **5253**
plain clothes officer **6261**
plane table operator – surveying **2254**
planer feeder – woodworking **9513**
planer grader – wood processing **9436**
planer mill grader – wood processing **9436**
planer operator – metal machining **9511**
planer operator – sawmill **9431**
planer operator – stone products **9414**
planer operator – woodworking **9513**
planer set-up operator – metal
    machining **9511**
planer – woodworking **9513**
planner, community recreation **2153**
planner, conference or event **1226**
planner, financial **1114**
planner, health care **4165**
planner, land use **2153**
planner, urban and regional **2153**
planning analyst, land use **2153**
planning co-ordinator, district health
    council program **4165**
planning consultant, health care **4165**
planning engineer, electrical systems **2133**
planning officer, administrative **1221**
planning officer, child care programs **4164**
planning officer, child health care
    programs **4165**
planning officer, health care **4165**
planning technician **2233**
planning vice-president – financial,
    communications and other business
    services **0013**
planning vice-president – goods
    production, utilities, transportation
    and construction **0016**
planning vice-president – health,
    education, social and community
    services and membership
    organizations **0014**
planning vice-president – trade,
    broadcasting and other services
    n.e.c. **0015**
plant accountant **1111**
plant breeder **2121**
plant breeding technician **2221**

plant care worker **8612**
plant carpenter **7271**
plant changer, manufacturing **7311**
plant cleaner **6663**
plant dispatcher **1475**
plant doctor **2225**
plant ecologist **2121**
plant electrician **7242**
plant engineer **2141**
plant engineer, electrical **2133**
plant equipment mechanic **7311**
plant gatekeeper **6651**
plant grower **8254**
plant guard **6651**
plant labourer – fish processing **9618**
plant layout technician **2233**
plant maintenance electrician **7242**
plant maintenance engineer, stationary **7351**
plant maintenance foreman/woman –
    manufacturing **7216**
plant maintenance mechanic **7311**
plant maintenance painter **7294**
plant maintenance superintendent **0722**
plant maintenance worker **6663**
plant manager, manufacturing **0911**
plant manager, plastic products
    manufacturing **0911**
plant manager – postal and courier
    service **0132**
plant manager – printing **0911**
plant manager, rubber products
    manufacturing **0911**
plant manager, sewage treatment **0912**
plant manager – telecommunications **0131**
plant nematologist **2121**
plant pathologist **2121**
plant pathology technician **2221**
plant pathology technologist **2221**
plant physiologist **2121**
plant population biologist **2121**
plant primary products inspector **2222**
plant products inspector **2222**
plant propagator **8432**
plant protection inspector **2222**
plant scientist **2121**
plant superintendent, manufacturing **0911**
plant superintendent – postal and courier
    service **0132**
plant taxonomist **2121**
plant tour guide **6441**
planting and cultivator contractor **8252**
planting crew foreman/woman **8211**
plantscape maintenance contractor **8255**
plantscape manager **8255**
plantscape technician **2225**
plasma physicist **2111**
plaster die maker **9414**
plaster model and mould maker **9414**

plaster moulder – dentures **3412**
plaster patternmaker – aircraft **7383**
plaster room attendant **3414**
plasterboard machine operator **9414**
plasterboard mixing machine tender **9414**
plasterer **7284**
plasterer apprentice **7284**
plasterer/decorator **7284**
plasterer, finish **7284**
plasterer, fireproofing **7284**
plasterer foreman/woman **7219**
plasterer helper **7611**
plasterer, moulding **7284**
plasterer, ornamental **7284**
plasterer, stucco **7284**
plastering and drywall contractor **7219**
plastering contractor **7219**
plastic aircraft parts assembly repairer **9495**
plastic and composite worker **9495**
plastic ankle patch moulder **9495**
plastic assembler **9495**
plastic bag machine operator **9422**
plastic bag maker operator **9422**
plastic bag production worker **9495**
plastic bottle trimmer **9495**
plastic casket maker **9495**
plastic casket moulder **9422**
plastic caster **9495**
plastic cellophane finisher **9495**
plastic centrifugal caster **9422**
plastic coagulation operator **9422**
plastic coagulator **9422**
plastic compounder **9422**
plastic extruder operator **9422**
plastic extrusion operator **9422**
plastic fibre extruding machine tender **9422**
plastic film extrusion machine operator **9422**
plastic fixture builder **9495**
plastic footwear moulder operator **9422**
plastic insulation applicator **7293**
plastic laminator – plastic products
    manufacturing **9495**
plastic laminator – woodworking **9513**
plastic material reeler and cutter **9495**
plastic mixer operator **9422**
plastic mould setter **9422**
plastic moulder, compression **9422**
plastic moulder, injection **9422**
plastic pack machine tender **9619**
plastic pipe production worker **9422**
plastic piping fabricator **9495**
plastic printer **9471**
plastic products buffer **9495**
plastic products inspector and tester **9495**
plastic products manufacturing
    inspector **9495**
plastic products sales representative –
    wholesale **6411**

plastic sheet finisher **9495**
plastic sheet worker **9495**
plastic sheets impregnator/corrugator **9422**
plastic shop foreman/woman **9214**
plastic spreading machine operator **9422**
plastic surgeon **3111**
plastic tank assembler **9495**
plastic tool maker **9495**
plastic toy assembler **9495**
plastic trimmer **9495**
plastic vacuum forming machine tender **9495**
plasticator operator **9422**
plastics and plastic products
    compounder **9422**
plastics and resins chemist **2112**
plastics assembly repairer **9495**
plastics blending machine tender **9422**
plastics blending machine tender helper **9613**
plastics caster **9495**
plastics cementer **9495**
plastics cutter **9495**
plastics engineer **2134**
plastics fabricator **9495**
plastics grinder **9495**
plastics inspector foreman/woman **9214**
plastics manufacturing technician **2233**
plastics masker **9619**
plastics mould maker **9422**
plastics moulding machine setter **9422**
plastics moulding technician **2233**
plastics press operator **9422**
plastics processing equipment mechanic **7311**
plastics set-up man/woman **9422**
plastics shredder **9495**
plastics strainer operator **9422**
plastics technician **2233**
plate burner – metal fabrication **9514**
plate file clerk **1413**
plate finisher – printing **9472**
plate fitter helper – construction **7611**
plate former, lead acid storage battery –
    electrical equipment manufacturing **9487**
plate glass installer **7292**
plate grainer – printing **9472**
plate grinder – metal fabrication **9612**
plate hanger – structural metal and
    platework **7263**
plate parting machine operator –
    electrical equipment manufacturing **9487**
plate processor – printing **9472**
plate roller – primary metal processing **9411**
plate shear operator – metal fabrication **9514**
plate worker helper – metal fabrication **9612**
platemaker – printing **9472**
platemaking supervisor – printing **7218**
platen press operator – printing **7381**
plater, bridge and girder **7263**
plater helper – metal fabrication **9612**

plater – shipbuilding **7263**
plater – structural metal and platework **7263**
plater, vacuum evaporation process – electronics manufacturing **9483**
plateroom supervisor – printing **7218**
platework fabricator **7263**
platework fabricator and fitter **7263**
platework fitter **7263**
platework foreman/woman **7214**
platform interpreter, sign language **5125**
platform superintendent – oil and gas drilling **8222**
plating room helper **9619**
plating tank operator **9497**
platoon chief – fire department **6262**
play ground maintenance man/woman **7621**
play therapist **3144**
playground leader **5254**
playground worker **5254**
playwright **5121**
pleat presser – laundry and dry cleaning **6682**
pleater, hand – garment manufacturing **9498**
pleater – textiles **9443**
pleating machine tender – garment manufacturing **9517**
pleats finisher – laundry and dry cleaning **6682**
plexiglass assembler **9495**
plexiglass former **9495**
plug cutting machine tender – tobacco processing **9464**
plug maker – tobacco processing **9464**
plug mill operator – primary metal processing **9411**
plug moulder, machine – tobacco processing **9464**
plug roller – tobacco processing **9464**
plugger – primary metal processing **9611**
plumber **7251**
plumber apprentice **7251**
plumber foreman/woman **7213**
plumber/gas fitter – military **7251**
plumber helper **7611**
plumber helper – utilities **7611**
plumber, maintenance and repair **7251**
plumber, pipefitting **7251**
plumber, residential construction **7251**
plumber's assistant **7611**
plumbing and heating services sales representative **6221**
plumbing contractor **7213**
plumbing estimator – construction **2234**
plumbing inspector **2264**
plumbing installer **7251**
plumbing mechanic **7251**
ply assembler, rubber **9423**
ply assembler – rubber products manufacturing **9423**

ply splicer – rubber products manufacturing **9423**
plywood and veneer matcher – wood processing **9436**
plywood and veneer, patcher and repairer **9434**
plywood boat veneer layer **9491**
plywood bundler **9434**
plywood drier feeder **9614**
plywood grader – wood processing **9436**
plywood inspection foreman/woman **9215**
plywood inspector – wood processing **9436**
plywood panel assembler **9434**
plywood panel groover operator – wood processing **9434**
plywood patcher **9434**
plywood sander feeder **9614**
plywood scarfer operator – wood processing **9434**
plywood sizing saw tender – wood processing **9434**
pneumatic drill operator – construction **7611**
pneumatic hammer operator **7611**
pneumatic tool repairer **7445**
pneumatic tube repairer **7445**
pneumatic unit tester and repairer **7445**
pocket feeder loader – printing **9619**
pocket marker **9619**
podiatric medicine, doctor of **3123**
podiatrist **3123**
poet **5121**
pointer operator – primary metal processing **9411**
pole cutter **8421**
pole distributor worker **7452**
pole framer, wood products **9513**
pole inspector – wood processing **9436**
pole shoe assembler – industrial electrical equipment **9485**
pole-up man/woman – rubber products manufacturing **9615**
police cadet **6261**
police captain **0641**
police chief **0641**
police chief, deputy **0641**
police college teacher **4131**
police constable **6261**
police constable – railway **6261**
police corporal **6261**
police department dispatcher **1475**
police diver **6261**
police inspector **0641**
police instructor **4131**
police lieutenant **0641**
police officer **6261**
police photographer **5221**
police salvage diver **6261**
police sergeant **6261**

police staff inspector **0641**
police station clerk **1441**
police superintendent **0641**
police surgeon **3111**
policeman/woman **6261**
policy analyst, child welfare **4164**
policy analyst, education **4166**
policy analyst, housing **4164**
policy analyst, immigration **4164**
policy analyst, natural and applied
     science **4161**
policy analyst, recreation, sport or
     fitness **4167**
policy analyst, social policy **4164**
policy analyst, unemployment insurance **4164**
policy analyst, women's directorate **4164**
policy change clerk – insurance **1434**
policy clerk – insurance **1434**
policy consultant, education **4166**
policy consultant, employment equity **4164**
policy consultant, labour mobility **4164**
policy consultant, social policy **4164**
policy consultant, women's employment **4164**
policy development officer, health **4165**
policy development officer, nursing
     homes **4165**
policy information clerk – insurance **1434**
policy officer, education **4166**
policy officer, labour **4164**
policy officer, visible minorities **4164**
polisher – clay products **9414**
polisher – granite products **9414**
polisher, jewellery **9498**
polisher, pottery and porcelain **9414**
polisher – spectacle frames **9517**
polisher – stone products **9414**
polisher – textiles **9441**
polishing filter tender – food and
     beverage processing **9461**
polishing machine operator – metal
     products **9516**
political analyst, radio or television **5123**
political cartoonist **5241**
political columnist **5123**
political geographer **4169**
political organization general manager **0014**
political organization manager **0314**
political organizer **4164**
political party president **0014**
political reporter **5123**
political science professor – university **4121**
political scientist **4169**
poll clerk **1454**
poll taker **1454**
pollster **4164**
pollution control engineer **2131**
pollution control inspector **2263**
pollution control technician **2231**

polygraph examiner **6465**
polygraph operator **6465**
polygraphist **6465**
polymer chemist **2112**
polymer engineer **2134**
polymer tester **2211**
polymerization engineer **2134**
polymerization kettle operator **9232**
polymerization unit operator **9232**
pond foreman/woman **8211**
pondman/woman **8616**
pony ride operator **6443**
pool and patio contractor **7217**
pool co-ordinator **4167**
pool equipment installer **7441**
pool installer – vinyl **7441**
pool parlour attendant **6671**
pool service routeman/woman **7441**
pop singer **5133**
popcorn candy maker **9461**
popcorn maker – food and beverage
     processing **9617**
popcorn vendor **6623**
population geneticist **2121**
porcelain cleaner **9619**
porcelain glazer – mineral products
     processing **9611**
pork cutter, retail and wholesale **6251**
pork grader **9465**
port captain, water transport **0713**
port manager **0721**
port meteorological inspector **2213**
port surveyor **2154**
portable appliance repairman/woman **7332**
portable diamond drill and saw operator
     helper **9619**
portable machine sander – woodworking **9513**
portable sawyer – woodworking **9513**
portable spot welder **9515**
porter **6672**
porter, baggage **6672**
porter – hospital **3413**
porter, sleeping car **6672**
portfolio manager **1112**
portrait painter **5136**
portrait photographer **5221**
Ports Canada police officer **6261**
position classifier **1121**
positive artist **5223**
post cutter **8421**
post-doctoral fellow **4122**
post hole driller **7611**
post-mortem attendant **3414**
post-mortem pathologist **3111**
post office clerk **1461**
post office manager **0132**
post-production technician **5225**
post-secondary research assistant **4122**

post-secondary teaching assistant **4122**
postal area manager **0132**
postal carrier **1462**
postal clerk **1461**
postal clerk – military **1461**
postal counter clerk **1461**
postal inspection officer **6465**
postal officer – military **0132**
postal services commercial sales
    representative **6411**
postal station superintendent **0132**
postal station supervisor **1214**
postal wicket clerk **1461**
postal zone manager **0132**
poster artist **5241**
poster layout designer **5223**
poster painter **5223**
posting machine operator **1461**
postman/woman **1462**
postmaster **1214**
pot fisherman/woman **8262**
pot liner – metal processing **9411**
pot room foreman/woman – primary
    metal processing **9211**
pot tender – primary metal processing **9411**
pot washer **6642**
potash miner **8231**
potato chip machine operator **9461**
potato chip sorter – food and beverage
    processing **9617**
potato farmer **8251**
potato peeling machine tender **9617**
potentiometer instrument assembler **9483**
potter **5244**
pottery and porcelain chipper **9414**
pottery and porcelain polisher **9414**
pottery and porcelain presser **9414**
pottery and porcelain sagger maker **9414**
pottery and porcelain sander **9414**
pottery and porcelain ware caster **9414**
pottery and porcelain ware inspector **9415**
pottery designer **5243**
pottery model maker **9414**
pottery trimmer **9414**
poultry boner **9462**
poultry breeder **8251**
poultry cooler worker – food and
    beverage processing **9617**
poultry culler **8431**
poultry dresser **9462**
poultry farm foreman/woman **8253**
poultry farm labourer **8431**
poultry farm manager **8251**
poultry farm worker **8431**
poultry grader **9465**
poultry hatching services contractor **8252**
poultry inspector **2222**
poultry operation supervisor **8253**

poultry packager **9617**
poultry plucker **8431**
poultry preparer **9462**
poultry scientist **2121**
poultry slaughterer – food and beverage
    processing **9462**
poultry specialty butcher **9462**
poultry technician **2221**
poultry technologist **2221**
poultry veterinarian **3114**
poultry worker – meat packing **9462**
poultry yard cleaner **8431**
pound attendant **6483**
pound net fisherman/woman **8262**
pound officer **6463**
pourer – metal processing **9411**
poverty researcher **4164**
powder blender **9421**
powder carrier – underground mining **8614**
powder keeper **1472**
powder security guard **6651**
powdered metal mixer – primary metal
    processing **9611**
powdered metal salvager – primary
    metal processing **9611**
powdered milk drier operator **9461**
powderman/woman – underground
    mining **8231**
power brake operator – metal
    fabrication **9514**
power cable ferry operator **7435**
power control room operator – electric
    power systems **7352**
power crane operator **7371**
power curber tender **7611**
power dispatcher – electric power
    systems **7352**
power dispatcher, journeyman/woman **7352**
power electrician **7243**
power engineer **7351**
power engineer apprentice **7351**
power engineer foreman/woman **9212**
power engineer helper **9613**
power engineer, mechanical **2132**
power grader operator **7421**
power hammer operator helper **9612**
power hammer operator – metal
    forgings **9512**
power lawn mower assembler **9486**
power line and cable workers
    foreman/woman **7212**
power line patrol pilot **2271**
power lineman/woman **7244**
power plant assembler – aircraft
    assembly **9481**
power plant engineer **2132**
power plant foreman/woman **9212**

power plant installation mechanic –
    aircraft assembly **9481**
power plant manager **0912**
power plant mechanic, aircraft **7315**
power plant mechanic – aircraft
    assembly **9481**
power plant operator – electric power
    systems **7352**
power plant stationary engineer **7351**
power press operator – metal fabrication **9514**
power press set-up operator – metal
    fabrication **9514**
power reactor operator – electric power
    systems **7352**
power saw operator – woodworking **9513**
power scheduling engineer **2133**
power sewing machine adjuster **7445**
power shear operator – metal
    fabrication **9514**
power shear tender – metal fabrication **9514**
power shovel mechanic **7312**
power shovel operator **7421**
power snow blower assembler **9486**
power station electrician – electric
    power systems **7243**
power station operator – electric power
    systems **7352**
power station operators foreman/woman **9212**
power sweeper operator – public works **7422**
power switchboard operator apprentice –
    electric power systems **7352**
power switchboard operator, chemical **9232**
power switchboard operator – electric
    power systems **7352**
power system electrician – electric
    power systems **7243**
power system operator **7352**
power system operator, offshore drilling **7352**
power system technician – electrical
    power **2241**
power tool repairer **7332**
power transformer assembler **9485**
power transformer core builder **9485**
power transformer repairer **7333**
power transmission assembly
    foreman/woman **9226**
power truck driver, material handling **7452**
powerhouse electrician – electric power
    systems **7243**
powerhouse electrician helper **7612**
powerhouse helper **9613**
powerhouse helper, coal **9613**
powerhouse mechanical repairer helper **7612**
powerhouse oiler **7612**
powerhouse operator **7351**
powerline maintainer – electric power
    systems **7244**

powerline patroller – electric power
    systems **7244**
practitioner, chinese medicine **3232**
practitioner, general **3112**
practitioner, herb **3232**
practitioner, herbal **3232**
practitioner, herbology **3232**
practitioner, holistic **3232**
practitioner, homeopathic **3232**
practitioner, homoeopathic **3232**
prawn fisherman/woman **8262**
preacher **4154**
preboarding security guard **6651**
precast concrete caulker **7611**
precast concrete erector **7264**
precast concrete finisher **7282**
precast concrete moulder **9414**
precast concrete slab maker **9414**
precast terrazzo maker **9414**
precious metal melter **9411**
precious metal recoverer **9411**
precious metals theft inspector – police **0641**
precious stone setter **7344**
precipitator helper – primary metal and
    mineral products processing **9611**
precipitator operator – chemical
    processing **9421**
precipitator – primary metal processing **9411**
precision grinder set-up operator **9511**
precision honing machine operator **9511**
precision instrument assembler **9483**
precision instrument assembly inspector **9498**
precision instrument machine shop
    foreman/woman **7211**
precision instrument mechanics and
    repairers foreman/woman **7216**
precision instrument technician –
    avionics **2244**
precision lapper – metal machining **9511**
precision lathe operator – metal
    machining **9511**
precision lens grinder –
    non-prescription **9517**
precision lens polisher –
    non-prescription **9517**
precision machinist **7231**
precision sheet metal fabricator **7261**
precision sheet metal mechanic **7261**
precision sheet metal worker **7261**
precision tool maker **7232**
precision welder **7265**
precooked sausage maker **9461**
prefab housing assembler **9493**
prefab housing assembler, wood **9493**
prefabricated housing worker, wood **9493**
prefitting machine feeder **9619**
preflight mechanic, mechanical systems **7315**

preform machine tender – plastic
    manufacturing **9422**
preheater tender – pipeline **7611**
premier **0011**
premium rater – insurance **1434**
preparation department foreman/woman
    – textiles **9216**
preparation plant foreman/woman –
    primary metal and mineral products
    processing **9211**
preparation upholsterer **7341**
preparator **5212**
preparatory supervisor – printing **7218**
prepress planner **1221**
prepress supervisor – printing **7218**
prepress technician **9472**
preprint coating machine tender **9472**
preretirement counsellor **4153**
presbyter **4154**
preschool helper **6473**
preschool supervisor **4214**
preschool teacher **4214**
prescription clerk, optical goods **1472**
prescriptionist **3131**
presentation co-ordinator – broadcasting **5226**
presentation technician **2213**
preshrinking process tester – textiles **9444**
president – academic association **0014**
president and general manager – health,
    education, social and community
    services and membership
    organizations **0014**
president and general manager – trade,
    broadcasting and other services
    n.e.c. **0015**
president – business association **0014**
president – computing service company **0013**
president – cultural association **0014**
president – department store **0015**
president – ethnic association **0014**
president – financial, communications
    and other business services **0013**
president – goods production, utilities,
    transportation and construction **0016**
president – government services **0012**
president – health care association **0014**
president – health, education, social and
    community services and membership
    organizations **0014**
president – labour organization **0014**
president – music guild **0014**
president – residential construction
    company **0016**
president – sports association **0014**
president – trade, broadcasting and other
    services n.e.c. **0015**
presiding steward – race track **5253**
press agent **5124**

press assistant, reel replacer **9619**
press brake operator – metal fabrication **9514**
press clipper **1452**
press feeder – printing **9619**
press floor attendant – printing **9619**
press helper – printing **9619**
press line operator, particle board **9434**
press line operator – rubber
    manufacturing **9423**
press operator assistant – printing **7381**
press operator – electrical equipment
    manufacturing **9487**
press operator – food and beverage
    processing **9461**
press operator, hardboard – wood
    processing **9434**
press operator, ink evaluation – printing **7381**
press operator, plastic **9422**
press operator – printing **7381**
press operator, rubber goods **9423**
press operator – tobacco processing **9464**
press reader **1452**
press reporter **5123**
press secretary **5124**
press supervisor – printing **7218**
press tender – plastic manufacturing **9495**
presser, artificial flowers **5244**
presser – laundry and dry cleaning **6682**
presser, pottery and porcelain **9414**
pressing machine feeder – garment
    manufacturing **9619**
pressing machine tender – laundry and
    dry cleaning **6682**
pressman/woman, ink evaluation –
    printing **7381**
pressman/woman, moulding – rubber
    manufacturing **9423**
pressman/woman – printing **7381**
pressroom foreman/woman – printing **7218**
pressroom supervisor – printing **7218**
pressroom worker, tire and tube – rubber
    products manufacturing **9615**
pressure control calibrator **7445**
pressure cooker operator – food and
    beverage processing **9461**
pressure sealer and tester – aircraft
    assembly **9481**
pressure-sensitive coater operator –
    plastic manufacturing **9422**
pressure switch tester **9498**
pressure tank tester **2261**
pressure tester **2261**
pressure vessel boilermaker **7262**
pressure vessel welder **7265**
pressurized container filler **9461**
prestidigitator **5232**
prestressed concrete inspector **2264**
pretzel baker **9461**

preventive medicine specialist **3112**
preventive medicine technician –
    military **2263**
price checker **6622**
price clerk – retail **6622**
price economist **4162**
price information clerk **1453**
price marker **6622**
price marker supervisor **6211**
priest **4154**
primary care nurse **3152**
primary grain elevator operator **6234**
primary metal labourer **9611**
primary products inspector, animals **2222**
primary products inspector, plants **2222**
primary school teacher **4142**
primary teacher **4142**
prime minister **0011**
primer inspector **9498**
primer sprayer **9496**
primer, tobacco **8431**
principal **0313**
principal – business school **0312**
principal clerk, house of commons **0414**
principal clerk, legislative assembly **0414**
principal clerk, legislative committees **0414**
principal – college or university **0312**
principal estimator – construction **2234**
print colour mixer **9421**
print developer **9474**
print finisher – photographic processing **9474**
print inspector – photographic
    processing **9474**
print retoucher – photographic
    processing **9474**
print tender – photographic processing **9474**
print transferrer – printing **9472**
printed circuit board assembler **9483**
printed circuit board etcher **9483**
printed circuit board fabrication
    foreman/woman **9222**
printed circuit board inspector and tester
    – electronics manufacturing **9483**
printed circuit board operator **9483**
printer **7381**
printer operator **9471**
printer, plastic **9471**
printer-slotter operator **9471**
printing and finishing machine operator **9471**
printing equipment assembly
    foreman/woman **9226**
printing machine operator **9471**
printing machinery mechanic **7311**
printing machinery sales representative **6221**
printing manager **0911**
printing operator – textiles **9443**
printing plant manager **0911**
printing plate engraver **9472**

printing plate moulder – printing **9472**
printing plate mounter – printing **9472**
printing plates order clerk **1474**
printing press assistant **7381**
printing press helper **9619**
printing press machinist **7231**
printing press operator **7381**
printing roller moulder – plastic
    manufacturing **9422**
printing services sales representative **6411**
printing shop foreman/woman **7218**
printing supervisor **7218**
printing technology teacher – college or
    vocational institute **4131**
printmaker **5136**
printmaking teacher **5136**
prism maker operator **9517**
prison guard **6462**
prison officer **6462**
prison warden **0314**
prisoner rehabilitation society director **0314**
private bailiff **6461**
private branch exchange inspector –
    telecommunications **7246**
private branch exchange installer –
    telecommunications **7246**
private branch exchange repairer –
    telecommunications **7246**
private chauffeur **7413**
private detective **6465**
private duty nurse **3152**
private investigation and security service
    manager **0123**
private investigator **6465**
private lands forester **2122**
private police agent and investigator
    supervisor **6465**
private practice occupational therapist **3143**
private school headmaster **0313**
private school principal **0313**
private secretary **1241**
private vocational school director **0312**
prize fighter **5251**
probate court judge **4111**
probation and parole officer **4155**
probation officer **4155**
process assistant **9613**
process cheese cooker **9461**
process cheese formulator **9461**
process clerk **1441**
process control checker – food and
    beverage processing **9465**
process control engineer, chemical **2134**
process control engineer, electrical **2133**
process control equipment mechanic **2243**
process control equipment repairer **2243**
process control operator – food and
    beverage processing **9461**

process engineer **2134**

process engineer, petroleum refineries **2134**

process inspector and tester – electrical equipment manufacturing **9484**

process inspector – electronics manufacturing **9483**

process instrumentation engineer **2133**

process lab operator – electronics manufacturing **9483**

process laboratory operator **2211**

process operator – food and beverage processing **9461**

process operator, liquid waste **9424**

process operator – primary metal and mineral products processing **9231**

process piping draftsman/woman **2253**

process refiner **9232**

process room operator, dry cell battery – electrical equipment manufacturing **9487**

process server **1443**

process technician – chemical processing **9232**

process technician – electronics manufacturing **9483**

process technician, refinery **9232**

process tester – electronics manufacturing **9483**

processing equipment cleaner **9619**

processing operator – chemical processing **9232**

proctologist **3111**

procurement clerk **1474**

procurement officer **1225**

produce buyer **6233**

produce clerk **6622**

produce clerk, supermarket **6421**

produce department supervisor **6211**

produce grader – food and beverage processing **9465**

produce inspector **2222**

produce manager, retail store **0621**

produce sampler – food and beverage processing **9617**

produce shipper **1471**

producer, broadcasting **5131**

producer/director **5131**

producer, motion picture **5131**

product checker – food and beverage processing **9465**

product designer **2252**

product inspector – furniture manufacturing **9492**

product marker **9619**

product painter **9496**

product stainer **9496**

product surface preparer – pre-finishing **9496**

product tester – food and beverage processing **9465**

product trimmer **9498**

production accountant **1111**

production and quality control technologist **2233**

production assembler, electrical equipment **9484**

production assembler – electrical equipment manufacturing **9484**

production assistant – motion pictures and broadcasting **5227**

production audio amplifier repairer **2241**

production boring machine operator – metal machining **9511**

production broaching machine tender **9511**

production brush stainer **9496**

production clerk **1473**

production clerk supervisor **1215**

production co-ordinator – manufacturing **1473**

production co-ordinator – motion pictures, broadcasting and stage productions **5226**

production control clerk **1473**

production control manager – postal service **0132**

production control technologist **2233**

production design assistant, advertising **5223**

production designer – motion pictures, broadcasting and stage productions **5131**

production editor **5122**

production electroplater **9497**

production engineer, manufacturing **2141**

production engineer, oil and gas **2145**

production engineering manager **0211**

production equipment fitter **7316**

production expediter **1473**

production foreman/woman – electronics manufacturing **9222**

production foreman/woman – fabric, fur and leather products manufacturing **9225**

production foreman/woman – mining and quarrying **8221**

production gear cutter **9511**

production general manager – goods production, utilities, transportation and construction **0016**

production grinder operator – metal machining **9511**

production helper – food and beverage processing **9617**

production helper – metal coating **9619**

production helper – primary metal and mineral products processing **9611**

production illustrator **2253**

production lapping machine tender **9511**

production lathe operator – metal machining **9511**

production line battery repairer –
    electrical equipment manufacturing **9487**
production line electrical appliance
    repairer **9484**
production line foreman/woman – motor
    vehicle manufacturing **9221**
production line set-up and service –
    electrical equipment manufacturing **9487**
production line solderer **9515**
production line welder **9515**
production machine fitter **7316**
production machine operator – electrical
    equipment manufacturing **9487**
production machine operator, plastic
    bags **9422**
production machine operator, plastic
    pipe **9422**
production machine shop
    foreman/woman **7211**
production machine tool operator **9511**
production machinery maintenance
    mechanics foreman/woman **7216**
production machinery mechanic **7311**
production maintenance mechanic **7311**
production manager, coal mining **0811**
production manager, logging **0811**
production manager, manufacturing **0911**
production manager, oil and gas fields **0811**
production manager – printing **0911**
production manager, raw materials **0811**
production mechanic **7311**
production miner **8231**
production operator, body – motor
    vehicle manufacturing **9482**
production operator – chemical
    processing **9232**
production operator – electronics
    manufacturing **9483**
production operator – motor vehicle
    manufacturing **9482**
production operator, paint **9496**
production operator, paint and mix
    control **9496**
production operator – rubber
    manufacturing **9423**
production operator, trim and final –
    motor vehicle manufacturing **9482**
production painter **9496**
production painter, brush **9496**
production painter, final colour **9496**
production painter helper **9619**
production petroleum engineer **2145**
production planning technician **2233**
production print applier **9496**
production repairer, electronics **2241**
production scheduler **1473**
production screw machine tender **9516**
production spot welder **9515**

production spray painter **9496**
production spray stainer **9496**
production superintendent **0911**
production supervisor, dry cleaning **6214**
production supervisor – electronics
    manufacturing **9222**
production supervisor – food and
    beverage processing **9213**
production supervisor, laundry **6214**
production supervisor – logging **8211**
production supervisor, pharmaceuticals **9212**
production supervisor – printing **7218**
production supervisor, specialty
    chemicals **9212**
production supply clerk **1473**
production support technician,
    electronics **2241**
production switcher **5224**
production technician – motion pictures,
    broadcasting and stage productions **5226**
production technologist – sawmill **2233**
production tester – electronics
    manufacturing **9483**
production tester, lead acid electric
    battery **9487**
production testing operator – oil and gas
    drilling **8232**
production upholsterer **7341**
production weigher **9619**
production worker – furniture
    manufacturing **9492**
professional agrologist **2123**
professional athlete **5251**
professional athletic team manager **0513**
professional dietitian **3132**
professional engineer, broadcasting **2133**
professional estimator – construction **2234**
professional football team manager **0513**
professional forester **2122**
professional hockey team manager **0513**
professional image consultant **6481**
professional land surveyor **2154**
professional sports scout **5252**
professional team coach **5252**
professor emeritus – university **4121**
professor of computer sciences **4121**
professor of medicine **4121**
professor, university **4121**
profile/pocket sewing machine operator **9451**
profile saw operator – jewellery **9517**
profile shaper operator – woodworking **9513**
profile trimmer – jewellery **9517**
profiling machine set-up operator **9511**
profit planning co-ordinator **1122**
program advisor, family violence
    prevention **4164**
program assistant – education **6472**
program co-ordinator, broadcasting **5226**

program co-ordinator – education **4166**

program co-ordinator, environmental
organization **4161**

program co-ordinator – recreation **4167**

program co-ordinator, recreational
activities **4167**

program co-ordinator – youth recreation
activities **4167**

program director, broadcasting **5131**

program manager, residential mental
health centre **0311**

program officer, education **4166**

program officer, energy **4161**

program officer, fisheries **4161**

program officer, health care association **4165**

program officer, health promotion **4165**

program officer, income maintenance **4164**

program officer, native employment **4164**

program officer, natural and applied
science **4161**

program officer, refugee affairs **4164**

program officer, social program **4164**

program planner, education **4166**

program planner, music **5226**

program planner, radio **5226**

program planner, social services **4164**

program planner, special events **1226**

program researcher, radio or television **5123**

program scheduler **1473**

program seller **6623**

program services manager, education **0413**

programmed-instruction writer **5121**

programmer analyst **2163**

programmer – computer systems **2163**

programming director, broadcasting **0512**

progress clerk, construction **1473**

project accountant **1111**

project co-ordinator, construction **0711**

project engineer, aeronautical **2146**

project engineer, chemical **2134**

project engineer, construction **2131**

project engineer, mechanical **2132**

project forester **2122**

project manager – computer systems **2162**

project manager, construction **0711**

project manager, interior design **5242**

project officer, international aid and
development **4164**

project officer, marketing **4163**

project officer, multiculturalism **4164**

project officer, sports **4167**

project superintendent, construction **0711**

projectionist **5227**

projector assembler **9498**

projector assembly inspector **9498**

promotion specialist **1122**

promotions manager **0611**

prompter **5227**

proof clerk – financial sector **1434**

proof machine operator **1431**

proof-press operator, gravure – printing **7381**

proof-press operator, letterpress –
printing **7381**

proof-press operator, offset lithographic
– printing **7381**

proof-press operator, photoengraved
plates – printing **7381**

proof pressman/woman – printing **7381**

proof teller, bank **1433**

proofmaker – printing **9472**

proofreader **1452**

prop maker **5227**

propane operator **9232**

propane refueler **6621**

propane tank attendant **6621**

propellant blender **9232**

propeller inspector, aircraft **7315**

propeller mechanic – aircraft assembly **9481**

properties custodian, stage or motion
pictures **5226**

property accountant **1111**

property adjuster – insurance **1233**

property administrator **1224**

property appraiser **1235**

property assessor **1235**

property clerk **1441**

property leasing co-ordinator **1224**

property management agent **1224**

property manager **1224**

property master – broadcasting **5226**

property master, motion pictures,
broadcasting and stage productions **5226**

property officer **1224**

property paralegal **4211**

property rental agent **1224**

property rental co-ordinator **1224**

property rentals manager **1224**

property standards inspector **6463**

property surveyor **2154**

property use inspector **6463**

property valuator **1235**

proprietor, retail store **0621**

proprietor, taxicab operation **7222**

props handler **5227**

props person **5227**

propulsion engineer, aerospace vehicles **2146**

propulsion shop technician **7315**

propulsion technician **7315**

prosecuting attorney **4112**

prosecutor **4112**

prospecting geologist **2113**

prospector **2212**

prosthesis maker – dental **3223**

prosthetic assistant **3219**

prosthetic technician **3219**

prosthetist **3219**

prosthetist-orthotist **3219**
prosthetist-orthotist technician **3219**
prosthodontist **3113**
protection co-ordinator – forestry **2223**
protection engineer, electrical systems **2133**
protection technologist **2241**
protective coatings chemist **2112**
protective relay engineer **2133**
protective services executive chief **0013**
protective signal installer helper **9619**
protective signal operator **1475**
protective signal servicer helper **7612**
protein chemist **2112**
prothonotary **1227**
protocol officer **4168**
prototype builder, heavy equipment **7316**
prototype fitter, locomotive **7316**
prototype machinist **7231**
prototype tester, outboard motors **9486**
protozoologist **2121**
provincial co-ordinator, social services **0314**
provincial court clerk **1443**
provincial court of appeal justice **4111**
provincial high court justice **4111**
provincial land surveyor **2154**
provincial secretary, deputy –
    government services **0012**
provincial supreme court justice **4111**
provincial team coach **5252**
provost, college **0312**
psychiatric aide **3413**
psychiatric nurse **3152**
psychiatric nursing supervisor **3151**
psychiatric social worker **4152**
psychiatrist **3111**
psychiatry, chief of **0311**
psychiatry nurse **3152**
psychiatry professor – university **4121**
psychic **6484**
psychic consultant **6484**
psychic reader **6484**
psychoanalyst **3111**
psycholinguist **4169**
psychological services director **0314**
psychologist **4151**
psychologist, educational **4151**
psychologist – military **4151**
psychology assistant – non-university **4164**
psychology, chief of **0311**
psychology, director **0311**
psychology professor – university **4121**
psychology research assistant –
    non-university **4164**
psychometrician **4169**
psychometrist **4169**
psychopharmacologist **3111**
psychotherapist **4151**
public accountant **1111**

public address announcer **5231**
public address servicer **2242**
public address system installer and
    repairer **2242**
public adjuster – insurance **1233**
public administration professor –
    university **4121**
public affairs director **0611**
public affairs officer **5124**
public affairs officer – military **5124**
public affairs program co-ordinator,
    broadcasting **5226**
public assistance advisor **4164**
public auditor **1111**
public auditor supervisor **1111**
public health bacteriologist **2121**
public health consultant – nurse **3152**
public health dentist **3113**
public health engineer **2131**
public health inspector **2263**
public health inspector supervisor **2263**
public health nurse **3152**
public health nursing director **0311**
public health nursing educational
    director **0411**
public health nursing supervisor **3151**
public health nutritionist **3132**
public health physician – medical **3112**
public health professor – university **4121**
public health statistician **2161**
public information director **0611**
public interviewer **1454**
public opinion collector **1454**
public opinion survey researcher **4164**
public relations agent **5124**
public relations clerk **1453**
public relations co-ordinator **5124**
public relations consultant **5124**
public relations director **0611**
public relations manager **0611**
public relations officer **5124**
public relations representative **5124**
public relations specialist **5124**
public rights co-ordinator **4164**
public speaking consultant **6481**
public speaking instructor **4131**
public trustee **1221**
public utilities manager **0912**
public welfare director **0314**
public works engineer **2131**
public works inspector, construction **2264**
public works labourer **7621**
public works maintenance equipment
    operator **7422**
public works maintenance labourer **7621**
public works superintendent **0414**
publication clerk **1452**
publication clerk supervisor **1213**

publication distributor **6411**
publication sales representative **6411**
publications editor **5122**
publications manager **0512**
publicist **5124**
publicity agent **5124**
publicity co-ordinator **5124**
publicity director **0611**
publisher **0016**
publisher's sales representative **6411**
publishing house general manager **0016**
publishing manager **0512**
puff gun operator – food and beverage
    processing **9461**
puffed cereal maker **9461**
pug mill operator – clay products **9414**
puisne judge **4111**
puller/laster – rubber manufacturing **9423**
pullman conductor **7362**
pulmonary disease specialist **3111**
pulmonary function technologist **3214**
pulp and paper engineer **2134**
pulp and paper liquor maker **9432**
pulp and paper machinery builder **7316**
pulp and paper manufacturing
    technologist **2233**
pulp and paper mill foreman/woman **9215**
pulp and paper products sales
    representative **6411**
pulp and paper technician **2233**
pulp and paper technologist **2233**
pulp baler – pulp and paper **9432**
pulp bleacher operator **9233**
pulp cook **9233**
pulp drier operator **9432**
pulp furnace tender – food and beverage
    processing **9461**
pulp grader **9432**
pulp maker **9233**
pulp mill equipment operator **9432**
pulp mill foreman/woman **9215**
pulp mill machine operator **9432**
pulp plant foreman/woman **9215**
pulp press tender **9433**
pulp processing foreman/woman **9215**
pulp refiner operator **9432**
pulp tester **9432**
pulp washer operator **9432**
pulp washer operator helper **9614**
pulper tender – food and beverage
    processing **9461**
pulping control operator **9233**
pulping group operator – pulp and paper **9233**
pulpstone builder **9414**
pulpwood buyer **6233**
pulpwood cutter **8421**
pulpwood harvester operator **8241**
pulpwood piler **8616**

pulverizing and sifting equipment tender
    – chemical processing **9421**
pulvi mixer operator **7421**
pump attendant **6621**
pump installer and repairer **7311**
pump installer and repairer helper **7612**
pump operator, well treatment – oil field
    services **8412**
pump repairer, industrial **7311**
pump runner, petroleum or gas wells **9232**
pump station operator, water treatment **9424**
pump tender – cement and concrete **7611**
pump tender, helper **9613**
pumper, oil pipeline **9232**
pumper, oilfield **9232**
pumper operator – oil field services **8412**
pumphouse operator, water treatment **9424**
pumping and supply engineer **2131**
pumping station foreman/woman **9212**
pumping station operator **9232**
pumpman/woman – oil field services **8412**
pumpman/woman – ship **7434**
pumps and compressors sales
    representative **6411**
punch and shear machine operator –
    metal fabrication **9514**
punch press operator helper – metal
    fabrication **9612**
punch press operator – metal fabrication **9514**
punch press operator – rubber
    manufacturing **9423**
punch press setter, metalworking **9514**
punched card equipment operator **1422**
puppeteer **5232**
purchase order clerk **1474**
purchaser **1225**
purchasing agent **1225**
purchasing assistant **1474**
purchasing buyer **1225**
purchasing chief **0113**
purchasing clerk **1474**
purchasing clerks supervisor **1215**
purchasing control clerk **1474**
purchasing director **0113**
purchasing expediter **1473**
purchasing manager **0113**
purchasing officer **1225**
purchasing supervisor **1225**
purification engineer **2131**
purification operator – chemical
    processing **9232**
purifier operator – food and beverage
    processing **9461**
purse seine fisherman/woman **8262**
purser, air transportation **6432**
purser, airline **6432**
purser instructor **4131**
purser, water transportation **6432**

purveyor – wholesale **6411**
pusher operator – primary metal processing **9411**
puttyman/woman, furniture and fixtures **9619**
pyrometallurgical engineer **2142**
pyrometallurgist **2142**
pyrotechnic assembler, fireworks **9498**

Q

quahoc digger **8613**
quahog digger **8613**
qualified operator, nondestructive testing **2261**
quality assurance manager **0211**
quality assurance officer **2262**
quality assurance technologist **2233**
quality control assembly inspector – automotive engines **9486**
quality control assembly inspector – marine engines **9486**
quality control chemist **2112**
quality control director, chemistry **0212**
quality control engineer **2141**
quality control foreman/woman – metal machining **7211**
quality control foreman/woman – rubber and plastic manufacturing **9214**
quality control foreman/woman – textiles **9216**
quality control inspector – food and beverage processing **9465**
quality control inspector, glass **9415**
quality control inspector – textiles **9444**
quality control manager **0211**
quality control technician – chemical processing **2211**
quality control technician (except chemical) **2233**
quality control technician – food processing **2211**
quality control technologist – chemical processing **2211**
quality control technologist, electrical and electronics **2241**
quality control technologist (except chemical) **2233**
quality control technologist – food processing **2211**
quality control tester, beer bottling line **9465**
quality control tester – textiles **9444**
quality control trouble shooter, electronics **2241**
quality controller – textiles **9444**
quality upgrader, paint – manufacturing **9496**
quantitative historian **4169**
quantity surveyor – construction **2234**

quantity surveyor, electrical and mechanical **2234**
quantity surveyor/estimator **2234**
quarantine officer – public health **2263**
quarry dump attendant **7611**
quarry labourer **7611**
quarry manager **0811**
quarry supervisor **8221**
quarry worker **7372**
quartermaster **7433**
quartz boat builder – stone products **9414**
quartz crystal etcher and plater – electronics manufacturing **9483**
quartz lamp assembler **9484**
quartzware fabricator – stone products **9414**
quaternary scientist **2113**
Quebec notary **4112**
Queen's Bench registrar **1227**
Queen's Counsel **4112**
quenching foreman/woman – mineral and metal processing **9211**
quick print machine tender **9474**
quill winder – textiles **9441**
quiller machine fixer – textile manufacturing **7317**
quiller – textiles **9441**
quilling machine tender, automatic – textiles **9441**
quilter, hand **5244**
quilter mechanic – textile manufacturing **7317**
quilting machine fixer – textile manufacturing **7317**
quilting machine operator **9442**

R

rabbi **4154**
race car driver **5251**
race relations officer **4164**
race track cashier **6611**
race track timer **5253**
racehorse exerciser **8431**
racehorse trainer **8253**
racetrack betting supervisor **6211**
racetrack finish photographer **5221**
racetrack steward **5253**
racing secretary and handicapper **5253**
racker – telecommunications **7246**
racquet stringer **9498**
radar engineer **2133**
radar indicator inspector – electronics manufacturing **9483**
radar plotter, sea – military **6464**
radar receiver assembler **9483**
radar systems technician – military **2241**
radar technician – military **2241**
radar technician, sea – military **2241**

radial arm saw operator – woodworking **9513**
radial drill operator **9511**
radial drill press operator **9511**
radial tire builder **9423**
radiation biophysicist **2111**
radiation detector assembler **9483**
radiation monitor **2263**
radiation oncologist **3111**
radiation oncology, chief of **0311**
radiation oncology simulator
    technologist **3215**
radiation oncology technologist **3215**
radiation technologist **3215**
radiation therapist **3215**
radiation therapy clinical co-ordinator **3215**
radiation therapy clinical instructor **3215**
radiation therapy technologist **3215**
radiator inspector – motor vehicle
    manufacturing **9482**
radiator installer – auto repair service **7443**
radiator installer – motor vehicle
    manufacturing **9482**
radiator maker **9486**
radiator plumber **7251**
radio advertising time sales
    representative **6411**
radio and electronic overhaul and repair
    mechanic – avionics **2244**
radio and music librarian **5111**
radio and radar inspector – avionics **2244**
radio and radar installer – avionics **2244**
radio and television broadcasting design
    engineer **2133**
radio and television field engineer **2133**
radio and television receiver aligner –
    electronics manufacturing **9483**
radio and television repair apprentice **2242**
radio announcer **5231**
radio assembler and installer **9483**
radio astronomer **2111**
radio commentator **5123**
radio communication equipment
    repairer **2242**
radio communication equipment
    repairman/woman – avionics **2244**
radio communications equipment
    repairer helper **9619**
radio director **5131**
radio dispatcher **1475**
radio frequency technologist **2241**
radio host/hostess **5231**
radio inspector **2262**
radio installation and repair technician **2242**
radio interference investigator **2262**
radio maintenance technician **2242**
radio master control room (MCR)
    technician **5224**
radio officer **1475**

radio operator **1475**
radio operator – drilling rig **1475**
radio operator – marine **1475**
radio operator – military **1475**
radio operator, sea – military **1475**
radio producer **5131**
radio programmer **5226**
radio programming manager **0512**
radio recorder **5225**
radio repair supervisor **2242**
radio repairer **2242**
radio research engineer **2133**
radio researcher **5123**
radio servicer **2242**
radio station general manager **0015**
radio station manager **0512**
radio systems engineer **2133**
radio technician **5225**
radio technician – military **2242**
radio telephone installer and repairer **7246**
radio-telephone operator, highways **1475**
radio time buyer **1225**
radio writer **5121**
radiographer, industrial **2261**
radiographer, medical **3215**
radiographic technician **2261**
radiographic technologist **3215**
radiographic tester **2261**
radiography clinical co-ordinator **3215**
radiography clinical instructor **3215**
radiography technologist **3215**
radioisotope technician **3215**
radiological technician **3215**
radiological technologist **3215**
radiologist **3111**
radiologist, diagnostic **3111**
radiologist, therapeutic **3111**
radiologist, veterinary **3114**
radiology aide **6631**
radiotelegraph operator **1475**
radiotherapeutic radiographer **3215**
radiotherapy technician **3215**
radiotherapy technologist **3215**
radome finisher – plastic manufacturing **9495**
rafter – logging **8616**
rafting guide **6442**
rag sorter and cutter – textiles **9616**
rail crane operator **7371**
rail dangerous goods inspector **2263**
rail express clerk **1461**
rail fence builder **7441**
rail lifter machine operator **7432**
rail lubricator **7622**
rail operations superintendent **0713**
rail sander **7432**
rail saw operator **7432**
rail traffic controller **2275**
rail transport electrician **7242**

rail transport equipment repairers
    foreman/woman **7216**
rail transportation traffic engineer **2131**
railroad claim adjuster – insurance **1233**
railroad commissioner **0012**
railway accident investigation officer **2262**
railway automatic anchor operator **7432**
railway car and locomotive pipefitter **7252**
railway car cleaner **6662**
railway car decal applier **7622**
railway car greaser **7431**
railway car inspector **7314**
railway car loader **7452**
railway car lubricator **7431**
railway car maintenance
    foreman/woman **7216**
railway car oiler **7431**
railway car production manager **0911**
railway car puller, crane **7371**
railway car repairer foreman/woman **7216**
railway car repairer helper **7612**
railway car trimmer **9486**
railway car truck assembler **9486**
railway car weigher **7622**
railway carman/woman **7314**
railway carman/woman, apprentice **7314**
railway carman/woman inspector **7314**
railway carmen/women supervisor **7216**
railway conductor **7362**
railway construction and maintenance
    superintendent **7217**
railway control tower operator **7431**
railway cook **6242**
railway dining car food service
    supervisor **6212**
railway division superintendent **0713**
railway engine attendant **7431**
railway engineer **7361**
railway engineer, freight **7361**
railway engineer, passenger train **7361**
railway engineer trainee **7361**
railway equipment inspector **7314**
railway express agent **6434**
railway freight manager **0713**
railway gang foreman/woman **7217**
railway gang labourer **7622**
railway hostler **7361**
railway inspector **2262**
railway labourer **7622**
railway locomotive engineer **7361**
railway mail clerk **1461**
railway maintenance equipment
    operator **7432**
railway manager **0713**
railway passenger agent **6434**
railway passenger operations manager **0713**
railway police chief **0641**
railway police constable **6261**

railway police officer **6261**
railway police supervisor **0641**
railway rolling stock manufacturing
    foreman/woman **7216**
railway signal installer **7242**
railway signal maintainer **7242**
railway surveyor **2154**
railway switchman/woman **7431**
railway tank car servicer **7431**
railway technician **2231**
railway tie injector operator **7432**
railway track grinder **7432**
railway track maintenance labourer **7622**
railway track maintenance worker **7432**
railway track tamper operator **7432**
railway tracks section boss **7217**
railway transport operations supervisor **7221**
railway yard labourer **7622**
railway yard worker **7431**
railway yardman/woman **7431**
raise borer helper – underground mining **8411**
raise boring machine operator –
    underground mining **8231**
raise miner **8231**
raise miner helper **8411**
raker, asphalt **7611**
ram press operator – clay products **9414**
ramp agent, air transport **7437**
ramp attendant, air transport **7437**
ramp lead hand, air transport **7437**
ramp manager, airline **0713**
ramp station attendant, air transport **7437**
ramp supervisor **1215**
ranch couple **8431**
ranch foreman/woman **8253**
ranch hand **8431**
ranch worker **8431**
rancher **8251**
range conservationist **2223**
range manager **2223**
rapid transit scheduler **1476**
rate reviewer **1431**
rate revision clerk, freight **1431**
rater – insurance **1434**
raw stock drier – textiles **9443**
raw stock dyer – textiles **9443**
RCMP commissioner **0641**
RCMP officer **6261**
RDMS technologist **3216**
reaction ferry operator **7435**
reactor operator, petroleum **9232**
reactor physicist **2111**
reader **1452**
reading clinician – elementary school **4142**
reading clinician – secondary school **4141**
ready mix operator – food and beverage
    processing **9461**
ready mix truck driver **7411**

reagent mixer, cellulose film **9421**
reagent tender helper – primary metal
     processing **9611**
reagent tender – primary metal
     processing **9411**
real estate agent **6232**
real estate analyst **1235**
real estate appraiser **1235**
real estate broker **6232**
real estate clerk **1434**
real estate dealer **6232**
real estate developer **0121**
real estate law clerk **4211**
real estate lawyer **4112**
real estate manager **0121**
real estate managing supervisor **0121**
real estate paralegal **4211**
real estate sales consultant **6232**
real estate sales manager **0121**
real estate sales representative **6232**
real estate sales supervisor **6232**
real estate salesperson **6232**
real estate secretary **1242**
realtime systems control analyst –
     computer systems **2147**
realtor **0121**
realty clerk **1434**
rebeamer – textiles **9441**
receiver **1471**
receiving barn custodian **6483**
receiving clerk **1471**
receiving clerk supervisor **1215**
receiving room clerk **1471**
reception clerk, hotel **6435**
reception clerk, office **1414**
receptionist **1414**
receptionist and enquiries clerk **1453**
receptionist/secretary **1414**
receptionist supervisor **1211**
receptionist/switchboard operator **1414**
receptionist/telephone operator **1414**
receptionist/typist **1414**
reclaim millman/woman – rubber
     manufacturing **9423**
reclaim operator – electronics
     manufacturing **9483**
reclaimed rubber inspector **9423**
reclaimer, abrasives – mineral products
     processing **9611**
reclaimer operator **7421**
reclamation engineer **2131**
reclamation foreman/woman – primary
     metal and mineral products
     processing **9211**
reconciliation clerk – banking **1434**
record library assistant **5211**
record press tender – plastic
     manufacturing **9495**

record producer **5131**
record store manager **0621**
record systems analyst **1122**
record systems analyst supervisor **1122**
recorder, court **1244**
recorder of deeds **1227**
recorder of wills **1227**
recorder, steel mill **1473**
recording artist **5133**
recording clerk **1473**
recording engineer **5225**
recording secretary **1241**
recording studio technician **5225**
recordings library clerk **1451**
records administrator **0114**
records and tapes sales clerk **6421**
records classifier **1413**
records clerk **1413**
records custodian **1413**
records management specialist **1122**
records management supervisor **1211**
records office supervisor **1211**
records officer **1413**
records support clerk **1413**
records system clerk **1413**
recovery equipment operator – chemical
     processing **9421**
recovery operator – pulp and paper **9432**
recovery plant operator helper – pulp
     and paper **9614**
recovery plant operator – pulp and
     paper **9233**
recreation administrator **0513**
recreation and sport director **0513**
recreation attendant **6671**
recreation centre director **0513**
recreation consultant **4167**
recreation equipment erector **7441**
recreation equipment installer **7441**
recreation leader **5254**
recreation manager **0513**
recreation planner **2153**
recreation policy analyst **4167**
recreation program leader **5254**
recreation programs co-ordinator **4167**
recreation programs director **0513**
recreation programs manager **0513**
recreation service manager **0513**
recreation structure erector **7441**
recreation supervisor **4167**
recreation vehicle assembler **9486**
recreation vehicle mechanic apprentice **7383**
recreation vehicle repairer **7383**
recreation vehicle service technician **7383**
recreational camp attendant **6671**
recreational campground manager **0632**
recreational co-ordinator, geriatric
     activities **4167**

recreational equipment installer **7441**
recreational equipment rental shop attendant **6421**
recreational facility attendant **6671**
recreational facility manager **0721**
recreational leadership teacher – college **4131**
recreational specialist **4167**
recreational therapist **3144**
recreologist **4167**
recreology professor – university **4121**
recruiter **1223**
recruiting manager **0112**
recruiting officer **1223**
recruitment and training constable **6261**
recruitment specialist **1223**
recruitment supervisor **1211**
rectifier, distilled liquors – food and beverage processing **9461**
rectifier operator – electric power systems **7352**
rector – education **0014**
recycled paper handler **7452**
recycling truck driver **7411**
red cross first aid director **0311**
red cross nurse **3152**
redcap, port **6672**
redraw operator – textiles **9441**
redryer operator – tobacco processing **9464**
redryer tender – tobacco processing **9464**
redrying machine operator – tobacco processing **9464**
reduction plant foreman/woman – primary metal and mineral products processing **9211**
reed cleaner – textiles **9616**
reel feeder – printing **9619**
reel man/woman – printing **9619**
reel oven operator – food and beverage processing **9461**
reel tender – textiles **9441**
reel winder – textiles **9441**
reel wrapper **9612**
reeled tubing helper – oil field services **8615**
reeled tubing operator – oil field services **8412**
reeler and cutter – plastic manufacturing **9495**
reeler – textiles **9441**
reeling machine operator – primary metal processing **9411**
reeling machine operator – textiles **9441**
reeve **0011**
referee, sports **5253**
referee, unemployment insurance appeals **1228**
reference assistant – library **5211**
reference clerk – library **1451**
reference librarian **5111**

refiner mill tender – rubber manufacturing **9423**
refiner, mint – primary metal processing **9411**
refiner operator – pulp and paper **9432**
refinery engineer **2134**
refinery fire chief **0642**
refinery helper – primary metal and mineral products processing **9611**
refinery operator **9232**
refinery process operator – primary metal processing **9231**
refinery superintendent **0911**
refining and metalworking engineer **2142**
refinisher technician – military **9496**
reflective sign fabricator **9498**
reflectoscope tester **2261**
reflexologist **3232**
reformatory guard **6462**
refractory brick repairer/mason **7281**
refractory bricklayer **7281**
refractory bricklayer foreman/woman **7219**
refractory builder **7281**
refractory mason **7281**
refractory mortar mixer **9414**
refractory tamp moulder – clay products **9414**
refrigerant gas leak tester **9484**
refrigeration and air conditioning equipment insulator **7293**
refrigeration and air conditioning mechanic **7313**
refrigeration and air conditioning mechanic apprentice **7313**
refrigeration and mechanical technician **7313**
refrigeration contractor **7216**
refrigeration engineer **2132**
refrigeration equipment gas charger **9484**
refrigeration foreman/woman **9212**
refrigeration mechanic **7313**
refrigeration mechanic apprentice **7313**
refrigeration mechanic foreman/woman **7216**
refrigeration mechanic helper **7612**
refrigeration mechanical technician – military **7313**
refrigeration operator helper **9613**
refrigeration plant operator **7351**
refrigeration system installer **7313**
refrigeration systems draftsman/woman **2253**
refrigeration unit inspector **9484**
refrigerator assembler, electric **9484**
refrigerator crater **9619**
refrigerator inspector – electrical appliance manufacturing **9484**
refrigerator installer, commercial and industrial **7313**
refrigerator servicer, domestic **7332**
refugee affairs program officer **4164**
refuse collector **7621**
refuse truck driver – public works **7422**

region service manager – postal and
    courier service **0132**
regional administration manager **0114**
regional administrator, social services **0314**
regional bank manager **0122**
regional claims and benefit officer –
    unemployment insurance **1228**
regional communications director **0611**
regional controller **0111**
regional correctional administrator **0314**
regional counsel **4112**
regional crown prosecutor **4112**
regional development analyst **4163**
regional director, education programs **0413**
regional director, social services –
    government services **0411**
regional economic development agency
    officer **4163**
regional inventory officer – forestry **2122**
regional library director **0511**
regional manager, administration **0114**
regional manager, agricultural
    representatives **0212**
regional manager, bank **0122**
regional manager, child welfare –
    government services **0411**
regional manager, income security –
    government services **0411**
regional manager, rural and native
    housing – government services **0411**
regional manager – telecommunications
    system **0131**
regional manager, unemployment
    insurance – government services **0411**
regional museum technician **5212**
regional planner **2153**
regional sales director **0611**
regional sales manager **0611**
regional sales representative **6411**
regional superintendent of education **0313**
regional superintendent, schools **0313**
regional transmitter technician **5224**
regional vice-president – financial,
    communications and other business
    services **0013**
regional vice-president – goods
    production, utilties, transportation
    and construction **0016**
regional vice-president – health,
    education, social and community
    services and membership
    organizations **0014**
regional vice-president – hotel chain **0015**
regional vice-president – petroleum
    production company **0016**
regional vice-president – trade,
    broadcasting and other services
    n.e.c. **0015**

regional vice-president – trust company **0013**
registered cardiology technologist **3217**
registered central service technician –
    medical **6631**
registered community health nurse **3152**
registered dental assistant **3411**
registered dental technician **3223**
registered diagnostic cardiac
    sonographer **3216**
registered diagnostic medical
    sonographer **3216**
registered dietitian **3132**
registered dietitian/nutritionist **3132**
registered electrocardiography
    technician **3217**
registered emergency paramedic **3234**
registered health nurse **3152**
registered mail clerk **1461**
registered massage therapist **3235**
registered nurse **3152**
registered nursing assistant **3233**
registered nutritionist **3132**
registered orthopaedic technologist **3414**
registered orthotic technician **3219**
registered patent agent **4161**
registered pharmacist **3131**
registered physical therapist **3142**
registered physiotherapist **3142**
registered professional dietitian **3132**
registered professional forester **2122**
registered prosthetic technician **3219**
registered psychiatric nurse **3152**
registered public health nurse **3152**
registered representative – investments **1113**
registered respiratory therapist **3214**
registered technologist – medical **3211**
registered technologist, nuclear
    medicine **3215**
registered technologist, radiation
    therapy **3215**
registered technologist, radiography **3215**
registered technologist, ultrasound **3216**
registered trade mark agent **4211**
registered vascular technologist **3218**
registrar clerk **1441**
registrar – college or university **0312**
registrar, community college **0312**
registrar – courts **1227**
registrar – museum **5212**
registrar of bankruptcy **1227**
registrar of court of appeal **1227**
registrar of deeds **1227**
registrar of probate **1227**
registrar of wills **1227**
registration clerk **1441**
registry clerk **1441**
registry supervisor **1211**

regulator and tester,
    telecommunications **7246**
regulatory officer, engineering **2262**
regulatory toxicologist **2121**
rehabilitation and renovation specialist **0712**
rehabilitation counsellor **4153**
rehabilitation engineer **2148**
rehabilitation housing inspector **2264**
rehabilitation nursing supervisor **3151**
rehabilitation services director –
    medical **0311**
rehabilitation specialist **4153**
rehabilitation worker, pipelines **7442**
rehabilitation worker – social services **4212**
rehabilitationist, aural **3141**
rehearsal musician **5133**
reinforced concrete inspector **2264**
reinforcing cage maker **9516**
reinforcing cage winding machine
    operator **9516**
reinforcing steel iron worker **7264**
reinforcing wire mesh worker **7611**
reinsurance clerk **1434**
reinsurance underwriter **1234**
relay engineer **2133**
relay tester and maintainer – electric
    power systems **7243**
relay tester and repairer – electric power
    systems **7243**
relay tester – telecommunications **7246**
relief officer **4212**
relief operator – telephone system **1424**
religion professor – university **4121**
religious and moral education high
    school teacher **4141**
religious education worker **4217**
relish maker **9461**
relocation consultant **4213**
relocation counsellor **4213**
remedial gymnast **3144**
remedial gymnast, supervisor **3144**
remedial herbalist **3232**
remedial herbologist **3232**
remedial therapist **3144**
remittance account clerk **1431**
remote broadcasting co-ordinator **5226**
remote sensing geologist **2113**
remote sensing technician **2255**
remote sensing technologist **2255**
renal technician **3212**
renderer, graphic arts **5223**
rendering equipment tender – food
    processing **9461**
renewal clerk – financial sector **1434**
renovation carpenter **7271**
renovation carpenter helper **7611**
renovation contractor **0712**
rental agent, apartments **1224**

rental agent, real estate **1224**
rental agent – retail **6421**
rental clerk – retail **6421**
rental clerk, storage space **6421**
rental service supervisor **6211**
rental shop attendant **6421**
repair clerk **1453**
repair dressmaker **7342**
repair lineman/woman – electric power
    systems **7244**
repair lineman/woman –
    telecommunications **7245**
repair seamstress **7342**
repair shop estimator, automotive **7322**
repairer, assembled wood products **9493**
repairer, automated processing
    equipment **2241**
repairer, bicycle **7445**
repairer – cable television **7247**
repairer, camera **7445**
repairer, central air conditioning **7313**
repairer, electric meter **7333**
repairer, electric motor **7333**
repairer, electric sign **7445**
repairer, electrical instruments **7333**
repairer, electronic equipment –
    avionics **2244**
repairer, electronic games **2242**
repairer, gas meter **7445**
repairer, household and business
    equipment **2242**
repairer, industrial process control
    equipment **2243**
repairer, leather glove **9451**
repairer, medical instruments **2241**
repairer, metal furniture **9494**
repairer, nucleonic controller **2243**
repairer, radio communication
    equipment – avionics **2244**
repairer, sewing machine – domestic **7445**
repairer, small engine apprentice **7335**
repairer, small engines **7335**
repairer, storage battery **7333**
repairer, switch network **7246**
repairer – telecommunications **7246**
repairer, television studio equipment –
    household and business equipment **2242**
repairer, televisions **2242**
repairer, upholstery **7341**
repairer, vending machine **7445**
repairer, water meter **7445**
repairman/woman, electric motor **7333**
repairman/woman paint, finished
    vehicle **9496**
repairman/woman, power transformer **7333**
repairman/woman, sash and door
    manufacturing **9493**
repairman/woman, transformer **7333**

repairman/woman, waterworks **7442**

repairs foreman/woman – power lines **7212**

repairs foreman/woman –
    telecommunications lines **7212**

repeater installer – telecommunications **7246**

repeater tester and adjuster –
    telecommunications **7246**

reporter, financial **5123**

reporter, foreign affairs **5123**

reporter, investigative **5123**

reporter, news **5123**

reporter, political **5123**

reporter, traffic **5231**

reporter, weather **5231**

representative, government agricultural
    service **2123**

requirements officer **1221**

rerecording mixer **5225**

resaw operator – sawmill **9431**

resaw operator – woodworking **9513**

resawyer – sawmill **9431**

research administrator – university **0312**

research analyst, health policy **4165**

research analyst – securities **1112**

research archaeologist **4169**

research assistant – forestry **2223**

research assistant – non-university **4164**

research assistant – post-secondary **4122**

research assistant, psychology –
    non-university **4164**

research assistant, university **4122**

research audiologist **3141**

research chemist **2112**

research department manager **0212**

research dietitian **3132**

research director, investments **0111**

research engineer, electrical and
    electronic **2133**

research forester **2122**

research home economist **4164**

research laboratory equipment repairer **2241**

research manager **0212**

research mathematician **2161**

research metallurgist **2115**

research nutritionist **3132**

research occupational therapist **3143**

research officer, education **4166**

research officer, social welfare **4164**

research pathologist, speech-language **3141**

research physiotherapist **3142**

research scientist, aerospace **2111**

research scientist, biochemistry **2112**

research scientist, ceramics **2115**

research scientist, chemistry **2112**

research scientist, communications **2111**

research scientist, composite materials **2115**

research scientist, electronics **2111**

research scientist, physics **2111**

research scientist, remote sensing **2111**

research technician, life sciences **2221**

researcher, dance/movement therapy **3144**

researcher, health care **4165**

researcher, international aid and
    development **4164**

researcher, legal **4211**

researcher, market **4163**

researcher, music therapy **3144**

researcher, organization and methods **1122**

researcher, radio or television **5123**

reservation administrator **1221**

reservation agent, railway **6434**

reservation agent, transportation (except
    airline) **6434**

reservation clerk, airline **6433**

reservation clerk, boat cruise **6434**

reservation clerk (except airline) **6434**

reservation clerk, wholesale travel **6434**

reservation sales agent, airline **6433**

reservations clerk, hotel **6435**

reservations manager **0632**

reservations supervisor – hotel **6216**

reserves clerk – financial sector **1434**

reservoir engineer, petroleum **2145**

reservoir engineering technician **2212**

residence cleaner **6661**

residence counsellor **4212**

resident physician, general practice **3112**

resident physician, specialist **3111**

resident, specialist **3111**

resident, surgeon **3111**

residential alarm specialist **6465**

residential architect **2151**

residential boarding home worker **6661**

residential cleaning service manager **0651**

residential construction company
    president **0016**

residential construction foreman/woman **7215**

residential construction manager **0711**

residential construction plumber **7251**

residential construction supervisor **7215**

residential construction wirer **7241**

residential counsellor **4212**

residential door installer **7441**

residential energy sales adviser **6221**

residential facility worker **6661**

residential floor and wall covering
    installer **7295**

residential home builder **0712**

residential life counsellor **4212**

residential painter **7294**

residential program manager, mental
    health centre **0311**

residential property manager **1224**

residential real estate agent **6232**

residential real estate salesperson **6232**

residential renovation contractor **0712**

residential services treatment centre
    director **0311**
residential shingler **7291**
residential wireman/woman **7241**
residual metal recoverer **9411**
resilient floor installer **7295**
resilient floor layer **7295**
resistance brazer **9515**
resistance welder **9515**
resistance welder, spot **9515**
resistance welder tender **9515**
resistance welding machine setter **7265**
resistance welding set-up man/woman **7265**
resistor assembler – electronics
    manufacturing **9483**
resistor machine feeder **9483**
resistor processing equipment operator **9483**
resort campground manager **0632**
resort manager **0632**
resource economist **4162**
resource management technician **2221**
resource officer, forest inventory **2223**
resource technician – forestry **2223**
resource technician, wildlife **2221**
resource technologist **2221**
respirator servicer and fitter **7445**
respiratory care practitioner **3214**
respiratory technician **3214**
respiratory technologist **3214**
respiratory therapist **3214**
respiratory therapy supervisor **3214**
respirologist **3111**
respirology, chief of **0311**
respooler – textiles **9441**
rest home worker **6661**
rest room attendant **6661**
rest room cleaner **6661**
restaurant assistant manager **0631**
restaurant cook **6242**
restaurant equipment sales
    representative **6411**
restaurant host/hostess **6451**
restaurant inspector – public health **2263**
restaurant manager **0631**
restaurant purchasing officer **1225**
restaurateur **0631**
restoration carpenter **7271**
restoration technician **5212**
restorer, antique vehicles **7322**
restrike hammer operator – metal
    forgings **9512**
retail analyst **4162**
retail butcher **6251**
retail buyer **6233**
retail establishment president **0015**
retail investigator **6465**
retail loss prevention officer **6465**

retail management teacher – college or
    vocational institute **4131**
retail manager **0621**
retail meat cutter **6251**
retail merchandiser **6233**
retail pharmacist **3131**
retail sales clerk **6421**
retail salesperson **6421**
retail space planner **5242**
retail store department head **6211**
retail store supervisor **6211**
retailer **0621**
retarder operator, railway **7431**
retort battery cook – food and beverage
    processing **9461**
retort tender – food and beverage
    processing **9461**
retort tender – mineral products
    processing **9411**
retort unloader **9613**
retoucher, photoengraving – printing **9472**
retread tire inspection foreman/woman **9214**
returning officer **4168**
revenue accounting clerk **1431**
revenue agent **1228**
revenue officer **1228**
revenue recovery officer **1228**
revenue supervisor **1228**
reverberatory furnace operator – primary
    metal processing **9411**
reversing mill operator – primary metal
    processing **9411**
review lawyer **4112**
review officer **4212**
rewarper – textiles **9441**
rewinder, processed paper **9433**
rewinder tender – pulp and paper **9433**
rewinder – textiles **9441**
rheologist **2111**
rheumatologist **3111**
rheumatology, chief of **0311**
rib knitter **9442**
ribber – meat packing **9462**
ribbing machine operator – textiles **9442**
ribbon looping machine tender **9517**
rice mill worker **9461**
rice miller **9461**
ride attendant **6671**
ride operator, amusement **6443**
riding instructor **5254**
riding master **5254**
rifle case maker – leather **9452**
rig electrician **7242**
rig manager – oil and gas drilling **8222**
rig mechanic **7311**
rig mechanic helper **7612**
rig welder **7265**
rigger – aircraft assembly **9481**

rigger (except shipbuilding and aircraft
    assembly) **7371**
rigger helper – ship **9612**
rigger – motion pictures, broadcasting
    and stage productions **5227**
rigger's helper **7611**
rigger, ship **7311**
rigger – telecommunications **7245**
rigging gaffer **5226**
rigging slinger **8241**
right of way agent **1225**
right of way inspector **6465**
rim bander, television picture tube **9483**
ring barker operator – wood processing **9434**
ring frame operator – textiles **9441**
ring mill operator – metal forgings **9512**
ring spinner – textiles **9441**
ringmaster, circus **5231**
rink attendant **6671**
rink icer **6671**
rinser – textiles **9443**
rip and groove machine tender –
    woodworking **9513**
rip-rap placer **7611**
ripper operator **7421**
ripsaw grader operator – woodworking **9513**
ripsaw matcher – woodworking **9513**
ripsaw operator – stone products **9414**
ripsaw operator – woodworking **9513**
ripsawyer – stone products **9414**
ritual slaughterer – meat packing **9462**
river and canal works engineer **2131**
river driver **8616**
river pilot **2273**
riverboat captain **2273**
rivet maker **9516**
rivet tester **9491**
riveter – ship building **9486**
riveting machine operator – electrical
    equipment manufacturing **9487**
riveting machine tender – electrical
    equipment manufacturing **9487**
RN **3152**
RNA **3233**
road and roll tester – motor vehicle
    manufacturing **9482**
road asphalt layer, manual **7611**
road boss, highway and bridge
    maintenance **7217**
road boss, paving gang **7217**
road clerk **1441**
road construction inspector **2264**
road foreman/woman, airport runways **7217**
road foreman/woman, freight train **7221**
road foreman/woman, passenger train **7221**
road form setter **7611**
road freight brakeman/woman **7362**
road freight conductor **7362**

road gang foreman/woman **7217**
road grader operator **7421**
road grading inspector **2264**
road maintenance foreman/woman **7217**
road maintenance worker – public
    works **7621**
road mixer operator **7421**
road mixer operator helper **7611**
road oiling truck driver – public works **7422**
road planer operator **7421**
road roller operator **7421**
road safety inspector **2262**
road spray truck helper **7611**
road test mechanic – motor vehicle
    manufacturing **9482**
road transport inspector **6463**
road worker, manual **7611**
roadheader operator – underground
    mining **8231**
roadmaker – underground mining **8411**
roadway lighting design engineer **2133**
roaster, chemical **9421**
roaster – mineral products processing **9411**
roaster operator – primary metal
    processing **9231**
robotic spray paint attendant **9496**
robotics service technician **2241**
robotics system installer and repairer **2241**
robotics technician **2241**
rock crusher foreman/woman – primary
    metal and mineral products
    processing **9211**
rock crusher helper – primary metal and
    mineral products processing **9611**
rock crusher – primary metal and
    mineral products processing **9411**
rock duster – underground mining **8614**
rock mechanics technician **2212**
rock singer **5133**
rock splitter **9619**
rock wool operator – stone products **9414**
rocket component mechanic – avionics **2244**
rod bending machine operator – metal
    fabrication **9514**
rod drawer helper – primary metal
    processing **9611**
rod drawer – primary metal processing **9411**
rod mill operator – primary metal
    processing **9411**
rod puller and coiler – primary metal
    processing **9611**
rodent control officer **2263**
rodent raiser **8251**
rodeo performer **5251**
rodman/woman, surveying **7612**
rolfer **3232**
rolfing movement teacher **3232**
roll builder/repairer – rolling mills **7311**

roll builder – rubber manufacturing **9423**

roll building foreman/woman – rubber manufacturing **9214**

roll catcher – primary metal processing **9611**

roll changer – rubber manufacturing **9615**

roll coater – metal processing **9497**

roll coverer – rubber manufacturing **9423**

roll finisher – paper **9433**

roll forger **9512**

roll forming machine setter, metalworking **9514**

roll grinder – rubber manufacturing **9423**

roll mat machine feeder – textiles **9616**

roll operator – metal fabrication **9514**

roll operator – plastic manufacturing **9422**

roll operator – rubber manufacturing **9423**

roll pipe and tube setter – primary metal processing **9411**

roll setter – rolling mills **7311**

roll slicing machine tender – paper converting **9435**

roll spacer – primary metal processing **9411**

roll table operator – primary metal processing **9411**

roll tender – printing **9619**

roll tester – motor vehicle manufacturing **9482**

roll threader operator **9516**

roll turner – textiles **9616**

roll wrapper – paper **9433**

roller bearing assembly inspector **9498**

roller cleaner – textiles **9616**

roller compactor operator, manual **7611**

roller engraver, printing **9472**

roller grinder, printing **9511**

roller leveler **9411**

roller machine tender – tannery **9453**

roller mill tender – food and beverage processing **9461**

roller operator **7421**

roller printer – textiles **9443**

roller repairer – garment **7317**

roller repairer – industrial equipment **7311**

roller repairer – plastic manufacturing **9495**

roller repairer – rubber manufacturing **9423**

roller repairman/woman – plastic manufacturing **9495**

roller repairman/woman – rubber manufacturing **9423**

roller room equipment tender – food and beverage processing **9461**

roller skating instructor **5254**

rollerman/woman, fishing vessel **8441**

rollerman/woman – wood processing **9614**

rolling machine operator – metal forgings **9512**

rolling machine tender – paper converting **9435**

rolling mill control operator – primary metal processing **9231**

rolling mill foreman/woman – primary metal processing **9211**

rolling mill operations helper – primary metal processing **9611**

rolling mill operator – primary metal processing **9231**

rolling mill worker – primary metal processing **9611**

rolling pin maker – woodworking **9513**

rollman/woman – printing **9619**

roof painter **7294**

roof tiler **7291**

roofer **7291**

roofer and waterproofer **7291**

roofer apprentice **7291**

roofer, asphalt and gravel **7291**

roofer foreman/woman **7219**

roofer helper **7611**

roofer helper, asphalt **7611**

roofer, metal **7291**

roofer, sheet metal **7291**

roofer supervisor **7219**

roofer trainee **7291**

roofer, wood shingle **7291**

roofing contractor **7219**

roofing mechanic **7291**

roofing supervisor **7219**

room attendant **6661**

room cleaner **6661**

room clerk **6435**

room service waiter/waitress **6453**

rooming house keeper **0632**

rooms manager **0632**

rooting machine operator – toy **9517**

rope coiling machine tender **9442**

rope machine setter – textile manufacturing **7317**

rope maker – textiles **9442**

rope twister **9442**

rope twisting machine tender **9442**

rose grower **8254**

rotary brush making machine operator **9517**

rotary driller helper – water-well **7611**

rotary drilling machine operator – surface mining and quarrying **7372**

rotary furnace tender – chemical processing **9232**

rotary kiln operator – primary metal and mineral products processing **9411**

rotary kiln tender – primary metal processing **9411**

rotary raise driller helper **8411**

rotary raise driller – underground mining **8231**

rotary shear operator – metal fabrication **9514**

rotary technician, aircraft mechanical systems **7315**
rotary tiller assembler **9486**
rotary trencher operator **7421**
rotating field coil assembler – industrial electrical equipment **9485**
rotisseur/meat chef **6241**
roto-lift operator – foundry **9412**
rotogravure cylinder technician **9472**
rotogravure foreman/woman **7218**
rotogravure press operator – printing **7381**
rotogravure press operator – textiles **9443**
rotogravure press operator, wallpaper **7381**
rotogravure pressman/woman – printing **7381**
rotoprinter **7381**
rotor assembler – industrial electrical equipment **9485**
rotor coil former – industrial electrical equipment **9485**
rotor core assembler – industrial electrical equipment **9485**
rough benchwork spray painter **9496**
rough carpenter **7271**
rough mill operator – woodworking **9513**
rough painter, construction **7294**
rough planer operator – woodworking **9513**
rough shellac sprayer, furniture **9494**
rough spray painter – manufacturing **9496**
roughing mill operator – metal processing **9411**
roughneck, offshore drilling rig **8615**
roughneck – oil and gas drilling **8615**
roughneck, service rig – oil field services **8615**
roundhouse foreman/woman – railway **7216**
rounding and backing machine operator – printing **9473**
roustabout, offshore drilling rig **8615**
roustabout – oil and gas drilling **8615**
route driver **7414**
route driver helper **7622**
route foreman/woman – motor transport **7222**
route planning analyst **2153**
route planning supervisor **1215**
route supervisor, retail sales **6211**
router operator – metal machining **9511**
router operator – woodworking **9513**
routing clerk **1461**
rover – textiles **9441**
roving frame tender – textiles **9441**
roving machine operator – textiles **9441**
Royal Canadian Mounted Police (RCMP) officer **6261**
royal commission officer **4168**
royalties manager **0512**
RPF **2122**
RPN **3152**
RRT **3214**

RS technician **2255**
RS technologist **2255**
RTNM **3215**
RTR **3215**
RTT **3215**
rubber abrasive wheel maker **9414**
rubber and vinyl coater – textiles **9443**
rubber balloon grader **9615**
rubber belt maker **9423**
rubber boot maker, moulded **9423**
rubber buffer **9423**
rubber cement mixer **9423**
rubber coater **9423**
rubber compounder **9615**
rubber cord cutter **9423**
rubber cord splicer **9423**
rubber curing press tender **9423**
rubber cushion inspector **9423**
rubber cutter **9423**
rubber cutting machine feeder **9615**
rubber foam cushion fabricator **9423**
rubber foam operator **9423**
rubber footwear checker and tester **9615**
rubber footwear foxer **9423**
rubber footwear hand bonder **9423**
rubber footwear maker **9423**
rubber footwear maker, hand **9423**
rubber footwear parts buffer **9423**
rubber footwear repairer **9423**
rubber footwear sub-assembler **9423**
rubber footwear tread machine tender **9423**
rubber fuel tank foreman/woman **9214**
rubber gasket making foreman/woman **9214**
rubber gear moulder **9423**
rubber glove maker **9423**
rubber goods batch tester **9615**
rubber goods cutter/finisher **9423**
rubber goods inspector **9423**
rubber goods machine operator **9423**
rubber goods press operator **9423**
rubber goods repairer **9423**
rubber goods seamer **9615**
rubber goods tester **9615**
rubber grinder **9423**
rubber hose checker **9615**
rubber hose foreman/woman **9214**
rubber hose inspection and testing foreman/woman **9214**
rubber inspectors foreman/woman **9214**
rubber lining installer **9423**
rubber mill operator **9423**
rubber moulder operator **9423**
rubber press operator **9423**
rubber products manufacturing inspector **9423**
rubber products manufacturing labourer **9615**
rubber products sales representative – wholesale **6411**

rubber products worker – tire and tube **9615**
rubber roll grinding inspector **9423**
rubber sheet inspector **9423**
rubber shoe cementer **9423**
rubber shoes strap maker **9423**
rubber snowtrack builder **9423**
rubber sole buffer, automatic **9423**
rubber stamp assembler **9423**
rubber stamp maker **9423**
rubber strap folding machine tender **9423**
rubber tester **9423**
rubber tire and tube cementer **9423**
rubber trimmer **9423**
rubber tubing splicer **9423**
rubber wading boot assembler **9423**
rubbish collector – public works **7621**
rug cleaner **6662**
rug cleaning foreman/woman – laundry
    and dry cleaning **6214**
rug coating machine operator **9443**
rug designer **5243**
rug installer **7295**
rug joiner **9451**
rug layer **7295**
rug maker, hand **5244**
rug repairer, oriental **7445**
rug setter – textiles **9441**
rug sewer **9451**
rug stretcher **9619**
rug underlay machine operator – rubber
    manufacturing **9423**
rug weaver **9442**
rughooker **5244**
ruling machine operator – printing **9471**
rulings officer, taxation **1111**
runner **1463**
runway paving foreman/woman **7217**
rural electrification engineer **2133**
rural mail carrier **1462**
rural sociologist **4169**
rural telephone maintainer **7246**
rustproof coater **9496**
rustproofer, automobile manufacturing **9496**

S

sack packer – textile **9619**
saddle cutter – leather products
    manufacturing **9452**
saddle machine tender – woodworking **9513**
saddle stitching machine operator –
    printing **9473**
saddle stitching machine set-up operator
    – printing **9473**
safe and vault servicer **7383**
safe expert **7383**
safe maker **7383**
safety and health inspector **2263**

safety and health officer **2263**
safety and health officer supervisor **2263**
safety and sanitary inspector – public
    and environmental health **2263**
safety deposit box clerk **1434**
safety deposits supervisor **1212**
safety director **0211**
safety earmuff assembler **9498**
safety engineer **2141**
safety equipment salesperson **6221**
safety goggle assembly repairer – plastic
    manufacturing **9495**
safety inspector, mines **2263**
safety inspector – occupational health
    and safety **2263**
safety officer **2263**
safety patrol officer – police **6261**
safety pin machine set-up operator **9516**
safety razor blade honer **9517**
safety razor blade maker **9517**
safety systems mechanic, aircraft
    mechanical systems **7315**
safety systems technician – military **7445**
safety valve repairer – pipelines **7445**
sagger maker, pottery and porcelain **9414**
sagger moulder – clay products **9414**
sagger packer – clay products **9611**
sail boat assembler **9491**
sail lay-out and patternmaker **5245**
sail maker **5245**
salad bar attendant **6641**
salad dressing finisher **9461**
salad maker **6641**
salary administration officer **1432**
salary analyst **1121**
sales agent – insurance **6231**
sales agent – securities **1113**
sales agent – wholesale **6411**
sales and advertising manager **0611**
sales and advertising vice president –
    trade, broadcasting and other services
    n.e.c. **0015**
sales and distribution manager **0611**
sales and marketing manager **0611**
sales associate – retail **6421**
sales auditor – financial **1111**
sales clerk **6421**
sales co-ordinator – wholesale **6411**
sales consultant – retail **6421**
sales consultant – wholesale **6411**
sales director (except retail) **0611**
sales engineer **6221**
sales executive, technical sales **6221**
sales executive – wholesale **6411**
sales general manager – trade,
    broadcasting and other services
    n.e.c. **0015**
sales manager (except retail) **0611**

sales manager, insurance sales **0121**
sales manager – real estate **0121**
sales manager – retail **0621**
sales planning manager **0611**
sales promotion administrator **1122**
sales promotion clerk **6421**
sales promotion manager **0611**
sales record supervisor **1212**
sales representative, courier services **6411**
sales representative, delivery services **6411**
sales representative – insurance **6231**
sales representative, real estate **6232**
sales representative – retail **6421**
sales representative, technical sales **6221**
sales representative – wholesale **6411**
sales statistician **2161**
sales supervisor – retail **6211**
sales, vice president – goods production, utilities, transportation and construction **0016**
sales vice president – trade, broadcasting and other services n.e.c. **0015**
salesman/woman – insurance **6231**
salesman/woman – securities **1113**
salesperson, new homes **6232**
salesperson, real estate **6232**
salesperson – retail **6421**
salesperson, technical sales **6221**
salesperson – wholesale **6411**
salmon grower **8257**
salt compactor operator **9411**
salt compressor operator **9411**
salt crusher **9411**
salt packer **9617**
salt processor **9411**
salt refiner **9411**
salt screening labourer **9611**
salt truck operator – public works **7422**
salvage buyer **6233**
salvage clerk **1472**
salvage dealer **0621**
salvage glass inspector **9415**
salvage operator – electronics manufacturing **9483**
salvage sawyer – woodworking **9513**
salvager, lumber – wood processing **9614**
salvager, storage battery **9485**
salvager, timber and steel props **8614**
salvation army captain **4217**
salvation army commissioned officer **4154**
salvation army field worker **4217**
sample clerk – fabric products **9619**
sample clerk – storage and warehousing **1472**
sample control clerk **1472**
sample cutter – fabric, fur and leather products manufacturing **9452**
sample distributor **1463**
sample garment maker **7342**

sample knitter **9442**
sample maker **9451**
sample maker, jewellery **7344**
sample preparer – chemical processing **9613**
sample preparer – textiles **9444**
sample printer – textiles **9443**
sample room foreman/woman – fabric, fur and leather products manufacturing **9225**
sample room supervisor – fabric, fur and leather products manufacturing **9225**
sample room worker **9619**
sample tester – primary metal and mineral products processing **9415**
sample weaver **9442**
sampler – chemical processing **9613**
sampler – food and beverage processing **9617**
sampler – primary metal and mineral products processing **9415**
sampler – textiles **9444**
sand and gravel tester **2264**
sand control man/woman – foundry **9412**
sand coremaker, manual – foundry **9412**
sand fill boss – underground mining **8221**
sand fill man/woman **8411**
sand mill operator – foundry **9412**
sand moulder – foundry **9412**
sand slinger operator – foundry **9412**
sand spreader operator – public works **7422**
sand system operator – foundry **9412**
sand tester, foundry **9415**
sandblast operator – stone products **9414**
sandblaster **6662**
sandblaster operator – metal fabrication **9612**
sandblasting building cleaner **6662**
sandblasting machine tender – metal fabrication **9612**
sander and finisher, floor **7441**
sander, drywall **7611**
sander, hand **9619**
sander, machine – woodworking **9513**
sander, portable machine – woodworking **9513**
sander, pottery and porcelain **9414**
sanding inspector – woodworking **9493**
sanding machine feeder – woodworking **9513**
sanding machine tender – food and beverage processing **9461**
sanding truck operator – public works **7422**
sandwich maker **6641**
sandwich, salad and dessert maker **6641**
sanitary department inspector – environmental health **2263**
sanitary engineer **2131**
sanitation engineer **2131**
sanitation man/woman **7621**
sanitation truck driver – public works **7422**
sanitation worker **7621**

santa claus **5232**
sash and door end matcher –
    woodworking **9513**
sash and door grader – wood **9493**
sash and door inspector – millwork
    manufacturing **9493**
sash and door repairman/woman **9493**
satellite antenna servicer **2242**
satellite instrumentation engineer **2133**
satellite technician **2241**
satin finisher – furniture finishing and
    refinishing **9494**
saturating machine feeder – chemical
    processing **9613**
saturating machine tender – chemical
    processing **9421**
saturator – textiles **9443**
sauce chef **6241**
saucier **6241**
sausage drier and smoker **9461**
sausage linker – food and beverage
    processing **9617**
sausage tier – food and beverage
    processing **9617**
sausage wrapper – food and beverage
    processing **9617**
savings account teller – financial
    services **1433**
savings accounts supervisor **1212**
savings clerk – financial sector **1434**
savings supervisor **1212**
saw edge fuser – metal machining **9511**
saw filer **7383**
saw fitter **7383**
saw knife miller **9516**
saw maker **7383**
saw operator – metal fabrication **9514**
saw operator – sawmill **9431**
saw repairer apprentice **7383**
saw tailer – wood processing **9614**
sawing machine operator –
    woodworking **9513**
sawing machine tender – woodworking **9513**
sawmill fire chief **0642**
sawmill foreman/woman **9215**
sawmill labourer **9614**
sawmill machine operator **9431**
sawmill worker **9614**
sawsmith **7383**
sawyer and assembler, wooden tank
    bottom **9493**
sawyer – woodworking **9513**
scaffold erector **7611**
scagliola caster – stone products **9414**
scale assembler **9498**
scale calibrator **7383**
scale inspector **9498**
scale maker **9498**

scale mechanic **7445**
scale operator, landfill **9613**
scale repairer **7445**
scaler – forestry **2223**
scaler – primary metal processing **9611**
scaler supervisor **2223**
scaler technician – logging **2223**
scaling co-ordinator – logging **2223**
scallop dredger **8262**
scallop shucker – fish processing **9463**
scalp treatment specialist **6482**
scalping helper – primary metal
    processing **9611**
scalping mill operating – primary metal
    processing **9411**
scanner operator – printing **9472**
scanner reader machine operator **1423**
scanning machine operator, colour
    corrections – printing **9472**
scanning machine operator, colour
    separations – printing **9472**
scarf gluer – wood processing **9434**
scarfing machine tender – wood
    processing **9434**
scarification equipment operator –
    forestry **8422**
scarifier operator **7421**
scene shifter **5227**
scenery artist **5136**
scenic constructor – motion pictures,
    broadcasting and stage productions **5227**
schedule analyst – air transport **0713**
schedule clerk **1473**
schedule clerk, transportation (except
    flights) **1476**
schedule clerks supervisor **1215**
schedule maker, transportation (except
    flights) **1476**
schedule writer **1476**
schedule writer, transportation **1476**
scheduler, flight **0713**
scheduler, flight crew **1476**
scheduler, transit system **1476**
scheduling clerk **1473**
scheduling technician, manufacturing **2233**
school adjustment officer **4143**
school aide **6472**
school board administrator **0313**
school board services manager **0413**
school board trustee **0011**
school bus driver **7412**
school counsellor **4143**
school crossing guard **6651**
school custodian **6663**
school for the blind, director **0313**
school for the deaf, director **0313**
school inspector **4166**
school janitor **6663**

school liaison officer – police **6261**
school librarian – elementary school **4142**
school librarian – secondary school **4141**
school maintenance manager **0722**
school nurse **3152**
school of nursing director **0312**
school principal **0313**
school psychologist **4151**
school safety officer – police **6261**
school secretary **1241**
school services director **0413**
school social worker **4152**
school teacher – elementary school **4142**
school teacher – secondary school **4141**
school vice-principal **0313**
science and technology curator **5112**
science co-ordinator – education **4166**
science teacher – secondary school **4141**
scientific consultant **4161**
scientific glass apparatus blower **5244**
scientific handwriting expert **4169**
scientific illustrator **5241**
scientific instruments sales
    representative **6221**
scientific librarian **5111**
scientific photographer **5221**
scientific programmer **2163**
scientific writer **5121**
scooptram operator – underground
    mining **8231**
scoreboard operator **5253**
scorer – paper converting **9435**
scouring machine operator **9441**
scout, professional sports **5252**
scow captain **7436**
scrap buyer **6233**
scrap metal crusher – primary metal
    processing **9411**
scrap metal dealer **0611**
scrap metal processor – primary metal
    processing **9611**
scrap metal salesperson **6421**
scrap metal shredder – primary metal
    processing **9411**
scrap piler – wood processing **9614**
scrap preparation foreman/woman –
    primary metal processing **9211**
scrap remelter – primary metal
    processing **9611**
scrap rubber grinder **9423**
scrap rubber grinder and dumper **9615**
scrap sorter and baler – primary metal
    processing **9611**
scrap yard worker – primary metal
    processing **9611**
scraper operator **7421**
screed operator, asphalt paving **7421**

screen aluminizer, picture tube
    assembly **9483**
screen and aperture mask assembly
    inspector **9483**
screen buffer, television picture tube **9483**
screen cleaner – pulp and paper **9614**
screen cleaner – rubber products
    manufacturing **9615**
screen print operator **9471**
screen printer, hand – textiles **9443**
screen printing artisan **5244**
screen printing machine feeder **9619**
screen printing machine operator –
    printing **9471**
screen printing machine operator –
    textiles **9443**
screen printing operator – textiles **9443**
screen printing paster **9619**
screen room operator – pulp and paper **9432**
screen stencil cutter, graphic arts **5223**
screen tender, chips – wood processing **9434**
screen tender – pulp and paper **9432**
screen writer **5121**
screener – chemical processing **9421**
screenmaker – printing **9472**
screenman/woman – pulp and paper **9432**
screw machine operator, custom **9511**
screw machine set-up operator **9511**
screw threader **9511**
screwdown operator – primary metal
    processing **9411**
screwmaker, automatic **9516**
script assistant **5227**
script editor **5122**
script supervisor **5227**
script writer **5121**
scroll machine tender **9516**
scroll quilting machine operator **9442**
scroll saw operator – woodworking **9513**
scrubber tender – mineral products
    processing **9611**
scuba diver, commercial **7382**
scuba diver – police **6261**
scuba specialist – police **6261**
scudder – hide and pelt processing **9453**
scullion **6642**
sculptor **5136**
sculptor, eskimo art **5136**
sculptor, metal **5136**
sculptor, monument **5136**
sculptor, wood **5136**
sculpture professor – university **4121**
sculpturing teacher **5136**
sea farm attendant **8613**
sea farm technologist **2221**
sea farm worker **8613**
sea food preparer – fish processing **9463**
seafood counter clerk **6421**

seal hunter **8442**

sealer – aircraft assembly **9481**

sealer, dry cell – electrical equipment
    manufacturing **9487**

sealer – hunting and trapping **8442**

sealer operator – motor vehicle
    manufacturing **9482**

sealing machine operator – electrical
    equipment manufacturing **9487**

sealing machine tender – electrical
    equipment manufacturing **9487**

sealing machine tender – paper
    converting **9435**

seam culker – construction **7611**

seaman/woman **7433**

seamer – rubber goods **9615**

seamless ball moulder **9517**

seamless hosiery knitter **9442**

seamless steel billet piercer – primary
    metal processing **9411**

seamless tube roller – primary metal
    processing **9411**

seamstress **7342**

seamstress, women's garments
    alterations **7342**

search and rescue technician – military **3234**

searchlight operator **5227**

seasonal resort manager **0632**

seasonal worker – public works **7621**

seasoning mixer – food and beverage
    processing **9617**

seat assembler – motor vehicle
    manufacturing **9482**

seat belt assembly inspector **9498**

seaweed dragger **8262**

seaweed gatherer **8613**

seaweed harvesting machine operator **8262**

second, boxing **6671**

second class power engineer **7351**

second class stationary engineer **7351**

second cook **6242**

second deck officer **2273**

second engineer, factory freezer trawler **2274**

second engineer, marine – water
    transport **2274**

second engineer, self-propelled drilling
    rig **2274**

second engineer – water transport **2274**

second hand, paper machine **9234**

second helper – primary metal
    processing **9611**

second language instructor – language
    school **4131**

second language program director **0413**

second mate, fishing vessel **8261**

second mate, foreign going **2273**

second mate, home trade **2273**

second mate, inland waters **2273**

second mate, ship **2273**

second officer **2271**

second pourer – primary metal
    processing **9611**

second secretary, foreign service **4168**

second watchkeeping engineer, coast
    guard vessel **2274**

second watchkeeping officer, coast
    guard vessel **2273**

secondary school education director **0413**

secondary school librarian **4141**

secondary school principal **0313**

secondary school reading clinician **4141**

secondary school teacher **4141**

secondary school teacher, special
    education **4141**

secondary school teacher, technical and
    vocational program **4141**

seconds inspector/grader **9454**

secret service man/woman **6261**

secretarial services teacher – college or
    vocational institute **4131**

secretarial stenographer **1241**

secretary **1241**

secretary, church **1241**

secretary, estate **1242**

secretary, executive **1241**

secretary, legal **1242**

secretary, litigation **1242**

secretary, medical **1243**

secretary, membership **1241**

secretary, real estate **1242**

secretary, school **1241**

secretary, social **1241**

secretary, technical **1241**

secretary to the council – government
    services **0012**

secretary, trademark **1242**

secretary, ward **1243**

section boss, railway tracks **7217**

section foreman/woman – railway **7217**

section leader, light fixture assembly **9484**

section lineman/woman –
    telecommunications **7245**

section manager, retail store **0621**

section worker, railway **7432**

securities analyst **1112**

securities clerk – financial sector **1434**

securities counsellor **1112**

securities research analyst **1112**

securities sales agent **1113**

securities sales director **0121**

securities trader **1113**

securities underwriter **1114**

security alarm consultant **6465**

security alarm installer **2242**

security alarm technician **2242**

security analysis officer – postal service **6465**

security and investigations officer **6465**
security constable – police **6261**
security consultant **6465**
security controller **6651**
security guard **6651**
security guard, chief **6651**
security investigator **6465**
security manager **0114**
security officer **6651**
security officer (enforcement) – military **6261**
security officer (management) – military **0641**
security officer – police **6261**
security officer, private **6465**
security service manager **0123**
security services sales consultant **6411**
security specialist **6465**
sedimentary geologist **2113**
sedimentologist **2113**
seed cleaning service contractor **8252**
seed cone collector **8422**
seed cone picker **8422**
seed corn grader **9465**
seed crop inspector **2222**
seed grower **8251**
seed packager **9619**
seed technologist **2221**
seeding contractor **8252**
seiner, fisherman/woman **8262**
seismic prospecting observer **2212**
seismic prospecting observer helper **8615**
seismic technician **2212**
seismologist **2113**
seismology technologist, petroleum geology **2212**
seismometer technician **2212**
selenium recovery helper – primary metal processing **9611**
self-propelled barge captain **2273**
self-propelled barge marine engineer **2274**
self-propelled drilling rig captain **2273**
self-propelled drilling rig chief engineer **2274**
self-propelled drilling rig engineer **2274**
self-serve gas bar attendant **6611**
self-serve gas bar cashier **6611**
semiconductor assembler **9483**
semiconductor assembly foreman/woman **9222**
semiconductor material gauger – electronics manufacturing **9483**
semiconductor mounter **9483**
semiconductor physicist **2111**
seminar leader, management **4131**
senate committee officer **4168**
senator **0011**
senior administrator, government agency **0012**
senior buyer – retail or wholesale **6233**

senior claims clerk **1434**
senior communications officer **5124**
senior computer operator **1421**
senior editor **5122**
senior engineer, coast guard vessel **2274**
senior engineer, marine – water transport **2274**
senior estimator – construction **2234**
senior extrusion operator – plastic manufacturing **9422**
senior financial analyst **1112**
senior fire control technician **2223**
senior industrial relations officer **1121**
senior investment officer **1112**
senior loan officer **1232**
senior MCR operator **5224**
senior motion picture camera operator **5222**
senior negotiating officer **1121**
senior operating technician **9232**
senior operator – chemical processing **9232**
senior planner, land use **2153**
senior pressman/woman – printing **7381**
senior probation officer **4155**
senior project manager, construction **0711**
senior schedule writer **1476**
senior staffing officer **1223**
senior teller – financial services **1433**
senior underwriter – insurance **1234**
septic system contractor **7219**
septic system installer **7441**
septic tank cleaner **6662**
septic tank service manager **0651**
sergeant-at-arms, house of commons **0012**
serger – garment manufacturing **9451**
serging machine operator **9451**
serologist **2121**
serology technologist **3211**
servant, domestic **6661**
server **6453**
service adviser **1453**
service assistant – telephone system **1424**
service attendant, gas station **6621**
service bartender **6452**
service centre technician – telecommunications **7246**
service contract negotiator – purchasing **1225**
service crew worker – underground mining **8411**
service dispatcher **1475**
service engineer, electrical power systems **2133**
service foreman/woman, electrical power lines **7212**
service foreman/woman – telecommunications **7212**
service inspector – telecommunications **7246**
service installation technician – cable television **7247**

service lineman/woman – electric power systems **7244**

service manager – retail **0621**

service mechanic, automotive **7321**

service monitor – telephone system **1424**

service observer – telephone system **1424**

service representative **1453**

service representative, business office **1453**

service representative – insurance **6231**

service representative – office machinery **2242**

service rig helper – oil field services **8615**

service rig operator – oil field services **8232**

service rig roughneck – oil field services **8615**

service station attendant **6621**

service station attendant apprentice **6621**

service station inspector **6463**

service station manager **0621**

service station representative **6411**

service station supervisor – automotive repair **7216**

service supervisor, telecommunication lines **7212**

service technician, domestic electrical appliances **7332**

service technician – household and business equipment **2242**

service technician, industrial instrument **2243**

service technician – motor vehicle repair **7321**

service technician, process control equipment **2243**

service technician supervisor – household and business equipment **2242**

service tracer – telecommunications **7245**

service truck driver, heavy equipment **7443**

service work order clerk **1473**

serviceman/woman, electric appliances **7332**

serviceman/woman, gas **7253**

servicer, cablevision **7247**

servicer, central air conditioning **7313**

servicer, heavy equipment **7443**

servicer – household and business equipment **2242**

servicer, locomotive **7431**

servicer, mobile home **7441**

servicer, photocopy machine **2242**

servicer, pipeline equipment **7443**

servicer, swimming pool **7441**

servicer, water conditioner **7441**

session musician **5133**

set builder **5227**

set decorator **5226**

set designer **5243**

set dresser **5227**

set electrician **5226**

set-up assembly line – electrical equipment **9484**

set-up assembly machine operator – electrical equipment manufacturing **9487**

set-up, coil winding machine – industrial electrical equipment **9485**

set-up man/woman, core room – foundry **9412**

set-up man/woman – dentures **3412**

set-up man/woman, electrical lamp making machines **9487**

set-up man/woman, machine tools **7231**

set-up man/woman, plastic processing **9422**

set-up man/woman, resistance welding **7265**

set-up operator, automated machine tools **7231**

set-up operator, electrostatic painting machine **9496**

set-up operator – plastic manufacturing **9422**

set-up production machines operator, electrical appliance and equipment manufacturing **9487**

set-up technician, flexographic press – printing **7381**

setter, artificial stone **7281**

setter, cathode ray tube processing **9483**

setter, core room – foundry **9412**

setter, exhaust equipment – electronics manufacturing **9483**

setter, marble **7281**

setter/operator, glass furnace **9413**

setter, simulated stone **7281**

setter, skids **7611**

setter-up, wood cooperage – woodworking **9513**

setter-up, wooden tank – woodworking **9513**

setting foreman/woman – logging **8211**

settlement liaison officer **4164**

sewage control engineer **2131**

sewage disposal foreman/woman **9212**

sewage disposal inspector – environmental health **2263**

sewage disposal manager **0912**

sewage pipelayer **7611**

sewage plant manager **0912**

sewage plant operator **9424**

sewage processing equipment tender **9424**

sewage treatment plant manager **0912**

sewage treatment plant mechanic **7311**

sewer construction foreman/woman **7217**

sewer construction inspector **2264**

sewer digger **7611**

sewer flusher operator driver – public works **7422**

sewer flushing truck operator – public works **7422**

sewer, fur goods **9451**

sewer – garment manufacturing **9451**

sewer installers foreman/woman **7217**
sewer jet cleaner operator – public
    works **7422**
sewer jet machine operator – public
    works **7422**
sewer maintenance worker **7621**
sewer pipe cleaner – manual **7621**
sewer pipe cleaning machine operator –
    public works **7422**
sewer, textile products **9451**
sewing instructor – non-vocational **4216**
sewing machine assembler **9486**
sewing machine assembly tester **9486**
sewing machine mechanic – domestic **7445**
sewing machine mechanic helper **7612**
sewing machine mender **9451**
sewing machine operator **9451**
sewing machine operator, automatic **9451**
sewing machine operator
    foreman/woman **9225**
sewing machine operator, fur **9451**
sewing machine operator supervisor **9225**
sewing machine repairer – domestic **7445**
sewing machine repairer helper **7612**
sewing machine salesperson **6421**
sewing machine servicer – domestic **7445**
sewing room supervisor **9225**
sewing teacher – non-vocational **4216**
sewing teacher – secondary school **4141**
sex therapist **4153**
sexton **6663**
shade matcher – textiles **9444**
shader – furniture finishing and
    refinishing **9494**
shaft miner **8231**
shake inspector – wood processing **9436**
shake maker **9431**
shake packer **9614**
shake sawyer **9431**
shake splitter **9431**
shakerhand – oil and gas drilling **8615**
shaman **3232**
shampooer **6683**
shaper operator – woodworking **9513**
shaper set-up operator **9511**
shaper – wood products manufacturing **9513**
shaver, hogs **9617**
shaver operator – woodworking **9513**
shaver sales clerk **6421**
shaving machine tender – hide and pelt
    processing **9453**
shear operator helper – metal
    fabrication **9612**
shear operator – metal fabrication **9514**
shear setter, metalworking **9514**
shearer, metalworking **9514**
shearer operator – underground mining **8231**

shearing machine fixer – textile
    manufacturing **7317**
shearing machine tender – textiles **9443**
sheather helper **7611**
sheathing extruder helper – primary
    metal processing **9611**
shed foreman/woman **7217**
sheep herdsperson **8253**
sheep relief **8253**
sheep shearer **8431**
sheep shearing contractor **8252**
sheet metal assembler – aircraft
    assembly **9481**
sheet metal brake tender **9514**
sheet metal contractor **7214**
sheet metal cutter – metal fabrication **9514**
sheet metal embossing machine operator **9514**
sheet metal erector **7261**
sheet metal fabricator **7261**
sheet metal installer **7261**
sheet metal instructor – secondary
    school **4141**
sheet metal layer-out **7261**
sheet metal lithographic press feeder **9619**
sheet metal mechanic **7261**
sheet metal model maker **7261**
sheet metal patternmaker **7261**
sheet metal polisher and buffer **9612**
sheet metal roll operator – metal
    fabrication **9514**
sheet metal roofer **7291**
sheet metal spinner – metal fabrication **9514**
sheet metal structures painter **9496**
sheet metal technician, aircraft **7315**
sheet metal worker **7261**
sheet metal worker apprentice **7261**
sheet metal worker helper –
    construction **7611**
sheet metal worker helper – industrial **9612**
sheet metal worker – maintenance **7261**
sheet metal worker – specialty
    manufacturing **7261**
sheet metalworking machine set-up
    operator **9514**
sheet metalworking machine tender –
    metal fabrication **9514**
sheet roller helper – primary metal
    processing **9611**
sheet roller – primary metal processing **9411**
sheet rougher – primary metal
    processing **9411**
sheet steel inspector – primary metal
    processing **9415**
sheeter helper – pulp and paper **9614**
sheeter operator – plastic manufacturing **9422**
sheeter operator – pulp and paper **9433**
sheeter – rubber manufacturing **9423**
sheetrock applicator **7284**

shelf stocker – retail **6622**
shelf stocker, supermarket **6622**
shell assembler **9498**
shell coremaker – foundry **9412**
shell maker, metal **9516**
shell mould bonder **9619**
shell moulder – foundry **9412**
shell trim operator, metal **9516**
shellac sprayer, furniture **9494**
shellacker **9496**
shellfish bed attendant **8613**
shellfish checker – fish processing **9618**
shellfish fisherman/woman **8262**
shellfish harvester **8613**
shellfish harvester deckhand **8441**
shellfish harvester operator **8262**
shellfish packer – fish processing **9618**
shellfish processing labourer **9618**
shellfish processing machine tender **9463**
shellfish processor, hand – fish
    processing **9463**
shellfish separator tender – fish
    processing **9463**
shellfish shucker – fish processing **9463**
sheltered workshop supervisor **4212**
shelving clerk – library **1451**
shepherd **8253**
sherardizer **9497**
sherardizer helper **9619**
sheriff **6461**
sheriff's bailiff **6461**
sheriff's officer **6461**
shiatsu therapist **3232**
shield operator **7421**
shielded metal arc welder **7265**
shift boss – mining and quarrying **8221**
shift foreman/woman – mining and
    quarrying **8221**
shift leader – mining and quarrying **8221**
shift operating supervisor – pulp and
    paper **9215**
shift supervisor, petroleum processing **9212**
shift supervisor, power station **9212**
shingle cutter **9431**
shingle inspector – wood processing **9436**
shingle maker **9431**
shingle mill foreman/woman – wood
    processing **9215**
shingle piler, material handling **7452**
shingle roofer **7291**
shingle roofing contractor **7219**
shingle sawyer **9431**
shingle trimmer **9614**
shingler **7291**
shingler, cedar shakes **7291**
shingler trainee **7291**
shingler, wood **7291**
ship boiler tender **7434**

ship broker **1236**
ship building plater **7263**
ship cargo agent **6434**
ship construction engineer **2148**
ship crane operator **7371**
ship engine greaser **7434**
ship engineer officer **2274**
ship inspector **2262**
ship joiner **7271**
ship loader operator **7451**
ship machinery fitter **7316**
ship machinery installer helper **7612**
ship master **2273**
ship passenger attendant **6672**
ship pilot **2273**
ship pipefitter foreman/woman **7213**
ship purser **6432**
ship repair technician **2232**
ship rigger **7311**
ship rigger foreman/woman **7214**
ship's captain **2273**
ship's chandler **0621**
ship's cook **6242**
ship's electrician – shipbuilding and
    repair **7242**
ship's electrician – water transport **7242**
ship's master, fishing vessel **8261**
ship's mate **2273**
ship's plater apprentice **7263**
ship's supply officer – military **0114**
ship storeman/woman **1472**
ship supply clerk **1474**
shipbuilding carpenter **7271**
shipbuilding electrician helper **7612**
shipfitter **7263**
shipfitter apprentice **7263**
shipfitter foreman/woman **7214**
shipfitter helper **9612**
shipfitter improver **7263**
shipment assembler **7452**
shipper **1471**
shipper/receiver **1471**
shipper supervisor **1215**
shipping agent **1471**
shipping and receiving clerk **1471**
shipping and receiving clerk supervisor **1215**
shipping clerk **1471**
shipping co-ordinator **1215**
shipping sales representative **6411**
shipwright apprentice **7263**
shipwright foreman/woman **7214**
shipwright helper **9612**
shipwright, metal **7263**
shipwright, wood **7271**
shipyard electrician helper **7612**
shipyard labourer **9619**
shipyard machine shop foreman/woman **7211**
shipyard painter **9496**

shipyard painter foreman/woman **9226**
shipyard painter helper **9619**
shirt finisher – laundry and dry cleaning **6682**
shirt folder – laundry and dry cleaning **6682**
shirt folding machine operator – laundry
 and dry cleaning **6682**
shirt inspector **9454**
shirt presser – laundry and dry cleaning **6682**
shock absorber installer **7443**
shoe cutter **9452**
shoe decoration assembler – footwear
 manufacturing **9498**
shoe designer **5243**
shoe dyer **7343**
shoe inspector **9454**
shoe last patternmaker **5245**
shoe mender **7343**
shoe parts cutter – footwear
 manufacturing **9452**
shoe parts dipper **9619**
shoe parts fastener **9517**
shoe parts folder – shoe manufacturing **9619**
shoe parts former **9619**
shoe parts sewer **9451**
shoe parts stock sorter **9619**
shoe patternmaker **5245**
shoe polisher – shoe manufacturing **9619**
shoe repair service manager **0651**
shoe repairer, factory **9498**
shoe repairer helper **7612**
shoe repairer – retail **7343**
shoe salesperson **6421**
shoe sewer **9451**
shoe shiner **6683**
shoe sprayer **9619**
shoe stitcher **9451**
shoe store manager **0621**
shoe trimming machine operator –
 footwear manufacturing **9517**
shoemaker **7343**
shoemaker, custom **7343**
shoemaker, orthopaedic **7343**
shohet – meat packing **9462**
shooter helper, seismic prospecting **8615**
shooting gallery operator **6443**
shop clerk **6421**
shop foreman/woman – appliance repair **7216**
shop foreman/woman, boiler making **7214**
shop foreman/woman – motor vehicle
 repair **7216**
shop inspector, aircraft mechanical
 systems repair **7315**
shop inspector, aircraft repair **7315**
shop inspector, avionics **2244**
shop inspector, avionics instruments **2244**
shop inspector, electrical accessories –
 avionics **2244**
shop manager **0621**

shop repairer – telecommunications **7246**
shop supervisor – automobile repair and
 service **7216**
shop supervisor – small equipment
 repair **7216**
shop tailor **7342**
shopping centre property administrator **1224**
shopping investigator – security **6465**
shopping mall maintenance manager **0722**
shopping mall manager **0721**
shore captain – fishing **0811**
shore captain – water transport **0713**
shore dredging labourer **7611**
shore fisherman/woman **8262**
short order cook **6242**
short story writer **5121**
shorthand reporter **1244**
shorthand teacher – college or
 vocational institute **4131**
shorthand teacher – secondary school **4141**
shortwave receiving station technician **5224**
shortwood harvester operator **8241**
shot bagger **9611**
shot firer – underground mining **8231**
shot foreman/woman – mining and
 quarrying **8221**
shot grinder – metal products **9612**
shotblast machine tender – metal
 fabrication **9612**
shotblast operator – metal fabrication **9612**
shotblaster – metal fabrication **9612**
shotgun shell maker **9516**
shovel handle assembler **9498**
shovel oiler **7443**
shovel operator **7421**
shoveller – underground mining **8614**
show and demonstration designer **5243**
show horse driver **5232**
show horseman/woman **8251**
showcase dresser **5223**
shower door and panel assembler **9498**
shredder operator – tobacco processing **9464**
shredder operator – woodworking **9513**
shredder, plastics **9495**
shrimp peeler tender – fish processing **9463**
shrimp processor – fish processing **9463**
shrinking machine operator – textiles **9443**
shrouder – food and beverage
 processing **9617**
shrub grower **8254**
shucker – fish processing **9463**
shunt assembler, small electric
 transformer **9484**
shuttle bus driver **7412**
shuttle car operator **8411**
shuttle filler – textiles **9616**
shuttle fixer – textile manufacturing **7317**
shuttle inspector – wood **9493**

shuttle maker – woodworking **9513**
shuttle planer – woodworking **9513**
sideboom mechanic **7312**
sideboom operator – pipeline construction **7421**
sideboom tractor operator **7421**
sider helper **7611**
siderographer – printing **9472**
sideseal operator, plastic bag **9422**
sidewalk cleaner – manual **7621**
sidewalk cleaning equipment operator **7621**
sidewalk concrete finisher **7282**
sidewall core sampler – oil field services **8232**
siding applicator **7441**
siding checker/messenger **7622**
siding contractor **7219**
siding installer **7441**
sightseeing boat operator **7436**
sightseeing bus driver **7412**
sightseeing guide **6441**
sightseeing tour driver **7412**
sign and display sales representative **6411**
sign carpenter **7271**
sign designer **5241**
sign erector – commercial **7441**
sign erector – highways **7611**
sign inspector **6463**
sign installer **7441**
sign language instructor **4215**
sign language interpreter **5125**
sign layout detailer **5223**
sign maker **9498**
sign painter **5223**
sign painter apprentice **5223**
sign panel primer **9496**
sign patternmaker **5223**
sign spray painter **9496**
sign trimmer and assembler, plastic **9495**
sign writer **5223**
signal engineer **2133**
signal gang helper **7622**
signal maintainer, railway **7242**
signal tower operator, railway **7431**
signaller, sea – military **6464**
signalman/woman, railway **7431**
silhouette artist **5136**
silicon wafer fabricator **9483**
silk finisher – laundry and dry cleaning **6682**
silk flower maker, hand **5244**
silkscreen artist **5136**
silkscreen assembler – printing **9472**
silkscreen printing machine operator **9471**
silkscreen printing machine operator – textiles **9443**
silkscreen stencil cutter **5223**
silkscreen technician **5223**
silkscreen tender – printing **9471**

silkscreening machine operator **9471**
silo erector/mason **7281**
silver chaser **7344**
silver plater operator **9497**
silver spray operator **9497**
silvering operator, glass **9413**
silversmith **5244**
silverware buffer **9517**
silverware cleaner **6642**
silverware department foreman/woman **9227**
silverware engraver **5244**
silverware salesperson **6421**
silviculture contractor **8211**
silviculture crew co-ordinator **2223**
silviculture forester **2122**
silviculture supervisor **8211**
silviculture technician **2223**
silviculture worker **8422**
silviculturist **2225**
simulated stone mason **7281**
simulated stone setter **7281**
simulation systems analyst – computer systems **2162**
simultaneous interpreter **5125**
singeing and boiling machine tender – textiles **9443**
singeing machine tender **9617**
singer **5133**
single end sewer **9619**
single needle sewing machine operator **9451**
singleply roofer **7291**
sink float equipment operator – metal processing **9411**
sintering machine operator – primary metal processing **9411**
sintering plant foreman/woman – mineral and metal processing **9211**
sintering press tender – foundry **9412**
site foreman/woman, construction **7217**
site planner **2153**
site superintendent, construction **0711**
sitter **6474**
sixth hand – pulp and paper **9614**
size maker – pulp and paper **9432**
size maker – textiles **9441**
sizing machine tender – textiles **9441**
sizing saw tender, plywood – wood processing **9434**
skate lining inserter **9619**
skate maker **9498**
skate press operator **9517**
skate shop attendant **6421**
skater **5251**
skating instructor **5254**
skein spooler – textiles **9441**
skein winder – textiles **9441**
skein yarn examiner – textiles **9444**
skeiner, hand – textiles **9616**

skeiner – textiles **9441**
sketch cartoonist **5241**
sketcher, ink **5136**
skewer machine feeder **9619**
ski coach **5252**
ski equipment repairer **7445**
ski host/hostess **6441**
ski instructor **5254**
ski lift attendant **6671**
ski lift operator **6671**
ski maker **9498**
ski patroller **5254**
ski resort manager **0632**
ski tow operator **6671**
skid setter – pipeline construction **7611**
skidder foreman/woman – logging **8211**
skidder, fruit packing **7452**
skidder operator – logging **8421**
skier **5251**
skiffman/woman, fishing vessel **8441**
skimmer, distillery **9461**
skin care consultant **6481**
skin care specialist **6481**
skin diver, commercial **7382**
skin fitter – aircraft assembly **9481**
skin specialist **3111**
skinner, animal – meat packing **9462**
skinning machine feeder – food and
    beverage processing **9617**
skinning machine setter – fish
    processing **9463**
skip loader – underground mining **8411**
skip tender – underground mining **8411**
skip tracer **1435**
skipper fishing vessel **8262**
skipper, gillnetter **8262**
skiver, machine – leather products **9517**
skiver – rubber manufacturing **9423**
skylight assembler – plastic
    manufacturing **9495**
slab inspector, rubber **9423**
slab machine operator – rubber
    manufacturing **9423**
slab off man/woman – rubber
    manufacturing **9615**
slab saw operator – sawmill **9431**
slabber **9421**
slabbing mill roller – primary metal
    processing **9231**
slasher loader operator **8241**
slasher operator helper – textiles **9616**
slasher operator – logging **8241**
slasher operator – sawmill **9431**
slasher operator – textiles **9441**
slasher sawyer operator **8241**
slasher – textiles **9441**
slat picker – woodworking **9513**
slat slicer, wood products **9513**

slate cutting and grinding machine
    tender **9415**
slate mixer **9414**
slate picker **8614**
slaughterer – meat packing **9462**
slaughterer, ritual – meat packing **9462**
slavonic studies professor – university **4121**
sleeping bag finisher **9498**
sleeping car conductor **7362**
sleeping car porter **6672**
sleeve machine tender – electrical
    equipment manufacturing **9487**
sleight-of-hand artist **5232**
sliced cheese maker **9461**
slicing machine tender – food and
    beverage processing **9461**
slickline operator – oil field services **8232**
slide fastener chain assembler **9498**
slide fastener inspector **9498**
slide forming machine set-up operator **9514**
slide forming machine setter – metal
    fabrication **9514**
slide forming machine tender – metal
    fabrication **9514**
slide maker – photographic processing **9474**
slime plant helper – primary metal
    processing **9611**
slime recovery operator – primary metal
    processing **9411**
slime treater – primary metal processing **9411**
slinger **7611**
slip form curb machine tender **7611**
slip seat coverer – furniture assembly **9619**
slipper maker **9451**
slitter and rewinder **9452**
slitter creaser feeder – paper converting **9435**
slitter creaser operator – paper
    converting **9435**
slitter operator – plastic manufacturing **9422**
slitter operator – rubber manufacturing **9423**
slitting machine operator helper **9619**
slitting machine operator – metal
    fabrication **9514**
sliver lapper – textiles **9441**
slotter operator – metal **9516**
slubber hand **9441**
slubber tender – textiles **9441**
sludge mill operator – primary metal
    processing **9411**
sludge worker – primary metal
    processing **9611**
slurry control operator – primary metal
    processing **9231**
slurry controller – primary metal
    processing **9231**
slurry equipment operator – primary
    metal and mineral products
    processing **9411**

slusher operator – underground mining **8231**
small animal veterinary specialist **3114**
small arms checkerer **9513**
small arms repairer **7383**
small claims court judge **4111**
small claims court registrar **1227**
small claims court supervisor **1227**
small craft operator **7436**
small electric motor assembler **9484**
small electric motor builder **9484**
small electrical appliances inspector **9484**
small electrical products assembler **9484**
small engine assembly foreman/woman **9226**
small engine mechanic **7335**
small engine mechanic, marine **7335**
small engine repairer **7335**
small equipment mechanic **7335**
small equipment mechanic apprentice **7335**
small equipment repairer **7335**
small fruit picker **8611**
small marine engine assembler **9486**
small parts assemblers – motor vehicle
    manufacturing **9482**
small power transformer coil winder **9485**
small transformer assembler – electrical
    equipment manufacturing **9484**
smelter and refinery mould maker –
    foundry **9412**
smelter engineer, minerals **2142**
smelter foreman/woman – primary metal
    and mineral products processing **9211**
smelter house mixer **9411**
smelter labourer **9611**
smelter liner **7611**
smelting furnace operator – primary
    metal processing **9411**
smoke house operator – food and
    beverage processing **9461**
smoke shop clerk **6421**
smoked meat preparer – food and
    beverage processing **9617**
smokestack repairer **7383**
smoking pipe air hole driller **9513**
smoking pipe burler **9513**
smoking pipe maker **9513**
smoking pipe repairer **7445**
smoking pipe sander **9513**
snack bar attendant **6421**
snag grinder – metal fabrication **9612**
sniper – military **6464**
snow blower operator, railway **7432**
snow blower repairer, gasoline powered **7335**
snow controller **2213**
snow fence erector **7441**
snow grooming machine operator **7421**
snow plough operator, road – public
    works **7422**
snow plough operator, sidewalk **7621**

snow removal equipment operator –
    public works **7422**
snow shoveler **6661**
snowblower driver – public works **7422**
snowmaker **6671**
snowmobile assembler **9486**
snowmobile assembly foreman/woman **9226**
snowmobile assembly supervisor **9226**
snowmobile final inspector **9486**
snowmobile inspector **9486**
snowmobile repairer **7334**
snowmobile repairman/woman **7334**
snowmobile test rider **9486**
snowshoe weaver **9498**
snowtrack builder, rubber **9423**
snowtrack foreman/woman – rubber
    manufacturing **9214**
snuff blending machine operator –
    tobacco processing **9464**
snuff drier – tobacco processing **9464**
snuff grinder – tobacco processing **9464**
soaking pit furnace operator – primary
    metal processing **9411**
soap and toilet goods inspector **9498**
soap boiler **9421**
soap cutter and stamper **9421**
soap maker **9421**
soccer player **5251**
social and cultural anthropologist **4169**
social animator **4212**
social assistance director **0314**
social case work consultant **4152**
social consultant **6481**
social development officer **4164**
social ecologist **4169**
social economist **4162**
social historian **4169**
social issues researcher **4164**
social policy researcher **4164**
social psychologist **4151**
social rehabilitation worker **4212**
social researcher **4164**
social science researcher **4164**
social science statistician **2161**
social sciences professor – university **4121**
social sciences teacher – secondary
    school **4141**
social secretary **1241**
social service program officer **4164**
social service worker **4212**
social services assistant **4212**
social services consultant **4164**
social services director **0411**
social services planning consultant **4164**
social services planning manager –
    government services **0411**
social services program planner **4164**
social services teacher – college **4131**

social survey researcher **4164**
social work director **0314**
social work officer **4152**
social work professor – university **4121**
social work supervisor **4152**
social worker **4152**
society columnist **5123**
society editor **5122**
society reporter **5123**
sociolinguist **4169**
sociologist **4169**
sociology professor – university **4121**
sock knitter **9442**
sock looper **9442**
sod farmer **8251**
sod layer **8612**
soda fountain attendant **6641**
soda solution maker **9421**
sofa inspector – furniture manufacturing **9492**
soft drink mixer **9617**
soft drink powder mixer **9461**
soft drinks driver/salesman/woman **7414**
soft rock miner **8231**
soft water serviceman/woman **7441**
soft water servicer **7441**
softtop trimmer – motor vehicle
    manufacturing **9482**
software analyst **2162**
software development programmer **2163**
software engineer **2147**
software programmer **2163**
software sales representative **6221**
software specialist **2162**
software systems programmer **2163**
soil and crop specialist **2123**
soil bacteriological technician **2221**
soil bacteriological technologist **2221**
soil bacteriologist **2121**
soil chemist **2112**
soil conservationist **2123**
soil engineer **2144**
soil fertility expert **2123**
soil inspector **2264**
soil preparation contractor **8252**
soil scientist **2115**
soil technologist, civil engineering **2231**
soil testing service contractor **8252**
soils testing technologist **2231**
solar heating equipment installer **7441**
solar heating technician **7441**
solderer **9515**
solderer/dipper **9515**
solderer, furnace **9515**
solderer, induction **9515**
solderer, jewellery **9498**
soldering machine feeder **9619**
soldering machine operator **9515**
sole edge stainer – shoe manufacturing **9619**

sole maker, rubber **9423**
sole moulding machine tender –
    footwear manufacturing **9517**
solenoid valve assembler **9498**
solicitor **4112**
solicitor general **0011**
solid fuel heating installer **7331**
solid fuel heating sales consultant **6221**
solid state assembler **9483**
solid state physicist **2111**
solid tire builder **9423**
solid tire finisher **9423**
solid tire mounter – toy manufacturing **9619**
solid waste disposal technician **2231**
solid waste manager **0912**
solution mixer – chemical processing **9421**
solution mixer operator – plastic
    manufacturing **9422**
solvent mixer operator – plastic
    manufacturing **9422**
solvent recovery tender – chemical
    processing **9421**
solvent treating plant operator **9232**
sonar operator – military **6464**
sonar technician – military **2241**
song writer **5132**
sonographer, medical **3216**
sonography technologist **3216**
sorter, boot and shoe **9454**
sorter, fruit – agriculture **8611**
sorter, garments **9619**
sorter, mail **1461**
sorter – rubber manufacturing **9615**
sorter, upholstery parts **9619**
sorter, vegetable – agriculture **8611**
sorting and routing clerk **1461**
sorting clerk – financial sector **1434**
sorting machine tender **1422**
sorting system operator, mail **1461**
sound cutter **5225**
sound editor **5225**
sound effects editor **5225**
sound engineer **5225**
sound engineer assistant **5225**
sound insulator **7293**
sound mixer **5225**
sound operator **5225**
sound recorder **5225**
sound recording equipment operator **5225**
sound recording supervisor **5225**
sound technician **5225**
soundproof material installer **7293**
sous-chef **6241**
sous-chef, first **6241**
soya mill operator **9461**
soyabean tester **9465**
space craft sub-assemblies
    foreman/woman **9226**

space officer **1224**
space physicist **2111**
space reliability specialist **2146**
space vision technologist **2241**
spacecraft communications systems
     engineer **2133**
spacecraft electronics engineer **2133**
spacer – pipeline construction **7611**
spacing saw operator – forestry **8422**
spanish teacher – high school **4141**
spar assembler – aircraft assembly **9481**
spark plug assembler **9484**
speaker assembler **9483**
speaker, legislative body **0011**
special assistant **1222**
special care aide – nursing **3413**
special care home attendant **3413**
special delivery mail carrier **1462**
special diet cook **6242**
special education assistant **6472**
special education co-ordinator –
     education **4166**
special education teacher – elementary
     school **4142**
special education teacher, mentally
     handicapped **4215**
special education teacher – secondary
     school **4141**
special effects assistant **5227**
special effects technician **5226**
special endorsement clerk – insurance **1434**
special events organizer **1226**
special features editor **5122**
special glass cutter **9413**
special librarian **5111**
special needs counsellor **4153**
special needs teacher – elementary
     school **4142**
special orders cook, hospital **6242**
special project manager, construction **0711**
special prosecutor **4112**
special services technician –
     telecommunications **7246**
specialist, advertising **1122**
specialist chef **6241**
specialist, child **3111**
specialist, community medicine **3111**
specialist, ear, nose and throat **3111**
specialist, emergency medicine **3111**
specialist, employment standards **4164**
specialist, environmental medicine **3111**
specialist, eye **3111**
specialist, foot **3123**
specialist, geriatric medicine **3111**
specialist, hearing **3141**
specialist, heart **3111**
specialist, herbal **3232**
specialist, HVAC systems **2232**

specialist in critical care medicine **3111**
specialist in epidemiology and
     community medicine **3111**
specialist in infectious diseases **3111**
specialist in medical genetics **3111**
specialist in nuclear medicine **3111**
specialist in occupational medicine **3111**
specialist, internal medicine **3111**
specialist, nerve **3111**
specialist, physical medicine and
     rehabilitation **3111**
specialist physician **3111**
specialist, preventive medicine **3111**
specialist, records management **1122**
specialist, rehabilitation **3111**
specialist, scalp treatment **6482**
specialist, skin **3111**
specialist, software **2162**
specialist, sports and spinal injury **3111**
specialist, telecommunications –
     computer systems **2147**
specialty transformer assembler **9484**
specification writer, construction **2231**
specifications writer (except
     construction) **5121**
spectacle frames polisher **9517**
spectroscopic technologist **2211**
spectroscopist **2211**
speech aide **3235**
speech and hearing clinician **3141**
speech and hearing therapist **3141**
speech clinician **3141**
speech consultant **3141**
speech correctionist – medical **3141**
speech language assistant **3235**
speech-language pathologist **3141**
speech pathologist **3141**
speech technician **3235**
speech therapist **3141**
speech therapy aide **3235**
speech therapy assistant **3235**
speech writer **5121**
speedometer repairer **7445**
spherical lens generator –
     non-prescription **9517**
spice miller **9461**
spice mixer **9461**
spike driver machine operator, railway **7432**
spike installer, golf shoe **9619**
spike machine feeder **9619**
spike machine operator – metal forgings **9512**
spike machine operator, railway **7432**
spike puller machine operator, railway **7432**
spin mould machine set-up operator,
     glass **9413**
spindle carver operator – woodworking **9513**
spinner – food and beverage processing **9461**
spinner, hand **5244**

spinner, metal **9514**

spinneret pack preparer – chemical processing **9421**

spinning frame fixer – textile manufacturing **7317**

spinning frame tender – textiles **9441**

spinning lathe operator – metal fabrication **9514**

spinning machine tender – textiles **9441**

spinning operator – textiles **9441**

spinning room foreman/woman – textiles **9216**

spinning supervisor – textiles **9216**

spiral binder machine operator – printing **9473**

spiral gear generator operator **9511**

spiral operator – rubber manufacturing **9423**

spiral weaving machine operator **9516**

spiral wound gasket maker – rubber manufacturing **9423**

splicer, cable – electric power systems **7244**

splicer helper – telecommunications **7612**

splicer, rubber **9423**

splicer technician – telecommunications **7245**

splicer technician, telephone **7245**

splicer – telecommunications **7245**

splicing machine tender – rubber manufacturing **9423**

splicing machine tender – textiles **9441**

splitter – hide and pelt processing **9453**

splitter operator – sawmill **9431**

splitter, rubber **9423**

splitter – woodworking **9513**

splitting machine tender – rubber manufacturing **9423**

spoke wheel assembler **9498**

sponge and dough mixer – food and beverage processing **9461**

sponge gasket assembler, rubber **9423**

sponge mop assembler **9498**

sponge press operator, rubber **9423**

sponge range operator – textiles **9443**

sponge rubber inspector **9423**

spontaneous art teacher **3144**

spool carrier – textiles **9616**

spool winder – textiles **9441**

spooler, latex threads – rubber manufacturing **9423**

spooler operator, automatic – textiles **9441**

spooler – textiles **9441**

spooler-twister operator – rubber manufacturing **9423**

spooling machine operator **9612**

spooling machine tender – textiles **9441**

sport administration director **0513**

sport attendant **6671**

sport policy analyst **4167**

sport psychologist **4151**

sporting goods repairer **7445**

sporting goods salesperson **6421**

sporting goods store manager **0621**

sports announcer **5231**

sports association director **0513**

sports ball inspector and repairer **9498**

sports ball moulder operator **9517**

sports cartoonist **5241**

sports co-ordinator **4167**

sports columnist **5123**

sports consultant **4167**

sports director, broadcasting **5131**

sports editor **5122**

sports equipment filler **9619**

sports equipment repairer **7445**

sports facility grounds keeper **8432**

sports facility manager **0721**

sports governing agency executive director **0513**

sports headgear assembler **9498**

sports instructor **5254**

sports medicine physician **3111**

sports official **5253**

sports program co-ordinator, broadcasting **5226**

sports program co-ordinator, sports and recreation **4167**

sports program director **0513**

sports program supervisors **4167**

sports supervisor **4167**

sports writer **5121**

sportscaster **5231**

spot welder, portable **9515**

spotlight operator **5227**

spotter – laundry and dry cleaning **6681**

spray booth cleaner **9619**

spray coating machine tender, hardboard **9496**

spray coating machine tender – textiles **9443**

spray drier tender – chemical processing **9421**

spray foam operator – electrical equipment manufacturing **9487**

spray gelcoat operator – plastic manufacturing **9422**

spray gun repairer **7445**

spray machine operator, paint **9496**

spray machine set-up man/woman, tinware **9496**

spray machine setter, tinware **9496**

spray paint crew leader **9496**

spray paint machine tender **9496**

spray paint operator **9496**

spray painter, benchwork **9496**

spray painter helper **9619**

spray painter, metal products **9496**

spray painter, production **9496**

spray painter, products **9496**

spray painter, rough **9496**

spray painter, signs **9496**
spray pilot **2271**
spray stainer – furniture finishing and refinishing **9494**
spray truck helper **7611**
sprayer, hand **8432**
sprayer, leather or suede, laundry and dry cleaning **6681**
sprayer – logging and forestry **8422**
spraying machine tender – textiles **9443**
sprayman/woman, finished enamel **9496**
spreader box tender **7611**
spreader machine tender – rubber manufacturing **9423**
spreader operator **7421**
spreader operator helper – plastic **9615**
spreader operator – rubber manufacturing **9423**
spring assembler – furniture manufacturing **9492**
spring assembler – motor vehicle manufacturing **9482**
spring inserter – furniture manufacturing **9619**
spring installer **7443**
spring machine operator **9516**
spring maker, clock **9498**
spring making machine set-up operator **9516**
spring tester **9516**
spring winding machine operator **9516**
springer – furniture assembly **9619**
sprinkler system installer **7252**
sprinkler system installer apprentice **7252**
sprinkler systems contactor **7213**
sprinkler systems fitter **7252**
sprinkler systems installer, foreman/woman **7213**
sprinkling truck driver – public works **7422**
sprinter **5251**
squeegee splicer, rubber **9423**
squeezer moulder – foundry **9412**
squeezer tender – woodworking **9513**
stabber – pipeline construction **7611**
stable boss **8253**
stable worker **8431**
stableman/woman **8431**
stacker operator – heavy equipment **7421**
stacker operator – material handling **7452**
stackerman/woman – printing **9619**
stacking machine operator – electrical equipment manufacturing **9487**
stacking machine tender – material handling **7452**
stadium manager **0721**
staff assistant – education **6472**
staff, chief of – hospital **0311**
staff counsel **4112**
staff inspector, police **0641**

staff lawyer **4112**
staff nurse **3152**
staff physiotherapist **3142**
staff relations administrator **1121**
staff relations manager **0112**
staff relations officer **1121**
staff sergeant **6261**
staff solicitor **4112**
staff superintendent, police **0641**
staff training and development manager **0112**
staff training and development supervisor **1121**
staff training officer **4131**
staff writer **5121**
staffing analyst **1223**
staffing assistant **1442**
staffing co-ordinator **1223**
staffing officer **1223**
stage carpenter **7271**
stage director **5131**
stage electrician **5226**
stage manager **5226**
stage musical director **5132**
stage producer **5131**
stage production worker **5227**
stage property foreman/woman **5226**
stage scenery designer **5243**
stage technician **5226**
stagehand **5227**
stager – printing **9472**
staging assistant **5227**
stained glass artist **5244**
stained glass glazier **7292**
stained glass painter **5244**
stained glass production worker **9413**
stainer **9494**
stair builder carpenter **7271**
stair builder helper **7611**
stairway carpenter **7271**
stake grader – wood processing **9436**
stakeman/woman, surveying **7612**
staking machine tender **9517**
stamp cancelling machine tender **1461**
stamp dealer **0621**
stamp pad maker **9517**
stampede performer **5251**
stamper, gold-leaf **9473**
stamper – primary metal processing **9611**
stamping die finisher **7232**
stamping die maker, bench **7232**
standards chemist **2112**
standards co-ordinator **1122**
standards engineer **2148**
standards specialist **1122**
staple cutter – glass products manufacturing **9413**
staple machine set-up operator **9516**

staple processing machine tender –
    textiles **9441**
stapling machine tender **9517**
stapling machine tender, box end **9517**
starch centrifuge tender **9617**
starch converter **9461**
starch factory labourer – food and
    beverage processing **9617**
starch maker – food and beverage
    processing **9461**
starch presser, corn products **9461**
starch separator operator **9461**
starch tester – food and beverage
    processing **9465**
starch washer – food and beverage
    processing **9461**
starter, harness racing **5253**
starter, horse racing **5253**
starting sheet maker – primary metal
    processing **9411**
station agent, airline **6433**
station agent, railway **6434**
station attendant, air transport **7437**
station duty officer – police **6261**
station manager, broadcasting **0512**
station officer – police **6261**
station operator – electric power
    systems **7352**
station services agent, airline **6433**
stationary engine oiler **7612**
stationary engineer **7351**
stationary engineer apprentice **7351**
stationary engineer, fifth class **7351**
stationary engineer, first class **7351**
stationary engineer foreman/woman **9212**
stationary engineer, fourth class **7351**
stationary engineer – military **7351**
stationary engineer, second class **7351**
stationary engineer, third class **7351**
stationary farm equipment mechanic **7311**
stationery store manager **0621**
stationmaster **7221**
statistical actuary **2161**
statistical analyst **2161**
statistical assistant **1454**
statistical clerk **1454**
statistical clerk supervisor **1213**
statistical consultant **2161**
statistical department director **0212**
statistical officer **2161**
statistical service manager **0212**
statistical technician **2161**
statistical typist **1412**
statistician **2161**
statistician, chief – government services **0012**
stator inspector – industrial electrical
    equipment **9485**
stave inspector, wood **9493**

stave jointer – woodworking **9513**
stave machine operator – woodworking **9513**
stave sawyer – woodworking **9513**
stayer machine tender – paper
    converting **9435**
steam cabinet attendant – garment
    manufacturing **9619**
steam cabinet operator – textiles **9443**
steam cleaner **6662**
steam cleaner – automotive **6662**
steam drier – food and beverage
    processing **9461**
steam engineer foreman/woman **9212**
steam engineer leader **9212**
steam finisher – laundry and dry
    cleaning **6682**
steam hammer operator – metal forgings **9512**
steam heating installer **7252**
steam kettle operator – food and
    beverage processing **9461**
steam main servicer **7252**
steam meter repairer **7445**
steam operator **7351**
steam oven operator – food and beverage
    processing **9461**
steam pipefitter **7252**
steam plant foreman/woman **9212**
steam plant maintenance mechanic **7311**
steam plant operator **7351**
steam power engineer, stationary **7351**
steam press operator **6682**
steam roller operator **7421**
steam room attendant **6683**
steam sponger – textiles **9443**
steam table attendant – food service **6641**
steam table operator – food and beverage
    processing **9461**
steam tank operator – stone products **9414**
steam tunnel operator – laundry and dry
    cleaning **6682**
steam turbine operator – electric power
    systems **7352**
steamblaster **6662**
steamer tender – textiles **9443**
steamer – tobacco processing **9464**
steamfitter **7252**
steamfitter foreman/woman **7213**
steamfitter/pipefitter **7252**
steamfitter's helper **7611**
steamship line manager **0713**
steamship passenger agent **6434**
steel chipper – metal fabrication **9612**
steel degasser process operator **9231**
steel die printer **9471**
steel engraver **5244**
steel erector helper **7611**
steel erector – underground mining **8411**
steel fabricator apprentice **7263**

steel fabricator – structural metal and
    platework **7263**
steel fitter – metal platework **7263**
steel fitter – structural metal **7263**
steel form setter – underground mining **8411**
steel form setting worker **7611**
steel forms setter helper **7611**
steel heater operator **9411**
steel inspector – primary metal
    processing **9415**
steel mill manager **0911**
steel mill recorder **1473**
steel plate caulker – ship building **9486**
steel pourer **9411**
steel production labourer **9611**
steel roller **9411**
steel rougher **9411**
steel rule die maker **7232**
steel sales representative **6221**
steel shot forge header operator **9512**
steel spar operator **8241**
steel straightener **9411**
steel structure erector **7264**
steel stud erector – nonbearing walls **7611**
steel tester – primary metal processing **9415**
steel wool machine operator **9516**
steeplejack **7383**
steepman/woman – food and beverage
    processing **9461**
steering box assembler **9486**
stem cutter – tobacco processing **9464**
stem flattening machine tender – tobacco
    processing **9464**
stem roller – tobacco processing **9464**
stemming machine operator – tobacco
    processing **9464**
stencil cutter – stone products **9414**
stencil maker, graphic arts **5223**
stenographer **1241**
stenographers and typists supervisor **1211**
stenotype operator **1244**
step and repeat camera operator **9472**
stereo equipment store manager **0621**
stereo repair technician **2242**
stereo repairer **2242**
stereo salesperson **6421**
stereo tape editor **5225**
stereoplotter, map **2255**
sterile products processor – chemical
    processing **9232**
sterile supply room attendant **6631**
sterilizer operator – food and beverage
    processing **9461**
sterilizer operator – surgical equipment **9517**
sterilizing machine operator – food and
    beverage processing **9617**
stevedore **7451**
stevedoring foreman/woman **7217**

steward, airline **6432**
steward, food service **6453**
steward (food service) – military **0631**
steward, kitchen **6212**
steward, racetrack **5253**
steward/stewardess, airline **6432**
steward (supervisor, distributing and
    scheduling) – military **1215**
steward (supervisor, mail distribution) –
    military **1214**
stewardess, airline **6432**
stewardess instructor **4131**
sticker, animal – meat packing **9462**
still cleaner – chemical processing **9613**
still tender **9421**
stitcher – garment manufacturing **9451**
stitcher operator – printing **9473**
stitcher operator, woodworking **9513**
stitcher/trimmer operator – printing **9473**
stitching department foreman/woman –
    fabric, fur and leather products
manufacturing **9225**
stitching department supervisor **9225**
stitching machine operator **9451**
stitching machine set-up operator –
    printing **9473**
stock attendant **8431**
stock broker **1113**
stock car racer **5251**
stock chaser **1473**
stock clerk, motor vehicle parts **1472**
stock clerk – retail **6622**
stock clerks supervisor **1215**
stock control clerk **1472**
stock control supervisor **1215**
stock cutter, woodworking **9513**
stock grader – furniture manufacturing **9492**
stock handler, food store **6622**
stock handler – manufacturing and
    warehousing **7452**
stock helper **7452**
stock herder **8431**
stock lay-up man/woman – rubber
    manufacturing **9615**
stock layer **9619**
stock market reporter **5123**
stock mixer – textiles **9441**
stock preparation foreman/woman –
    rubber manufacturing **9214**
stock preparer – rubber manufacturing **9615**
stock receiver **1471**
stock records clerk **1472**
stock supervisor – retail **6211**
stock tester – pulp and paper **9432**
stock tracer **1473**
stock washer – pulp and paper **9432**
stocking inspector **9444**
stocking stitcher **9451**

stockkeeper's helper 7452
stockpiler 7452
stockroom clerk – retail 6622
stockyard and herdsmen
    foreman/woman 8253
stockyard attendant 8431
stoker erector 7331
stoker – ship 7434
stone bed setter – mineral products
    processing 9611
stone beveler 9414
stone carver, hand 5244
stone driller – stone products 9414
stone duster – underground mining 8614
stone grinder tender 9414
stone lay out marker 9414
stone machine operator – woodworking 9513
stone mason chimney repair 7281
stone mason foreman/woman 7219
stone masonry contractor 7219
stone planer 9414
stone polisher, hand 9414
stone polisher, machine 9414
stone processing foreman/woman 9211
stone sandblaster 9414
stone saw setter 7445
stone sawyer – stone products 9414
stone setter 7281
stone splitter, hand 9619
stone splitter tender 9414
stone spreader operator, manual 7611
stonecutter, building 9414
stonecutter, hand 9414
stonecutter – jewellery 7344
stonecutter – stone products 9414
stonemason 7281
stonesetter – jewellery 7344
stonework block maker 9414
stonework drill press operator 9414
stonework engraver – stone products 9414
stonework filler – mineral products
    processing 9611
stonework grader – mineral products
    processing 9415
stonework inspector – mineral products
    processing 9415
stonework moulder 9414
stonework patternmaker 7383
stonework sandblast operator 9414
stonework saw operator 9414
stonework stencil cutter 9414
stope driller – underground mining 8231
stope foreman/woman 8221
stopper grinder, glass 9413
storage battery assembler 9487
storage battery charger – electrical
    equipment manufacturing 9487

storage battery tube filler – electrical
    equipment manufacturing 9487
storage facility rental clerk 6421
storage foreman/woman 7217
storage man/woman 7452
storage service sales representative 6411
storage worker 7452
store clerk 6421
store detective 6465
store display designer 5243
store manager – retail 0621
storekeeper 1472
storekeeper, drilling rig 1472
storekeeper, ship 1472
storeman/woman 1472
stores and receiving supervisor 1215
story board artist 5241
story teller 5135
stove assembler, electric 9484
stove refinisher 9496
stove repairman/woman, electric 7332
stove serviceman/woman, electric 7332
stowage clerk 6434
straddle truck operator 7452
straightening press operator – metal
    fabrication 9514
straightening roll operator – primary
    metal processing 9411
strainer tender – rubber manufacturing 9423
strand forming machine tender – textiles 9441
stranding machine operator 9516
strap maker, rubber shoes 9423
strapping machine operator – glass
    manufacturing 9413
stratigrapher 2113
street cleaner – manual 7621
street flusher operator – public works 7422
street light repairer – electric power
    systems 7244
street light servicer – electric power
    systems 7244
street musician 5133
street paver, asphalt 7421
street paver operator 7421
street sprinkler operator – public works 7422
street sweeper – manual 7621
street sweeper operator – public works 7422
street vendor 6623
streetcar and subwaycar mechanic 7383
streetcar cleaner 6662
streetcar conductor 7412
streetcar mechanic 7383
streetcar operator 7412
stress engineer, aerospace 2146
stretcher, bedspring 9619
stretcher drier – laundry and dry
    cleaning 6682

stretcher leveller operator – primary
    metal processing **9411**
stretching machine operator – hide and
    pelt processing **9453**
stretching machine tender – textiles **9443**
strike off machine tender **9443**
stringed instrument maker **5244**
stringed instrument repairer **7445**
stringing machine feeder **9517**
strip cutters and blending operator –
    tobacco processing **9464**
strip cutting machine tender – tobacco
    processing **9464**
strip machine operator – rubber
    manufacturing **9423**
strip roll forming machine operator –
    metal fabrication **9514**
strip-tease dancer **5232**
striper, hand – shoe manufacturing **9619**
stripper/assembler – printing **9472**
stripper, hand – furniture manufacturing **9619**
stripper/image assembler – printing **9472**
stripper/layout specialist – printing **9472**
stripper, moulded products – plastic and
    rubber manufacturing **9615**
stripper – printing **9472**
stripping machine tender – leather
    products manufacturing **9452**
stripping machine tender – tobacco
    processing **9464**
stripping shovel oiler **7443**
structural and ornamental metalwork
    inspector **9514**
structural design engineer **2131**
structural design technologist **2231**
structural draftsman/woman **2253**
structural draftsperson **2253**
structural engineer, aerospace **2146**
structural engineer, civil **2131**
structural engineering technician **2231**
structural geologist **2113**
structural glass glazier **7292**
structural glass installer **7292**
structural hydraulic jack operator **7421**
structural investigator **2231**
structural iron erector **7264**
structural iron worker **7264**
structural metal and platework fabricator
    apprentice **7263**
structural metal and platework layer-out **7263**
structural metal erector **7264**
structural metal fabricator **7263**
structural metal fitter **7263**
structural metal fitter helper **9612**
structural plate fitter helper –
    construction **7611**
structural steel contractor **7214**
structural steel draftsman/woman **2253**

structural steel erecting contractor **7214**
structural steel erector **7264**
structural steel erector helper **7611**
structural steel fitter **7263**
structural steel inspector **2264**
structural steel plate shaper **7263**
structural steel shop foreman/woman **7214**
structure seat installer **7441**
structures aerospace engineer **2146**
structures technician, aircraft **7315**
structures technician (drywalling) –
    military **7284**
structures technician (floor installation)
    – military **7295**
stucco lather **7284**
stucco plasterer **7284**
student activities adviser **4212**
student activities dean **0312**
student, CA **1111**
student cardiology technologist **3217**
student counsellor **4143**
student dental mechanic **3221**
student denturist **3221**
student loan officer **1232**
student optician **3231**
student placement officer **1223**
student residence cleaner **6661**
student residence manager **0632**
student sonographer, medical **3216**
studio administrator **5226**
studio camera operator **5222**
studio carpenter **7271**
studio control operator, transmission **5224**
studio electrician **5226**
studio image processing system operator
    – printing **9472**
studio operator, audio recording **5225**
studio operator, video transmission **5224**
stuffing machine tender – toys **9517**
stummel turner – woodworking **9513**
stunt co-ordinator **5226**
stunt rider **5232**
stuntman/woman **5135**
stylist, hair **6271**
sub-sheriff **6461**
subassembler – aircraft assembly **9481**
subassembler, electrical control panel **9485**
subassembler, electronic equipment **9483**
subassembler – furniture manufacturing **9492**
subassembler – motor vehicle
    manufacturing **9482**
subdivision control officer **6463**
subject consultant – education **4166**
submerged arc welder **7265**
subscription clerk **1441**
subsea engineer **2145**
subsea equipment engineer, offshore
    drilling rig **2145**

substance abuse worker **4212**

substation electrician – electric power
    systems **7243**

substation inspector – electric power
    systems **7352**

substation operator – electric power
    systems **7352**

substation operator, helper **9613**

substitute high school teacher **4141**

substitute teacher – elementary school **4142**

substitute teacher – secondary school **4141**

subway car cleaner **6662**

subway scheduler **1476**

subway traffic controller **7222**

subway train operator **7412**

succession duty auditor – taxation **1228**

suede cleaner – laundry and dry
    cleaning **6681**

sugar boiler **9461**

sugar boiler helper **9617**

sugar bush labourer **8431**

sugar tester **9465**

suggestion program clerk **1441**

suit maker **7342**

sulky driver **5251**

sulphuric acid plant operator **9232**

sun-tan studio attendant **6683**

superannuation clerk – financial sector **1434**

supercalender operator helper – pulp and
    paper **9614**

supercalender operator – pulp and paper **9433**

supercargo clerk **1471**

superintendent, bridge construction **0711**

superintendent, building **6663**

superintendent, city **0012**

superintendent, construction **0711**

superintendent couple **6663**

superintendent, electrical **0722**

superintendent, engineering **0211**

superintendent, factory **0911**

superintendent, general construction **0711**

superintendent, greens **2225**

superintendent, historical park **0511**

superintendent, maintenance **0722**

superintendent, maintenance and service **0722**

superintendent, marine operations **0713**

superintendent, mechanical services **0722**

superintendent, mill **0911**

superintendent of academic affairs **0313**

superintendent of education programs **0313**

superintendent of elementary schools **0313**

superintendent of operations,
    maintenance **0722**

superintendent of operations, schools **0313**

superintendent of production **0911**

superintendent of professional
    development and supervision,
    schools **0313**

superintendent of secondary schools **0313**

superintendent of special education **0313**

superintendent of student services **0313**

superintendent of transportation **0713**

superintendent, pipeline construction **0711**

superintendent – police **0641**

superintendent, race track maintenance **7219**

superintendent, refinery **0911**

superintendent, regional schools **0313**

superintendent, schools **0313**

superior court justice **4111**

supermarket butcher **6251**

supermarket clerk **6622**

supermarket department supervisor **6211**

supermarket manager **0621**

supermarket meat cutter **6251**

supervising chef **6241**

supervising engineer, power systems
    operations **2133**

supervising engineer, rock sciences **2144**

supervisor, accountants **1111**

supervisor, accounting clerks **1212**

supervisor, accounts **1212**

supervisor, advertising art **5241**

supervisor, advertising clerks **1213**

supervisor, agricultural products
    inspection **2222**

supervisor, air craft maintenance
    mechanics **7216**

supervisor, air pilots, flight officers and
    flight engineers **2271**

supervisor, air transport operating
    support occupations **1215**

supervisor, aircraft assembly **9226**

supervisor, aircraft maintenance –
    mechanical systems **7216**

supervisor, airline sales and service
    agents **6216**

supervisor, ambulance service **3234**

supervisor, animal control **6463**

supervisor, appliance repair shop **7216**

supervisor, art **5241**

supervisor, art therapists **3144**

supervisor, assembly and test –
    electronics manufacturing **9222**

supervisor, assembly – motor vehicle
    manufacturing **9221**

supervisor, assessment clerks **1212**

supervisor, athletic club attendants **6216**

supervisor, attendance records **1211**

supervisor, audio visual equipment
    repair **2242**

supervisor, auditors **1111**

supervisor, automotive body repair shop **7216**

supervisor, automotive service
    mechanics **7216**

supervisor, baggage porters **6216**

supervisor, baggage porters and
    bellhops **6216**
supervisor, bartenders **6452**
supervisor, bicycle assembly **9227**
supervisor, billing **1212**
supervisor, bindery – printing **7218**
supervisor, bingo hall workers **6216**
supervisor, body shop – motor vehicle
    manufacturing **9221**
supervisor, boilermakers **7214**
supervisor, bookkeepers and accounting
    clerks **1212**
supervisor, bottling **9213**
supervisor, bricklaying **7219**
supervisor, budget **1212**
supervisor, budget accounting **1111**
supervisor, building insulation **7219**
supervisor, bus drivers **7222**
supervisor, buyers **6233**
supervisor, by-law enforcement officers **6463**
supervisor, cable installation **7212**
supervisor, cablevision technicians **7212**
supervisor, car wash **6215**
supervisor, cardiology **3217**
supervisor, cardiovascular perfusion **3214**
supervisor, carpenters **7215**
supervisor, carpentry **7215**
supervisor, cashiers **6211**
supervisor, cement finishing **7219**
supervisor, cement manufacturing **9211**
supervisor, central supply room –
    hospital **6631**
supervisor, chassis assembly – motor
    vehicle manufacturing **9221**
supervisor, chauffeurs **7222**
supervisor, chemical processing **9212**
supervisor, city **0012**
supervisor, claims adjusters **1212**
supervisor, clay, glass and stone furnace
    and kiln operators **9211**
supervisor, cleaners **6215**
supervisor, cleaning and maintenance **6215**
supervisor, clinical perfusion **3214**
supervisor, clock and watch assembly **9227**
supervisor, club house attendants **6216**
supervisor, collection clerks **1212**
supervisor, commissionaires **6216**
supervisor, composing – printing **7218**
supervisor, computer operations **1211**
supervisor, computer operators **1211**
supervisor, construction electricians **7212**
supervisor, construction painters **7219**
supervisor, contract clerks **1211**
supervisor, copyright clearance **1213**
supervisor, correctional officers **6462**
supervisor, correspondence clerks
    (clerical) **1213**
supervisor, cost **1212**

supervisor, cost accounting **1111**
supervisor, counselling program **4153**
supervisor, couriers **1214**
supervisor, court reporters **1211**
supervisor, credit clerks **1212**
supervisor, criminal/traffic registry **1227**
supervisor, crushing and grinding –
    primary metal and mineral products **9211**
supervisor, customer service, bank or
    financial institution **1212**
supervisor, customer service clerks
    (except financial institutions) **1213**
supervisor, customs brokerage clerks **1212**
supervisor, customs clerks **1211**
supervisor, customs inspection **1228**
supervisor, dance therapists **3144**
supervisor, data control **1211**
supervisor, data entry clerks **1211**
supervisor, dental technician **3223**
supervisor, desk-top publishing **1211**
supervisor, dispatchers **1215**
supervisor, display **5243**
supervisor, distribution **1215**
supervisor, door-to-door sales **6211**
supervisor, drafting occupations **2253**
supervisor, drafting office **2253**
supervisor, dressmakers **9225**
supervisor, dressmaking shop **9225**
supervisor, driver/salesmen/women **7222**
supervisor, dry cleaning **6214**
supervisor, drywall installers **7219**
supervisor, dye department – textiles **9216**
supervisor, dyeing – textiles **9216**
supervisor, economic research **4162**
supervisor, education policy **4166**
supervisor, electric power inspectors and
    testers **7212**
supervisor, electrical appliance
    assembly **9223**
supervisor, electrical equipment
    manufacturing **9223**
supervisor, electrical installation **7212**
supervisor, electrical wiring inspectors **7212**
supervisor, electricians **7212**
supervisor, electronic data processing
    equipment operators **1211**
supervisor, electronic equipment
    installation and repair **2242**
supervisor, electroplating **9226**
supervisor, employment counsellors **4213**
supervisor, engine assembly (except
    aircraft) **9226**
supervisor, engine dress – motor vehicle
    manufacturing **9221**
supervisor, environmental program
    development **4161**
supervisor, equipment department –
    railway **7216**

supervisor, excise tax officers **1228**
supervisor, export traffic **1215**
supervisor, factory electricians **7212**
supervisor, file clerks **1211**
supervisor, filing services **1211**
supervisor, film processing **7218**
supervisor, final assembly – motor
    vehicle manufacturing **9221**
supervisor, financial accounting **1212**
supervisor, fingerprint classifiers **1215**
supervisor, finishing – printing **7218**
supervisor, finishing – textiles **9216**
supervisor, fish products inspection **2222**
supervisor, fisheries inspectors **2224**
supervisor, fishery officers **2224**
supervisor, floor covering **7219**
supervisor, food and beverage
    processing **9213**
supervisor, food products testers **9213**
supervisor, food services **6212**
supervisor, forest management **2223**
supervisor, forest products processing **9215**
supervisor, forestry **8211**
supervisor, forestry technicians **2223**
supervisor, foundry **9211**
supervisor, freight forwarding unit **1215**
supervisor, furniture and fixture
    manufacturing **9224**
supervisor, furniture finishers **9224**
supervisor, gambling tables **6443**
supervisor, garden tractor assembly **9226**
supervisor, gas field **9212**
supervisor, gas fitters **7213**
supervisor, gas transmission **9212**
supervisor, general office clerks **1211**
supervisor, glass cutters **9211**
supervisor, glazing **7219**
supervisor, halfway house **4212**
supervisor, hat and cap manufacturing
    workers **9225**
supervisor, health officers **2263**
supervisor, health record unit **1211**
supervisor, health records technicians **1211**
supervisor, heavy equipment mechanics **7216**
supervisor, heavy equipment operators **7217**
supervisor, helicopter assembly **9226**
supervisor, hospital admitting clerks **1211**
supervisor, hotel clerks **6216**
supervisor, human resources **1121**
supervisor, human rights commission
    officers **4164**
supervisor, immigration officers **1228**
supervisor, import traffic **1215**
supervisor, industrial electricians **7212**
supervisor, industrial mechanics **7216**
supervisor, information clerks **1213**
supervisor, injection moulding – rubber
    and plastic manufacturing **9214**

supervisor, insurance agents **6231**
supervisor, internal auditors **1111**
supervisor, inventory clerks **1215**
supervisor, ironworks **7214**
supervisor, janitors **6215**
supervisor, jewellery assembly **9227**
supervisor, job evaluation **1121**
supervisor, knitting **9216**
supervisor, laboratory maintenance –
    anatomical pathology **3414**
supervisor, latherers **7219**
supervisor, laundry **6214**
supervisor, lens manufacturing –
    non-prescription **9227**
supervisor, letter carriers **1214**
supervisor, library **5111**
supervisor, library clerks **1213**
supervisor, licence clerks **1211**
supervisor, light rail transit operators **7222**
supervisor, line and cable workers **7212**
supervisor, loading testers **7212**
supervisor, logging **8211**
supervisor, logistics **1215**
supervisor, machine fitters **7216**
supervisor, machine shop **7211**
supervisor, machinery inspectors **7211**
supervisor, machinists **7211**
supervisor, mail and postal clerks **1214**
supervisor, mail carriers **1214**
supervisor, maintenance electricians **7212**
supervisor, manufacturing plant
    electricians **7212**
supervisor, meat packing **9213**
supervisor, medical laboratory **3211**
supervisor, medical radiation
    technologists **3215**
supervisor, medical records unit **1211**
supervisor, medical sonographers **3216**
supervisor, merchandising clerks **1212**
supervisor, messengers **1214**
supervisor, metal mould and pattern
    makers **7211**
supervisor, methods and procedures
    analysts **1122**
supervisor, millwork assembly **9227**
supervisor, mine **8221**
supervisor, mobile home assembly **9226**
supervisor, mobile radio broadcast **5224**
supervisor, money market investments **1212**
supervisor, mortuary **3414**
supervisor, motor vehicle assembly –
    motor vehicle manufacturing **9221**
supervisor, motor vehicle repair shop **7216**
supervisor, moving van drivers **7222**
supervisor, municipal law enforcement
    officers **6463**
supervisor, music therapists **3144**
supervisor, night clerks **6216**

supervisor, nuclear medicine
    technologists **3215**
supervisor, nursery workers **8256**
supervisor – nursing **3151**
supervisor, nursing registry **1211**
supervisor, occupational health **2263**
supervisor of chambermaids **6215**
supervisor of ultrasound **3216**
supervisor, office machine operators **1211**
supervisor, office services **1211**
supervisor, open pit mine **8221**
supervisor, organization and methods
    analysts **1122**
supervisor, paint shop – motor vehicle
    manufacturing **9221**
supervisor, paper converting **9215**
supervisor, paper mill **9215**
supervisor, park labourers **8256**
supervisor, parking lot **6216**
supervisor, parts clerks **1215**
supervisor, passport office **1211**
supervisor, payment processing unit **1212**
supervisor, payroll **1212**
supervisor, personnel clerks **1211**
supervisor, petroleum refining **9212**
supervisor, photocopy unit **1211**
supervisor, photographic and film
    processing **7218**
supervisor, photography **5221**
supervisor, pipefitters **7213**
supervisor, pipeline operation **9212**
supervisor, plastering **7219**
supervisor, plastic products
    manufacturing **9214**
supervisor, platemaking – printing **7218**
supervisor, platwork fabricators **7214**
supervisor, plumbers **7213**
supervisor, postal clerks **1214**
supervisor, postal station **1214**
supervisor, power station **9212**
supervisor, power system electricians **7212**
supervisor, press – printing **7218**
supervisor, pressroom – printing **7218**
supervisor, price markers **6211**
supervisor, primary metal and mineral
    products processing **9211**
supervisor, printing **7218**
supervisor, private police agents and
    investigators **6465**
supervisor, private policemen/women
    and investigators **6465**
supervisor, production clerks **1215**
supervisor, public auditors **1111**
supervisor, public health inspectors **2263**
supervisor, public opinion interviewers **1213**
supervisor, public works maintenance
    equipment operators **7217**
supervisor, publication clerks **1213**

supervisor, purchasing **1225**
supervisor, purchasing clerks **1215**
supervisor, quarry **8221**
supervisor, radiation therapists **3215**
supervisor, radio or television
    broadcasting equipment operators **5224**
supervisor, radio repair **2242**
supervisor, radiography technologist **3215**
supervisor, railway car maintenance **7216**
supervisor, railway station clerks **6216**
supervisor, real estate **6232**
supervisor, real estate agents **6232**
supervisor, receiving **1215**
supervisor, receptionists **1211**
supervisor, record systems analysts **1122**
supervisor, records clerks **1211**
supervisor, records office **1211**
supervisor, recruitment **1211**
supervisor, registered representatives **1113**
supervisor, registration unit **1211**
supervisor, remedial gymnasts **3144**
supervisor, reservations – hotel **6216**
supervisor, respiratory therapy **3214**
supervisor – retail **6211**
supervisor, roof shingling **7219**
supervisor, roofers and shinglers **7219**
supervisor, rubber products
    manufacturing **9214**
supervisor, safety and health officers **2263**
supervisor, sales clerks **6211**
supervisor, salt milling **9211**
supervisor, sawmill **9215**
supervisor, scheduling clerks **1215**
supervisor, school bus drivers **7222**
supervisor, school lunch room **6472**
supervisor, security guards **6216**
supervisor, service technicians –
    household and business equipment **2242**
supervisor, sewage treatment plant **9212**
supervisor, sheet metal workers **7214**
supervisor, shingle mill – wood
    processing **9215**
supervisor, shipping **1215**
supervisor, shipping and receiving **1215**
supervisor, shipping and receiving
    clerks **1215**
supervisor, shoe makers and repairers –
    leather, fur and fabric products
manufacturing **9225**
supervisor, silverware manufacturing **9227**
supervisor, small engine assembly **9226**
supervisor, small engine repair shop **7216**
supervisor, snowmobile assembly **9226**
supervisor, social service program
    officers **4164**
supervisor, social survey researchers **4164**
supervisor, sound recording **5225**

supervisor, sports equipment
    manufacturing **9227**
supervisor, sprinkler system installers **7213**
supervisor, staff training and
    development **1121**
supervisor, stationary engineers **9212**
supervisor, statistical clerks **1213**
supervisor, steamfitters **7213**
supervisor, stenographers and typists **1211**
supervisor, stock clerks **6211**
supervisor, street railway operators **7222**
supervisor, subway and street railway
    operators **7222**
supervisor, subway operators **7222**
supervisor, surface mine **8221**
supervisor, survey **2154**
supervisor, survey interviewers **1213**
supervisor, switchboard operators **1211**
supervisor, systems – computer systems **2162**
supervisor, tailors **7342**
supervisor, taxi drivers and chauffeurs **7222**
supervisor, telecommunication installers
    and repairers **7212**
supervisor, telegraph operators **1215**
supervisor, telemarketers **6211**
supervisor, telephone installation **7212**
supervisor, telephone operators **1211**
supervisor, telephone sales clerks **6211**
supervisor, television repair **2242**
supervisor, tellers **1212**
supervisor, textile mechanics **7216**
supervisor, textile processing **9216**
supervisor, theatre attendants **6216**
supervisor, ticket clerks – recreation **6216**
supervisor, ticket sellers – recreation **6216**
supervisor, ticket takers – recreation **6216**
supervisor, tilesetting **7219**
supervisor, tire building **9214**
supervisor, tobacco processing **9213**
supervisor, tobacco processing machine
    operators **9213**
supervisor, toll bridge attendants **6216**
supervisor, tool and die inspectors **7211**
supervisor, tool and die makers **7211**
supervisor, tour guides **6216**
supervisor, toy manufacturing **9227**
supervisor, traffic and distribution **1215**
supervisor, training **1121**
supervisor, travel clerks **6216**
supervisor, tree service **8256**
supervisor, trim and hardware – motor
    vehicle manufacturing **9221**
supervisor, truck drivers **7222**
supervisor, truck trailer assembly **9226**
supervisor, typesetting **1211**
supervisor, typing **1211**
supervisor, unit clerks **1211**
supervisor, ushers **6216**

supervisor, vegetable canning **9213**
supervisor, vegetable packing **9213**
supervisor, watch and clock assembly
    repairers **9227**
supervisor, water treatment plant **9212**
supervisor, water well drilling **7217**
supervisor, weaving **9216**
supervisor, welders **7214**
supervisor, welfare policy analysts **4164**
supervisor, well services crew – oil field
    services **8222**
supervisor, wharf clerks **1215**
supervisor, wholesale trade
    representative **6411**
supervisor, window washers **6215**
supervisor, woodworking machine
    operators **9224**
supervisor, word processing unit **1211**
supervisor, work study analysts **1122**
supervisor, yarn preparation – textiles **9216**
supervisors, railway transport
    operations **7221**
supplies attendant, beauty salon **6683**
supply clerk **1474**
supply clerk, ship **1474**
supply control co-ordinator **1215**
supply high school teacher **4141**
supply officer, government **1225**
supply officer – military **0114**
supply officer, ship **6432**
supply, processing and distribution aide
    – medical **6631**
supply teacher – elementary school **4142**
supply teacher – high school **4141**
supply technician (purchasing and
    inventory) – military **1474**
supply technician (storekeeping and
    parts) – military **1472**
supply technician supervisor – military **1215**
support services vice-president –
    financial, communications and other
    business services **0013**
support services vice-president – goods
    production, utilities, transportation
    and construction **0016**
support services vice-president – health,
    education, social and community
    services and membership
    organizations **0014**
support services vice-president – trade,
    broadcasting and other services
    n.e.c. **0015**
supreme court justice **4111**
supreme court registrar **1227**
surface grinder operator, production **9511**
surface mounted assemblies operator –
    electronics manufacturing **9483**

surface plate finisher – concrete, clay and stone products **9414**
surface weather observer **2213**
surgeon **3111**
surgeon, dental **3113**
surgeon, oral **3113**
surgeon, oral and maxillofacial **3113**
surgeon, veterinary **3114**
surgery, chief of **0311**
surgery, director of **0311**
surgery professor – university **4121**
surgical aide **3413**
surgical appliances fitter **3219**
surgical assistant – non-nursing **3414**
surgical assistant – nursing **3233**
surgical belt maker **3219**
surgical co-ordinator – nursing **3151**
surgical fitter **3219**
surgical pad knitter **9442**
surgical pathologist **3111**
surgical supplies salesperson **6221**
surgical technician – non-nursing **3414**
surgical technician – nursing **3233**
surgical ward supervisor – nursing **3151**
surplus assets officer **1221**
surrogate court judge **4111**
surrogate court registrar **1227**
surveillance manager – telecommunications **0131**
survey compiler **1454**
survey draftsperson **2253**
survey engineer **2131**
survey interviewer **1454**
survey notekeeper **1454**
survey pilot **2271**
survey research director – government services **0411**
survey research manager – government services **0411**
survey research service manager **0123**
survey statistician **2161**
survey supervisor **2154**
survey taker **1454**
survey technician **2254**
survey technologist **2254**
surveying and optical instrument repairer **7445**
surveying and optical instrument repairer helper **7612**
surveying and optical instrument technician **7445**
surveying engineer **2131**
surveyor, cargo **2262**
surveyor, gas leaks **7442**
surveyor helper **7612**
surveyor, land **2154**
surveyor, marine cargo **2262**
survival equipment repairer **7445**

swamper – logging and forestry **8422**
swamper, seasonal – logging **8616**
swatch checker – textiles **9444**
sweatband roller **9619**
sweep moulder – foundry **9412**
sweeper **6661**
swim coach **5252**
swimming instructor **5254**
swimming pool cleaner **6662**
swimming pool contractor **7219**
swimming pool installer **7441**
swimming pool maintenance service manager **0651**
swimming pool servicer **7441**
swine herdsperson **8253**
swine relief **8253**
swing type lathe operator – woodworking **9513**
switch engineer, railway **7361**
switch network installer & repairer – telecommunications **7246**
switch tender, railway **7431**
switchboard operator – clerical **1414**
switchboard operator, generating station – electric power systems **7352**
switcher, broadcasting **5224**
switcher, railway **7431**
switchgear assembler – industrial electrical equipment **9485**
switchgear fitter/wirer – industrial electrical equipment **9485**
switchman/woman helper – telecommunications **7612**
switchman/woman – telecommunications **7246**
swordfish fisherman/woman **8262**
synthesizer repairer **2242**
synthetic marble production worker **9422**
synthetic textiles technician **2211**
syrup kettle operator **9461**
syrup maker **9461**
system control centre operator – electric power systems **7352**
system controller – electric power systems **7352**
system development co-ordinator – computer systems **2162**
system electrician – electric power systems **7243**
system operator – computer **1421**
system operator – electric power systems **7352**
system planning technician – electrical power **2241**
systematist, biology **2121**
systems analysis technical counsellor – computer systems **2162**
systems analyst – computer systems **2162**

systems analyst, EDP **2162**

systems analyst, electronic data processing **2162**

systems application engineer **2147**

systems assurance and optimization, programmer **2163**

systems design engineer **2147**

systems designer – computer systems **2162**

systems development manager – computer systems **0213**

systems engineer, aerospace **2146**

systems engineer, computer **2147**

systems manager – computer systems **0213**

systems programmer **2163**

systems software programmer **2163**

systems software support representative **6221**

systems specialist, business – computer systems **2162**

systems specialist – computer systems **2162**

systems test foreman/woman – electronics manufacturing **9222**

systems tester **2241**

T

table assembler **9492**

table assembler, wood **9492**

table dancer **5232**

table top edger – woodworking **9513**

table top laminator – woodworking **9513**

tablet coating machine operator **9517**

tablet making machine tender **9517**

tabulating machine operator **1422**

tabulating supervisor **1212**

tack maker **9516**

tack welder/assembler **9515**

tacker – footwear manufacturing **9517**

tacker sewing machine operator **9451**

tag machine tender – paper converting **9435**

tag printing machine tender **9471**

tagger, laundry and dry cleaning **6681**

tai-chi instructor **5254**

tail-end brakeman/woman **7362**

tail sawyer – sawmill **9431**

tailings labourer – primary metal processing **9611**

tailings thickener tender – primary metal processing **9411**

tailor, made to measure garments **7342**

tailor, men's garments alterations **7342**

tailor, ready to wear garments **7342**

tailor/tailoress **7342**

takeout pizza driver **7414**

takeout service attendant **6641**

talent co-ordinator **5226**

talent representative **6411**

talk show host/hostess **5231**

tall oil operator **9432**

tallow extractor tender – food processing **9461**

tallow refiner **9617**

tally clerk **1473**

tallyman/woman **1473**

tamper-aligner machine operator, railway **7432**

tamper, asphalt – manual **7611**

tamper operator **7611**

tamping machine operator, railway **7432**

tank assembler, wood **9493**

tank builder helper **7611**

tank car cleaner **6662**

tank cleaner **6662**

tank driver – military **6464**

tank farm operator **9232**

tank gunner – military **6464**

tank house operator – food and beverage processing **9461**

tank liner – rubber manufacturing **9423**

tank stave assembler, wood **9493**

tank truck driver **7411**

tank truck loader **7452**

tanker loader – marine cargo handling **7451**

tanker pumper – ship **7434**

tankerman/woman – marine cargo handling **7451**

tankhouse equipment operator – primary metal processing **9411**

tankhouse foreman/woman – primary metal and mineral products processing **9211**

tankhouse helper – primary metal processing **9611**

tanner – hide and pelt processing **9453**

tannery foreman/woman – hide and pelt processing **9225**

tannery machinery repairer **7311**

tanning salon attendant **6683**

tanning salon manager **0651**

tanning solution preparer **9453**

tap dancer **5134**

tap-dancing teacher **5134**

tape cartridge and cassette assembler **9483**

tape cartridge and cassette inspector **9483**

tape control multi-purpose machine operator – metal machining **9511**

tape-controlled drill press operator **9511**

tape-controlled jig boring machine operator **9511**

tape-controlled riveting machine operator **9516**

tape duplicator **5227**

tape librarian, computer **1421**

tape recorder repairer **2242**

tape rule printer **9471**

taper, drywall **7284**

taper operator – electrical equipment manufacturing **9487**
taper, shoe parts **9619**
taping machine tender – electrical equipment manufacturing **9487**
tapman/woman **6452**
tapper, glass – mineral products processing **9611**
tapper labourer - metal processing **9611**
tapping machine tender **9516**
tar and gravel roofer **7291**
tar roofer **7291**
tare assessor – food and beverage processing **9617**
tariff clerk **1431**
tariff counsel **4112**
tarot card reader **6484**
tarpaulin finisher **9498**
tarpaulin maker **5245**
tart maker **9461**
task force officer **4168**
tassel machine tender – textiles **9442**
taster and buyer, beverages **6233**
tattoo artist **6482**
tattooer **6482**
tax accountant **1111**
tax adviser **1111**
tax analyst **1111**
tax appeal officer **1228**
tax assessor **1228**
tax attorney **4112**
tax auditor **1111**
tax clerk **1431**
tax collection officer **1228**
tax consultant **1111**
tax court judge **4111**
tax economist **4162**
tax enforcement officer **1228**
tax evaluator **1111**
tax examiner **1111**
tax expert **1111**
tax interpretation officer **1228**
tax law clerk **4211**
tax lawyer **4112**
tax legal assistant **4211**
tax paralegal **4211**
tax recovery officer **1228**
tax return preparer **1431**
tax specialist **1111**
taxation manager **0412**
taxi dispatcher **1475**
taxi driver **7413**
taxi inspector **6463**
taxicab operation proprietor **7222**
taxidermist **5212**
taximeter repairer **7445**
taxonomist **2121**
taxonomist, biology **2121**

tea blender **9617**
tea leaf reader **6484**
tea room manager **0631**
teacher, acting – private or studio **5135**
teacher, agricultural school **4131**
teacher, art therapy **3144**
teacher, ballet **5134**
teacher, ballroom dancing **5134**
teacher, bible college **4131**
teacher, bible school **4131**
teacher, business college **4131**
teacher, CÉGEP **4131**
teacher, college of applied arts and technology **4131**
teacher, commercial college **4131**
teacher, community college **4131**
teacher, consultant **4166**
teacher, dancing **5134**
teacher, day-care **4214**
teacher, dramatic arts – private or studio **5135**
teacher, elementary school **4142**
teacher, English as a second language – (except elementary, high school or university) **4131**
teacher, folk dancing **5134**
teacher for the hearing impaired **4215**
teacher, French as a second language – not elementary, high school or university **4131**
teacher, high school **4141**
teacher, kindergarten **4142**
teacher, legal assistant program **4131**
teacher librarian – elementary school **4142**
teacher, music – private, conservatory or studio **5133**
teacher of the blind **4215**
teacher of the deaf **4215**
teacher of the mentally handicapped **4215**
teacher of the physically disabled **4215**
teacher, orientation and mobility of the blind **4215**
teacher, painting **5136**
teacher, physically disabled **4215**
teacher, police college **4131**
teacher, preschool **4214**
teacher, primary school **4142**
teacher, printmaking **5136**
teacher, rehabilitation of the blind **4215**
teacher, rolfing movement **3232**
teacher's aide **6472**
teacher's assistant **6472**
teacher's helper **6472**
teacher, sculpturing **5136**
teacher, secondary school **4141**
teacher – seminary **4131**
teacher, spontaneous art **3144**
teacher, tap dancing **5134**
teacher, teacher's college **4121**

teacher, technical institute **4131**

teacher, technological institute **4131**

teacher, university **4121**

teacher, vocational institute **4131**

teacher, vocational school **4131**

teachers' federation executive director **0314**

teaching assistant, college **4122**

teaching assistant – post-secondary **4122**

teaching assistant, university **4122**

teaching homemaker **6471**

teaching orthoptist **3123**

team supervisor, flour milling **9213**

techer, art (except primary, secondary, post-secondary education) **5136**

technical advisor, welding **2212**

technical and vocational teacher – secondary school **4141**

technical assistant, geology **2212**

technical assistant – medical laboratory **3212**

technical assistant, pharmacy **3414**

technical assistant, statistics **1454**

technical attendant – pathology **3211**

technical co-ordinator, nuclear medicine **3215**

technical co-ordinator, radiography **3215**

technical co-ordinator, radiotherapy **3215**

technical counsellor, systems analysis – computer systems **2162**

technical director – motion pictures, broadcasting and the performing arts **5131**

technical director, nuclear medicine **3215**

technical director, radiography **3215**

technical editor **5122**

technical high school principal **0313**

technical illustrator **2253**

technical indexer – library **5211**

technical indexer – records and file management **1413**

technical inspector, mechanical **2232**

technical institute instructor **4131**

technical institute teacher **4131**

technical officer – museum **5212**

technical producer **5131**

technical records clerk **1413**

technical sales representative **6221**

technical sales specialist **6221**

technical sales supervisor **6221**

technical salesperson **6221**

technical salesperson, telecommunications **6221**

technical school director **0312**

technical school manager **0312**

technical secretary **1241**

technical service representative – household and business equipment **2242**

technical service sales consultant **6221**

technical services and automation librarian **5111**

technical services clerk – library **1451**

technical services engineer, electrical **2133**

technical services officer, statistics **2161**

technical supervisor, medical laboratory **3211**

technical translator **5125**

technical writer **5121**

technician, aerospace engineering **2232**

technician, agricultural **2221**

technician, aircraft engine **7315**

technician, aircraft hydraulics shop **7315**

technician, aircraft instruments **2244**

technician, aircraft maintenance, mechanical systems **7315**

technician, ambulance **3234**

technician, animal care **3213**

technician, animal health **3213**

technician, architectural **2251**

technician, assistive listening device **3235**

technician, audiology **3235**

technician, audiometric **3235**

technician, autopsy – health support services **3414**

technician, autopsy – medical laboratory **3211**

technician, bacteriological **2221**

technician, biochemistry, except medical **2211**

technician, biological **2221**

technician, cable television **7247**

technician, cardiology **3217**

technician, cartographic **2255**

technician, cast room **3414**

technician, central supply room – hospital **6631**

technician, chemical **2211**

technician, chemical engineering **2211**

technician, civil engineering **2231**

technician, conservation **5212**

technician, construction **2231**

technician, contact lens **3231**

technician, dairy products **2221**

technician, dental **3223**

technician, dental laboratory **3223**

technician, denture **3221**

technician, design **2253**

technician, diagnostic radiological **3215**

technician, dietary **3219**

technician, echoencephalographic **3218**

technician, electrocardiographic **3217**

technician, electrocardiography **3217**

technician, electrocardiology **3217**

technician, electroencephalographic **3218**

technician, electromyography **3218**

technician, emergency medical **3234**

technician, EMG **3218**

technician, EMG lab **3218**

technician, engineering design **2253**

technician, engineering survey **2254**

technician, fish roe **2221**

Index   251

technician, fisheries **2221**
technician, food **2211**
technician, forest engineering **2223**
technician, forestry **2223**
technician, geochemical **2211**
technician, geodetic survey **2254**
technician, geographic information
    system (GIS) **2255**
technician, geological **2212**
technician, geological engineering **2212**
technician, geophysical **2212**
technician, graphic arts **5223**
technician, health records **1413**
technician, hearing aid **3235**
technician, hearing assessment **3235**
technician, household and business
    equipment **2242**
technician, incoming inspection **2241**
technician, industrial engineering **2233**
technician, laboratory animal **3213**
technician, land survey **2254**
technician, library **5211**
technician, loom – textile
    manufacturing **7317**
technician, manufacturing **2233**
technician, marine engineering **2232**
technician, mechanical engineering **2232**
technician, medical records **1413**
technician, metallurgical engineering **2212**
technician, microbiology (except
    medical) **2221**
technician, mineral **2212**
technician, mining engineering **2212**
technician, morgue **3414**
technician, museum **5212**
technician, nondestructive evaluation **2261**
technician, nondestructive examination **2261**
technician, nondestructive inspection **2261**
technician, nuclear medicine **3215**
technician, nurse **3152**
technician, occupational therapy **6631**
technician, open-end – textile
    manufacturing **7317**
technician, operating room – nursing **3233**
technician, ophthalmic (except retail) **3235**
technician, ophthalmic – retail **3414**
technician, optical lab – retail **3414**
technician, orthodontic **3223**
technician, orthopaedic **3414**
technician, orthotic **3219**
technician, pathology **3211**
technician, petroleum engineering **2212**
technician, pharmacy **3414**
technician, physical rehabilitation **3235**
technician, physiotherapy **3235**
technician, planning **2233**
technician, plastic and synthetic resins **2211**
technician, plastics **2233**

technician, propulsion **7315**
technician, prosthetic **3219**
technician, prosthetist/orthotist **3219**
technician, pulp and paper **2233**
technician, quality control – chemical **2211**
technician, quality control –
    manufacturing **2233**
technician, radioisotope **3215**
technician, radiological therapeutic **3215**
technician, radiotherapy **3215**
technician, real estate appraisal **1235**
technician, registered central service –
    medical **6631**
technician, remote sensing **2255**
technician, resource **2221**
technician, restoration **5212**
technician, ship repair **2232**
technician, silviculture **2223**
technician, sound **5225**
technician, speech **3235**
technician, surgical – nursing **3233**
technician, survey **2254**
technician, synthetic textiles **2211**
technician, telecommunications **7246**
technician, telephone line **7245**
technician, television maintenance **2242**
technician, terminal equipment –
    military **7246**
technician, textile **2233**
technician, topographic survey **2254**
technician, traffic **2231**
technician, ultrasound **3216**
technician, veterinary **3213**
technician, veterinary laboratory **3213**
technician, water well drilling **7373**
technician, wildlife **2221**
technician, X-Ray **3215**
technological institute instructor **4131**
technological institute teacher **4131**
technologist, aerospace engineering **2232**
technologist, agricultural **2221**
technologist, anaesthesia **3214**
technologist, anatomical pathology **3211**
technologist, animal care **3213**
technologist, animal health **3213**
technologist, architectural **2251**
technologist, autopsy – health support
    services **3414**
technologist, autopsy – medical
    laboratory **3211**
technologist, bacteriological **2221**
technologist, biochemistry (except
    medical) **2211**
technologist, biological **2221**
technologist, brachytherapy **3215**
technologist, cardiology **3217**
technologist, cardiovascular perfusion **3214**
technologist, cartographic **2255**

technologist, chemical **2211**
technologist, chemical engineering **2211**
technologist, civil engineering **2231**
technologist, construction **2231**
technologist, design **2253**
technologist, diagnostic medical
  radiation **3215**
technologist, diagnostic radiography **3215**
technologist, diagnostic radiological **3215**
technologist, dietary **3219**
technologist, ECG **3217**
technologist, EEG **3218**
technologist, electrocardiographic **3217**
technologist, electroencephalograph **3218**
technologist, electroencephalographic **3218**
technologist, electroencephalographic,
  chief **3218**
technologist, electromyography **3218**
technologist, EMG **3218**
technologist, EMG, chief **3218**
technologist, engineering design **2253**
technologist, engineering survey **2254**
technologist, evoked potential **3218**
technologist, extracorporeal circulation **3214**
technologist, fisheries **2221**
technologist, food **2211**
technologist, forest engineering **2223**
technologist, forestry **2223**
technologist, geochemical **2211**
technologist, geodetic survey **2254**
technologist, geographic information
  system (GIS) **2255**
technologist, geological **2212**
technologist, geological engineering **2212**
technologist, geophysical **2212**
technologist, industrial engineering **2233**
technologist, industrial hygiene **2211**
technologist, inhalation **3214**
technologist, inhalation therapy **3214**
technologist, land survey **2254**
technologist, mammography **3215**
technologist, manufacturing **2233**
technologist, marine engineering **2232**
technologist, mechanical engineering **2232**
technologist, medical laboratory **3211**
technologist, medical radiation **3215**
technologist, metallurgical engineering **2212**
technologist, microbiology (except
  medical) **2221**
technologist, mineral **2212**
technologist, mining **2212**
technologist, mining engineering **2212**
technologist, nuclear **2232**
technologist, nuclear engineering **2232**
technologist, nuclear medicine **3215**
technologist, oncology **3215**
technologist, ophthalmic **3235**
technologist, orthopaedic **3414**

technologist, oxygen therapy **3214**
technologist, petroleum engineering **2212**
technologist, pulmonary function **3214**
technologist, pulp and paper **2233**
technologist, quality control **2233**
technologist, radiation oncology **3215**
technologist, radiation oncology
  simulator **3215**
technologist, radiation therapy **3215**
technologist, radiographic **3215**
technologist, radiography **3215**
technologist, radiological **3215**
technologist, radiotherapy **3215**
technologist, RDMS **3216**
technologist, remote sensing **2255**
technologist, residential building **2251**
technologist, resource **2221**
technologist, respiratory **3214**
technologist, silviculture **2223**
technologist, survey **2254**
technologist, textile **2233**
technologist, topographic survey **2254**
technologist, traffic **2231**
technologist, ultrasound **3216**
technologist, vascular **3218**
technologist, veterinary **3213**
technologist, welding **2212**
technologist, wildlife **2221**
technology teacher, community college
  or technical institute **4131**
teen club program co-ordinator **4167**
telecine operator **5227**
telecommunications contractor **7212**
telecommunications engineer **2133**
telecommunications equipment
  inspector **7246**
telecommunications equipment installer **7246**
telecommunications equipment
  technician **7246**
telecommunications general manager **0013**
telecommunications line installer **7245**
telecommunications manager **0131**
telecommunications sales representative **6221**
telecommunications service tester **7246**
telecommunications services manager **0131**
telecommunications specialist **2147**
telecommunications specialist –
  computer systems **2147**
telecommunications splicer **7245**
telecommunications supervisor **7212**
telegram messenger **1463**
telegraph and cable systems traffic
  manager **0131**
telegraph dispatcher **1475**
telegraph operator **1475**
telegraph operator supervisor **1215**
telemarketer **6623**
telemarketing supervisor **6211**

telephone adjuster – insurance **1233**
telephone answering service operator **1414**
telephone assembler **9483**
telephone cable splicer **7245**
telephone cable splicer helper **7612**
telephone clerk **1414**
telephone company chief executive
  officer **0013**
telephone company district manager **0131**
telephone engineer **2133**
telephone enquiries clerk **1453**
telephone equipment installer &
  repairer **7246**
telephone equipment sales representative
  – wholesale **6411**
telephone equipment salesperson **6421**
telephone equipment tester **7246**
telephone facilities evaluator **7246**
telephone installer **7246**
telephone line and cableman/woman **7245**
telephone line installer/repairer –
  military **7245**
telephone line technician **7245**
telephone messenger, telegrams **1463**
telephone operator assistant **1424**
telephone operator, chief **1211**
telephone operator supervisor **1211**
telephone operator – telephone system **1424**
telephone repairer **7246**
telephone sales agent **6623**
telephone service assistant – telephone
  system **1424**
telephone service monitor – telephone
  system **1424**
telephone service observer – telephone
  system **1424**
telephone servicer **7246**
telephone shop repairer **7246**
telephone solicitor **6623**
telephone station installer **7246**
telephone station repairer **7246**
telephone survey clerk **1454**
telephone switchboard installer and
  repairer **7246**
telephone switchman/woman **7246**
telephone system control board operator
  – telephone system **1424**
telephone system relay adjuster **7246**
telephone system traffic manager **0131**
telephone technician **7246**
telephone tester **7246**
telephone traffic inspector **7246**
telephone traffic observer – telephone
  system **1424**
teleprinter installer –
  telecommunications **7246**
teleprocessing software programmer **2163**
teleprompt operator **5227**

telereceptionist **1414**
teletype and cipher technician – military **7246**
teletype installer – telecommunications **7246**
teletype operator **1412**
teletype operator – military **1412**
teletype repairer – telecommunications **7246**
teletypist **1412**
television advertising time salesperson **6411**
television and stereo equipment store
  manager **0621**
television antenna installer **7441**
television assembler **9483**
television assembly chief inspector **9483**
television cabinet maker **7272**
television cable service salesperson **6421**
television camera operator **5222**
television camera repairer – household
  and business equipment **2242**
television director **5131**
television evangelist **4154**
television host/hostess **5231**
television installation and repair
  technician **2242**
television installer **2242**
television maintenance technician **2242**
television musical director **5132**
television news camera operator **5222**
television picture tube laminator **9483**
television picture tube rim bander **9483**
television picture tubes tester –
  electronics manufacturing **9483**
television producer **5131**
television programmer **5226**
television receiver inspector and tester –
  electronics manufacturing **9483**
television rental attendant **6421**
television repair supervisor **2242**
television repairer **2242**
television repairer, production **2241**
television researcher **5123**
television salesperson **6421**
television servicer **2242**
television station manager **0512**
television studio equipment repairer –
  household and business equipment **2242**
television systems engineer **2133**
television time buyer **1225**
television tube assembler **9483**
television writer **5121**
telex operator **1412**
teller – financial services **1433**
teller supervisor **1212**
teller trainee – financial services **1433**
temper mill roller – primry metal
  processing **9411**
temperature actuated controls tester **9484**
temperature regulator **9613**

tempering bin operator – food and beverage processing **9461**

tempering foreman/woman – primary metal processing **9211**

tempering furnace operator, glass **9413**

tempering operator, glass furnace **9413**

template maker **7383**

template maker – shipbuilding **7383**

template maker – structural steel **7383**

template maker, tool and die **7232**

tender, egg processing machine **8431**

tender, heating and ventilation equipment **7351**

tender, milking machine **8431**

tender, washing machine extractor – laundry and dry cleaning **6681**

tennis ball maker operator **9517**

tennis coach **5252**

tennis court attendant **6671**

tennis court manager **0721**

tennis instructor **5254**

tennis player **5251**

tennis pro **5254**

tenoner operator – woodworking **9513**

tensile strength tester – primary metal processing **9415**

tension drying machine tender – textiles **9443**

tension meter assembler – electronics manufacturing **9483**

tent finisher **9498**

tent frame machine operator **9516**

tent maker **5245**

tenter machine tender – textiles **9443**

teppan chef **6241**

terminal and repeater tester – telecommunications **7246**

terminal attendant, ferry **7435**

terminal equipment technician – military **7246**

terminal supervisor, motor transport **7222**

terminologist **5125**

terra cotta mason **7281**

terrazzo finisher **7611**

terrazzo finishing contractor **7219**

terrazzo floor layer **7283**

terrazzo grinder, manual **7611**

terrazzo layer **7283**

terrazzo layer helper **7611**

terrazzo machine grinder **7611**

terrazzo mason **7283**

terrazzo mechanic **7283**

terrazzo mechanic helper **7611**

terrazzo polisher **7283**

terrazzo polisher helper **7611**

terrazzo setter **7283**

terrazzo, tile and marble setter **7283**

terrazzo worker **7283**

terrazzo worker helper **7611**

territorial commissioner **0011**

territorial judge **4111**

territory manager, sales **0611**

test and trim operator – electronics manufacturing **9483**

test baker – food and beverage processing **9465**

test clerk **1441**

test desk operator – telecommunications **7246**

test driver – motor vehicle manufacturing **9482**

test engineer, aerospace **2146**

test engineer, electronics **2133**

test equipment repairer, oil exploration **2241**

test machine operator – electronics manufacturing **9483**

test pilot **2271**

test supervisor – electronics manufacturing **9222**

test technician **2241**

tester, air conditioning unit **9484**

tester and inspector – primary metal and mineral products processing **9415**

tester and regulator – telecommunications equipment **7246**

tester, ballast transformers **9484**

tester, boiler **2261**

tester, cable – telecommunications **7245**

tester, control panel **2241**

tester, control systems **2241**

tester, electric battery **9487**

tester, electric light bulb **9487**

tester, electrical appliance assembly **9484**

tester, electrical continuity **9484**

tester, electrical dry cell battery **9487**

tester, electrical lead acid storage battery **9487**

tester, electrical light fixtures **9484**

tester, electrical wire insulation **9484**

tester, electronic components **9483**

tester – electronics manufacturing **9483**

tester, feed – food and beverage processing **9465**

tester, glass **9415**

tester, gravel and sand **2264**

tester, motors and controls **9485**

tester, packaging **9498**

tester, small electric motors **9484**

tester, small electric transformers **9484**

tester, systems **2241**

tester, telephone exchange **7246**

tester, temperature actuated controls **9484**

tester, terminal and repeater **7246**

tester, transmission – telecommunications **7246**

testing and analysis foreman/woman **9213**

testing mechanic, automotive vehicle **7321**

textbook sales representative **6411**

textile and clothing consultant **4164**
textile bags turner operator **9517**
textile chemist **2112**
textile colour technologist **2211**
textile colourist **9443**
textile designer **5243**
textile dyer **9443**
textile engineer **2148**
textile grader **9444**
textile inspector **9444**
textile machine cleaner **9616**
textile machine feeder **9616**
textile machine fixer **7317**
textile machine mechanic **7317**
textile machine offbearer **9616**
textile machine overhauler **7317**
textile machine repairer **7317**
textile machinery assembly
    foreman/woman **7216**
textile machinery fitter **7316**
textile machinery mechanic **7317**
textile machinery repairer **7317**
textile machinery salesperson **6221**
textile mill manager **0911**
textile printer **9443**
textile processing supervisor **9216**
textile products inspector **9444**
textile products mender **9451**
textile products patternmaker **5245**
textile sampler **9444**
textile shader **9444**
textile spinner **9441**
textile technician **2233**
textile technologist **2233**
textile tester **9444**
textile twisting frame operator **9441**
textile washer **9443**
textile weaver **9442**
textiles conservator **5112**
textiles finishing inspector **9444**
texturing machine tender – textiles **9443**
thallium recoverer **9411**
theatre attendant **6683**
theatre cashier **6611**
theatre company manager **0512**
theatre manager **0651**
theatre technician **5226**
theatre usher **6683**
theatrical agent **6411**
theatrical designer **5243**
theatrical manager **6411**
theoretical chemist **2112**
theoretical nuclear physicist **2111**
therapeutic diet cook **6242**
therapeutic dietitian **3132**
therapeutic radiological technician **3215**
therapeutic radiologist **3111**
therapeutic recreationist **3144**

therapeutic services administrator **0311**
therapeutic services director **0311**
therapist, art **3144**
therapist, athletic **3144**
therapist, counselling **4153**
therapist, dance **3144**
therapist, dance/movement **3144**
therapist, dental **3222**
therapist, denture **3221**
therapist, home care **3143**
therapist, inhalation **3214**
therapist, marriage **4153**
therapist, massage **3235**
therapist, movement **3144**
therapist, music **3144**
therapist, occupational **3143**
therapist, oxygen **3214**
therapist, physical **3142**
therapist, remedial **3144**
therapist, respiratory **3214**
therapist, shiatsu **3232**
therapist, speech **3141**
therapist, speech and hearing **3141**
thermal acid equipment operator **9232**
thermal design engineer **2132**
thermal physicist **2111**
thermal power engineer **2132**
thermal station technician **2232**
thermite welder **7265**
thermo mechanical pulp assistant
    operator – pulp and paper **9432**
thermo mechanical pulp operator **9233**
thermoforming foreman/woman – plastic
    manufacturing **9214**
thermographer, nondestructive **2261**
thermographer tester **2261**
thermographic printer **7381**
thermospray operator **9497**
thermostat assembler **9484**
thermostat calibrator **9484**
thermostat capillary sealer **9619**
thermostat inspector **9484**
thermostat repairer **7445**
thermovacuum technologist **2232**
thickener equipment tender – primary
    metal processing **9411**
thinning saw operator – forestry **8422**
thiokol operator – plastic manufacturing **9422**
third class power engineer **7351**
third class stationary engineer **7351**
third cook **6242**
third engineer – water transport **2274**
third hand – pulp and paper **9433**
third mate, ship **2273**
third secretary, foreign service **4168**
third watchkeeping engineer, coast guard
    vessel **2274**

third watchkeeping officer – coast guard vessel **2273**

thoracic surgeon **3111**

thread cutter, metal machining **9511**

thread doubler **9441**

thread grinder operator **9511**

thread grinder set-up operator **9511**

thread inspector – textiles **9444**

thread spinner **9441**

thread spooler **9441**

thread trimmer – garment manufacturing **9619**

thread winder **9441**

threader – textiles **9442**

threading machine tool operator **9511**

threshing machine operator **8431**

thrill performer **5232**

throat specialist **3111**

ticket agent, airline **6433**

ticket agent, boat cruise **6434**

ticket and information clerk (except airline) **6434**

ticket clerk (except airline) **6434**

ticket clerk, railway **6434**

ticket clerk supervisor – recreation **6216**

ticket seller **6611**

ticket taker **6683**

ticket taker and usher **6683**

tie and timber inspector **9436**

tie axe machine operator, railway **7432**

tie bed scarifier machine operator, railway **7432**

tie crane operator, railway **7432**

tie cutting machine operator, railway **7432**

tie dye artisan **5244**

tie end remover operator, railway **7432**

tie injector machine operator, railway **7432**

tie inspector, railway **7432**

tie maker **9619**

tie plate inserter operator, railway **7432**

tie plate placer operator, railway **7432**

tie saw operator, railway **7432**

tie shearer operator, railway **7432**

tie tamper operator, railway **7432**

tier lift truck operator **7452**

tiffany lamp maker **9413**

tig welder **7265**

tile burner – clay products **9414**

tile designer **5243**

tile fitter **7283**

tile grader, clay – mineral products processing **9415**

tile installer **7283**

tile layer **7283**

tile layer helper **7611**

tile maker – clay products **9414**

tile mason **7283**

tile mechanic **7283**

tile moulder, hand – clay products **9414**

tile roofer **7291**

tilesetter **7283**

tilesetter apprentice **7283**

tilesetter helper **7611**

tilesetter, lead hand **7283**

tilesetters foreman/woman **7219**

tilesetting contractor **7219**

tilting table tender – metal processing **9411**

timber and steel prop salvager **8614**

timber buyer **6233**

timber cruiser **2223**

timber cut off sawyer – sawmill **9431**

timber foreman/woman **8211**

timber marker **2223**

timber rider **2223**

timber scaler **2223**

timber technician **2223**

timber treating tank operator **9434**

timber treating tank operator helper **9614**

timberman/woman helper – underground mining **8614**

timberman/woman – underground mining **8411**

time clerk **1432**

time lock expert **7383**

time study analyst **2233**

time study engineer **2141**

time study technologist **2233**

timekeeper, payroll **1432**

tin can coating machine tender **9496**

tin can inspector **9516**

tin plater operator **9497**

tin roofer **7291**

tinner's helper **9619**

tinplate inspector and grader **9415**

tinsel maker operator **9517**

tinsmith roofer **7291**

tinsmith, sheet metal **7261**

tinter – chemical processing **9421**

tinware beader **9516**

tinware dipping enameller **9496**

tinware spray machine set-up man/woman **9496**

tinware worker **9619**

tip banding machine tender **9496**

tipman/woman, surface coal mine **7452**

tipping machine tender – tobacco processing **9464**

tire and tube pressroom worker – rubber manufacturing **9615**

tire assembler **9423**

tire bagger **9423**

tire bagging machine tender **9423**

tire balance checker – rubber manufacturing **9615**

tire band wrapper – rubber manufacturing **9615**

tire breaker operator **9423**
tire buffer **9423**
tire builder **9423**
tire building foreman/woman **9214**
tire changer – automotive service **7443**
tire classifier **9423**
tire cleaner and painter – rubber
    manufacturing **9615**
tire coverer **9423**
tire cureman/woman **9423**
tire curer **9423**
tire dealer **0621**
tire finisher **9423**
tire finishing foreman/woman **9214**
tire inspection foreman/woman **9214**
tire inspector **9423**
tire maker **9423**
tire measurer – rubber manufacturing **9615**
tire mould dresser **7232**
tire mould repairer **7232**
tire plant manager **0911**
tire rebuilder **9423**
tire recapper **9423**
tire repairer, assembly line **9423**
tire repairer – automotive service **7443**
tire repairer/vulcanizer **9423**
tire retread foreman/woman **9214**
tire retreader **9423**
tire retreading inspector **9423**
tire retreading machine tender **9423**
tire salesperson **6421**
tire stock preparation foreman/woman **9214**
tire touch-up and buff worker **9423**
tire tread moulder **9423**
tire trimmer, hand **9423**
tire tube foreman/woman **9214**
tire valve worker **9423**
tire vulcanizer **9423**
tissue technologist **3211**
title and administration clerk **4211**
title and lease clerk **4211**
title artist **5241**
title examiner **4211**
title lawyer **4112**
title searcher **4211**
toaster assembler **9484**
tobacco baler **9617**
tobacco blender **9464**
tobacco blending line attendant **9464**
tobacco blending machine operator **9464**
tobacco buyer **6233**
tobacco carton packaging machine
    tender **9617**
tobacco conditioner tender **9464**
tobacco curer **8431**
tobacco curing room foreman/woman **9213**
tobacco cutter – tobacco harvesting **8611**
tobacco cutter – tobacco processing **9464**

tobacco cutting machine tender **9464**
tobacco dressing machine operator –
    tobacco processing **9464**
tobacco drier **9464**
tobacco farm foreman/woman **8253**
tobacco farm worker **8431**
tobacco farmer **8251**
tobacco flavourer **9464**
tobacco grader **9465**
tobacco harvesting machine operator **8431**
tobacco hogshead liner **9617**
tobacco leaf blender **9464**
tobacco leaf inspector **9465**
tobacco machine tender **9464**
tobacco packaging machine tender **9464**
tobacco packing machine tender **9617**
tobacco picker **8611**
tobacco processing foreman/woman **9213**
tobacco processing machine mechanic **7311**
tobacco processing machine operator **9464**
tobacco processing supervisor **9213**
tobacco products clerk **6421**
tobacco products sales representative **6411**
tobacco roller **9464**
tobacco shredder **9464**
tobacco stripper – tobacco harvesting **8611**
tobacco stripper – tobacco processing **9464**
tobacco warehouse manager **0721**
tobacco weigher **9617**
toe and heel sprayer – shoe
    manufacturing **9619**
toggle switch assembler – electrical
    equipment manufacturing **9484**
toll booth attendant **6683**
toll bridge attendant supervisor **1212**
toll captain **1212**
toll collector **6683**
toll equipment man/woman –
    telecommunications **7246**
toll line inspector – telecommunications **7245**
toll line repairman/woman –
    telecommunications **7245**
toll lineman/woman –
    telecommunications **7245**
toll operator – telephone system **1424**
toll supervisor, telephone system **1211**
toll switchman/woman –
    telecommunications **7246**
toll tester, telephone exchange **7246**
tomato grower **8251**
tomato juice extractor **9461**
tomato picker **8611**
tombstone erector **7611**
tombstone setter **7611**
tonnage compilation clerk **1431**
tool and cutlery assembly inspector **9498**
tool and die designer **2232**
tool and die engineer **2132**

tool and die inspector **7231**
tool and die maker **7232**
tool and die maker apprentice **7232**
tool and die maker foreman/woman **7211**
tool and die maker, injection moulds **7232**
tool and die making supervisor **7211**
tool and die making teacher – college or
    vocational institute **4131**
tool and die repairer **7232**
tool and die welder **7265**
tool and equipment rental clerk **6421**
tool and gauge inspector **7231**
tool clerk **1472**
tool clerk foreman/woman **1215**
tool crib attendant **1472**
tool crib supervisor **1215**
tool cutter and grinder **9511**
tool design draftsman/woman **2253**
tool designer **2232**
tool drawing checker **2253**
tool dresser operator **9511**
tool engineer **2132**
tool fitter **7232**
tool grinder/labourer **9612**
tool grinder, machining **9511**
tool lapper – metal machining **9511**
tool machine shop foreman/woman **7211**
tool machinist **7231**
tool maintainer **7232**
tool maintenance man/woman **7232**
tool maker **7232**
tool maker, bench **7232**
tool production department manager **0911**
tool programming technologist **2233**
tool pusher, offshore drilling rig **8222**
tool pusher – oil and gas drilling **8222**
tool repairer **7232**
tool repairman/woman **7232**
tool room attendant **1472**
tool room machinist **7231**
tool room storeman/woman **1472**
tooling inspector **7231**
toolsmith **7266**
tooth grinder, metal saw **9511**
tooth pick lathe operator **9513**
toothbrush maker operator **9517**
toothpick chopping machine tender **9513**
top cager – underground mining **8411**
top capping machine tender – electrical
    equipment manufacturing **9487**
top dyer – textiles **9443**
top knitter **9442**
topographic survey technician **2254**
topographic survey technologist **2254**
topographical equipment salesperson **6221**
topographical surveyor – military **2254**
torch brazer **9515**
torch welder **7265**

torque wrench calibrator **7445**
total style co-ordinator **6481**
totalizator systems technician **2242**
totem pole carver **5244**
touch-up cleaner – furniture finishing
    and refinishing **9619**
touch-up painter, production **9496**
touch-up person – furniture finishing **9494**
tour and travel manager **0621**
tour escort **6441**
tour foreman/woman – pulp and paper **9215**
tour guide **6441**
tour guide supervisor **6216**
tour operator, wholesale **6411**
tour package sales representative –
    wholesale **6411**
tour packages sales manager **0611**
tourism co-ordinator – government **4163**
tourism consultant – government **4163**
tourism development manager –
    government services **0412**
tourism development officer –
    government **4163**
tourism industry consultant –
    government **4163**
tourism information officer **5124**
tourist booth attendant **6441**
tourist camp attendant **6671**
tourist camp worker **6661**
tourist guide **6441**
tourist home operator **0632**
tourist information clerk **1453**
tow-motor driver (except airlines) **7452**
tow-truck dispatcher **1475**
tow truck driver **7411**
tower controller, air traffic **2272**
tower crane erector **7264**
tower crane operator **7371**
tower line maintainer – electric power
    systems **7244**
tower lineman/woman – electric power
    systems **7244**
tower loader operator – marine cargo
    handling **7451**
tower operator, railway **7431**
towerman/woman, railway **7431**
town clerk **0012**
town planner **2153**
township clerk **0012**
toxicologist **2121**
toy assembler **9498**
toy assembly foreman/woman **9227**
toy designer **5243**
toy gun cleaner **9619**
toy inspector **9498**
toy maker **9498**
toy manufacturing foreman/woman **9227**
toy store manager **0621**

tracer, drafting **2253**
tracer – telecommunications **7245**
tracer transferrer – printing **9472**
tracing clerk (except mail) **1441**
tracing clerk, mail **1461**
track aligner operator, railway **7432**
track athlete **5251**
track boss, railway **7217**
track boss – underground mining **8221**
track broom machine operator, railway **7432**
track dresser, railway **7432**
track fitter, railway **7432**
track foreman/woman, railway **7217**
track foreman/woman, streetcar lines **7217**
track greaser, railway **7622**
track grinder operator, railway **7432**
track inspector, railway **7432**
track labourer **7622**
track labourer, railway **7622**
track layer, railway **7432**
track laying foreman/woman **7217**
track liner operator, railway **7432**
track liner, railway **7432**
track loader operator **7421**
track maintenance machine operator,
    railway **7432**
track patroller, railway **7432**
track repairer, railway **7432**
track surfacing machine operator,
    railway **7432**
track sweeper, railway **7622**
track walker, railway **7432**
tracked reconnaissance vehicle driver –
    military **6464**
trackman/woman, railway **7432**
trackmobile operator, railway **7432**
traction belt builder – rubber
    manufacturing **9423**
tractor crane operator **7371**
tractor mechanic **7312**
tractor mechanic, farm **7312**
tractor operator – construction **7421**
tractor operator – farming **8431**
tractor operator, side-boom **7421**
tractor repairer, farm **7312**
tractor trailer truck driver **7411**
trade analyst **4162**
trade association manager **0314**
trade commissioner **0012**
trade development director –
    government services **0412**
trade economist **4162**
trade instructor – secondary or
    vocational high school **4141**
trade mark agent **4211**
trade mark lawyer **4112**
trade school general manager **0014**
trade school manager **0312**

trade show planner **1226**
trademark secretary **1242**
trader – investments **1113**
trader, stocks and bonds **1113**
trades helper – construction **7611**
traffic checker **1454**
traffic chief – telecommunications **0131**
traffic clerk **1473**
traffic clerk, broadcasting **1473**
traffic control clerk **1473**
traffic control supervisor **1215**
traffic controller, air **2272**
traffic controller, subway system **7222**
traffic counter **1454**
traffic engineer **2131**
traffic engineer, rail transportation **2131**
traffic engineering manager **0211**
traffic engineering manager –
    telecommunications **0211**
traffic inspector – police **0641**
traffic inspector, public transit system **7222**
traffic light installer **7441**
traffic manager – telecommunications **0131**
traffic manager – transportation **0713**
traffic manager, water transport **0713**
traffic observer – telephone system **1424**
traffic operations engineer **2131**
traffic patrol officer **6261**
traffic rate clerk **1431**
traffic reporter **5231**
traffic safety administrator **0411**
traffic scheduling supervisor, freight **1215**
traffic sign painter **5223**
traffic signal repairer **7441**
traffic superintendent – police **0641**
traffic supervisor – by-law enforcement **6463**
traffic supervisor – motor transport **7222**
traffic technician – civil engineering **2231**
traffic technician – military **7437**
traffic technologist **2231**
trailer assembler **9486**
trailer finisher, exterior **9486**
trailer finisher, interior **9486**
trailer frame assembler **9486**
trailer mechanic **7321**
trailer mechanical systems repairer **7321**
trailer park attendant **6671**
train conductor **7362**
train depot agent **6434**
train dispatch operator **2275**
train dispatcher **2275**
train dispatcher supervisor **2275**
train engineer **7361**
train operator **2275**
train scheduler **1476**
train service attendant **6672**
trainee adjuster – insurance **1233**
trainee instructor **4131**

trainee, nondestructive test **2261**
trainer, athletic (except boxing) **3144**
trainer, company **4131**
trainer, computer **4131**
trainer, horse **8253**
trainer – vocational **4131**
training and development manager **0112**
training clerk **1442**
training consultant **4131**
training development officer – military **4131**
training institute director **0312**
training instructor **4131**
training officer **4131**
training representative, computer **4131**
training supervisor **1121**
trainman/woman – underground mining **8411**
trainman/woman, yard **7431**
trainmaster **7221**
transcriber **1244**
transcriber, medical **1244**
transcribing machine operator **1244**
transcribing machine servicer **7445**
transcriptionist **1244**
transcriptionist, medical **1244**
transfer clerk **1431**
transfer company agent **6411**
transfer knitter **9442**
transfer machine tender – metal
    machining **9511**
transfer man/woman – wood processing **9614**
transfer tender – wood processing **9614**
transferer – printing **9472**
transformer assembler **9485**
transformer assembly clamper **9485**
transformer builder **9485**
transformer coil impregnator – electrical
    equipment manufacturing **9484**
transformer coil repairer **7333**
transformer coil winder **9485**
transformer core assembler **9485**
transformer core maker **9485**
transformer department lead hand **9485**
transformer fitter **9485**
transformer fitter/wirer **9485**
transformer inspector **9485**
transformer maker **9485**
transformer repair shop foreman/woman **7216**
transformer repairer **7333**
transformer static plate assembler **9484**
transformer sub-assembler **9485**
transformer tapgear assembler **9485**
transformer winder **9485**
transistor assembler **9483**
transit man/woman – surveying **2254**
transit operator – surveying **2254**
transit operator – transportation **7412**
transit scheduler **1476**
transit station ticket agent **6434**

transit system general manager **0016**
translation clerk **1452**
translator **5125**
translator, foreign broadcast **5125**
translator, literature **5125**
translator, official languages **5125**
translator, technical documents **5125**
transmission assembler **9486**
transmission assembly inspector **9486**
transmission assembly tester **9486**
transmission engineer **2133**
transmission engineering technologist –
    electrical power **2241**
transmission installer – motor vehicle
    manufacturing **9482**
transmission lineman/woman – electric
    power systems **7244**
transmission lines manager **0912**
transmission mechanic apprentice **7321**
transmission operations director **0912**
transmission operator **5224**
transmission planning engineer **2133**
transmission protection engineer **2133**
transmission rebuilding shop
    foreman/woman **9226**
transmission tester – motor vehicle
    manufacturing **9482**
transmission tester –
    telecommunications **7246**
transmitting operator **5224**
transmix operator – rubber
    manufacturing **9423**
transplanter **8612**
transport and communications general
    manager **0016**
transport compliance officer **6463**
transport department manager **0713**
transport driver **7411**
transport economist **4162**
transport program analyst **4161**
transport terminal attendant **1453**
transportation agent (except airline) **6434**
transportation clerk **1476**
transportation co-ordinator **1215**
transportation crew scheduler **1476**
transportation director **0713**
transportation enforcement officer **6463**
transportation engineer **2131**
transportation logistics manager **0713**
transportation manager **0713**
transportation planner **2153**
transportation planning co-ordinator **1215**
transportation policy director –
    government services **0412**
transportation route scheduler **1476**
transportation safety analyst **4161**
transportation vehicle scrubber **6662**
trap boss – fishing **8262**

trap fisherman/woman **8262**
trapper **8442**
trapping guide **6442**
travel agency manager **0621**
travel agent **6431**
travel and relocation department manager **0713**
travel clerk supervisor **6216**
travel consultant **6431**
travel counsellor **6431**
travel guide **6441**
travel information clerk **6431**
travelling salesperson – wholesale **6411**
trawl boss, factory freezer trawler **8261**
trawler captain **8261**
trawlerman/woman **8441**
tray line worker, hospital **6641**
tread cutter machine operator – rubber manufacturing **9423**
tread cutter, truck tires **9423**
treadle saw operator – woodworking **9513**
treasurer **0111**
treasury board president **0011**
treasury clerk **1431**
treasury vice-president – banking **0013**
treated pole tester – wood processing **9436**
treater, petroleum **9232**
treating worker, wood preserving **9434**
treatment plant mechanic **7311**
tree and shrub specialist **2225**
tree grafter **8432**
tree grower **8254**
tree harvester operator **8241**
tree nursery operator **8254**
tree planter, seasonal **8616**
tree processor operator **8241**
tree pruner – forestry **8422**
tree removal contractor **8255**
tree service contractor **8255**
tree service supervisor **8256**
tree service technician **2225**
tree spacer – forestry **8422**
tree sprayer **8612**
tree surgeon helper **8612**
tree trimmer **8612**
treelength forwarder operator **8241**
treelength harvester operator **8241**
trench digger **7611**
trench digging machine operator **7421**
trenching machine operator **7421**
trial co-ordinator – courts **1227**
trial court judge **4111**
tribologist **2132**
tribunal judge **0411**
tribunal officer **4168**
tricologist **6482**
trim and hardware inspector – motor vehicle manufacturing **9482**

trim lathe operator – rubber manufacturing **9423**
trim machine adjuster **9516**
trim operator, laser – electronics manufacturing **9483**
trim saw operator – sawmill **9431**
trim saw operator – woodworking **9513**
trim sawyer – sawmill **9431**
trimmer, fish **9463**
trimmer, footwear parts – footwear manufacturing **9517**
trimmer – furniture finishing **9494**
trimmer – leather products manufacturing **9452**
trimmer loader – wood processing **9614**
trimmer, meat **9462**
trimmer, moulded plastic products **9495**
trimmer operator – rubber manufacturing **9423**
trimmer operator – sawmill **9431**
trimmer operator – woodworking **9513**
trimmer, plastic **9495**
trimmer, rubber products **9423**
trimmer, soft top – motor vehicle manufacturing **9482**
trimmerman/woman – sawmill **9431**
trimming and boring machine operator – woodworking **9513**
trimming machine operator – sawmill **9431**
trimming machine operator – woodworking **9513**
trip hammer operator – metal forgings **9512**
troller **8262**
troller fisherman/woman **8262**
trolley bus operator **7412**
trolley coach driver **7412**
trolley operator **7412**
trophy assembler **9498**
trophy designer **5243**
tropical fish breeder **8251**
trouble foreman/woman – telecommunications **7212**
trouble man/woman, gas works **7253**
trouble shooter, electrical service **7241**
trouble shooter, electrician **7241**
trouble shooter, gas works **7253**
trouble shooter, incoming inspection **2241**
trouble shooter, pipeline **7442**
trout farmer **8257**
truck and transport mechanic **7321**
truck and transport mechanic apprentice **7321**
truck assembler **9486**
truck assembly foreman/woman **9226**
truck body builder **9486**
truck body building apprentice **9486**
truck crane operator **7371**
truck dispatcher **1475**
truck driver **7411**

truck driver, bulk milk **7411**
truck driver, dangerous goods **7411**
truck driver, heavy truck **7411**
truck driver helper **7622**
truck driver supervisor **7222**
truck driver, tractor-trailer **7411**
truck farmer **8251**
truck fleet foreman/woman **7222**
truck hostler **7443**
truck leasing representative **6421**
truck loader **7452**
truck mechanic **7321**
truck owner/contractor **7222**
truck salesperson **6421**
truck scheduler **1476**
truck tire builder **9423**
truck tire tread cutter **9423**
truck trailer assembler **9486**
truck trailer assembly foreman/woman **9226**
truck trailer builder **9486**
truck trailer builder apprentice **9486**
truck trailer final inspector **9486**
truck trailer mechanic **7321**
truck trailer repairer apprentice **7321**
truck wash manager **0651**
truck washer **6662**
truck weigher **7452**
trucker **7411**
trucking company general manager **0016**
trucking contractor **7222**
trucks and trailers sales representative – wholesale **6411**
trumpeter **5133**
trunk inspector – leather products **9454**
trunk maker, leather **9452**
trunk panel finisher – woodworking **9513**
truss maker, wood **9493**
trust company branch manager **0122**
trust company general manager **0013**
trust company investment manager **0122**
trust company manager **0122**
trust company teller **1433**
trust officer **1114**
trustee, school board **0011**
tub filler – food and beverage processing **9617**
tube balancer – rubber manufacturing **9615**
tube bending machine operator – metal fabrication **9514**
tube checker – rubber manufacturing **9615**
tube drawer helper – primary metal processing **9611**
tube drawer – primary metal processing **9411**
tube finisher, rubber **9423**
tube fitter – structural metal and platework **7263**
tube machine operator – paper converting **9435**

tube mounter **9483**
tube roller helper – primary metal processing **9611**
tube roller – primary metal processing **9411**
tube skiver, rubber **9423**
tube sorter, rubber reclaiming **9423**
tube splicer machine operator, rubber **9423**
tube splicer operator, rubber **9423**
tube splicer, rubber **9423**
tube straightener – primary metal processing **9411**
tube tester **9483**
tube vulcanizer tender, rubber **9423**
tube winding machine operator – paper converting **9435**
tuber extrusion operator – rubber manufacturing **9423**
tuber machine operator helper – rubber manufacturing **9615**
tuber operator – plastic manufacturing **9422**
tuber operator – rubber manufacturing **9423**
tubing folder – textiles **9616**
tubing machine tender – electrical equipment manufacturing **9487**
tubing machine tender – primary metal processing **9411**
tubular heating element maker **9484**
tubular metal products fabricator **9514**
tufted carpet mender **9451**
tufting machine operator **9442**
tufting operator – textiles **9442**
tufting supervisor – textiles **9216**
tug boat skipper **2273**
tugboat captain **2273**
tugboat deck hand **7433**
tugboat deck hand, log boom **7433**
tugboat dispatcher **1475**
tugboat engineer **2274**
tugboat master **2273**
tumbler operator – laundry and dry cleaning **6681**
tumbler operator – rubber manufacturing **9423**
tumbler tender – food and beverage processing **9617**
tumbler tender – rubber manufacturing **9423**
tumbler tender – textiles **9443**
tumbling barrel painter **9496**
tumbling barrel tender – metal fabrication **9612**
tune-up mechanic – motor vehicle **7321**
tune-up specialist – motor vehicle **7321**
tuner technician – piano **7445**
tungsten inert gas welder **7265**
tunnel construction inspector **2264**
tunnel engineer **2131**
tunnel kiln operator – clay products **9414**
tunnel kilnman/woman – clay products **9414**

tunneling machine operator **7421**
tunneling machine operator helper **7611**
tunnelman/woman – ship **7433**
turbine assembly foreman/woman **7216**
turbine assembly inspector and tester **9486**
turbine blade machinist **7231**
turbine fitter **7316**
turbine machinery mechanic – gas **7311**
turbine machinery mechanic – steam **7311**
turbine operator – stationary engines **7351**
turbine operator, steam – electric power
    systems **7352**
turbine pipefitter **7252**
turkey farm foreman/woman **8253**
turkey producer **8251**
turner – garment manufacturing **9619**
turner, pottery and porcelain – clay
    products **9414**
turner – woodworking **9513**
turning machine operator – textile bags **9517**
turning machine operator –
    woodworking **9513**
turning sander tender – woodworking **9513**
turnip waxer – food and beverage
    processing **9461**
turnstile attendant **6683**
turntable tender, railway **7431**
turret lathe operator – metal machining **9511**
turret lathe set-up operator **9511**
turret machine tender – tobacco
    processing **9464**
turret punch press operator – metal
    fabrication **9514**
tutor, correspondence school **4131**
tutor – elementary school subjects **4142**
tutor, modern languages – language
    school **4131**
tutor – secondary school **4141**
twine dyer **9443**
twine maker **9441**
twist maker, tobacco leaves **9464**
twisted wire brush assembler **9498**
twister, hand – tobacco leaves **9464**
twister tender – textiles **9441**
twisting foreman/woman – textiles **9216**
twisting frame operator – textiles **9441**
twisting operator – textiles **9441**
tying machine tender **9619**
type compositor **1423**
typesetter **1423**
typesetter operator **1423**
typesetter, page make-up **1423**
typesetter, photocomposition **1423**
typesetting input operator **1423**
typesetting machine operator **1423**
typesetting machine tender **1423**
typesetting output operator **1423**
typesetting supervisor **1211**

typewriter assembly tester **9498**
typewriter inspector, parts and
    assemblies **9483**
typewriter repairer **7445**
typewriter servicer **7445**
typing clerk **1412**
typing pool supervisor **1211**
typing supervisor **1211**
typing teacher – commercial college **4131**
typing teacher – secondary school **4141**
typist **1412**
typographer **1423**

U

ultrasonic equipment salesperson **6221**
ultrasonic immersion tester **2261**
ultrasonic technician **2261**
ultrasonic tester **2261**
ultrasonographer **3216**
ultrasound specialist **3216**
ultrasound supervisor **3216**
ultrasound technician **3216**
ultrasound technologist **3216**
ultraviolet light inspector **2261**
umbrella inspector **9498**
umbrella maker **9498**
umpire **5253**
uncured hose cutter operator – rubber
    manufacturing **9423**
uncured tire inspector **9423**
uncured tire repairer **9423**
under secretary of state **0012**
undercoater, motor vehicle **9496**
undercutter operator – underground
    mining **8231**
underground cable helper **7612**
underground cable splicer – electric
    power systems **7244**
underground cable splicer helper **7612**
underground cable splicer –
    telecommunications **7245**
underground distribution engineer **2133**
underground distribution technologist –
    electrical power **2241**
underground labourer – construction **7611**
underground lineman/woman – electric
    power systems **7244**
underground lines inspector, utilities **7442**
underground splicer – electric power
    systems **7244**
underground superintendent – mining **0811**
undertaker **6272**
undertaker assistant **6272**
underwater contractor **7382**
underwater vehicle pilot, remote control **2255**
underwater welder **7382**
underwater worker **7382**

underwear sewer **9451**
underwriter, insurance **1234**
underwriter, investment **1114**
underwriter, life – insurance **6231**
underwriter, marine and aircraft **1234**
underwriter, property **1234**
underwriter, securities **1114**
underwriting department manager **0121**
unemployment insurance agent **1228**
unemployment insurance appeals board
    chairperson **0012**
unemployment insurance appeals
    referee **1228**
unemployment insurance claims
    investigator **1228**
unemployment insurance commissioner **0012**
unemployment insurance officer **1228**
unemployment insurance policy analyst **4164**
unemployment insurance services
    advisor **4164**
union organizer **1121**
union representative **1121**
unit administrator – nursing **3151**
unit chief, ambulance service **3234**
unit clerk **1441**
unit forester **2122**
unit manager – motion pictures and
    broadcasting **5226**
unit operator, petroleum **9232**
unit supervisor, food services **6212**
university academic dean **0312**
university department head **4121**
university instructor, engineering **4121**
university laboratory assistant **4122**
university maintenance manager **0722**
university president **0014**
university professor **4121**
university professor, English **4121**
university registrar **0312**
university research assistant **4122**
university research director **0312**
university residence manager **0632**
university teacher **4121**
university teaching assistant **4122**
upfitter – furniture manufacturing **9492**
upholsterer **7341**
upholsterer, aircraft **7341**
upholsterer helper **9619**
upholsterer/patternmaker **7341**
upholsterer, railway car **7341**
upholstery and furniture repair
    salesperson **6421**
upholstery cleaner **6662**
upholstery cleaner and finisher **9619**
upholstery cutting and sewing
    foreman/woman **9225**
upholstery moulder – plastic
    manufacturing **9495**

upholstery parts sorter **9619**
upholstery repairer **7341**
upholstery trimmer **9619**
upsetter helper **9612**
upsetter – metal forgings **9512**
upsetter operator – metal forgings **9512**
upsetting machine operator – metal
    forgings **9512**
uptwister tender – textiles **9441**
uranium classifier operator **9411**
uranium ore evaluator **9415**
uranium processing foreman/woman **9211**
urban and regional planner **2153**
urban forester **2122**
urban geographer **4169**
urban planner **2153**
urban planning professor – university **4121**
urban planning technician **2231**
urban renewal planner **2153**
urban road system engineer **2131**
urban snow removal equipment operator
    – public works **7422**
urban sociologist **4169**
urban transit operator **7412**
urban transit system manager **0713**
urologist **3111**
urology, chief of **0311**
used car renovator **7322**
used car salesperson **6421**
user support analyst – computer systems **2162**
usher **6683**
utilities billing clerk **1431**
utilities clerk **1441**
utilities instrument mechanic **2243**
utilities instrument mechanic helper **7612**
utilities maintenance crew dispatcher **1475**
utility clerk **1441**
utility clerk, bank **1434**
utility labourer – primary metal and
    mineral products processing **9611**
utility locator, pipes **7442**
utility machine worker – primary metal
    and mineral products processing **9611**
utility man/woman, electrical equipment
    manufacturing **9484**
utility man/woman – pulp and paper **9614**
utility operator, electrical equipment
    manufacturing **9484**
utility operator – electronics
    manufacturing **9483**
utility operator – motor vehicle
    manufacturing **9482**
utility plant maintenance mechanic **7311**
utility plant maintenance worker **7442**
utility pole installer **7612**
utility repair – motor vehicle
    manufacturing **9482**
utilization engineer **2132**

A/V assistant **5227**

V

v-belt builder, rubber **9423**
v-belt coverer, rubber **9423**
v-belt curer, rubber **9423**
v-belt finisher, rubber **9423**
v-belt foreman/woman – rubber
  manufacturing **9214**
v-belt skiver, rubber **9423**
vacation farm operator **0632**
vaccine technician **2221**
vacuum bottle assembler **9498**
vacuum cleaner assembler **9484**
vacuum cleaner repairman/woman **7332**
vacuum cleaner salesperson,
  door-to-door **6623**
vacuum cleaner servicer **7332**
vacuum degasser process operator –
  primary metal processing **9231**
vacuum evaporation process plater –
  electronics manufacturing **9483**
vacuum furnace operator – primary
  metal processing **9411**
vacuum kettle cook – food and beverage
  processing **9461**
vacuum wrapper, meat **9617**
valet, parking **6683**
valuation clerk – financial sector **1434**
valuation consultant **1235**
valuator/appraiser **1235**
valve buffer – rubber products
  manufacturing **9423**
valve repairer – pipelines **7445**
vamp stitcher **9451**
van assembler **9482**
van loader **7452**
vanity and kitchen cupboard installer **7441**
vanity and kitchen cupboard installer
  helper **7611**
vapourizer – plastic manufacturing **9422**
variable capacitor tester **9483**
variable resistor assembler **9483**
variety saw operator – woodworking **9513**
variety store manager **0621**
varnish maker **9421**
varnish maker helper **9613**
varnishing machine tender **9435**
vascular plants curator **5112**
vascular sonographer **3216**
vascular surgeon **3111**
vascular technologist **3218**
vat tender, logs – wood processing **9434**
vat washer **6662**
vault attendant – financial sector **1434**
vault custodian **6651**
vault custodian, furs **6683**

vault repairer **7383**
vault servicer **7383**
vegetable canner – food and beverage
  processing **9461**
vegetable drier tender **9461**
vegetable farm foreman/woman **8253**
vegetable farm worker **8431**
vegetable grower **8251**
vegetable inspector **2222**
vegetable oil extractor **9461**
vegetable packer – agriculture **8611**
vegetable packing supervisor **9213**
vegetable picker **8611**
vegetable sorter – agriculture **8611**
vegetable thinner **8431**
vehicle cleaner **6662**
vehicle cleaner/coater **9496**
vehicle safety officer, base – military **0713**
vehicle service scheduler **1473**
vehicle spring repairer – metal forgings **9512**
vehicle technician – military **7321**
vehicle upholstery repairer **7341**
velvet steamer – laundry and dry
  cleaning **6682**
vending machine assembler **9486**
vending machine assembly
  foreman/woman **9226**
vending machine driver/servicer **7414**
vending machine driver/supplier **7414**
vending machine mechanic **7445**
vending machine repairer **7445**
vending machine sales representative **6411**
vending machine tester **9486**
vendor **6623**
veneer and plywood grader – wood
  processing **9436**
veneer bricklayer **7281**
veneer clipper tender, automatic – wood
  processing **9434**
veneer clipper – wood processing **9434**
veneer cutter – wood processing **9434**
veneer drier tender – wood processing **9434**
veneer dryer feeder **9614**
veneer foreman/woman – wood
  processing **9215**
veneer grader – wood processing **9436**
veneer jointer – wood processing **9434**
veneer lathe operator – wood processing **9434**
veneer layer, plywood boat **9491**
veneer matcher – wood processing **9434**
veneer patcher – wood processing **9434**
veneer reel tender – wood processing **9434**
veneer sander – woodworking **9513**
veneer slicing machine operator – wood
  processing **9434**
veneer splicer tender – wood processing **9434**
veneer strip cut off sawyer – wood
  processing **9434**

veneer taper – wood processing **9434**

venetian blind assembler **9498**

venetian blind cleaner and repairer **6662**

venetian blind installer **7441**

venetian blind maker **9498**

ventilation man/woman – underground
  mining **8411**

ventilation system cleaner **6662**

ventriloquist **5232**

verifier **1422**

verifier operator **1422**

vertebrate zoology curator **5112**

vertical boring mill operator **9511**

vertical kiln operator **9411**

vertical press operator – metal
  fabrication **9514**

vertical resaw operator – woodworking **9513**

vertical roll operator – metal fabrication **9514**

vestibular technician **3235**

veterans' services director **0314**

veterans' services officer **4212**

veterinarian **3114**

veterinarian's assistant **3213**

veterinary anatomist **3114**

veterinary attendant **6483**

veterinary bacteriologist **3114**

veterinary dentist **3114**

veterinary epidemiologist **3114**

veterinary equipment and supplies
  salesperson **6221**

veterinary inspector **3114**

veterinary internist **3114**

veterinary laboratory diagnostician **3114**

veterinary laboratory technician **3213**

veterinary medicine professor –
  university **4121**

veterinary microbiologist **3114**

veterinary parasitologist **3114**

veterinary pathologist **3114**

veterinary pharmacologist **3114**

veterinary physiologist **3114**

veterinary radiologist **3114**

veterinary surgeon **3114**

veterinary technician **3213**

veterinary technologist **3213**

veterinary virologist **3114**

vibration analysis technician **2261**

vibration technologist **2232**

vibrator operator, seismic prospecting **8615**

vibrator roller operator **7611**

vibratory compactor operator **7611**

vice-consul **0012**

vice-president, engineering – television
  broadcasting service **0015**

vice-president, finance – food
  wholesaler **0015**

vice-president, finance – holding
  company **0013**

vice president, finance – mining
  company **0016**

vice-president – financial,
  communications and other business
  services **0013**

vice-president, general sales manager –
  trade, broadcasting and other services
  n.e.c. **0015**

vice-president – goods production,
  utilities, transportation and
  construction **0016**

vice-president – government services **0012**

vice-president – health, education, social
  and community services and
  membership organizations **0014**

vice-president, marketing – airline **0016**

vice-president, marketing – grocery
  store chain **0015**

vice-president, marketing – office
  personnel service **0013**

vice-president, operations – electric
  power company **0016**

vice-president, operations – radio
  broadcasting service **0015**

vice-president, operations – satellite
  communication service **0013**

vice-president, personnel – bank **0013**

vice-president, sales – pulp and paper
  manufacturing **0016**

vice-president – trade, broadcasting and
  other services n.e.c. **0015**

vice-principal, school **0313**

victorian order nurse **3152**

video and sound recorder **5225**

video archivist **5113**

video artist **5136**

video camera operator **5222**

video camera repairer – household and
  business equipment **2242**

video cassette recorder repairer **2242**

video control operator **5224**

video director **5131**

video editing equipment operator **5225**

video equipment installation and repair
  technician – household and business
  equipment **2242**

video producer **5131**

video production company manager **0512**

video recorder **5225**

video recording equipment operator **5225**

video recording technician **5225**

video rental clerk **6421**

video rental store manager **0621**

video technician **5225**

video transmission operator **5224**

videographer **5222**

videotape recording (VTR) editor **5225**

videotape technician **5225**

videotex operator **1423**
videotex page designer **5241**
village clerk **0012**
vinegar maker **9461**
vinegar maker helper **9617**
vineyard foreman/woman **8253**
vineyard manager **8251**
vineyard pruner **8431**
vintage car restorer **7322**
vinyl asbestos blending machine tender **9421**
vinyl floor installer **7295**
vinyl floor layer **7295**
vinyl paperhanger **7294**
vinyl roof installer – motor vehicle
    manufacturing **9482**
vinyl tile layer **7295**
violin maker **5244**
violin repairer **7445**
violin teacher **5133**
violinist **5133**
virologist **2121**
virology technologist **2221**
viscose filter operator **9421**
visiting homemaker **6471**
visiting professor – university **4121**
visiting scholar – university **4121**
visiting teacher – elementary school
    subjects **4142**
visiting teacher – high school subjects **4141**
visual artist **5136**
visual arts teacher (except primary,
    secondary, post-secondary
    education) **5136**
visual language interpreter **5125**
vital statistician **2161**
vocal music teacher – private,
    conservatory or studio **5133**
vocal soloist **5133**
vocalist **5133**
vocational counsellor **4213**
vocational high school principal **0313**
vocational high school teacher **4141**
vocational high school trade instructor **4141**
vocational institute teacher **4131**
vocational instructor, technical subjects **4131**
vocational instructor, technological
    subjects **4131**
vocational psychologist **4151**
vocational rehabilitation consultant **4153**
vocational rehabilitation counsellor **4153**
vocational school administrator **0312**
vocational school director **0312**
vocational school manager **0312**
vocational school teacher **4131**
vocational school teacher, appliance
    repair **4131**
vocational secondary school teacher **4141**
vocational teacher, applied arts subjects **4131**

vocational teacher, business subjects **4131**
vocational teacher – secondary school **4141**
vocational training school teacher **4131**
voice teacher, music **5133**
volcanologist **2113**
voltage regulator maintainer – electric
    power systems **7243**
volunteer co-ordinator, social services **4212**
volunteer services director **0314**
VON nurse **3152**
votator tender – food and beverage
    processing **9461**
voucher clerk **1431**
VTR editor **5225**
vulcanizer – rubber manufacturing **9423**
vulcanizer tender, rubber tube **9423**

W

wafer fabrication operator – electronics
    manufacturing **9483**
wafer machine tender – electrical
    equipment manufacturing **9487**
wafer technician – electronics
    manufacturing **9483**
waferboard press operator – wood
    processing **9434**
wage analyst **1121**
wage and salary administration manager **0112**
wagon drill operator – underground
    mining **8231**
waiter/waitress **6453**
walking bridge crane operator **7371**
walking tour guide **6441**
wall and ceiling installer **7284**
wall and floor covering installer,
    residential **7295**
wall washer **6661**
wallboard installer **7284**
wallboard laminator – stone products **9414**
wallboard taper **7284**
wallpaper designer **5241**
wallpaper inspector **9498**
wallpaper lapper – paper converting **9435**
wallpaper printer **9471**
wallpaper printer helper **9619**
wallpaper salesperson **6421**
ward aide – hospital **3413**
ward clerk **1441**
ward nurse **3152**
ward secretary **1243**
ward supervisor – nursing **3151**
warden **0314**
wardrobe assistant **5227**
wardrobe attendant **5227**
wardrobe co-ordinator **5226**
wardrobe supervisor **5226**

ware dresser – concrete, clay and stone products **9414**
warehouse and distribution manager **0721**
warehouse checker **1472**
warehouse clerk **1472**
warehouse distribution supervisor **1215**
warehouse foreman/woman **1215**
warehouse manager **0721**
warehouse receiver **1471**
warehouse stock picker **6622**
warehouse superintendent **0721**
warehouse supervisor **1215**
warehouse worker **7452**
warehouseman/woman **7452**
warm-up millman/woman – rubber manufacturing **9423**
warp beamer helper – textiles **9616**
warp beamer – textiles **9441**
warp drawer – textiles **9442**
warp dresser – textiles **9441**
warp knitting machine tender **9442**
warp placer – textiles **9442**
warp spinner – textiles **9441**
warp tension tester – textiles **9444**
warp tier-in – textiles **9442**
warp twister tender – textiles **9441**
warp tying machine tender – textiles **9442**
warper tender, automatic – textiles **9441**
warper – textiles **9441**
warping operator – textiles **9441**
warranty clerk **1441**
wash-off operator – furniture finishing **9494**
washer and drier – chemical processing **9421**
washer/drier, rubber products **9423**
washer, hand – laundry and dry cleaning **6681**
washer, machine – laundry and dry cleaning **6681**
washer operator – pulp and paper **9432**
washerman/woman – pulp and paper **9432**
washing and waxing machine tender – food and beverage processing **9617**
washing machine assembler – electrical equipment manufacturing **9484**
washing machine extractor operator – laundry and dry cleaning **6681**
washing machine operator – laundry and dry cleaning **6681**
washing machine repairman/woman **7332**
washing machine servicer **7332**
washing machine tender – textiles **9443**
washroom cleaner **6661**
waste machine feeder – textiles **9616**
waste management co-ordinator **4161**
waste management director **0912**
waste plant operator **9424**
waste treatment engineer **2134**
waste water plant operator **9424**
waste water treatment plant operator **9424**

watch and clock assembly repairers foreman/woman **9227**
watch assembly inspector **9498**
watch balance wheel adjuster **9517**
watch crystal edge grinder **9517**
watch inspector **9498**
watch repairer **7344**
watch repairer apprentice **7344**
watch repairman/woman **7344**
watch salesperson **6421**
watchkeeping mate, ship **2273**
watchkeeping officer, coast guard vessel **2273**
watchkeeping officer – water transport **2273**
watchmaker **7344**
watchman/woman – ship **7433**
water and sewer engineer **2131**
water bomber pilot **2271**
water chemist **2112**
water conditioner servicer **7441**
water distribution director **0912**
water distribution systems technician **2231**
water extractor, peat moss **9411**
water filtration plant manager **0912**
water filtration plant mechanic **7311**
water filtration plant operator **9424**
water gate operator **9424**
water heater installer **7441**
water heater servicer **7441**
water inspector – public health **2263**
water intake tender – utilities **9613**
water leak examiner – motor vehicle manufacturing **9482**
water leak inspector – motor vehicle manufacturing **9482**
water mains maintenance man/woman **7442**
water management engineer **2131**
water meter installer **7441**
water meter reader **7442**
water meter repairer **7445**
water pipe installer **7611**
water plant operator **9424**
water plant pump operator **9424**
water pollution control director **0912**
water pump assembler **9486**
water purification chemist **2112**
water purification plant foreman/woman **9212**
water purification plant operator **9424**
water purification technician **2211**
water quality control technician **2231**
water resources engineer **2131**
water, sanitation and POL technician – military **9424**
water service dispatcher **1475**
water softener installer **7441**
water supervisor **9212**
water supply director **0912**
water supply maintenance worker **7442**
water systems engineer **2131**

water taxi operator **7436**
water transport manager **0713**
water treatment engineer **2131**
water treatment plant operator **9424**
water utilities plant maintenance
    man/woman **7442**
water well driller **7373**
water well driller apprentice **7373**
water well driller helper **7611**
water well driller journeyman/woman **7373**
water well drilling contractor **7217**
water well drilling foreman/woman **7217**
water well drilling technician **7373**
waterproofer, construction **7611**
waterproofer, garments **9619**
waterproofer helper **7611**
waterproofers foreman/woman **7219**
waterslide attendant **6671**
waterway traffic checker **2275**
waterworks construction
    foreman/woman **7217**
waterworks construction inspector **2264**
waterworks labourer – utilities **9613**
waterworks maintenance worker **7442**
waterworks manager **0912**
waterworks operations manager **0912**
waterworks pumphouse operator **9424**
waterworks superintendent **0912**
waterworks utility servicer **7442**
wave soldering machine operator –
    electronics manufacturing **9483**
wax bleacher **9421**
wax depilation specialist **6482**
waxer – textiles **9443**
weapons operator, surface – military **6464**
weapons operator, underwater – military **6464**
weapons technician, air – military **6464**
weapons technician, land – military **6464**
weapons technician, surface – military **6464**
weapons technician, underwater –
    military **6464**
weaponsman/woman, surface – military **6464**
weaponsman/woman, underwater –
    military **6464**
weather briefer **2213**
weather chart plotter **2213**
weather forecaster **2114**
weather reporter **5231**
weather service specialist **2213**
weather strip installer **7441**
weather stripper **7441**
weave room supervisor – textiles **9216**
weaver **9442**
weaver, carpet **9442**
weaver, chair seat **9492**
weaver, cloth **9442**
weaver, hand **5244**
weaver, jacquard loom **9442**

weaver, metalworking **9516**
weaving foreman/woman **9216**
weaving inspector **9444**
weaving inspector foreman/woman **9216**
weaving instructor **5244**
web press operator – printing **7381**
web pressman/woman – printing **7381**
wedding cake decorator **6252**
wedding consultant **6481**
weed control foreman/woman **8256**
weft straightener – textiles **9443**
weigh scale attendant, landfill **9613**
weigh tank tender – food and beverage
    processing **9461**
weigher – chemical processing **9421**
weigher, drug and toilet goods **9421**
weigher, livestock **8431**
weigher, production **9619**
weigher, railway car **7622**
weigher, truck **7452**
weighing station operator **6463**
weight analyst, aircraft design **2146**
weight and balance engineer **2146**
weight lifting instructor **5254**
weight loss advisor **6481**
weight loss clinic manager **0651**
weight loss consultant **6481**
weights and measures inspector **2262**
weir fisherman/woman **8262**
welcome wagon agent **6623**
weld inspector **2261**
weldability test inspector **2261**
welder, aircraft **7265**
welder apprentice **7265**
welder, arc **7265**
welder, combination **7265**
welder, drilling rig **7265**
welder/fitter **7265**
welder/fitter helper – construction **7611**
welder/fitter helper – manufacturing **9619**
welder foreman/woman **7214**
welder, gas **7265**
welder, gas and arc **7265**
welder, gas-shielded arc **7265**
welder, general **7265**
welder, heliarc **7265**
welder, laser beam **7265**
welder, oxy-acetylene **7265**
welder, oxy-hydrogen **7265**
welder, pipeline **7265**
welder, precision **7265**
welder, pressure vessels **7265**
welder, production line **9515**
welder, resistance **9515**
welder, seam resistance **9515**
welder/setter, resistance **7265**
welder, shielded-metal arc **7265**
welder, spot **9515**

welder, submerged arc **7265**
welder, tool and die **7265**
welder, underwater **7382**
welding contractor **7214**
welding engineer **2142**
welding equipment mechanic **7311**
welding equipment repairman/woman **7311**
welding equipment salesperson **6221**
welding fit-up man/woman **7265**
welding lay-out man/woman **7265**
welding machine operator, automatic **9515**
welding machine operator helper **9612**
welding rod extruder helper – primary metal processing **9611**
welding rod extruder operator **9516**
welding rod extruder tender **9516**
welding supervisor **7214**
welding teacher – vocational training school **4131**
welding technical advisor **2212**
welding technician **2212**
welding technologist **2212**
welfare and compensation officer **4212**
welfare department director **0314**
welfare economist **4162**
welfare institute inspector – public health **2263**
welfare manager **0314**
welfare organization counsellor **4153**
welfare organization director **0314**
welfare organization manager **0314**
welfare organization supervisor **4212**
welfare program officer, corrections **4155**
welfare worker **4212**
well acidizer – oil field services **8412**
well logging engineer **2145**
well puller helper – oil field services **8615**
well puller – oil field services **8232**
well services crew supervisor – oil and gas drilling **8222**
well testing operator – oil and gas drilling **8232**
well treatment blender operator – oil field services **8412**
well treatment helper – oil field services **8615**
well treatment pump operator – oil field services **8412**
wellsite co-ordinator – geology **2113**
welt maker – hat manufacturing **9452**
welt trimming machine tender – hat manufacturing **9452**
wet end tender, cellulose film **9421**
wet process miller – food and beverage processing **9461**
wet suit maker **9517**
wharf clerk **1431**
wharf clerk supervisor **1215**

wharf worker – fishing **8613**
wharfinger **1431**
wharfman/woman **7451**
wheat farmer **8251**
wheat starch maker **9461**
wheel and axle inspector – railway **7314**
wheel and tire installer – motor vehicle manufacturing **9482**
wheel shop foreman/woman – railway equipment **7216**
wheelabrator operator – metal fabrication **9612**
wheeled reconnaissance vehicle driver – military **6464**
wheelsman/woman – ship **7433**
wheelwright, farm machinery **7312**
whisk assembler **9498**
white lead mixer **9421**
white metal caster – foundry **9412**
whitener – furniture finishing and refinishing **9494**
whitewater rafting guide **6442**
wholesale buyer **6233**
wholesale establishment manager **0611**
wholesale sales representative **6411**
wholesaler **0611**
wig assistant – motion pictures, broadcasting and stage productions **5227**
wig maker, hand **9498**
wig stylist **6271**
wildlife biologist **2121**
wildlife biology technician **2221**
wildlife technician **2221**
wildlife technologist **2221**
willow operator – textiles **9441**
wills and estates law clerk **4211**
wills and estates legal assistant **4211**
wills and estates paralegal **4211**
wind instrument repairer **7445**
wind tunnel test technician **2232**
wind tunnel test technologist **2232**
winder, AC and DC armatures – industrial electrical equipment **9485**
winder, automatic – textiles **9441**
winder/fixer – textile manufacturing **7317**
winder, large transformer coils **9485**
winder operator, paper machine **9433**
winderman/woman – pulp and paper **9433**
winding frame cleaner – textiles **9616**
winding inspector – industrial electrical equipment **9485**
winding technician – industrial electrical equipment **9485**
windmill repairman/woman **7311**
window air conditioner installer **7441**
window air conditioner repairer **7332**
window air conditioner repairer helper **7612**
window and door installer, aluminum **7441**

window and screen assembler **9498**
window caulker **7611**
window cleaner **6662**
window display designer **5243**
window installer **7441**
window shade installer **7441**
window washer **6662**
window washer, head **6215**
window washing service manager **0651**
window washing supervisor **6215**
windshield autoclave operator, glass **9413**
windshield plastic processor **9422**
wine cellar attendant **1472**
wine fermenter – food and beverage processing **9461**
wine finisher **9461**
wine maker **0911**
wine maker – food and beverage processing **9461**
wine pasteurizer **9461**
wine sales representative, wholesale **6411**
wine steward **6453**
wine store manager **0621**
wine store sales clerk **6421**
wine tester **9465**
wineries fermentation inspector **9465**
wineries gauger **9465**
wineries skimmer **9461**
winery cellarman/woman – food and beverage processing **9461**
winery cellarmaster **9213**
winery press operator **9461**
wing inspector – aircraft assembly **9481**
wing marry up mechanic – aircraft assembly **9481**
wing tank mechanic – aircraft assembly **9481**
wink cutter – rubber manufacturing **9423**
winterizer tender – food and beverage processing **9461**
wire and assembly operator **9483**
wire basket maker **9516**
wire bender, hand **9619**
wire bonder – electronics manufacturing **9483**
wire border assembler – furniture assembly **9619**
wire cable stretcher and tester **9516**
wire coating equipment operator **9497**
wire coiner operator **9516**
wire communications engineer **2133**
wire connector – electrical equipment manufacturing **9484**
wire conveyor belt builder **9498**
wire crimping machine operator **9516**
wire cutting machine operator – electronics manufacturing **9483**
wire drawer **9516**
wire drawer helper **9612**
wire drawer operator **9516**

wire drawing machine operator **9516**
wire editor **5122**
wire fence erector **7441**
wire finisher **9612**
wire lamp shade frame maker **9516**
wire lather **7284**
wire loom helper **9619**
wire loom setter **9516**
wire loop machine operator **9516**
wire mesh gate assembler **9516**
wire mesh knitter **9516**
wire mesh setter **7611**
wire netting machine operator **9516**
wire numbering machine tender – electrical equipment manufacturing **9487**
wire paint coating machine tender **9496**
wire pairing machine tender **9516**
wire products inspector **9516**
wire roller – primary metal processing **9411**
wire rope maker **9516**
wire saw operator – concrete, clay and stone products **9414**
wire screen former **9516**
wire screen maker **9516**
wire screen weaver **9516**
wire splicer – electric power systems **7244**
wire splicer – telecommunications **7245**
wire spooler **9612**
wire stripper – electrical equipment manufacturing **9487**
wire tester and inspector – primary metal processing **9415**
wire tinner operator **9497**
wire weaver, bench loom **9516**
wire weaver helper **9619**
wire weaving loom setter **9516**
wire welder **7265**
wire wound resistor calibrator – electronics manufacturing **9483**
wire wound resistor inspector – electronics manufacturing **9483**
wire wrapping machine operator – electronics manufacturing **9483**
wireline operator – oil field services **8232**
wireman/woman, electrical switchgear **9485**
wireman/woman – industrial electrical equipment **9485**
wireperson, electrical switchgear **9485**
wirer, electrical lighting fixtures **9484**
wirer, electrical switchgear panels **9485**
wirer, residential **7241**
wirer – telecommunications **7246**
wiring and soldering operator – electronics manufacturing **9483**
wiring electrician **7241**
wiring inspector, domestic installation **2264**
wiring inspector, industrial installation **2264**
wobble saw operator – woodworking **9513**

women's centre co-ordinator **4212**
women's directorate policy analyst **4164**
women's fashion designer **5243**
women's hat maker – milliner **7342**
women's issues lobbyist **4164**
women's shelter co-ordinator **4212**
wood blank sawyer **9513**
wood block artist **5136**
wood burner installer **7331**
wood burner maintainer **7331**
wood burning appliance installer **7331**
wood burning system installer **7331**
wood carver **5244**
wood carving machine operator **9513**
wood caulker – boat building **9491**
wood chemist **2112**
wood chip unloader **9614**
wood cutter – logging **8421**
wood driller – woodworking **9513**
wood finisher – furniture finishing and
    refinishing **9494**
wood flask maker, foundry **9493**
wood floor covering layer **7295**
wood frame building foreman/woman **7215**
wood frame carpenter **7271**
wood frame house carpenter **7271**
wood furnace installer **7331**
wood furniture and fixtures
    patternmaker **7272**
wood furniture assembler **9492**
wood furniture assembly repairer **9492**
wood furniture polisher **9494**
wood grainer – furniture finishing and
    refinishing **9494**
wood lathe turner – woodworking **9513**
wood lather **7284**
wood machining inspector **9493**
wood machinist – woodworking **9513**
wood measurer – wood processing **9436**
wood model maker **7272**
wood mould maker **7271**
wood particle dryer tender **9434**
wood pattern inspector **7272**
wood patternmaker **7272**
wood preserving plant labourer **9614**
wood processing grader **9436**
wood processing inspector **9436**
wood product graders foreman/woman **9227**
wood product inspector **9493**
wood products assembler **9493**
wood products assembling inspector **9493**
wood products foreman/woman **9227**
wood pulp caustic liquor maker **9432**
wood room foreman/woman – pulp and
    paper **9215**
wood rubber – furniture manufacturing **9619**
wood sander – woodworking **9513**
wood sash and door assembler **9493**

wood saw operator – woodworking **9513**
wood sawyer – sawmill **9431**
wood sculptor **5136**
wood shingle roofer **7291**
wood shingle roofing contractor **7219**
wood shipwright **7271**
wood siding applicator **7441**
wood stock cutter **9513**
wood technologist **2221**
wood treater **9434**
wood treating plant foreman/woman –
    wood processing **9215**
wood turner – woodworking **9513**
wood turning lathe operator –
    woodworking **9513**
wooden boat assembly inspector **9491**
wooden boat inspector **9491**
wooden boatbuilder **9491**
wooden bowl lathe operator **9513**
wooden bowl lathe tender **9513**
wooden box assembler **9493**
wooden box bander **9619**
wooden box hinger **9493**
wooden box maker **9493**
wooden box maker foreman/woman **9227**
wooden case maker **9493**
wooden coat hanger shaper machine
    feeder **9619**
wooden door maker **9493**
wooden fence erector **7441**
wooden products machine feeder **9619**
wooden products machine tender **9513**
wooden reel assembler **9493**
wooden truss maker **9493**
woodenware assembler **9493**
woodlands manager **0811**
woodroom labourer – pulp and paper **9614**
woods foreman/woman **8211**
woods superintendent **0811**
woodsawyer – woodworking **9513**
woodworker, hand **5244**
woodworking drill press operator **9513**
woodworking flarer **9513**
woodworking machine cutter sharpener **9511**
woodworking machine feeder **9619**
woodworking machine operator **9513**
woodworking machine operator
    foreman/woman **9224**
woodworking machine set-up apprentice **9513**
woodworking machine set-up
    man/woman **9513**
woodworking machine set-up operator **9513**
woodworking machine setter **9513**
woodworking shop helper **9619**
woodworking splitter **9513**
woodworking stitcher operator **9513**
wool batcher **9441**
wool blender **9441**

wool grader **9444**
wool mixer **9441**
wool opener and duster **9441**
wool puller – hide and pelt processing **9619**
wool scourer **9441**
wool shearing contractor **8252**
wool sorter **9441**
wool sorting and grading
    foreman/woman **9216**
wool washer **9441**
word processing equipment repairer **2242**
word processing operator **1412**
word processing supervisor **1211**
word processor clerk **1412**
word processor operator **1412**
work measurement engineer **2141**
work-over rig operator – oil field
    services **8232**
work study analyst **1122**
work study analyst supervisor **1122**
workboat operator **7436**
worker, forestry **8422**
worker, silviculture **8422**
workers' compensation officer **4164**
workers' compensation policy analyst **4164**
working head chef **6241**
working sous-chef **6241**
works manager, metal fabrication **0911**
worksheet clerk – financial sector **1434**
worm picker **8431**
wort cooler – food and beverage
    processing **9461**
wort maker – food and beverage
    processing **9461**
wrangler, dude ranch **6442**
wrapper – laundry and dry cleaning **6681**
wrapper stacker operator – electrical
    equipment manufacturing **9487**
wrapping machine operator **9612**
wrapping machine tender – electrical
    equipment manufacturing **9487**
wreath maker **5244**
wrecker, building **7611**
wrecker, buildings and houses **7611**
wrestler **5251**
wringer tender – textiles **9443**
wrinkle remover – shoe manufacturing **9619**
writ server – bailiff **6461**
writer **5121**
writer, advertising **5121**
writer, fiction **5121**
writer, handbook **5121**
writer, music **5132**
writer, newspaper **5123**
writer, newspaper editorial **5123**
writer, scientific **5121**
writer, short story **5121**
writer, song **5132**

writer, speeches **5121**
writer, technical **5121**
writer, television or radio **5121**

X

X-Ray equipment salesperson **6221**
X-Ray film developer **9474**
X-Ray physicist **2111**
X-Ray plate developer **9474**
X-Ray technician **3215**
X-Ray technician – military **3215**

Y

yacht broker **1236**
yard attendant – livestock **8431**
yard attendant, used building materials **7452**
yard boss – mining and quarrying **8221**
yard conductor **7362**
yard coupler, railway **7431**
yard engineer, railway **7361**
yard foreman/woman – pulp and paper **9215**
yard foreman/woman – railway **7221**
yard labourer – pulp and paper **9614**
yard labourer, railway **7622**
yard locomotive engineer **7361**
yard supervisor – mining and quarrying **8221**
yard worker, railway **7431**
yardage controller – glass products
    manufacturing **9413**
yarder operator **8241**
yarding engineer – logging **8241**
yardman – livestock **8431**
yardmaster, railway **7221**
yarn conditioner **9443**
yarn doubler – textiles **9441**
yarn drier **9443**
yarn dyer **9443**
yarn examiner **9444**
yarn finisher **9443**
yarn handler **9616**
yarn inspector **9444**
yarn linker **9616**
yarn mercerizer **9443**
yarn plaiting equipment tender **9441**
yarn salvager **9616**
yarn soaker **9441**
yarn spinner **9441**
yarn tester **9444**
yarn texturing machine tender **9441**
yarn weigher **9616**
yarn winder **9441**
yarn winder, automatic **9441**
yeast drier **9461**
yeast emulsifier tender – food and
    beverage processing **9461**

yeast maker **9461**
yeast room operator **9461**
yeast sampler – food and beverage
    processing **9617**
yeast separator – food and beverage
    processing **9617**
yoga instructor **5254**
yogurt maker **9461**
youth counsellor **4153**
youth court clerk **1443**
youth court judge **4111**
youth hostel manager **0632**
youth services worker **4212**
youth worker, corrections **4155**
youth worker, social services **4212**

Z

zamboni driver **6671**
zinc cathode puller **9611**
zinc cell operator **9411**
zinc chloride tender **9411**
zinc drosser **9611**
zinc dust maker **9611**
zinc galvanizer **9497**
zinc vapour condenser **9411**

zipper assembler **9498**
zipper chain assembler **9498**
zipper chain machine tender **9517**
zipper inspector **9498**
zipper machine tender **9517**
zipper repairer **9619**
zipper sewing machine operator **9451**
zone manager, postal facilities **0132**
zone manager, sales **0611**
zone supervisor, assembly – motor
    vehicle manufacturing **9221**
zoning inspector **6463**
zoning officer **2153**
zoning officer, land use **2153**
zoo attendant **6483**
zoo director **0212**
zoo foreman/woman **2221**
zoo supervisor **2221**
zoo veterinarian **3114**
zoological park director **0212**
zoological technician **2221**
zoological technologist **2221**
zoologist **2121**
zoology professor – university **4121**
zyglo inspector **2261**
zyglo tester **2261**